Your opinion matters. It matters to us. It matters to your fellow Fodor's travelers, too. And we'd like to hear it. In fact, we *need* to hear it.

When you share your experiences and opinions, you become an active member of the Fodor's community. That means we'll not only use your feedback to make our books better, but we'll publish your names and comments whenever possible. Throughout our guides, look for "Word of Mouth," excerpts of your unvarnished feedback.

Here's how you can help improve Fodor's for all of us.

Tell us when we're right. We rely on local writers to give you an insider's perspective. But our writers and staff editors—who are the best in the business—depend on you. Your positive feedback is a vote to renew our recommendations for the next edition.

Tell us when we're wrong. We're proud that we update most of our guides every year. But we're not perfect. Things change. Hotels cut services. Museums change hours. Charming cafés lose charm. If our writer didn't quite capture the essence of a place, tell us how you'd do it differently. If any of our descriptions are inaccurate or inadequate, we'll incorporate your changes in the next edition and will correct factual errors at fodors.com *immediately.*

Tell us what to include. You probably have had fantastic travel experiences that aren't yet in Fodor's. Why not share them with a community of like-minded travelers? Maybe you chanced upon a café or bistro or B&B that you don't want to keep to yourself. Tell us why we should include it. And share your discoveries and experiences with everyone directly at fodors.com. Your input may lead us to add a new listing or highlight a place we cover with a "Highly Recommended" star or with our highest rating, "Fodor's Choice."

Give us your opinion instantly at our feedback center at www.fodors.com/feedback. You may also e-mail editors@fodors.com with the subject line "Moscow & St. Petersburg Editor." Or send your nominations, comments, and complaints by mail to Moscow & St. Petersburg Editor, Fodor's, 1745 Broadway, New York, NY 10019.

You and travelers like you are the heart of the Fodor's community. Make our community richer by sharing your experiences. Be a Fodor's correspondent.

Happy traveling!

Tim Jarrell, Publisher

CONTENTS

PLANNING YOUR TRIP

About this Book F6
What's Where F8
Quintessential Moscow &
  St. Petersburg F10
If You Like F12
Great Itinerary F14
When to Go F16
On the Calendar F17
Smart Travel Tips F20

MOSCOW & ST. PETERSBURG

1 MOSCOW 1
Exploring Moscow 4
Where to Eat 72
Where to Stay 87
Nightlife & the Arts 96
Sports & the Outdoors 104
Shopping 109
Moscow Excursions 116
Moscow A to Z 121

2 MOSCOW ENVIRONS &
THE GOLDEN RING 131
Moscow Environs 134
The Northern Golden Ring 143
The Eastern Golden Ring 149
Moscow Environs &
  the Golden Ring A to Z 155

3 ST. PETERSBURG 158
Exploring St. Petersburg 160
Where to Eat 212
Where to Stay 227
Nightlife & the Arts 234
Sports & the Outdoors 252
Shopping 253
St. Petersburg A to Z 259

4 SUMMER PALACES &
HISTORIC ISLANDS 270
The Summer Palaces 273
Kronshtadt & Valaam 291
Summer Palaces & Historic
  Islands A to Z 294

UNDERSTANDING MOSCOW & ST. PETERSBURG

Russia at a Glance 298
English-Russian Vocabulary 300
INDEX 306
ABOUT OUR WRITERS 316

CLOSEUPS

Moscow's Magnificent Metro 37
The Seven Gothic Sisters 41
Rules of the Banya 106
St. Petersburg in Literature 169
Vodka: A Taste of Russia 226
The Story of the Amber Room 283

MAPS

European Russia F7

Exploring Moscow 8-9

The Kremlin .10

Kitai Gorod .23

Tverskaya to the Arbat 32

South of the Kremlin 52

Where to Stay &
  Eat in Moscow 74-75

Moscow Environs &
  the Golden Ring 135

Troitsa-Sergieva Lavra 139

St. Petersburg 166-167

Where to Stay &
  Eat in St. Petersburg 214-215

Summer Palaces &
  Historic Islands 274

Peterhof (Petrodvorets) 276

Pushkin (Tsarskoye Selo) 282

ABOUT THIS BOOK

Our Ratings

Sometimes you find terrific travel experiences and sometimes they just find you. But usually the burden is on you to select the right combination of experiences. That's where our ratings come in.

As travelers we've all discovered a place so wonderful that its worthiness is obvious. And sometimes that place is so unique that superlatives don't do it justice: you just have to be there to know. These sights, properties, and experiences get our highest rating, Fodor's Choice ★, indicated by orange stars throughout this book.

Black stars highlight sights and properties we deem Highly Recommended ★, places that our writers, editors, and readers praise again and again for consistency and excellence.

By default, there's another category: any place we include in this book is by definition worth your time, unless we say otherwise. And we will.

Disagree with any of our choices? Care to nominate a place or suggest that we rate one more highly? Visit our feedback center at www. fodors.com/feedback.

Budget Well

Hotel and restaurant price categories from ¢ to $$$$ are defined in the opening pages of each chapter. For attractions, we always give standard adult admission fees; reductions are usually available for children, students, and senior citizens. Want to pay with plastic? **AE, D, DC, MC, V** following restaurant and hotel listings indicate whether American Express, Discover, Diner's Club, MasterCard, and Visa are accepted.

Restaurants

Unless we state otherwise, restaurants are open for lunch and dinner daily. We mention dress only when there's a specific requirement and reservations only when they're essential or not accepted—it's always best to book ahead.

Hotels

Hotels have private bath, phone, TV, and air-conditioning and operate on the European Plan (aka EP, meaning without meals), unless we specify that they use the Continental Plan (CP, with a continental breakfast), Breakfast Plan (BP, with a full breakfast), or Modified American Plan (MAP, with breakfast and dinner) or are all-inclusive (including all meals and most activities). We always list facilities but not whether you'll be charged an extra fee to use them, so when pricing accommodations, find out what's included.

Many Listings

★	Fodor's Choice
★	Highly recommended
✉	Physical address
✛	Directions
⌖	Mailing address
☎	Telephone
🖶	Fax
⊕	On the Web
✍	E-mail
🎫	Admission fee
☉	Open/closed times
►	Start of walk/itinerary
Ⓜ	Metro stations
⊟	Credit cards

Hotels & Restaurants

🏨	Hotel
🛏	Number of rooms
⌂	Facilities
❙❙❙	Meal plans
✕	Restaurant
⌔	Reservations
🏛	Dress code
↘	Smoking
🍷	BYOB
✕🏨	Hotel with restaurant that warrants a visit

Other

♺	Family-friendly
🚹	Contact information
⇨	See also
✉	Branch address
☞	Take note

European Russia

SWEDEN

Nike

Murmansk

Barents Sea

0   300 miles

0   400 km

Pechora

Kozhva

KEY

· · · · *Rail lines*

White Sea

Arkhangelsk

Vendenga

Mikun

Syktyvkar

Yushkozero

Kimasozero

Severnaya Dvina

Kotlas

FINLAND

Petrozavodsk

RUSSIA

Kirov

Vyatka

Lake Ladoga

Helsinki

St. Petersburg

Vologda

Tallinn

Gulf of Finland

Cherepovets

Baltic Sea

ESTONIA

Novgorod

Yaroslavl

Nizhniy Novgorod

Volga

Kazan

Gulf of Riga

Riga

Pskov

Tver

Vladimir

Simbirsk

LATVIA

Saransk

LITHUANIA

Kaunas

Moscow

Oka

Kaliningrad

RUSSIA

Vitsyebsk

Ryazan

Penza

Vilnius

Smolensk

Kaluga

Tambov

Warsaw

Minsk

Mahilyow

Saratov

BELARUS

Bryansk

Oka

Lipetsk

KAZAKHSTAN

Homyel

Orel

Kursk

POLAND

Voronezh

Volga

L'viv

UKRAINE

Kiev

Belgorod

Don

Volgograd

Kharkiv

Donets

Vinnytsya

Dnieper

Dnipropetrovsk

MOLDOVA

Rostov na Donu

Chisinau

Kherson

Sea of Azov

Stavropol

ROMANIA

Odesa

Krasnodar

Bucharest

Sevastopol

Danube

Black Sea

GEORGIA

BULGARIA

WHAT'S WHERE

MOSCOW	Cosmopolitan in flavor, Moscow exudes prosperity and vigor, at least in the center. In the Russian capital things tend to be done on the grand scale. In contrast to reserved and self-contained St. Petersburg, Moscow seeks to capture rather than captivate, to welcome with a rough bearlike hug. There's a festive spirit about the ornate churches with shiny golden cupolas, as well as the no-nonsense ambition of the six-lane highways and monumental Stalinist architecture. Even the metro stations are carved in marble. All shades of human nightlife are here—from trendy raves to large-scale popular entertainment.
	Russian provincials liken the city to Babylon, denouncing its crowded streets, its galloping break-neck pace, its refusal to sleep, and its unfortunate penchant for going over the top. A merchant capital by birth, Moscow was fashioned for big spenders, and money always made the wheels go round here. In postcommunist times, it has easily won a place among the world's most expensive cities. The only possible limit is the size of your wallet.
MOSCOW ENVIRONS & THE GOLDEN RING	The Golden Ring is a chain of medieval Russian towns northeast of Moscow. In the 12th to 14th centuries, they were the most important political, religious, and commercial centers in Russia until Moscow usurped all power. Nowadays these ancient enclaves, with no political clout and minimal commercial activity apart from tourism, are great destinations for rolling back the centuries. Their medieval convents, churches, gates, trade chambers, and kremlins form a living encyclopedia of Russian culture.
	These provincial towns are largely populated by the elderly. Although in Vladimir there are some modern five-story concrete apartment buildings, in the smaller Golden Ring towns like Suzdal many people still live in wooden houses. These are called *izba,* and their interiors and the lifestyle of their occupants differ little from that of their 19th-century ancestors.
ST. PETERSBURG	Serenity and reflection reign in this city. Tsars don't rush—it would be undignified. St. Petersburg was founded as the new capital of the Russian Empire in 1703 by Peter the Great and still carries itself with austere regal grace. So much so that energetic and impatient Muscovite visitors pull faces at the slow and—to them at least—sleepy pace of life.

Many 18th-century European critics mocked Peter the Great for imitating Western cities, suggesting that "the artificial city" would never become the real thing. Now, it attracts more tourists than anywhere else in Russia. A brilliant fusion created by Italian and French architects, St. Petersburg invites comparisons with Amsterdam, Venice, and Stockholm. And yet compared with them it makes surprisingly little use of its abundant waterways. The compact historical center is best explored on foot or from the water and it enthralls with a decadent, aristocratic flair. The delicate classical center has been preserved in its original form, with no ugly modern blocks intruding.

The big attractions here are the pastimes of the nobility—classical concerts, ballet, fine dining, and idyllic promenading in the 19th-century landscape.

SUMMER PALACES & HISTORIC ISLANDS

A sense of St. Petersburg's Imperial history is greatly enhanced by a visit to one of the city's splendid outlying summer residences. Though all enjoy the same aristocratic origins, the fortunes of these places, which are the size of small towns, varied enormously after the Bolshevik revolution. As result, there are big differences in their appearances and state of repair.

Peterhof (Petrodvorets) and Pushkin (Tsarskoye Selo) have become much-visited museums with impressive promotion budgets. Peterhof's gorgeous park is Russia's answer to Versailles. The most sumptuous country seat of all is Pushkin's Catherine Palace, housing the legendary Amber Room.

Though a UNESCO world cultural heritage site, the former royal estate of Lomonosov (Oranienbaum) has attracted little attention from tourists and little care from authorities. The headquarters of a Soviet defense center until 1983, the marvelous palaces were off-limits to visitors and crumbled into ruins. But a revival plan backed by massive state funding is set to launch a renaissance. Konstantine Palace languished in a similar state of neglect until Russian businesspeople sponsored its reconstruction, turning the venue into a residence for President Vladimir Putin.

QUINTESSENTIAL MOSCOW & ST. PETERSBURG

Porcelain

When Catherine the Great ordered her elaborate dinner service from the renowned Imperial Porcelain Manufacturer, porcelain was the exclusive preserve of aristocrats. But since then it has become almost every Russian's favorite gift.

After the Bolshevik Revolution, Soviet spin doctors skillfully used porcelain as propaganda. Potteries put all those idyllic shepherds out to pasture and switched to turning out figurines of earnest pioneers by the million. They produced china chess sets pitching aristocrats against peasants and fashioned ink pots in the shape of women embroidering the Soviet flag.

The country is hugely proud of its ancient and still thriving porcelain tradition. Inevitable as a wedding present, it also makes a gift fit for many other occasions. At St. Petersburg's 300th anniversary celebrations, President Vladimir Putin presented every head of state who attended with a specially made teacup and saucer.

Shrovetide (Maslenitsa)

Rio and Venice may have their colorful carnivals, but Russians have something no less amazing up their sleeve—Maslenitsa, or Shrovetide. It's the brightest surviving Slavic feast, and although it eventually gained acceptance by the Orthodox Church, its roots go back to pagan times.

Today Shrovetide is a rambunctious outdoor spring festival, when Russians indulge in dressing-up and wild singing and dancing. Russian bliny are served in virtually every eatery across the nation during Shrovetide week. Hot, buttery, and delicious, the round, golden bliny represent the sun. Russians fill themselves full of bliny and burn a handmade effigy like a scarecrow symbolizing winter.

To celebrate Shrovetide, arrange to visit for the last week before Lent. Remember that

Experience Russia with all your senses and discover what "Russianness" means. We guide you through some of the most exciting pursuits, basic rituals, and beloved symbols of this country.

Russian Lent follows the Julian calendar (in other words, two weeks later than in Catholic countries).

Epic Food

In Russian folk tales, amorous admirers ply their sweethearts with *pryaniki pechatnie* (printed ginger breads). This ancient Russian culinary delight, named after aromatic *pryanosti* (spices), is a baked sweet pastry filled with honey or jam and flavored with ginger, cinnamon, cardamom, and other spices. It's easily found at any bakery and at many coffee shops.

Another longstanding favorite is *kvas,* a refreshing nonalcoholic drink. Many Russians would say kvas beats modern colas hands down. Coca-Cola got the message: they now produce vast quantities of their own brand of kvas. Kvas, which literally translates as "sour drink," is made with fermented rye bread and is a renowned hangover remedy. In summertime people buy it by the liter from large wagons on the street.

Rye bread itself is quite a treat, too: don't miss *karelsky* with raisins, *borodinsky* with coriander, and *rizhsky* with cumin.

Banya

Sweaty people applying wet bundles of birch twigs to each others' bodies in a room full of steam may sound like purgatory or sadomasochism. But for Russians the banya experience is the way to nirvana and longevity. Most people in Russia believe the excruciating wet heat of the banya makes you shed toxins ultrafast, through heavy sweating, and that it rejuvenates the internal organs.

The banya also appears in an ancient Russian legend. In the year 945, Olga, widow of Kievan Prince Igor, lured his murderers—the elite corps of a whole of East Slavic tribe of Drevlyane—into a banya and set the bathhouse on fire. Meet Russia's first saint.

IF YOU LIKE

Imperial Balls & Palaces

Sumptuous Imperial balls, which flourished in prerevolutionary Russia, are enjoying an impressive renaissance, returning to the country's famous royal palaces. The management at the palaces, which house some of Russia's finest museums, at first had their doubts. Given the poverty and shortages endured by many, critics branded such extravagance as "a feast during the plague." But financial benefits and imperial nostalgia, and the desire to make use of such grand locations, won out.

Most contemporary St. Petersburg balls are organized by musicians and revive Russia's musical, cultural, and historical traditions. These date back to the reign of Peter the Great, when aristocrats put on carnivals, masquerades, and musical performances in their family palaces. Russian ministers and wealthy businesspeople also rent palaces for weddings and Western millionaires present their daughters with birthday balls. The less well-heeled get their palatial experience at classical chamber concerts, gourmet dinners, and fashion shows.

- **New Year's Eve Balls.** Renowned Russian conductor Yury Temirkanov hosts the Temirkanov Ball held in the mysterious Yusupov Palace. The luxurious Tsar's Ball takes place in Tsarskoye Selo.

- **White Nights Ball.** The Mariinsky Theater runs its own annual ball during its summer festival "Stars of the White Nights," in one of the suburban royal residences surrounding St. Petersburg.

- **Strauss Ball.** This annual event is held in early June in one of St. Petersburg's suburban palaces, as part of the classical music festival "Musical Olympus."

Ballet

Classical ballet is the only art form that never really went dissident in Russia. Russia's last tsar, Nicholas II, fell for the charms of ballerina Matilda Kshessinskaya, and from then on, through the Communist era and into the Putin years, ballet and especially ballerinas have been beyond criticism and free of oppression. As ballet has continued to thrive under state sponsorship, it has become an essential part of any official visit, as much a part of protocol as a trip to the war memorials.

Russian ballet is known for its exquisite blend of expressiveness, razor-sharp technique, and ethereal flair. Visiting ballet professionals envy both coordination and torso, the two strongest elements of Russian ballet training. Russian classical ballet, with its antique poetic charm, has preserved its precious legacy without becoming old-fashioned.

- **Swan Lake.** See this signature ballet at the Bolshoi (Moscow) or Mariinsky (St. Petersburg) theaters.

- **Sleeping Beauty.** This marvel of 19th-century choreography has been meticulously restored in its original form at the Mariinsky Theater in St. Petersburg.

- **The Nutcracker.** The Bolshoi, Mariinsky, and other companies perform this Christmas classic year round.

- **Vaganova Ballet Academy in St. Petersburg.** Formerly the Imperial Ballet School, Russia's most prestigious classical ballet academy is alma mater to Anna Pavlova, George Balanchine, and Mikhail Baryshnikov. It has a wonderful museum.

Exploring the Communist Legacy

Since the downfall of the Soviet empire, Russia has been struggling to get over its totalitarian past. The monument to Felix Dzerzhinsky, the "Iron Felix" who established the country's first security service under Lenin, was pulled down in 1991. But it survived that humiliating setback and was reinstalled outside the headquarters of Russia's federal security service on Moscow's Lubyanska Ploschad.

Soviet culture is still very much alive. Some of the things bequeathed by the Soviets fill Russians with pride, and a number of Soviet icons also serve commercial purposes.

- **Lenin's Mausoleum, Moscow.** Many Russians have demanded that the Russian parliament remove Lenin's tomb to a place where it can rest in peace.

- **Kirov Museum, St. Petersburg.** Sergei Kirov's unsolved murder in 1936 marked the start of the full-scale Stalinist Terror. This gripping and deeply personal collection offers fresh insights into the horrific way in which Stalin consolidated his power.

- **Russian Political History Museum, St. Petersburg.** The only gallery of its kind documents all aspects of the Communist past, from Soviet realism to the paraphernalia of spying to propaganda.

- **Moscow Metro.** The sumptuously ornate stations are palaces for the public.

Ice-Skating

Perhaps naturally for a wintry place like Russia, the most popular sport is ice-skating. The entire country is glued to the TV during ice-skating tournaments, to witness Russians winning ever more medals.

It seems that almost everything becomes a skating rink in Russia in winter. While the big freeze is on, iced-over ponds in city parks, outdoor stadiums and playgrounds, and brand-new ice palaces all welcome inexhaustible flocks of skaters.

As usual, there's a downside. Thanks to street-cleaning services that sometimes fail to complete the job, a surprise skating excursion could happen at any time. Cases of broken arms and legs leap dramatically during the snowy season. Snow boots, or shoes with nonslip rubber soles are strongly advised. Leather can be lethal.

- **Gorky Park, Moscow.** However gloomy and forbidding this place may sound from the novel of that name by Martin Cruz Smith, the picturesque park, packed with skating rinks, cafés, and other entertainment is Moscow's top venue for a family day out.

- **Moscow Ice Ballet.** Russia's answer to "Stars On Ice" is famous for adapting classical ballets, fairy tales, and even drama for the ice.

- **Moscow Circus on the Ice.** Under threat in the Arctic, the polar bears on ice here are in good shape and are both elegant and loads of fun.

- **The Cup of Russia, St. Petersburg.** Part of ISU Grand Prix of Figure Skating, this prestigious international competition is held every December.

GREAT ITINERARY

Day 1: The Kremlin

Devote this day to exploration of the Kremlin museums and cathedrals. Stroll through Red Square, St. Basil's Cathedral, and the shopping arcades of GUM. Admire the crowns of the Russian tsars at the Armory Palace. If you're into treasures, don't miss the notorious 190-carat Orlov diamond at the Diamond Fund. Lenin's Mausoleum is entirely optional. Take a ride on the world's most opulent and ornate metro, with its marble columns, mosaic panoramas, elaborate chandeliers, and quirky Soviet-era monuments. If you have any energy left, spend the evening at the Bolshoi theater.

Logistics: The most fascinating metro stations are on the circle line. Mayakovskaya and Ploshchad Revolutsii are also exciting. The Armory is closed on Thursday, and the Mausoleum, open Tuesday through Sunday, closes at 1 PM.

Day 2: Old Moscow

Discover old Moscow: wander through the winding narrow streets and visit the ancient churches of Kitai-Gorod and pass through the cheerful Old Arbat. Make a pilgrimage to the sad and stately 1524 New Maiden's Convent, a refuge for exiled noble women in the tsarist era. Be sure to see the Romanov Palace Chambers in Zaryadye, the impressive 16th century palace of the Romanov boyars and the home of the Romanov family before they made it to the throne. End your day with a bath at the palatial, venerable Sandunovskaya banya.

Logistics: The Romanov palace is open to groups with reservations during the week

and Saturday; Sunday is the best day for individual visitors. It costs from 500 to 1,000 rubles per person to visit Sandunovskaya banya.

Day 3: Tretyakov Gallery & Cathedral of Christ Our Savior

Spend the morning at the Tretyakov Gallery, which has one of the finest collections of Russian art. To feel the vigor of the new Moscow, head to the resurrected Cathedral of Christ Our Savior, demolished in 1931 and rebuilt from scratch. Travel to St. Petersburg on the stylish Nikolayevsky Express, fashioned to resemble an early-20th-century train and named after Russia's last tsar, Nicholas II.

Logistics: Nikolayevsky Express leaves from Moscow daily at 11:30 PM, and gets to St. Petersburg at 7 AM. The train departs from St. Petersburg at 11:24 PM and arrives in Moscow at 7:10 AM.

Day 4: St. Petersburg from Above & the Hermitage

For an invigorating start, climb the 260 steps to the colonnade of St. Isaac's Cathedral for a fabulous all-around panorama of the historical center. Then head to the State Hermitage Museum. But don't try to rush through this huge place all in one go. Make a list of your favorite things and return when you can. In the evening attend a performance at the Mariinsky Theater, and take a short detour before the start of the show to visit the magnificent 18th-century St. Nicholas (patron saint of sailors) Cathedral.

Logistics: The Hermitage is free on the first Thursday of every month.

Day 5: Icons, Onion Domes & Peter & Paul Fortress

Culture vultures should begin the day at the State Museum of Russian Art, home to the world's largest collection of Russian art, from icons to avant-garde to socialist realism. The brightly colored onion domes of the Church of the Savior on Spilled Blood, the dramatic scene of the murder of Tsar Alexander I, are just round the corner. In good weather, spend an hour observing the city from the water, taking one of the many boat trips, or a water bus. Visit the Peter and Paul Fortress in the late afternoon. Sightseeing can be continued even during a meal. The Bessonnitsa ("Insomnia") restaurant next to the fortress overlooks the Hermitage, Admiralty, and the Strelka.

Logistics: The quickest way to get to the Peter and Paul Fortress from Nevsky prospect is to travel one stop by metro and get off at Gorkovskaya. When you get out of the station, turn right and walk through a little park until you reach the fortress.

Day 6: A Palace Visit

Devote the day to a trip to one of the former royal residences. Choose Pushkin (Tsarskoye Selo) in winter and Peterhof in summer.

Logistics: It takes 30 minutes to get to Peterhof by hydrofoils departing from several quays along Dvortsovaya embankment, near the Hermitage and the Bronze Horseman.

TIPS

❶ All top tourist sights and central metro stations in both cities are notorious for pickpockets. Be extra careful.

❷ To save time and money, buy tickets for Moscow's Bolshoi and St. Petersburg's Mariinsky theaters online at www.bolshoi.ru and www.mariinsky.ru.

❸ To prepare best for the Russian banya, go to the Sandunovskaya banya's Web site (www.sanduny.ru) and read the expertly written "secrets" section (available in English).

❹ Be sure to bring an umbrella. According to the latest research, St. Petersburg boasts a pathetic maximum of 30 cloudless days a year.

❺ Consider staying in one of St. Petersburg's more than 200 minihotels. Most are centrally located, reasonably priced, and if you travel in a group, you could have the entire property just for yourselves.

WHEN TO GO

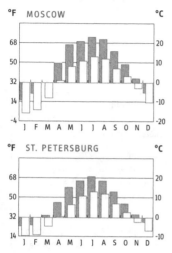

The climate in Russia changes dramatically with the seasons. Both Moscow and St. Petersburg are best visited in late spring or early autumn, just before and after the peak tourist season. The weather is always unpredictable, but you are most apt to encounter pleasantly warm and sunny days in late May and late August. In Moscow, summers tend to be hot, and thunderstorms and heavy rainfall are common in July and August. In St. Petersburg, on the other hand, it rarely gets very hot, even at the height of summer, though you'll likely need an umbrella. If this maritime city is your only destination, try to visit St. Petersburg during the White Nights (June to early July), when the northern day is virtually endless.

In winter months both cities are covered in an attractive blanket of snow, but only the hardiest tourists should visit between late November and early February, when the days are short and dark—extremely so in St. Petersburg—and the weather is often bitterly cold. St. Petersburg is flooded with tourists in the summer months but a foreign language is barely heard in town in winter. The city's most famous cultural institutions have teamed up with leading hotels to offer discounted arts packages under the brand "White Days." New art festivals are launched in winter in an effort to show that St. Petersburg is not a deserted place totally obscured by snow.

Climate
🛈 Forecasts Weather Channel Connection ☎ 900/932–8437 95¢ per minute ⊕ www.weather.com.

With the demise of the Soviet Union and the accompanying religious revival, church holy days are now more widely celebrated than traditional political holidays. These days, November 7, the anniversary of the Bolshevik Revolution, merits only a rally of the Communist supporters. But within St. Petersburg, November 7 is now celebrated as the anniversary of the city's renaming from Leningrad back to St. Petersburg. Listed below are major holidays celebrated in Russia.

WINTER	
Dec.	**December Nights** is a monthlong festival of music, dance, theater, and art held in Moscow.
	New Year's Eve is a favorite holiday marked by merrymaking and family gatherings. Friends and family exchange small gifts, putting them under a New Year's tree, a tradition that began when Christmas and other religious holidays were not tolerated by the Soviet authorities.
Dec.–Jan.	The **International Arts Square Festival** is a classical music festival at the St. Petersburg Philharmonic.
Jan.	New Year's Eve is celebrated twice—first on December 31, with the rest of the world, and then again on January 13, **"Old" New Year's Eve** (according to the Julian calendar used in Russia until the revolution).
	Russian Orthodox Christmas has become an increasingly important holiday and is celebrated on January 7 with lights, *yolkas* (fir trees), and modest gifts under the tree.
Feb.	February 23, **Defenders of the Fatherland Day** (formerly Soviet Army and Navy Day), is somewhat similar to Father's Day in the United States. Even though not every man ends up in the army, the holiday traditionally honors all men, not just members of the military. The day ends with fireworks in the evening.
Feb.–Mar.	**Shrovetide (Maslenitsa)** (Butter Week) is a Slavic version of carnival that takes place the week before Lent. It's largely a celebration of the sun and spring—hence the round, sun-shape blini that are consumed in massive amounts this week.
	St. Petersburg Tennis Cup, Russia's second-largest tennis tournament, is held in the waning days of winter.
Mar.	March 8, **International Women's Day,** is a popular holiday similar to Mother's Day, but honoring all women, especially wives. Giving a gift of flowers or a torte to female friends is de rigueur for men.

ON THE CALENDAR

SPRING	
Mar.–Apr.	**Orthodox Easter,** which generally falls a few weeks after Easter in the West, is a major national holiday in Russia. Festive church services begin at midnight and run through the night.
Apr.	St. Petersburg's **Spring Jazz Festival** brings together the finest jazz performers from across Russia.
May	*Prazdnik Vesny,* on May 1, is a celebration of spring; in Soviet times this holiday was observed as International Labor Day.
	May 9, **Victory Day,** is one of the country's most important holidays; World War II veterans appear on the streets decked out in their medals and are honored throughout the day at open-air festivals and parades.
	The Mariinsky's Valery Gergiev started the **Easter Festival** in Moscow. The program, played by top classical musicians, devotes special attention to spiritual–religious music (orthodox chants and bell-ringing concerts).
	St. Petersburg City Day is May 27.
	May 30, the **Day of Kostroma,** celebrates the anniversary of this city northeast of Moscow; the celebration usually stretches for three days.
	Yaroslavl celebrates its founding on May 31, the **Day of Yaroslavl.**
SUMMER	
June	The first Sunday of June is the **Festival of Pushkin's Poetry,** celebrated in the poet's hometown of Pskov.
	June 12 is **Russian Independence Day.**
	The International Moscow Film Festival is an annual event showcasing both international and Russian film offerings.
	Ivan Kupala Day (June 24) is based on a pagan celebration of the summer solstice that has had Christian tones superimposed on it.
	In St. Petersburg, the **White Nights Music Festival**—with jazz, fine arts, and film events—is held during the whole of June.
July	The last Sunday in July in St. Petersburg is **Fleet Day,** with wonderful naval parades and celebrations at the mouth of the Neva.
Late Aug.–early Sept.	Moscow's **International Chekhov Theater Festival** highlights but is not limited to plays by Chekhov.

FALL	
Sept.	Thousands of Muscovites take to the streets the first weekend of September to celebrate **Moscow City Day,** with parades, performances, competitions, and sports events. Local motorists rue the day the capital was founded, since City Day events close most of the main thoroughfares.
	September 12, **Day of Alexander Nevsky,** which is centered on St. Petersburg's Alexander Nevsky Square, is an annual festival with a typically Russian flavor, featuring brass bands and choruses.
	The **New Drama Festival** in Moscow showcases cutting-edge Russian plays staged by prominent Moscow companies.
Oct.	The **Kremlin Cup,** Russia's biggest tennis tournament, is held every October at Moscow's Olympisky Sports Complex.
Nov.	November 7, **Day of Reconciliation and Agreement,** formerly celebrated as the anniversary of the Bolshevik Revolution, is mainly now an excuse for a day off, and for pro- and anti-Communist demonstrations.
Nov.–Dec.	**The Cup of Russia,** an international ice-skating competition and part of ISU Grand Prix of Figure Skating, is held in St. Petersburg.

SMART TRAVEL TIPS

Addresses
Air Travel
Airports
Bus Travel
Business Hours
Cameras & Photography
Car Rental
Car Travel
Children in Moscow & St. Petersburg
Computers on the Road
Concierges
Consumer Protection
Cruise Travel
Customs & Duties
Disabilities & Accessibility
Discounts & Deals
Eating & Drinking
Electricity
Embassies & Consulates
Emergencies
English-Language Media
Etiquette & Behavior
Gay & Lesbian Travel
Health
Holidays
Insurance
Language
Lodging
Mail & Shipping
Money Matters
Packing
Passports & Visas
Restrooms
Safety
Senior-Citizen Travel
Shopping
Student Travel
Taxes
Telephones
Time
Tipping
Tours & Packages
Train Travel
Transportation
Travel Agencies
Visitor Information
Web Sites

Finding out about your destination before you leave home means you won't spend time organizing everyday minutiae once you've arrived. You'll be more streetwise when you hit the ground as well, better prepared to explore the aspects of Moscow and St. Petersburg that drew you here in the first place. The organizations in this section can provide information to supplement this guide; contact them for up-to-the-minute details, and consult the A to Z sections that end each chapter for facts on the various topics as they relate to the different regions. Happy landings!

ADDRESSES

The main Russian terms for addresses are *bulvar,* or boulevard; *korpus,* or building; *naberezhnaya,* or embankment (abbreviated as nab.); *pereulok,* or side street (abbreviated as per.); *Ploshchad,* or square (abbreviated as Pl.); *prospekt,* or prospect (abbreviated as pr.); *proyezd,* or passage or thoroughfare; *shosse,* or highway; and *ulitsa,* or street (abbreviated as ul., which can come before or after the proper street name).

AIR TRAVEL

Nonstop flights from the United States to Russia are available only to Moscow, originating in New York or Los Angeles. To St. Petersburg, either a direct flight, which requires at least one stop, or a connecting flight, which requires a change of airplanes, will be your only choices if you're coming from the United States. Some flights, especially those that are nonstop, may be scheduled only on certain days of the week. Depending on your destination and the originating city, you may need to make more than one connection. Your best bet is to use Helsinki or Frankfurt, which have the greatest number of connecting flights. Helsinki is less than an hour from St. Petersburg and less than two hours from Moscow.

Travelers coming from the United Kingdom have plenty of options including overnight "red-eye" flights. British Airways and Transaero are popular choices. There are no direct flights from Australia and New Zealand. A popular way is to fly on the national flag carrier to Singapore and then change to Aeroflot or some other European airline to finish the journey. Aeroflot flies directly from Singapore to Moscow but with two or three stops for refueling. Travel with a European airline will mean transferring again in Europe.

BOOKING

Two airlines may operate a connecting flight jointly, so ask whether your airline operates every segment of the trip; you may find that the carrier you prefer flies you only part of the way. To find more booking tips and to check prices and make online flight reservations, log on to www.fodors.com.

If you're flying as an independent traveler within the CIS (Commonwealth of Independent States), a quasi-confederation of states including most of the former Soviet Union), it's best to **purchase your ticket with a credit card via an agent in your home country or a reputable one in Russia.** This will allow you the best chance for refunds if your flight is canceled. Russian airlines have a habit of permitting refunds only at the office at which the ticket was purchased. If you book from abroad, you should reconfirm your reservation in person as soon as you arrive in the country.

CARRIERS

When flying internationally, you must usually choose among a domestic carrier, the national flag carrier of the country you are visiting (Aeroflot-Russian International Airlines), and a foreign carrier from a third country. National flag carriers have the greatest number of nonstop flights. Domestic carriers may have better connections to your hometown and serve a greater number of gateway cities. Third-party carriers may have a price advantage.

Within Russia, in addition to Aeroflot, there are several smaller, regional airlines (sometimes called "babyflots"). Aeroflot offers good international service between Russia and some 140 destinations, and it also flies some domestic routes. The babyflots are slowly bringing their service up to international standards and service to and from St. Petersburg and Moscow is far better than that between smaller cities.

Although the older Russian aircraft are being phased out in favor of Boeing and Airbus planes, they're still much in use. On the better airlines, this is nothing to worry about, but the state of the cabin may be shabbier than what you're used to.

Two airlines that stand head and shoulders above the rest are Transaero, which flies to several destinations in Europe and the CIS, and has internal flights to major Russian cities; and Pulkovo, which also has a number of international flights as well as good domestic service. Both have established partnerships with international airlines in order to increase their reach—Transaero has links to the United States with Continental, Virgin, and Lufthansa, for example. A third domestic airline that will take you into the heart of Siberia (and elsewhere) is Sibir, which coordinates some of its routes with Aeroflot.

Delays and cancellations are more frequent in winter, particularly in those places where the climate is severe. The farther east you go from Moscow, the more unreliable air travel can be. If possible, stick to the airlines mentioned above.

To & From Russia Aeroflot-Russian International Airlines ✉ 630 5th Ave., New York, NY 10011 ☎ 800/995-5555 in U.S., 495/753-5555 in Moscow, 812/718-5555 in St. Petersburg ⊕ www.aeroflot.org. **Air France** ☎ 800/237-2747 in U.S., 495/937-3839 in Moscow, 812/336-2900 in St. Petersburg ⊕ www.airfrance.com. **British Airways** ☎ 800/247-9297 in U.S., 495/363-2525 in Moscow, 812/380-0626 in St. Petersburg ⊕ www.britishairways.com. **Czech Airlines** ☎ 212/765-6545 in U.S., 495/973-1847 in Moscow ⊕ www.csa.cz. **Delta** ☎ 800/241-4141 in U.S., 495/937-9090 in Moscow, 812/571-5820 or 812/571-5819 in St. Petersburg ⊕ www.delta.com. **Finnair** ☎ 800/950-5000 in U.S., 495/933-0056 in Moscow, 812/303-9898 in St. Petersburg ⊕ www.finnair.com. **KLM** ☎ 800/374-7747 in U.S., 495/258-3600 in Moscow, 812/346-6868 in St. Petersburg ⊕ www.klm.com. **Lufthansa** ☎ 800/645-3880 in U.S., 495/737-6400 in Moscow, 812/320-1000 in St. Petersburg ⊕ www.lufthansa.com. **SAS** ☎ 800/221-2350 in U.S., 495/775-4747 in Moscow, 812/326-2600 in St. Petersburg.

Within Russia Pulkovo ☎ 812/704-3428 international flights, 495/995-2025 in Moscow, 812/723-8345 in St. Petersburg for domestic flights. **Sibir** ☎ 495/777-9999 in Moscow. **Transaero** ☎ 212/

582–0505 or 312/917–3200 in U.S., 495/788–8080 in Moscow, 812/727–8449 or 812/579–1274 in St. Petersburg ⊕ www.transaero.ru.

CHECK-IN & BOARDING

Always **find out your carrier's check-in policy.** Plan to arrive at the airport about two hours before your scheduled departure time for domestic flights and 2½ to 3 hours before international flights. You may need to arrive earlier if you're flying from one of the busier airports or during peak air-traffic times. Note that in Russia, check-in officially ends 40 minutes before departure, and if you arrive late you may need to do some serious begging to be allowed onto the plane. At St. Petersburg's Pulkovo I, there is a separate check-in for flights to Moscow—take the entrance on the right-hand side of the upper floor of the building.

To avoid delays at airport-security checkpoints, try not to wear any metal. Jewelry, belt and other buckles, steel-toe shoes, barrettes, and underwire bras are among the items that can set off detectors.

Assuming that not everyone with a ticket will show up, airlines routinely overbook planes. When everyone does, airlines ask for volunteers to give up their seats. In return, these volunteers usually get a several-hundred-dollar flight voucher, which can be used toward the purchase of another ticket, and are rebooked on the next available flight out. If there are not enough volunteers, the airline must choose who will be denied boarding. The first to get bumped are passengers who checked in late and those flying on discounted tickets, so get to the gate and check in as early as possible, especially during peak periods.

Always **bring a government-issued photo ID** to the airport; even when it's not required, a passport is best.

CUTTING COSTS

The least expensive airfares to Moscow and St. Petersburg are often priced for round-trip travel and must usually be purchased in advance. Airlines generally allow you to change your return date for a fee; most low-fare tickets, however, are nonre-

fundable. It's smart to call a number of airlines and check the Internet; when you are quoted a good price, book it on the spot—the same fare may not be available the next day, or even the next hour. Always check different routings and look into using alternate airports. Also, price off-peak flights and red-eye, which may be significantly less expensive than others. Travel agents, especially low-fare specialists (⇨ Discounts & Deals), are helpful.

Consolidators are another good source. They buy tickets for scheduled flights at reduced rates from the airlines, then sell them at prices that beat the best fare available directly from the airlines. (Many also offer reduced car-rental and hotel rates.) Sometimes you can even get your money back if you need to return the ticket. Carefully read the fine print detailing penalties for changes and cancellations, purchase the ticket with a credit card, and confirm your consolidator reservation with the airline.

When you fly as a courier, you trade your checked-luggage space for a ticket deeply subsidized by a courier service. There are restrictions on when you can book and how long you can stay. Some courier companies list with membership organizations, such as the Air Courier Association and the International Association of Air Travel Couriers; these require you to become a member before you can book a flight.

Many airlines, singly or in collaboration, offer discount air passes that allow foreigners to travel economically in a particular country or region. These visitor passes usually must be reserved and purchased before you leave home. Information about passes often can be found on most airlines' international Web pages, which tend to be aimed at travelers from outside the carrier's home country. Also, try typing the name of the pass into a search engine, or search for "pass" within the carrier's Web site.

🚩 **Consolidators** AirlineConsolidator.com ⊕ www.airlineconsolidator.com; for international tickets. **Best Fares** ⊕ www.bestfares.com; $59.90 annual membership. **Cheap Tickets** ⊕ www.cheaptickets.com. **Expedia** ⊕ www.expedia.com.

Hotwire ⊕ www.hotwire.com. **Onetravel.com**
⊕ www.onetravel.com. **Orbitz** ⊕ www.orbitz.com.
Priceline.com ⊕ www.priceline.com. **Travelocity**
⊕ www.travelocity.com.
**⁊ Courier Resources Air Courier Association/
Cheaptrips.com** ☏ 800/461-8856 or 800/282-1202
⊕ www.aircourier.org or www.cheaptrips.com; $39
annual membership. **International Association of
Air Travel Couriers** ☏ 308/632-3273 ⊕ www.
courier.org; $45 annual membership.
⁊ Discount Passes FlightPass EuropebyAir
☏ 888/387-2479 ⊕ www.europebyair.com. **SAS Air
Passes** Scandinavian Airlines ☏ 800/221-2350,
0870/6072-7727 in U.K., 1300/727707 in Australia
⊕ www.scandinavian.net.

ENJOYING THE FLIGHT

State your seat preference when purchasing your ticket, and then repeat it when
you confirm and when you check in. For
more legroom, you can request one of the
few emergency-aisle seats at check-in, if
you're capable of moving obstacles comparable in weight to an airplane exit door
(usually between 35 pounds and 60
pounds)—a Federal Aviation Administration requirement of passengers in these
seats. Seats behind a bulkhead also offer
more legroom, but they don't have under-
seat storage. Don't sit in the row in front
of the emergency aisle or in front of a
bulkhead, where seats may not recline.
SeatGuru.com has more information
about specific seat configurations, which
vary by aircraft.

Ask the airline whether a snack or meal is
served on the flight. If you have dietary
concerns, request special meals when
booking. These can be vegetarian, low-
cholesterol, or kosher, for example. It's a
good idea to pack some healthful snacks
and a small (plastic) bottle of water in
your carry-on bag. On long flights, try to
maintain a normal routine, to help fight jet
lag. At night, get some sleep. By day, eat
light meals, drink water (not alcohol), and
move around the cabin to stretch your
legs. For additional jet-lag tips consult
Fodor's FYI: Travel Fit & Healthy (available at bookstores everywhere).

Smoking policies vary from carrier to carrier. Most airlines, including smaller Russian ones, prohibit smoking on all of their
flights; others allow smoking only on certain routes or certain departures. Ask your
carrier about its policy.

FLYING TIMES

Flying time to Moscow is 8½ hours from
New York, 10–11 hours from Chicago, 12
hours from Los Angeles, 4 hours from
London and 24–30 hours from Sydney, depending on which airline you choose.

HOW TO COMPLAIN

If your baggage goes astray or your flight
goes awry, complain right away. Most carriers require that you **file a claim immediately.** The Aviation Consumer Protection
Division of the Department of Transportation publishes *Fly-Rights*, which discusses
airlines and consumer issues and is available online. You can also find articles and
information on mytravelrights.com, the
Web site of the nonprofit Consumer Travel
Rights Center.
⁊ Airline Complaints Aviation Consumer Protection Division ⊠ U.S. Department of Transportation,
Office of Aviation Enforcement and Proceedings, C-
75, Room 4107, 400 7th St. SW, Washington, DC
20590 ☏ 202/366-2220 ⊕ airconsumer.ost.dot.gov.
**Federal Aviation Administration Consumer Hot-
line** ⊠ For inquiries: FAA, 800 Independence Ave.
SW, Washington, DC 20591 ☏ 866/835-5322
⊕ www.faa.gov.

RECONFIRMING

Check the status of your flight before you
leave for the airport. You can do this on
your carrier's Web site, by linking to a
flight-status checker (many Web booking
services offer these), or by calling your carrier or travel agent. Always confirm international flights at least 72 hours ahead of
the scheduled departure time. Within Russia, you do not normally need to reconfirm
your outbound flight or intra-destination
flights.

AIRPORTS

The major international airports are
Sheremetyevo II Airport in Moscow and
Pulkovo II Airport in St. Petersburg.

For domestic travel, Moscow has three airports in addition to Sheremetyevo II:

Sheremetyevo I (for flights to the north and west), Domodedovo (for eastern destinations and the airport for British Airways and Transaero), and Vnukovo (for southern destinations). In St. Petersburg, there's one airport other than Pulkovo II: Pulkovo I, which handles domestic flights. Even though the departing or arriving airport may be printed on your ticket, double-check this information with your local travel agent.

⚑ Airport Information Domodedovo Airport (DME) ☎ 495/933–6666. Pulkovo I Airport ☎ 812/ 704–3822. Pulkovo II Airport ☎ 812/704–3444. Sheremetyevo I Airport ☎ 495/232–6565. Sheremetyevo II Airport ☎ 495/956–4666 or 495/ 578–9101. Vnukovo Airport ☎ 495/436–2813.

BUS TRAVEL

Traveling by bus can be daunting in Russia if you do not speak the language. But for some smaller towns and suburban destinations, this may be the only way to travel. And it's generally cheaper than train travel. Take note, however, that shrinking city budgets have made all surface transport less reliable, and when you can, you should travel by train or suburban train (*elektrichka*).

Ticket offices tend to have long hours of operation and you can typically purchase your bus ticket before departing. If you have any contact who will help negotiate the purchase for you, avail yourself of him or her. Handwritten seating charts and tickets are the norm, but tickets are sold even when there are no seats left (even for longer rides). This leads to some very crowded conditions (and, on hot days, quite stuffy situations, as these buses, although reasonably comfortable, do not have air-conditioning and only sometimes do their windows open). Payment is with rubles *only.*

RESERVATIONS

It's recommended that you buy advance tickets for peak long-distance travel days—Friday, Saturday, and Sunday.

BUSINESS HOURS

BANKS & OFFICES

General hours for most businesses and banks are from 10 AM to 6 PM. They are usually closed on weekends, and many take an hour off for lunch.

Consulates, government offices, ticket agencies, and exchange offices tend to close for an hour in the afternoon for lunch. Nothing stands between Russian businesses and public holidays, and the major holidays often involve a break of at least two days—three if they coincide with a weekend. See Holidays *(below)* for national holidays and Mail & Shipping for post office hours.

GAS STATIONS

Most gas stations are open 24 hours.

MUSEUMS & SIGHTS

Museum hours vary, but many are closed on Monday. Many museums close for one extra day (on which they'd normally be open) at the end of the month.

PHARMACIES

In general, pharmacies are open from 9 or 10 AM until 9 PM. There are, however, some 24-hour pharmacies in the major cities.

SHOPS

Most shops and department stores are open from 10 AM until 7 PM or even as late as 9 PM seven days a week. Fewer and fewer break for lunch for an hour in the afternoon. Restaurants and shopping arcades rarely have days off.

CAMERAS & PHOTOGRAPHY

When you enter any museum or church in Russia, take a look around the entrance for signs regarding photography. Even if you don't see any signs, ask someone before starting to snap away. Museums and churches essentially adhere to one of three different sets of rules. If taking pictures is completely forbidden, you'll most likely see a sign with a camera icon and a red line through it. If you fail to respect this warning, the consequences could range from simply having an attendant yell at you to having your film or camera confiscated by a security guard. Other places may allow you to take pictures, but without using your flash—basically to protect artworks and preserve the sanctity of a church. The third option is that photography—with or without flash—is allowed, but at a price, which can be even higher than the cost of an entrance ticket. If you decide not to pay the extra charge, you may not be allowed to enter with your camera.

Photography devotees will find plenty to keep them busy during a trip to Russia. Every visitor to Moscow wants a shot of the onion-domed St. Basil's Cathedral on Red Square, and the entire square is particularly striking when lit up at night—an exceptionally beautiful effect in winter. St. Petersburg is best photographed during the White Nights season—June to early July—when the sky never really gets dark. Stay up late with your camera to join the city's residents on the embankment of the Neva River to watch as, one by one, the bridges are raised to let sea traffic through. For great photographs of the suburbs of St. Petersburg, there's really no time like the fall. When the trees change color, the parks of Pushkin, Pavlovsk, Peterhof, and Gatchina really come to life.

The *Kodak Guide to Shooting Great Travel Pictures* (available at bookstores everywhere) is loaded with tips.

🖪 **Photo Help Kodak Information Center** ☎ 800/242-2424 ⊕ www.kodak.com.

EQUIPMENT PRECAUTIONS

Don't pack film or equipment in checked luggage, where it is much more susceptible to damage. X-ray machines used to view checked luggage are extremely powerful and therefore are likely to ruin your film. Try to ask for hand inspection of film, which becomes clouded after repeated exposure to airport X-ray machines, and keep videotapes and computer disks away from metal detectors. Always keep film, tape, and computer disks out of the sun. Carry an extra supply of batteries, and be prepared to turn on your camera, camcorder, or laptop to prove to airport security personnel that the device is real.

Winter in Moscow and St. Petersburg can reach minus 35°F; you may be able to stand these temperatures, but odds are your camera won't—especially your batteries. Winter in St. Petersburg is not photography-friendly by any means. The city

endures a long period of near-perpetual dusk, the complete opposite of the White Nights season. If the cold doesn't encourage you to leave your camera at home, the lack of available light probably will. In Moscow, however, you'll probably want to take some winter shots, in which case you should bring an insulated camera bag and lots of spare batteries.

FILM & DEVELOPING

All standard kinds of film are available in Russia, including products from Fuji and Kodak, and the latter's Advantix. A standard roll of 36-exposure, color print film costs between $2 for ISO 100 and $4 for ISO 400. Just about every photo shop now offers 24-hour, one-hour, and even 30-minute service for color print film—but, like many places in the United States, don't go looking for top-quality work. If your photos are important to you, wait until you get back home and work with a trusted developer. There are plenty of fully stocked photo shops in the center of Moscow and St. Petersburg that sell a large selection of cameras and accessories such as lenses, cases, tripods, and filters.

VIDEOS

The Russian standard for videotape, like Europe's, is Pal.

CAR RENTAL & HIRING A DRIVER

Due to road quality, dangerous drivers, and unwanted police attention, it's not recommended to drive around Russia, particularly in Moscow and St. Petersburg, if you don't speak Russian and lack local knowledge. To explore parts that are off the beaten path, or visit nearby towns in warmer weather, a car is certainly convenient, but can be very expensive. Car-rental rates are all over the map in Russia, but if you shop around you should be able to get rates from the major chains for as low as $60 a day for a Russian car (manual, no air) with at least 100 free km (60 mi) per day. Foreign cars, automatic transmission, and air-conditioning cost extra. These prices usually include the tax on car rentals, which is 20%. Insurance is mandatory (Russian rentals usually include the cost of insurance).

All agencies require advance reservations (at least two to three days is a good idea), and you'll have to show your driver's license, an international license, and a credit card.

Another option is to hire a car with driver for about $15–$35 per hour, which will help you circumvent some of the problems with driving in Russia (⇨ Car Travel). Major hotels will arrange this service for their guests. Some local tour companies, such as Patriarshy Dom Tours, or Western travel agents specializing in independent travel, such as Mir Corporation, can arrange daily-rate car-and-driver options, which are less expensive.

🄵 **Major Agencies Alamo** ☎ 800/522-9696 ⊕ www.alamo.com. **Avis** ☎ 800/331-1084, 800/272-5871 in Canada, 0870/606-0100 in U.K., 02/9353-9000 in Australia, 09/526-2847 in New Zealand ⊕ www.avis.com. **Budget** ☎ 800/527-0700 ⊕ www.budget.com. **Hertz** ☎ 800/654-3001, 800/263-0600 in Canada, 0870/844-8844 in U.K., 02/9669-2444 in Australia, 09/256-8690 in New Zealand ⊕ www.hertz.com. **National Car Rental** ☎ 800/227-7368 ⊕ www.nationalcar.com.

🄵 **Car & Driver Hire Mir Corporation** ☎ 800/424-7289 in U.S. ⊕ www.mircorp.com. **Patriarshy Dom Tours** ☎ 495/795-0927 in Moscow ✉ alanskaya@co.ru ⊕ www.russiatravel-pdtours.netfirms.com.

INSURANCE

When driving a rented car you are generally responsible for any damage to or loss of the vehicle. Collision policies that car-rental companies sell for European rentals typically do not cover stolen vehicles. Before you rent—and purchase collision or theft coverage—see what coverage you already have under the terms of your personal auto-insurance policy and credit cards.

SURCHARGES

Before you pick up a car in one city and leave it in another, ask about drop-off charges or one-way service fees, which can be substantial. Also inquire about early-return policies; some rental agencies charge extra if you return the car before the time specified in your contract while others give you a refund for the days not used. Most agencies note the tank's fuel level on your contract; to avoid a hefty refueling fee, return the car with the same tank level. If the tank was full, refill it just before you turn in the car, but be aware that gas stations near the rental outlet may overcharge. It's almost never a deal to buy a tank of gas with the car when you rent it; the understanding is that you'll return it empty, but some fuel usually remains.

CAR TRAVEL

Your own driver's license is not acceptable in Russia. You'll need an International Driver's Permit and, if traveling into the country by car, an international certificate of registration of the car in the country of departure. You'll also need a certificate of obligation (which should be registered with customs at the point of entry; consult your rental company about this) if you have plans for driving a rental car in over the border. International Driving Permits (IDPs) are available from the American and Canadian automobile associations and, in the United Kingdom, from the Automobile Association and Royal Automobile Club.

Driving in Russia is not for the faint-hearted. You must first be comfortable driving on roads marked only with Cyrillic and/or international symbology; you must be willing to deal with the bribe-hungry traffic inspectors; and you must be prepared for the poor and sometimes even dangerous road conditions. Even the main highways are potholed and in poor condition. Repair stations are few and far between, and many places sell poor-quality gasoline. In addition, you should not underestimate the risk of crime: highway robbery and car theft are on the rise, and foreign drivers are the number-one targets. **Do not stop to help motorists** whose cars appear to have broken down, even if they wave at you for help—this is a classic ambush technique. Never leave anything of value inside your car.

In light of these concerns, you may wish to hire a car and driver rather than driving yourself (⇨ Car Rental).

EMERGENCY SERVICES

Because service stations are few and poorly stocked, it's recommended that for long distances you carry a complete emergency repair kit, including a set of tools, a towing cable, a pressure gauge, a pump, a spare tire, a repair outfit for tubeless tires, a good jack and one or two tire levers, a gasoline can, a spare fan belt, spare windshield-wiper blades, and spark plugs. You should also have a set of headlight bulbs and fuses, a set of contact-breaker points for the ignition distributor, a spare condenser, a box of tire valve interiors, and a roll of insulating tape. There's no national emergency service to call, but if you're in the Moscow area, call the service Angel ☎ 495/747–0022.

GASOLINE

More and more stations, bearing the names of major oil companies, are opening, and nowadays it's easy to find somewhere to fill up, even outside of major towns. Gas prices are comparable to those in the United States. It's also fairly easy to find unleaded gasoline; for leaded gas, foreign cars should be filled only with 95 octane gas. Russian-made cars run on 92 octane.

ROAD CONDITIONS

 Around Moscow and St. Petersburg, most of the country roads have been paved with asphalt. Nonetheless, driving in winter can be dangerously slippery, and the spring thaw can turn roadways into lakes. Driving in snowy conditions in the cities is only for the experienced—Russian drivers see fallen snow as an obstacle to be overcome, not as a reason to take the metro.

ROAD MAPS

If you do decide to drive by yourself, be sure to get adequate road and street atlases (sold in major bookstores and sometimes even on the street) and plan your travel out ahead of time.

RULES OF THE ROAD

Driving regulations are strict, but they're often broken by local drivers; a good rule of thumb is to **drive defensively.** Traffic keeps to the right. The speed limit on highways is 90 kph (56 mph); in towns and populated areas it's 60 kph (37 mph), although on the wide streets of Moscow few people observe this rule. You can proceed at traffic intersections only when the light is green—this includes left and right turns. You must wait for a signal—an arrow—permitting the turn, and give way to pedestrians crossing. Wearing front seat belts is compulsory; driving while intoxicated carries very heavy fines, including imprisonment. Do not consume any alcohol at all if you plan to drive. You should also keep your car clean—you can be fined for having a dirty car.

Traffic control in Russia is exercised by traffic inspectors (GIBDD, but still commonly known as GAI), who are stationed all over cities and at permanent posts out of town; they also patrol in cars and on motorcycles and like to sit in ambush. They may stop you for no apparent reason other than to check your documentation. In this event, you're not required to exit your vehicle. Do not ignore attempts by a traffic cop—known colloquially as *gaishnik*—to flag you over. Remember that the GIBDD is regarded as a confounded nuisance by most Russians, and the friendly cop who will provide directions to gas stations or garages is rare. Traffic cops are also good at finding *something* wrong with your documentation and/or your driving; this may be nothing more than an attempt to secure a bribe.

CHILDREN IN MOSCOW & ST. PETERSBURG

Moscow and St. Petersburg have plenty of museums, parks, and recreation facilities that are kid-friendly and often offer free admission for children. Both cities have great circuses (ask your hotel concierge or service bureau to get tickets for you) and great riverboat rides.

Outbreaks of common infectious diseases have been rare in Russia lately, but you should still make sure all immunizations are up-to-date. Children (and adults) should be immunized against diphtheria, measles, mumps, rubella, and polio, as well as hepatitis A and typhus. A flu shot is also recommended for winter travel.

If you are renting a car, don't forget to arrange for a car seat when you reserve. For general advice about traveling with children, consult *Fodor's FYI: Travel with Your Baby* (available in bookstores everywhere).

FLYING

If your children are two or older, ask about children's airfares. As a general rule, infants under two not occupying a seat fly at greatly reduced fares or even for free. But if you want to guarantee a seat for an infant, you have to pay full fare. Consider flying during off-peak days and times; most airlines will grant an infant a seat without a ticket if there are available seats. When booking, confirm carry-on allowances if you're traveling with infants. In general, for babies charged 10% to 50% of the adult fare you are allowed one carry-on bag and a collapsible stroller; if the flight is full, the stroller may have to be checked or you may be limited to less.

Experts agree that it's a good idea to use safety seats aloft for children weighing less than 40 pounds. Airlines set their own policies: if you use a safety seat, U.S. carriers usually require that the child be ticketed, even if he or she is young enough to ride free, because the seats must be strapped into regular seats. And even if you pay the full adult fare for the seat, it may be worth it, especially on longer trips. Do **check your airline's policy about using safety seats during takeoff and landing.** Safety seats are not allowed everywhere in the plane, so get your seat assignments as early as possible.

When reserving, request children's meals or a freestanding bassinet (not available at all airlines) if you need them. But note that bulkhead seats, where you must sit to use the bassinet, may lack an overhead bin or storage space on the floor.

LODGING

Most hotels in Moscow and St. Petersburg allow children under a certain age to stay in their parents' room at no extra charge, but others charge for them as extra adults; be sure to find out the cutoff age for children's discounts.

SIGHTS & ATTRACTIONS

Places that are especially appealing to children are indicated by a rubber-duckie icon (🐥) in the margin.

SUPPLIES & EQUIPMENT

Most supermarkets and reasonably large pharmacies will have *detskoe pitanie* (baby formula) and diapers, which are known widely by the name "Pampers."

COMPUTERS ON THE ROAD

Checking your e-mail or surfing the Web can often be done in the business centers of major hotels, which usually charge an hourly rate. Web access is also available at many fax and copy centers, many of which are open 24 hours and on weekends. During business hours and in Moscow and St. Petersburg, local Internet service providers often allow hourly rate e-mail access at their offices, and the number of Internet cafés is increasing, as is the availability of Wi-Fi. Rates for Internet use run from about 60 rubles or $2 an hour and up.

CONCIERGES

Concierges, found in many hotels, can help you with theater tickets and dinner reservations: a good one with connections may be able to get you seats for a hot show or prime-time dinner reservations at the restaurant of the moment. You can also turn to your hotel's concierge for help with travel arrangements, sightseeing plans, services ranging from aromatherapy to zipper repair, and emergencies. **Always tip** a concierge who has been of assistance (⇨ Tipping).

CONSUMER PROTECTION

Whether you're shopping for gifts or purchasing travel services, **pay with a major credit card** whenever possible, so you can cancel payment or get reimbursed if there's a problem (and you can provide documentation). If you're doing business with a particular company for the first time, contact your local Better Business Bureau and the attorney general's offices in your state and (for U.S. businesses) the company's home state as well. Have any complaints been filed? Finally, if you're buying a package or tour, always consider travel insurance that includes default coverage (⇨ Insurance).

🔲 **BBBs Council of Better Business Bureaus** ✉ 4200 Wilson Blvd., Suite 800, Arlington, VA 22203 ☎ 703/276-0100 📠 703/525-8277 ⊕ www.bbb.org.

CRUISE TRAVEL

International cruise lines offering tours to Russia usually disembark in St. Petersburg and continue to Moscow by land. Some cruises follow the Volga River between Moscow and St. Petersburg on a journey of up to two weeks. To learn how to plan, choose, and book a cruise-ship voyage, consult *Fodor's FYI: Plan & Enjoy Your Cruise* (available in bookstores everywhere). See the A to Z sections in the Moscow and St. Petersburg chapters for information.

🚢 **Cruise Lines Cunard** ☎ 800/728-6273 ⊕ www.cunard.com. **Holland America** ☎ 877/724-5425 ⊕ www.hollandamerica.com. **Norwegian Cruise Lines** ☎ 305/436-4000 or 800/327-7030 ⊕ www.norwegiancruiselines.com. **Princess** ☎ 800/774-6237 ⊕ www.princess.com. **Royal Caribbean** ☎ 800/398-9819 ⊕ www.royalcaribbean.com.

🚢 **River Cruises Cruise Marketing International** ✉ 3401 Investment Blvd., Suite 3, Hayward, CA 94545 ☎ 800/578-7742 ⊕ www.cruiserussia.com. **GlobalQuest** ✉ 185 Willis Ave., 2nd fl., Mineola, NY 11501 ☎ 516/739-3690 or 800/221-3254 🖷 516/739-8022 ⊕ www.globalquesttravel.com. **Smithsonian Journeys** ✉ Box 23293, Washington, DC 20026 ☎ 202/357-4700 or 800/338-8687 🖷 202/633-9250 ⊕ www.smithsonianjourneys.org. **Uniworld** ✉ 17323 Ventura Blvd., Encino, CA 91316 ☎ 818/382-7820 or 800/733-7820 🖷 818/461-1777 ⊕ www.uniworld.com.

CUSTOMS & DUTIES

When shopping abroad, keep receipts for all purchases. Upon reentering the country, **be ready to show customs officials what you've bought.** Pack purchases together in an easily accessible place. If you think a duty is incorrect, appeal the assessment. If you object to the way your clearance was handled, note the inspector's badge number. In either case, first ask to see a supervisor. If the problem isn't resolved, write to the appropriate authorities, beginning with the port director at your point of entry.

IN AUSTRALIA

Australian residents who are 18 or older may bring home A$900 worth of souvenirs and gifts (including jewelry), 250 cigarettes or 250 grams of cigars or other tobacco products, and 2.25 liters of alcohol (including wine, beer, and spirits). Residents under 18 may bring back A$450 worth of goods. If any of these individual allowances are exceeded, you must pay duty for the entire amount (of the group of products in which the allowance was exceeded). Members of the same family traveling together may pool their allowances. Prohibited items include meat products. Seeds, plants, and fruits need to be declared upon arrival.

🛂 **Australian Customs Service** ⌂ Customs House, 10 Cooks River Dr., Sydney International Airport, Sydney, NSW 2020 ☎ 02/6275-6666 or 1300/363263, 02/8334-7444 or 1800/020-504 quarantine-inquiry line 🖷 02/8339-6714 ⊕ www.customs.gov.au.

IN CANADA

Canadian residents who have been out of Canada for at least seven days may bring in C$750 worth of goods duty-free. If you've been away fewer than seven days but more than 48 hours, the duty-free allowance drops to C$200. If your trip lasts 24 to 48 hours, the allowance is C$50; if the goods are worth more than C$50, you must pay full duty on all of the goods. You may not pool allowances with family members. Goods claimed under the C$750 exemption may follow you by mail; those claimed under the lesser exemptions must accompany you. Alcohol and tobacco products may be included in the seven-day and 48-hour exemptions but not in the 24-hour exemption. If you meet the age requirements of the province or territory through which you reenter Canada, you may bring in, duty-free, 1.5 liters of wine *or* 1.14 liters (40 imperial ounces) of liquor *or* 24 12-ounce cans or bottles of beer or ale. Also, if you meet the local age requirement for tobacco products, you may bring in, duty-free, 200 cigarettes, 50 cigars or cigarillos, and 200 grams of tobacco. You may have to pay a minimum duty on tobacco products, regardless of whether or not you exceed your personal exemption. Check ahead of time with the Canada Border Services Agency or the Department of Agriculture for policies regarding meat products, seeds, plants, and fruits.

You may send an unlimited number of gifts (only one gift per recipient, however) worth up to C$60 each duty-free to Canada. Label the package UNSOLICITED GIFT—VALUE UNDER $60. Alcohol and tobacco are excluded.

🛄 **Canada Border Services Agency** ✉ Customs Information Services, 191 Laurier Ave. W, 15th fl., Ottawa, Ontario K1A 0L5 ☎ 800/461-9999 in Canada, 204/983-3500, 506/636-5064 ⊕ www.cbsa.gc.ca.

IN NEW ZEALAND

All homeward-bound residents may bring back NZ$700 worth of souvenirs and gifts; passengers may not pool their allowances, and children can claim only the concession on goods intended for their own use. For those 17 or older, the duty-free allowance also includes 4.5 liters of wine or beer; one 1,125-ml bottle of spirits; and either 200 cigarettes, 250 grams of tobacco, 50 cigars, *or* a combination of the three up to 250 grams. Meat products, seeds, plants, and fruits must be declared upon arrival to the Agricultural Services Department.

🛄 **New Zealand Customs** ✉ Head office: The Customhouse, 17–21 Whitmore St., Box 2218, Wellington ☎ 04/473-6099 or 0800/428-786 ⊕ www.customs.govt.nz.

IN RUSSIA

Upon arrival in Russia, you first pass through passport control, where a border guard will carefully examine your passport and visa, and retain one sheet of your Russian visa. You can speed your transit through passport control by bringing along a photocopy of your visa and handing this, along with the original, to the border guard.

It's of great importance that you fill out a migration card and get it stamped while passing though passport control. These white cards are automatically issued on some flights, but not all. It's possible to enter the country without one, but lack of a card can cause all manner of headaches, from hotel registration problems to document checks by police. If you're not given a card, ask for one (*migratsionnaya karta* for one, *migratsionnye karty* for several) or look for them on stands in the arrivals hall.

If you haven't been given a customs form on the plane, look for the forms on a table or stand at customs after retrieving your luggage. You must keep it until your departure, when you'll be asked to present it again (along with a second, identical form noting any changes). You may import free of duty and without special license any articles intended for personal use, including clothing, food, tobacco, and cigarettes, alcoholic drinks, perfume, sports equipment, and camera equipment. One video camera and one laptop computer per person are allowed. Importing weapons and ammunition, as well as opium, hashish, and pipes for smoking them, is prohibited. The punishment for carrying illegal substances is severe. You should write down on the customs form the exact amount of currency you're carrying (in cash as well as traveler's checks); you may enter the country with any amount of money, but **you cannot leave the country with more money than you had when you entered.** You should also include on your customs form any jewelry (particularly silver, gold, and amber) as well as any electronic goods (cameras, personal tape recorders, computers, etc.) you have. It's important to **include any valuable items on the customs form** to ensure that you'll be allowed to export them, but be aware that you're expected to take them with you, so you cannot leave them behind as gifts. (If an item included on your customs form is stolen, you should obtain a police report to avoid being questioned upon departure.) Technically you're allowed to bring into the country up to $2,000 of consumer items for personal use and gifts. But customs agents at the airport have been enforcing this rule sporadically at best, and will not likely challenge you on this front unless you have an excessive amount of luggage.

IN THE U.K.

From countries outside the European Union, including Russia, you may bring home, duty-free, 200 cigarettes, 50 cigars, 100 cigarillos, or 250 grams of tobacco; 1 liter of spirits or 2 liters of fortified or sparkling wine or liqueurs; 2 liters of still table wine; 60 ml of perfume; 250 ml of toilet water; plus £145 worth of other goods, including gifts and souvenirs. Prohibited items include meat and dairy products, seeds, plants, and fruits.

⚡ HM Customs and Excise ✉ Portcullis House, 21 Cowbridge Rd. E, Cardiff CF11 9SS ☎ 0845/010-9000 or 0208/929-0152 advice service, 0208/929-6731 or 0208/910-3602 complaints ⊕ www.hmce.gov.uk.

IN THE U.S.

U.S. residents who have been out of the country for at least 48 hours may bring home, for personal use, $800 worth of foreign goods duty-free, as long as they haven't used the $800 allowance or any part of it in the past 30 days. This exemption may include 1 liter of alcohol (for travelers 21 and older), 200 cigarettes, and 100 non-Cuban cigars. Family members from the same household who are traveling together may pool their $800 personal exemptions. For fewer than 48 hours, the duty-free allowance drops to $200, which may include 50 cigarettes, 10 non-Cuban cigars, and 150 ml of alcohol (or 150 ml of perfume containing alcohol). The $200 allowance cannot be combined with other individuals' exemptions, and if you exceed it, the full value of all the goods will be taxed. Antiques, which U.S. Customs and Border Protection defines as objects more than 100 years old, enter duty-free, as do original works of art done entirely by hand, including paintings, drawings, and sculptures. This doesn't apply to folk art or handicrafts, which are in general dutiable.

You may also send packages home duty-free, with a limit of one parcel per addressee per day (except alcohol or tobacco products or perfume worth more than $5). You may mail up to $200 worth of goods for personal use; label the package PERSONAL USE and attach a list of its contents and their retail value. If the package contains your used personal belongings, mark it AMERICAN GOODS RETURNED to avoid paying duties. You may send up to $100 worth of goods as a gift; mark the package UNSOLICITED GIFT. Mailed items do not affect your duty-free allowance on your return.

To avoid paying duty on foreign-made high-ticket items you already own and will take on your trip, register them with a local customs office before you leave the country. Consider filing a Certificate of Registration for laptops, cameras, watches, and other digital devices identified with serial numbers or other permanent markings; you can keep the certificate for other trips. Otherwise, bring a sales receipt or insurance form to show that you owned the item before you left the United States.

For more about duties, restricted items, and other information about international travel, check out U.S. Customs and Border Protection's online brochure, *Know Before You Go*. You can also file complaints on the U.S. Customs and Border Protection Web site, listed below.

⚡ U.S. Customs and Border Protection ✉ For inquiries and complaints, 1300 Pennsylvania Ave. NW, Washington, DC 20229 ⊕ www.cbp.gov ☎ 877/227-5551 or 202/354-1000.

DISABILITIES & ACCESSIBILITY

In Russia, provisions for travelers with disabilities are extremely limited. Some of the new, foreign-built hotels have rooms that can accommodate people who use wheelchairs, but beyond that, special facilities at public buildings are rare. Public transportation is especially difficult to use. Given cobblestone streets and the fact that most wheelchair users must be carried up and down steps, a folding, narrow chair with push handles and tubeless tires is preferable to a power wheelchair.

RESERVATIONS

When discussing accessibility with an operator or reservations agent, ask hard questions. Are there any stairs, inside *or* out? Are there grab bars next to the toilet *and* in the shower/tub? How wide is the doorway to the room? To the bathroom? For the most extensive facilities meeting the latest legal specifications, opt for newer accommodations. If you reserve through a toll-free number, consider also calling the hotel's local number to confirm the information from the central reservations office. Get confirmation in writing when you can.

TRANSPORTATION

The U.S. Department of Transportation Aviation Consumer Protection Division's online publication *New Horizons: Information for the Air Traveler with a Disability* offers advice for travelers with a disability, and outlines basic rights. Visit DisabilityInfo.gov for general information.

⚑ Information & Complaints Aviation Consumer Protection Division (⇨ Air Travel) for airline-related problems; ⊕ airconsumer.ost.dot.gov/publications/horizons.htm for airline travel advice and rights. **Departmental Office of Civil Rights** ✉ For general inquiries, U.S. Department of Transportation, S-30, 400 7th St. SW, Room 10215, Washington, DC 20590 ☎ 202/366–4648, 202/366–8538 TTY 🖷 202/366–9371 ⊕ www.dotcr.ost.dot.gov. **Disability Rights Section** ✉ NYAV, U.S. Department of Justice, Civil Rights Division, 950 Pennsylvania Ave. NW, Washington, DC 20530 🖷 ADA information line 202/514–0301, 800/514–0301, 202/514–0383 TTY, 800/514–0383 TTY ⊕ www.ada.gov. **U.S. Department of Transportation Hotline** 🖷 For disability-related air-travel problems, 800/778–4838 or 800/455–9880 TTY.

TRAVEL AGENCIES

In the United States, the Americans with Disabilities Act requires that travel firms serve the needs of all travelers. Some agencies specialize in working with people with disabilities. Liberty Tours Ltd. is a St. Petersburg company that arranges airport transfers, tours, and dinners for travelers with disabilities. Tours range from city highlights to particular churches and museums.

⚑ Local Agency Liberty Tours Ltd. ✉ St. Petersburg ⊕ www.libertytour.ru ✎ info@libertytour.ru. **⚑ Travelers with Mobility Problems Access Adventures/B. Roberts Travel** ✉ 1876 East Ave., Rochester, NY 14610 ☎ 800/444–6540 ⊕ www.brobertstravel.com, run by a former physical-rehabilitation counselor. **CareVacations** ✉ No. 5, 5110–50 Ave., Leduc, Alberta, Canada T9E 6V4 ☎ 780/986–6404 or 877/478–7827 🖷 780/986–8332 ⊕ www.carevacations.com, for group tours and cruise vacations. **Flying Wheels Travel** ✉ 143 W. Bridge St., Box 382, Owatonna, MN 55060 ☎ 507/451–5005 🖷 507/451–1685 ⊕ www.flyingwheelstravel.com.

DISCOUNTS & DEALS

CREDIT-CARD BENEFITS

When you use your credit card to make travel purchases you may get free travel-accident insurance, collision-damage insur-ance, and medical or legal assistance, depending on the card and the bank that issued it. American Express, MasterCard, and Visa provide one or more of these services, so get a copy of your credit card's travel-benefits policy. If you're a member of an auto club, always ask hotel and car-rental reservations agents about auto-club discounts. Some clubs offer additional discounts on tours, cruises, and admission to attractions.

DISCOUNT RESERVATIONS

To save money, look into discount reservations services with Web sites and toll-free numbers, which use their buying power to get a better price on hotels, airline tickets (⇨ Air Travel), even car rentals. When booking a room, always **call the hotel's local toll-free number** (if one is available) rather than the central reservations number—you'll often get a better price. Always ask about special packages or corporate rates.

When shopping for the best deal on hotels and car rentals, look for guaranteed exchange rates, which protect you against a falling dollar. With your rate locked in, you won't pay more, even if the price goes up in the local currency.

⚑ Hotel Rooms Accommodations Express ☎ 800/444–7666 or 800/277–1064. **Hotels.com** ☎ 800/219–4606 or 800/364–0291 ⊕ www.hotels.com. **Steigenberger Reservation Service** ☎ 800/223–5652 ⊕ www.srs-worldhotels.com. **Turbotrip.com** ☎ 800/473–7829 ⊕ w3.turbotrip.com.

PACKAGE DEALS

Don't confuse packages and guided tours. When you buy a package, you travel on your own, just as though you had planned the trip yourself. Fly–drive packages, which combine airfare and car rental, are often a good deal. In cities, ask the local visitor's bureau about hotel and local transportation packages that include tickets to major museum exhibits or other special events.

EATING & DRINKING

The restaurants we list are the cream of the crop in each price category. Properties indicated by ✕⊞ are lodging establishments whose restaurant warrants a special trip.

If you're traveling on an organized tour, you can expect your hotel meals to be hearty and ample but far from deluxe (except, of course, in finer hotels). Moscow and St. Petersburg have been enjoying a restaurant boom in the past few years and the dining-out options have expanded enormously (be sure to reserve ahead for more upscale restaurants, particularly on the weekends). Be prepared to set aside an entire evening for your restaurant meal; Russians consider dining out to be a form of entertainment, and table turnover is virtually an unknown concept in more traditional restaurants.

CUTTING COSTS

Getting a cheap, quick snack on the go is easy to do in both cities. Yolki Palki is a good budget-priced Russian chain. Taras Bulba Korchma is a good, affordable Ukrainian chain. There are also many TGI Friday's outlets. Il Patio is the most widespread Italian chain.

MEALS & SPECIALTIES

At traditional Russian restaurants, the main meal of the day is served in midafternoon and consists of a starter, soup, and a main course. Russian soups are excellent, including borscht, *shchi* (cabbage soup), and *solyanka,* a spicy, thick stew made with vegetables and meat or fish. Delicious and filling main courses include Siberian *pelmeni* (tender dumplings, usually filled with minced pork and beef, and sometimes also lamb) or beef Stroganoff. If you're looking for Russian delicacies, try the excellent smoked salmon, blini with caviar, or the famous *kotlety po-Kievski* (chicken Kiev), a garlic-and-butter-filled chicken breast encased in a crispy crust. Consider ordering a shot of vodka, a glass of local beer, or a bottle of Georgian wine to accompany your meal.

MEALTIMES

Restaurants are typically open from noon until midnight, and late at night many nightclubs serve good food. There are also several 24-hour restaurants in both cities. During the week, many restaurants are nearly empty, but there's no hard and fast rule for this—an ordinary Wednesday can find even an off-the-beaten-path eatery

packed. Unless otherwise noted, the restaurants listed in this guide are open daily for lunch and dinner.

PAYING

Many restaurants list their prices in "conditional units" (*YE* in Cyrillic), which are pegged to an exchange rate of their own devising (usually the dollar or euro). Even when prices are listed in conditional units, cash payment is only accepted in rubles. Many restaurants accept credit cards, though you should always double-check with the staff, even if the restaurant has a sign indicating it accepts cards.

RESERVATIONS & DRESS

It's best to reserve ahead for Saturday-evening dining, whether you are planning a quick Chinese meal or a gourmet splash. In general, reservations are always a good idea; we mention them only when they're essential or not accepted. Book as far ahead as you can, and reconfirm as soon as you arrive. (Large parties should always call ahead to check the reservations policy.) We mention dress only when men are required to wear a jacket or a jacket and tie.

WINE, BEER & SPIRITS

Drinks are normally ordered by milliliter (50, 100, or 200) or by the bottle. An average bottle holds about three-quarters of a liter. In upscale establishments you'll often find an impressive wine list with imported wine and foreign liquors. Most hotel restaurants and smaller restaurants have some imported wines, as well as cheaper wines from Moldova, Georgia, and Eastern Europe. Georgian wines can be excellent—as a rule of thumb, go for the more expensive brands costing around $10 to $20 in shops, though the markup in restaurants can double or triple that. Even the less-expensive restaurants can serve a bewildering array of vodkas and other spirits. Make any alcohol purchases from a proper shop, as wine and spirits counterfeiting is a problem. The beverage that has really taken off in Russia in the past few years, however, is beer. Perhaps the most famous national brand is Baltika, which produces numbered beers—0 being the lightest, and 9 being difficult to distinguish from rocket fuel. But there are dozens of other companies producing ales, lagers, porters, and flavored and unfiltered beers, making it a drink that's become almost as ubiquitous as vodka. Note that public intoxication is strictly punished. It's okay to become inebriated within an establishment as long as you don't fall over or become aggressive. However, if you walk along the streets in a drunken state, you'll be a target for police document checks and could possibly be arrested for public drunkeness.

ELECTRICITY

To use electric-powered equipment purchased in the U.S. or Canada, **bring a converter and adapter.** The electrical current in Russia is 220 volts, 50 cycles alternating current (AC); wall outlets take Continental-type plugs, with two round prongs.

If your appliances are dual-voltage, you'll need only an adapter. Don't use 110-volt outlets marked FOR SHAVERS ONLY for high-wattage appliances such as blow-dryers. Most laptops operate equally well on 110 and 220 volts and so require only an adapter.

EMBASSIES & CONSULATES

See Embassies *under* Moscow A to Z *in* Chapter 1 *and* Consulates *under* St. Petersburg A to Z *in* Chapter 3.

EMERGENCIES

See Emergencies *under* Moscow A to Z *in* Chapter 1 *and* St. Petersburg A to Z *in* Chapter 3.

🚑 **Emergency Services** Ambulance ☎ 03. Fire ☎ 01. Police ☎ 02.

ENGLISH-LANGUAGE MEDIA

In many hotels and the few English-language bookstores, you can pick up Western newspapers and local English-language publications, including full-fledged newspapers, lifestyle journals, and magazines. These are often an excellent source of information on cultural events, and they can give you a good feel for Russian politics and business and the expatriate community.

BOOKS

English-language books are for the most part relegated to a few specialized book-

stores, such as Anglia, which has stores in both Moscow and St. Petersburg. Although the selection is not bad, the books tend to be much more expensive than they would be in English-speaking countries (⇨ English-Language Media *under* Moscow A to Z *in* Chapter 1 *and* St. Petersburg A to Z *in* Chapter 3.)

NEWSPAPERS & MAGAZINES

The main English-language newspaper in Russia is the *Moscow Times* (⊕ www. themoscowtimes.com), published five times a week, covering mostly news and business, with a guide to cultural events and nightlife as well.

In St. Petersburg the main source of news is the *St. Petersburg Times* (⊕ www. sptimes.ru), a sister paper to the *Moscow Times* published every Tuesday and Friday. Besides covering local news and business, the Friday issue also features an arts section with a preview of events during the upcoming week. *Pulse* is a monthly journal that publishes separate Russian and English editions and focuses mainly on the world of entertainment.

In addition to these papers, there are many publications, widely available in restaurants and hotels, that claim to be home-grown tourist or cultural guides to Moscow and St. Petersburg. The major problem is that they were originally written in Russian and their translations are for the most part incomprehensible. Their only value is that they may be able to give you some accurate addresses or phone numbers (or even hours of entertainment if you happen to be a philologist or professional translator).

ETIQUETTE & BEHAVIOR

In general, there's no such thing as being overdressed in Russia. Travelers who dress as if they're about to go camping stand out like a sore thumb. Bring some nice, urban, dressy clothes. Shoes are particularly important and must be kept clean, even when the weather conditions make this difficult. Women are expected to look feminine.

Russia is far stricter about enforcing dress codes at religious sites than are most similar places in Europe. Men are expected to

remove their hats, and women are required to wear below-knee-length skirts or
slacks (*never* shorts, even walking shorts)
and bring something to cover their heads.
Note that it's considered disrespectful to
put your hands inside your pockets when
visiting an Orthodox church.

If you're invited to a home, be ready to remove your shoes and put on some of the
household's communal slippers.

If you meet any Russians socially, chances
are they'll give you something; Russians
tend to give small gifts even on short acquaintance. You may want to be prepared
to reciprocate with souvenirs from your
hometown or state, such as postcards,
pens, or decorative pins. One of the great
taboos, however, is to present someone
with a gift, shake hands, or kiss across the
threshold or doorway. Wait until you're
inside.

BUSINESS ETIQUETTE

Gift-giving is also the norm in business relations—as is drinking. Personal trust and
personal relations are more important in
Russian business than in the West, so businesspeople should be willing to take part
in any sorts of bonding sessions, from
vodka drinking to visiting the *banya,* or
Russian-style sauna. That said, vodka-
drinking sessions with strangers should be
avoided, especially on trains.

DRINKING ETIQUETTE

At a dinner, usually a carafe or bottle of
vodka will be ordered for the whole table
and shots will be gulped down whole (not
sipped) after repeated toasts throughout
the meal. Shots will usually be poured for
women even if they don't want any. Although it's quite acceptable for a woman
to not drink vodka and to have wine or
champagne instead, men are obliged. It's
not good form to drink vodka without
food. There are particular sorts of food
that are ideal with vodka, notably pickles,
which are really obligatory for any vodka-
drinking session. Lightly salted herrings
with potatoes and onions is another good
choice. The correct way to drink vodka is

to inhale, drink the whole shot, then exhale and bite a salted pickle as a chaser.

GAY & LESBIAN TRAVEL

One carryover from the Soviet era—when
homosexuality was officially banned and
punishable with one to five years in
prison—is that there's little social and cultural acceptance of gay people in Russia
today. Being gay is still widely seen as a
mental deviation in Russia, and the older
generation in particular is likely to look at
a gay person with an unpleasant mixture
of compassion and contempt. Attitudes are
slowly changing among young urbanites
and there are just a few openly gay service
providers or establishments. Your best bet
is to contact some of the international organizations below for the latest news and
information. One good resource is
⊕ www.gay.ru, with English-language information on the gay scene in Moscow
and St. Petersburg.

🇫 Gay- & Lesbian-Friendly Travel Agencies Different Roads Travel ✉ 155 Palm Colony, Palm
Springs, CA 92264 ☎ 310/289-6000 or 800/429-
8747 🖷 310/855-0323 ✎ lgernert@tzell.com.
Skylink Travel and Tour/Flying Dutchmen Travel
✉ 1455 N. Dutton Ave., Suite A, Santa Rosa, CA
95401 ☎ 707/546-9888 or 800/225-5759 🖷 707/
636-0951; serving lesbian travelers.

HEALTH

A visit to Russia poses no special health
risk, but the country's medical system is
far below world standards, a fact you
should consider if you have chronic medical conditions that may require treatment
during your visit. There are, however,
Western-style clinics in Moscow and St.
Petersburg (⇨ Emergencies *under*
Moscow A to Z *in* Chapter 1 *and* St. Petersburg A to Z *in* Chapter 3). Still, you
may want to purchase traveler's health insurance, which would cover medical evacuation. Sometimes even minor conditions
cannot be treated adequately because of
the severe and chronic shortage of basic
medicines and medical equipment. Tuber-
culosis is a serious problem in Russian

prisons, but the short-term visitor to Russia needn't worry about infection.

FOOD & DRINK

You should **drink only boiled or bottled water.** The water supply in St. Petersburg is thought to contain an intestinal parasite called Giardia lamblia, which causes diarrhea, stomach cramps, and nausea. The gestation period is two to three weeks, so symptoms usually develop after an infected traveler has already returned home. The condition is easily treatable, but be sure to let your doctor know that you may have been exposed to this parasite. Avoid ice cubes and use bottled water to brush your teeth. In Moscow and St. Petersburg, imported, bottled water is widely available in shops. It's a good idea to buy a liter of this water whenever you can. Hotel floor attendants always have a samovar in their offices and will provide boiled water if asked. Many top-end hotels filter their water, but it's best to double-check with reception. Mild cases of traveler's diarrhea may respond to Imodium (known generically as loperamide) or Pepto-Bismol, both of which can be purchased over the counter. Drink plenty of purified water or tea—chamomile is a good folk remedy. In severe cases, rehydrate yourself with a saltsugar solution—½ teaspoon salt and 4 tablespoons sugar per quart of water.

Fruits and vegetables served in restaurants are generally washed with purified water and are thus safe to eat. However, food poisoning is common in Russia, so be wary of dairy products and ice cream that may not be fresh. The pierogi (meat- and cabbage-filled pies) sold everywhere on the streets are cheap and tasty, but they can give you a nasty stomachache.

MEDICAL PLANS

No one plans to get sick while traveling, but it happens, so consider signing up with a medical-assistance company. Members get doctor referrals, emergency evacuation or repatriation, hotlines for medical consultation, cash for emergencies, and other assistance.

🚩 **Medical-Assistance Companies International SOS Assistance** ⊕ www.internationalsos.com

⊠ 3600 Horizon Blvd., Suite 300, Trevose, PA 19053 ☎ 215/942-8000 or 800/523-6586 🖷 215/354-2338 ⊠ Landmark House, Hammersmith Bridge Rd., 6th fl., London, W6 9DP ☎ 20/8762-8008 🖷 20/8748-7744 ⊠ 12 Chemin Riantbosson, 1217 Meyrin 1, Geneva, Switzerland ☎ 22/785-6464 🖷 22/785-6424 ⊠ 331 N. Bridge Rd., 17-00, Odeon Towers, Singapore 188720 ☎ 6338-7800 🖷 6338-7611.

OVER-THE-COUNTER REMEDIES

Just about everything is available in pharmacies without a prescription, and many pharmacies stock Western painkillers and cold medicines, which mostly come from Germany and France. If you can't find your favorite brand, just ask for either aspirin or Panadol, which is the equivalent of Tylenol or Advil. However, there's a good chance of buying a counterfeit medicine as well. According to official statistics, up to 30% of most popular drugs in Russian pharmacies are fake or made illegally with inadequate technology. Large chains—including PetroFarm, Natur Produkt, Pharmacy Doctor, and Pervaya Pomoshch—as well as the pharmacies of international clinics are believed to be free of such fakes and also stock Western brands.

SHOTS & MEDICATIONS

Foreigners traveling to Russia are often advised to get vaccinated against diphtheria—not so long ago, both Moscow and St. Petersburg had outbreaks of this disease, along with cases of cholera. These outbreaks are now rare, but in particular, children should be immunized against diphtheria, measles, mumps, rubella, and polio, as well as hepatitis A and typhus. A flu shot is also recommended for winter travel for people of all ages.

🚩 **Health Warnings National Centers for Disease Control and Prevention** (CDC) ⊠ Office of Health Communication, National Center for Infectious Diseases, Division of Quarantine, Travelers' Health, 1600 Clifton Rd. NE, Atlanta, GA 30333 ☎ 877/394-8747 international travelers' health line, 800/311-3435 other inquiries, 404/498-1600 Division of Quarantine and international health information 🖷 888/232-3299 ⊕ www.cdc.gov/travel. **Travel Health Online** ⊕ tripprep.com. **World Health Organization** (WHO) ⊕ www.who.int.

HOLIDAYS

Below is a list of Russia's major holidays, most of which entail closures of many businesses; note that religious holidays like Christmas and Easter are celebrated according to the Russian Orthodox calendar. In addition, from May 1 through May 9 and from December 31 through January 13, the entire country shuts down. These are major holiday periods when absolutely nobody does anything: even clinics close. These weeks can pose a real problem for visitors, so try not to travel to Russia during these special holiday periods. Be aware that on the day before a public holiday, everything tends to close early.

January 1–5 (New Year's), January 7 (Christmas), February 23 (Defenders of the Fatherland Day), March 8 (International Women's Day), May 1 (Day of Spring and Labor), May 9 (Victory Day), June 12 (Independence Day), November 4 (Day of Reconciliation and Agreement).

INSURANCE

The most useful travel-insurance plan is a comprehensive policy that includes coverage for trip cancellation and interruption, default, trip delay, and medical expenses (with a waiver for preexisting conditions).

Without insurance you'll lose all or most of your money if you cancel your trip, regardless of the reason. Default insurance covers you if your tour operator, airline, or cruise line goes out of business—the chances of which have been increasing. Trip-delay covers expenses that arise because of bad weather or mechanical delays. Study the fine print when comparing policies.

If you're traveling internationally, a key component of travel insurance is coverage for medical bills incurred if you get sick on the road. Such expenses aren't generally covered by Medicare or private policies. U.K. residents can buy a travel-insurance policy valid for most vacations taken during the year in which it's purchased (but check preexisting-condition coverage). British and Australian citizens need extra medical coverage when traveling overseas.

Always **buy travel policies directly from the insurance company**; if you buy them from a cruise line, airline, or tour operator that goes out of business you probably won't be covered for the agency or operator's default, a major risk. Before making any purchase, review your existing health and home-owner's policies to find what they cover away from home.

🛈 **Travel Insurers** In the U.S.: **Access America** ✉ 2805 N. Parham Rd., Richmond, VA 23294 ☎ 800/729–6021 🖷 804/673–1469 or 800/346–9265 ⊕ www.accessamerica.com. **Travel Guard International** ✉ 1145 Clark St., Stevens Point, WI 54481 ☎ 800/826–4919 or 715/345–1041 🖷 800/955–8785 or 715/345–1990 ⊕ www.travelguard.com.
🛈 In the U.K.: **Association of British Insurers** ✉ 51 Gresham St., London EC2V 7HQ ☎ 020/7600–3333 🖷 020/7696–8999 ⊕ www.abi.org.uk. In Canada: **RBC Insurance** ✉ 6880 Financial Dr., Mississauga, Ontario L5N 7Y5 ☎ 800/565–3129 ⊕ www.rbcinsurance.com. In Australia: **Insurance Council of Australia** ✉ Level 3, 56 Pitt St. Sydney, NSW 2000 ☎ 02/9253–5100 🖷 02/9253–5111 ⊕ www.ica.com.au. In New Zealand: **Insurance Council of New Zealand** ✉ Level 7, 111–115 Customhouse Quay, Box 474, Wellington ☎ 04/472–5230 🖷 04/473–3011 ⊕ www.icnz.org.nz.

LANGUAGE

If you make an effort to learn the Russian (Cyrillic) alphabet, you'll be able to decipher many words; a rudimentary knowledge of the alphabet can help you to navigate the streets and subways on your own. You may want to learn a few basic words, but don't expect to become conversant overnight. Hotel staff almost always speak good English, and many of the restaurants and shops catering to foreigners often have English-speaking staff. Outside these places a good grasp of English is uncommon.

The following terms pop up in this book and may help you in your travels: *dom,* or house; *dvor,* or courtyard; *dvorets,* or palace; *khram,* or church; *monastyr,* or monastery or convent; *muzey,* or museum; *palata,* or palace; *passazh,* or arcade; *sobor,* or cathedral; *stantsiya,* or metro station; *teatr,* or theater; *tserkov,* or church; *vokzal,* or train/bus station; and *vorota,* or gateway.

Refer to the English-Russian Vocabulary section at the back of this book for helpful Russian phrases and words.

LODGING

Assume that hotels operate on the European Plan (EP, with no meals) unless we specify that they use the Continental Plan (CP, with a continental breakfast), Modified American Plan (MAP, with breakfast and dinner), or the Full American Plan (FAP, with all meals).

The lodgings we list are the cream of the crop in each price category. We always list the facilities that are available, but we don't specify whether they cost extra; when pricing accommodations, always ask what's included and what costs extra. Properties are assigned price categories based on the range between their least and most expensive standard double rooms at high season (excluding holidays). Unless otherwise indicated, assume that the hotels listed operate on the European Plan (without meals). Properties marked ✕☑ are lodging establishments whose restaurants warrant a special trip.

In most instances you can book reservations (and request visa support for your Russian visa) directly with the hotel, but you may encounter problems. In addition to the language barrier, placing a call to Russia can be time-consuming. International telephone lines are occasionally overloaded, and once you get through, you may find that no one answers the phone. To save time and avoid language problems, book your hotel through a travel agent or sign on for an organized tour.

APARTMENT RENTALS

If you want a home base that's roomy enough for a family and comes with cooking facilities, consider a furnished rental. These can save you money, especially if you're traveling with a group. Home-exchange directories sometimes list rentals as well as exchanges.

🛈 **International Agents Hideaways International** ✉ 767 Islington St., Portsmouth, NH 03801 ☎ 603/430-4433 or 800/843-4433 🖷 603/430-4444 ⊕ www.hideaways.com, annual membership $185.

HOSTELS

No matter what your age, you can save on lodging costs by staying at hostels. In some 4,500 locations in more than 70 countries around the world, Hostelling International (HI), the umbrella group for a number of national youth-hostel associations, offers single-sex, dorm-style beds and, at many hostels, rooms for couples and family accommodations. Membership in any HI national hostel association, open to travelers of all ages, allows you to stay in HI-affiliated hostels at member rates; one-year membership is about $28 for adults in the United States (C$35 for a two-year minimum membership in Canada, £15.95 in the U.K., A$52 in Australia, and NZ$40 in New Zealand); hostels charge about $10–$30 per night. Members have priority if the hostel is full; they're also eligible for discounts around the world, even on rail and bus travel in some countries.

🛈 **Organizations Hostelling International–USA** ✉ 8401 Colesville Rd., Suite 600, Silver Spring, MD 20910 ☎ 301/495-1240 🖷 301/495-6697 ⊕ www.hiusa.org. **Hostelling International–Canada** ✉ 205 Catherine St., Suite 500, Ottawa, Ontario K2P 1C3 ☎ 613/237-7884 or 800/663-5777 🖷 613/237-7868 ⊕ www.hihostels.ca. **YHA England and Wales** ✉ Trevelyan House, Dimple Rd., Matlock, Derbyshire DE4 3YH, U.K. ☎ 0870/870-8808, 0870/770-8868, or 01629/592-600 🖷 0870/770-6127 ⊕ www.yha.org.uk. **YHA Australia** ✉ 422 Kent St., Sydney, NSW 2001 ☎ 02/9261-1111 🖷 02/9261-1969 ⊕ www.yha.com.au. **YHA New Zealand** ✉ Level 1, Moorhouse City, 166 Moorhouse Ave., Box 436, Christchurch ☎ 03/379-9970 or 0800/278-299 🖷 03/365-4476 ⊕ www.yha.org.nz.

HOTELS

The hotel scenes are slowly improving in Moscow and St. Petersburg, but they still fall short of what you'll find in major cities in Western Europe or North America. St. Petersburg in particular is short on quality hotels, although a number of small, independent hotels and bed-and-breakfasts have opened in recent years. Though service is also improving, in many cases it still leaves much to be desired. Cheaper hotels and hostels may not have hot water in summer. In general, hotels are overpriced for what you get, particularly in St. Petersburg.

All hotels listed have private bath unless otherwise noted.

Old-fashioned Soviet-style hotels have key attendants stationed on each floor. You are expected to relinquish your room key to this person every time you leave the hotel. Since only one key is given out for a double room, you may actually find this a convenient system. But the key attendant often leaves the key unattended (in an open box on the desk in front of the stairwell), so if you can coordinate your schedule with your roommate, you're better off "attending" to the key yourself. These attendants—usually stern-looking elderly women—can be quite friendly and helpful, however. They can provide extra blankets or help get a leaky faucet fixed. They almost always have a samovar in their offices and will provide hot water for tea or coffee.

RESERVING A ROOM

Here are some helpful terms and sentences you can use to request room reservations. The bracket spaces below are for filling in the date (note that the "s [_]" indicates the first night and the "po[_]" is for the last night).

For a room with a bath for two people: *Zdravstvuite, ya khochu zakazat' dvukhmestny nomer s vannoi v Vashei gostinitse s [_], 2007 po [_], 2007. S yvazheniem,* Name here.

On a high floor with a view: *Zdravstvuite, ya khochu zakazat' dvukhmestny nomer na vysokom etazhs khoroshim vidom goroda v Vashei gostinitse s [_], 2007 po [ ], 2007. S yvazheniem,* Name here.

A quiet room: *Zdravstvuite, mne khotelos by zakazat dvukhmestny nomer v spokoinom meste v Vashei gostinitse s [_], 2007 po [_], 2007. S yvazheniem.* Name here.

If you would like to reserve a room for one person instead of two, simply replace the word "dvukhmestny" with "odnomestny" in any of the above letters. A renovated room is "yevrostandart" or "eurostandard."

Important terms to keep in mind are: *konditsioner* (air-conditioning), *lichnaya vannaya* or *vannaya v nomere* (private bath), *vannaya* (tub, but also means bathroom), *dush* (shower), *dvukhmestnye krovati* (double beds), *odnomestnye krovati* (twin beds), *otdelno* (separate), *vmeste* (pushed

together), *ochen' bolshaya krovat'* (queen or king bed).

F **Toll-Free Numbers** Best Western ☎ 800/528-1234 ⊕ www.bestwestern.com. Choice ☎ 800/424-6423 ⊕ www.choicehotels.com. Holiday Inn ☎ 800/465-4329 ⊕ www.ichotelsgroup.com. Marriott ☎ 800/228-9290 ⊕ www.marriott.com. Le Meridien ☎ 800/543-4300 ⊕ www.lemeridien.com. Radisson ☎ 800/333-3333 ⊕ www.radisson.com. Renaissance Hotels & Resorts ☎ 800/468-3571 ⊕ www.marriott.com. Sheraton ☎ 800/325-3535 ⊕ www.starwood.com/sheraton.

MAIL & SHIPPING

The postal system in all parts of Russia is notoriously inefficient, and mail is often lost. Postcards generally have a better chance of reaching their destination than letters. The best option for mail is to go to a branch of WestPost, which whisks mail off to Finland and sends it from there, guaranteeing you European service. There are also DHL and Federal Express offices in Moscow and St. Petersburg.

You can buy international envelopes and postcards at post offices and in hotel-lobby kiosks.

F WestPost ☎ 495/234-9038 ⊕ www.westpost.ru.

POSTAL RATES

Sending mail from Russia to the United States, Europe, or Australia costs 16.50R for a postcard and 20.40R for a letter.

RECEIVING MAIL

Mail from outside Russia takes approximately four weeks to arrive, sometimes longer, and sometimes it never arrives at all. If you absolutely must receive something from home during your trip, consider using an express-mail service, such as DHL or Federal Express.

MONEY MATTERS

Today the ruble is reasonably stable at around 29 to the dollar. Talk of a renascent middle class aside, the majority of Russians can only dream of buying Western-made cars and clothes, dining out, and traveling abroad for their holidays.

Goods and services aimed at foreigners are as expensive as anywhere in Western Europe. A cup of coffee in a foreign-run hotel will cost $3–$5. There is, however, a growing number of bars and cafés that provide comfort and quality at a cost somewhere between these extremes. Public transport is cheap; a ride on the metro costs about 50¢. Taxi rates are generally low, but as soon as the driver realizes that you're a foreigner, the rate goes up. In general, it's best to deal only with taxis that have been ordered for you by the staff of your hotel. Some museums and theaters, such as the Armory Palace in the Kremlin and the Hermitage Museum in St. Petersburg, have instituted special, higher fees for foreign tourists, whereas tickets for Russians are incredibly inexpensive. For example, a "foreign ticket" for an opera or ballet at the Mariinsky (Kirov) Theater costs around $55, whereas a Russian can get a seat for a tenth of that, or even less. Expect to pay higher prices at any of the major cultural institutions—only foreigners who can prove they live in Russia can get "Russian" tickets.

Prices throughout this guide are given for adults. Substantially reduced fees are almost always available for children, students, and senior citizens. For information on taxes, *see* Taxes, *below*.

ATMS

Bankomaty (bank machines) have cropped up all over the place in Moscow and St. Petersburg, and in the city centers they are not difficult to find: hotels and banks are the most obvious (and safest) places to look, but there are some on the streets as well. In addition, many metro stations now have them—but have a partner watch your back when you take money out, and remember what kind of nimble-fingered people hang around such places. All ATMs have an English option, and some also have options for French and German. Each individual bank machine also clearly shows what cards (Plus, Cirrus, Visa, and such) it accepts. Some machines dispense dollars and euros as well as rubles. Some serve only their own customers. For use in Russia, your PIN must be four digits long.
🔢 **ATM Locations Cirrus** ☎ 800/424-7787. **Plus** ☎ 800/843-7587.

CREDIT & DEBIT CARDS

Many shops, restaurants, and hotels within Moscow and St. Petersburg accept credit cards (American Express, Diners Club, MasterCard, and Visa), though you should always double-check with the staff, despite any signs you may see. If you can use your credit card or a debit card, the benefits are several. A credit card allows you to delay payment and gives you certain rights as a consumer (⇨ Consumer Protection). Establishments outside the cities are less likely to accept credit cards.

Throughout this guide, the following abbreviations are used: **AE**, American Express; **DC**, Diners Club; **MC**, MasterCard; and **V**, Visa.

To report lost or stolen credit cards, the U.S. Embassy in Russia advises that you can call your credit company collect through AT&T Direct. From Moscow, dial ☎ 755–5042; from St. Petersburg dial ☎ 325–5042.
🔢 **Reporting Lost Cards American Express** ☎ 800/327-2177, from outside the U.S. **Diners Club** ☎ 800/234-6377. **MasterCard** ☎ 800/307-7309. **Visa** ☎ 800/847-2911.

CURRENCY

The national currency in Russia is the ruble (R). There are paper notes of 10, 50, 100, 500, and 1000, and there are 1-, 2-, and 5-ruble coins. There are 100 kopeks in a ruble and there are coins for 1, 5, 10, and 50 kopeks.

On August 17, 1998, a Russian government debt freeze and payments crisis sent the ruble into a tailspin. As a result, the ruble finished the year at 27 to the dollar, further obliterating savings that had, out of habit, been stuffed under the mattress. Several major banks folded and their clients lost almost everything. The conversion rate has since crept up, hovering at around 28R to the dollar.

Russians and resident expats have gotten used to thinking in both rubles and dollars—that is, talking in rubles but mentally pegging prices to the dollar. This can create a certain amount of confusion for the tourist, so bear the following in mind. First, remember that payment, by law, can only be made in rubles or by credit card. Nonetheless, many stores, restaurants, travel agencies, and retailers list prices in dollars, or "conditional units" (*uslovnyE yedinitsy,* often marked on menus and price lists as *YE*), a euphemism for the dollar (or in some cases the euro). In this book prices are listed in rubles for sights and attractions, as this is the more common practice, particularly for museum entrance fees and concert tickets (though some museums and sights do list prices in conditional units). For hotels and restaurants, however, prices are listed in dollars because that's the going rate at which the prices are pegged. For hotels, bear in mind that the sum in rubles will be high, and seeing prices in dollars can spare you some heavy-duty math (it's not much fun converting 2,376R into dollars in your head).

CURRENCY EXCHANGE

At this writing (spring 2006) one U.S. dollar equaled 28 rubles; one euro equaled 33 rubles; one U.K. pound equaled 49 rubles; one Canadian dollar equaled 24 rubles; one Australian dollar equaled 21 rubles; and one New Zealand dollar equaled 19 rubles.

Rubles cannot be obtained at banks outside Russia, but if you somehow acquire them (through friends or acquaintances) it's legal to import or export them, although you'll need to declare them and you cannot bring out of Russia more money (however valuated) than you brought in. There's no limit, however, on the amount of foreign currency you may bring in with you. It's safest to carry your money in traveler's checks, but you should have at least $100 in cash (in 10s and 20s). If you don't mind the risk of theft or loss, bring more; you're bound to need it. For the most favorable rates, **change money through banks.** Although ATM transaction fees may be higher abroad than at home, ATM rates are excellent because they're based on wholesale rates offered only by major banks. You can also exchange foreign currency for rubles (and vice versa) at state-run exchange offices—where you'll get the worst rate—or at any of the numerous currency exchange booths (*obmen valyuty*). Try to bring newer bills with you to Russia, as older versions (as well as worn or torn foreign bills) are frequently rejected by exchange offices. On your way out of Russia you can change

excess rubles back into dollars at any bank or at the airport. For this you will need your passport.

TRAVELER'S CHECKS

It's safest to bring your money into the country in traveler's checks, which can be cashed at the state-run offices, at private banks, and at most major hotels within the cities (note that some exchange counters and many stores will not accept traveler's checks). If you're going to rural areas and small towns, convert your traveler's checks to rubles before you go. Lost or stolen checks can usually be replaced within 24 hours. To ensure a speedy refund, buy your own traveler's checks—don't let someone else pay for them: irregularities like this can cause delays. The person who bought the checks should make the call to request a refund.

PACKING

No matter what time of year you visit, bring a sweater. St. Petersburg especially can be unexpectedly cold in summer. A raincoat and fold-up umbrella are also musts. You'll probably be doing a lot of walking outdoors, so bring warm, comfortable clothing, and be sure to pack a pair of sturdy walking shoes.

Russians favor fashion over variety in their wardrobes, and it's perfectly acceptable to wear the same outfit several days in a row. Be sure to pack one outfit for dress-up occasions, such as theater events. Coat-check attendants at theaters and restaurants will scold you if you do not have a loop sewn into the back of your coat for hanging. The layer system works well in the unpredictable weather of fall and spring; wear a light coat with a sweater that you can put on and take off as the weather changes. In winter, bring heavy sweaters, warm boots, a wool hat, a scarf and mittens, and a heavy coat. Woolen tights or long underwear are essential during the coldest months. Russian central heating can be overly efficient, so again, use the layer system to avoid sweltering in an overheated building or train.

Russian pharmacies, supermarkets, and hotels all have reasonable stocks of the essential toiletries and personal hygiene products, but bring your own supplies of medicines and prescription drugs you take regularly. Although some well-known Western brands are easily available, you may not recognize the Russian equivalent of certain medicines. Consider whether you might want any of the difficult-to-find items: insect repellent (in summer and fall mosquitoes can be a serious problem), camera batteries, laxatives, antidiarrhea pills, travel-sickness medicine, and the like.

Toilet paper is plentiful in hotels but less so in public buildings, so **bring small packages of tissues** to carry around with you. If you're a stickler for cleanliness and you're staying in one of the older hotels, bring disinfectant spray for the bathroom. Premoistened cleansing tissues will also come in handy, especially if you're traveling by train. A small flashlight may also prove useful, particularly if visiting someone's apartment—stairwells are often dimly lit. Laundry facilities in hotels are unpredictable, so you'll probably end up washing some clothes by hand. Bring your own laundry detergent and a round sink stopper (not always provided in hotel rooms).

In your carry-on luggage, pack an extra pair of eyeglasses or contact lenses and enough of any medication you take to last a few days longer than the entire trip. You may also ask your doctor to write a spare prescription using the drug's generic name, as brand names may vary from country to country. In luggage to be checked, **never pack prescription drugs, valuables, or undeveloped film.** And don't forget to carry with you the addresses of offices that handle refunds of lost traveler's checks. Check *Fodor's How to Pack* (available at online retailers and bookstores everywhere) for more tips.

To avoid customs and security delays, carry medications in their original packaging. Don't pack any sharp objects in your carry-on luggage, including knives of any size or material, scissors, nail clippers, and corkscrews, or anything else that might arouse suspicion.

To avoid having your checked luggage chosen for hand inspection, don't cram bags full. The U.S. Transportation Security Administration suggests packing shoes on top and placing personal items you don't want touched in clear plastic bags.

CHECKING LUGGAGE

You're allowed to carry aboard one bag and one personal article, such as a purse or a laptop computer. Make sure what you carry on fits under your seat or in the overhead bin. Get to the gate early, so you can board as soon as possible, before the overhead bins fill up. Within Russia, the rules regulating carry-on luggage are strict but often disregarded. Checked luggage is frequently lost and/or pilfered, so **pack as much as you can in your carry-on, including all of your valuables,** for internal flights.

Baggage allowances vary by carrier, destination, and ticket class. On international flights, you're usually allowed to check two bags weighing up to 50 pounds (23 kilograms) each, although a few airlines allow checked bags of up to 88 pounds (40 kilograms) in first class. Some international carriers don't allow more than 66 pounds (30 kilograms) per bag in business class and 44 pounds (20 kilograms) in economy. If you're flying to or through the United Kingdom, your luggage cannot exceed 70 pounds (32 kilograms) per bag. On domestic flights, the limit is usually 50 to 70 pounds (23 to 32 kilograms) per bag. In general, carry-on bags shouldn't exceed 40 pounds (18 kilograms). Most airlines won't accept bags that weigh more than 100 pounds (45 kilograms) on domestic or international flights. Expect to pay a fee for baggage that exceeds weight limits. Check baggage restrictions with your carrier before you pack.

Airline liability for baggage is limited to $2,500 per person on flights within the United States. On international flights it amounts to $9.07 per pound or $20 per kilogram for checked baggage (roughly $540 per 50-pound bag), with a maximum of $634.90 per piece, and $400 per passenger for unchecked baggage. You can buy additional coverage at check-in for about $10 per $1,000 of coverage, but it often excludes a rather extensive list of items, shown on your airline ticket.

Before departure, itemize your bags' contents and their worth, and label the bags with your name, address, and phone number. (If you use your home address, cover it so potential thieves can't see it readily.) Include a label inside each bag and **pack a copy of your itinerary.** At check-in, make sure each bag is correctly tagged with the destination airport's three-letter code. Because some checked bags will be opened for hand inspection, the U.S. Transportation Security Administration recommends that you leave luggage unlocked or use the plastic locks offered at check-in. TSA screeners place an inspection notice inside searched bags, which are resealed with a special lock.

If your bag has been searched and contents are missing or damaged, file a claim with the TSA Consumer Response Center as soon as possible. If your bags arrive damaged or fail to arrive at all, file a written report with the airline before leaving the airport.

🛈 **Complaints** U.S. Transportation Security Administration Contact Center ☎ 866/289-9673 ⊕ www.tsa.gov.

PASSPORTS & VISAS

Within Russia you should carry your passport, visa, and migration card at all times. **Make two photocopies of the data page** of your passport (one for someone at home and another for you, carried separately from your passport). If you lose your passport, promptly call the nearest embassy or consulate and the local police.

U.S. passport applications for children under age 14 require consent from both parents or legal guardians; both parents must appear together to sign the application. If only one parent appears, he or she must submit a written statement from the other parent authorizing passport issuance for the child. A parent with sole authority must present evidence of it when applying; acceptable documentation includes the child's certified birth certificate listing only the applying parent, a court order specifically permitting this parent's travel with the child, or a death certificate for the nonapplying parent. Application forms and instructions are available on the Web

site of the U.S. State Department's Bureau of Consular Affairs (⊕ travel.state.gov).

ENTERING RUSSIA

U.S. citizens, even infants, need a valid passport to enter Russia for stays of any length, plus a visa. You'll need to submit the following items to the Russian Consulate at least 21 days before departure: a completed visa application, a copy of the signed page(s) of your passport, three photos, reference numbers from the hotels you'll be staying at (to prove that you have confirmed reservations) or a properly endorsed business invitation from a host organization, a self-addressed stamped envelope, and a $65 application fee. The fee is higher if you need a faster turnaround time ($75 for seven days, $105 for four business days, $145 for next-day service). Requirements vary slightly if you'll be staying as a guest in a private home or if you're traveling on business. Travel agencies have ways of getting around the advanced hotel reservations requirement, but usually you must pay for at least one night's accommodation. Go To Russia (⊕ www.gotorussia.net) is a useful resource for obtaining a visa.

Citizens of Australia, Canada, and the United Kingdom must also obtain a visa to enter Russia. The procedures are similar to those outlined above for American citizens.

🛈 **Russian Consulates General** Australia ✉ 7-9 Fullerton St., Woollahra, NSW 2025, Australia ☎ 2/9326-1188 or 2/9326-1866 ⊠ **Canada** ✉ 3685 ave. du Musée, Montréal, Québec, H3G 2E1, Canada ☎ 514/843-5901 ✉ **New Zealand** ✉ 57 Messines Rd., Karori, Wellington, New Zealand ☎ 4/476-6742 or 4/381-3101 ✉ **U.K** ✉ Kensington Palace Gardens 5, London W8, UK ☎ 0171/229-3215; £10 for a single-entry visa ✉ **U.S.** ✉ 9 E. 91st St., New York, NY 10128, United States ☎ 212/348-0926 or 800/634-4296 ⊕ www.ruscon.org.

PASSPORT OFFICES

The best time to apply for a passport or to renew is in fall and winter. Before any trip, check your passport's expiration date, and, if necessary, renew it as soon as possible.

🛈 **Australian Citizens** Passports Australia Australian Department of Foreign Affairs and Trade ☎ 131-232 ⊕ www.passports.gov.au.

Canadian Citizens Passport Office ✉ to mail in applications: Foreign Affairs Canada, Gatineau, Québec K1A 0G3 ☎ 800/567-6868 ⊕ www.ppt.gc.ca.
New Zealand Citizens New Zealand Passports Office ☎ 0800/22-5050 or 04/474-8100 ⊕ www.passports.govt.nz.
U.K. Citizens U.K. Passport Service ☎ 0870/521-0410 ⊕ www.passport.gov.uk.
U.S. Citizens National Passport Information Center ☎ 877/487-2778, 888/874-7793 TDD/TTY ⊕ travel.state.gov.

RESTROOMS

Public restrooms do exist, but they're mostly poorly marked and difficult to spot, and many are crumbling and not up to Western standards of hygiene. Your best bet, if you're unwilling or unable to buy a snack in a café or bar and avail yourself of its facilities, is to head for a mainline train station. If you do spot a restroom, have some small change ready, such as 1R, 2R, and 5R coins, to use for tips and convenience machines. It's also a good idea to carry a package of tissues with you into public restrooms.

SAFETY

Travel to Russia is fraught with many unusual challenges, plus the normal safety and security issues you would associate with travel to any large city. Terrorist acts such as bombings have occurred in large Russian cities. In late 2003 a small bomb exploded outside the National Hotel in Moscow, and a suicide bomber killed 39 people in a Moscow metro car in early 2004. Be alert for any unusual behavior or packages left unattended in public. Consult government-issued travel advisories (⇨ Visitor Information) before your trip.

Tourists are a common target for thieves in Moscow and St. Petersburg, so stay alert, particularly in places commonly frequented by visitors (outside hotels, for example, and at bars). Don't wear a money belt or a waist pack, both of which peg you as a tourist. Distribute your cash and any valuables (including your credit cards and passport) between a deep front pocket, an inside jacket or vest pocket, and a hidden money pouch. Do not reach for the money pouch once you're in public.

If you get in trouble, don't expect much help from the police, who are often maligned by natives as *bandity* (gangsters). If you do find yourself in any tricky situations with the police, show your passport and visa and be polite. Even when willing to help, it's rare that anyone in law enforcement speaks a word of any foreign language. Most likely, they won't be able to understand your complaint and may wave you off, suggesting you were drunk or careless. Beware that if you venture to outlying suburbs, the risk of being robbed or attacked by skinheads or hooligan gangs increases significantly.

LOCAL SCAMS

Never change money on the street; as with con artists everywhere, counterfeit money, sleights of hand, and the old folded-note trick are practiced by people standing outside official exchange offices. As well as avoiding taxis that already have occupants, **never allow your driver to stop to take an extra passenger after you have gotten in.** It's possible that this is indeed a random passerby; it's also possible that he is an accomplice of the driver who has been waiting around the corner. Unlike the driver, he has his hands free to cause whatever mischief the two have planned. This is particularly applicable to lone travelers seeking a ride from the airport who are clearly foreigners and loaded with luggage. If your driver attempts to take another fare, say "*nyet*" (no) and/or "*nye nado*" (literally "not necessary," meaning here "I'd rather not"). Better still, team up with a fellow lone traveler and split the fare. A new scam has appeared recently, known as the "turkey drop." Don't pick up money that you find lying on the ground or that you see somebody drop, because you're likely to become embroiled with scam artists in an awkward saga that ends up with you having to cover the difference between the amount allegedly lost and the amount found. Also, when using money-exchange booths, thoroughly check that you have received the full amount—sometimes bills can mysteriously get "stuck" to the least visible side of the exchange drawer.

Sadly, whereas police in the West are considered keepers of the peace, those in uniform do not enjoy this image in Russia. The reason is partly because of their habit of shaking people down to supplement their meager salaries. Foreigners make appetizing targets. **Carry your passport, migration card, and visa** at all times. Regardless of whether this is a legal requirement (the law is hazy on the subject), a crooked cop will use it as an excuse to demand a "fine." Pay special attention when leaving a nightclub—the cops know that these are hangouts for foreigners and have been known to lie in wait to extract "fines" for alleged drunken behavior. There's no sure way of avoiding this—other than not setting foot outside—and every expat has a story of finding himself or herself in the ridiculous situation of haggling with a cop over the size of the bribe to be handed over. In all situations, be polite, allow the police to search you if they require, and stay cool; physical resistance only leads to a spell in the cells until the police think you'll crumble and hand over your money. This is by no means the case with all Russian police, but it happens too frequently to be dismissed as the actions of a minority. One thing you can do is ask to see the policeman's identification, but this may only serve to irritate him—in any case, stories of criminals dressing up as cops to demand bribes are getting rarer.

WOMEN IN RUSSIA

Exercise the same precautions you would in any major city. It's best to stick with a companion if you're out at night. If you carry a purse, choose one with a zipper and a thick strap that you can drape across your body; adjust the length so that the purse sits in front of you at or above hip level. (Don't wear a money belt or a waist pack.) Store only enough money in the purse to cover casual spending. Distribute the rest of your cash and any valuables between deep front pockets, inside jacket or vest pockets, and a concealed money pouch.

SENIOR-CITIZEN TRAVEL

Russia is often a difficult place to travel for people of any age. For senior citizens who have any special medical needs, have reduced mobility, or are not able to handle the greater-than-average travel discomforts that still come with visiting Russia, this is not the ideal destination. Still, many senior citizens can and do travel to Russia and have enjoyable trips by and large—even if there are no age-related discounts for foreigners in the country.

To qualify for age-related discounts, mention your senior-citizen status up front when booking hotel reservations (not when checking out) and before you're seated in restaurants (not when paying the bill). Be sure to have identification on hand. When renting a car, ask about promotional car-rental discounts, which can be cheaper than senior-citizen rates.

🚺 **Educational Programs Elderhostel** ✉ 11 Ave. de Lafayette, Boston, MA 02111 ☎ 877/426–8056, 978/323–4141 international callers, 877/426–2167 TTY 🖷 877/426–2166 ⊕ www.elderhostel.org.

SHOPPING

It's illegal in Russia to accept payment in currency other than rubles. Most "nice" food and consumer goods stores, however, will accept credit cards, with payment being calculated at something close to that day's ruble exchange rate. (Be sure to check this rate, as stores often set very high rates; it may well be better to pay in cash rubles, acquired at a bank's more favorable rate.) Keep in mind that stores do not accept traveler's checks.

There are still some "old-style" Russian stores hanging on, particularly outside the big cities. They tend to be denoted by their primary products (milk, bread, lights, women's shoes) but often carry more than the name implies, including a spate of imported Western goods, such as soft drinks, liquor, and chewing gum. The main stumbling block for foreigners in these places is the arduous method of purchase; it's time-consuming and quite trying. First you look for the item you want to buy and note its price (often asking the sales assistant to wrap it up), then you go to the cashier and pay for it, indicating merely the price and department (*otdel*). Then, you take your receipt back to the sales assistant, who gives you your goods in exchange. If you do not speak Russian and want to avoid this type of shopping (once the only way things were done), stick to Western-style stores or to street purchases, where you can use the universal language of finger-pointing and cash paid directly to the vendor.

Russian-style service may be surlier than what you are accustomed to, also. A few words spoken in Russian and a composed countenance from you may soften the vendor, but in any case, don't take it personally. On the bright side, when you do encounter good manners, they are impeccable.

WATCH OUT

If you buy any artwork in Russia other than a standard souvenir, ask the shop to provide you with the necessary documentation to let you take it out of the country, which should be presented to customs on departure. (Art stores and antiques shops should be able to handle the paperwork.) Remember that anything more than 100 years old cannot be taken out of the country—art, books, sculptures, and other such items of this age are deemed "cultural valuables." You're also unlikely to be allowed to export items less than a century old if they are things such as original Shostakovich scores or Manevich paintings unless you have extremely good contacts within the Russian government.

Alcohol counterfeiting is a big problem in Russia, so be careful when purchasing vodka. Your best bet on price and safety is to buy at outlet shops of vodka distilleries or at supermarkets. Every bottle of vodka sold in Russia must bear a white excise stamp, glued over the cap, and those sold in Moscow must also bear a bar-code stamp.

STUDENT TRAVEL

A student ID may get you discounts at some museums and sights. To save money, look into deals available through student-oriented travel agencies.

🚩 **IDs & Services STA Travel** ✉ 10 Downing St., New York, NY 10014 ☎ 212/627-3111, 800/781-4040 24-hr service center in the U.S. ⊕ www.sta.com.

Travel Cuts ✉ 187 College St., Toronto, Ontario M5T 1P7, Canada ☎ 800/592-2887 in U.S., 416/979-2406, 888/359-2887 and 888/359-2887 in Canada 🖷 416/979-8167 ⊕ www.travelcuts.com.
🚩 **Student Tours Contiki Holidays** ✉ 801 E. Katella Ave., 3rd fl., Anaheim, CA 92805 ☎ 888/266-8454 🖷 714/935-2579 ⊕ www.contiki.com.

TAXES

Airport departure taxes are almost always included in the price of the airline ticket. Hotels charge a 18% value-added tax if you pay in cash or by credit card upon arrival; if you pay in advance, then you don't get charged these taxes (at least that's the general rule). Moscow hotels add an additional 1% tax to your bill.

VALUE-ADDED TAX

Russia currently has an 18% value-added tax (V.A.T.) charged on most everything and refundable on almost nothing (interestingly, the V.A.T. law specifically says the V.A.T. does not apply to exported goods, but there's simply no mechanism worked out for handling refunds at the airport, nor do stores have V.A.T. refund forms). Goods bought at duty-free shops in the airport are free of V.A.T.

TELEPHONES

Direct dialing is the only way to go. Russian phone numbers have 10 digits (including the area code). To use your North American cell phone in Russia, it must be tri or quad band. If it's an unlocked GSM cell phone, purchase a SIM card to install so that you'll be charged Russian rates for usage while there.

AREA & COUNTRY CODES

The country code for Russia is 7. The city code for Moscow is 495, for St. Petersburg 812. When dialing a Russian number from abroad, drop the initial 0 from the local area code.

The country code is 1 for the United States and Canada, 61 for Australia, 64 for New Zealand, and 44 for the United Kingdom.

DIRECTORY & OPERATOR ASSISTANCE

Throughout the country you can dial 09 for directory assistance. However, because directory workers and operators are underpaid, overworked, and speak only Russian, you probably have a better chance of getting telephone information from your hotel concierge or a friendly assistant at a business center.

INTERNATIONAL CALLS

Most hotels have satellite telephone booths where, for several dollars a minute, you can make an international call in a matter of seconds. If you want to economize, you can visit the main post or telegraph office and order a call for rubles (but you'll still pay about a dollar or two a minute). From your hotel room or from a private residence, you can dial direct. To place your call, dial 8, wait for the dial tone, then dial 10, then the country code (1 for the United States) followed by the number you're trying to reach. In the Western-managed hotels, rooms are usually equipped with international, direct-dial (via satellite) telephones, but beware that the rates are hefty.

If you want to save money, you can set up an international callback account in the United States before you go. These services can often save you as much as half off the rates of the big carriers. You simply dial a preestablished number in the United States from any phone in Moscow or St. Petersburg, let the call ring a few times, then hang up. In a few minutes, a computer calls you back and makes a connection, giving you a U.S. dial tone, from which you dial any number in the United States.

Callback Company Kallback ☎ 877/777-5242 ⊕ www.kallback.com.

LONG-DISTANCE CALLS

For long-distance calls within Russia, simply dial 8, wait for another dial tone, and then dial the rest of the number as listed.

LONG-DISTANCE SERVICES

AT&T, MCI, and Sprint access codes make calling long-distance relatively convenient, but you may find the local access number blocked in many hotel rooms. First ask the hotel operator to connect you. If the hotel operator balks, ask for an international operator, or dial the international operator yourself. One way to improve your odds of getting connected to

your long-distance carrier is to travel with more than one company's calling card (a hotel may block Sprint, for example, but not MCI). If all else fails, call from a pay phone. If you are traveling for a longer period of time, consider renting a cell-phone from a local company.

Some hotels have credit-card "swipe" telephones.

Access Codes AT&T Direct ☎ 8/755-5042 or 8/10800-497-7211 from Moscow to U.S., 325-5042 from St. Petersburg to U.S., 800/435-0812 for other areas. **MCI WorldPhone** ☎ 747-3320 or 747-3322 from Russia to U.S., 800/444-4141 for other areas. **Sprint International Access** ☎ 8/108-001-102011 from Russia to U.S., 800/877-4646 for other areas.

PHONE CARDS

Phone cards can be bought at any metro station. You stick the card in the pay phone (there's a picture showing you the right way) and wait for the dial tone. Then press 8 and wait for another dial tone, then dial the number. A number will flash up on the screen showing you how many units you have left; as you speak, units are subtracted from your total.

PUBLIC PHONES

Public phones are similar to those found in most other European countries. There are two types: card- and coin-operated. If the phone takes coins, just drop in some change and dial the number. In Russia, the longer you speak, the more you pay, so perhaps drop in a 5R coin just to be safe.

The old coin-operated telephones in Moscow and St. Petersburg that take plastic subway tokens (*zhetony*) have been replaced by phone cards, also available at subway stations as well as many kiosks. City centers have telephone centers handy for making all sorts of calls: in Moscow, try the Central Telegraph office at 7 Tverskaya ulitsa, and St. Petersburg has one located at 2 Bolshaya Morskaya ulitsa.

TIME

Russia is the largest country in the world and has 11 time zones. Moscow and St. Petersburg share one and are both 3 hours ahead of London, 8 hours ahead of New York City, 11 hours ahead of Los Angeles, and 6–8 hours behind Sydney, depending on daylight savings. Daylight Savings Time is in sync with the rest of the northern hemisphere.

TIPPING

Tipping is the norm in Russia. Cloakroom attendants, waiters, porters, and taxi drivers will all expect a tip, but tour guides, ushers, restroom attendants will not. Whether you should tip the bartender depends on the establishment. Add an extra 10% to 15% to a restaurant bill, and round up taxi fares. Some restaurants add a service charge to the bill automatically, so double-check before you leave a big tip. If you're paying by credit card, leave the tip in cash—the waiter is less likely to see it if you add it to the credit-card charge. Moreover, some restaurants actively refuse to allow tips being added on to the bill by credit card. The only places with bellhops who carry your bags are Moscow and St. Petersburg's five-star hotels; in such establishments, a 100R tip is a decent thank you.

TOURS & PACKAGES

Because everything is prearranged on a prepackaged tour or independent vacation, you spend less time planning—and often get it all at a good price.

Operators that handle several hundred thousand travelers per year can use their purchasing power to give you a good price. Their high volume may also indicate financial stability. But some small companies provide more personalized service; because they tend to specialize, they may also be more knowledgeable about a given area.

BOOKING WITH AN AGENT

Travel agents are excellent resources. But it's a good idea to collect brochures from several agencies, as some agents' suggestions may be influenced by relationships with tour and package firms that reward them for volume sales. If you have a special interest, find an agent with expertise in that area. The American Society of Travel Agents (ASTA) has a database of specialists worldwide; you can log on to the group's Web site to find one near you.

Make sure your travel agent knows the accommodations and other services of the place being recommended. Ask about the hotel's location, room size, beds, and whether it has a pool, room service, or programs for children, if you care about these. Has your agent been there in person or sent others whom you can contact?

Do some homework on your own, too: local tourism boards can provide information about lesser-known and small-niche operators, some of which may sell only direct.

BUYER BEWARE

Each year consumers are stranded or lose their money when tour operators—even large ones with excellent reputations—go out of business. So check out the operator. Ask several travel agents about its reputation, and try to **book with a company that has a consumer-protection program.** (Look for information in the company's brochure.) In the United States, members of the U.S. Tour Operators Association are required to set aside funds (up to $1 million) to help eligible customers cover payments and travel arrangements in the event that the company defaults. It's also a good idea to choose a company that participates in the American Society of Travel Agents' Tour Operator Program; ASTA will act as mediator in any disputes between you and your tour operator.

Remember that the more your package or tour includes, the better you can predict the ultimate cost of your vacation. Make sure you know exactly what is covered, and beware of hidden costs. Are taxes, tips, and transfers included? Entertainment and excursions? These can add up.

Tour-Operator Recommendations American Society of Travel Agents (⇨ Travel Agencies). CrossSphere–The Global Association for Packaged Travel ✉ 546 E. Main St., Lexington, KY 40508 ☎ 859/226-4444 or 800/682-8886 🖷 859/226-4414 ⊕ www.CrossSphere.com. United States Tour Operators Association (USTOA) ✉ 275 Madison Ave., Suite 2014, New York, NY 10016 ☎ 212/599-6599 🖷 212/599-6744 ⊕ www.ustoa.com.

GROUP TOURS

Among companies that sell tours to Moscow and St. Petersburg, the following are nationally known, have a proven reputation, and offer plenty of options. The classifications used below represent different price categories, and you'll probably encounter these terms when talking to a travel agent or tour operator. The key difference is usually in accommodations, which run from budget to better, and better-yet to best.

🎫 **Super-Deluxe Abercrombie & Kent** ✉ 1520 Kensington Rd., Suite 212, Oak Brook, IL 60523 ☎ 630/954–2944 or 800/554–7016 🖷 630/954–3324 ⊕ www.abercrombiekent.com. **Travcoa** ✉ Box 2630, 2350 S.E. Bristol St., Suite 310, Newport Beach, CA 92660 ☎ 946/476–2800 or 800/992–2003 🖷 946/476–2538 ⊕ www.travcoa.com.

🎫 **Deluxe Exeter International** ✉ 25 Davis Blvd., Tampa, FL 33606 ☎ 813/251–5355 or 800/633–1008 🖷 813/251–6685 ⊕ www.exeterinternational.com. **Globus** ✉ 5301 S. Federal Circle, Littleton, CO 80123-2980 ☎ 866/755–8581 🖷 303/347–2080 ⊕ www.globusandcosmos.com. **Maupintour** ✉ 10650 W. Charleston Blvd., Summerlin, NV 89135 ☎ 800/255–4266 🖷 702/260–3787 ⊕ www.maupintour.com.

🎫 **First-Class Brendan Tours** ✉ 21625 Prairie St., Chatsworth, CA 91311-5833 ☎ 818/428–6000 or 800/421–8446 🖷 818/772–6492 ⊕ www.brendantours.com. **General Tours** ✉ 53 Summer St., Keene, NH 03431 ☎ 603/357–5033 or 800/221–2216 🖷 603/357–4548 ⊕ www.generaltours.com. **Insight International Tours** ✉ 801 Katella Ave., Anaheim, CA 92805 ☎ 800/582–8380 🖷 714/935–2570 ⊕ www.insightvacations.com. **Intourist** ✉ 12 S. Dixie Hwy., Suite 201, Lake Worth, FL 33460 ☎ 561/585–5305 or 800/556–5305 🖷 561/582–1353 ⊕ www.intourist.com. **Isram World of Travel** ✉ 630 3rd Ave., New York NY 10017 ☎ 212/661–1193 or 800/223–7460 🖷 212/370–1477 ⊕ www.isram.com. **Mir Corporation** ✉ 85 S. Washington St., Suite 210, Seattle, WA 98104 ☎ 206/624–7289 or 800/424–7289 🖷 206/624–7360 ⊕ www.mircorp.com. **Norvista** (⇨ Deluxe). **Trafalgar Tours** ✉ 11 E. 26th St., New York, NY 10010 ☎ 800/854–0103 🖷 800/457–6644 ⊕ www.trafalgartours.com.

🎫 **Budget Cosmos** (⇨ Globus *in* Deluxe).

PACKAGES

Like group tours, independent vacation packages are available from major tour operators and airlines. The companies listed below offer vacation packages in a broad price range.

🎫 **Air-Hotel Abercrombie & Kent** (⇨ Group Tours). **Exeter International** (⇨ Group Tours).

General Tours (⇨ Group Tours). **Intourist** (⇨ Group Tours). **ITS Tours & Travel** ✉ 707 Texas Ave., Suite 101A, College Station, TX 77840 ☎ 979/764–0518 or 800/533–8688 🖷 979/693–9673. **Mir Corporation** (⇨ Group Tours).

THEME TRIPS

🎫 **Art Mir Corporation** (⇨ Group Tours).

🎫 **Home Stays American-International Homestays** ✆ Box 1754, Nederland, CO 80466 ☎ 303/258–3234 or 800/876–2048 🖷 303/258–3264 ⊕ www.aihtravel.com. **Host Family Association** ☎ 202/333–9343 🖷 812/275–1992 in St. Petersburg. **Mir Corporation** (⇨ Group Tours).

🎫 **Learning Earthwatch** ✉ 3 Clock Tower Pl., Suite 100, Maynard, MA 01754 ☎ 978/461–0081 or 800/776–0188 🖷 978/461–2332 ⊕ www.earthwatch.org, for research expeditions. **Smithsonian Journeys** ✉ Box 23293, Washington, DC 20026 ☎ 202/357–4700 or 800/338–8687 🖷 202/633–9250 ⊕ www.smithsonianjourneys.org.

🎫 **Music & Literature Dailey-Thorp Travel** ✉ Box 670, Big Horn, WY 82833 ☎ 307/673–1555 or 800/998–4677 🖷 307/674–7474 ⊕ www.daileythorp.com. **Mir Corporation** (⇨ Group Tours).

TRAIN TRAVEL

In Russia trains are the most reliable, convenient, and comfortable form of transportation. Remarkably, most trains leave exactly on time; there's a broadcast warning five minutes before departure, but no whistle or "all aboard!" call, so be careful not to be left behind.

There are numerous day and overnight trains between St. Petersburg and Moscow. The old favorite *Avrora* train makes the trip in just under six hours; the ER-200 trains are even faster at around 4 hours, 45 minutes. A new overnight service, the Grand, has showers in the compartments of the higher classes, and hand basins in lower classes, as well as satellite television and other luxuries.

Train travel in Russia offers an unrivaled opportunity to glimpse the quaint Russian countryside, which is dotted in places with colorful wooden cottages. If you're traveling by overnight train, set your alarm and get up an hour or so before arrival so that you can watch at close hand the workers going about their morning rounds in the rural areas just outside the cities.

To make your train trip more comfortable, be sure to **bring along bottled water,** both for drinking and brushing your teeth on longer journeys. Vendors run up and down train cars at and between stops, selling drinks and sandwiches. You may, however, want to bring a packed meal; most Russians do so, and your compartment mates may offer to share (beware of offers of vodka, however; poison bootleg vodka is a big problem in Russia). The communal bathrooms at both ends of each car are notoriously dirty, so bring premoistened cleansing tissues for washing up. Definitely pack toilet paper. Also be sure to pack a heavy sweater. The cars are often overheated and toasty warm, but sometimes they're not heated at all, so in winter it can get very cold.

Train travel to most major cities inside Russia is fairly painless, but you should stick to the usual precautions when it comes to security. The safest options are the day trains. If you're traveling alone on an overnight train, you should take extra security precautions. The doors to the compartments can be locked, but the locks can be picked, so you might consider bringing a bicycle chain or securing the door tightly shut with a strong leather belt. You may also want to buy out the entire compartment so as not to risk your luck with unknown compartment-mates. Conductors who find out you have done this will often insist this is not permissible, and threaten to put a cabin-mate in with you. Do not allow this. Show the tickets to all the berths, and be firm. To be on the safe side you should stow your luggage in the bin under the lower bunk, and you should sleep with your money, passport, and other important items.

For more information, *see* Train Travel *under* Moscow A to Z *in* Chapter 1 *and* St. Petersburg A to Z *in* Chapter 3.

CLASSES

Trains are divided into four classes. The highest class, "deluxe," is usually available only on trains traveling international routes. The deluxe class offers two-berth compartments with soft seats and private washrooms; the other classes have washrooms at the end of the cars. First-class service—the highest class for domestic routes—is called "soft-seat," with spring-cushioned berths (two berths to a compartment). When buying your ticket, ask for "SV." There's no segregation of the sexes, and no matter what class of service you choose, you could end up sharing a compartment with someone of the opposite sex. Second-class service, or "hard-seat" service—ask for *coupé*—has a cushion on wooden berths, with four berths to a compartment. The third class—wooden berths without compartments—is rarely sold to foreigners unless specifically requested. Known in Russian as *platzkart,* this class entails an almost complete surrender of privacy, not to mention the risk of being robbed while you're asleep or in the lavatory.

Most compartments have a small table, limited room for baggage (including under the seats) and a radio that can be turned down, but not off. In soft-seat compartments there are also table lamps. The price of the ticket may or may not include use of bedding; sometimes this fee (which will not be much more than $3) is collected by the conductor.

All of the cars are also equipped with samovars. Back in the days of Communism, the conductor would offer tea to passengers before bedtime. This was interrupted for a few years, but train service is definitely on the mend, and it's not uncommon in soft-seat class to be offered tea in the evening and morning, plus a small boxed meal. For second- or third-class travel, you may want to bring some tea bags or instant coffee and a mug, since you can take hot water from the samovar at any time.

CUTTING COSTS

To save money, **look into rail passes.** But be aware that if you don't plan to cover many miles, you may come out ahead by buying individual tickets.

FARES & SCHEDULES

Purchasing a domestic train ticket outside the CIS can be difficult, but tickets are easily purchased within the country. Tickets go on sale 10 days prior to departure.

Note that you must show your passport when purchasing train tickets. Your best bet is to go to Moscow or St. Petersburg's central booking office. Telephone inquiries for train services are characterized by poor lines and clerks who speak only Russian. Try and get your hotel, a Russian acquaintance, or an independent travel agency to help you book tickets. A one-way ticket between Moscow and St. Petersburg on an overnight train costs slightly less than $50.

TRANSPORTATION

In general, the best, safest, and most efficient way to get around Russia is by train. You can travel in relative comfort, and there are plenty of trains between Moscow and St. Petersburg. Travel by bus is quite a bit sketchier and is best handled by people who can speak some Russian or who have some experience traveling in Russia. Travel by car can be convenient, but less safe, given the poor road conditions and the sometimes-dangerous drivers. Travel by plane within Russia is best for longer distances, but only if you can get on flights of the most reputable and safe carriers

TRAVEL AGENCIES

A good travel agent puts your needs first. Look for an agency that has been in business at least five years, emphasizes customer service, and has someone on staff who specializes in your destination. In addition, **make sure the agency belongs to a professional trade organization.** The American Society of Travel Agents (ASTA) has more than 10,000 members in some 140 countries, enforces a strict code of ethics, and will step in to mediate agent-client disputes involving ASTA members. ASTA also maintains a directory of agents on its Web site; ASTA's TravelSense.org, a trip planning and travel advice site, can also help to locate a travel agent who caters to your needs. (If a travel agency is also acting as your tour operator, *see* Buyer Beware *in* Tours & Packages.)

🛂 Local Agent Referrals **American Society of Travel Agents (ASTA)** ✉ 1101 King St., Suite 200, Alexandria, VA 22314 ☎ 703/739-2782, 800/965-2782 24-hr hotline 🖷 703/684-8319 ⊕ www.astanet.com and www.travelsense.org. **Association**

of British Travel Agents ✉ 68-71 Newman St., London W1T 3AH ☎ 0901/201-5050 ⊕ www.abta.com. **Association of Canadian Travel Agencies** ✉ 350 Sparks St., Suite 510, Ottawa, Ontario K1R 7S8 ☎ 613/237-3657 🖷 613/237-7052 ⊕ www.acta.ca. **Australian Federation of Travel Agents** ✉ Level 3, 309 Pitt St., Sydney, NSW 2000 ☎ 02/9264-3299 or 1300/363-416 🖷 02/9264-1085 ⊕ www.afta.com.au. **Travel Agents' Association of New Zealand** ✉ Level 5, Tourism and Travel House, 79 Boulcott St., Box 1888, Wellington 6001 ☎ 04/499-0104 🖷 04/499-0786 ⊕ www.taanz.org.nz.

VISITOR INFORMATION

Learn more about foreign destinations by checking government-issued travel advisories and country information. For a broader picture, consider information from more than one country.

🛂 City & Government Offices **Moscow City Tourist Office** ✉ 53 W. 36th St., Suite 204, New York, NY 10018 USA ☎ 212/868-8700 or 800/755-3080 🖷 212/868-8588 ✉ 21/5 Kuznetsky Most, Suite 2-022, Bely Gorod, Moscow ☎ 495/926-0391 🖷 495/928-9837 Ⓜ Kuznetsky Most ⊕ www.moscowcity.com. Russian Consulates General (⇗ Passports & Visas).

🛂 Russian National Tourist Office **In the U.S.** ✉ 800 3rd Ave., Suite 3101, New York, NY 10022 ☎ 212/758-1162 🖷 212/758-0933 ⊕ www.russia-travel.com. **In Canada** ✉ 1801 McGill Ave., Suite 930, Montréal, Québec H3A 2N4 ☎ 514/849-6394 🖷 514/849-6743 **In the U.K.** ✉ Kennedy House, 115 Hammersmith Rd., London W14 OQH ☎ 0171/603-1000 🖷 0171/602-4000.

🛂 Government Advisories **U.S. Department of State** ✉ Bureau of Consular Affairs, Overseas Citizens Services Office, 2201 C St. NW Washington, DC 20520 ☎ 888/407-4747 or 202/501-4444 from overseas ⊕ www.travel.state.gov. **Consular Affairs Bureau of Canada** ☎ 800/267-6788 or 613/944-6788 ⊕ www.voyage.gc.ca. **U.K. Foreign and Commonwealth Office** ✉ Travel Advice Unit, Consular Directorate, Old Admiralty Bldg., London SW1A 2PA ☎ 0870/606-0290 or 020/7008-1500 ⊕ www.fco.gov.uk/travel. **Australian Department of Foreign Affairs and Trade** ☎ 300/139-281 travel advisories, 02/6261-1299 Consular Travel Advice ⊕ www.smartraveller.gov.au or www.dfat.gov.au. **New Zealand Ministry of Foreign Affairs and Trade** ☎ 04/439-8000 ⊕ www.mft.govt.nz.

WEB SITES

Do check out the World Wide Web when planning your trip. You'll find everything from weather forecasts to virtual tours of famous cities. Be sure to visit Fodors.com (⊕ www.fodors.com), a complete travel-planning site. You can research prices and book plane tickets, hotel rooms, rental cars, vacation packages, and more. In addition, you can post your pressing questions in the Travel Talk section. Other planning tools include a currency converter and weather reports, and there are loads of links to travel resources.

Friends and Partners (⊕ www.friends-partners.org/friends) should be your first stop for any Russia-related information. Entirely database-driven, it pulls together tons of links and keeps them organized by area of interest. *Russian Life* magazine's Web site (⊕ www.rispubs.com) includes archives of articles from the magazine and links to other useful sites. The EIN News site (⊕ www.einnews.com/russia) is one of the best online sources for news about Russia, with late-breaking information on Russia, particularly politics. The *Newsline* site (⊕ www.rferl.org/newsline) reports news gathered by Radio Free Europe correspondents throughout the region. You can also sign up for the e-mail newswire from here. The Web sites of the *St. Petersburg Times* (⊕ www.sptimes.ru) and the *Moscow Times* (⊕ www.themoscowtimes.com) are great starting points for information on either of the two cities. You can even read a daily online version of the papers.

The official online guide (⊕ www.moscow-city.ru) put out by the Moscow City Tourist Office is in Russian, but a sidebar menu offers English downloads. For St. Petersburg, check out the official city Web site (⊕ www.spb.ru/eng). Russian Passport (⊕ www.russia-rail.com), an online travel service specializing in Russia's railways, can handle everything from rail reservations to visas. City.ru (⊕ www.city.ru) is a rather random mix of Web sites, some in English, on dozens of towns and cities in Russia. With a little patience, you can find some useful news and tourism sites.

Culture of Russia (⊕ www.russianculture.ru) is a Russian-only resource so far, though a few sections of the site have been translated into English. It provides an enormous amount of information on the cultural scene and history. The Bucknell Russian Program's site (⊕ www.departments.bucknell.edu/russian) includes a great chronology of Russian history as well as links to other sites about Russia. About.com's language-learning source (⊕ www.russian.about.com) is good for both beginners and for those looking to hone their skills in the finer points of Russian's lethal verbs of motion. Crossword puzzles, quizzes, dictionaries, and a listening lab are also available.

Check your country's legislation first, but if you're allowed to download music, Zvuki.ru (⊕ www.zvuki.ru) will introduce you to the best and worst of Russian pop (*zvuki* means "sounds").

Moscow

WORD OF MOUTH

"In Moscow, definitely visit Rod Square in the evening (a much different feel than during the daytime)."

—ms_go

"Novodevichy Monastyr [New Maiden's Convent] is delightful with its moving cemetery containing the resting places of Stanislavsky and Chekhov (and don't miss Restaurant U Pirosmani across the pond)."

—Andrea

". . . take the Metro and visit some stations—they are so beautiful with many statues, pictures, decorations, and lights."

—valtor

By Lauri del
Commune

Updated by
Anna Malpas,
Kevin O'Flynn,
and Oksana
Yablokova

IT MAY BE DIFFICULT FOR WESTERNERS to appreciate what an important place Moscow holds in the Russian imagination as a symbol of spiritual and political power. Throughout much of its history the city was known as Holy Moscow, and was valued as a point of pilgrimage not unlike Jerusalem, Mecca, or Rome. Founded in the 12th century as the center of one of several competing minor principalities, Moscow eventually emerged as the heart of a unified Russian state in the 15th century. One hundred years later it had grown into the capital of a strong and prosperous realm, one of the largest in the world. Although civil war and Polish invasion ravaged the city in the early 17th century, a new era of stability and development began with the establishment of the Romanov dynasty in 1613.

The true test for Moscow came under Peter the Great (1672–1725). Profoundly influenced by his exposure to the West, Peter deliberately turned his back on the old traditions and established his own capital—St. Petersburg—on the shores of the Baltic Sea. Yet Western-looking St. Petersburg never succeeded in replacing Moscow as the heart and soul of the Russian nation. Moscow continued to thrive as an economic and cultural center, despite its demotion. More than 200 years later, within a year of the Bolshevik Revolution in 1917, the young Soviet government restored Moscow's status as the nation's capital. In a move just as deliberate as Peter the Great's, the new Communist rulers transferred the seat of government back to the Russian heartland, away from the besieged frontier and Russia's imperial past.

Moscow thus became the political and ideological center of the vast Soviet empire. And even though it has been nearly two decades since that empire broke apart, the city retains its political, industrial, and cultural sway as Russia's capital. With a population of more than 10 million, Moscow is Russia's largest city and the site of some of the country's most renowned cultural institutions, theaters, and film studios. It's also the country's most important transportation hub—even today most flights to the former Soviet republics are routed through Moscow's airports. To salvage and propel Russia's giant economy, the government and business communities of Moscow are actively pursuing outside investment and setting their own economic plans and agendas. For visitors this translates into a modern, fast-paced city with increased availability of Western-style services and products. Even as Moscow becomes a hub of international business activity, however, the metropolis is determinedly holding onto its Russian roots.

As Russia enters the 21st century, development and reconstruction are at an all-time high. Parts of the city, especially within the Bulvarnoye Koltso (Boulevard Ring), are now sparkling clean and well kept. Although the Russians are protecting some of their architectural heritage, they're also creating a new, often controversial legacy, in the form of skyscrapers, shopping malls, and churches. Many of these buildings are designed to be harmonious with the ancient Russian style, but there's a

To see all of the main sights of Moscow and its environs you need at least two weeks. Add another week to that if you want to do a thorough job of exploring the city's many museums along the way. If your time is limited, you'll have to be very selective in planning excursions.

If you have 3 days

Start with a stroll across Red Square, a tour of St. Basil's Cathedral, the shopping arcades of GUM, and, if you're a devoted student of Soviet history and/or embalming techniques, the Lenin Mausoleum. Then walk through Alexander Garden to reach the tourist entrance to the Kremlin. Plan on spending the better part of your first day exploring the churches, monuments, and exhibits within the grounds of this most famous of Russian fortresses. On the second day, spend the morning sightseeing and shopping on Tverskaya ulitsa. In the afternoon, head to Kitai Gorod; this neighborhood has churches and historic buildings on Varvarka ulitsa, which extends from the eastern edge of Red Square, just behind St. Basil's. Try also, toward the end of the day, to squeeze in a stroll across Teatralnaya Ploshchad to see the Bolshoi and Maly theaters. Devote the third morning to the Tretyakov Gallery, which has the finest collection of Russian art in the country. In the afternoon stroll down the Arbat, where you can find plenty of options for haggling over Russian souvenirs.

If you have 7 days

Follow the three-day itinerary above. On the fourth day explore Bolshaya Nikitskaya ulitsa, with its enchanting mansions. Devote the fifth day to the Pushkin Museum of Fine Arts and an exploration of some of the streets in the surrounding Kropotkinsky District. Come back the next day and walk from the Russian State Library to the Kropotkinsky District. Be sure to include the Pushkin Memorial Museum and a walk along the Kremlyovskaya naberezhnaya (the embankment of the Moskva River) in the late afternoon for the spectacular views of the cupolas and towers of the Kremlin. Depending on whether your interests tend toward the religious or the secular, you could spend your last day visiting either the New Maiden's Convent and the adjoining cemetery or Gorky Park and the Tolstoy House Estate Museum, where Tolstoy once lived.

If you have 10 days

After following the seven-day itinerary above, plan on traveling farther afield on day trips to visit the cathedrals and museums of Arkhangelskoye, Ostankino, Kolomenskoye, and the Golden Ring towns. Depending on your interests, you could also use this extra time to visit some of the numerous smaller museums devoted to the lives and accomplishments of prominent Russians, such as Pushkin Apartment Museum and Lermontov House Museum, the former homes of the writers Pushkin and Lermontov, respectively.

---

growing number of shockingly modern steel-and-glass office towers, particularly in central Moscow. The 21st century promises growth, excitement, and hurdles to overcome. Moscow is ready. It's a city very much on the move, as well as a city that holds interesting views of both the past and present of Russia.

Exploring Moscow

Moscow is an in-your-face metropolis that can often overwhelm with monstrous-sized avenues, unbearable traffic jams, and a 24-hour lifestyle à la New York or London that seems to exclude any peace and harmony. But behind that brash facade is a city that has been built up and knocked down and built up again for centuries and where, with a little guidance, a visitor can find those quiet moments of serenity and beauty.

Moscovites often find themselves in new corners of the city that they have never before seen. Don't be afraid to wander off the beaten track, for the city, despite its disorganized and chaotic edge, is organized in a clear manner. Russians often call Moscow a *bolshaya derevnya* or "big village" and the center itself is more compact and vital a place than many other world capitals.

The Kremlin, the heart of Moscow, is encircled twice, first by the Bulvarnoye Koltso or Boulevard Ring, a leafy greeny boulevard, split into 10 sections with different names. The next embracing ring is the Sadovoe Koltso (Garden Ring), a huge road that unfortunately holds no resemblance to its name. Moscow's downtown proper, and most of the city's famous sights, are within the Boulevard Ring.

Despite their destruction during Soviet times, numerous churches remain in the center, and the sound of church bells resonates on the deserted streets on Sunday morning. If you want to go inside some churches, most are generally open from 8 AM to 8 PM, with exceptions for early or late masses. You can walk most of the areas below on foot, but to be efficient in your tour of the city, especially if you have only a few days, familiarize yourself with the metro system.

Most restaurants and hotels in Moscow quote their prices in "conditional units" (YE in Cyrillic; usually the day's dollar or euro rate) so prices for dining and lodging establishments are provided in dollars in this chapter. Admission prices are in rubles. See the Money Matters section *in* Smart Travel Tips for more information.

Getting Your Bearings

As you move out from the center of Moscow you'll encounter historic neighborhoods no longer known by their names, but referred to by main streets or the nearest metro stations. Northeast of the Kremlin–Red Square area is Kitai Gorod, the historic center of the city, rich with palaces and churches. North of the Kremlin is Bely Gorod, or the White City, named after the white-stone ramparts that encircled the area in the 16th century. This neighborhood runs in a semicircle between Kitai Gorod and the Boulevard Ring north of the Moskva River (approximately between the Pushkin Museum of Fine Art and the Yauza River to the east). Bely Gorod includes the first half of Tverskaya ulitsa, Moscow's main shopping street; Kuznetsky Most, a street famous for its designer shops; and the sights around the Tchaikovsky Conservatory on Bolshaya Nikitskaya.

The next main neighborhood is Zemlyanoi Gorod, or "earth city," historically a humbler area that encircles Bely Gorod running north of the Boulevard Ring to the Garden Ring. The term Zemlyanoi Gorod is never

The Arts

Gone are the days when the Bolshoi Theater and the Moscow Art Theater ruled the cultural life of Russia's capital. Moscow's arts scene has taken a decidedly adventurous turn, with smaller, innovative theater companies and musical ensembles giving the old standbys a run for their money. Musicians, writers, and directors have long since flung off their rigid, state-imposed chains and are now creating everything from glitzy musicals to experimental dramas. Several theater troupes are also restaging Russian classics in an effort to inject new life into the pieces. Moscow now also hosts the International Chekhov Theater Festival, an innovative and increasingly popular competition.

Churches & Monasteries

All over Moscow, churches are being painted, refurbished, polished, resurfaced, and, in some cases, rebuilt from the ground up. At almost every turn you'll run into a church surrounded by scaffolding on which diligent artisans are tending to the rebirth of Orthodoxy. Many of these restoration projects are already finished, and one of the joys of meandering through the city is suddenly happening upon the gleaming cupolas and brightly painted facade of a church from the Moscow baroque period. Brief services are conducted throughout the day in many of these churches, most of which are open to the public from 8 AM to 8 PM. There are also several splendid monastery complexes within the city limits; others, including the venerated Sergiev-Posad (Zagorsk), are just a day trip away.

A Dining Scene on the Rise

From the state-run restaurants (once the only choice available), to the collectively-owned cooperatives that followed perestroika, to the present era in which thousands of restaurants now proliferate, the changes in the dining scene have been nothing short of astonishing. Whereas in the early to mid-'90s you would have been hard-pressed to find any decent—let alone outstanding—food, there's no such shortage now. You can pick and choose from a cornucopia of cafés, restaurants, and food-serving bars. The contrasts, however, may leave you a bit wobbly. At a small restaurant you might experience the discomforts of Soviet management techniques, but right up the same street there may be an establishment so elegant it could compete in Paris or New York.

Nightlife

Moscow's nightlife scene exploded in the mid-'90s with stories of debauchery and excess. After-hours life has mellowed and matured since then; clubs have become safer, and service has improved. Evenings on the town are still wild, however, and Russians love to cut a rug, regardless of whether they can dance. The sleazy casinos and seedy erotic clubs that gave the city its off-color reputation are still plentiful, but Moscow is attempting to emulate Paris, New York, and London by developing a chic clubbing scene with an emphasis on exotic, expensive interiors and rigid face control. Plenty of plain old bars and live-music clubs also continue to crop up around town, as do places playing international Top 40 and Russian pop hits. A fledgling gay-and-lesbian scene has slowly been gaining steam, but these clubs tend to fold more frequently than those on the mainstream entertainment circuit.

used by locals, who refer to parts of this area by what metro station is closest. Within this neighborhood are the second half of Tverskaya ulitsa, the pedestrian Arbat area, ever popular for strolling, and the U.S. embassy.

South of the Moskva River, the main area of interest is the Zamoskvorechye neighborhood. Among other sights here are the Tretyakov Gallery and several beautiful churches.

Most of Moscow's major sights, hotels, and restaurants can be found within the above-mentioned neighborhoods. Two other notable neighborhoods are Krasnaya Presnya and Taganka. The former lies to the west and contains the Bely Dom, Victory Park, and, in the southwest, New Maiden's Convent. Taganka lies in the east and has some beautiful churches.

Numbers in the text correspond to numbers in the margin and on the Kremlin, Kitai Gorod, Tverskaya to the Arbat, and South of the Kremlin maps.

Heart of Russia: The Kremlin & Red Square
Кремль и Красная Площадь

FodorsChoice
★

Few places in the world possess the historic resonance of the **Kremlin,** the walled ancient heart of Moscow and the oldest part of the city. The first wooden structure was erected on this site sometime in the 12th century. As Moscow grew, the city followed the traditional pattern of Russian cities, developing in concentric circles around the elevated fortress at its center (*kreml* means "citadel" or "fortress"). After Moscow emerged as the center of a vast empire in the late 15th century, the Kremlin came to symbolize the mystery and power of Russia, as it has ever since. Before the black-suited men of the Bolshevik Revolution took over, tsars were ceremoniously crowned and buried here. In the 20th century the Kremlin became synonymous with the Soviet government, and "Kremlinologists," Western specialists who studied the movements of the politicians in and around the fortress, made careers out of trying to decipher Soviet Russian policies. Much has changed since the Soviet Union broke up, but the Kremlin itself remains mysteriously alluring. A visit to the ancient Kremlin grounds reveals many signs of the old—and new—Russian enigma.

You can buy tickets for the Kremlin grounds and cathedrals at the two kiosks on either side of the Kutafya Tower. Tickets, which cost 300R, grant you access to all the churches and temporary exhibits within the Kremlin. Tickets to the Armory Palace (Oruzheynaya Palata) and Diamond Fund (Almazny Fond) cost extra (350R each); you can buy them at the kiosks or at the entrances to these buildings. Tickets for the Diamond Fund are limited in number and are sold 1½ hours before the four showings each day. Between May and September tickets are also available for a changing-of-the-guard ceremony, which takes place on Saturday at noon. Tickets cost 1,000R and include entry to all the churches and temporary exhibits. Ignore scalpers selling tickets. Keep in mind that you need to buy a 50R ticket if you wish to take pictures with your camera, and that video cameras are not allowed. All heavy bags must be checked for about 60R at the *kamera khraneniya,* which is in Aleksandrovsky Sad (Alexander Garden), to the right down and behind the stairs from the ticket kiosks.

a good walk

The Kremlin sits at the very center of Moscow, atop Borovitsky (Pine Grove) Hill. Start at the Aleksandrovsky Sad or Teatralnaya metro station, both outside the fortress walls, to visit a few sights on your way to the Kremlin gates. To the right as you emerge from the Teatralnaya station are the Kremlin's battlement walls. In some places 65 feet high and 10 to 20 feet thick, the walls have stood practically unchanged since the end of the 15th century. At the northernmost point of the battlements stands the **Sobakina Tower** ❶ ▐▔. Adjacent to the tower is the monumental wrought-iron gate that marks the entrance to the **Alexander Garden** that runs along the northwest wall of the Kremlin. Just beyond the garden entrance, to your left against the Kremlin wall, is the **Tomb of the Unknown Soldier** ❷. To your right is the underground Manezh shopping mall and plaza. Looking up from the garden to the Kremlin walls, you can see a large yellow building, the Arsenal.

Walking south along the garden's path takes you to a double bastion lined by a stone bridge on nine pillars, including the white, outer **Kutafya Tower** ❸, and the massive **Troitskaya Tower** ❹ near the wall. Up to the right is the exit for the Aleksandrovsky Sad metro station, and farther up, as you ascend to the left going away from the tower, you can find the kiosks where you purchase tickets to the Kremlin grounds and cathedrals. Enter the Kremlin through the Kutafya Tower. Cross the bridge to pass through the Troitskaya Tower. The big gray building to your right as you enter is the **State Kremlin Palace** ❺. The yellow building to your left is the **Arsenal** ❻. Straight ahead, the **Tsar Cannon** ❼ sits in front of the **Cathedral of the Twelve Apostles** ❽. Continue on to the **Tsar Bell** ❾, which is the world's largest bell.

Take a left at the bell and enter the historic heart of the Kremlin, **Sobornaya Ploshchad** ❿—Cathedral Square. As you enter the square note the massive **Ivan the Great Bell Tower** ⓫. Continuing around the square in a counterclockwise manner, you'll encounter several cathedrals. The dominating one is the mammoth **Assumption Cathedral** ⓬, which is next to the smaller, single-domed **Church of the Deposition of the Virgin's Robe** ⓭. Looking across the square from Assumption Cathedral you'll see the **Cathedral of the Archangel** ⓮, and to the right, **Annunciation Cathedral** ⓯. Exit the square by this last cathedral.

You'll come out to the road where vehicular traffic passes; across the road are the working buildings of the Russian government. These buildings are off-limits to the public, and uniformed police officers blow whistles at anyone who goes off the main path. Walk down the hill to the **Great Kremlin Palace** ⓰, a cluster of buildings that includes the Terem and the 15th-century Granovitaya Palata. Although most of the buildings are closed to the public, a portion of the Granovitaya Palata's facade is visible from Cathedral Square. The yellow building to your left houses the **Armory Palace** ⓱, the oldest and richest museum in the

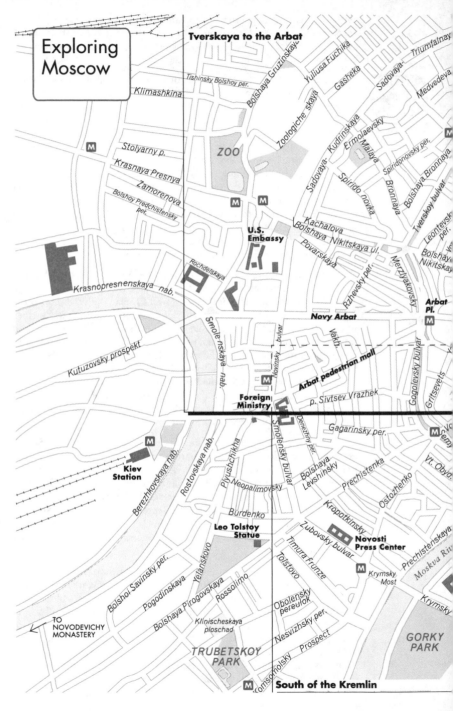

Exploring Moscow

Tverskaya to the Arbat

Klimashkina

Tishinsky Bolshoy per.

Bolshaya Gruzinskaya

Yuliusa Fuchika

Gasheka

Sadovaya- Triumfalnay

Medvedeva

ZOO

Zoologiche skaya

Sadovaya- Kudrinskaya

Ermolaevsky

Malaya

Spiridonovsky per.

Bolshaya Bronnaya

Stolyarny p.

Krasnaya Presnya

Zamorenova

Bolshoy Predchistensky per.

Spirido novka

Tverskoy bulvar

Leontevsk per.

U.S. Embassy

Kachalova

Bolshaya Nikitskaya ul.

Povarskaya

Bolshaya Nikitskay

Krasnopresnenskaya nab.

Rochdelskaya

Merzlyakovsky

Rzhevsky per.

Arbat Pl.

Novy Arbat

Smolenskaya nab.

bulvar

Novinsky

Vakh.

Kutuzovsky prospekt

Arbat pedestrian mall

Gogolevsky bulvar

Gritsevets

Foreign Ministry

p. Sivtsev Vrazhek

Denezhny per.

Gagarinsky per.

V

Sery

Kiev Station

Berezhkovskaya nab.

Rostovskaya nab.

Plyushchikha

Neopalimovsky

Smolensky bulvar

Bolshaya Levshinsky

Prechistenka

Ostozhenko

Vt. Obya

Burdenko

Kropotkinsky

Novosti Press Center

Leo Tolstoy Statue

Yelanskovo

Timura Frunze

Zubovsky bulvar

Tolstovo

Krymsky Most

Prechistenskaya

Moskva Riv

TO NOVODEVICHY MONASTERY

Bolshoi Savinsky per.

Pogodinskaya

Bolshaya Pirogovskaya

Rossolimo

Obolensky pereulok

Krymsky

Klinischeskaya ploschad

Nesvizhsky per.

Prospect

GORKY PARK

TRUBETSKOY PARK

Komsomolsky Prospect

South of the Kremlin

Mokena Community Public Library District
Phone: 708-479-9663
Fax: 708-479-9684

patron's name:Nelson, Caroline

title:Rick Steves'. Germany & S
item id:30050058939199
due:4/2/2008,23:59

title:15-minute workouts for du
item id:31985001612337
due:4/2/2008,23:59

title:Fodor's San Diego
author:Fodor, Eugene.
item id:31985001619357
due:4/2/2008,23:59

title:Fodor's Moscow and St. Pe
item id:31985001578272
due:4/2/2008,23:59

www.Mokena.lib.il.us
Check Us Out: We're More Than Books

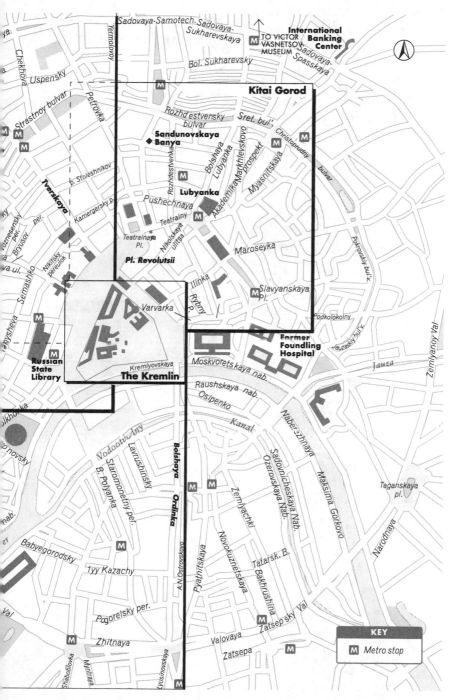

International Banking Center

TO VICTOR VASNETSOV MUSEUM

Sadovaya-Samotech. Sadovaya-Sukharevskaya

Sadovaya-Spasskaya

Bol. Sukharevsky

Kitai Gorod

Rozhdestvensky bulvar

Sret. bul.

Sandunovskaya Banya

Christoprudny bulvar

Myasnitskaya

Lubyanka

Pushechnaya

Akademika Markhlevskovo prospekt

Teatralny

Maroseyka

Teatralnaya Pl.

Nikolskaya ulitsa

Pl. Revolutsii

Ilinka

Rybny p.

Slavyanskaya Pl.

Varvarka

Podkolokolny

Former Foundling Hospital

Jauzsky bul'v.

Russian State Library

Kremlyovskaya

The Kremlin

Moskvoretskaya nab.

Raushskaya nab.

Osipenko

Kanal

Naberezhnaya

Jauza

Zemlyanoy Val

Vodootvodny

Lavrushinsky

Staromonetny per.

B. Polyanka

Bolshaya Ordinka

Zemlyachki

Sadovnicheskaya Nab.

Ozerovskaya Nab.

Maksima Gorkovo

Taganskaya pl.

Babvegorodsky

Tyy Kazachy

A.N.Ostrovskogo

Pyatnitskaya

Novokuznetskaya

Tatarsk. B.

Bakhrushina

Narodnaya

Pogorelsky per.

Zhitnaya

Lyusinovskaya

Valovaya

Zatsepsky Val

Zatsepa

Chekhova

Uspensky

Yermolovoy

Strastnoy bulvar

Petrovka

b. Stoleshnikov

Tverskaya

Kamergersky p.

Nikitsky pereulok

Bryusov

Semashko

Vozresensky per.

va ul.

Shabolovka

Myntnaya

Val

KEY

M *Metro stop*

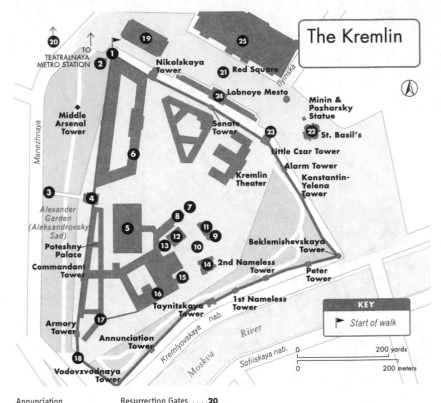

The Kremlin

Annunciation
Cathedral **15**

Armory Palace **17**

Arsenal **6**

Assumption
Cathedral **12**

Borovitskaya Tower **18**

Cathedral of the
Archangel **14**

Cathedral of the
Twelve Apostles **8**

Church of the
Deposition of the
Virgin's Robe **13**

Great Kremlin
Palace **16**

GUM **25**

Historical Museum **19**

Ivan the Great
Bell Tower **11**

Kutafya Tower **3**

Lenin Mausoleum **24**

Red Square **21**

Resurrection Gates **20**

St. Basil's Cathedral . . .**22**

Sobakina Tower **1**

Sobornaya Ploshchad . .**10**

State Kremlin Palace **5**

Tomb of the Unknown
Soldier **2**

Tower of the Savior **23**

Troitskaya Tower **4**

Tsar Bell **9**

Tsar Cannon **7**

Kremlin. In the same building is the **Diamond Fund**, which houses an extraordinary collection of diamonds and precious gems. Farther down stands the pyramid-shape **Borovitskaya Tower** ⑱. To exit the Kremlin retrace your steps to Kutafya Tower.

Turn right after exiting through Kutafya Tower and walk back down to the Aleksandrovsky Sad. Retrace your steps through the garden past the Tomb of the Unknown Soldier. Turn right once again, following the wall of the Kremlin. Walk through the ornate wrought-iron gates topped with gold past the rear of the redbrick **Historical Museum** ⑲. After passing by the statue of General Zhukov astride a horse, take a right to reach the awesome multicolor **Resurrection Gates** ⑳, which front a small chapel. The bronze plaque in the ground in front of the chapel marks kilometer zero for the Russian highway system. Pass through the gates to reach **Red Square** ㉑.

As you enter the square, the stunning multicolor onion domes of **St. Basil's Cathedral** ㉒ slowly come into view. Outside the cathedral doors are the **Lobnoye Mesto** and the **Minin and Pozharsky statue;** to the right is the **Tower of the Savior** ㉓. Opposite St. Basil's, at the north end of Red Square, stands the Historical Museum. Running along the Kremlin wall is the **Lenin Mausoleum** ㉔, the world-famous and much-visited resting place of Communism's greatest icon. Facing it across the square is the long facade of the **GUM** ㉕ department store.

TIMING Plan to spend a half day, at the very least, touring the Kremlin; budget a full day or more if you want to linger at the museums. The Kremlin grounds and cathedrals are open 10 to 5 every day except Thursday. The Armory Palace and Diamond Fund are also closed on Thursday. Note that the Kremlin occasionally closes on other days for official functions. Check with your hotel concierge.

If you don't want to tackle all of this solo, you should consider a tour of the Kremlin grounds, which includes the Armory Palace, available from virtually any tour service in Moscow. A tour is particularly helpful because there are no signs, in any language, explaining the displays.

If you wish to see Red Square in all its splendor, come back in the evening, when the square and its surrounding buildings are beautifully illuminated.

What to See
Alexander Garden (Aleksandrovsky Sad, Александровский Сад). Laid out in the 19th century by the Russian architect Osip Bove, this garden named after Alexander I stretches along the northwest wall of the Kremlin, where the Neglinnaya River once flowed. The river now runs beneath the garden, through an underground pipe. Bove added the classical columns topped with an arc of chipped bricks; in the 19th century such "romantic" imitation ruins were popular in gardens. Today this mock ruin is blocked by a gate, but in eras past it was a famous place for winter sledding. A few pleasant outdoor cafés open in the garden in summer provide a nice place to rest after a tour of the Kremlin. ⊠ *Manezhnaya ul., Kremlin/Red Square* ☎ *No phone* ✍ *300R Kremlin ticket* ⊙ *Fri.–Wed. 10–5* Ⓜ *Aleksandrovsky Sad.*

⑮ Annunciation Cathedral (Blagoveshchensky Sobor, Благовещенский Собор). This remarkable monument of Russian architecture, linking three centuries of art and religion, was the private chapel of the royal family. Its foundations were laid in the 14th century, and in the 15th century a triangular brick church in the early Moscow style was erected on the site. Partially destroyed by fire, it was rebuilt in the 16th century during the reign of Ivan the Terrible, when six gilded cupolas were added. Tsar Ivan would enter the church by the southeast-side porch entrance, built especially for him. He was married three times too many (for a total of six wives) and was therefore, under the bylaws of the Orthodox religion, not allowed to enter the church through its main entrance. The interior is decorated by brilliant frescoes painted in 1508 by the Russian artist Feodosy. The polished tiles of agate jasper covering the floor are said to be a gift from the Shah of Persia. Most striking of all is the chapel's iconostasis. The fine icons of the second and third tiers were painted by some of Russia's greatest masters—Andrei Rublyov, Theophanes the Greek, and Prokhor of Gorodets. ⊠*Kremlin, Square* ☎*495/203–0349* ☒*300R Kremlin Ticket* ☉ *Fri.–Wed. 10–5* Ⓜ *Aleksandrovsky Sad or Borovitskaya.*

⑰ Armory Palace (Oruzheynaya Palata, Оружейная Палата). The Armory
Fodor'sChoice Palace is the oldest and richest museum in the Kremlin. It was originally
★ founded in 1806 as the Imperial Court Museum, which was created out of three royal treasuries: the Court Treasury, where the regalia of the tsars and ambassadorial gifts were kept; the Stable Treasury, which contained the royal harnesses and carriages used by the tsars during state ceremonies; and the Armory, a collection of arms, armor, and other valuable objects gathered from the country's chief armories and storehouses. The Imperial Court Museum was moved to the present building in 1851. It was further enhanced and expanded after the Bolshevik Revolution with valuables confiscated and nationalized from wealthy noble families as well as from the Patriarchal Sacristy of the Moscow Kremlin. The roughly 4,000 artifacts here date from the 12th century to 1917, and include a rare collection of 17th-century silver. The museum tour (at this writing you could only visit the museum by taking one of these tours, though this may change) begins on the second floor. Halls (*zal*) VI–IX are on the first floor, Halls I–V on the second.

Hall I displays the works of goldsmiths and silversmiths of the 12th through 19th centuries, and **Hall II** contains a collection of 18th- to 20th-century jewelry. One of the most astounding exhibits is the collection of Fabergé eggs on display in Hall II (Case 23). Among them is a silver egg whose surface is engraved with a map of the Trans-Siberian Railroad. The "surprise" inside the egg, which is also on display, was a golden clockwork model of a train with a platinum engine, windows of crystal, and a headlight made of a tiny ruby.

Hall III contains Asian and Western European arms and armor, including heavy Western European suits of armor from the 15th to 17th centuries, pistols, and firearms.

Hall IV showcases a large collection of Russian arms and armor from the 12th to early 19th centuries, with a striking display of helmets. The earliest helmet here dates from the 13th century and is ascribed to Prince Yaroslav, father of military hero and saint Alexander Nevsky (circa 1220–63). Here, too, is the helmet of Prince Ivan, the son of Ivan the Terrible. The prince was killed by his father at the age of 28, an accidental victim of the tsar's unpredictable rage. The tragic event has been memorialized in a famous painting by Ilya Repin now in the Tretyakov Gallery, showing the frightened tsar holding his mortally wounded son. Russian chain mail, battle-axes, maces, harquebuses, ceremonial armor, and Russian and Asian sabers are also in this hall. A highlight of the collection is the large Greek quiver belonging to Tsar Alexei (Peter the Great's father), his Asian saber, and a heavy golden mace presented to him by the Persian shah Abbas. Among the sabers on display here are those of Kuzma Minin and Dmitry Pozharsky, the national heroes who ousted the Polish forces from Moscow in the early 17th century; a statue on Red Square pays tribute to them.

Hall V is filled with foreign gold and silver objects, mostly ambassadorial presents to the tsars. Among the displays is the "Olympic Service" of china presented to Alexander I by Napoléon after the signing of the Treaty of Tilsit in 1807. **Hall VI** holds vestments of silk, velvet, and brocade, embroidered with gold and encrusted with jewels and pearls. These were once worn by the tsars, patriarchs, and metropolitans.

Hall VII contains regalia and the imperial thrones. The oldest throne, veneered with carved ivory, belonged to Ivan the Terrible. The throne of the first years of Peter the Great's reign, when he shared power with his older brother Ivan, has two seats in front and one hidden in the back. The boys' older sister, Sophia (1657–1704), who ruled as regent from 1682 to 1689, sat in the back, prompting the young rulers to give the right answers to the queries of ambassadors and others. Another throne, covered with thin plates of gold and studded with more than 2,000 precious stones and pearls, was presented to Tsar Boris Godunov by Shah Abbas of Persia. The throne of Tsar Alexei, also from Persia, is decorated with 876 diamonds and 1,223 other stones. Among the crowns, the oldest is the sable-trimmed Cap of Monomakh, which dates to the 13th century. Ukraine is now asking for it back because it originally belonged to the Kievan prince Vladimir Monomakh. It was a gift to the prince from his grandfather, the Byzantine emperor, and is revered as a symbol of the transfer of religious power from Byzantium to Russia. Also on display in this section are several coronation dresses, including the one Catherine the Great wore in 1762.

Hall VIII contains dress harnesses of the 16th through 18th centuries. On display are Russian saddles, including one used by Ivan the Terrible, and other items once belonging to the Moscow Kremlin Equestrian Department.

Hall IX has a marvelous collection of court carriages. The oldest one came from England and is believed to have been presented to Tsar Boris Godunov by King James I at the turn of the 17th century. Here you'll find the Winter Coach that carried Elizaveta Petrovna (daughter of Peter the Great and someone who clearly liked her carriages; 1709–62) from St. Petersburg to Moscow for her coronation. Catherine the Great's French carriage, painted by François Boucher, is arguably the most attractive of the collection. ⊠ *Kremlin* ☎ *495/202–4631* 🖅 *350R; tickets sold 90 min before each tour* 🕓 *Fri.–Wed. tours at 10, 12:30, 2:30, 4:30* Ⓜ *Aleksandrovsky Sad or Borovitskaya.*

⑥ Arsenal (Арсенал). Commissioned in 1701 by Peter the Great, the weapons arsenal was partially destroyed by the fire that greeted Napoléon as he stormed the city in 1812 (some say the Russian army set fire to the city intentionally). Its present form dates from the early 19th century, when it was given its yellow color and simple, but impressive form by Osip Bove (the same architect who designed the Alexander Garden). Today it houses government offices and is closed to the public. ⊠ *Kremlin* ☎ *495/203–0349* Ⓜ *Aleksandrovsky Sad or Borovitskaya.*

⑫ Assumption Cathedral (Uspensky Sobor, Успенский Собор). The dominating structure of Cathedral Square is one of the oldest edifices of the Kremlin. Designed after the Uspensky Sobor of Vladimir, it was built in 1475–79 by the Italian architect Aristotle Fiorovanti, who had spent many years in Russia studying traditional Russian architecture. Topped by five gilded domes, the cathedral is both austere and solemn. The ceremonial entrance faces Cathedral Square; the visitor entrance is on the west side (to the left). After visiting the Archangel and Annunciation cathedrals, you may be struck by the spacious interior here, unusual for a medieval church. Light pours in through two rows of narrow windows. The cathedral contains rare ancient paintings, including the icon of the Virgin of Vladimir (the work of an 11th-century Byzantine artist), the 12th-century icon of St. George, and the 14th-century Trinity icon. The carved throne in the right-hand corner belonged to Ivan the Terrible, and the gilt wood throne to the far left was the seat of the tsarina. Between the two is the patriarch's throne. Until the 1917 revolution, Uspensky Sobor was Russia's principal church. This is where the crowning ceremonies of the tsars took place, a tradition that continued even after the capital was transferred to St. Petersburg. Patriarchs and metropolitans were enthroned and buried here. After the revolution the church was turned into a museum, but in 1989 religious services were resumed here on major church holidays. ⊠ *Kremlin* ☎ *495/203–0349* 🖅 *300R Kremlin Ticket* 🕓 *Fri.–Wed. 10–5* Ⓜ *Aleksandrovsky Sad or Borovitskaya.*

⑱ Borovitskaya Tower (Borovitskaya Bashnya, Боровицкая Башня). The main entrance to the Kremlin rises to more than 150 feet. At its base a gate pierces its thick walls, and you can still see the slits for the chains of the former drawbridge. Black Volgas and, now, top-of-the-line Mercedes and BMWs whiz through the vehicular entrance, carrying government employees to work. Uniformed security guards stand at the separate pedestrian entrance. ⊠ *Kremlin Manezhnaya ul.* ☎ *No phone* Ⓜ *Borovitskaya.*

⑭ Cathedral of the Archangel (Arkhangelsky Sobor, Архангельский Собор). This five-dome cathedral was commissioned by Ivan the Great (1440–1505), whose reign witnessed much new construction in Moscow and in the Kremlin in particular. The cathedral was built in 1505–09 to replace an earlier church of the same name. The architect was the Italian Aleviso Novi, who came to Moscow at the invitation of the tsar; note the distinct elements of the Italian Renaissance in the cathedral's ornate decoration, particularly in the scallop-shape gables on its facade. Until 1712, when the Russian capital was moved to St. Petersburg, the cathedral was the burial place of Russian princes and tsars. Inside there are 46 tombs, including that of Ivan Kalita (Ivan "Moneybags"; circa 1304–40), who was buried in the earlier cathedral in 1340. Ivan Moneybags, who earned his nickname because he was so good at collecting tribute, was the first Russian ruler to claim the title of grand prince. The tomb of Ivan the Terrible (1530–84) is hidden behind the altar; that of his young son Dmitry is under the stone canopy to your right as you enter the cathedral. Dmitry's death at the age of seven is one of the many unsolved mysteries in Russian history. He was the last descendant of Ivan the Terrible, and many believe he was murdered because he posed a threat to the ill-fated Boris Godunov (circa 1551–1605), who at the time ruled as regent. A government commission set up to investigate Dmitry's death concluded that he was playing with a knife and "accidentally" slit his own throat. The only tsar to be buried here after 1712 was Peter II (Peter the Great's grandson; 1715–30), who died of smallpox while visiting Moscow.

The walls and pillars of the cathedral are covered in frescoes that tell the story of ancient Russian history. The original frescoes, painted right after the church was built, were repainted in the 17th century by a team of more than 50 leading artists from several Russian towns. Restoration work in the 1950s uncovered some of the original medieval frescoes, fragments of which can be seen in the altar area. The pillars are decorated with figures of warriors; Byzantine emperors; the early princes of Kievan Rus' (the early predecessor of modern-day Russia and Ukraine), Vladimir, and Novgorod; as well as the princes of Moscow, including Vasily III, the son of Ivan the Great. The frescoes on the walls depict religious scenes, including the deeds of Archangel Michael. The carved baroque iconostasis is 43 feet high and dates from the 19th century. The icons themselves are mostly 17th century, although the revered icon of Archangel Michael is believed to date to the 14th century. ✉ *Kremlin* ☎ *495/203–0349* 🎟 *300R Kremlin Ticket* ⊙ *Fri.–Wed. 10–5* Ⓜ *Aleksandrovsky Sad or Borovitskaya.*

❽ Cathedral of the Twelve Apostles (Sobor Dvenadtsati Apostolov, Собор Двенадцати Апостолов). Built in 1655–56 by Patriarch Nikon, this was used as his private church. An exhibit here displays icons removed from other Kremlin churches destroyed by the Soviets. The silver containers and stoves were used to make holy oil. Next door to the church is the Patriarch's Palace. ✉ *Kremlin* ☎ *495/203–0349* 🎟 *300R Kremlin Ticket* ⊙ *Fri.–Wed. 10–5* Ⓜ *Aleksandrovsky Sad or Borovitskaya.*

⓭ Church of the Deposition of the Virgin's Robe (Tserkov Rizopolozheniya, Церковь Ризоположения). This single-dome church, once the private church of the Moscow patriarch, was built in 1484–86 by masters from Pskov. It was rebuilt several times and restored to its 15th-century appearance by Soviet experts in the 1950s. Brilliant frescoes dating to the mid-17th century cover the church's walls, pillars, and vaults. The most precious treasure is the iconostasis by Nazary Istomin. On display inside the church is an exhibit of ancient Russian wooden sculpture from the Kremlin collection. ⊠ *Kremlin* ☎ *495/203–0349* ☜ *300R Kremlin Ticket* ☉ *Fri.–Wed. 10–5* Ⓜ *Aleksandrovsky Sad or Borovitskaya.*

★ **Diamond Fund** (Almazny Fond, Алмазный Фонд). In 1922 the fledgling Soviet government established this amazing collection of diamonds, jewelry, and precious minerals. The items on display within the Armory Palace date from the 18th century to the present. Highlights of the collection are the Orlov Diamond, a present from Count Orlov to his mistress, Catherine the Great (1729–96); and the Shah Diamond, which was given to Tsar Nicholas I (1796–1855) by the Shah of Persia as a gesture of condolence after the assassination in 1829 of Alexander Griboyedov, the Russian ambassador to Persia and a well-known poet. ⊠ *Armory Palace, Kremlin/Red Square* ☎ *495/229–2036* ☜ *350R* ☉ *Fri.–Wed. 10–5* Ⓜ *Aleksandrovsky Sad or Borovitskaya.*

⑯ **Great Kremlin Palace** (Bolshoi Kremlyovsky Dvorets, Большой Кремлевский Дворец). The palace actually consists of a group of buildings. The main section is the newest, built between 1838 and 1849. Its 375-foot-long facade faces south, overlooking the Moskva River. This was for centuries the site of the palace of the grand dukes and tsars, but the immediate predecessor of the present building was badly damaged in the 1812 conflagration. It's currently closed to the general public.

The other buildings of the Great Kremlin Palace include the 17th-century **Terem** (Tower Chamber), where the tsarina received visitors, and the 15th-century **Granovitaya Palata** (Palace of Facets). Both of these buildings are also closed to the public. ⊠ *Kremlin* ☎ *495/203–0349* Ⓜ *Aleksandrovsky Sad or Borovitskaya.*

㉕ **GUM** (ГУМ). Pronounced "goom," the initials are short for Gosudarstvenny Universalny Magazin, or State Department Store. This staggeringly enormous emporium, formerly called the Upper Trading Rows, was built in 1889–93 and has long been one of the more famous sights of Moscow. Three long passages with three stories of shops run the length of the building. A glass roof covers each passage, and there are balconies and bridges on the second and third tiers. Another series of passages runs perpendicular to the three main lines, creating a mazelike mall. In feel, it resembles a cavernous turn-of-the-20th-century European train station. There are shops (both Western and Russian) aplenty here now, and a saunter down at least one of the halls is enjoyable. The elegant Bosco restaurant on the ground floor has a small summer garden that looks out onto Red Square. ⊠ *3 Red Sq.* ☎ *495/929–3470* ☉ *Mon.–Sat. 9–9, Sun. 10–8* Ⓜ *Ploshchad Revolutsii.*

⑲ **Historical Museum** (Istorichesky Muzey, Исторический Музей). This red-brick museum was built in 1874–83 in the pseudo-Russian style, which combined a variety of architectural styles. You may recognize the building's twin towers if you've ever caught clips of Soviet military parades on television. Against the backdrop of the towers' pointed spires, the tanks and missiles rolling through Red Square seemed to acquire even more potency. The museum's extensive archaeological and historical collections and interesting temporary exhibits outline the development of Russia. Also here are a rich collection of Russian arms and weaponry and a restaurant called Krasnaya Ploshchad that uses 200-year-old recipes, including dishes from tsars' coronation menus. ⊠ *1/2 Red Sq.* ☎ *495/692–3731* 💰 *150R* 🕐 *Wed.–Sat. 10–8, Sun. 11–6* Ⓜ *Ploshchad Revolutsii.*

⓫ Ivan the Great Bell Tower (Kolokolnya Ivana Velikovo, Колокольня Ивана Великого). The octagonal main tower of this, the tallest structure in the Kremlin, rises 263 feet—3 feet higher than the Rossiya hotel (on the opposite side of Red Square), which was built in accordance with the tradition established by Boris Godunov that the bell tower remain the tallest building in Moscow. The first bell tower was erected on this site in 1329. It was replaced in the early 16th century, during the reign of Ivan the Great (hence the bell tower's name). But it was during the reign of Boris Godunov that the tower received its present appearance. In 1600 the main tower was rebuilt, crowned by an onion-shape dome and covered with gilded copper. For many years it served as a watch-tower; Moscow and its environs could be observed for a radius of 32 km (20 mi). Altogether, the towers have 52 bells, the largest weighing 70 tons. The annex of the bell tower is used for temporary exhibits of items from the Kremlin collection; tickets may be purchased at the entrance. At the time of writing, the bell tower itself was being restored, with the aim of making it available to climb. ⊠ *Kremlin* ☎ *495/203–0349* 💰 *300R Kremlin Ticket* 🕐 *Fri.–Wed. 10–5* Ⓜ *Aleksandrovsky Sad or Borovitskaya.*

❸ Kutafya Tower (Kutafya Bashnya, Кутафья Башня). This white bastion, erected in 1516, once defended the approach to the drawbridge that linked Aleksandrovsky Sad to the Kremlin. In Old Slavonic *kutafya* means "clumsy" or "confused"; this adjective was applied to the tower because it so differs in shape and size from the other towers of the Kremlin. Kutafya Tower marks the main public entrance to the Kremlin, which opens promptly at 10 AM every day except Thursday. You can buy tickets to the Kremlin grounds and cathedrals at the kiosks on either side of the tower. The guards may ask where you're from and check inside your bags; there's a small security checkpoint to walk through, similar to those at airports. ⊠ *Manezhnaya ul., Kremlin/Red Square* ☎ *No phone* 💰 *300R Kremlin Ticket* 🕐 *Fri.–Wed. 10–5* Ⓜ *Aleksandrovsky Sad or Borovitskaya.*

㉔ Lenin Mausoleum (Mavzolei Lenina, Мавзолей Ленина). Except for a brief interval during World War II, when his body was evacuated to the Urals, Vladimir Ilyich Lenin (1870–1924) has lain in state here since his death in 1924. Whether it's really Lenin or a wax look-alike is probably one of those Russian mysteries that will go down in history unanswered. From 1924 to 1930 there was a temporary wooden mausoleum, which has been replaced by the pyramid-shape mausoleum you see now. It's made of red, black, and gray granite, with a strip of black granite near the top level symbolizing a band of mourning. Soviet leaders watched parades from the balcony. Both versions of the mausoleum were designed by one of Russia's most prominent architects, Alexei Shchusev, who also designed the grand Kazansky train station near Komsomolskaya metro station.

In the past, there were notoriously endless lines of people waiting to view Lenin's body, but this is no longer the case. A visit to the mausoleum, however, is still treated as a serious affair. The surrounding area is cordoned off during visiting hours, and all those entering are observed by uniformed police officers. It's forbidden to carry a camera or any large bag, although for a small fee some tour guides break the rules and offer the chance to take photographs. Inside the mausoleum it's cold and dark. It's considered disrespectful to put your hands inside your pockets (the same applies when you visit an Orthodox church), and the guards have been known to reprimand people for unbuttoned collars or sweaters. If you're inclined to linger at all, they will gently but firmly move you along.

Before you know it you are ushered out of the mausoleum to the special burial grounds outside the mausoleum. When Stalin died in 1953, he was placed inside the mausoleum alongside Lenin, but in the early 1960s, during Khrushchev's tenure, the body was removed and buried here, some say encased in heavy concrete. There has been talk of finally burying Lenin, but even in today's Russia this would be a very controversial move, so he is likely to remain in Red Square for some time. Also buried here are such Communist leaders as Zhdanov, Dzerzhinsky, Brezhnev, Chernenko, and Andropov. The American journalist John Reed, friend of Lenin and author of *Ten Days That Shook the World,* an account of the October revolution, is buried alongside the Kremlin wall. Urns set inside the wall contain ashes of the Soviet writer Maxim Gorky; Lenin's wife and collaborator, Nadezhda Krupskaya; Sergei Kirov, the Leningrad Party leader whose assassination in 1934 (believed to have been arranged by Stalin) was followed by enormous purges; the first Soviet cosmonaut, Yury Gagarin; and other Soviet eminences.

The hourly changing of the guard outside Lenin's tomb, once a staggeringly formal event, has been eliminated. Local police officers, much more jocular in demeanor, have replaced the ramrod-stiff soldiers who once guarded the way into the tomb. ⊠ *Red Sq.* ☎ *495/923–5527* 🖃 *Free* ⊙ *Tues.–Thurs. and Sat. 10–1, Sun. 10–1* Ⓜ *Ploshchad Revolutsii.*

Lobnoye Mesto (Лобное Место). The name of the strange, round, whitestone dais in front of St. Basil's Cathedral literally means "place of the brow," but it has come to mean "execution site," for it was next to the spot where public executions were carried out. Built in 1534, the dais was used by the tsars as a podium for public speeches and the proclamation of imperial *ukazy* (decrees). When the heir apparent reached the age of 16, he was presented to the people from this platform. ⊠ *Red Sq.* ☎ *No phone* Ⓜ *Ploshchad Revolutsii.*

Minin and Pozharsky statue (Памятник Минину и Пожарскому). In 1818 sculptor Ivan Martos built this statue, which honors Kuzma Minin (a wealthy Nizhni-Novgorod butcher) and Prince Dmitry Pozharsky, who drove Polish invaders out of Moscow in 1612 during the Time of Troubles. This period of internal strife and foreign intervention began in approximately 1598 with the death of Tsar Fyodor I and lasted until

1613, when the first Romanov was elected to the throne. This was the first monument of patriotism funded by the public. The inscription on the pedestal reads, "To citizen Minin and prince Pozharsky from a thankful Russia 1818." The statue originally stood in the center of the square, but was later moved to its current spot in front of St. Basil's. In 2005 November 4th was named a new public holiday in honor of Minin and Pozharsky and to replace the old communist November 7 holiday. ✉ *Red Sq.* ☎ *No phone* Ⓜ *Ploshchad Revolutsii.*

Patriarch's Palace (Patriarshy Dvorets, Патриарший Дворец). Adjoining the Cathedral of the Twelve Apostles, the Patriarch's Palace has housed the **Museum of 17th-Century Applied Art** since 1963. The exhibits here were taken from the surplus of the Armory Palace and include books, tableware, clothing, and household linen. A taped explanation in English is available. ✉ *Kremlin* ☎ *495/921–4720, 495/203–8817, or 495/202–0347* 🎟 *300R Kremlin Ticket* ☉ *Fri.–Wed. 10–5* Ⓜ *Aleksandrovsky Sad or Borovitskaya.*

Poteshny Dvorets (Amusement Palace, Потешный Дворец). Behind the State Kremlin Palace stands the Amusement Palace—so called because it was used by *boyarin* (nobleman) Alexei in the 17th century as a venue for theatrical productions. Later, both Stalin and Trotsky had apartments here. ✉ *Kremlin* ☎ *495/203–0349* 🎟 *300R Kremlin Ticket* ☉ *Fri.–Wed. 10–5* Ⓜ *Aleksandrovsky Sad.*

㉑ Red Square (Krasnaya Ploshchad, Красная Площадь). World famous for the grand military parades staged here during the Soviet era, this was originally called the Torg, the Slavonic word for marketplace. Many suppose that the name "Red Square" has something to do with Communism or the Bolshevik Revolution. In fact, however, the name dates to the 17th century. The adjective *krasny* originally meant "beautiful," but over the centuries the meaning of the word changed to "red," hence the square's present name. The square is most beautiful and impressive at night, when it's entirely illuminated by floodlights, with the ruby-red stars atop the Kremlin towers glowing against the dark sky. There are five stars in all, one for each of the tallest towers. They made their appearance in 1937 to replace the double-headed eagle, a tsarist symbol that is again finding favor as an emblem of Russia. The glass stars, which are lighted from inside and designed to turn with the wind, are far from dainty: the smallest weighs a ton. ☎ *No phone* Ⓜ *Ploshchad Revolutsii.*

⓴ Resurrection Gates (Voskresenskiye Vorota, Воскресенские Ворота). These gates, which formed part of the Kitai Gorod defensive wall, were named for the icon of the Resurrection of Christ that hangs above them. However, the gates are truly "resurrection" gates; they have been reconstructed many times since they were first built in 1534. In 1680 the gates were rebuilt and a chapel honoring the Iberian Virgin Mary was added. In 1931 they were destroyed by the Soviets. They were most recently rebuilt in 1994–95. Today the redbrick gates with the bright-green-and-blue chapel dedicated to the Iberian Virgin are truly a magnificent sight and a fitting entrance to Red Square. The bronze compass inlaid in the ground in front of the chapel marks kilometer zero on the Rus-

Fodor'sChoice ★

sian highway system. ✉ *Red Sq.* ☎ *No phone* 🎫 *300R Kremlin Ticket* ⊙ *Chapel daily 8 AM–10 PM* Ⓜ *Ploshchad Revolutsii.*

㉒ **St. Basil's Cathedral** (Pokrovsky Sobor, Покровский Собор). Although

Fodor'sChoice it's popularly known as St. Basil's Cathedral, the proper name of this

★ whimsical structure is Church of the Intercession. It was commissioned by Ivan the Terrible to celebrate his conquest of the Tatar city of Kazan on October 1, 1552, the day of the feast of the Intercession. The central chapel, which rises 107 feet, is surrounded by eight towerlike chapels linked by an elevated gallery. Each chapel is topped by an onion dome carved with its own distinct pattern and dedicated to a saint on whose day the Russian army won battles against the Tatars. The cathedral was built between 1555 and 1560 on the site of the earlier Trinity Church, where the Holy Fool Vasily (Basil) had been buried in 1552. Basil was an adversary of the tsar, publicly reprimanding Ivan the Terrible for his cruel and bloodthirsty ways. He was protected, however, from the tsar by his status as a Holy Fool, for he was considered by the Church to be an emissary of God. Ironically, Ivan the Terrible's greatest creation has come to be known by the name of his greatest adversary. In 1558 an additional chapel was built in the northeast corner over Basil's remains, and from that time on the cathedral has been called St. Basil's.

Very little is known about the architect who built the cathedral. It may have been the work of two men—Barma and Postnik—but now it seems more likely that there was just one architect, Postnik Yakovlyev, who went by the nickname Barma. Legend has it that upon completion of the cathedral, the mad tsar had the architect blinded to ensure that he would never create such a masterpiece again.

After the Bolshevik Revolution, the cathedral was closed and in 1929 turned into a museum dedicated to the Russian conquest of Kazan. Although services are held here on Sunday at 10 AM, the museum is still open. The antechamber houses displays outlining the various stages of the Russian conquest of Kazan as well as examples of 16th-century Russian and Tatar weaponry. Another section details the history of the cathedral's construction, with displays of the building materials used. After viewing the museum exhibits, you're free to wander through the cathedral. Compared with the exotic exterior, the dark and simple interiors are somewhat disappointing. The brick walls are decorated with faded flower frescoes. The most interesting chapel is the main one, which contains a 19th-century baroque iconostasis. There's some concern about the cathedral's future after renovation work uncovered serious damage to the foundation, perhaps due to nearby construction work and concerts, such as the Paul McCartney performance that took place on Red Square in 2003. ✉ *Red Sq.* ☎ *495/298–3304* 🎫 *100R* ⊙ *Weekdays 11–5, Sun. 11–6; closed 1st Mon. of month* Ⓜ *Ploshchad Revolutsii.*

► **❶** **Sobakina Tower** (Sobakina Bashnya, Собакина Башня). More than 180 feet high, the Sobakina (formerly Arsenal) Tower at the northernmost part of the thick battlements that encircle the Kremlin was an important part of the Kremlin's defenses. It was built in 1492 and its thick walls concealed a secret well, which was of vital importance during times of siege. It isn't open for touring. ⊠ *Manezhnaya ul., Kremlin* ☎ *No phone* 🎟 *300R Kremlin Ticket* Ⓜ *Ploshchad Revolutsii.*

❿ Sobornaya Ploshchad (Cathedral Square, Соборная Площадь). This paved square, the ancient center of the Kremlin complex, is framed by three large cathedrals in the old Russian style, the imposing Ivan the Great Bell Tower, and the Palace of Facets. A changing-of-the-guard ceremony takes place in the square every Saturday at noon in the summer months. ⊠ *Kremlin* ☎ *No phone* Ⓜ *Aleksandrovsky Sad or Borovitskaya.*

❺ State Kremlin Palace (Gosudarstvenny Kremlyovsky Dvorets, Государственный Кремлевский Дворец). In 1961 this rectangular structure of glass and aluminum was built as the *Dvorets Syezdov* (Palace of Congresses) to accommodate meetings of Communist Party delegates from across the Soviet Union. Today it's affiliated with the Bolshoi Theater and is used for concerts, fashion shows, and ballets. Big names such as Tom Jones, Bryan Adams, and Rod Stewart have played here. A sizable portion of the palace is underground: the architect designed the structure this way so that it wouldn't be higher than any of the other Kremlin buildings. Apart from attending a concert, the building is of no real interest. ⊠ *Kremlin* ☎ *495/917–2396* Ⓜ *Aleksandrovsky Sad.*

❷ Tomb of the Unknown Soldier (Mogila Neizvestnovo Soldata, Могила Неизвестного Солдата). Dedicated on May 9, 1967, the 22nd anniversary of the Russian victory over Germany in World War II, this red granite monument within Alexander Garden contains the body of an unidentified Soviet soldier, one of those who, in autumn 1941, stopped the German attack at the village of Kryukovo, just outside Moscow. To the right of the grave there are six urns holding soil from the six "heroic cities" that so stubbornly resisted the German onslaught: Odessa, Sevastopol, Stalingrad, Kiev, Brest, and Leningrad (St. Petersburg). Very likely, no matter what time of year you are visiting, you'll see at least one wedding party. The young couple in full wedding regalia, along with friends and family, customarily stops here after getting married, leaving behind flowers and snapping photographs along the way. The gray obelisk just beyond the Tomb of the Unknown Soldier was erected in 1918 to commemorate the Marxist theoreticians who contributed to the Bolshevik Revolution. It was created out of an obelisk that had been put up three years earlier, in honor of the 300th anniversary of the Romanov dynasty. ⊠ *Manezhnaya ul., Aleksandrovsky Sad, Kremlin/Red Square* ☎ *No phone* 🎟 *300R Kremlin Ticket* ☉ *Fri.–Wed. 10–5* Ⓜ *Ploshchad Revolutsii.*

㉓ Tower of the Savior (Spasskaya Bashnya, Спасская Башня). Until Boris Yeltsin's presidency (1991–99) this 1491 tower served as the main entrance to the Kremlin. Indeed, in the centuries before Communist rule, all who passed through it were required to doff their hats and bow before the icon of the Savior that hung on the front of the tower. The icon was removed, but you can see the outline of where it was. The embellished roof and the first clock were added in 1625. President Vladimir Putin uncharacteristically used the Spasskaya Tower exit in May 2003 when hurrying to the Paul McCartney concert on Red Square. ⊠ *Red Sq.* ☎ *495/203–0349* 🎫 *300R Kremlin Ticket* ◷ *Fri.–Wed. 10–5* Ⓜ *Ploshchad Revolutsii.*

❹ Troitskaya Tower (Troitskaya Bashnya, Троицкая Башня). Rising 240 feet above the garden, this is the tallest *bashnya* (tower) in the Kremlin wall and is the passage to the Kremlin territory. This tower is linked to the Kutafya Tower by a bridge that once spanned a moat. Its deep, subterranean chambers were once used as prison cells. Napoléon supposedly lost his hat when he entered the Kremlin through this gate in 1812. ⊠ *Aleksandrovsky Sad, Kremlin* ☎ *495/203–0349* 🎫 *300R Kremlin Ticket* ◷ *Fri.–Wed. 10–5* Ⓜ *Aleksandrovsky Sad.*

❾ Tsar Bell (Tsar Kolokol, Царь-Колокол). The world's largest bell is also the world's most silent: it has never rung once. Commissioned in the 1730s, the bell was damaged when it was still in its cast. It weighs more than 200 tons and is 20 feet high. The bas-reliefs on the outside show Tsar Alexei Mikhailovich and Tsarina Anna Ivanovna. ⊠ *Kremlin* ☎ *No phone* Ⓜ *Aleksandrovsky Sad or Borovitskaya.*

❼ Tsar Cannon (Tsar Pushka, Царь-Пушка). This huge piece of artillery (*pushka*) has the largest caliber of any gun in the world, but like the Tsar Bell that has never been rung, it has never fired a single shot. Cast in bronze in 1586 by Andrei Chokhov, it weighs 40 tons and is 17½ feet long. Its present carriage was cast in 1835, purely for display purposes. ⊠ *Kremlin* ☎ *No phone* Ⓜ *Aleksandrovsky Sad or Borovitskaya.*

Kitai Gorod

Китай-Город

Kitai Gorod, with its twisting and winding streets, is the oldest section of Moscow outside the Kremlin. The literal translation of Kitai Gorod is "Chinatown," but there has never been a Chinese settlement here. The origin of the word *kitai* is disputed; it may come from the Tatar word for fortress, but most likely it derives from the Russian word *kita,* in reference to the bundles of twigs that were used to reinforce the earthen wall that once surrounded the area.

Kitai Gorod begins where Red Square ends. Settlement of this area began in the 12th century, around the time that the fortified city of Moscow was founded on Borovitsky Hill (the site of the present-day Kremlin). By the 14th century Kitai Gorod was a thriving trade district, full of shops and markets. At that time it was surrounded by earthen ramparts, which were replaced in the 16th century by a fortified wall, remnants of which still remain. As Moscow grew, so did Kitai Gorod. At the time of the Bolshevik Revolution it was the city's most important financial and commercial district, with major banks, warehouses, and trading companies concentrated here. These days the multitude of shops, restaurants, and banks demonstrates the area's reasserted role as an energized commercial center.

Bolshoi Theater .**44**
Cathedral of the
Epiphany **28**
Cathedral of Our
Lady of Kazan .**26**
Cathedral of the
Sign **34**
Church of All-
Saints **38**
Church of St.
George **36**
Church of St.
Maxim **33**
Church of the
Trinity in
Nikitniki **37**
English Court .**32**
Lubyanskaya
Ploshchad ..**42**
Maly Theater .**45**
Mayakovsky
Museum **41**
Merchants'
Arcade **30**
Metropol **43**
Monastery
Savior Behind
Icons **27**
Museum of the
History of
Moscow **39**
Polytechnical
Museum **40**
Romanov Palace
in Zaryadye ..**35**
Ryabushinsky
Bank **29**
St. Barbara's
Church **31**
V.I. Lenin
Museum **46**

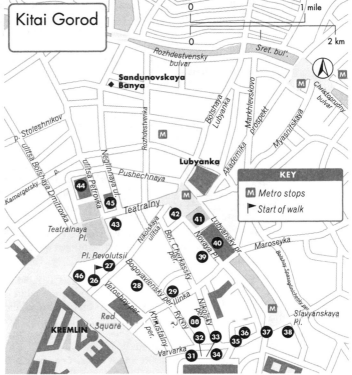

A good starting point for your tour is Nikolskaya ulitsa, which begins at the corner opposite the redbrick Historical Museum and runs along the north side of GUM. If you're coming from St. Basil's, walk alongside GUM toward the Historical Museum. If you're coming from outside of Red Square, get to Nikolskaya by way of Teatralnaya Ploshchad (Theater Square). If you're standing with your back to the Bolshoi on this square, walk straight ahead, cross the street, and enter one of the narrow passageways to the right or left of the Teatralnaya metro station (as you're facing it). Taking a right out of either passageway will bring you to Nikolskaya ulitsa. Go a short way farther to the right, to the cobblestone edge of Red Square, to begin your walk.

Nikolskaya ulitsa, which is named after the Kremlin's Nikolskaya Gate Tower, is one of the oldest streets in Moscow. At the corner with Red Square is the **Cathedral of Our Lady of Kazan** ㉖ ☞. Leaving it, take a left to make your way through the teeming crowds of shoppers on Nikolskaya ulitsa to No. 7, the **Monastery of the Savior Behind the Icons** ㉗, a former Slavonic-Greco-Latin Academy now undergoing a slow restoration. Farther down the street, also on the left-hand side, is a once brightly painted white-and-aqua building with an elaborate facade (No. 15). The building was erected between 1810–14 on the site of the 16th-century Pechatny Dvor (Printing Yard), where Russia's first printed book was assembled in 1553. Today the building houses the Moscow Institute of Historical Records and the Moscow Humanitarian University. Cross the street to go down Bogoyavlensky pereulok. Halfway down the block, opposite the entrance to the Ploshchad Revolutsii metro, is the **Cathedral of the Epiphany** ㉘. Continue down the street to where it intersects with ulitsa Ilinka. Before the 1917 revolution this was Moscow's Wall Street, and it's still lined with the impressive facades of former banks. On the left-hand corner stands the former **Ryabushinsky Bank** ㉙. Turn right onto ulitsa Ilinka and you'll see it leads directly to the Kremlin's Spasskaya Tower. At No. 3 stands the Tserkov Svyatoi Ilii church from which the street takes its name. The church, which dates to 1520, is in disrepair except for its facade. Opposite the church is one of the border streets of the **Merchants' Arcade** ㉚. Turn left and walk the length of Khrustalny pereulok to reach one of the oldest streets in Moscow, Varvarka ulitsa. The opposite side of the street is lined with quaint old churches and buildings, but the first thing you'll likely notice is the gray bulk of the massive, concrete-and-glass Rossiya, one of Europe's largest and most unattractive hotels, which is scheduled to be knocked down in 2006.

At the farthest corner of the street, to your left, is **St. Barbara's Church** ㉛. Adjacent is the **English Court** ㉜. Next comes the white-stone **Church of St. Maxim the Blessed** ㉝. The pointed bell tower just before the semicircle sidewalk leading to the upper-level entrance of the Rossiya hotel was once attached to the redbrick **Cathedral of the Sign** ㉞ on the other side of the sidewalk; with its foundation on the slope below, it's set back from the street. At No. 10 is the **Romanov Palace Chambers in Zaryadye** ㉟, believed to be the birthplace of Tsar Mikhail Romanov. Before leaving Varvarka ulitsa take note of the last church, the blue **Church of St. George on Pskov Hill** ㊱ at No. 12. If you stand to the left of the church (on the walkway leading to the Rossiya hotel) you can glimpse a remnant of Kitai Gorod's 16th-century brick fortification wall. It's to your left, opposite the hotel's eastern facade. Cross to the other side of Varvarka ulitsa and walk a short hop past the final church. Make a right and climb up the narrow Ipatevsky pereulok, which leads to several government and administrative buildings. At the top of the incline to the right is one of Moscow's best-preserved 17th-century churches, the **Church of the Trinity in Nikitniki** ㊲.

Continue down the lane to the right of the church to reach Novaya Ploshchad, or New Square, which is more like a boulevard than a square. To your right, at the far bottom of the hill, Slavyanskaya Ploshchad opens up. At the bottom of the hill is the redbrick **Church of All-Saints in Kulishki** ㊳. From Novaya Ploshchad stroll for a long block or two past the government buildings, where the Central Committee of the Communist Party once sat. Now these buildings house the Duma of the Moscow Region. Soon you'll come to the beginning of a busy intersection. To your right, in the median strip that divides Novaya Ploshchad, is a park that holds the Plevna Memorial, an octagonal, towerlike monument commemorating the Russian soldiers who fell in the

Battle of Plevna in the Russo-Turkish War (1878). Keep walking up the street on the left side to go to the **Museum of the History of Moscow** ㊲.

On the opposite side of the street is a museum of science and technology that takes up the entire block, the **Polytechnical Museum** ㊵. Directly north is yet another museum, **Mayakovsky Museum** ㊶, which includes a re-creation of the study of the great revolutionary poet. A short distance from here, Novaya Ploshchad intersects with the circular **Lubyanskaya Ploshchad** ㊷, where you can behold the Lubyanka Prison and the former KGB headquarters, which now house the FSB—the New Russia's federal security service. On the west side of the square is Detsky Mir, a large department store that used to specialize in toys but now carries all sorts of items.

Walk past Lubyanskaya Ploshchad to the west side, down to where it converges with the broad street of Teatralny proyezd, Moscow's most elite shopping street. On a side street to your right stands the ornate and luxurious Savoy hotel (3 Rozhdestvenka ulitsa), which, like the nearby Metropol hotel, was built in connection with the celebrations in the early 20th century honoring 300 years of the Romanov dynasty. On the left-hand side of the street you will pass a statue of Ivan Fyodorov, the printer who produced Russia's first book at the old Printing Yard on Nikolskaya ulitsa. The arched gateway just to the right of the statue links Teatralny proyezd with Nikolskaya ulitsa, the street on which you started the tour. Teatralny proyezd leads into Teatralnaya Ploshchad, site of three of Moscow's most important theaters.

Taking up the block on the southeast corner, the first building you'll encounter to your left as you approach Teatralnaya Ploshchad is the **Metropol** ㊸, an art nouveau hotel. Reaching the square, you'll see at the center a large monument to Karl Marx, carved on the spot from a 200-ton block of granite and unveiled in 1961. Across the boulevard stands the **Bolshoi Theater** ㊹, flanked on the left, on the corner farthest away from you, by the Central Children's Theater, and, to the right, by the **Maly Theater** ㊺. Turn left at the corner of the Metropol, and walk by the park and the hotel's main entrance. The large redbrick wall ahead is the other surviving remnant of the 16th-century fortification wall that once surrounded Kitai Gorod. The wall has been heavily rebuilt, and a new tower has been added. Inside the tower are a couple of restaurants and bars. When you reach the Teatralnaya–Ploshchad Revolutsii metro station, take a moment to admire the exterior of the massive redbrick building on the corner—the **V. I. Lenin Museum** ㊻. If you still have some time but not much energy, consider hopping on Trolleybus 2, which can be caught at the bus stop opposite the Bolshoi Theater. The trolley ride takes about 45 minutes and makes a loop passing by Lubyanskaya Ploshchad, Ploshchad Pobedi (Victory Square—note the obelisk topped by an angel), the Borodino Battle Panorama (in a circular blue pavilion), Kievsky vokzal (train station), the Novy Arbat, and Alexander Garden, before returning to Teatralnaya Ploshchad. You can purchase a ticket for 15R from the driver. Try to have exact change. Make sure to punch the ticket on board the bus.

TIMING Taken at a leisurely pace, with stops at least to glance at the interiors of the many churches along the route, this walk should take about five hours. If you intend to take a quick look at the exhibits in the museums along the way, you'll need an entire day. Both the Polytechnical Museum and the Museum of the History of Moscow are worth coming back to for a longer look at their holdings.

What to See

🕙 ⓜ **Bolshoi Theater** (Большой Театр). Moscow's "big" (*bolshoi* means "big")
Fodor'sChoice and oldest theater, formerly known as the Great Imperial Theater, was
★ completely rebuilt after a fire in 1854. Its main building is closed for a renovation and is expected to reopen in 2009 but you can still see performances at the Novaya Stsena (New Stage) to the left of it. The building itself is remarkable: its monumental colonnade is topped by a statue of bronze horses pulling the chariot of Apollo, patron of music. Its crimson-and-gold interior is similarly grand. All of this splendor is matched by the quality of the resident opera and ballet troupes—two of the most famous performing-arts companies in the world. If you want to have the pleasure of seeing a performance at the Bolshoi, be sure to book one of its 2,155 seats as far as possible in advance, because performances can sell out quickly. Tickets can be bought in advance on the Bolshoi's Web site, and touts sell tickets outside the theater just before performances, sometimes at reasonable prices (though more often at exorbitant prices). An interesting footnote in the theater's and the Soviet Union's history: Lenin made his last public speech here, in 1922. Also to the left of the Bolshoi is the **Tsentralny Detsky Teatr** (Central Children's Theater), which puts on traditional performances for a younger audience. This is where you'll find the Bolshoi's main ticket office. The plaza, with fountains and fine wooden benches, is a nice spot for a relaxing look at the theater. ⊠ *1 Teatralnaya Pl.* ☎ *495/292–9986, 495/250–7317 tickets* ⊕ *www.bolshoi.ru* Ⓜ *Teatralnaya.*

need a break? The small café-bar at the **Metropol** (⊠ 4 Teatralny proyezd ☎ 495/927–6010 Ⓜ Teatralnaya) is a sophisticated spot for tea, coffee, and a selection of delicious cakes and pastries. In this busy part of town its expense is worth the calming effect of comfy, padded seats and intimate service. The hotel also has a famous (and even pricier) restaurant with an enormous dining hall in art nouveau style. The entrance to the café is on the right hand side of the hotel. Moscow's best Mexican restaurant, **Hola Mexico** (⊠ 7/5 Pushechnaya ul. ☎ 495/925–8251 Ⓜ Kuznetsky Most) is just around the corner from the Bolshoi theater. Huge portions and reasonable prices make it a favorite spot with Moscow's foreign community.

❷❽ **Cathedral of the Epiphany** (Bogoyavlensky Sobor, Богоявленский Собор). This church is all that remains of the monastery that was founded on this site in the 13th century by Prince Daniil of Moscow. A good example of the Moscow baroque style, the late-17th-century cathedral is now undergoing a long-overdue and very slow renovation, and some of the structure has remained hidden by scaffolds for a number of years. It is, however, open for services. There's a shop in the foyer that sells icon cards, religious objects, and books about the Russian Orthodox faith (entry is from the courtyard around back). Services are at 8:30 AM on Saturday and 7:30 AM on Sunday. ✉ *2/4 Bogoyavlensky per., Kitai Gorod* ☎ *495/ 298–3771* 🚇 *Free* ⊙ *Daily 8–8* Ⓜ *Ploshchad Revolutsii.*

📌 ㉖ **Cathedral of Our Lady of Kazan** (Kazansky Sobor, Казанский Собор). Built between 1633–36 to commemorate Russia's liberation from Polish occupation during the Time of Troubles, this church was purposely blown up in 1936, and then rebuilt and fully restored in 1993. Its salmon-and-cream painted brick and gleaming gold cupolas are now a colorful magnet at the northeast corner of Red Square, between the Historical Museum and GUM. Inside and outside hang icons of Our Lady of Kazan. The small chapel affords an excellent look at the traditional iconostasis and interior design of Russian churches. In the front vestibule, you can buy candles to light a prayer; you'll also find other religious articles for sale. Many worshippers visit throughout the day. ✉ *8 Nikolskaya ul., at Red Sq., Kitai Gorod* 🚇 *Free* ⊙ *Daily 8–7, except Mon., when it closes at end of 5 PM vespers service. Sun. services at 7 and 10 AM* Ⓜ *Ploshchad Revolutsii.*

㉞ **Cathedral of the Sign** (Znamensky Sobor, Знаменский Собор). This was part of the monastery of the same name, built on the estate of the Romanovs in the 16th century, right after the establishment of the Romanov dynasty. After the death of the last heir to Ivan the Terrible, a dark period set in, marked by internal strife and foreign intervention. That period, commonly known as the Time of Troubles, ended in 1613, when the Boyar Council elected the young Mikhail Romanov tsar. ✉ *8a Varvarka ul., Kitai Gorod* ☎ *495/298–0490* ⊙ *Daily 8–8. Services daily at 8 AM and 5 PM* Ⓜ *Kitai Gorod.*

㉟ **Church of All-Saints in Kulishki** (Tserkov Vsekh Svyatykh na Kulishkakh, Церковь Всех Святых на Кулишках). A fine example of 17th-century religious architecture, this graceful church is one of the few survivors of the Soviet reconstruction of the area. It's open for services. ✉ *2 Slavyansky Pl., Kitai Gorod* Ⓜ *Kitai Gorod.*

㊱ **Church of St. George on Pskov Hill** (Tserkov Georgiya na Pskovskoy Gorke, Церковь Георгия на Псковской Горке). This graceful five-dome church with blue cupolas studded by gold stars, built in 1657 by merchants from Pskov, stands right next to the Romanov Palace Chambers in Zaryadye. The bell tower is an addition from the 19th century. The interior of the church is mostly bare, though an art boutique on the premises is open daily 11–7. ✉ *12 Varvarka ul., Kitai Gorod* Ⓜ *Kitai Gorod.*

㉝ **Church of St. Maxim the Blessed** (Tserkov Maksima Blazhennovo, Церковь Максима Блаженного). In 1698 this white-stone church was built on the site where the Holy Fool Maxim was buried. It's between St. Barbara's and the Cathedral of the Sign (in front of the northern side of the Rossiya). An art boutique here is open daily 11–6. ✉ *6 Varvarka ul., Kitai Gorod* Ⓜ *Kitai Gorod.*

㊲ **Church of the Trinity in Nikitniki** (Tserkov Troitsy v Nikitnikakh, Церковь Троицы в Никитниках). Painted with white trim and topped by five green cupolas, this lovely redbrick creation—one of the most striking churches in the city—mixes baroque decoration with the principles of ancient Russian church architecture. The church was built between 1628–34 for the merchant Grigory Nikitnikov; the private chapel on the south side was the family vault. The murals and iconostasis were the work of Simon Ushakov, a famous icon painter whose workshop was nearby in the brick building across the courtyard. Although surrounded with barriers and still under reconstruction, it's a working church. Services are at 8:30 AM on Sunday and 5 PM on Saturday. Times of masses are also posted on the barriers. ✉ *3 Nikitnikov per., Kitai Gorod* ☎ *495/298–5018* Ⓜ *Kitai Gorod.*

㉜ **English Court** (Anglisky Dvor, Английский Двор). Built in the mid-16th century, this white-stone building with a steep shingled roof and narrow windows became known as the English Court because Ivan the Terrible—wanting to encourage foreign trade—presented it to English merchants trading in Moscow. In 1994 Queen Elizabeth II presided over the opening of the building as a branch of the Museum of the History of Moscow. Its displays about Russian-British trade relations over the centuries may be particularly interesting to visitors from the United Kingdom. Phone ahead for information on tours in English. ✉ *4 Varvarka ul., Kitai Gorod* ☎ *495/298–3952* 💴 *50R* ☉ *Tues., Thurs., and weekends 10–5:30, Wed. and Fri. 11–6* Ⓜ *Ploshchad Revolutsii or Kitai Gorod.*

㊷ **Lubyanskaya Ploshchad** (Лубянская Площадь). Now called by its pre-revolutionary name again, this circular "square" had been renamed Dzerzhinsky Square in 1926 in honor of Felix Dzerzhinsky, a Soviet revolutionary and founder of the infamous CHEKA, the forerunner of the KGB. His statue once stood in the center of the square but was toppled in August 1991, along with the old regime. A huge round flower bed has replaced it. In 2003 Moscow mayor Yuri Luzhkov suggested returning the statue of Dzerzhinsky to its previous spot, but the idea was shelved after public outcry. The large yellow building facing the square, with bars on the ground-floor windows, was once the notorious Lubyanka Prison and KGB headquarters. Ⓜ *Lubyanka.*

㊺ **Maly Theater** (Малый Театр). Writer Maxim Gorky (1868–1936), known as the father of Soviet socialist realism, once called this theater famous for its productions of Russian classics "the Russian people's university." It opened in 1824 and was originally known as the Little Imperial Theater (*maly* means "little"). Out front stands a statue of a beloved and prolific playwright whose works are often performed here, the 19th-century satirist Alexander Ostrovsky. ✉ *1/6 Teatralnaya Pl.* ☎ *495/923–2621* Ⓜ *Teatralnaya.*

㊶ **Mayakovsky Museum** (Muzey Mayakovskovo, Музей Маяковского). The museum for one of Russia's great revolutionary poets is suitably among the most imaginative and revolutionary installations in the city. The museum, which is housed in the building the poet inhabited opposite the headquarters of the KGB, relies on symbols to explain Vladimir Mayakovsky's (1893–1930) life. The entrance gate is shaped like a rib cage. Emblems of the life and loves of the poet hang everywhere inside, tracing his early revolutionary activities, complicated love affairs, and death. The collection includes archival documents, photos, manuscripts, paintings, and posters of and by the poet, including his handwritten suicide note. ✉ *3/6 Lyubansky proyezd* ☎ *495/928–2569* 💴 *100R* ☉ *Tues. and Fri.–Sun. 10–5, Thurs. 1–8* Ⓜ *Lubyanka.*

㉚ Merchants' Arcade (Gostinny Dvor, Гостиный Двор). This market, which takes up an entire block between ulitsa Ilinka and Varvarka ulitsa, just east of Red Square, is made up of two imposing buildings. Running the length of Khrustalny pereulok is the Old Merchant Arcade, erected by the Italian architect Quarenghi between 1791 and 1805; on the other side of the block, bordering Rybny pereulok, is the New Merchant Arcade, built between 1838 and 1840 on the site of the old fish market. The entire complex has been renovated and is filled with all manner of restaurants and shops. ✉ *Ul. Ilinka, Kitai Gorod* Ⓜ *Ploshchad Revolutsii or Kitai Gorod.*

㊸ Metropol (Метрополь). Built at the turn of the 20th century in preparation for the celebrations commemorating 300 years of the Romanov dynasty, the Metropol underwent reconstruction in the late 1980s to restore its brilliant art nouveau facade to its original colorful guise. The ceramic mosaics are especially arresting as the sun bounces off the tiles. Look for the Princess "Greza" panel made by Mikhail Vrubel, which was inspired by the plays of Edmond Rostand. On the main facade of the building is a mosaic depicting the four seasons. The hotel was the focus of heavy fighting during the revolution, and it was also the venue of many historic speeches, including a few by Lenin. For some time the Central Committee of the Russian Soviet Federal Republic met here under its first chairman, Yakov Sverdlov. ✉ *1/4 Teatralny proyezd* ☎ *495/927–6061 or 495/927–6000* Ⓜ *Ploshchad Revolutsii or Teatralnaya.*

㉗ Monastery of the Savior Behind the Icons (Zaikonospassky Monastyr, Заиконоспасский Монастырь). The monastery was founded at the beginning of the 17th century by Boris Godunov. Russia's first institution of higher learning, the Slavonic-Greco-Latin Academy, was opened in this building in 1687. Many an illustrious scholar studied here, including scientist and poet Mikhail Lomonosov (1711–65) from 1731 to 1735. Hidden inside the courtyard is the monastery's cathedral, **Spassky Sobor,** built in 1600–61 in the Moscow baroque style. Although the church is currently under ongoing renovation, services are held here daily. ✉ *7 Nikolskaya ul., Kitai Gorod* Ⓜ *Ploshchad Revolutsii.*

Monetny Dvor (The Mint, Монетный Двор). Built in 1697, the former mint, near the Cathedral of Our Lady of Kazan, is an excellent example of old baroque architecture. Its facade can be seen through the courtyard of an 18th-century building immediately next to the cathedral. ✉ *Nikolskaya ul. at Red Sq., Kitai Gorod* Ⓜ *Ploshchad Revolutsii.*

㊴ Museum of the History of Moscow (Muzey Istorii Goroda Moskvy, Музей Истории Города Москвы). This small, manageable museum, housed in the former Church of St. John the Baptist (1825), presents Moscow's architectural history through paintings and artifacts. It's worth stopping in for a brief visit to get a fuller view of the Moscow history only hinted at in older neighborhoods. ✉ *12 Novaya Pl., Kitai Gorod* ☎ *495/924–8490* ⊕ *www.museum-city-moscow.ru* 💰 *50R* ⊙ *Tues., Thurs., weekends 10–6, Wed. and Fri. 11–7; closed last day of month* Ⓜ *Lubyanka.*

40 **Polytechnical Museum** (Politekhnichesky Muzey, Политехнический Музей). The achievements of science and technology, including an awesome collection of old Russian cars, fill an entire Moscow block. When this museum opened in 1872 it was originally called the Museum of Applied Knowledge. There are many good temporary exhibits. ✉ *3/4 Novaya Pl., Kitai Gorod* ☎ *495/923–0756* ⊕ *www.polymus.ru* 💰 *150R* ⊙ *Tues.–Sun. 10–6; closed last Thurs. of month* Ⓜ *Lubyanka.*

35 **Romanov Palace Chambers in Zaryadye** (Palaty Romanovykh v Zaryadye, Палаты Романовых в Зарядье). It's believed that Mikhail Romanov (1596–1645), the first tsar of the Romanov dynasty, was born in this house. Today the mansion houses a lovely museum devoted to the boyar lifestyle of the 16th and 17th centuries. Period clothing, furniture, and household items furnish the rooms, illustrating how the boyars lived. During the week the museum is generally open only to groups with advance reservations, but if you ask, you may be allowed to join a group. On Sunday the museum is open to the general public; as during the rest of the week, you can only visit in groups, but after a short wait, enough individuals will gather here to form a tour. Tours are available in English, but you must make reservations two months ahead. The entrance is downstairs, opposite the lower doorway of the Rossiya hotel. ✉ *10 Varvarka ul., Kitai Gorod* ☎ *495/298–3706* 💰 *150R* ⊙ *Mon. and Wed.–Sat. 10–6, Sun. 11–5* Ⓜ *Kitai Gorod.*

29 **Ryabushinsky Bank** (Рябушинский Банк). Fyodor Shekhtel designed this turn-of-the-20th-century art nouveau masterpiece for the rich merchant Ryabushinsky. The pale-orange building on the opposite side of the street, built in the classical style at the end of the 19th century, is the former Birzha (Stock Exchange); it now houses the Russia Chamber of Commerce and Industry. ✉ *Birzhevaya Pl. at ul. Ilinka, Kitai Gorod* Ⓜ *Ploshchad Revolutsii.*

31 **St. Barbara's Church** (Tserkov Velikomuchenitsy Varvary, Церковь Великомученицы Варвары). This peach-and-white church, built in the classical style at the end of the 18th century, lends its name to the street. ✉ *Varvarka ul. off Red Sq., Kitai Gorod* ⊙ *Services daily at 5 PM* Ⓜ *Ploshchad Revolutsii.*

St. John's Convent (Ivanovsky Monastyr, Ивановский Монастырь). This convent, which was built in the 16th century and restored in the 19th century, was used as a prison in the Stalinist era and was in shambles for many years after that. It's again being refurbished, but the convent is open for limited services. Among the noblewomen who were forced to take the veil here were Empress Elizabeth's illegitimate daughter, Princess Augusta Tarakanova, and the mad serf owner Dariya Saltykova, who was imprisoned here after she murdered 138 of her serfs, most of them young women. ✉ *Zabelina ul. and Maly Ivanovsky per.* 💰 *Free* ⊙ *Services weekdays at 6 AM and 10:30 PM, weekends at 7 AM and 5 PM* Ⓜ *Kitai Gorod.*

Sandunovskaya Banya. The Sandunovsky *banya* (sauna) has been popular ever since it was built in the late 19th century, and it's still one of the places to be seen around town. The ornate interior has appeared in several classic Russian films. ⊠ *14 Neglinniy ul.* ☎ *495/925–4631 or 495/928–4633* ⊕ *www.sanduny.ru* ▧ *600R–1,000R* ⏱ *Daily 8 AM–10 PM* Ⓜ *Teatralnaya.*

⓯ **V. I. Lenin Museum** (Muzey V. I. Lenina, Музей В.И. Ленина). Although during the time of Soviet Russia this was a solemn and sacred place, the museum is now closed. The magnificent redbrick exterior is well worth a look, however. Former disciples of Lenin usually congregate outside the museum selling pamphlets, books, and old badges, and arguing the wrongs of the world away. ⊠ *Ploshchad Revolutsii, Kitai Gorod* Ⓜ *Teatralnaya.*

Tverskaya Ulitsa: Moscow's Fifth Avenue
Тверская Улица

Tverskaya ulitsa is Moscow's main shopping artery, attracting shoppers hungry for the latest trends, as well as foreign investors looking for a lucrative place to set up shop. The lovely, wide boulevard is lined with perfumeries, banks and exchanges, eateries, and bookshops. Some of the city's best and biggest stores are on the ground floors of massive apartment buildings, some quite attractive and graced by a fine art nouveau style. On a sunny day, Tverskaya is an especially pleasant walk. Keep an eye out for plaques (in Russian) etched in stone on building walls. These will tell you about the famous people, usually artists, politicians, or academicians, who lived or worked here.

As the line of the road that led from the northern tip of the Kremlin to the ancient town of Tver, Tverskaya ulitsa had been an important route for centuries. Later that road was extended all the way to the new capital on the Baltic Sea, St. Petersburg. Tverskaya ulitsa was given its present form in the mid-1930s, and from 1932 to 1990 the road was known as Gorky Street, in honor of the writer Maxim Gorky, the father of Soviet socialist realism. In 1990 the first section of the street, leading from the heart of town to Triumfalnaya Ploshchad, was given back its prerevolutionary name of Tverskaya ulitsa. A year later, the second section, ending at the Belorussian Railway Station, was also returned to its old name—Tverskaya-Yamskaya. Until the rebuilding in the 1930s, Tverskaya ulitsa was narrow and twisting, lined in places with wooden houses. Today it's a broad, busy avenue, a tribute to the grandiose reconstruction projects of the Stalinist era.

a good walk

Walking away from the northern side of the Kremlin up the left-hand side of the street, you pass the **Yermolova Theater** ▶ ㊻, a theater with an arched entrance at No. 5. One short block farther stands the **Central Telegraph** ㊽, with a striking semicircular entrance. On the opposite side of the avenue, the pedestrianized Kamergersky pereulok, with a few interesting bookshops and lots of good cafés, leads off to the right. The small green building on the left-hand side of this street houses the **Moscow Art Theater** ㊾.

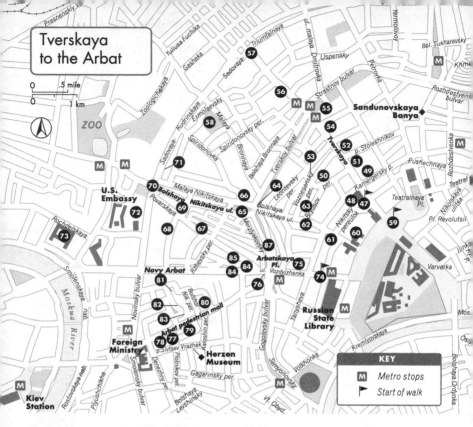

Tverskaya to the Arbat

0   .5 mile
0   1 km

ZOO

U.S. Embassy

Sandunovskaya Banya

Novy Arbat

Arbatskaya Pl.

Foreign Ministry

Arbat pedestrian mall

Herzen Museum

Kiev Station

Russian State Library

KEY

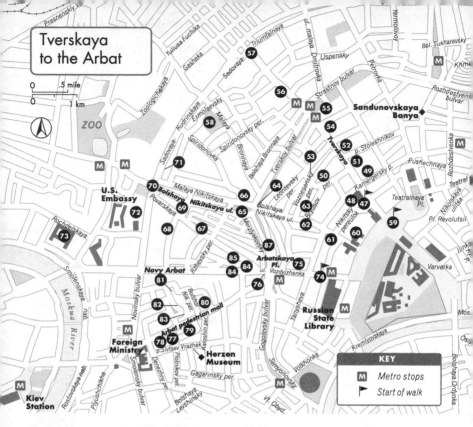 Metro stops

▶ Start of walk

Tverskaya Ulitsa ▼

Central Telegraph **48**

Church of the Resurrection **50**

Moscow Art Theater **49**

Moscow City Council **51**

Museum of the Contemporary History of Russia **56**

Patriarch's Pond **58**

Pushkinskaya Ploshchad **55**

Stanislavsky Museum ...**53**

Triumfalnaya Ploshchad **57**

Tverskaya Ploshchad **52**

Yeliseyevsky's **54**

Yermolova Theater **47**

Bolshaya Nikitskaya Ulitsa ▼

Bely Dom **73**

CDL: Central House of Writers **69**

Chaliapin House Museum **72**

Chekhov House Museum **71**

Church of the Great Ascension **65**

Episcopal Church **63**

Gorky Literary Museum **67**

Kudrinskaya Ploshchad **70**

Manezhnaya Ploshchad **59**

Moscow State University **60**

Nikitskiye Vorota **64**

Ryabushinsky Mansion **66**

Tchaikovsky Conservatory **62**

Tsvetaeva House Museum **68**

Zoological Museum **61**

The Arbat, Old & New ▼

Andrei Bely Apartment Museum **78**

Arbatskaya Ploshchad ...**76**

Church of St. Simon the Stylite **85**

Church of the Transfiguration on the Sands **82**

Dom Druzhby **75**

Dom Knigi **84**

Gogol statue **87**

Lermontov House Museum **86**

Melnikov House **79**

Pushkin Apartment Museum **77**

Scriabin Museum **83**

Shchusev Architecture Museum **74**

Spaso House **81**

Vakhtangov Theater **80**

Continue along the left-hand side of Tverskaya. If you want to take a break from the hustle and bustle, wander down Bryusov pereulok, a side street to the left. You enter the street through the arched passageway of No. 11, which is the Russian Federation of Science and Technology. This street has long been home to many of Moscow's successful artists. At the end of the block, you come upon the pretty **Church of the Resurrection** ⑤⓪. After visiting, head back to Tverskaya ulitsa. Just ahead, the handsome red building with impressive iron gates leading to its adjacent side street is the **Moscow City Council** ⑤①. Across the street, another short stretch brings you to the small square **Tverskaya Ploshchad** ⑤②. Farther north on the street, again on the left-hand side, you pass Leontyevsky pereulok. Wander down this street to reach the **Stanislavsky Museum** ⑤③ at No. 6 and to see many graceful 18th- and 19th-century buildings housing embassies. Retrace your steps to Tverskaya and head north again. At No. 14 stands **Yeliseyevsky's** ⑤④, the most dazzling of all of Moscow's stores. Head farther up the street, toward **Pushkinskaya Ploshchad** ⑤⑤, named after the revered poet and writer. Bordering the west side of the square is the Pushkinskaya Cinema, which stands on the site of the former Strastnoi Monastery (Convent of the Lord's Passion), which dated to the mid-17th century. The monastery was destroyed in 1937, and all that remains today is the white-stone Church of the Nativity near the corner with ulitsa Chekhova (to the far left as you face the theater).

Bordering the square to the right and left of the park are the offices of some of Russia's largest and most influential newspapers. Easily spotted is *Izvestia* (*News*), once the mouthpiece of the Soviet government and now considered a liberal newspaper. Between 18 and 20 Tverskaya, if you look down the alley, you'll see the striking facade of *Trud* (*Labor*), the official newspaper of the trade unions and a conservative voice. Looking back to the far corner that you came from, you'll see the building that once held *Moskovskie novosti* (*Moscow News*), the newspaper that helped give glasnost (openess) true meaning back in the early years of perestroika (restructuring). Its brave editor allowed articles on topics then considered extremely controversial, from Stalinist collectivization to the ethnic strife in Armenia and Azerbaijan. Although the newspaper has left the building its sign is still visible on top of the roof.

Continuing along Tverskaya ulitsa, you reach the attractive railings of **Museum of the Contemporary History of Russia** ⑤⑥ and then pass the Stanislavsky Theater. The next major intersection is **Triumfalnaya Ploshchad** ⑤⑦. On the north side of Triumfalnaya Ploshchad, Tverskaya ulitsa becomes **Tverskaya-Yamskaya ulitsa.** Walk on the left-hand side of Triumfalnaya Ploshchad on Bolshaya Sadovaya ulitsa. Take a left on Malaya Bronnaya ulitsa. After 10 minutes, **Patriarch's Pond** ⑤⑧, a shady park with a pond, will be just a few steps away on your right.

TIMING Allow at least three hours for this tour, five or six if you plan to visit the museums along the route.

What to See

 Central Telegraph (Tsentralny Telegraf, Центральный Телеграф). The striking semicircular entrance is adorned with a large, illuminated, and constantly revolving globe and a huge digital clock. Inside, you can buy stamps, send a fax home, make a phone call abroad, or use the Internet (although the Net City Internet café on nearby Kamergersky pereulok is a more convenient and more comfortable choice). There are also currency-exchange counters and ATMs in the lobby, plus the main post office. ⊠ *7 Tverskaya ul.* ☎ *495/504–4444* ⊙ *Daily 9–8* Ⓜ *Okhotny Ryad.*

50 **Church of the Resurrection** (Tserkov Voskreseniya, Церковь Воскресения). Built in 1629, this is one of the few lucky churches to have stayed open throughout the years of Soviet rule. As a survivor, the church was the recipient of many priceless icons from less fortunate churches destroyed or closed by the Soviets. Services are still held here daily. Be sure to look at the beautiful ceilings in the chapels on either side of you as you enter. Two famous icons, depicting the Coronation of the Virgin Mary and the Assumption of the Blessed Virgin Mary, hang in the vaults on either side of the vestibule. ⊠ *2 Bryusov per.* ☎ *495/229–6616* Ⓜ *Tverskaya.*

49 **Moscow Art Theater** (MKhAT, Московский Художественный Театр). One of Moscow's most historically important theaters, this performance space is renowned for its productions of the Russian classics, especially those of Anton Chekhov (1860–1904). Founded in 1898 by the celebrated actor and director Konstantin Stanislavsky (1863–1938) and playwright and producer Vladimir Nemirovich-Danchenko (1858–1943), the theater staged the first productions of Chekhov's and Gorky's plays. It was here that Stanislavsky developed the "Stanislavsky Method," based on the realism in traditional Russian theater. After the successful production of Chekhov's *The Seagull* (the first staging in St. Petersburg had bombed), the bird was chosen as the theater's emblem. An affiliated, more modern theater, with a seating capacity of 2,000, also confusingly called the Moscow Art Theater, was opened in 1972 on Tverskoi bulvar, near Stanislavsky's home. The mural opposite the old theater depicts Anton Chekhov, as does the statue at the start of Kamergersky pereulok. ⊠ *3 Kamergersky per.* ☎ *495/692–6748* ⊕ *www.art.theatre. ru* Ⓜ *Okhotny Ryad.*

51 **Moscow City Council** (Mossoviet, Моссовет). This impressive structure was built at the end of the 18th century by Matvey Kazakov for the Moscow governor-general. During the reconstruction of Tverskaya ulitsa in the 1930s, the building was moved back about 45 feet in order to widen the street. The top two stories—a mirror image of the mansion's original two stories—were added at that time. ⊠ *22 Tverskaya ul.* Ⓜ *Tverskaya.*

off the beaten path

CENTRAL ARMED FORCES MUSEUM (Centralny Muzey Vooruzhennikh Sil, Центральный Музей Вооруженных Сил) – The museum is a playground for any lover of army hardware. The museum and its grounds hold a huge collection of Soviet and prerevolutionary arms from tanks to intercontinental missiles. The museum also takes you through a compelling tour through the wars and battles that Soviet and Russian forces have fought, from the Civil War to the Afghan War. ⊠ *2 ul. Sovietskoi Armii, Northern Outskirts* ☎ *495/681–4877* ⊕ *www.armymuseum.ru* ✉ *50R* ⊙ *Wed.–Sun. 10–5* Ⓜ *Novoslobodskaya.*

off the beaten path

DOSTOYEVSKY MEMORIAL APARTMENT (Muzey-Kvartira Dostoevskovo, Музей-квартира Достоевского) – This small, museum is devoted to the great Russian novelist. It's on the grounds of the hospital where he was born and where his father, Mikhail Andreevich, resided and worked as a doctor. Fyodor Dostoyevsky (1821–81) lived here until he was 16. The museum has kept things much as they were, from family pictures to the neat, middle-class furniture. ✉ *2 ul. Dostoevskovo, Northern Outskirts* ☎ *495/681–1085* *30R* ⏲ *Wed. and Fri. 2–8, Thurs. and weekends 11–6; closed last day of month* Ⓜ *Novoslobodskaya.*

56 **Museum of the Contemporary History of Russia** (Muzey Sovremennoi Istorii Rossii, Музей Современной Истории России). The onetime social center of the Moscow aristocracy has an entrance flanked by two smirking lions. Originally built by Giliardi in 1787, the mansion was rebuilt in the classical style after the Moscow Fire of 1812. The building housed the Museum of the Revolution from 1926 to the late 20th century, at which time the museum was converted to its present purpose. Although it retains many of its former exhibits—heavily imbued with Soviet propaganda—the museum has been updated to reflect the changing political climate in Russia and exhibits cover events up to 2000. The permanent exhibit, on the second floor, begins with a review of the first workers' organizations in the 19th century. The exhibits outlining the 1905 and 1917 revolutions include the horse-drawn machine-gun cart of the First Cavalry Army, the texts of the first decrees of the Soviet government on peace and land, dioramas and paintings portraying revolutionary battles, and thousands of other relics. The next rooms outline the history of Soviet rule, with extensive material devoted to Stalin's rise to power before whizzing through the short post-Soviet history.

With a huge archive and the country's best collection of political posters and medals, the museum has a reputation for hosting excellent temporary exhibits. Explanations are only in Russian, but you can arrange a tour in English by calling ahead. The fine gift shop sells Russian souvenirs (including some beautiful amber) and great vintage items like flags and political-rally posters. ✉ *21 Tverskaya ul.* ☎ *495/299–6724* 🌐 *www.sovr.ru* *150R* ⏲ *Tues.–Sun. 10–6; closed last Fri. of month* Ⓜ *Tverskaya.*

58 **Patriarch's Pond** (Patriarshy Prudy, Патриаршие Пруды). The beginning of Russian satirist and novelist Mikhail Bulgakov's (1891–1940) novel *The Master and Margarita* is set in this small park. Bulgakov is most famous for this novel and his hilarious play *Heart of a Dog*. The park and pond were named after the patriarch of the Orthodox Church, who once owned the area. Shaded by trees and with plenty of benches, it's a nice spot for a break, and there are several good restaurants nearby. In winter the pond is used as a skating rink. Cafe Margarita is nearby at 28 Malaya Bronnaya, and its lively musical performers and Bulgakov mural make it worth a visit, especially if you've read any Bulgakov. ✉ *Malaya Bronnaya ul. at Yermoleyevsky per.* Ⓜ *Mayakovskaya.*

55 **Pushkin Square** (Pushkinskaya Ploshchad, Пушкинская Площадь). The city's first McDonald's is at this site, where Moscow's innermost ring, the Boulevard Ring, crosses Tverskaya ulitsa. There are rarely lines anymore at this McDonald's, as there were when it first opened in 1990 (branches have opened throughout the city), but it remains very popular. The counters are always crowded, with disorganized but swiftly moving lines. The menu hews to the original, and prices are cheaper than in the States. A park next to McDonald's is a nice place to sit and is particularly festive with kebab stands and army brass bands in summer. On the opposite side of the street is the most popular meeting place in town for Muscovites: a fountain in the center of a terraced park, which is lined with benches. A bronze statue of Alexander Pushkin (1799–1837) stands at the top of the park. It's the work of Alexander Opekushin and was erected by public subscription in 1880. Summer and winter, fresh flowers on the pedestal prove that the poet's admirers are still ardent and numerous. Ⓜ *Pushkinskaya.*

Russian Folk Art Museum (Muzey Narodnovo Iskusstva, Музей Народного Искусства). At this writing the museum was closed for a lengthy renovation. It does have an interesting matryoshka shop, which is worth looking at if you're nearby; call ahead to see if it has reopened. The museum displays a rich collection of Russian folk art dating from the 17th century to the present, including antique and modern pottery, ceramics, glassware, metalwork, wood, bone, embroidery, lace, and popular prints. Theater director Konstantin Stanislavsky, founder of the Moscow Art Theater, lived for a time in the building at No. 6. ✉ *7 Stanislavskovo ul.* ☎ *495/290–2114* Ⓜ *Tverskaya.*

53 **Stanislavsky Museum** (Muzey Stanislavskovo, Музей Станиславского). Konstantin Stanislavsky was a Russian actor, director, and producer, as well as the founder of the Stanislavsky Method, the catalyst for method acting. He was also one of the founders of the Moscow Art Theater. Stanislavsky lived and worked in this house during the last 17 years of his life. The house, which has been kept as it was while he lived here, showcases photos and theater memorabilia. ✉ *6 Leontyevsky per.* ☎ *495/ 229–2442 or 495/229–2855* 💰 *50R* ☉ *Wed. and Fri. 2–7, Thurs. 11–5, weekends 11–3; closed last Thurs. of month* Ⓜ *Pushkinskaya.*

57 **Triumphal Square** (Triumfalnaya Ploshchad, Триумфальная Площадь). This major intersection is where the grand boulevard of Moscow, the Garden Ring, crosses Tverskaya ulitsa. Traffic here also passes through a tunnel running below Tverskaya ulitsa, and there's an underpass for pedestrians. A statue of the revolutionary poet Vladimir Mayakovsky (1893–1930) stands in the center of the square. It's generally believed that Mayakovsky committed suicide out of disillusionment with the revolution he had so passionately supported.

The square is a center of Moscow's cultural life. The **Tchaikovsky Concert Hall,** opened in 1940, stands on the corner nearest you. In its foyer are various food outlets, where you can get anything from pizza at Pizza Hut to croissants and coffee at the dependable Brioche. The **Satire Theater** is right next door, on the Garden Ring. On the far side of the

MOSCOW'S MAGNIFICENT METRO

EVEN IF YOU DON'T PLAN *on using the metro to get around Moscow, it's still worth taking a peek at this wonder of the urban world. The first line opened in 1935 and the earliest stations—in the city center and along the ring line—were built as public palaces. Many of the millions of commuters using the system each day bustle past chandeliers, sculptures, stained-glass windows, beautiful mosaics, and pink, white, and black marble. With its rich collection of decorative materials, the metro has often been called a museum; it's even been said that no geological museum in the world has such a peculiar stone library.*

Mayakovskaya station, opened in 1938, may well be the jewel in the crown of the Moscow metro. The vaulted ceiling of the grand central hall has 33 mosaic panels, based on the theme "One Day of Soviet Skies," by Russian artist Alexander Deineka. Novoslobodskaya, opened in

*1952, sparkles, thanks to its light-backed stained glass. With their Soviet-inspired designs, several other stations—such as **Ploshchad Revolutsii**, with its bronze figures from the socialist world order (farmers, soliders, and such)—are tourist attractions in their own right.*

In the past, Moscow's metro architects won international architecture awards for their designs. Designs of new stations, however, have departed somewhat from these grand old stations; they lack brass sculptures and intricate stained glass, for example. But with indirect lighting, exquisite marble, and an open, airy feeling, these new stations reflect modern life in a way that the monumental Soviet displays of past glories do not. As of October 2005, Moscow's was the most heavily used metro system in the world. It also has the most miles of track (299 km), but Madrid is expected to inch past it in 2007.

square stands the **Moskva Cinema**, the popular **Mossoviet Theater** is also nearby, at 16 Bolshaya Sadovaya. To your far left is the multitiered tower of the imposing **Peking Hotel,** opened in 1956 as a mark of Sino-Soviet friendship. Looking to your right, you'll see the **American Bar and Grill** and **City Grill,** popular with Russians as well as the foreign community.

While you're here, it's worth riding the escalator down for a peek at the spectacular interior of the **Mayakovskaya metro station,** which like many early stations, lies deep underground (it doubled as a bomb shelter during World War II). Stalin made a famous speech here on the 24th anniversary of the Bolshevik Revolution, at the height of the Siege of Moscow. Colorful, pastel mosaics depicting Soviet achievements in outer space decorate the ceiling. The main entrance of the metro is closed for repairs and is expected to reopen in 2007. A new one lies approximately 100 yards up Tverskaya-Yamskaya ulitsa. Ⓜ *Mayakovskaya.*

🔵52 **Tverskaya Ploshchad** (Тверская Площадь). This square, which dates to 1792, was named for the street, but in 1918 it was renamed Sovetskaya (Soviet) Ploshchad. In 1994 its historical name, Tverskaya, was reinstated. In the small park here stands a statue of Prince Yuri Dolgoruky, the founder of Moscow in 1147. The equestrian statue was erected in 1954, shortly after the celebrations marking Moscow's 800th anniversary. Ⓜ *Tverskaya.*

Tverskaya-Yamskaya ulitsa (Тверская-Ямская улица). This last section of Tverskaya ulitsa has little of historical interest. The street ends at the Belorussky Railway Station, which also has two interconnecting metro stations. A statue of Maxim Gorky, erected in the 1950s, stands in a small park outside the station. It's near the site of the former Triumphal Gates, built in the 19th century by the architect Osip Bove to commemorate the Russian victory in the war with Napoléon. The gates were demolished in a typical fit of destruction in the 1930s. Fragments can be found on the grounds of the Donskoy Monastery. A replica of the original gates was erected in 1968 near Poklonnaya Hill, at the end of Kutuzovsky prospekt. Ⓜ *Mayakovskaya.*

❺❹ **Yeliseyevsky's** (Елисеевский). Of all the stores and boutiques on Tverskaya ulitsa, this grocery store at No. 14, in a Matvei Kazakov–designed, late-18th-century, classical mansion, has the most dazzling interior, with chandeliers, stained glass, and gilt wall decorations. Under Communist administration, the store had the official, generic title Gastronom No. 1, but it once again carries the name that most people continued to call it even then—Yeliseyevsky's, after the rich merchant from St. Petersburg who owned the store before the revolution. The store sells loads of good cognac and Georgian wine (including Stalin's favorite, Khvanchkara—still much touted despite its unsavory stamp of approval). The large alcohol section in the back room includes a number of vodkas, some in bottles shaped as bears or, for one brand, Pushkin's head. Coffee beans, caviar, and candy are other items you can buy here. One of the few food stores in the city center, and open 24 hours, it's a good place to stock up on items. ✉ *14 Tverskaya ul.* ☎ *495/209–0760* ⏰ *Daily, 24 hrs* Ⓜ *Tverskaya or Pushkinskaya.*

▶ ❹❼ **Yermolova Theater** (Teatr imeni Yermolovoi, Театр имени Ермоловой). The theater housed in this short building with an arched entrance was founded in 1937 and named after the Russian actress Maria Yermolova (1853–1928). ✉ *5 Tverskaya ul.* ☎ *495/203–9032* Ⓜ *Okhotny Ryad.*

The Old Moscow of Bolshaya Nikitskaya Ulitsa
Большая Никитская Улица

Bolshaya Nikitskaya ulitsa is one of the many old streets radiating from the Kremlin, spokelike as Tverskaya ulitsa to the northeast and Novy Arbat to the southwest. The street was laid out along the former road to Novgorod, an ancient town northwest of Moscow, and is divided into two sections. The first part is lined with 18th- and 19th-century mansions; it begins at Manezhnaya Ploshchad, across from the fortification walls of the Kremlin. The second section, notable for its enchanting art nouveau mansions, starts at Nikitskiye Vorota square, where Bolshaya Nikitskaya ulitsa intersects with Bulvarnoye Koltso (the Boulevard Ring). Like most Moscow streets, Bolshaya Nikitskaya has been through a few name changes. Before the 1917 revolution, it was named Bolshaya

Nikitskaya, after the Nikitsky Convent, which was founded in the 16th century. In 1920 it was renamed ulitsa Gertsena in honor of the 19th-century philosopher Alexander Herzen, who exerted a tremendous influence on Russian sociopolitical thought in the mid-19th century as a progressive writer and fierce advocate of liberal reform.

a good walk

Start at **Manezhnaya Ploshchad** ⑤ ▶, which you can walk to from the Okhotny Ryad metro stop. Take the exit to the Okhotny Ryad shopping mall. Wander through the shopping mall at your leisure and leave the building through any exit to your left. This will lead you to lower Manezhnaya Ploshchad, where the Russian sculptor Zurab Tsereteli's bronze statues of Russian fairy-tale characters stand in a long fountain (the fountain is supposed to represent the Neglinnaya River, which once ran here, but has since been relegated underground). Make your way up the stairs on either side of the fountain to reach Manezhnaya Ploshchad. Walk across the square away from the Kremlin and cross the street. You'll come to the old campus of **Moscow State University** ⑥, Russia's oldest university. Pass the university and make a right onto Bolshaya Nikitskaya ulitsa. Turn right and walk one block up to the **Zoological Museum** ⑥, at the corner of ulitsa Belinskovo. Farther up, on the left-hand side of the street at No. 13, is the **Tchaikovsky Conservatory** ⑥, where the famous Tchaikovsky Music Competition takes place. Just past the conservatory is Voznesensky pereulok; make a right onto this street and walk to Moscow's **Episcopal Church** ⑥, at No. 8. Return to Bolshaya Nikitskaya ulitsa and walk 10 minutes to the square **Nikitskiye Vorota** ⑥.

The busy road in front of you, intersecting Bolshaya Nikitskaya ulitsa, is the Boulevard Ring, which forms a semicircle around the city center. On the other side of the boulevard, facing the square, is the classical **Church of the Great Ascension** ⑥. Bolshaya Nikitskaya ulitsa veers sharply to the left here, so that if you continue straight ahead, keeping to the right of the square, you'll end up on Malaya Nikitskaya ulitsa. About half a block down, near the corner, is a marvelous example of Moscow art nouveau, the **Ryabushinsky Mansion** ⑥. Follow the road behind the Church of the Great Ascension and continue straight onto Nozhovyi pereulok (which leads to the left off Bolshaya Nikitskaya ulitsa). As you walk down, Nozhovyi turns into Maly Rzhevsky pereulok and passes several side streets with names like Stolovy (Dining Room), Skatertny (Tablecloth), and Khlebny (Bread). The streets are named after the servants of the tsar (the waiters, the linen makers, the bakers) who lived in this area. Today the district houses many foreign embassies. Walk down Paliashvili ulitsa until you reach the busy intersection with **Povarskaya ulitsa**, where you should turn right. The mansion at No. 25 (on the left-hand side of the street) houses the **Gorky Literary Museum** ⑥, a must-see only for admirers of Maxim Gorky.

Walk along Povarskaya and take the first road on the left, Borisoglebsky pereulok. On the right you'll reach **Tsvetaeva House Museum** ⑥. Retrace your steps to Povarskaya ulitsa for another literary sight, the **CDL: Central House of Writers** ⑥. Continue along Povarskaya ulitsa until it comes out onto Novinsky bulvar; in front of you is **Kudrinskaya Ploshchad** ⑦. Turn right and you'll find **Chekhov House Museum** ⑦ on your right after about 100 yards. Walk south on Novinsky bulvar to reach the **Chaliapin House Museum** ⓱, at one time the home of one of the world's great opera singers. Farther down on the right side of the street you can see the U.S. embassy and the **Bely Dom** ⓮.

TIMING Because this walk covers quite a bit of territory and includes detours down crooked streets in picturesque neighborhoods, it's best to allow a full day to see everything at a leisurely pace. The tour runs from the Okhotny Ryad metro station to the Barrikadnaya station—roughly 3 km (2 mi) in a straight line—save this walk for a day when you're well rested.

What to See

⓮ **Bely Dom** (White House, Белый Дом). This large, white, modern building perched along the riverbank, across the river from the Ukraina hotel, is one of the seven "Stalin Gothic" skyscrapers built in Moscow in the mid-20th century. Before the August 1991 coup the White House was the headquarters of the Russian Republic of the USSR. You may have first seen the building on television when it was shelled in October 1993 in response to the rioting and near-coup by Vice President Alexander Rutskoi and parliamentarians. They had barricaded themselves in the White House after Yeltsin's decision to dissolve parliament and hold new elections. Today the building houses the prime minister's and the Russian government's offices and is called the Dom Pravitelstva, or Government House. ⊠ *2 Krasnopresnenskaya nab., Krasnaya Presnya* ☎ *495/205–5735* Ⓜ *Barrikadnaya or Krasnaya Presnya.*

⓰ **CDL: Central House of Writers** (Tsentralny Dom Literatorov). The CDL is an exclusive club for members of the Writers' Union. The club (at 53 Bolshaya Nikitskaya; it's the same building, but the club entrance is on another street) is off-limits, but the dining room is open to the public and is now one of the city's very best restaurants. There's also an art-house cinema on the floor above the restaurant. Next door (No. 52) is a large mansion, enclosed by a courtyard, that houses the administrative offices of the Writers' Union. It's commonly believed that Leo Tolstoy (1828–1910) used this mansion as a model for his description of the Rostov home in *War and Peace*. A statue of Tolstoy stands in the courtyard. Mikhail Bulgakov (1891–1940) set part of his wonderful satire of Soviet life, *The Master and Margarita*, here. ⊠ *50 Povarskaya ul.* ☎ *495/291–1515* Ⓜ *Barrikadnaya.*

⓱ **Chaliapin House Museum** (Dom-muzey Chaliapina, Дом-музей Шаляпина). Fyodor Chaliapin (1873–1938), one of the world's greatest opera singers, lived in this beautifully restored manor house from 1910 to 1922. Chaliapin was stripped of his Soviet citizenship while on tour in France in 1922; he never returned to Russia again. The Soviets turned his home into an apartment building, and until restorations in the 1980s, the building contained 60 communal apartments. With help from Chaliapin's family in France, the rooms have again been arranged and furnished as they were when the singer lived here. The walls are covered with works of art given to Chaliapin by talented friends, such as the artists Mikhail Vrubel and Isaac Levitan. Also on display are Chali-

THE SEVEN GOTHIC SISTERS

WITH THEIR SPOOKILY LIT *cornices dominating the skyline since the mid-20th century, the "Seven Sisters" (also known as the "Stalin Gothics") are as much a part of the Moscow experience as the Empire State Building is in New York. The neo-Gothic buildings are often called "wedding cake" skyscrapers because their tiered construction creates a sense of upward movement and grandeur, like a rocket on standby.*

The seven buildings—the White House (Bely Dom) at the end of the Arbat; the Ukraina and Leningradskaya hotels; the residential buildings at Kudrinskaya Ploshchad (Kudrinsky Square), Kotelnicheskaya naberezhnaya (Kotelnicheskaya Embankment), and Krasniye Vorota; and the imposing Moscow State University on Sparrow Hills—were constructed when the country lay in ruins, just after World War II, intended as a symbol of Soviet power at the beginning of the Cold War. Inspired, perhaps, by news of U.S. president Harry Truman laying the first stone for the United Nations building in New York, Stalin ordered the skyscrapers to be built in 1947, on the 800th anniversary of Moscow's founding. He took a personal interest in their design, insisting, for example, that each building have a central tower and spire. German prisoners of war were forced to work on several of the buildings.

An eighth skyscraper was planned (before the others were started) but never built: the grandiose Palace of Soviets, which was meant to replace the Kremlin as the seat of government power. It was intended to be the tallest building in the world, with a height of 1,378 feet topped by a 300-foot statue of Lenin. The site of the Cathedral of Christ Our Savior on the Moskva River was chosen, and the church was demolished in 1931. Only later did builders realize that the ground was too wet to support such an enormous structure. The plans were abandoned, and the area was turned into a swimming pool until the cathedral was rebuilt in 1997.

According to the Soviet propaganda of the time, most of the new buildings were part of the government's drive to replace slums with better housing. In truth, residents were mainly party members, actors, writers, and other members of the elite. With few ordinary people living in or having access to the buildings, legendary stories developed around the Seven Sisters. The Ukraina's spire was said to hide a nuclear-rocket launcher, while Moscow State University was rumored to have a secret tunnel leading to Stalin's dacha. The university was also said to run as deep underground as it did above, concealing secret study centers and a metro connection. The building at Kudrinskaya Ploshchad overlooks the U.S. embassy. It was said that KGB spies kept an eye on the embassy compound from certain windows.

Today you can easily visit most of the skyscrapers, particularly the Ukraina and Leningradskaya hotels. The White House may still be off-limits, but a determined manner is often all you need to get past the doorman at the university or the residential buildings. You may also notice a new stepsister on the drive in from Sheremetyevo II airport. Triumph Palace, near the Sokol metro station, is a modern copy of the original skyscrapers. This expensive block of flats, the tallest residential building in Europe at 866 feet, has been criticized by architects, but its huge size and similarity to the original Seven Sisters will likely make it in time another city symbol.

apin's colorful costumes, which were donated to the museum by his son. When you reach the piano room, you're treated to original recordings of Chaliapin singing his favorite roles. Entrance is from inside the courtyard. English-language tours are available and should be reserved ahead of time. ⊠ *25–27 Novinsky bulvar* ☎ *495/252–2530* ✉ *25R* ☉ *Tues. and Sat.10–6, Wed. and Thurs. 11:30–6:30, Sun. 10–4; closed last day of month* Ⓜ *Barrikadnaya.*

🟤 **Chekhov House Museum** (Dom-muzey Chekhova, Дом-музей Чехова). The sign DR. CHEKHOV still hangs from the door of this home where Chekhov resided from 1886 to 1890. The rooms are arranged as they were when he lived here, and his manuscripts, letters, photographs, and personal effects are exhibited. ⊠ *6 Sadovaya-Kudrinskaya ul.* ☎ *495/ 291–6154 or 495/291–3837* ✉ *30R* ☉ *Wed.–Fri. 2–6, weekends 11–4* Ⓜ *Barrikadnaya.*

🟤 **Church of the Great Ascension** (Tserkov Bolshovo Vozneseniya, Церковь Большого Вознесения). Like Moscow State University, this classical church was designed by Matvei Kazakov and built in the 1820s. For years it stood empty and abandoned, but after major repair, religious services have resumed here. The church is most famous as the site where the Russian poet Alexander Pushkin married the younger Natalya Goncharova; Pushkin died outside St. Petersburg six years after their wedding, in a duel defending her honor. (History has judged Natalya harshly; she was probably not guilty of adultery, although she did enjoy flirting.) The statue in the park to the left of the church as you face it is of Alexey Tolstoy, a relative of Leo's and a well-known Soviet writer of historical novels. A house museum dedicated to him is next to the Ryabushinsky Mansion. ⊠ *36 Malaya Nikitskaya ul.* Ⓜ *Arbatskaya.*

🟤 **Episcopal Church** (Episcopalnaya tserkov, Епископальная Церковь). Moscow's only Episcopal church is inside this attractive red-sandstone building. Built in 1884, it served the British-expatriate community for more than 40 years, including a mass for Queen Victoria after her death in 1901. No bells were rung then, however, because only Orthodox churches were allowed to have them in the city. Instead the tower was used as a strong room for the rich British merchant community. The 1917 revolution ended spiritual and secular functions, however, and the church was closed. The pews are believed to have been subsequently burned in the harsh winters of the early 1920s, and the stained glass was replaced when the building was converted into a recording studio. Today the English have reacquired the property, and it's again a working church and gathering place for the community. ⊠ *8 Voznesensky per.* Ⓜ *Okhotny Ryad.*

🟤 **Gorky Literary Museum** (Literaturny Muzey Gorkovo, Литературный Музей Горького). For Gorky buffs only, this museum is packed with the letters, manuscripts, and pictures of the great proletarian writer. There are also portraits of him by Nesterov and Serov. Gorky never lived here, but there is a red wooden reproduction of his childhood home, complete with village yard and outbuildings. You probably won't be able to leave without the kindly but fierce matrons who protect this place compelling you to sign the guestbook. Phone ahead for individual or group tours in English. ✉ *25a Povarskaya ul.* ☎ *495/290–5130* 🖃 *Free* 🕙 *Mon., Tues., and Thurs. 10–5, Wed. and Fri. noon–6; closed 1st Thurs. of month* Ⓜ *Barrikadnaya.*

70 **Kudrinskaya Ploshchad** (Kudrinsky Square, Кудринская Площадь). Along one side of this square, cars race along the Garden Ring, the major circular road surrounding Moscow. If you approach the ring from Bolshaya Nikitskaya ulitsa or Povarskaya ulitsa, the first thing to catch your eye will be the 22-story skyscraper directly across Novinsky bulvar. One of the seven Stalin Gothics, this one is 525 feet high. The ground floor is taken up by shops and the rest of the building contains apartments. This area saw heavy fighting during the uprisings of 1905 and 1917 (the plaza was previously called Ploshchad Vosstaniya, or Insurrection Square). The Barrikadnaya (Barricade) metro station is very close by. Cross the ulitsa Barrikadnaya and bear right and down the hill; you'll see people streaming into the station to your right. Ⓜ *Barrikadnaya.*

▶ **59** **Manezhnaya Ploshchad** (Manezh Square, Манежная Площадь). When the Soviets razed this square in 1938, many of the area's old buildings were lost. The plan, which never came to pass, was to build a superhighway through the area. In 1967 the square was renamed "50th Anniversary of the October Revolution Square." In the 1990s the square reverted to its original name and construction of an underground shopping mall was begun. Construction was halted in 1993 to let archaeologists excavate the area. The team found a plethora of artifacts dating from as far back as the 13th century. In 1997 the Manezh shopping mall was finally opened, much to the chagrin of most Muscovites, who saw it as an eyesore. The present (and prerevolutionary) name comes from the Imperial Riding School, or Manezh, that stands on the opposite side of the square from the Moskva Hotel. The 1817 structure was gutted by a fire in early 2004, but has since been restored.

Opened in 1935, the **Moskva Hotel** was one of the first buildings erected as part of Stalin's reconstruction plan for Moscow. Despite protests, the hotel that's featured on Stolichnaya vodka labels was demolished in late 2003 to make way for a new Moskva, which is planned to exactly replicate the facade of the original structure; the new hotel was under construction at this writing.

60 **Moscow State University** (Moskovsky Gosudarstvenny Universitet, Московский Государственный Университет). Russia's oldest university was founded in 1755 by the father of Russian science, Mikhail Lomonosov. The neoclassical buildings here were originally designed by Matvei Kazakov in 1786–93. They were rebuilt and embellished in the mid-19th century, after the 1812 fire. The law and journalism schools are still housed in these quarters. The university's main campus is on Sparrow Hills (formerly Lenin Hills), southwest of the city center, in the largest of the so-called Stalin Gothic skyscrapers. ✉ *19 Mokhovaya ul.* Ⓜ *Okhotny Ryad.*

National Hotel (Гостиница Националь). The ornate art nouveau splendor of the National Hotel, built in 1903, belies its revolutionary function as the pre-Kremlin residence for Lenin, and subsequent home for Communist Party operatives and fellow travelers, such as author John Reed. Beautiful mosaics adorn the hotel facade; inside, the luxurious rooms and restaurants conjure up the National's prerevolutionary dominance in elegance. ✉ *15/1 Mokhovaya ul.* ☎ *495/258–7000* ⊕ *www. national.ru* Ⓜ *Okhotny Ryad.*

64 **Nikitskiye Vorota** (Никитские Ворота). This square was named after the gates (*vorota*) of the white-stone fortification walls that once stood here. One side of the square is a modern building with square windows; this is the office of TASS, once the official news agency of the Soviet Union and the mouthpiece of the Kremlin. In the park in the center of the square stands a monument to Kliment Timiryazev, a famous botanist.

The busy road intersecting Bolshaya Nikitskaya ulitsa is the **Bulvarnoye Koltso** (Boulevard Ring), which forms a semicircle around the city center. It begins at the banks of the Moskva River, just south of the Kremlin, running in a northeastern direction. After curving eastward, and then south, it finally reaches the riverbank again after several miles, near the mouth of the Yauza River, northeast of the Kremlin. Its path follows the lines of the 16th-century white-stone fortification wall that gave Moscow the name "White City." The privilege of living within its walls was reserved for the court nobility and craftsmen serving the tsar. The wall was torn down in 1775, on orders from Catherine the Great, and was replaced by the current Boulevard Ring. The perfect way to get a good view of the inner city is to slowly walk along the ring. Running along its center is a broad strip of trees and flowers, dotted with playgrounds and benches. Summer brings out a burst of outdoor cafés, ice-cream vendors, and strolling lovers along the boulevard. Ⓜ *Arbatskaya.*

Oriental Art Museum (Muzey Iskusstva Narodov Vostoka, Музей Искусства Народов Востока). Glass cases filled to capacity with artwork and clothing from the Central Asian republics, China, Japan, and Korea make up the museum's large permanent collection. The museum itself is a cool and calm place to take a leisurely look at the magnificent holdings. Most of the museum is strictly in Russian, but there are a few annotations in English. ✉ *12a Nikitsky bulvar* ☎ *495/202–4555* 💴 *100R* ⊗ *Tues.–Sun. 11–8* Ⓜ *Arbatskaya.*

Cook Street (Povarskaya ulitsa, Поварская улица). This is where the tsar's cooks lived. After the revolution the street was renamed Vorovskovo, in honor of a Soviet diplomat who was assassinated by a Russian, but it has returned to its prerevolutionary name. Povarskaya ulitsa is an important center of the Moscow artistic community, with the film actors' studio, the Russian Academy of Music (the Gnesin Institute), and the Tsentralny Dom Literatorov (Central House of Writers, Центральный Дом Литераторов) all located here. Many of the old mansions have been preserved, and the street retains its prerevolutionary tranquillity and charm. In the first flush days of summer your walk is likely to be accompanied by a rousing drum set or tinkling piano sonata issuing from the open windows of the music school. Ⓜ *Arbatskaya.*

66 **Ryabushinsky Mansion** (Dom Ryabushinskovo, Дом Рябушинского). This marvelous example of Moscow art nouveau was built in 1901 for a wealthy banker and designed by the architect Fyodor Shektel. (If you arrived in Moscow by train, you may have noticed the fanciful Yaroslav Station, another of his masterpieces, just opposite the Leningrad Railway Station.) The building has been wonderfully preserved. This was thanks in part to the fact that Maxim Gorky lived here from 1931 until his death in 1936. Although Gorky was a champion of the proletariat, his home was rather lavish. Gorky himself apparently hated the *style moderne,* as art nouveau was termed back then. Those who don't, however, are charmed by this building of ecru brick and stone painted pink and mauve atop gray foundations. On the exterior, a beautiful mosaic of irises forms a border around the top of most of the house, and a strangely fanciful yet utilitarian iron fence matches the unusual design of the window frames. The spectacular interior is replete with a stained-glass roof and a twisting marble staircase that looks like a wave of gushing water. Tours in English are available; call ahead for more information. ⊠ *6/2 Malaya Nikitskaya ul.* ☎ *495/290–0535* ☒ *Free* ☉ *Wed.–Fri. and Sun. noon–7, Sat. 10–5; closed last Thurs. of month* Ⓜ *Arbatskaya.*

62 **Tchaikovsky Conservatory** (Konservatoriya imeni Chaykovskovo, Консерватория имени Чайковского). The famous Tchaikovsky Music Competition takes place every four years in this conservatory's magnificent concert hall (the next one is scheduled for 2006). The conservatory was founded in 1866 and moved to its current location in 1870. Rachmaninoff, Scriabin, and Tchaikovsky are among the famous composers who worked here. There's a statue of Tchaikovsky in the semicircular park outside the main entrance. It was designed by Vera Mukhina, a famous Soviet sculptor. You can buy reasonably priced tickets to excellent concerts of classical music in the lobby ticket office in the main building. You can also just sit back with a coffee and listen to rehearsals and concerts from the summer garden of the Coffeemania here, near the Tchaikovsky statue. ⊠ *13 Bolshaya Nikitskaya ul.* ☎ *495/229–9401 or 495/229–8745* ⊕ *www.mosconsv.ru* Ⓜ *Okhotny Ryad or Arbatskaya.*

68 **Tsvetaeva House Museum** (Dom-muzey Tsvetaevoy, Дом-музей Цветаевой). Marina Tsvetaeva (1892–1941), the renowned poet, lived in an apartment on the second floor of this building from 1914 to 1922. Today the building houses not only a museum dedicated to her but also a cultural center that arranges international literary evenings, musical events, and annual conferences covering the Silver Age (1890s–1917) and Tsvetaeva. You must ring the bell to enter the museum, which begins on the second floor. Although the rooms are decorated in the style of the early 1900s, they are not as they were when Tsvetaeva lived here. The poetry written on the wall in her bedroom has been re-created. The children's room has some stuffed animals in place of the real animals—a dog, a squirrel, and a turtle, to name a few—Tsvetaeva kept in her home. This place is well worth a visit even if you're not familiar with Tsvetaeva's work, because the staff is enthusiastic and the apartment is well representative of the period. Tours can be arranged in English if you call ahead. ⊠ *6 per. Borisoglebski* ☎ *495/202–3543* ☒ *Free* ☉ *Daily noon–5* Ⓜ *Arbatskaya.*

🕊 **Zoo** (Zoopark, Зоопарк). Zurab Tsereteli, Moscow's most ubiquitous sculptor, designed the statues and gates of Moscow's small zoo. Some people appreciate the whimsical design, which looks as if it came out of a fairy-tale land envisioned by Walt Disney. Others consider it yet another one of Tsereteli's outrageous creations. Visit on a weekday to avoid the large crowds on weekends. ⊠ *1 Bolshaya Gruzinskaya ul.* ☎ *495/255–5375* ⊕ *www.zoo.ru/* ☜ *100R* ⊘ *Apr.–Sept., Tues.–Sun. 10–8; Oct.–Mar., Tues.–Sun. 10–5* Ⓜ *Barrikadnaya.*

🕊 ⓺ **Zoological Museum** (Zoologichesky Muzey, Зоологический Музей). This museum, founded in 1902, is always swarming with schoolchildren, who take a special delight in its huge collection of stuffed mammals, birds, amphibians, and reptiles. The museum also has a collection of more than 1 million insects, including more than 100,000 butterflies donated by a Moscow resident. ⊠ *6 Bolshaya Nikitskaya ul.* ☎ *495/ 203–8923* ⊕ *www.zoo.ru* ☜ *30R* ⊘ *Tues.–Sun. 10–5; closed last Tues. of month* Ⓜ *Okhotny Ryad.*

The Arbat, Old & New
Арбат

Two of downtown Moscow's most interesting and important avenues are the Arbat (also known as the Stary Arbat, or Old Arbat) and Novy Arbat (New Arbat), which are two more spokelike routes leading away from the Kremlin. Stary Arbat is closed to all traffic and revered by Muscovites, who usually refer to it simply as "the Arbat." The area is an attractive, cobbled pedestrian precinct with many gift shops, cafés in restored buildings, and kiosks selling all manner of souvenirs. It's a carnival of portrait artists, poets, and musicians, as well as the enthusiastic admirers of their work. One of the oldest sections of Moscow, the Arbat dates from the 16th century, when it was the beginning of the road that led from the Kremlin to the city of Smolensk. At that time it was also the quarter where court artisans lived, and several of the surrounding streets still recall this in such names as Plotnikov (Carpenter), Serebryany (Silversmith), and Kalashny (Pastry Cook). Early in the 19th century the Arbat became a favorite district of the aristocracy, and a century later it became a favorite shopping street.

Novy Arbat has both a different history and spirit. For almost 30 years it was named Kalinin prospekt, in honor of Mikhail Kalinin, an old Bolshevik whose prestige plummeted after 1991. The stretch from the Kremlin to Arbatskaya Ploshchad has been given back its prerevolutionary name of ulitsa Vozdvizhenka. The second section—which begins where Vozdvizhenka ends and runs west for about a mile to the Moskva River—is now called Novy Arbat. In contrast to ulitsa Vozdvizhenka, which has retained some of its prerevolutionary charm, and the Arbat, which is actively re-creating the look of its past, Novy Arbat is a modern thoroughfare. Once a maze of narrow streets and alleys, the avenue was widened and modernized in the 1960s, with the goal of making it the showcase of the Soviet capital. In typical Soviet fashion, concrete-and-glass skyscrapers were erected. Now these eyesores house apartments and department stores. Novy Arbat is now also something of an entertainment area, with flashy casinos and lots of decent restaurants.

a good
walk

Take the metro to Biblioteka Imeni Lenina. When you come out of the station, bear left, walking away from the Kremlin. The large gray building on the corner of ulitsa Vozdvizhenka and ulitsa Mokhovaya is the Russian State Library, Moscow's main library. The square in front of it, adorned with a huge statue of Fyodor Dosteovsky, is a favorite meeting place. Ulitsa Vozdvizhenka is lined with plenty of prerevolutionary buildings, most of which were renovated during the mid-1990s. However, the drawings and photographs at the **Shchusev Architecture Museum** ⓐ ▶, at No. 5, can give you an idea of what the area used to look like. Continue walking west, away from the Kremlin. Using the underpass, cross to the right-hand side of the street to get a closer look at the curious **Dom Druzhby** ⓑ. Just beyond this eccentric mansion is the busy intersection of **Arbatskaya Ploshchad** ⓒ. To your left as you emerge from the crowded underpass is the Arbat; to your right, Novy Arbat. In the distance to your far left stands a statue erected in the 1950s of the 19th-century Russian writer Nikolai Gogol. Head to the left to start your stroll down the lively Arbat, the end of which is marked by the Ministry of Foreign Affairs, one of the Stalin Gothic skyscrapers.

Continuing down the Arbat, almost to the end, you'll come to the **Pushkin Apartment Museum** ⓓ and the **Andrei Bely Apartment Museum** ⓔ, former homes of Alexander Pushkin and Andrei Bely; they're both on the left-hand side of the street and share an entrance. Backtrack eastward to turn right down Plotnikov pereulok; make a left onto Krivoarbatsky pereulok to take a look at the Constructivist-style **Melnikov House** ⓕ, on the left-hand side at No. 10. Continue on Krivoarbatsky pereulok to reach the Arbat once again. You'll now be standing in front of an impressive building with columns at No. 26—the **Vakhtangov Theater** ⓖ. Take a right onto narrow Bolshoi Nikolopeskovsky pereulok. Continue along the left-hand side of the street until you reach No. 7. Walk through the archway and head straight back to see **Spaso House** ⓗ, the residence of the American ambassador, and, to the garden's left, the lovely **Church of the Transfiguration on the Sands** ⓘ. The garden here has plenty of benches and is surrounded by tall trees, making it a pleasant spot for a break. Retrace your path to Bolshoi Nikolopeskovsky pereulok and turn left to continue. A few doors up, on the left-hand side of the street, you come to the **Scriabin Museum** ⓙ, dedicated to the composer Alexander Scriabin; continue up the street past the museum for approximately one block, then take the stairs in the narrow passageway between the two skyscrapers to reach the busy and noisy Novy Arbat.

Turn right as you come out onto Novy Arbat and make your way back toward the Kremlin. As you elbow your way through the crowds of shoppers and vendors, you may want to keep an eye out in particular for the country's largest bookstore, **Dom Knigi** ⓚ, on the left-hand side near the street's end at Arbatskaya Ploschad. Past Dom Knigi, at the corner of Povarskaya ulitsa, on a tiny grassy knoll, stands the charming, 17th-century **Church of St. Simon the Stylite** ⓛ. To get to the **Lermontov House Museum** ⓜ, for a time the home of poet and novelist Mikhail Lermontov, take a left on Povarskaya ulitsa, then another left on Bolshaya Molchanovka ulitsa. The street will turn into Malaya Molchanovka, and on the right-hand side is the house-museum. Return to Arbatskaya Ploshchad and turn left up Nikitsky bulvar. Inside the first courtyard to your left is a **Gogol statue** ⑧⑦ worth seeing.

TIMING Without stops at any of the museums, this tour should take only about two hours to complete. If you're interested in souvenir shopping at the numerous shops and street kiosks you'll see along the way, however, you'll want to allot an additional few hours. In fact, you could easily spend a whole day on the Old Arbat alone, browsing through its stores, exploring the numerous side streets, and stopping for a break in any of its cafés. If you want to avoid crowds, do this tour on a weekday; the pedestrian zone on the Old Arbat, in particular, draws big crowds on the weekends. The museums included on this tour are all fairly small; you'll need no more than an hour for each of them.

What to See

⑦⑧ **Andrei Bely Apartment Museum** (Muzey-kvartira Andreya Belovo, Музей-квартира Андрея Белого). On display are artifacts from the life of the writer Andrei Bely (1880–1934), considered to be one of the great Russian Symbolists and most famous for his novel *Petersburg*. The "Lines of Life" drawing on the wall of the first room shows the "energy" of Bely's life (the blue line in the middle) marked by dates and names of people he knew during specific times. The keepers of the museum offer exhaustive tours of the apartment in Russian. The general entrance to the museum is through the souvenir shop. ⊠ *55 Arbat* ☎ *495/241–7702* 🔤 *50R* ◷ *Wed.–Sun. 11–7* Ⓜ *Smolenskaya.*

⑦⑥ **Arbatskaya Ploshchad** (Arbat Square, Арбатская Площадь). At this busy intersection, ulitsa Vozdvizhenka crosses the Boulevard Ring. The pedestrian underpass here has become a bustling marketplace (before you head underground take a look behind you at one of Russia's oldest movie theaters, the Kinoteatr Khudozhestvenny, which was opened in 1912). The stairs are lined with women selling tiny kittens and puppies; the animals' furry heads stick out from a bag or from underneath a coat, and they are nearly irresistible, so it's best not to stop and look. In the underpass itself, artists set up their easels, trying to entice passersby into having their portraits painted. And in spring and summer you'll find lots of impromptu flower vendors with the season's latest blooms (usually homegrown) for sale. Later in the evening musicians gather to play pretty good rock, foreign, and Russian, in the underpass. When you emerge from the dizzying minimarket, you will be in front of the Praga restaurant, a three-story neoclassical building. Ⓜ *Arbatskaya.*

need a break?

Among the numerous cafés along the Arbat where you can take a break and have a drink is **Zhiguli** (⊠ 11/1 Novy Arbat, off Arbatsky per. ☎ 495/291–4144 Ⓜ Arbatskaya), which feeds on a new wave of nostalgia for the Soviet Union. Fortunately the service and the food are better than they were in the old days. The café is not very far from the brightly tiled **Stena Mira** (Peace Wall). Carolyna Marks created the first World Wall for Peace in Berkeley, California, in 1988. A Russian woman then set about bringing Marks to Moscow. Marks worked with thousands of Russian teens to build this one in 1990.

85 **Church of St. Simon the Stylite** (Tserkov Simeona Stolpnika, Церковь Симеона Столпника). This 17th-century church stands out in stark contrast to the modern architecture dominating the area. During the reconstruction of Novy Arbat in the 1960s, many old churches and buildings were destroyed, but this one was left purposely standing as a "souvenir" of the past. For years it housed a conservation museum, but now it's been returned to the Orthodox Church and is active. Nothing remains, however, of the original interiors. ✉ *4 ul. Novy Arbat* Ⓜ *Arbatskaya.*

82 **Church of the Transfiguration on the Sands** (Khram Spasa Preobrazheniya na Peskakh, Храм Спаса Преображения на Песках). Built in the 17th century, this elegant church was closed after the 1917 revolution and turned into a cartoon-production studio. Like many churches throughout Russia, it has been returned to its original purpose. The church is depicted in Vasily Polenov's well-known canvas *Moskovsky Dvornik* (*Moscow Courtyard*), which now hangs in the Tretyakov Gallery. Services are at 10 on Sunday. ✉ *4 Spasopeskovsky per.* ☎ *495/241–6203* 🎟 *Free* ◷ *Daily 8–8* Ⓜ *Smolenskaya.*

75 **Dom Druzhby** (Friendship House, Дом Дружбы). One of Moscow's most interesting buildings—it looks like a Moorish castle—was built in the late 19th century by the architect V. A. Mazyrin for the wealthy (and eccentric) industrialist Savva Morozov (Tolstoy mentions this home in his novel *Resurrection*). The building's name is a holdover from the Soviet days, when Russians and foreigners were supposed to meet only in officially sanctioned places. Today its more popular name is Dom Evropy, because the Federation Internationale Maisons de l'Europe is headquartered here. The interior is a veritable anthology of decorative styles, ranging from imitation Tudor to classical Greek and baroque, but, unfortunately, the building is not open to the public. ✉ *16 Vozdvizhenka ul.* Ⓜ *Arbatskaya.*

84 **Dom Knigi** (House of Books, Дом Книги). The country's largest bookstore has an English-language section on the second floor, and there's also often a good selection at the individual vendors' stalls outside the store. Keep in mind that some parts of the bookstore still subscribe to the cashier system. To actually purchase a book or map involves some patience. First find what you want, then determine the price. Look above the counter where you found the book to see at which *kassa* (cashier) you must pay. Wait in line at the cashier, and tell the salesperson the price of your book and the number of the counter. You'll be issued a receipt upon payment; then you must return to the counter. Give the salesperson there the receipt, which will allow you to receive your book. ✉ *26 Novy Arbat* ☎ *495/789–3591* ◷ *Weekdays 10–7:30, Sat. 10–6* Ⓜ *Arbatskaya.*

87 **Gogol statue** (Памятник Гоголю). This statue of a melancholy Nikolai Gogol (1809–52) originally stood at the start of Gogolevsky bulvar but was replaced by a more "upbeat" Gogol. The statue now stands inside a courtyard near the apartment building where the writer spent the last months of his life. The statue actually captures Gogol's sad disposition perfectly. He gazes downward, with his long, flowing cape draped over his shoulder, protecting him from the world. Gogol is perhaps best known in the West for his satirical drama *Revizor* (*The Inspector General*), about the unannounced visit of a government official to a provincial town. Characters from this and other Gogol works are engraved on the pedestal. ⊠ *7 Nikitsky bulvar* Ⓜ *Arbatskaya.*

Herzen Museum (Muzey Gertsena, Музей Герцена). Here you can learn not only about the writer, philosopher, and revolutionary Alexander Herzen (1812–70), but also about life in the 1840s in Russia and the Decembrists who rebelled against tsarist rule in 1825. Herzen himself may be most famous for his novel *Who Is to Blame?* as well as his short stories *Magpie the Thief* and *Dr. Krupov.* Explanations in English are available. You'll have to ring the bell to enter the museum, and you'll be given slippers to wear inside. ⊠ *27 Sivtsev Vrazhek* ☎ *495/241–5859* 🖂 *30R* 🕑 *Tues., Thurs., and Sat. 11–6, Wed. and Fri. 1–6; closed last day of month* Ⓜ *Arbatskaya.*

86 **Lermontov House Museum** (Dom-muzey Lermontova, Дом-музей Лермонтова). The Romantic poet and novelist Mikhail Lermontov (1814–41) lived in this house with his grandparents from 1830 to 1832. Several rooms are on display, including a small salon where Lermontov wrote poetry and drew pictures of his love interest. You can see these artifacts on the writing desk here. In the big salon in which the family entertained guests, there are family portraits and four small friezes depicting the War of 1812 hanging on the walls. Another room displays remarkably good pen-and-ink drawings by Lermontov. A steep staircase leads up to Lermontov's bedroom, complete with a guitar on the bed, a sketch on an easel, and portraits of Pushkin and others he admired. ⊠ *2 Malaya Molchanovka ul.* ☎ *495/291–5298* 🖂 *30R* 🕑 *Tues., Thurs., and Sat. 11–4, Wed. and Fri. 2–5* Ⓜ *Arbatskaya.*

79 **Melnikov House** (Dom Melnikova, Дом Мельникова). This cylindrical concrete building was designed by the famous Constructivist architect Konstantin Melnikov in the late 1920s. The house is as remarkable outside with its wall-length windows as it's inside with its spiral staircases linking the three floors. Plans to open it as a museum have been in motion for years but sadly look nowhere near completion. The architect's elderly son still lives in the house. ⊠ *10 Krivoarbatsky per.* Ⓜ *Smolenskaya.*

77 **Pushkin Apartment Museum** (Muzey-kvartira Pushkina, Музей-квартира Пушкина). The poet Alexander Pushkin lived here with his bride, Natalya Goncharova, for several months in 1831, right after they were married. Experts have re-created the original layout of the rooms and interior decoration. The first floor presents various trinkets and poems, plus information on Pushkin's relationship with Moscow; the second floor is a reconstruction of a typical early-19th-century room. ⊠ *53 Arbat* ☎ *495/241–9295* 🖂 *50R* 🕑 *Wed.–Sun. 11–7* Ⓜ *Smolenskaya.*

83 **Scriabin Museum** (Muzey Scriabina, Музей Скрябина). This charming, dusty house-museum is in the composer Alexander Scriabin's (1872–1915) last apartment, where he died of blood poisoning in 1915. Visitors are scarce because foreign tourist groups are not usually brought here. The rooms are arranged and furnished just as they were when Scriabin lived here. Downstairs there's a concert hall where accomplished young musicians perform his music, usually on Tuesday and Wednesday evenings. Call for more information. ⊠ *11 Bolshoi Nikolopeskovsky per.* ☎ *495/ 241–1901* 💷 *150R* ☼ *Thurs. and weekends 10–5, Wed. and Fri. noon–6; closed last Fri. of month* Ⓜ *Smolenskaya.*

▶ ❼❹ **Shchusev Architecture Museum** (Muzey Arkhitektury imeni Shchuseva, Музей Архитектуры имени Щусева). This museum, in an 18th-century neoclassical mansion, has a good reputation for displaying works by some of the best and most controversial architects in Russia and from around the world. The temporary exhibits cover Moscow architecture from ancient through contemporary times. ⊠ *5 Vozdvizhenka ul.* ☎ *495/291–2109* ⊕ *www.muar.ru* 💷 *50R* ☼ *Weekdays 11–6, weekends 11–4* Ⓜ *Biblioteka Imeni Lenina.*

❽❶ **Spaso House** (Спасо-Хаус). The yellow neoclassical mansion behind the iron gate is the residence of the American ambassador. It was built in the early 20th century for a wealthy merchant. From Nikolopeskovsky pereulok, what you first see of this mansion is actually the back side of the building; it's much more impressive from the front. To get there, bear right at the small park, which is usually filled with neighborhood kids and their grandmothers. It's a pleasant place to take a break. ⊠ *Spasopeskovskaya Pl.* Ⓜ *Smolenskaya.*

❽❶ **Vakhtangov Theater** (Teatr imeni Vakhtangova, Театр имени Вахтангова). An excellent traditional theater is housed within this impressive structure named after Stanislavsky's pupil Evgeny Vakhtangov (1883–1922). The gold statue of Princess Turandot and stone fountain to the right of the theater were created in honor of the 850th anniversary of Moscow in 1997; they are loved and hated by an equal proportion of Muscovites. ⊠ *26 Arbat* 📞 *495/241–1679* Ⓜ *Arbatskaya.*

The Kropotkinsky District
Район Кропоткинской

This picturesque old neighborhood, still commonly known as the Kropotkinsky District, takes its name from its main street, which was called Kropotkinskaya ulitsa under the Soviets but has now been returned to its 16th-century name: ulitsa Prechistenka. It's yet another ancient section of Moscow whose history dates back nearly to the foundation of the city itself. Almost none of its earliest architecture has survived, but this time the Soviets are not entirely to blame. The area suffered badly during the 1812 conflagration of Moscow, so most of its current buildings date to the postwar period of reconstruction, when neoclassicism and the so-called Moscow Empire style were in vogue. Before the revolution, the Kropotkinsky District was the favored residence of Moscow's old nobility, and it's along its thoroughfares that you'll find many of their mansions and homes, often called "nests of the gentry." It was also the heart of the literary and artistic community, and there were several famous literary salons here. Prince Kropotkin, for whom the street was named, compared it to the Saint-Germain quarter of Paris.

The Kropotkinsky District ▼

Cathedral of Christ
Our Savior **91**

Monastery of the
Conception **94**

Pashkov
House **89**

Pertsov
House **95**

Pushkin Memorial
Museum **92**

Pushkin Museum
of Fine Arts ...**90**

Russian State
Library **88**

Tolstoy Memorial
Museum **93**

**Gorky Park to
the Tretyakov
Gallery** ▼

Central House
of Artists **99**

Church of St.
Nicholas of the
Weavers **96**

Gorky Park **98**

Peter the Great
Statue **101**

Tolstoy House
Estate
Museum **97**

Tretyakov
Gallery **100**

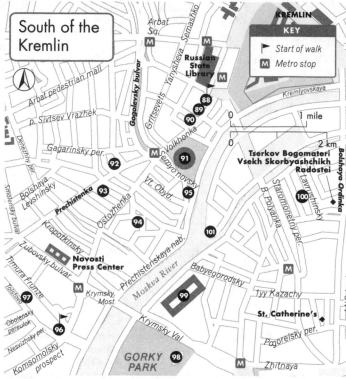

a good
walk

Start at Russia's largest library, the **Russian State Library** 88 ▶, at the bottom of ulitsa Vozdvizhenka, at the corner of Mokhovaya ulitsa (Moss Street, where moss used for wall caulking was once sold). To get here, take the metro to the Biblioteki Imeni Lenina station, which is directly beneath the library. Walk south from the library along broad Mokhovaya ulitsa to reach Borovitskaya Ploshchad, where several old streets converge. To your left, ulitsa Znamenka descends toward the Borovitsky Gate of the Kremlin and then continues across the Great Stone Bridge of the Moskva River; to your right the street leads up a steep incline in the direction of the Arbat. Ulitsa Volkhonka, which leads into the Kropotkinsky District, is straight ahead. On the hillock to your right, facing the Kremlin gates, is one of Moscow's most beautiful old mansions, **Pashkov House** 89. Cross the square and continue straight onto ulitsa Volkhonka, which was first laid out sometime in the late 12th or early 13th century. It received its current name in the mid-18th century, in honor of Prince Volkhonsky, who lived in the mansion at No. 8. After a block you reach Moscow's museum of foreign paintings, the **Pushkin Museum of Fine Arts** 90, in the middle of a small park to your right.

Just past the Pushkin museum is **Cathedral of Christ Our Savior** 91, a gigantic cathedral covering an entire block between Volkhonka and the quay of the Moskva River. Just beyond this cathedral, ulitsa Volkhonka intersects with the Boulevard Ring. To your right, across the street, is the entrance to the Kropotkinskaya metro station. At this point ulitsa Volkhonka ends, splitting into ulitsa Prechistenka (to the right) and ulitsa Ostozhenka (to the left). A small park between the two streets holds a statue of Friedrich Engels and, behind it, a restored 17th-century bo-yars' chamber. Cross the square and walk up ulitsa Prechistenka. At the corner with Prechistensky pereulok stands the **Pushkin Memorial Museum** 92, dedicated to the poet. Not far from this museum, on the opposite side of the street, is a museum honoring another giant of Russian literature: the **Tolstoy Memorial Museum** 93.

If you're feeling energetic and want to see more of the area's mansions, continue walking straight along ulitsa Prechistenka. No. 17, on the left-hand side, belonged to the poet Denis Davidov; a bit farther, at No. 19, is the former mansion of Prince Dolgoruky. No. 21 now houses the Rus-sian Academy of Arts. This mansion originally belonged to Count Potemkin and then later to the wealthy merchant Savva Morozov, whose private art collection was one of the largest in Moscow (you can see it in the Pushkin Museum of Fine Arts).

For a shorter walk, turn left after you exit the Tolstoy Memorial Mu-seum onto Lopukhinsky pereulok, and walk one block to ulitsa Os-tozhenka. Across the street and down to the right are the remnants of the **Monastery of the Conception** 94. Returning to ulitsa Ostozhenka, you could break for something to eat at Genatsvale VIP, a tasty Georgian restaurant. Otherwise turn right, walk two blocks back in the direction of the Cathedral of Christ Our Savior, and then turn right onto Vtoroy (2nd) Obydensky pereulok. Soon you'll come to the pretty St. Prophet Elijah Church, built in one day in 1702. Continue past the church and turn left onto Kursovoy pereulok. At the bottom of the street, to the right on Soymonovsky proyezd, is the steep-roofed art nouveau **Pertsov House** 95. From here continue around the house by taking a left and then crossing the street to reach the Cathedral of Christ Our Savior. Walk toward the embankment of the Moskva River. The views from the Prechistenskaya naberezhnaya (Prechistenska Embankment) and its ex-tension, the Kremlyovskaya naberezhnaya, are spectacular. This river walk takes you along the southern wall of the Kremlin to the Moskvoret-sky Bridge. Walk out onto the bridge for one of the best views of St. Basil's Cathedral and Red Square. From here you can either walk back to Red Square (the nearest metro stop here is Ploshchad Revolutsii), or, if this walk has worn you out, continue across the bridge and settle into the comfy, if not cheap, Café Kranzler at the Baltschug Kempinski hotel for some coffee and incredibly rich pastry, or beer and sandwiches.

If you still have energy you may want to linger in the Kropotkinsky Dis-trict; there are several interesting houses along ulitsa Ostozhenka that are worth seeing. The 19th-century anarchist Mikhail Bakunin was raised at No. 49. No. 38 was a governor's home in the 1700s; later it became a school, where one of its students was Ivan Goncharov, author of *Oblomov*. Today it's the Institute of Foreign Languages. One of Rus-sia's greatest writers, Ivan Turgenev, lived and worked at No. 37, a small rustic house. He set his famous story *Mu Mu* at this location. The private home of the art nouveau architect Lev Kekushev stands at No. 21.

Leaving from the upper end of ulitsa Ostozhenka, you come out at the Park Kultury metro station. At the other end (back at Soymonovsky proyezd) is the Kropotkinskaya station.

TIMING Taken at a leisurely pace, this walk could easily take three to four hours; add an extra half hour if you plan on taking the walk along the riverbank at the end. With stops at any of the various museums along this route, though, your exploration could easily expand to two days (the Pushkin Museum of Fine Arts alone is worth a day). If you're definitely interested in visiting some of the museums in this district, do *not* do this tour on a Monday, as most of the museums are closed that day.

What to See

91 Cathedral of Christ Our Savior (Khram Khrista Spasitelya, Храм Христа Спасителя). This cathedral carries an amazing tale of destruction and reconstruction. Built between 1839 and 1883 as a memorial to the Russian troops who fell fighting Napoléon's forces in 1812, the cathedral was the largest single structure in Moscow and dominated the city's skyline. It had taken almost 50 years to build what only a few hours would destroy. On December 5, 1931, the cathedral was blown up. Under Stalin, the site had been designated for a mammoth new "Palace of Soviets," intended to replace the Kremlin as the seat of the Soviet government. Plans called for topping the 1,378-foot structure with a 300-foot statue of Lenin, who, had the plans ever materialized, would have spent more time above the clouds than in plain view. World War II delayed construction, and the entire project was scrapped when it was discovered that the land along the embankment was too damp to support such a heavy structure.

The site lay empty and abandoned until 1958, when the Moscow Pool, one of the world's largest outdoor swimming pools, was built. Divided into several sections, for training, competition, diving, and public swimming, it was heated and kept open all year long, even in the coldest days of winter. The pool was connected to the locker rooms by covered tunnels, and you could reach it by swimming through them. The pool was dismantled in 1994. Then—in perhaps one of architectural history's stranger twists—the cathedral was resurrected in 1997 from the ruins at a cost of more than $150 million. Today the giant cathedral is complete, with a stunning interior. ⊠ *Ul. Volkhonka* Ⓜ *Kropotkinskaya.*

need a break? Superb cakes and pastries, an à la carte menu, and alcoholic refreshments await you at **Cafe Kranzler** (⊠ 1 Balchug ul., Zamoskvoreche ☎ 495/230–6500 Ⓜ Novokuznetskaya) inside the luxurious Balchug hotel. It is not cheap but it's the perfect place to relax after a long walk.

94 Monastery of the Conception (Zachatievsky Monastyr, Зачатьевский Монастырь). Founded in the 16th century, this working monastery is the oldest complex in the district, though nothing remains of the original buildings. Only the 17th-century redbrick Gate Church survives, and even that has been carefully renovated. It was built by the last surviving son of Ivan the Terrible, in what amounted to a plea to God for an heir (hence the monastery's name). He and his wife failed to have a son, however, and Boris Godunov became the next Russian leader. ✉ *Zachatievsky per.* Ⓜ *Kropotkinskaya.*

❽❾ Pashkov House (Dom Pashkova. Дом Пашкова). Designed by Vasily Bazhenov, one of Russia's greatest architects, this mansion was erected between 1784 and 1786 for the wealthy Pashkov family. The central building is topped by a round belvedere and flanked by two service wings. In the 19th century it housed the Rumyantsev collection of art and rare manuscripts. Following the 1917 revolution, the museum was closed and the art collection was transferred to the Hermitage in St. Petersburg and the Pushkin Museum of Fine Art. The manuscripts were donated to the Russian State Library which now owns this building. Pashkov House is off-limits to the general public, but after years of neglect, the government finally pledged funds for restoration work, which began in 2003. ✉ *Mokhovaya ul. and ul. Znamenka* Ⓜ *Borovitskaya.*

❾❺ Pertsov House (Dom Pertsova, Дом Перцова). One of the finest examples of Moscow art nouveau was built in 1905–07 by the architects Schnaubert and Zhukov. The facade of the steep-roofed and angled building, which is closed to the public, is covered in colorful mosaics. Walk all the way to the end of Soymonovsky pereulok, coming out at the river, and straight across you'll see a large, redbrick compound. This is the Krasny Oktyabr (Red October) candy factory, which sometimes fills the neighborhood with the smell of chocolate early in the morning. To your left, the buildings of the Kremlin line the distance, the golden cupolas of its churches all agleam. To the right you can see the behemoth Peter the Great statue. ✉ *Soymonovsky per. and Kropotkinskaya nab.* Ⓜ *Kropotkinskaya.*

❾❷ Pushkin Memorial Museum (Muzey Pushkina, Музей Пушкина). Aleksandr Pushkin (1799–1837) never lived here and probably never even visited this fine yellow mansion built in the 19th century by architect Afanasy Grigoriev, but don't let that put you off. A redesign in 1999 that coincided with the 200th anniversary of Pushkin's birth made this one of the smartest museums in town and an increasingly popular place for conferences and business bashes. Upon first entering the museum you'll step into a beautiful atrium that floods the building with light. Beyond the atrium are several rooms showcasing Pushkin's sketches, letters, and personal effects. ✉ *12 ul. Prechistenka* ☎ *495/201–5674* 🎟 *80R* 🕐 *Tues.–Sun. 10–6* Ⓜ *Kropotinskaya.*

❾⓪ Pushkin Museum of Fine Arts (Muzey Izobrazitelnykh Iskusstv imeni Pushkina, Музей Изобразительных Искусств имени Пушкина). One of the finest art museums in Russia, the Pushkin is famous for its Gauguin, Cézanne, and Picasso paintings, among other masterpieces. Founded by Ivan Vladimirovich Tsvetayev (1847–1913) of Moscow State University, father of poet Marina Tsvetaeva, the museum was originally established as a teaching aid for art students, which explains why a large part of its collection is made up of copies. The original building dates from 1895 to 1912 and was first known as the Alexander III Museum.

Fodor's Choice
★

It was renamed for Pushkin in 1937, on the centennial of the Russian poet's death. Next door, the **Muzey Chastnykh Kollektsiy** (Museum of Private Collections) hosts some of the museum's most famous works and has separate hours and a small entrance fee.

The first-floor exhibit halls in the original building contain a fine collection of ancient Egyptian art (Hall 1); Greece and Rome are well represented, though mostly by copies (Room 7). The Italian school from the 15th century (Room 5) is represented by Botticelli's *The Annunciation,* Tomaso's *The Assassination of Caesar,* Guardi's *Alexander the Great at the Body of the Persian King Darius,* and Sano di Pietro's *The Beheading of John the Baptist,* among others. When you reach the Dutch School of the 17th Century (Hall 10), look for Rembrandt's *Portrait of an Old Woman,* whose subject may have been the artist's sister-in-law. Flemish and Spanish art from the 17th century are also well represented, with paintings by Murillo, Rubens, and Van Dyck (Hall 11).

The Museum of Private Collections (☎ 495/203–1546 🎫 40R ☉ Wed.–Sun. noon–6) houses a stunning assortment of impressionist, postimpressionist, and modern art. There are many fine canvases by Picasso (Hall 17), including several from his "blue" period. The same hall contains fascinating works by Henri Rousseau, including *Jaguar Attacking a Horse.* There are 10 works by Gauguin, mainly in Hall 18, which also houses Cézanne's *Pierrot* and *Harlequin.* The museum owns several works by Matisse (Hall 21), although they're not all on display. In the same hall hangs the poignant *Landscape at Auvers After the Rain* by Vincent van Gogh. The collection ends at Hall 23, which has works by Degas, Renoir, and Monet, including Monet's *Rouen Cathedral at Sunset.* ✉ *12 and 14 ul. Volkhonka* ☎ *495/203–7998 or 495/203–9578* ⊕ *www.museum.ru/gmii* 🎫 *300R* ☉ *Tues.–Sun. 10–7* Ⓜ *Kropotinskaya.*

▶ 🔵88 **Russian State Library** (Rossiyskaya Gosudarstvennaya Biblioteka, Российская Государственная Библиотека). Still called Biblioteka Imeni Lenina, or the Lenin Library, this is Russia's largest library, with more than 30 million books and manuscripts. The modern building was built between 1928 and 1940. Bronze busts of famous writers and scientists adorn the main facade. The portico, supported by square black pillars, is approached by a wide ceremonial staircase. A 12-foot statue of the great Dostoyevsky was erected in front of the library in 1997 in honor of the 850th anniversary of Moscow. Dostoyevsky, sculpted by Alexander Rukavishnikov, sits where the Soviets once considered erecting a giant Lenin head. In theory, anyone can visit the library as a day visitor, but you may need some persistence to fill in forms and deal with the bureaucracy (bring your passport). It's worth it, though, to see the grand main hall. ✉ *3 ul. Vozdvizhenka* ☎ *495/202–5790* ⊕ *www.rsl.ru* ☉ *Mon.–Sat. 9–9* Ⓜ *Biblioteki Imeni Lenina.*

🔵93 **Tolstoy Memorial Museum** (Muzey Tolstovo, Музей Толстого). Architect Afanasy Grigoriev designed this mansion, a fine example of the Moscow Empire style (1822–24). The minor poet Lopukhin, a distant relative of Tolstoy's, lived here, and the mansion was converted into a museum in 1920. The exhibit halls contain a rich collection of manuscripts and photographs of Tolstoy and his family, as well as pictures and paintings of Tolstoy's Moscow. Even if you don't know Russian, you can read the writer's life story through the photographs, and in each room there's a typed handout in English to help explain its holdings. Note the picture of 19th-century Moscow in the second hall (on the left-hand wall). The huge cathedral taking up more than half the photograph is the Cathedral of Christ Our Savior—the original 19th-century structure that was subsequently replaced by the Moscow Pool. ⊠ *11 ul. Prechistenka* ☎ *495/201–3811* ⊕ *www.tolstoymuseum.ru* ✉ *50R* ☺ *Tues.–Sun. 11–5* ☺ *Closed last Fri. of month* Ⓜ *Kropotkinskaya.*

Gorky Park to the Tretyakov Gallery
От Парка Горького до Третьяковской Галереи

Gorky Park, popularized by Martin Cruz Smith's Cold War novel of the same name, is situated along the right bank of the Moskva River, just beyond Krymsky most (Crimea Bridge). The highlights of this area are Moscow's famous Tretyakov Gallery, Bolshaya Ordinka ulitsa lined with Russian Orthodox churches, and the park itself and its various surrounding sites of interest.

a good walk

Gorky Park lies between two major metro stations, Oktyabrskaya and Park Kultury, both on the circle line. This walk begins at the Park Kultury stop, but if your only destination is Gorky Park, head to the Oktyabrskaya station, which is closer.

Leave the Park Kultury metro station, turn right (as you face the bridge ahead), and walk along Komsomolsky prospekt one long block. When you reach the corner with ulitsa Lva Tolstovo you'll see the striking **Church of St. Nicholas of the Weavers** ㉖ ▶ ; turn right here to go around to the church's entrance, which is on the side. The next stop is the **Tolstoy House Estate Museum** ㉗, Tolstoy's winter home. As you start your walk up the street named in his honor, ulitsa Lva Tolstovo, look for an old whitestone building with a wood-shingle roof, on your right. Tolstoy's estate is a bit farther up the street, on the left-hand side, behind a long, redwood fence.

Retrace your steps to the Park Kultury metro stop. Catch Trolleybus 10 or B to be delivered across the Moskva River to the main entrance of **Gorky Park** ㉘, or walk down busy Zubovsky bulvar to cross the Krymsky most, which offers a fine vantage point. Directly across the street from the park is the **Central House of Artists** ㉙, with three floors of exhibit halls and a sculpture garden. The **New Tretyakov Gallery** is in the same building—the entrance is on the sculpture-garden side.

After looking at the galleries, walk away from the bridge on Krymsky Val ulitsa to Kaluzhskaya Ploshchad, which has a giant Lenin statue. Almost directly opposite Lenin is the entrance to the Oktyabrskaya metro station. Take the orange-colored radial line one stop to the Tretyakovskaya station. When you reach the street, turn left past the McDonald's, cross the road and go straight along a small alley. This will open up onto a pedestrian alleyway on the right. Following it, you'll see the spires of the Moscow baroque **Church of the Resurrection in Kadosh.** Stop at No.

12 to reach the famous Russian art musem, the **Tretyakov Gallery** ⑩. From the museum, make your way to the river and cross the pedestrian bridge. From here you'll see the behemoth **Peter the Great statue** ⑩. The gardens on the other side of the bridge are a perfect spot for a well-deserved break. The statue in the gardens is a Soviet-era sculpture of the famous Russian painter Ilya Repin, whose paintings hang in the Tretyakov. To get back to the center of town you can continue walking to the left of the statue through the garden. Crossing the street to your right you'll see a bridge that stretches to the Kremlin. Great views can be had from here. The Cathedral of Christ Our Savior is to the left and the Kremlin is to the right.

TIMING   This tour covers a fair amount of territory, and if you do it all on foot, it could easily take four to five hours just to see the sights. Allow another two hours to visit the Tolstoy House Estate Museum. To truly enjoy the Tretyakov Gallery, it's probably best to plan a separate visit. A full exploration of Gorky Park could also easily take an afternoon. Note that many of the sights on this tour are closed on Monday.

What to See

Bolshaya Ordinka ulitsa. Russian Orthodox churches, many in states of dilapidation, line this north-south street that runs for more than a mile. Near the Dobrininskaya metro, the white classical-style **St. Catherine's Church** (Tserkov Ekaterini, Церковь Екатерины; ⊠ No. 60) sits on the corner of Pogorelsky pereulok. It was commissioned by Catherine the Great in 1763 and designed by Karl Blank. The interior is in a bad state, but you can still make out some frescoes. Walk farther north to reach **Martha and Mary Convent** (Marfo-Mariinskaya Obitel, Марфо-Мариинская Обитель; ⊠ No. 34), which opened in 1909 and is most noted for its white Church of the Intercession of the Virgin Mary. It's open for services on Sunday at 8:30 AM, otherwise, you can get a glimpse of it through an arch in the convent's white-stone wall. The religious order of the convent is now across the street.

A few doors from the convent is **Church of St. Nicholas in Pyzhi** (Tserkov Nikoly v Pyzhakh, Церковь Николы в Пыжах; ⊠ No. 27а ☎ 495/231–3742 ⊙ Mon., Tues., and Thurs. noon–6:30, weekends 10–6:30 Ⓜ Dobrininskaya), an ornate, bright-white building with five gold cupolas, dating from 1670.

Continue up Bolshaya Ordinka ulitsa and take a right on Klimentovsky pereulok. Push your way through the throngs exiting the metro to the middle of the small alleyway to view the baroque **St. Clement's Church** (Tservkov Klimenta, Церковь Климента; ⊠ 26 Klimentovsky per. Ⓜ Tretyakovskaya). The construction of this church, begun in 1743 and designed by Pietro Antonio Trezzini, took three decades. Today it sits in moldering glory, completely abandoned and derelict; however, its star-studded cupolas and redbrick baroque building are still impressive.

Retrace your steps to Bolshaya Ordinka ulitsa and cross the street and take a right. A few steps away is the yellow **Church of the Virgin of All Sorrows** (Tserkov Bogomateri Vsekh Skorbyashchikh Radostei; ⊠ No. 20 Ⓜ Tretyakovskaya). Designed by Osip Bove and built between 1828 and 1835, the neoclassical-era church is an excellent example of the Empire style popular in the early 19th century. It replaced one that had burned down in the fire of 1812. The interior, filled with icons and gold, is nothing earth-shattering, but is good for getting the feel of a typical working church. Sunday services are often at 10 AM, but the church is usually open daily. From here, you're not far from the famous Tretyakov Gallery. ✉ *Bolshaya Ordinka ul. Zamoskvoreche* Ⓜ *Oktyabrskaya or Dobrininskaya.*

99 **Central House of Artists** (TsDKh; Tsentralny Dom Khudozhnikov, Центральный Дом Художников). The street entrance of this huge, modern building leads to the exhibit halls of the Artists' Union, where members display their work on three floors. This is a great place to find a sketch or watercolor to take home with you. The building also houses the modern branch of the Tretyakov Gallery. Next door is the **Art Park,** where contemporary sculpture and old statues of Soviet dignitaries stand side by side. It's a pleasant place for a stroll. ✉ *10 Krymsky Val, Zamoskvoreche* ☎ *495/238–9843 or 495/238–9634* 📠 *70R* 🕐 *Tues.–Sun. 11–7* Ⓜ *Park Kultury or Oktyabrskaya.*

Church of the Resurrection in Kadosh (Tserkov Voskreseniya v Kadashakh, Церковь Воскресения в Кадашах). Because a high fence surrounds it, this colorful church is best viewed from far away. Look for a red-and-white brick bell tower and a large green-blue onion dome surrounded by three smaller ones. Built in 1687, the church, which is undergoing a very slow renovation process, is an excellent example of the Moscow baroque style. ✉ *7 Vtoroi (2nd) Kadshovksy per., Zamoskvoreche* Ⓜ *Tretyakovskaya.*

▶ 96 **Church of St. Nicholas of the Weavers** (Tserkov Nikoly v Khamovnikakh, Церковь Николы в Хамовниках). This church, which was built between 1679 and 1682 and remained open throughout the years of Communist rule, has been wonderfully preserved and its elegant bell tower is particularly impressive. Five gilded domes top the church, and the saucy colorfulness of the orange and green trim against a perfectly white facade makes it look like a frosted gingerbread house. In fact, the design was meant to suggest a festive piece of woven cloth, for it was the weavers who settled in considerable numbers in this quarter in the 17th century who commissioned the building of this church. Morning and evening services are held daily, and the church, with its wealth of icons, is as handsome inside as out. ✉ *Komsomolsky pr. and ul. Lva Tolstovo, Zamoskvoreche* Ⓜ *Park Kultury.*

🍃 98 **Gorky Park** (Парк Горького). Muscovites usually refer to this park made famous by Martin Cruz Smith's Cold War novel *Gorky Park* as Park Kultury (Park of Culture); its official title is actually the Central Park of Culture and Leisure. The park was laid out in 1928 and covers an area of 275 acres. It's the city's most popular all-around recreation center, and in summer, especially on weekends, it's crowded with children and adults enjoying its many attractions. A giant Ferris wheel dominates the park's green; if you're brave enough to ride it, you'll be rewarded with great views of the city. The even braver may want to venture onto the roller coaster. Note that the park's admission price does not include individual rides. Stretching along the riverside, the park includes the Neskuchny Sad (Happy Garden) and the Zelyony Theater (Green Theater), an open-air theater with seating for 10,000. The park also has a boating pond, a fairground, sports grounds, a rock club, and numerous stand-up cafés. In summer, boats leave from the pier for excursions along the Moskva River, and in winter the ponds are transformed into skating rinks. ⊠ *9 Krymsky Val, Zamoskvoreche* 📧 *50R in summer, free in winter* ☉ *Daily 10–10* Ⓜ *Oktyabrskaya.*

New Tretyakov Gallery (Novaya Tretyakovskaya Galereya, Новая Третьяковская Галерея). This branch of the Tretyakov Gallery is in the same building, through a side entrance, as the Tsentralny Dom Khudozhnikov (Central House of Artists) across from Gorky Park. Often called the "New Branch," it has a permanent exhibit titled "Art of the 20th Century" that spans from prerevolutionary work by Chagall, Malevich, and Kandinsky to the Socialist Realist, Modern, and Postmodern periods. ⊠ *10 Krymsky Val, through sculpture-garden side entrance, Zamoskvoreche* 📧 *495/238–1378 or 495/238–2054* 📧 *225R* ☉ *Tues.–Sun. 10–7* Ⓜ *Park Kultury.*

⑩ Peter the Great statue (Памятник Петру Великому). The enormous statue of the tsar stands atop a base made in the form of a miniature ship. He's holding the steering wheel of a ship, symbolizing his role as the founder of the Russian naval force in the 1700s. The statue, measuring 90 feet high, has been a source of controversy since construction started on it in 1996. Most Muscovites agree that the statue, made by Moscow mayor Yuri Luzhkov's favorite sculptor, Zurab Tsereteli, is not only an eyesore but also has no place in Moscow since Peter the Great was the one who moved the capital of Russia from Moscow to St. Petersburg. After citizens complained, a board of art experts was formed to decide if the statue would stay. They decided to keep it. The decision was made mostly in light of the fact that erecting the statue cost $20 million and dismantling it would cost half that amount. There's now a city ordinance that statues and public monuments must be approved by a board of experts before construction starts, although this tends to get ignored if the city really wants to put up something. When you finally set eyes on the statue you'll probably understand why common nicknames for it are "Cyclops" and "Gulliver." The colossal statue is so tall that a red light had to be put on its head to warn planes. ⊠ *Krymskaya nab., Zamoskvoreche* Ⓜ *Park Kultury.*

㊷ Tolstoy House Estate Museum (Muzey-usadba Tolstovo, Музей-усадьба Толстого). Tolstoy bought this house in 1882, at the age of 54, and spent nine winters here with his family. In summer he preferred his country estate in Yasnaya Polyana. The years here were not particularly happy ones. By this time Tolstoy had already experienced his "religious conversion," which prompted him to disown his earlier great novels, including *War and Peace* and *Anna Karenina.* His conversion sparked a feud among his own family members, which manifested itself even at the dining table: Tolstoy's wife, Sofia Andreevna, would sit at one end with their sons, while the writer would sit with their daughters at the opposite end.

The ground floor has several of the children's bedrooms and the nursery where Tolstoy's seven-year-old son died of scarlet fever in 1895, a tragedy that haunted the writer for the rest of his life. Also here are the dining rooms and kitchen, as well as the Tolstoys' bedroom, in which you can see the small desk used by his wife to meticulously copy all of her husband's manuscripts by hand.

Upstairs you'll find the Tolstoys' receiving room, where they held small parties and entertained guests, who included most of the leading figures of their day. The grand piano in the corner was played by such greats as Rachmaninoff and Rimsky-Korsakov. When in this room, you should ask the attendant to play the enchanting recording of Tolstoy greeting a group of schoolchildren, followed by a piano composition written and played by him. Also on this floor is an Asian-style den and Tolstoy's study, where he wrote his last novel, *Resurrection*.

Although electric lighting and running water were available at the time to the lesser nobility, Tolstoy chose to forgo both, believing it better to live simply. The museum honors his desire and shows the house as it was when he lived there. Tickets to the museum are sold in the administrative building to the far back left. Inside the museum, each room has signs in English explaining its significance and contents, but you might want to consider a guided tour (which must be booked in advance). You can also arrange a tour of the museum's attractive gardens, which include a number of trees from Tolstoy's time. ⊠ 9 *ul. Lva Tolstovo, Krasnaya Presnya* ☎ 495/246–9444 ☜ 200R ☉ *Tues. Sun. 10 5; closed last Fri. of month* Ⓜ *Park Kultury.*

need a break? Delicious Georgian delights await you at **Guriya** (⊠ 7/3 Komsomolsky pr., side entrance, on right, Krasnaya Presnya ☎ 495/246–0738 Ⓜ Park Kultury), a longtime favorite of expats and locals alike for its cheap prices, down-home style, and authentic food.

⑩ **Tretyakov Gallery** (Tretyakovskaya Galereya, Третьяковская Галерея). FodorsChoice The Tretyakov Gallery—now often called the "Old Tretyakov" in light ★ of the annex, the New Tretyakov—is the repository of some of the world's greatest masterpieces of Russian art. Spanning the 11th through the 20th centuries, the works include sacred icons, stunning portrait and landscape art, the famous Russian Realists' paintings that culminated in the Wanderers' Group, and the splendid creations of Russian Symbolism, impressionism, and art nouveau.

The Tretyakov was officially opened in 1892 as a public state museum, but its origins predate that time by more than 35 years. In the mid-1800s, a successful young Moscow industrialist, Pavel Mikhailovich Tretyakov, was determined to amass a collection of national art that would be worthy of a museum of fine arts for the entire country. In pursuit of this high-minded goal, he began to purchase paintings, drawings, and sculpture, adjudged both on high artistic merit and on their place within the various important canons of their time. For the most part undeterred by critics' disapproval and arbiters of popular taste, he became one of the—if not *the*—era's most valued patrons of the arts, with honor and gratitude conferred upon him still to this day.

Up until six years before his death, Tretyakov maintained his enormous collection as a private one, but allowed virtually unlimited free access to the public. In 1892 he donated his collection to the Moscow city government, along with a small inheritance of other fine works collected by his brother Sergei. The holdings have been continually increased by subsequent state acquisitions, including the nationalization of privately owned pieces after the Communist revolution.

There are no English-language translations on the plaques here, but you can rent an audio guide or buy an English-language guide book. The first floor, which houses the icon collection, also holds drawings and watercolors from the 18th to the 20th centuries. Among the many delights here are icons painted in the late 14th and early 15th centuries by the master Andrei Rublyov, including his celebrated *Holy Trinity.* Also on display are icons of his disciples, Daniel Chorny among them, as well as some of the earliest icons to reach ancient Kievan Rus', such as the 12th-century *Virgin of Vladimir,* brought from Byzantium.

The second floor holds 18th-, 19th-, and 20th-century paintings and sculpture and is where indefatigable Russian art lovers satisfy their aesthetic longings. A series of halls of 18th-century portraits, including particularly fine works by Dmitry Levitsky, acts as a time machine into the country's noble past. Other rooms are filled with works of the 19th century, embodying the burgeoning movements of romanticism and naturalism in such gems of landscape painting as Silvester Shchedrin's *Aqueduct at Tivoli* and Mikhail Lebedev's *Path in Albano* and *In the Park.* Other favorite pieces to look for are Karl Bryullov's *The Last Day of Pompeii,* Alexander Ivanov's *Appearance of Christ to the People,* and Orest Kiprensky's well-known *Portrait of the Poet Alexander Pushkin.*

It may be the rich collection of works completed after 1850, however, that pleases museum goers the most, for it comprises a selection of pieces from each of the Russian masters, sometimes of their best works. Hanging in the gallery are paintings by Nikolai Ge (*Peter the Great Interrogating the Tsarevich Alexei*), Vasily Perov (*Portrait of Fyodor Dostoyevsky*), Vasily Polenov (*Grandmother's Garden*), Viktor Vasnetsov (*After Prince Igor's Battle with the Polovtsy*), and many others. Several canvases of the beloved Ivan Shishkin, with their depictions of Russian fields and forests—including *Morning in the Pine Forest,* of three bear cubs cavorting—fill one room. There are also several paintings by the equally popular Ilya Repin, whose most famous painting, *The Volga Boatmen,* also bedecks the walls. Later works, from the end of the 19th century, include an entire room devoted to the Symbolist Mikhail Vrubel (*The Princess Bride, Demon Seated*); Nestorov's glowing *Vision of the Youth Bartholomew,* the boy who would become St. Sergius, founder of the monastery at Sergeyev-Posad; and the magical pieces by Valentin Serov (*Girl with Peaches, Girl in Sunlight*). You'll also see turn-of-the-20th-century paintings by Nikolai Konstantinovich Roerikh (1874–1947), whose New York City home is a museum.

When you leave the gallery, pause a moment to look back on the fanciful art nouveau building itself, which is quite compelling. Tretyakov's original home, where the first collection was kept, still forms a part of the gallery. As the demands of a growing collection required additional space, the house was continually enlarged, until finally an entire annex was built to function as the gallery. In 1900 when there was no longer a family living in the house, the artist Viktor Vasnetsov undertook to create the wonderful facade the gallery now carries, and more space was later added. Keep in mind that the ticket office closes at 6:30 PM. ✉ *12 Lavrushinsky per., Zamoskvoreche* ☎ *495/951–1362* ⊕ *www.tretyakov. ru* 🚏 *225R* ☉ *Tues.–Sun. 10–7:30* Ⓜ *Tretyakovskaya.*

Donskoy Monastery & New Maiden's Convent
Донской Монастырь и Новодевичий Монастырь

The New Maiden's Convent, southwest of the city center, is one of Moscow's finest and best-preserved ensembles of 16th- and 17th-century Russian architecture. It's interesting not only for its impressive cathedral and charming churches but also for the dramatic chapters of Russian history that have been played out within its walls. It stands in a wooded section bordering a small pond, making this a particularly pleasant place for an afternoon stroll. After the Bolshevik Revolution, the convent was made into a museum. One of the convent's churches is open for services. Attached to the convent is a fascinating cemetery where some of Russia's greatest literary, military, and political figures are buried. A few metro stops away is another fabled religious institution, Donskoy Monastery, founded in the 16th century by Boris Godunov, with a cathedral commissioned a century later by the regent Sophia, Peter the Great's half-sister.

a good walk

To reach **New Maiden's Convent,** take the metro to the Sportivnaya station. Leave the metro via the stadium exit, and then follow ulitsa Frunzensky Val to your right. It will lead you through a small park and eventually to the southeast corner of the convent. When you come out onto Luzhnetsky proyezd, you should see the convent's whitewashed walls to your right. Turn right and walk up the street; the main entrance is at the other end, off Bolshaya Pirogovskaya ulitsa.

After visiting the convent, retrace your steps, walking back down Luzhnetsky proyezd to the right. The entrance to the **Novodevichy cemetery** is marked by a pair of green gates. After touring the cemetery, return to the Sportivnaya metro station and ride two stops to Park Kultury station. Switch to the ring line (your only choice for a transfer), ride one stop to Oktyabrskaya station, then go south one stop to Shabolovskaya to visit the **Donskoy Monastery.** When you exit the metro, turn right and walk one block to Donskaya ulitsa. Turn right again and follow the street until you see the copper-top domes of the monastery's churches above the trees to your left. Follow the path along the redbrick fortification wall until you reach the main entrance on the other side.

TIMING   Reserve an entire day to explore these monasteries. You could even easily devote two full days to these beautiful and historic sites. Note that it will take you about 45 minutes' travel time each way from downtown Moscow.

What to See

★

Donskoy Monastery (Donskoy Monastyr, Донской Монастырь). The 16th-century Donskoy Monastery, situated in a secluded, wooded area in the southwest section of Moscow, is a fascinating memorial to Russian architecture and art. From 1934 to 1992, a branch of the Shchusev Architecture Museum, keeping architectural details of churches, monasteries, and public buildings destroyed under the Soviets, was located—more or less secretly—inside its walls. Today the monastery is once again functioning as a religious institution, and the museum is slowly removing its exhibits from inside the churches. But the bits and pieces of demolished churches and monuments remain, forming a graveyard of destroyed architecture from Russia's past.

The monastery grounds are surrounded by a high defensive wall with 12 towers, the last of the defense fortifications to be built around Moscow. The monastery was built on the site where, in 1591, the Russian army stood waiting for an impending attack from Tatar troops grouped on the opposite side of the river. According to legend, the Russians awoke one morning to find the Tatars gone. Their sudden retreat was considered a miracle, and Boris Godunov ordered a monastery built to commemorate the miraculous victory. Of course, it didn't happen quite like that, but historians confirm that the Tatars did retreat after only minor skirmishes, which is difficult to explain. Never again would they come so close to Moscow. The victory was attributed to the icon of the Virgin of the Don that Prince Dimitry Donskoy had supposedly carried previously, during his campaign in 1380 (in which the Russians won their first decisive victory against the Tatars). The monastery was named in honor of the wonder-working icon.

When you enter the grounds through the western gates, an icon of the Virgin of the Don looks down on you from above the entrance to the imposing **New Cathedral.** The brick cathedral was built in the late 17th century by Peter the Great's half-sister, the regent Sophia. It has been under restoration for decades; services are held in the gallery surrounding the church, where the architectural exhibits were once housed. The smaller **Old Cathedral** stands to the right of the New Cathedral. The attractive red church with white trim was built between 1591and 1593, during the reign of Boris Godunov. It's open for services.

One of the most fascinating sections of the monastery is its graveyard, with many fine examples of memorial art. After the plague swept through Moscow in 1771, Catherine the Great forbade any more burials in the city center. The Donskoy Monastery, at that time on the city's outskirts, became a fashionable burial place for the well-to-do. The small **Church of the Archangel** built against the fortification wall on the far right was the private chapel and crypt of the prominent Golitsyn family (original owners of the Arkhangelskoye estate). Many leading intellectuals, politicians, and aristocrats were buried here in the 18th, 19th, and 20th centuries. ✉ *1 Donskaya Pl., Southern Outskirts* ☎ *495/ 952–1646* ✇ *Free* ☉ *Daily 7:20–6* Ⓜ *Shabolovskaya.*

Novodevichy cemetery (Новодевичье кладбище). The Novodevichy cemetery (*kladbishche*) contains a fascinating collection of memorial art, but it's difficult for non-Russian speakers to identify the graves. You may wonder how a cemetery could be controversial, but this one was. For more than a generation, the cemetery was closed to the general public in large part because the controversial Nikita Khrushchev (1894–1971) is buried here, rather than on Red Square, like other Soviet leaders. Thanks to glasnost, the cemetery was reopened in 1987, and now anyone is welcome to visit its grounds, the final resting place for national luminaries from all walks of life.

Khrushchev's grave is near the rear of the cemetery, at the end of a long tree-lined walkway. If you can't find it, any of the *babushki* (a colloquial term used throughout Russia to refer to museum caretakers, often hearty grandmothers who wear babushka head coverings of the same name) will point out the way. (They almost certainly will not speak English, but you can often figure out their opinion of him in the way they gesture.) Krushchev was deposed in 1964 and lived his next and last seven years in disgrace, under virtual house arrest. The memorial consists of a stark black-and-white slab, with a curvilinear border marking the separation of the two colors. The contrast of black and white symbolizes the contradictions of his reign. The memorial caused a great furor of objection among the Soviet hierarchy when it was unveiled. It was designed by the artist Ernst Neizvestny, himself a controversial figure. In the 1960s Khrushchev visited an exhibit of contemporary art that included some of Neizvestny's works. Khrushchev dismissed Neizvestny's contributions as "filth," and asked the name of their artist. When Neizvestny (which means "Unknown") answered, Khrushchev scornfully said that the USSR had no need for artists with such names. To this the artist replied, "In front of my work, I am the premier." Considering the times, it was a brave thing to say to the leader of the Soviet Union. Neizvestny eventually joined the ranks of the émigré artists; he now lives in the United States.

Many of those buried in the cemetery were war casualties in 1941 and 1942. The memorials often include a lifelike portrait or a photograph of the person remembered, or convey a scene from that person's life. Flowers and photographs of the dead are at almost all the graves. Among the memorials you might want to look for are those to the composers Prokofiev and Scriabin and the writers Chekhov, Gogol, Bulgakov, and Mayakovsky. Chekhov's grave is decorated with the trademark seagull of the Moscow Art Theater, the first to successfully produce his plays. Along the right-hand wall (the southwest wall of the monastery) is a memorial where all the crew members from a huge Soviet aircraft that crashed are interred. The grave of Stalin's wife, Nadezhda Aliluyeva, is marked by a simple tombstone and her bust. She supposedly committed suicide, and many hold Stalin responsible for her death. Fyodor Chaliapin, the opera singer who was stripped of his Soviet citizenship while on tour in France in the 1920s, is also buried here. His remains were transferred here in 1984. His grave is marked by a marvelous lifelike representation of him that conveys the fervor and passion that characterized his singing. You can request a tour in English from the cemetery's excursion bureau; it's best to call and reserve ahead. In light of the bountiful history and scant English translations, these tours can be very rewarding. ✉ *Luzhnetsky proyezd, Krasnaya Presnya* ☎ *495/ 246–6614 or 495/246–7527* 🖰 *Free* ☉ *Daily 10–6* Ⓜ *Sportivnaya.*

New Maiden's Convent (Novodevichy Monastyr, Новодевичий Монастырь). Enclosed by a crenellated wall with 12 colorful battle towers, the convent comprises several groups of buildings. Tsar Vasily III (1479–1533) founded the convent in 1524 on the road to Smolensk and Lithuania—a strategic way to commemorate Moscow's capture of Smolensk from Lithuania. Due to the tsar's initiative, it enjoyed an elevated position among the many monasteries and convents of Moscow and became a convent primarily for ladies of noble birth. Little remains of the original structure. The convent suffered severely during the Time of Troubles (approximately 1598–1613), concluding when the first Romanov was elected to the throne. Its current appearance dates largely from the 17th century, when the convent was significantly rebuilt and enhanced. Until the middle of the 20th century, when Moscow's population expanded rapidly, the convent effectively marked the city's southern edge.

Among the first of the famous women to take the veil here was Irina, wife of the feebleminded Tsar Fyodor and the sister of Boris Godunov, in the 16th century. Opera fans may be familiar with the story of Boris Godunov, the subject of a well-known work by Mussorgsky. Godunov was a powerful nobleman who exerted much influence over the tsar. When Fyodor died, Godunov was the logical successor to the throne, but rather than proclaim himself tsar, he followed his sister to Novodevichy. Biding his time, Godunov waited until the clergy and townspeople begged him to become tsar. His election took place at the convent, inside the Cathedral of Smolensk. But his rule was ill-fated, touching off the Time of Troubles.

In the next century, Novodevichy became the residence of yet another royal: Sophia, the half-sister of Peter the Great, who ruled as his regent from 1682 through 1689, while he was still a boy. During this time there was much new construction at the convent. The power-hungry Sophia, who did not wish to give up her position when the time came for Peter's rule, had to be deposed by him. He then kept her prisoner inside Novodevichy. Even that was not enough to restrain the ambitious sister, and from her cell at the convent she organized a revolt of the *streltsy* (Russian militia). The revolt was summarily put down, and to punish Sophia, Peter had the bodies of the dead streltsy hung up along the walls of the convent and outside Sophia's window. Despite his greatness, Peter had a weakness for the grotesque, especially when it came to punishing his enemies. He left the decaying bodies hanging for more than a year. Yet another of the convent's later "inmates" was Yevdokiya Lopukhina, Peter's first wife. Peter considered her a pest and rid himself of her by sending her to a convent in faraway Suzdal. She outlived him, though, and eventually returned to Moscow. She spent her final years at Novodevichy, where she is buried.

You enter the convent through the arched passageway topped by the **Preobrazhensky Tserkov** (Gate Church of the Transfiguration), widely considered one of the best examples of Moscow baroque. To your left as you enter is the ticket booth, where tickets are sold to the various exhibits housed in the convent. Exhibits include rare and ancient Russian paintings, both ecclesiastical and secular; woodwork and ceramics; and fabrics and embroidery. There's also a large collection of illuminated and illustrated books, decorated with gold, silver, and jewels. The building to your right is the Lophukin House, where Yevdokiya lived from 1727 to 1731. Sophia's prison, now a guardhouse, is to your far right, in a corner of the northern wall.

The predominant structure inside the convent is the huge five-dome **Sobor Smolenskoy Bogomateri** (Cathedral of the Virgin of Smolensk), dedicated in 1525 and built by Alexei Fryazin. It was closely modeled after the Kremlin's Assumption Cathedral. Inside, there's a spectacular iconostasis with 84 wooden columns and icons dating from the 16th and 17th centuries. Simon Ushakov, a leader in 17th-century icon art, was among the outstanding Moscow artists who participated in the creation of the icons. Also here are the tombs of Sophia and Yevdokiya. Yet another historic tale connected to the convent tells how the cathedral was slated for destruction during the War of 1812. Napoléon had ordered the cathedral dynamited, but a brave nun managed to extinguish the fuse just in time, and the cathedral was spared.

To the right of the cathedral is the **Uspensky Tserkov** (Church of the Assumption) and **Refectory,** originally built in 1687 and then rebuilt after a fire in 1796. It was here that the blue-blooded nuns took their meals.

If a convent can have a symbol other than an icon, then Novodevichy's would be the ornate belfry towering above its eastern wall. It rises 236 feet and consists of six ornately decorated tiers. The structure is topped by a gilded dome that can be seen from miles away. ⊠ *1 Novodevichy proyezd, Krasnaya Presnya* ☎ *495/246–8526 or 495/246–2201* ☜ *30R* ☾ *Museum Thurs –Tues. 10–5; convent daily 10 6; closed last Mon. of month* Ⓜ *Sportivnaya.*

┌─────────┐
│ **need a** │ **U Pirosmani** (⊠ 4 Novodevichy proyezd, Krasnaya Presnya ☎ 495/
│ **break?** │ 247–1926 Ⓜ Sportivnaya), a well-known restaurant specializing in
└─────────┘ the spicy cuisine of Georgia, is across the pond from the convent. If
you're visiting on a weekend, you may want to book ahead.

The Monasteries of Southeast Moscow
Монастыри Юго-Запада Москвы

There are three ancient monasteries along the banks of the Moskva River, in the southeast section of Moscow. Their history dates to Moscow's earliest days, when it was the center of a fledgling principality and constantly under threat of enemy attack. A series of monasteries was built across the river from the Kremlin to form a ring of defense fortifications. Two of the monasteries here were once part of that fortification ring.

Formerly suburban, this area did not fare well as the city grew. Beginning in the 19th century, factories were built along the banks of the river, including the famous Hammer and Sickle metallurgical plant. Today this is one of Moscow's bleaker sections, marked by busy highways, monolithic residential high-rises, and factories. Street crossings are complicated and, to Westerners unskilled in Muscovite ways, slightly treacherous. Always look for the pedestrian underpasses and crossing signs. But in the midst of this bit of urban blight are the quaint monasteries of Moscow's past, not always in the best condition but nevertheless lasting reminders of Moscow's origins.

Andrei Rublyov Museum of Ancient Russian Culture and Art (Muzey Drevnerusskoi Kultury i Iskusstva imeni Andreya Rubleva, Музей Древнерусской Культуры и Искусства имени Андрея Рублева). Located within the Andronik Monastery, the museum is named after the monastery's most celebrated monk, the icon painter Andrei Rublyov, who is believed to be buried here. Rublyov lived in the early 15th century, a time of much bloodshed and violence. Russia was slowly loosening the Mongol-Tatar yoke, and people lived in constant fear as the divided Russian principalities fought among themselves and against the Mongol-Tatar invaders. Rublyov's icons—amazing creations of flowing pastels conveying peace and tranquillity—seem even more remarkable when viewed against the backdrop of his turbulent era. His most famous work, *Holy Trinity,* is now housed in the Tretyakov Gallery. The museum in the monastery, strangely enough, does not contain a single Rublyov work. Its collection of ancient religious art is nevertheless a fine one and well worth a visit. Tickets to the exhibits are sold in the office around the corner to the right as you enter the monastery grounds. The museum is divided into three sections, and you must purchase a ticket for each part that you want to see. To get here from Ploshchad Ilyicha metro, take ulitsa Sergiya Radonezhskovo one long block and when you get to the square with four roads running into it, turn right. ⊠ *10 Andronevskaya Pl., Southern Outskirts* ☎ *495/678–1467* ☞ *100R* ☉ *Thurs.–Tues. 11–6; closed last Fri. of month* Ⓜ *Ploshchad Ilyicha.*

Andronik Monastery (Andronikov Monastyr, Андроников Монастырь). A stroll inside the heavy stone fortifications of this monastery, which is in far better condition than Novospassky Monastyr or Krutitskoye Podvorye, is an excursion into Moscow's past. The loud crowing of birds overhead drowns out the rumble of the city. Even the air seems purer here, perhaps because of the old birch trees growing on the monastery grounds and just outside its walls. The monastery was founded in 1360 by Metropolitan Alexei and named in honor of its first abbot, St. Andronik. The site was chosen not only for its strategic importance—on the steep banks of the Moskva River—but also because, according to legend, it was from this hill that Metropolitan Alexei got his first glimpse of the Kremlin.

The dominating structure on the monastery grounds is the **Spassky Sobor** (Cathedral of the Savior), Moscow's oldest stone structure. Erected in 1420–27 on the site of an earlier, wooden church, it rests on the mass grave of Russian soldiers who fought in the Battle of Kulikovo

(1380), the decisive Russian victory that eventually led to the end of Mongol rule in Russia. Unfortunately, the original interiors, which were painted by Andrei Rublyov and another famous icon painter, Danil Chorny, were lost in a fire in 1812. Fragments of their frescoes have been restored, however. The cathedral is open for services at 5:30 PM on Saturday and 9 AM on Sunday.

The building to your immediate left as you enter the monastery is the former abbot's residence. It now houses a permanent exhibit titled "Masterpieces of Ancient Russian Art," with works from the 13th through 16th centuries. The exhibit includes icons from the Novgorod, Tver, Rostov, and Moscow schools. A highlight of the collection is the early-16th-century *St. George Smiting the Dragon,* from the Novgorod School.

The next building, to the left and across the pathway from the Cathedral of the Savior, is the **Refectory.** Like the Novospassky Monastyr, it was built during the reign of Ivan the Great, between 1504 and 1506. Today it houses an exhibit of the monastery's newer acquisitions, primarily icons from the 19th to 20th centuries. Attached to the Refectory is the **Tserkov Archangela Mikhaila** (Church of St. Michael the Archangel), another example of the style known as Moscow baroque. It was commissioned by the Lopukhin family—relatives of Yevdokiya Lopukhina, the first, unloved wife of Peter the Great—as the family crypt in 1694. But there are no Lopukhins buried here, as Peter had Yevdokiya banished to a monastery in faraway Suzdal before the church was even finished, and her family was exiled to Siberia.

The last exhibit is in the former monks' residence, the redbrick building just beyond the Church of St. Michael the Archangel. The exhibit is devoted to Nikolai the Miracle Worker and contains icons depicting his life and work. From Ploshchad Ilyicha, follow Sergiya Radonezhskovo until you come out onto a square with tramlines. On your right you will find the monastery. ✉ *10 Andronevskaya Pl., Southern Outskirts* 🕾 *495/678–1467* ✉ *Free* 🕓 *Daily 8–8* Ⓜ *Ploshchad Ilyicha.*

Church of St. Martin the Confessor (Tserkov Svyatitelya Martina Ispovednika, Церковь Святителя Мартина Исповедника). This lovely church dates from the late 18th century and is in need of full restoration; its cupola is rusted and little trees are growing on its roof, but it remains a working church. Farther down the street, at No. 29, is another building of historic importance: the apartment house where the theater director Stanislavsky was born in 1863. After exiting Taganskaya station, you'll be in a huge square with a series of roads leading off it. In the northwest corner look for the opposite metro station, currently closed for repairs. Head for that station in a clockwise direction and after the station, keep going clockwise and take the second road on the left and you will reach St. Martin. ✉ *15 Bolshaya Kommunisticheskaya ul., Southern Outskirts* Ⓜ *Taganskaya.*

Krutitskoye Ecclesiastical Residence (Krutitskoye Podvorye, Крутицкое Подворье). The first cathedral on this hill was erected sometime in the 13th century. Its name comes from the word *kruta,* meaning "hill." This was originally a small monastery, a site of defense in the 14th century against the Tatar-Mongol invaders. At the end of the 16th century the monastery's prestige grew when it became the suburban residence of the Moscow metropolitan. The church and grounds were completely rebuilt, and the current structures date from this period. As monasteries go, Krutitskoye's period of flowering was short-lived; it was closed in 1788 on orders from Catherine the Great, who secularized many church buildings. In the 19th century it was used as army barracks, and it's said that the Russians accused of setting the Moscow fire of 1812 were tortured here by Napoléon's forces. In the 20th century, the Soviets turned the barracks into a military prison. Although the buildings have been returned to the Orthodox Church, the prison, now closed, remains on the monastery grounds. There's also a police station right outside the main gate, so do not be alarmed if you're greeted by a small band of uniformed police officers as you enter.

To your left as you enter the monastery grounds is the five-dome, redbrick **Uspensky Sobor** (Assumption Cathedral), erected at the end of the 16th century on the site of several previous churches. It's a working church, undergoing restoration like many of its counterparts throughout the city. Still very attractive inside, it has an assemblage of icons, lovely frescoes that have been half-restored, and an impressive all-white altar and iconostasis. Services take place on the weekend and on all holidays. The cathedral is attached to a gallery leading to the **Teremok** (Gate Tower), a splendid example of Moscow baroque. It was built between 1688 and 1694, and its exterior decoration is the work of Osip Startsev. Except for the carved, once-white columns, the walls are completely covered with colorful mosaics. Framed in the redbrick of the adjoining buildings, the red, green, and white tiles—all of different sizes and shapes—despite the verging frenzy of the decoration, give an overall effect of a compositional whole. The gallery and Teremok originally served as the passageway for the metropolitan as he walked from his residence (to the right of the Teremok) to the cathedral. Passing through the gate tower, you will see the military prison, replete with lookout towers, on the opposite side of the Teremok gates. Film crews often come to shoot inside the now-defunct prison.

You should go through the gate tower to take a full walk around the tranquil grounds. From this side, you can enter the bell tower, which dates from 1680. Taking the stairs inside, through the door off its first level, you'll have access to the gallery itself and can walk along the walls. As you go around the complex, you may encounter young artists who have chosen this quiet place to make sketches for their school assignments. To get here from Proletarskaya station, take only lefts out of the station to emerge on Sarinsky proyezd. With your back to the metro, walk toward Trety (3rd) Krutitsky pereulok, the busy street a short distance ahead. Turn right to reach the older, tree-lined street leading up an incline. This is the Chetvyorty (4th) Krutitsky pereulok. Climb to the top of the hill and you'll see the five-dome Uspensky Sobor. ⊠ *Pervyi (1st) Kruititsky per., Southern Outskirts* ☏ *495/676–9256, 495/676–3093 information about tours* ☉ *Wed.–Mon. 9–6; closed 1st Mon. of month* Ⓜ *Proletarskaya.*

New Savior Monastery (Novospassky Monastyr, Новоспасский Монастырь). The monastery was built in 1462, but its history dates to the 13th century. It was originally inside the Kremlin, and it's called the *New* Savior Monastery because its new site on the banks of the Moskva River was a transfer ordered by Ivan III, also known as Ivan the Great, who wanted to free up space in the Kremlin for other construction. Ivan was the first Russian leader to categorically (and successfully) renounce Russia's allegiance to the khan of the Golden Horde. It was during his reign that a unified Russian state was formed under Moscow's rule. This monastery was just one of the numerous churches and monasteries built during the prosperous time of Ivan's reign. None of the monastery's original 15th-century structures has survived. The present fortification wall and most of the churches and residential buildings on the grounds date from the 17th century. In uglier modern history, a site just outside the monastery's walls was one of the mass graves for those executed during Stalin's purges.

You enter the monastery at the near entrance to the left of the **Bell Tower Gate,** which was erected in 1786. It's now closed from the outside, though once inside the complex you can walk beneath its archway. The entire monastery is, sadly, in a state of semi-disrepair. Reconstruction *is* being done, but slowly; it has already taken more than 30 years. Since the early 1990s, however, when the monastery was returned to the Orthodox Church, the pace has picked up. Still, except on Sunday and church holidays, the monastery grounds are often virtually deserted. A stroll among its decaying buildings can therefore be a very private, and perhaps eerie, experience.

The first thing you see as you enter the grounds is the massive white **Sobor Spasa Preobrazheniya** (Transfiguration Cathedral). You may notice a resemblance, particularly in the domes, to the Kremlin's Assumption Cathedral, which served as this cathedral's model. The structure was built between 1642 and 1649 by the Romanov family, commissioned by the tsar as the Romanov family crypt. The gallery leading to the central nave is decorated with beautiful frescoes depicting the history of Christianity in Kievan Rus'. It's worth timing your visit with a church service (weekdays at 8 AM and 5 PM, Saturday at 8 AM, Sunday at 7 and 9 AM) to see the interior. Even if the church is closed, the doors may be unlocked. No one will stop you from taking a quick peek at the gallery walls.

In front of the cathedral, on the right-hand side, is the small red **Nadmogilnaya Chasovnya** (Memorial Chapel), marking the grave of Princess Augusta Tarakanova, the illegitimate daughter of Empress Elizabeth and Count Razumovsky. The princess lived most of her life as a nun in Moscow's St. John's Convent, forced to take the veil by Catherine the Great. During her lifetime her identity was concealed, and she was known only as Sister Dofiya. The chapel over her grave was added in 1900, almost a century after her death. In an odd twist, Princess Tarakanova had an imposter who played a more visible role in Russian history. The imposter princess appeared in Rome in 1775, to the alarm of Catherine, who dispatched Count Alexei Orlov to lure the imposter back to Russia. Orlov was successful, and the imposter Tarakanova was imprisoned in St. Petersburg's Petropavlovskaya Krepost (Peter and Paul Fortress). A mysterious character of European origin, the imposter never revealed her true identity. The false Princess Tarakanova died of consumption in 1775. Her death in her flooded, rat-infested cell was depicted in a famous painting by Konstantin Flavitsky in 1864.

To the right as you face Transfiguration Cathedral stands the tiny **Pokrovsky Tserkov** (Church of the Intercession). Directly behind the cathedral is the **Tserkov Znamenia** (Church of the Sign). Painted in the dark yellow popular in its time, with a four-column facade, the church was built between 1791 and 1808 by the wealthy Sheremetyev family and contains the Sheremetyev crypt. In the rear right-hand corner of the grounds, running along the fortification walls, are the former monks' residences.

Proletarskaya station is the closest metro stop. Take only lefts to get out of the station, and you will emerge on Sarinsky proyezd. With your back to the metro, walk toward Trety (3rd) Krutitsky pereulok, the busy street a short distance ahead. This will take you in the direction of the Moskva River, and as you head to where the streets intersect, the yellow belfry of the monastery gate church will appear in the distance to your right (southwest). When you reach the intersection, use the underground passageway to cross to the other side. From here it's just a short walk up a slight incline to the monastery's entrance. ⊠ *Bolshie Kamenshchiki at Novospassky per., Southern Outskirts* ☎ *495/676–9570* ⌕ *Free* ☉ *Daily 7–7* Ⓜ *Proletarskaya.*

WHERE TO EAT

The Moscow restaurant world is slowly growing into the dining scene that a metropolis deserves.

Restaurants of all classes and styles are opening every week, with imported foreign chefs battling it out for Moscow's upper and middle classes. There's a new breed of restaurants serving Russian fare as the fad for Western food loses some, but by no means all, of its glamour. Ethnic restaurants have arrived as well, and you can sample Tibetan, Indian, Chinese, Latin American, or Turkish any night of the week. Be warned, however, that chef turnover is high in Moscow and that a restaurant can swiftly go downhill or uphill.

Reserve plenty of time for your meal. In Russia dining out is an occasion, and Russians often make an evening (or an afternoon) out of going out to eat, especially at those Moscow showplaces replete with gilded cornices, hard-carved oak, and tinkling crystal. An unhurried splendor is definitely the order of the day.

Prices

Prices at high-class restaurants are more expensive than what you'd expect to pay in the United States, although they're probably comparable to London prices. Almost all the expensive hotel restaurants serve a Sunday brunch, when you can enjoy their haute cuisine and elegant surroundings at greatly reduced prices, usually between $30–$90. Restaurants generally post their prices in conditional units though payment is expected in rubles. Most restaurants link the units to the course of the dollar although linking their prices to the euro is becoming much more common. Some even fix it to their own imaginary course somewhere between that of the dollar and the euro. It's best to check before you order.

WHAT IT COSTS In U.S. dollars					
	$$$$	**$$$**	**$$**	**$**	**¢**
AT DINNER	over $35	$25–$35	$18–$25	$10–$18	under $10

Prices are per person for a main course at dinner.

Kremlin–Red Square

Italian

$–$$$$ ✕ **Bosco.** On the first floor of GUM, this Italian restaurant has the enviable advantage of being the only place in Moscow with a terrace on Red Square. Bosco charges for the view with very expensive Italian food, but it's tasty. You can get the view as well and still escape with a full wallet by just ordering a coffee. The terrace closes once it gets too cold. ⊠ 3 *Red Sq.* ☎ *495/929–3182* ▤ *AE, DC, MC, V* Ⓜ *Ploshchad Revolutsii.*

Kitai Gorod

Barbecue

$$ ✕ **The Conservatory.** Head to the top floor of the Ararat Park Hyatt to enjoy the view over part of the Kremlin and the Bolshoi Theater and a glass of wine. The balcony, very popular with tourists and open late April–mid-September, stretches around three sides of the hotel for a great panorama of the city. The food and service, however, don't always match the view. Service can be slow and befuddled, and the food—meats and seafood grilled on an outdoor barbecue—is unexciting. Drinks, especially cocktails, are pricey. ⊠ *4 Neglinnaya ul.* ☎ *495/783–1234* ▤ *AE, DC, MC, V* Ⓜ *Okhotny Ryad or Teatralnaya.*

Central Asian

$$$–$$$$ ✕ **Beloye Solntse Pustyni.** Named after a legendary Soviet film, *Beloye Solntse Pustyni* (White Sun of the Desert) is a theme restaurant that specializes in delicious Uzbek food, which incorporates Russian, Persian, and Chinese elements. The restaurant's sun-bleached walls instantly sweep you down to Central Asia. Inside the illusion continues: a diorama with a ship marooned in the desert, waitresses dressed as Uzbek maidens, and intricately carved wooden doors. Make sure you try the salad bar's mouthwatering vegetables. The Dastarkhan, a set meal, overwhelms you with food—unlimited access to the salad bar, a main course such as mutton kebabs and *manty* (large mutton ravioli), *plov* (a Central Asian rice pilaf), and numerous desserts. ⊠ *29/14 Neglinnaya ul.* ☎ *495/209–7525* ⌦ *Reservations essential* ▤ *AE, DC, MC, V* Ⓜ *Kuznetsky Most.*

Contemporary

$$–$$$$ ✕ **Bulvar.** Bulvar has developed a reputation both for its clientele—the rich and fashionable—and for chef Thomas Chiarelli's experimental fu-

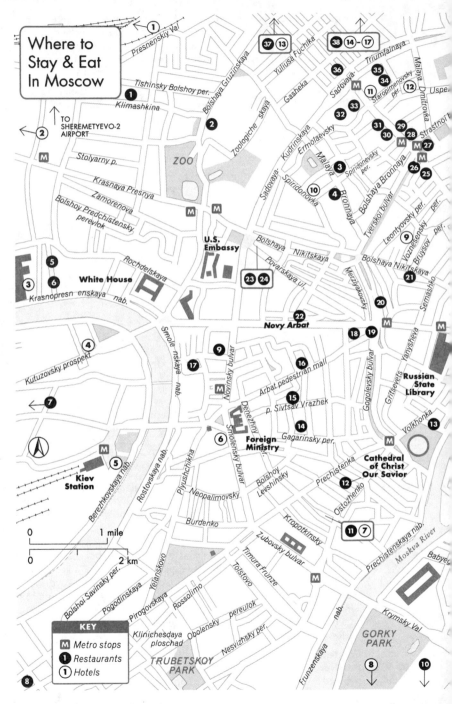

Where to Stay & Eat In Moscow

TO SHEREMETYEVO-2 AIRPORT

ZOO

U.S. Embassy

White House

Novy Arbat

Foreign Ministry

Russian State Library

Cathedral of Christ Our Savior

Kiev Station

KEY
Ⓜ Metro stops
① Restaurants
① Hotels

GORKY PARK

TRUBETSKOY PARK

0   1 mile

0   2 km

Restaurants ▼

American Bar and Grill **36, 42**
Bavarius **35**
Beloye Solntse Pustyni **51**
Bochka **6**
Bosco **50**
Brioche **33**
Bulvar **56**
Café des Artistes **57**
Cafe Margarita **3**
Café Pushkin **26**
Carré Blanc **40**
CDL **24**
Coffeehouse **18, 59**
Coffemania **21**
Coffee Bean **29, 46, 53, 60**
The Conservatory **47**
Correa's **2, 61**
Donna Klara **4**
Dzhagannat Express ...**54**
Five Spices **15**
Galereya **39**
Genatsvale VIP **12**
Goodman's Steakhouse **9, 31**
Grand Imperial **14**
Il Patio **13, 34**
Jean Jacques **20**
Karetny Dvor **23**
Krasny Bar **7**
Marin's   **1**
Mesto Vstrechi **25**
Metropol **49**
Petrovich **43**
Pirogi na Nikolskoy **48**
Poslednyaya Kaplya **16, 27**
Praga **19**
Project O.G.I. **44**
Propaganda **45**
Pyramida **58**
Rytzarsky Klub **10**
Scandinavia **30**
Shinok **5**
Sirena **41**
Starlite Diner **32, 62**
Tiflis **11**
Tinkoff **17**

The Tsar's Hunt **38**
U Pirosmani **8**
Vogue Café **55**
Yakitoria **22, 37, 52**
Yolki-Palki Po... .....**28**

Hotels ....▼

Ararat Park Hyatt **27**
Arte **1**
Baltschug Kempinski **30**
Courtyard Marriott **9**
Gamma-Delta Izmailova **22**
Golden Apple **12**
Golden Ring **6**
Holiday Inn Lesnaya ...**13**
Hotel Budapest **24**
Hotel Danilovskaya **8**
Iris **15**
Katerina **31**
Kosmos **18**
Marco Polo Presnya **10**
Marriott Grand **11**
Marriott Royal Aviora **25**
Marriott Tverskaya **14**
Metropol **29**
Mezhdunarodnaya **3**
National Hotel **28**
Novotel Moscow Center **19**
Novotel Sheremetyevo 2 Moscow Airport **16**
Radisson Slavyanskaya **5**
Renaissance Moscow **20**
Savoy **26**
Sheraton Palace **17**
Sretenskaya **23**
Soyuz **2**
Swissôtel **32**
Tiflis **7**
Travelers Guest House Moscow **21**
Ukraina **4**

sion cuisine. Despite the sometimes unusual combinations, dishes such as hot sashimi or lobster ravioli come out well. The restaurant is fairly small and service can be snooty, but it's well worth a visit. A covered summer veranda looks out onto the boulevard. ⊠ *30/7 ul. Petrovka* ☎ *495/209–6798* ▤ *AE, DC, MC, V* Ⓜ *Kuznetsky Most.*

Continental

$$–$$$$ ✕ **Metropol.** Recalling the splendor of prerevolutionary Russia, the op-
Fodor'sChoice ulent interiors of the Metropol hotel's grand dining hall are a stunning
★ memorial to Russian art nouveau. The nearly three-story-high dining room is replete with stained-glass windows, marble pillars, and a leaded-glass roof. The beautifully set tables and formally dressed waiters are impressive. The chefs prepare French and Russian delicacies, such as the popular fried duck with wild-cherry sauce and a baked apple. A special chef's menu has a different theme each season. The Metropol has a wine cellar, and many diners cap their meal with wine and cheese. A grand $25 breakfast is served here daily. ⊠ *1/4 Teatralny proyezd* ☎ *495/927– 6061* ⌂ *Reservations essential* ⌂ *Jacket and tie* ▤ *AE, DC, MC, V* Ⓜ *Ploshchad Revolutsii or Teatralnaya.*

$–$$$ ✕ **Vogue Cafe.** As the name suggests, Vogue is one of the most fashion-able restaurants in town but it does it in a distinctly Russian way. The interior is sophisticated and understated, drawing models and the well heeled. However, the menu is a throwback to Soviet times with items such as Russian salami and kefir, a sour milk drink. It's cool to con-sume these retro oldies here. The rest of the menu is a mix of Russian, Italian, and French dishes. ⊠ *7/9 Kuznetsky Most* ☎ *495/923–1701* ▤ *AE, DC, MC, V* Ⓜ *Kuznetsky Most.*

Eclectic

¢ ✕ **Propaganda.** Propaganda is one of Moscow's most popular clubs but before it opens up the dance floor, it lays out the tables for its own hearty food. The club has some of the tastiest food and most reasonable prices in the city center. The cuisine ranges over all the continents from Indian to Thai to Russian, but the dishes are kept simple and service is quick. Reservations are essential. ⊠ *7 Bolshoi Zlatoustinsky per.* ☎ *495/923– 3494* ▤ *No credit cards* Ⓜ *Kitai Gorod.*

Japanese

¢–$ ✕ **Yakitoria.** Yakitoria has proved the most reliable of Moscow's many sushi restaurants. The food may not be the most genuine article (the real thing goes for bank-breaking prices in Moscow and you can count on the fish coming from a freezer here), but the service is quick, most in-gredients fresh, and the menu comprehensive. There are several branches of the restaurant, including this one nearly opposite the Marriott Royal Avrora hotel and one on Novy Arbat. Lines are common, so reserva-tions are a good idea. ⊠ *16 Petrovka ul.* ☎ *495/924–0609* ▤ *DC, MC, V* Ⓜ *Kuznetsky Most.*

Russian

¢–$ ✕ **Pirogi na Nikolskoy.** Cheap and bohemian, Pirogi na Nikolskoy is part of the O.G.I. chain of inexpensive restaurant–clubs popular among the students, the hip, and those who never grow old. The chain is open 24 hours and usually has a small, upmarket bookshop attached. This cellar location is simple but cheerful. Don't expect great service or a smoke-free zone but do expect a good atmosphere, decent food—the beef stroganoff is worth a try—and a pleasant surprise when you get the bill. The best O.G.I. for location is this one at the end of Tretyakovsky Proyezd, a fine juxtaposition as it's one of Moscow's most expensive streets, a few hundred yards from the Kremlin. ⊠ *19/21 Nikolskaya ul., Kitai Gorod* ☎ *495/921–5827* ▤ *MC, V* Ⓜ *Ploshchad Revolutsii.*

Vegetarian

¢–$ ✕ **Dzhagannat Express.** This new age café is one of the few respites for vegetarians in the heavily meat-oriented Moscow restaurant world. Also known as the Center for Healthy Eating and Living, the restaurant serves Indian-inspired cuisine that is not very spicy. Apart from the curries, the huge salad bar is the best bet, along with the various tofu and dried wheat protein dishes. In keeping with the healthful eating ethos, no alcohol is served, although nonalcoholic beer, wine, and champagne are available. There are also freshly squeezed juices and exotic fruit cocktails. ⊠ *11 Kuznetsky Most* ☎ *495/928–3580* ▤ *No credit cards* Ⓜ *Kuznetsky Most.*

Tverskaya Ulitsa

American

$–$$$ ✕ **American Bar and Grill.** One of the original American bars in Moscow, the Bar and Grill goes for the pseudo–Wild West look that is especially popular with anyone who has never been to the United States. Buffalo heads hang on walls beside leather saddles and old American road signs. The only really genuine American thing are the huge portions. The 24-hour bar always seems to be busy with clients feeding on its popular chicken wings or downing margaritas. Although the Mayakovskaya branch is more popular, the bigger Taganka restaurant has pool rooms, a larger summer garden, and bands regularly rocking its main room. ⊠ *2/1 Pervaya (1st) Tverskaya-Yamskaya ul.* ☎ *495/251–7999* ▤ *AE, DC, MC, V* Ⓜ *Mayakovskaya* ⊠ *59 Zemlyanoi Val, Taganka* ☎ *495/912–3615* ▤ *AE, DC, MC, V* Ⓜ *Taganskaya.*

$–$$$ ✕ **Goodman's Steakhouse.** If you have an urge for steak in Moscow, then Goodman's Steakhouse is a sure-fire bet for high-quality meat and good service. Steaks are of course the specialty, but the lamb shank is not to be spurned. Goodman's has two restaurants with the original on Tverskaya winning on atmosphere. At Tverskaya there's a small summer garden that's also open in winter; you'll be provided with coats and hot drinks to ward off the cold. ⊠ *23 ul. Tverskaya* ☎ *495/937–4684* ▤ *AE, DC, MC, V* Ⓜ *Tverskaya.*

¢–$ ✕ **Starlite Diner.** The two branches of this round-the-clock diner are identical to those back in the United States, with brightly lighted 1950s design, large portions of sandwiches and burgers, and great value for the price. In Moscow these spots are popular with late workers, exhausted early-morning party goers, and old friends getting together for a weekend brunch. It's always full of boisterous first-timers to Russia and expats looking for a taste of home. This location is busier because of its city-center location and its secluded summertime patio. Waiters are young and friendly, speak English, and serve fast. ✉ *16 Bolshaya Sadovaya, in garden by Mossoviet Theater* ☎ *495/290–9638* ▭ *AE, DC, MC, V* Ⓜ *Mayakovskaya.*

Cafés & Coffee Shops

$–$$$ ✕ **Donna Klara.** Comfy window seats, a laid-back staff, and a selection of sticky cakes make this a cozy place to eat. The wine list may not be very big—and you're better off sticking to the cakes, anyway—but the friendliness of the staff makes this a pleasant family eatery in which to relax the afternoon away. Always busy, so book ahead. It's a few minutes away from Patriarch's Pond. ✉ *21/13 Malaya Bronnaya ul.* ☎ *495/ 290–3848* ▭ *AE, DC, MC, V* Ⓜ *Mayakovskaya.*

¢ ✕ **Brioche.** Closeted inside the Tchaikovsky Concert Hall on Triumfalnaya Ploshchad, Brioche is a good pre- or postconcert stop for cake and coffee. There's always a decent selection of sandwiches, the pastries are fresh, and you can buy croissants and baguettes here as well. Ingredients are brought in from France as is, seemingly, the convivial spirit. ✉ *4/ 31 Triumfalnaya Pl.* ☎ *495/299–4284* ▭ *No credit cards* Ⓜ *Mayakovskaya.*

¢ ✕ **Coffee Bean.** In a grand 19th-century building, the Tverskaya ulitsa branch is the most convenient of this coffee chain, one of the first and better of the many Seattle-style coffee chains that have opened in Moscow. Try to nab a sofa by the window for the best seat. Giant cappuccinos and some of the best coffee in town are brewed here and served with a smile. There's a sparse selection of sandwiches and lots of desserts, though the latter aren't very good. The Pokrovka site is big and has a small summer garden ideal for watching Pokrovkans walk by. ✉ *10 Tverskaya ul.* ☎ *495/788–6357* ▭ *MC, V* Ⓜ *Tverskaya.* ✉ *18 Pokrovka* ☎ *495/923–9793* ▭ *MC, V* Ⓜ *Chistiye Prudy* ✉ *5 Pyatnitskaya ul.* ☎ *495/953–6726* ▭ *MC, V* Ⓜ *Novokuznetskaya.*

¢ ✕ **Coffeehouse.** This is one of Moscow's biggest coffee chains, and there seems to be a branch within a coffee bean's throw no matter where you are in the city center. It does all the things a good coffeehouse should and has the added advantage of Internet access in several of its branches (including the Gogolevsky bulvar and Malaya Dmitrovka branches). In addition to lattes and cappuccinos, Coffeehouse serves beer, wine, toasted sandwiches, and a huge list of coffee cocktails. ✉ *3 Malaya Dmitrovka ul.* ☎ *495/299–9728* ▭ *No credit cards* Ⓜ *Pushkinskaya* ✉ *3/2 Gogolevsky bulvar* ☎ *495/923–0219* ▭ *No credit cards* Ⓜ *Kropotkinskaya.*

Continental

$$$–$$$$ ✕ **Café des Artistes.** Just off Tverskaya ulitsa and opposite the Moscow Art Theater, this is the perfect spot for a pre- or post-theater dinner. The restaurant, which specializes in French, Swiss, and Italian cuisine, comes into its own in summer with its outdoor café. Entrées might include tiger prawns à la provencale or risotto with black truffle. The business lunch, which costs 540R for a three-course meal, is one of the best in the city center. ✉ *5/6 Kamergersky per.* ☎ *495/692–4042* ▭ *AE, DC, MC, V* Ⓜ *Okhotny Ryad.*

$–$$$$ ✕ **Galereya.** Most nights of the week, large Mercedes, Hummers, and Bentleys are parked outside of Galereya, one of Moscow's hippest restaurants. Owned by Moscow's restaurant magnate Arkady Novikov, Galereya has sophisticated contemporary food, which rarely hits a false note. The lamb dishes are always tender. People mostly come to Galereya to be seen and to watch the crowds of beautiful people who cram the restaurant. ⊠ *27 Petrovka ul.* ☎ *495/937–4544* ▭ *DC, MC, V* Ⓜ *Tverskaya.*

Eclectic

$–$$ ✕ **Pyramida.** Despite being housed in a stunningly ugly and vulgar pyramid-shape building, this is one of the trendiest restaurants in the city. Pyramida always seems to be busy (in summer look for the bikers parading their expensive motorbikes and spotlessly clean leather bike wear just outside). Inside, modern, slick lines meet pseudo–ancient Egyptian decor. The food is a mixture of the trendiest items in Moscow: a bit of sushi, some weird fusion concoctions, and lots of salads. ⊠ *18a Tverskaya ul.* ☎ *495/200–3603* ▭ *AE, DC, MC, V* Ⓜ *Pushkinskaya.*

German

$–$$ ✕ **Bavarius.** Bavarius looks as if it has been transported straight from Munich's Oktoberfest. Oompah music plays in the background, dirndl-clad waitresses carry fistfulls of liter-size beer mugs, and the smell of sauerkraut lingers in the air. Whether you fancy a snack of knockwurst (a mild pork sausage) or just want to sample German and Czech beers, this is the place. Instead of sitting indoors, head through the arch to the left of the main entrance to reach the quiet courtyard that holds the biggest beer garden in Moscow. Food is served in both areas, but credit cards are accepted as payment only in the restaurant. ⊠ *2/30 Sadovaya-Triumfalnaya* ☎ *495/299–4211* ▭ *MC, V* Ⓜ *Mayakovskaya.*

Mongolian

¢ ✕ **Yolki-Palki Po . . .** Choose your own ingredients, hand them over to a chef, and watch them sizzle on hot Mongolian barbecue plates. Yolki-Palki Po . . . is a more proletarian, fast-food version of the normal Mongolian dining experience. Tribal Mongolian banners hang overhead in the dining room of this glass building in the center of Moscow, on Pushkinskaya Ploshchad. Salads, good Russian pies, and Central Asian soups are also on the menu, as is loud, not Mongolian, pop music. The place is extremely popular, and lines form outside even in the dead of winter. ⊠ *18a Tverskaya ul.* ☎ *495/287–8127* ▭ *No credit cards* Ⓜ *Pushkinskaya.*

Pizza

¢–$$ ✕ **Il Patio.** This branch sits opposite the statue of Mayakovsky on Triumfalnaya Ploshchad and is one of the most popular in the city. The menu runs the gamut of pizzas, with a real salad bar and Italian entrées. ⊠ *2 (1st) Tverskaya-Yamskaya ul.* ☎ *495/930–0815* ▭ *AE, DC, MC, V* Ⓜ *Mayakovskaya.*

Russian

$$–$$$$ ✕ **Café Pushkin.** Imagine traveling back in time to when Pushkin strolled
Fodor'sChoice the boulevards of 19th-century Moscow. That's what the designers of
★ this high-class Russian restaurant intended when they created a replica

mansion not far from the statue of Pushkin. Staff members dress like 19th-century servants; the menu resembles an old newspaper, with letters no longer used in the Russian alphabet; and the food is fit for a tsar. All the favorites can be found here—blini, caviar, pelmeni—and there's a fine wine list. Prices rise with each floor (there are three) of the restaurant. Open daily, 24 hours, Pushkin is popular among the business elite and the golden youth who come for breakfast after a night of clubbing. In summer you can dine on the rooftop patio. ⊠ *26a Tverskoi bulvar* ☎ *495/229–5590* ⌖ *Reservations essential* ▭ *AE, DC, MC, V* Ⓜ *Pushkinskaya.*

$–$$$ ✕ **Mesto Vstrechi.** In a cool cellar setting a few minutes from Pushkinskaya Ploshchad, this restaurant is ideal for a relaxing meal before hitting the town. There are plenty of nooks to hide in if you want to have some peace and quiet. Although never amazing, the mix of European and Russian food is well crafted and satisfying, and you'll find probably the best pelmeni in town here. The place also has an unusually good choice of foreign beers. Mesto Vstrechi, which means "meeting place," is the name of a famous Russian police film, set after World War II. ⊠ *9/8 Maly Gnezdnikovsky per., Bldg. 7* ☎ *495/229–2373* ▭ *AE, DC, MC, V* Ⓜ *Pushkinskaya.*

¢–$$$ ✕ **Petrovich.** Petrovich is a place that revels in nostalgia. Objets d'art from the Soviet era are scattered around the huge cellar bar-club-restaurant; the menu of filling Russian food is full of insider jokes about life under the old regime; beer is served in the old mugs that were the only thing, apart from jam jars, that beer was once served in; and Soviet pop plays in the background. Try the pelmeni, sturgeon kebabs, or Georgian dishes such as *sulguni* (breaded fried cheese). This place often claims to be a private club, but if you call beforehand you can usually get in. ⊠ *24/3 Myasnitskaya ul., head into courtyard behind kiosk at 24 Myasnitskaya ul. and look for metal door on left* ☎ *495/923–0082* ⌖ *Reservations essential* ▭ *No credit cards* Ⓜ *Chistiye Prudy.*

¢–$ ✕ **Cafe Margarita.** Set by picturesque Patriarch's Pond, this intimate café is marked by a colorful mural depicting a scene from Mikhail Bulgakov's classic novel *The Master and Margarita,* part of which takes place beside the pond. This has long been a favorite with tourists and locals, but not because of the basic, somewhat overpriced Russian food such as borscht soup and potato-and-mushroom dumplings. Instead, people come to hear the musicians—some students, some professionals—who play every night, creating a wonderful, sing-along atmosphere with a repertoire of classical music, Russian folk songs, and popular hits. A 100R charge is added to each bill for the music. ⊠ *28 Malaya Bronnaya ul.* ☎ *495/299–6534* ▭ *No credit cards* Ⓜ *Mayakovskaya.*

¢–$ ✕ **Poslednyaya Kaplya.** The Last Drop, which roughly translates as "the last straw" in English, is one of the better bars in the city. Just slip into one of the leather armchairs and order a portion of the excellent pelmeni, some herring, and potatoes, plus the tipple of your choice. There's a decent menu of Russian favorites, with a few modern bar snacks thrown in. Be warned: if you ask the bartender for a shot, he will ring the ship bell and get you to down the drink in one. The bar is in a gloomy, yet cozy, cellar off Pushkinskaya. ⊠ *4 Strastnoi bulvar, Bldg. 3* ☎ *495/692–7549* ▭ *No credit cards* Ⓜ *Chekhovskaya.*

¢–$ ✕ **Project O.G.I.** The original O.G.I (the initials stand for United Humantiarian Publisher), this cheap and cheerful hangout has regular concerts, a bookstore, readings, and 24-hour cheap food and drink. It's in a courtyard off one of Moscow's most charming streets. ✉ *8/21 Potapovsky per.* ☎ *495/927–5366* 🖃 *AE, DC, MC, V* Ⓜ *Chisty Prudy.*

Scandinavian

$$–$$$$ ✕ **Scandinavia.** Cozy and relaxing, this is one of the most serene dining rooms in the city, with comfortable wooden chairs, upholstered benches, and dried-flower arrangements on deep window ledges. The Swedish chef mixes modern European and Scandinavian cooking. If you're out for a purely Scandinavian selection, try the herring with boiled potatoes, which comes with a shot of aquavit. The burgers are the highest ranked in Moscow. Despite being near the bustle of Tverskaya ulitsa, Scandinavia's balcony and summer beer garden are the city's most tranquil and popular places for outdoor dining. There's a slightly cheaper menu for the summer garden. ✉ *7 Maly Palashevsky per.* ☎ *495/937–5630* 🖃 *AE, DC, MC, V* Ⓜ *Pushkinskaya.*

Bolshaya Nikitskaya Ulitsa

American

$–$$$ ✕ **Goodman's Steakhouse.** If you have an urge for steak in Moscow, then Goodman's Steakhouse is a sure fire bet for high-quality meat and good service. This restaurant is perfect for a business lunch. It's next to one of the "Stalin Sisters" by the Barrikadnaya metro station. ✉ *31 Novinsky bulvar* ☎ *495/981–4941* 🖃 *AE, DC, MC, V* Ⓜ *Barrikadnaya.*

Azeri

¢–$ ✕ **Karetny Dvor.** Popular among the new rich and the new middle class, Karetny Dvor serves an enormous selection of Azeri (from Azerbeijan) and Caucasian dishes. Waiters are quite good at recommending a selection if it all gets a bit bewildering. Do try the fresh Azeri tomatoes to accompany the dozens of kebabs, including the hard-to-find potato version. Seating is either in a rustic main room or smaller ones that resemble hideaways within an old farmer's barn. In summer there's seating outside. ✉ *52 Povarskaya ul., Zemlyanoi Gorod* ☎ *495/291–6376* 🖃 *No credit cards* Ⓜ *Barrikadnaya.*

Cafés & Coffee Shops

¢–$$$ ✕ **Coffeemania.** Tucked into the side of the Tchaikovsky Conservatory, this is the perfect place to come for a snack before or after a concert or just to eavesdrop on the musicians rehearsing during the day. There's a huge indoor area, good coffee, and a decent summer garden overlooking the statue of Tchaikovsky. Apart from the usual coffee assortments, Coffeemania has a large menu with well-prepared Italian, Russian, and Japanese dishes. ✉ *13/6 Bolshaya Nikitskaya ul., Bldg. 1* ☎ *495/229–3901* 🖃 *AE, DC, MC, V* Ⓜ *Biblioteka imeni Lenina.*

Contemporary

¢–$$ ✕ **Correa's.** Originally from the United States, chef Isaac Correa has stood out throughout his long Moscow career. His latest venture is an intimate family place that's a firm favorite on the restaurant scene, especially the cozy Bolshaya Gruzinskaya address, which has only seven tables. Great pizzas, simple good Italian food, but with lots of contemporary touches, come in large portions and with very friendly service. Breakfast for 230 rubles is one of the most civilized in the city. ⊠ *32 Bolshaya Gruzinskaya ul.* ☎ *495/933–4684* ▭ *AE, DC, MC, V* Ⓜ *Barrikadnaya.*

Russian

$$–$$$$ ✕ **CDL.** Inside this elegant mansion is one of the city's most beautiful
Fodor'sChoice dining rooms—and one of the best places to sample authentic Russian
★ cuisine. In the 19th century the house served as the headquarters for Moscow's Freemasons; more recently it was a meeting place for members of the Soviet Writers' Union. Crystal chandeliers, rich-wood paneling, fireplaces, and antique balustrades place CDL among the warmest and most sumptuous eateries in Moscow. The food is extremely well prepared; try the *ukha* (fish soup) or *pelmeni* (meat dumplings) for starters, and move on to the beef Stroganoff. If you're feeling adventurous, cleanse your palate between courses with *kvas* (bread-beer). There's also a less luxurious Italian restaurant here. ⊠ *50 Povarskaya ul.* ☎ *495/291–1515* ▭ *AE, DC, MC, V* Ⓜ *Barrikadnaya.*

The Arbat, Old & New

Eclectic

$$$$ ✕ **Praga.** In a handsome prerevolutionary building, a prior restaurant here once hosted Leo Tolstoy and Ilya Repin. During the Soviet era it was the most prestigious restaurant in town before slipping into near terminal decline. It now has a new lease on life with three separate restaurants—Brazilian, Italian, and European—operating inside. All in all, it's a vast, brash, extravagant, often tasteless, yet curiously appealing place. You could spend days wandering about the luxurious interior—gold and marble abound (even the metal detector is covered in marble). The Brazilian buffet is the best all-around bargain. ⊠ *2 Arbat* ☎ *495/290–6171* ⌂ *Reservations essential* ▭ *AE, DC, MC, V* Ⓜ *Arbatskaya.*

¢–$$$ ✕ **Tinkoff.** A few yards from the controversial British-embassy building (some think it's a design miracle, others an abomination) is a plain brick building that holds this stylish Russian microbrewery. The series of bars and rooms has a brick-and-glass design. Although there are four cuisines on offer in different areas of the brewery—Japanese, German, Italian, and modern European—people come for the beer, not the food. Ten very different beers are brewed on the premises, with prices starting at less than $4 for a half liter. ⊠ *11 Protochny per.* ☎ *495/777–3300* ▭ *AE, DC, MC, V* Ⓜ *Smolenskaya.*

French

¢–$ ✕ **Jean Jacques.** You may not be able to smoke in Parisian restaurants any more, but Jean Jacques, a cheap and cheerful 24-hour French bistro, is a copy of the old smoky Parisian classic. The café is nearly always busy and has one of the best selections of reasonably priced wines by the glass in Moscow. ⊠ *12 Nikitsky Bulvar* ☎ *495/290–3886* ▭ *MC, V* Ⓜ *Arbatskaya.*

Japanese

¢–$ ✕ **Yakitoria.** Yakitoria has proved the most reliable of Moscow's many sushi restaurants for inexpensive, good-quality sushi. This branch is halfway down the Novy Arbat. ✉ *Novy Arbat ul.* ☎ *495/250–5385* ▤ *DC, MC, V* Ⓜ *Arbatskaya.*

Kropotkinsky District

Georgian

¢–$$ ✕ **Genatsvale VIP.** An offshoot of its neighbor Genatsvale, the VIP branch is designed to look like an old Georgian country home. After entering through a tunnel of vine leaves, you're seated at oak tables in a somewhat Disney-esque version of Georgia (the country). The food is genuine, however, and in the evenings you can enjoy an authentic Georgian choir and traditional dancing. If you come in a group, you may want to share the special kebab combination. Complement your food with one of the various Georgian wines served in 1-liter clay bottles. Service can be brusque. ✉ *14/2 ul. Ostozhenka* ☎ *495/203–1242* ▤ *MC, V* Ⓜ *Kropotkinskaya.*

$ ✕ **Tiflis.** Named after the old name for the Georgian capital, Tbilisi, Tiflis is one of the city's oldest Georgian restaurants. Long popular among the expat Georgian community, it's the perfect place on a hot summer evening. One of best balconies in the city sweeps you away to the romantic old town of Tbilisi. The menu has all of the best of Georgian cuisine: piping hot *khachapuris* or cheese pancakes, kebabs cooked over charcoal, and sweet red Georgian wine. ✉ *32 ul. Ostozhenka* ☎ *495/290–2897* ▤ *MC, V* Ⓜ *Kropotkinskaya.*

Pan-Asian

¢–$$$$ ✕ **Five Spices.** The interior of this place may resemble an Asian house of ill repute, but the food is as classy as you can get. In addition to Chinese food, Five Spices serves a good number of Tandoori dishes. For starters try the crispy lamb or the honey-glaze pork and then move on to any of the many prawn dishes. This is one of the few places in Moscow where you can get tofu and a good selection of vegetarian dishes. ✉ *3/18 Sivtsev Vrazhek* ☎ *495/203–1283* ▤ *AE, DC, MC, V* Ⓜ *Kropotkinskaya.*

Pizza

¢–$$ ✕ **Il Patio.** An airy place to find pizza bliss, this cheerful restaurant has a huge back room with a ceiling and walls of glass, letting the sun pour in all day. This original location is a stone's throw from the Pushkin Museum of Fine Arts. The gamut of pizzas have a thin and dusty crust, and daily specials include such dishes as lasagna and cannelloni. There's also a salad bar. A speedy two-course lunch costs 190R and the three-course, 280R. A soft drink is included. Pop music plays softly, and the rooms are always filled with a pleasantly bustling crowd. ✉ *13a ul. Volkhonka* ☎ *495/298–2530* ▤ *AE, DC, MC, V* Ⓜ *Kropotkinskaya.*

Russian

$–$$$$ ✕ **Grand Imperial.** Superbly prepared and often Croesus-rich Russian

Fodor'sChoice dishes, such as the rich meat stew à la Romanoff or fried quail wrapped

★ in bacon, are well matched by the surroundings—double-headed imperial eagles, gilded Empire-style chairs worthy of a tsar, original art, crystal chandeliers, bouquets of flowers, and antique silver. The dining room is relatively small, and made even more intimate by a fountain and an old grand piano. A pianist plays daily, and is joined in the evening by a guitarist singing Old Russia tunes. The Grand Imperial's secretive banquet hall is a favorite dining place for Russia's oligarchs, who cherish the grandeur and privacy it offers. ✉ *9/5 Gagarinsky per.* ☎ *495/291–6063* ⚓ *Reservations essential* 🏛 *Jacket and tie* ⊟ *AE, MC, V* Ⓜ *Kropotkinskaya.*

Zamoskvoreche (Gorky Park, Tretyakov Gallery)

American

¢–$ ✕ **Starlite Diner.** A round-the-clock diner identical to those back in the United States, this branch is a hundred yards or so behind the largest Lenin statue left in Moscow. Amidst brightly lighted 1950s decor, large sandwiches and burgers are served at a great value. The speedy waiters are young and friendly, and speak English. ✉ *9a Korovy Val, Zamoskvoreche* ☎ *495/959–8919* ⊟ *AE, DC, MC, V* Ⓜ *Oktyabrskaya.*

Cafés & Coffee Shops

¢ ✕ **Coffee Bean.** This branch of the Seattle-style chain is just over the bridge from the Kremlin on an old street that, when not full of traffic, is one of Moscow's most charming. It's also nearly opposite a lovely 18th-century baroque church complete with bell tower. ✉ *5 Pyatniyskaya, Zamoskvoreche* ☎ *495/951–7037* ⊟ *MC, V* Ⓜ *Novokuznetskaya.*

Contemporary

¢–$$ ✕ **Correa's.** Originally from the United States, chef Isaac Correa has stood out throughout his long Moscow career. His latest venture is an intimate family place that's now a firm favorite. There are always some Italian dishes on the contemporary menu. It's much roomier and sophisticated than the other Correa's, although it loses some of the charm due to the officelike surroundings. ✉ *40 ul. Bolshaya Ordynka, Bldg. 2, Zamoskvoreche* ☎ *725–5878* ⊟ *AE, DC, MC, V* Ⓜ *Tretyakovskaya.*

Tverskaya-Yamskaya ul., Krasnaya Presnya ul. & Novoslobodskaya ul.

French

★ $$$$ ✕ **Carré Blanc.** The city's most praised restaurant, Carré Blanc has captured the hearts of Moscow gourmets. A group of expatriates established the place, which magically melds exquisite French cooking, probably Moscow's best wine collection, and a relaxed, convivial atmosphere. Try the French onion soup and if you can splurge, then go for the rack of lamb for a hefty $84. Also here are a bar and a bistro with somewhat, if not significantly, lower prices. ✉ *19/2 Seleznyovskaya ul., Northern Outskirts* ☎ *495/258–4403* ⊟ *AE, DC, MC, V* Ⓜ *Novoslobodskaya.*

Italian

★ $–$$$$ ✕ **Mario's.** Mario's has always ranked as one of the top Italian restaurants in Moscow, but some foodies say the resident Italian chef has turned it into the best restaurant in town. Using ingredients flown in twice a week from Italy, the kitchen creates consistently wonderful pasta dishes, such as a splendid tagliatelle with cream, mushrooms, and fresh truffles. The carpaccio never fails. The meat and fish dishes are also excellent. The restaurant has one of the best (and most private) summer gardens in town, favored by many a Russian star and nouveau riche millionaire, bodyguards in tow. ⊠ *17 Klimashkina ul., Krasnaya Presnya* ☎ *495/253–6505* ⊸ *Reservations essential* ▤ *AE, DC, MC, V* Ⓜ *Ulitsa 1905 Goda.*

Japanese

¢–$ ✕ **Yakitoria.** Yakitoria has proved the most reliable of Moscow's many sushi restaurants for cheap, good-quality sushi. This branch, close to Belorusskaya train station, is one of its most popular with an enclosed terrace. ⊠ *29 Pervaya (1st) Tverskaya-Yamskaya ul., Northern Outskirts* ☎ *495/250–5385* ▤ *DC, MC, V* Ⓜ *Belorusskaya.*

Russian

$$–$$$$ ✕ **Bochka.** One of Moscow's numerous round-the-clock restaurants, Bochka, opposite the Mezhdunarodnaya hotel, is a dependable place for good Russian food, even if the prices are somewhat high. It attracts its fair share of New Russians, businesspeople, and the after-rave set. If you're brave turn up on Friday, when a giant spit is assembled for the roasting of wild game, including bulls and goats. If that doesn't appeal, the salads are all well worth a try, although the *kholodets*, a portion of meat served wobbling in its own jelly, may inspire doubt. ⊠ *2 ul. 1905 Goda, Krasnaya Presnya* ☎ *495/252–3041* ▤ *AE, DC, MC, V* Ⓜ *Ulitsa 1905 Goda.*

Ukrainian

$–$$$$ ✕ **Shinok.** Half-zoo, half-collective farm, the 24-hour Shinok is a faux-Ukrainian farmyard complete with goats, cow, hens, and a knitting granny. The enclosure is completely sound- and smell-proof, and the animals don't really impinge on the meal. Ukrainian cuisine doesn't differ that much from Russian, sharing dishes such as borsht, *vareniki* (Ukrainian-style pelmeni stuffed with cottage cheese), and *solyanka* (a spicy, thick stew made with vegetables and meat or fish). For an unusual taste from the Ukraine, try *salo* (thin slices of fat) and the Ukrainian beer Starokiyevskoye. The helpful servers can give advice, although not all speak English. Go on an empty stomach, because the food can be very filling. ⊠ *2a ul. 1905 Goda, Krasnaya Presnya* ☎ *495/255–0204* ▤ *AE, MC, V* Ⓜ *Ulitsa 1905 Goda.*

Near New Maiden Convent

Contemporary

$$ ✕ **Krasny Bar.** From the 27th floor of this modern skyscraper you can see the city stretching out in front of you. Nighttime views are particularly fine. Many jokes have been made about the men's bathroom's unique view of the White House, where the government works. The restaurant serves what it calls "modern European" cuisine, which means lots of small salads and fusion. But it's a better bet to just sit with a cocktail and stare out of the window. Open until 3 AM, it's perfect for late-night carousing. ⊠ *22–24 Kutuzovsky pr., Krasnaya Presnya* ☎ *495/730–0808* ▤ *AE, DC, MC, V* Ⓜ *Kievskaya.*

Georgian

¢–$$$$ ✕ **U Pirosmani.** Whitewashed walls and wood-panel ceilings inside this popular restaurant named for Georgian artist Niko Pirosmani re-create the aura of an artist's studio. Copies of Pirosmani's art decorate the walls. Try to sit by the window in the main hall or on the balcony so you can enjoy beautiful views of New Maiden's Convent, across the pond from the restaurant. The menu reads like a Georgian cookbook. The specialties are *shashlyk po-mirzaansky* (shish kebab with mushrooms) and *adzhakhuri* (pork cutlet and potatoes, with pomegranate seeds). The kitchen also serves delightful *khinkali*, Georgian meat dumplings. Order a bottle of Georgian wine to accompany your meal. ⊠ *4 Novodevichy proyezd, Krasnaya Presnya* ☎ *495/247–1926* ▭ *MC, V* Ⓜ *Sportivnaya.*

Northern Outskirts

Russian

$$–$$$ ✕ **The Tsar's Hunt.** A traditional log structure houses this fashionable restaurant designed in country style. The carved-wood decorations, bear and wolf skins on the floors and chairs, and an antique Russian stove create an environment so warm it feels as if you've just returned from an ermine-covered troika ride. Though this spot is far from the city center, diners flock here for simple and good food, like the pork ribs with hot sauce and the *winter schchi,* a warming winter cabbage soup. Start with *zakuski*— Russian appetizers, traditionally enjoyed with vodka—displayed on a cart. Work your way through the various wild animals offered, including seasonal Russian bear. ⊠ *186a Rublevo-Uspenskoye shosse, Zhukovka village, Northern Outskirts* ☎ *495/418–7983* ⌂ *Reservations essential* ▭ *AE, DC, MC, V* Ⓜ *By car or train from Belorussia Station.*

Seafood

$$$–$$$$ ✕ **Sirena.** There are probably as many live fish as dead denizens of the deep at this seafood showplace, a longtime favorite of the famous, including Sting and Liza Minnelli. One room has a glass floor beneath which huge sturgeon squirm; in another, aquariums surround you with numerous fish who watch you eat their brethren. Waiters dressed like sailors greet you as you enter the restaurant via the stern of a ship. The wide selection of fish main courses, such as the mixed seafood cooked in parchment, rarely disappoints but Sirena is still far too expensive. ⊠ *15 Bolshaya Spasskaya, Northern Outskirts* ☎ *495/208–1412* ▭ *AE, DC, MC, V* Ⓜ *Sukharevskaya.*

Southern Outskirts

Georgian

$–$$$ ✕ **Rytzarsky Klub.** Under the ski jump at Sparrow Hills and overlooking most of Moscow, this restaurant has one of the best views in the city. In summer you can dine on the wood balcony. Rytzarsky Klub, which means the "Knight Club," was designed to imitate the style of the Middle Ages, with knight paraphernalia on display throughout the rooms and heavy oak chairs and a fireplace in the Knight Room. The elegant White Room displays the works of 19th-century Russian artists. As for the hearty Georgian food, start with the eggplant stuffed with walnuts.

For the main course try the *kuchmachi,* a dish made from cow tongue, heart, and liver. It's a long walk from the metro to the restaurant. ⊠ *28 ul. Kosygina, Southern Outskirts* ☎ *495/930–0726* ▭ *MC, V* Ⓜ *Leninsky Prospekt or Universitet.*

WHERE TO STAY

You might think that a world capital with a population of more than 10 million would have a large number of hotels, but this is not yet the case in Moscow. As Russia comes in from the cold, the city's hotel scene is expanding slowly, with on average one new major hotel opening a year. A Ritz-Carlton is under construction (scheduled to open in spring 2006) on Tverskaya ulitsa on the site of the former landmark Intourist hotel, demolished in 2002. Another icon of Moscow, the Moskva hotel featured on the label of Stolichnaya vodka—was torn down in 2003. A deluxe hotel is to rise on the same site with a replica facade of the original by 2006.

For travelers able and willing to splurge, Moscow's top hotels offer a level of amenities and pampering that were unavailable a decade ago. Fine restaurants, business centers, cafés and cocktail bars, health clubs, and attentive service are now the norm at hotels geared to business travelers. Mid-level establishments are improving their facilities and service, too. For example, most now have card keys, and it's rare to find rooms that are not clean, even if they are a bit tattered.

That noted, the city suffers from a dearth of decent mid-range hotels, and old-style hangovers are still evident at many of these lodgings. Some mid-range spots retain their Soviet decor—mouse-brown carpet, tarnished gold-patterned polyester upholstery, and plywood furniture. Competition among hotels is slowly leading to improvements, but be prepared for a lower level of service than you might expect at home. When reserving, it really pays to ask for a room that has been renovated; the cost is usually the same and the difference can be startling, particularly in the lower-price hotels. If it matters, you should also ask whether your double room has twin beds or one large one; either is possible.

Prices

The city's best hotels can—and do—charge high rates that are mostly paid by travelers with expense accounts. Many of these hotels often offer steeply discounted weekend rates. Budget properties are available, though they generally have few amenities and are some distance from the city center. Hotels generally list their prices in conditional units (linked to that day's dollar rate).

	$$$$	$$$	$$	$	¢
WHAT IT COSTS In U.S. dollars					
FOR 2 PEOPLE	over $275	$200–$275	$150–$200	$75–$150	under $75

Prices are for a standard double room in high season, excluding taxes and service charge.

Kitai Gorod

$$$$ 🏨 **Ararat Park Hyatt.** One of the most luxurious of Moscow's hotels combines the traditional and modern. You enter through gigantic stone pillars into a sparkling (occasionally gaudy) interior with glass-and-steel elevators and a dark-wood reception area. Rooms are light and spacious, with elegant beige-fabric furniture, glass tables, and powerful showers in the bathrooms. Café Ararat, a replica of the landmark café of the same name that stood on this site in the 1940s, serves Armenian cuisine and has design elements based on ancient Armenian culture. The hotel is a short walk from the Bolshoi Theater and the Kremlin. ⊠ *4 Neglinnaya ul., 109012* ☎ *495/783–1234* 🖷 *495/783–1235* ⊕ *www.moscow.park. hyatt.com* ⇰ *219 rooms, 16 suites* ⚭ *2 restaurants, cable TV, health club, 4 bars, Internet, meeting rooms* ⊟ *DC, MC, V* Ⓜ *Okhotny Ryad or Teatralnaya.*

$$$$
Fodor'sChoice
★
🏨 **Metropol.** Originally built between 1899 and 1903, this first-class hotel has been the stage for some fabled events: Lenin spoke frequently in the assembly hall of the building, and David Lean filmed part of *Doctor Zhivago* in the restaurant. The hotel is one of Moscow's most elegant, with outstanding service and amenities. The lobby and restaurants transport you back a century, and the guest rooms have hardwood floors, Oriental rugs, and modern furnishings. Antiques grace all the suites, and the two presidential suites come with private saunas. The location, opposite the Bolshoi Theater and a five-minute walk from the Kremlin, is top-notch. ⊠ *1/4 Teatralny proyezd, 103012* ☎ *495/927–6000, 7501/927–6000 outside Russia* 🖷 *495/927–6010, 7501/927–6010 outside Russia* ⊕ *www.metropol-moscow.ru* ⇰ *292 rooms, 76 suites* ⚭ *3 restaurants, café, room service, cable TV, gym, sauna, 3 bars, casino, Internet, business services, meeting room, travel services, no-smoking rooms* ⊟ *AE, DC, MC, V* Ⓜ *Ploshchad Revolutsii or Teatralnaya.*

$$$$ 🏨 **Savoy.** The Savoy opened in 1913 in connection with celebrations commemorating the 300th anniversary of the Romanov dynasty. Recent renovations enlarged guest rooms and made the hotel facade more distinguished. Interiors of gilded chandeliers, ceiling paintings, and polished paneling invoke the spirit of pre-revolutionary Russia. The ornate dining room, where a complimentary breakfast is served, exudes romance: there's a pianist, fountain, and painted cherubs that float amongst clouds. The rooms have new spacious marble bathrooms, some with hydro massage baths. The bedrooms are equipped with king-size beds with orthopedic mattresses and antiallergenic pillows. Views are negligible, owing to the hotel's side-street location, but this gives the advantage of quiet. The hotel is just off Teatralnaya Ploshchad and within walking distance of the Kremlin. ⊠ *3 ul. Rozhdestvenka, 103012* ☎ *495/929–8500* 🖷 *495/230–2186* ⊕ *www.savoy.ru* ⇰ *70 rooms, 17 suites* ⚭ *Restaurant, room service, minibars, cable TV, bar, casino, business services, travel services* ⊟ *AE, DC, MC, V* Ⓜ *Kuznetsky Most.*

$$$$ 🏨 **Sretenskaya.** Indulge yourself in the atmosphere of an old Russian fairytale with massive carved oak furniture, stained glass windows, and wall paintings depicting popular tales like "Little Red Flower." The lobby bar is nicely set in the winter garden with rich vegetation. Guest rooms are quite modern, with all amenities. Though centrally located, Sretenskaya is a 25-minute walk to the Red Square. Moscow's famous boulevards and the Garden Ring are only steps away. ⊠ *15 ul. Sretenka, Kitai Gorod, 103045* ☎ *495/933–5544* 🖷 *495/933–5545* ⊕ *www.hotel-sretenskaya.ru* ↘ *38 rooms* ♨ *Restaurant, sauna, lobby bar, meeting rooms* ▤ *AE, DC, MC, V* Ⓜ *Sukharevskaya Kitai Gorod.*

$$$ 🏨 **Hotel Budapest.** Opened in 1876 as a club for noblemen, this city-center hotel later became an accommodation in Soviet days for those visiting Moscow on official business. Now it's a comfortable hotel with a homey old style: high ceilings, Oriental rugs, leather chairs, and small touches such as the wrought-iron mailbox in the lobby. Although the hotel has no restaurant, it serves complimentary breakfast in guest rooms. Just up the block there's a trendy and inexpensive café, Gogol, that serves traditional Russian dishes. ⊠ *2/18 Petrovsky Linii, 103051* ☎ *495/923–2356* 🖷 *495/921–1266, 7502/221–1665 outside Russia, 7502/921–5210 reservations outside Russia* ⊕ *www.hotel-budapest.ru* ↘ *86 rooms, 30 suites* ♨ *Minibars, cable TV, pub, business services, meeting room, no-smoking rooms* ▤ *AE, DC, MC, V* Ⓜ *Kuznetsky Most.*

Tverskaya Ulitsa, the Arbat

★ **$$$$** 🏨 **Courtyard Marriott.** The location of this newly built hotel is probably the best of any hotel in its class. In the heart of the historical center, across from St. Andrew's Anglican Church and near the Moscow Conservatory, this hotel consists of three interconnected buildings including a two-story historical building facing Voznesensky Pereulok and a cozy atrium. The guest rooms, some of which have views of the Kremlin, are spacious, combining comfort and functionality. In addition to high-speed Internet, the rooms have large desks with conveniently placed lighting and outlets and ergonomic chairs. Bathrooms are equipped with illuminated make-up mirrors. ⊠ *7 Voznesensky per., 125009* ☎ *495/981–3300* 🖷 *495/981–3301* ⊕ *www.marriott.com* ↘ *218 rooms* ♨ *2 restaurants, lobby lounge, gym, Internet* ▤ *AE, DC, MC, V* Ⓜ *Pushkinskaya or Tverskaya.*

$$$$ 🏨 **Golden Apple.** Catching up with the global obsession, Moscow finally
Fodor'sChoice got a boutique hotel in fall 2004. Cozy, stylish, quirky, and upmarket, ★ Golden Apple indeed embodies the definition of boutique. Shiny metallic panels clash with bright, oddly shaped armchairs in the lobby bar. The enormous golden apple next to the front desk turns out to be a comfortable sofa on closer inspection. Each of the hotel's seven floors is painted different colors. In a reference to the Chekhov play, some rooms have huge propellerlike iron seagulls hanging from the ceiling. Though the hotel's building has some connection to the great playwright, the staff could not elaborate on it. ⊠ *11, ul. Malaya Dmitrovka, 103006* ☎ *495/980–7000* 🖷 *495/980–7001* ⊕ *www.goldenapple.ru* ↘ *92 rooms* ♨ *Restaurant, lobby bar, gym, sauna, business center* ▤ *MC, V* Ⓜ *Chekhovskaya or Pushkinskaya.*

$$$$ 🏨 **Golden Ring.** Although the name refers to the "ring" of ancient Russian towns northeast of Moscow, there's nothing provincial about this towering hotel just across the Garden Ring from the Foreign Affairs Ministry skyscraper. Business travelers check in for the friendly staff, appealing and spacious guest rooms, and excellent city views, particularly from the hotel's upper floors. The 22nd-floor bar's observation point is stunning at night, and the Mediterranean restaurant on the top (23rd floor) has panoramic views. ⊠ *5 Smolenskaya ul., 119121* ☎ *495/725–0100* 🖨 *495/725–0101* ⊕ *www.hotel-goldenring.ru* ⤵ *166 rooms, 81 suites* ⚷ *2 restaurants, health club, bar, casino, business services, meeting rooms, travel services, parking (fee)* ⊟ *AE, DC, MC, V* Ⓜ *Smolenskaya.*

$$$$ 🏨 **Marco Polo Presnya.** Opened in 1904 as a residence for English teachers and later the exclusive domain of the Communist Party, this hotel is an intriguing choice for those interested in the Soviet era. For instance, the auditorium was once the movie house where party insiders came to see Western films unavailable to most Muscovites. The hotel is in a prestigious residential neighborhood near Patriarch's Pond, and many rooms have balconies overlooking the quiet green surroundings. In warm months, the inner courtyard is an attractive place to relax. Gray and light-blue walls make the small rooms a bit dark, but multicolor bedspreads add a homey touch. The service is friendly and efficient. ⊠ *9 Spiridonevsky per., 103104* ☎ *495/244–3631* 🖨 *495/926–5404 or 495/926–5402* ⊕ *www.presnja.ru* ⤵ *48 rooms, 20 suites* ⚷ *Restaurant, café, room service, minibars, cable TV, gym, sauna, lobby lounge, Internet, business services, meeting room* ⊟ *AE, DC, MC, V* Ⓜ *Mayakovskaya or Pushkinskaya.*

$$$$ 🏨 **Marriott Grand.** Once you step inside past the renovated turn-of-the-20th-century art nouveau facade, you'll likely feel very much at home—if home is the United States. You'll even find eggs Benedict on the breakfast buffet. Marriott opened its nine-story hotel amid the bustle of Tverskaya ulitsa in 1997, just in time to celebrate Moscow's 850th anniversary. The Western-style rooms are spacious, and some overlook a peaceful courtyard. A round central staircase ascends from the lobby's sunny atrium. Service is pleasant. Red Square is 1 km (½ mi) away. ⊠ *26 Tverskaya ul., 103050* ☎ *495/935–8500, 7502/935–8500 outside Russia* 🖨 *495/935–8501* ⊕ *www.marriotthotels.com* ⤵ *377 rooms, 13 suites* ⚷ *3 restaurants, room service, minibars, cable TV, pool, gym, hair salon, massage, sauna, 2 bars, concierge, Internet, business services, meeting rooms, no-smoking floor* ⊟ *AE, DC, MC, V* Ⓜ *Mayakovskaya or Tverskaya.*

$$$$ 🏨 **Marriott Royal Avrora.** On the corner of ulitsa Petrovka and pedestrianized Stoleshnikov pereulok, the Marriott Royal Avrora is close to the Kremlin, Tverskaya ulitsa, and the Bolshoi Theater, which is some three minutes' walk away. Together with the Marriott Grand on Tverskaya ulitsa, the Marriott Royal, constructed in art nouveau style, symbolizes the Moscow of Mayor Yuri Luzhkov's era and his construction boom. Full butler service for all guests is unique to the city. Each room has three direct telephone lines, individual climate control, and excellent bathroom amenities. ⊠ *11/20 ul. Petrovka, 103050* ☎ *495/937–1000* 🖨 *495/937–0801* ⊕ *www.marriotthotels.com* ⤵ *227 rooms, 38 suites* ⚷ *2 restaurants, in-room safes, cable TV, pool, gym, sauna, bar, shop, Internet* ⊟ *AE, DC, MC, V* Ⓜ *Okhotny Ryad.*

$$$$
Fodor'sChoice
★
🏨 **National Hotel.** If you seek luxury and elite service, this 1903 hotel is the place for you. It's the city's most elegant accommodation, right across a plaza from Red Square and at the foot of Tverskaya ulitsa. Inside the stunning landmark art nouveau building are a great marble staircase, elevators topped by silvered twists of ivy, and a Viennese-style café. Most

rooms are plush with polished-oak furniture upholstered in silk. Though a bit small, the modern white-tile bathrooms sparkle. For $800 a night you can stay in a two-room suite where Lenin lived for a time in 1918. ✉ *15/1 Mochovaya ul., 103012* ☎ *495/258–7000* 🖷 *495/258–7100* 🌐 *www.national.ru* 📠 *195 rooms, 36 suites* ⚖ *2 restaurants, café, room service, minibars, cable TV, pool, gym, hair salon, massage, sauna, 2 bars, casino, Internet, business services, meeting room* 🖃 *AE, DC, MC, V* Ⓜ *Okhotny Ryad.*

Kropotkinsky District

$$$ 🏨 **Tiflis.** Taking the old name of the Georgian capital Tbilis, this small, attractive hotel is built in a style of an old Tbilisi townhouse. It's a little more than a mile south of the Kremlin and close to some of the finest restaurants in town, Christ the Savior Cathedral, and Pushkin Museum of Fine Arts. The rooms with views of a small square and a fountain are big and light thanks to wall-size windows, all in different styles. Two suites have Jacuzzis, and one two-story supersuite has a Jacuzzi and sauna. ✉ *32 ul. Ostozhenka, 119034* ☎ *495/733–9070* 🖷 *495/203–3536* 🌐 *www.hoteltiflis.com* 📠 *60 rooms, 7 suites* ⚖ *Restaurant, room service, Wi-Fi, pool, cable TV, bar* 🖃 *MC, V* Ⓜ *Kropotkinskaya.*

Zamoskvoreche (Gorky Park, Tretyakov Gallery)

$$$$ 🏨 **Baltschug Kempinski.** On the banks of the Moskva River opposite the Kremlin and Red Square, this deluxe hotel has extraordinary views—and prices, too. The building dates to the 19th century, but the sparkling interior is modern. The rooms are stately, equipped with all sorts of amenities, including bedroom slippers. Rooms with a view cost more but are preferable; request one or you could end up staring at the factory bordering the hotel's eastern side. The hotel is central but not particularly convenient—it's a 15-minute walk from the nearest metro station and the city's main attractions. ✉ *1 Baltchug ul., Zamoskvoreche, 113035* ☎ *495/230–6500, 7501/230–6500 outside Russia* 🖷 *495/230–6502, 7501/230–6502 outside Russia* 🌐 *www.kempinski-moscow.com* 📠 *202 rooms, 30 suites* ⚖ *2 restaurants, café, room service, cable TV, pool, gym, sauna, 2 bars, casino, Internet, business services, meeting room, no-smoking floor* 🖃 *AE, DC, MC, V* Ⓜ *Novokuznetskaya, Ploshchad Revolyutsii, or Tretyakovskaya.*

$$$$ 🏨 **Katerina.** Near the river and Riverside Towers, one of the city's main business centers, this small Swedish-run hotel is popular with European business travelers. The hotel occupies a renovated prerevolutionary mansion and a modern eight-story annex. In the comfortable modern rooms, dark-blue furniture complements the yellow-fabric-covered walls, which are lined with watercolors. The staff is friendly and helpful. Views of the picturesque Moskva River and New Savior Monastery are splendid. Guests who stay on the Privileged Floor can relax in a cozy lounge with a fireplace and cigars. The Stockholm restaurant, serving traditional Scandinavian and Russian cuisine, is a big plus. ✉ *6 Shlyuzovaya nab., Zamoskvoreche* ☎ *495/795–2444* 🖷 *495/795–2443* 🌐 *www.katerina.msk.ru* 📠 *110 rooms, 9 suites* ⚖ *Restaurant, cable TV, gym, sauna, library, Internet* 🖃 *AE, DC, MC, V* Ⓜ *Paveletskaya.*

$$$$ 🏨 **Swissôtel.** Rising 34 stories above the city, this sleek glass and metal cylinder is the newest and the tallest member of Moscow's family of luxury hotels, as well as a conspicuous addition to a skyline dominated by Stalin's seven towers. In the heart of a booming business district not far from Pavetetsky train station and next to Moscow House of Music, the hotel opened in summer 2005. The hotel is visible from Red Square but many Muscovites have complained that it ruined one of the city's best views. Guest rooms are among the largest in the city and include espresso coffee machines and electronic safes. Bathrooms are large and modern, with small tiles, glass and chrome, and a heated floor. A shower and tub are enclosed in glass in a space bigger than a walk-in closet. The shower heads are as large as a plate. Swissôtel's greatest attraction: a bar inside an inverted glass bowl on the 34th floor. ⊠ *52 Kosmodamianskaya nab., Bldg. 6, Zamoskvoreche, 115054* ☎ *495/787–9800* 🖷 *495/787–9898* ⊕ *www.swissotel.com* ☞ *235 rooms* ⟁ *2 restaurants, 2 bars, gym, pool, spa center, Internet, business services, meeting rooms, business center* ▭ *AE, DC, MC, V* Ⓜ *Paveletskaya or Taganskaya.*

$ 🏨 **Hotel Danilovskaya.** Within the walls of the Orthodox Danilovsky (St.
Fodor$Choice Daniel) Monastery—the official residence of Patriarch Alexei II of
★ Moscow and All Russia—this hotel is serene and lovely, with fountains, religious-theme paintings, and domed monastery buildings. The church holds conferences here, and also sponsors concerts and exhibitions. Though basic, the rooms (breakfast included) are clean and spacious; some rooms have showers, but no tubs. Standard double rooms have two twin beds, and suites have double beds. The restaurant's Russian menu is affordable, but the green decor feels institutional. The hotel is just a five-minute walk from the metro station. ⊠ *5 Bolshoi Starodanilovsky per., Zamoskvoreche, 113191* ☎ *495/954–0503* 🖷 *495/954–0750* ☞ *103 rooms, 13 suites* ⟁ *Restaurant, room service, refrigerators, cable TV, pool, massage, sauna, bar, business services, meeting room* ▭ *AE, DC, MC, V* Ⓜ *Tulskaya.*

Tverskaya-Yamskaya ul., Krasnaya Presnya ul. & Novoslobodskaya ul.

$$$$ 🏨 **Holiday Inn Lesnaya.** The 12-story hotel opened in 2005 and its big advantage is its conference facilities and central location on Lesnaya Ulitsa, near Belorussky Station and just steps away from Tverskaya Ulitsa. Rooms are spacious with walls stylishly decorated in beige, ivory, and terra-cotta. All standard rooms have high-speed Internet and tea and coffeemakers. The hotel offers guests "a pillow menu" from which to choose various types and sizes of pillows. ⊠ *15 Lesnaya ul., Krasnaya Presnya, 123456* ☎ *495/101–4105* ⊕ *holiday.bookin.ru/* ☞ *284 rooms, 17 suites* ⟁ *Restaurant, snack bar, gym, Internet, meeting rooms* ▭ *AE, MC, V* Ⓜ *Belorusskaya.*

★ **$$$$** 🏨 **Marriott Tverskaya.** After a stroll from Red Square along bustling Tverskaya ulitsa, you may find comfort in the coziness of this eight-story art nouveau building. The small, peaceful lobby is complemented by a four-story atrium, which is overlooked by the alcove booths of the Italian restaurant Gratzi. A sunny guests-only lounge offers coffee and tea in the morning, and drinks at the end of the day. The rooms are understated—ivory, rose, and olive make up the palette, with darker notes provided by wood furniture. Old black-and-white prints of Moscow scenes line the walls on some floors. ✉ *34 Pervaya (1st) Tverskaya-Yamskaya ul., Krasnaya Presnya, 125047* ☎ *495/258–3000, 7501/258–3000 outside Russia* 🖷 *495/258–3099, 7501/258–3099 outside Russia* ⊕ *www. marriotthotels.com* ⤴ *115 rooms, 7 suites* ⚹ *Restaurant, room service, cable TV, gym, sauna, bar, Internet, business services, meeting rooms, no-smoking floor* ⊟ *AE, DC, MC, V* Ⓜ *Belorusskaya.*

$$$$ 🏨 **Mezhdunarodnaya.** With a name that means "international," this big gray hotel, nicknamed "the Mezh" by foreign residents, is part of the huge World Trade Center complex, which also includes a shopping center and two buildings for offices and apartments. Although it has lost some of its original prestige, the Mezh is near the city exposition center and is a frequent site for conferences. The rooms are spacious, with elegant dark-wood furniture and cream-color walls. The hotel is within sight of the city center but far from the metro, and only one city bus stops near here. ✉ *12 Krasnopresnenskaya nab., Krasnaya Presnya, 123610* ☎ *495/258–2122* 🖷 *495/253–2051* ⊕ *mezhdunarodnaya. bookin.ru* ⤴ *547 rooms, 33 suites* ⚹ *5 restaurants, room service, minibars, cable TV, pool, gym, hair salon, sauna, 3 bars, casino, shop, Internet, business services, meeting room, travel services* ⊟ *AE, DC, MC, V* Ⓜ *Ul. 1905 Goda.*

$$$$ 🏨 **Novotel Moscow Center.** This 18-floor hotel just a few metro stops from the Kremlin is one of the best mid-price options in the city for business travelers. It's a typical Novotel creation—functional and efficient, if a bit unimaginative. Rooms come with all the usual amenities, and some of them have rather interesting shapes because the building itself is cylindrical. The hotel stands next door to the Meyerhold complex, which includes a theatrical center, offices, and retail space. ✉ *23 Novoslobodskaya ul., Krasnaya Presnya, 127055* ☎ *495/780–4000* 🖷 *495/780–4001* ⊕ *www.novotel.com* ⤴ *255 rooms, 1 suite* ⚹ *Restaurant, cable TV, health club, bar, Internet, business services* ⊟ *AE, DC, MC, V* Ⓜ *Mendeleyevskaya.*

$$$$ 🏨 **Sheraton Palace.** The European business community loves this place, thanks to its amenities, which include a chauffeur-driven fleet of cars. However, the rooms are small for the amount and size of furniture put into them. The real winners are those who can afford the duplexes (starting at $335) that are on the Towers Floor, a hotel within a hotel with its own reception and lounge. The hotel's location at the far upper end of Tverskaya ulitsa is excellent, and the soundproof windows keep things quiet. Moscow was one of the first European cities to get a taste of Sheraton's new beds, when they were installed in all rooms during the refurbishment in fall 2004. ✉ *19 Pervaya (1st) Tverskaya-Yamskaya ul., Krasnaya Presnya, 125047* ☎ *495/931–9700, 7502/256–3000 outside Russia* 🖷 *495/931–9708, 7502/256–3008 outside Russia* ⊕ *www. starwood.com/sheraton* ⤴ *221 rooms, 18 suites* ⚹ *3 restaurants, café, room service, minibars, cable TV, health club, massage, 2 bars, concierge, Internet, business services, meeting room, free parking, no-smoking rooms* ⊟ *AE, DC, MC, V* Ⓜ *Belorusskaya.*

Near New Maiden Convent

★ **$$$$** 🏨 **Radisson Slavyanskaya.** Designed for business travelers, the Radisson offers every modern American-style amenity and no-nonsense comfort. Its huge, two-story lobby—great for people-watching—is lined with restaurants, luxury shops, a popular English-language theater with first-run movies, a casino, and a health club. The hotel's location is not quite central, but alongside the Kiev Station, with its transients and homeless population. There are security guards at the hotel entrance, and some businesspeople rarely leave the hotel during their stays. This is a good choice for people who favor comfort and service over character. ✉ *2 Berezhkovskaya nab., Krasnaya Presnya, 121059* 🕾 *495/941–8020, 800/ 333–3333 in U.S.* 🖷 *495/941–8000, 7502/224–1225 outside Russia* 🌐 *www.radisson.com* 🛏 *410 rooms, 20 suites* ♨ *4 restaurants, café, room service, refrigerators, cable TV, indoor pool, health club, massage, sauna, lobby lounge, casino, theater, Internet, business services, meeting room, car rental, travel services* ▭ *AE, DC, MC, V* Ⓜ *Kievskaya.*

$$ 🏨 **Ukraina.** One of the seven Stalin Gothic skyscrapers, this hotel is a familiar landmark on the banks of the Moskva River. It has all the hallmarks of the Stalinist era inside, including red carpeting, grandiose socialist-realist decor (note the foyer's ceiling), redwood and oak furnishing, and fancy chandeliers. The rooms are worn but clean. Rooms on the higher floors have great views, particularly of the White House, where the government and prime minister work, across the river. The almost-central location places you where Kutuzovsky prospekt (a chic place to shop) meets up with the Novy Arbat. The nearest metro is a 10-minute trek away. ✉ *2/1 Kutuzovsky pr., Krasnaya Presnya, 121249* 🕾 *495/ 933–5652, 495/243–3030 reservations* 🖷 *495/243–3001* 🌐 *www. ukraina-hotel.ru* 🛏 *1,600 rooms* ♨ *4 restaurants, café, room service, refrigerators, massage, sauna, bar, casino, business services* ▭ *AE, DC, MC, V* Ⓜ *Kievskaya.*

Northern Outskirts

$$$$ 🏨 **Arte.** The proprietor of this hotel also owns a gallery in Berlin, and he has covered the hotel walls with contemporary Russian artwork. At the edge of a park and away from the urban crush, this hotel can make you feel as if you're in the country. Some rooms overlook the park and the hotel beer garden, which has live music and a weekend brunch. Guest rooms are clean and basic, and breakfast is included in the price. Twenty minutes by car from Red Square, Arte is far from public transportation, and necessitates a 20-minute walk or a trolley ride from the metro station. ✉ *2 Tretya (3rd) Peschannaya ul., Northern Outskirts, 125252* 🕾 *495/725–0905* 🖷 *495/725–0904* 🌐 *www.arthotel.ru* 🛏 *81 rooms, 2 suites* ♨ *Restaurant, room service, cable TV, 2 tennis courts, gym, massage, sauna, beer garden, meeting rooms, no-smoking rooms* ▭ *AE, DC, MC, V* Ⓜ *Sokol.*

$$$$ 🏨 **Novotel Sheremetyevo 2 Moscow Airport.** If you need a room near Sheremetyevo II airport, try this hotel. The rooms and beds are comfortable, the halls quiet. In addition, the staff is eager to please, and the modern facilities are well maintained. A 24-hour shuttle bus runs to the airport, which is ¼ mi away, and there's a complimentary bus to the city center as well. Clients are, predictably, primarily businesspeople and airline personnel, though the Novotel also happens to be popular with professional European soccer teams because of its few distractions. Day rates of less than half the normal prices are available. ⊠ *Sheremetyevo II airport, Northern Outskirts, 103339* ☎ *495/926–5900, 7502/926–5900 outside Russia* ☒ *495/926–5903 or 495/926–5904, 7502/220–6604 outside Russia* ⊕ *www.novotel.com* ⇆ *466 rooms, 22 suites* ♧ *2 restaurants, cable TV, pool, gym, sauna, lobby lounge, Internet, meeting rooms* ▭ *AE, DC, MC, V.*

$$$ ⌕ **Iris.** Iris's dismal views and distant location—in a bleak residential district on the northern outskirts of town, adjacent to the world-famous Fyodorov Eye Institute and about halfway between the city center and the airport—are unfortunate, because this is a fine French-run hotel with spacious, cheery rooms that have lots of closet space, large bathrooms, and balconies. Complimentary shuttle buses run hourly until 11 PM to two central stops. The hotel also provides free bus tours of the city and excursions to the popular weekend Izmailovsky flea market. ⊠ *10 Korovinskoye shosse, Northern Outskirts, 103051* ☎ *495/488–8000* ☒ *495/488–8888, 7502/220–8888 outside Russia* ⊕ *www.iris-hotel.ru* ⇆ *155 rooms, 40 suites* ♧ *2 restaurants, room service, minibars, cable TV, pool, gym, sauna, bar, business services, meeting room, no-smoking floor* ▭ *AE, DC, MC, V.*

★ $ ⌕ **Kosmos.** This huge, 26-story hotel built by the French for the 1980 Olympics is popular with tour groups, for good reason: it's one of the city's better bargains. Years of heavy tourist traffic have dulled the shine on the French-furnished interiors, but the rooms are adequate, clean, and fairly inexpensive. The spacious, two-story lobby is decorated with a sculpture strongly reminiscent of the molecule models typically found in a sixth-grade science class. The hotel stands across the street from the All-Russian Exhibition Center, a part of town that has interesting sights, but is far from downtown; however, the metro is right across the street. ⊠ *150 Prospekt Mira, Northern Outskirts, 129366* ☎ *495/234–1212, 495/234–1000, 495/234–1206, or 495/234–1256* ☒ *495/215–8880* ⇆ *1,300 rooms* ♧ *4 restaurants, cable TV, hair salon, bowling, 2 bars, casino, nightclub* ▭ *AE, DC, MC, V* Ⓜ *VDNKh.*

Eastern Outskirts

$$$$ ⌕ **Renaissance Moscow.** Rooms are large and equipped with every amenity at this hotel, a busy place for conferences and meetings. There's even an English-language movie theater. An executive floor has a lounge for breakfast, butler service, and a separate reception area. The hotel is far from the city center, but it's a good value and convenient to all major arterial roads, and the Prospekt Mira metro stop is a 15-minute walk away. Athletes competing or musicians performing in the nearby Olympic Sports Stadium—used for volleyball, tennis, swimming, and other sporting events, as well as large-scale concerts—often stay here. ⊠ *18/1 Olympisky pr., Eastern Outskirts, 129110* ☎ *495/931–9000* ☒ *495/931–9076* ⊕ *www.renaissancehotels.com* ⇆ *475 rooms, 13 suites* ♧ *4 restaurants, café, room service, minibars, cable TV, pool, gym, sauna,* bar, Internet, business services, meeting room, no-smoking floor ⊟ AE, DC, MC, V Ⓜ Prospekt Mira.

¢ ⊞ **Gamma-Delta Izmailovo.** At one time this mammoth hotel complex included five buildings, making it Europe's largest lodging, with thousands of rooms. Now it's four hotels, Alfa, Beta, Gamma, and Delta, with the latter most commonly used by foreigners. A two-minute walk from the lively Izmailovsky flea market, this is a convenient place for the serious souvenir shopper. It's also adjacent to a metro station, close to Izmailovo Royal Estate (where Peter the Great learned to sail), and near Izmailovsky Park, one of the biggest in the city; otherwise this is a trek from most tourist sights. The rooms are basic. ⊠ 71 Izmailovskoye shosse, Eastern Outskirts, 105613 ☎ 495/166–4490 or 495/737–7000 🖷 495/166–7486 ➯ 2,000 rooms ⚘ 3 restaurants, room service, sauna, 6 bars, meeting room ⊟ AE, DC, V Ⓜ Partizanskaya.

¢ ⊞ **Travelers Guest House Moscow.** For those on a tight budget, this is the place. It's clean and friendly, with four- and five-person rooms, doubles, and singles. You can use the kitchen to cook your own meals, but there are few dishes and not much equipment. As in most Russian apartments, the hot water is turned off for three weeks in the summer for system maintenance. Typically, more than half the guests here are young Americans, and the staff speaks English. It's a 10-minute walk to the metro. ⊠ 50 Bolshaya Pereyaslavskaya, 10th fl., Taganka, 129041 ☎ 495/631–4059 🖷 495/680–7686 ⊕ www.tgh.ru ➯ 33 rooms ⚘ Laundry service; no room phones, no room TVs ⊟ MC, V Ⓜ Prospekt Mira.

NIGHTLIFE & THE ARTS

A city of classical culture, Moscow also offers plenty of glamour and glitz. Ballet at the Bolshoi, concerts at the Tchaikovsky Conservatory, and theaters packed for Chekhov plays are among the highlights of the intense arts scene, while the nightlife takes in cozy cellar bars and glittering clubs for the elite.

Ticket booths on city streets testify to Muscovites' love of theater, and low prices ensure that high culture remains a mass pursuit. This enthusiasm means that the most popular shows can sell out weeks ahead, but smaller arts events, such as the regular free concerts at the Conservatory are often equally rewarding. Although the Bolshoi's famous columned theater has been closed for repairs, the troupe still performs in a newly built venue whose elaborate interior rivals the original. On a much smaller scale, the Helikon Opera's innovative productions of classics such as Carmen gain critical raves, notwithstanding the theater's tiny stage.

The neon facades of downtown casinos and the ranks of Mercedes cars outside certain city clubs make it clear that Moscow is a city for big spenders. But you don't have to be an oligarch to have a good time. A more bohemian crowd gathers at bars and clubs that offer live concerts by local bands, cheap beers, and tasty eats. The city is too far off the beaten track to attract the top-name Western stars, but it can be a wonderful place to catch blues and jazz by Russian musicians and even ethnic folk acts from the regions, such as the Tuvan throat singers who frequently appear at festivals.

The Arts

St. Petersburg may be most well known as Russia's cultural capital, but Moscow easily rivals its northern neighbor. Estimates differ, but the city has anywhere from 60 to 200 theaters, not to mention several prestigious acting schools and the increasingly popular International Chekhov Theater Festival, which usually takes place late-August through early-September. Every Thursday the English-language newspaper *Moscow Times* publishes a schedule of cultural events for the coming week.

Most theaters' tickets can be obtained at the theaters themselves or at the box offices (*teatralnaya kassa*) scattered throughout the city. Note that some theaters charge different prices for Russians and foreigners. If you're intimidated by the language barrier, avail yourself of your hotel's concierge. The prices are inflated, but a concierge can often get you tickets to otherwise sold-out performances. Scalpers usually can be found selling tickets outside theaters immediately prior to performances, but they have been known to rip off tourists, either charging exorbitant prices or selling fake tickets.

Art Galleries

Numerous private galleries sell Russian artwork, a nice alternative to the kitsch available at most of the tourist and riverside markets. The Friday edition of the *Moscow Times* carries a review of current exhibits. At group shows and festivals, watch out for the one-man Coat Gallery (aka Alexander Petrelli), who has paintings hidden within his overcoat. Just go up to him and ask and he'll open up and show you his wares. For opening hours, check with the galleries themselves; some are open only by appointment, and most are closed on Sunday and Monday.

Aidan Gallery. The artists displayed in this central gallery that was founded in 1992 are young, little known, and very stylish. ☒ *22 (1st) Tverskaya-Yamskaya ul., 3rd fl., Kitai Gorod* ☎ *495/251 3731* ⊕ *www.aidan-gallery.ru* Ⓜ *Mayakovskaya*.

ArtStrelka. This bohemian arts center houses 11 galleries displaying contemporary art, photographs, and designer clothes. Cross the pedestrian bridge opposite the Church of Christ the Savior and turn right. ☒ *14 Bersenevskaya nab., Bldg. 5* ☎ *8/916–112–7180 cell phone* ⊕ *www.artstrelka.ru* Ⓜ *Kropotkinskaya*.

Dom Nashchokina Gallery. This established show space makes its name with a mixture of classic Russian art and crowd-pulling exhibitions by celebrity artists. ☒ *12 Vorotnikovsky per., Kitai Gorod* ☎ *495/299–1178* ⊕ *www.domnaschokina.ru* Ⓜ *Mayakovskaya*.

Fine Art. This was one of the first private galleries in post-Soviet Russia. Today it displays contemporary art from the best of the previous generation's nonconformists to the most current names. ☒ *3/10 Bolshaya Sadovaya, Bldg. 10* ☎ *495/251–7649* Ⓜ *Mayakovskaya*.

★ **Guelman Gallery.** One of Moscow's first galleries, this is also one of its most controversial, due to the attention-loving nature of owner Marat Guelman. There's a definite shock value to many of the modern and avant-garde exhibits. It's a good bet for performance art. ☒ *7/7 ul. Malaya Polyanka, Bldg. 5, Zamoskvoreche* ☎ *495/238–8492* ⊕ *www.guelman.*

ru Ⓜ *Polyanka.*

Krokin Gallery. This gallery focuses on modern art, particularly photography and graphic art. ✉ *15 Bolshaya Polyanka, Zamoskvoreche* ☎ *495/959–0141* ⊕ *www.krokingallery.com* Ⓜ *Polyanka.*

NB Gallery. In the unlikely event that none of the contemporary landscape paintings displayed here catches your eye, proprietor Natalya Bykova, a friendly English-speaking art lover, is happy to offer advice on other top art venues in Moscow. The gallery is within an apartment, so it's best to call ahead. ✉ *6/2 Sivtsev Vrazhek, Apartment 2* ☎ *495/ 203–4006 or 495/737–5298* Ⓜ *Kropotkinskaya.*

★ **Stella Art.** Work by top names such as Andy Warhol is exhibited at this commercial gallery that opened in 2003. The art here can go for millions of dollars. ✉ *7 Skaryatinksy per.* ☎ *495/291–3407* ⊕ *www.stella-art.ru* Ⓜ *Krasnopresnenskaya.*

★ **Stella Art Russian.** Veteran Russian conceptual artists are featured at this sister of Stella Art. In 2004 it invited prominent, New York-based artist Ilya Kabakov for his first Moscow exhibition since emigrating. ✉ *62 Mytnaya ul.* ☎ *495/954–0253* ⊕ *www.stella-art.ru* Ⓜ *Tulskaya.*

Tsentralny Dom Khudozhnika (TsDKh). Many different galleries are housed within this vast exhibition center, the Central House of Artists, and if you wander long enough you're sure to find something to fit your tastes, from traditional landscapes to the latest avant-garde outrage. In front of TsDKh a huge painting market snakes its way along the river. Among the piles of kitsch and tedious landscapes you can find some real gems. Be prepared to bargain. ✉ *10 Krymsky Val, Zamoskvoreche* ☎ *495/238– 9843 or 495/238–9634* ⊕ *www.cha.ru* Ⓜ *Park Kultury or Oktyabrskaya.*

XL-Gallery. Russia's most renowned conceptual artists exhibit drawings, photographs, installations, and occasionally put on performance art in this intimate space. ✉ *16/2 Podkolokolny per.* ☎ *495/917–8508 or 495/916–8235* Ⓜ *Kitai Gorod.*

Movies

American House of Cinema. Only English-language movies are shown at this one-screen cinema. ✉ *Radisson Slavyanskaya hotel, 2 Ploshchad Yevropy, Krasnaya Presnya* ☎ *495/941–8747 or 495/941–8895* ⊕ *www. america-cinema.ru* Ⓜ *Kievskaya.*

Dome Cinema. A hotel movie house, Dome Cinema caters to the expatriate community with recent Hollywood releases. ✉ *Renaissance Moscow hotel, 18/1 Olympiisky pr., Eastern Outskirts* ☎ *495/931–9873* ⊕ *www.domecinema.ru* Ⓜ *Prospekt Mira.*

35mm. An artsy crowd frequents this simple theater with top-quality projection and sound. The films are always shown in their original language, usually with Russian subtitles. ✉ *47/24 Pokrovka, Kitai Gorod* ☎ *495/ 917–5492 or 495/917–1883* Ⓜ *Krasniye Vorota.*

Music

Moscow's musical life has always been particularly rich; the city has several symphony orchestras as well as song-and-dance ensembles. Moiseyev's Folk Dance Ensemble is well known in Europe and America, but the troupe is on tour so much of the year that when it performs in Moscow (generally at the Tchaikovsky Concert Hall), tickets are very difficult to obtain. Other renowned companies include the State Symphony Orchestra and the Armed Forces Song and Dance Ensemble. With the exception of special performances, tickets are usually easily available and inexpensive.

Glinka Music Museum Hall. This is one of many small concert halls scattered throughout the city. ✉ *4 ul. Fadeyeva* ☎ *495/251–1066* Ⓜ *Mayakovskaya.*

Moscow International House of Music. Opened in 2002, this architecturally striking center stages major classical concerts in its Svetlanov Hall, which contains Russia's largest organ. ✉ *52 Kosmodamianskaya nab., Bldg. 8* ☎ *495/730–4350 or 495/730–1860* ⊕ *www.mmdm.ru* Ⓜ *Paveletskaya.*

Russian Army Theater. The Armed Forces Song and Dance Ensemble calls this venue home. ✉ *2 Suvorovskaya Pl., Northern Outskirts* ☎ *495/681–2110 or 495/681–5120* Ⓜ *Novoslobodskaya.*

Scriabin Museum Hall. Performances are held usually on Wednesday in a small concert hall in the apartment building where the composer Alexander Scriabin lived. ✉ *11 Bolshoi Nikolopeskovsky per.* ☎ *495/241–1901* Ⓜ *Smolenskaya.*

Tchaikovsky Concert Hall. With seating for more than 1,600, this huge hall is home to the State Symphony Orchestra. ✉ *4/31 Triumfalnaya Pl.* ☎ *495/299–0378* Ⓜ *Mayakovskaya.*

Fodor'sChoice
★ **Tchaikovsky Conservatory.** Rachmaninoff, Scriabin, and Tchaikovsky are among the famous composers who have worked here. The acoustics of the magnificent Great Hall are superb, and portraits of the world's great composers hang above the high balcony. The adjacent Small Hall is usually reserved for chamber-music concerts. ✉ *13 Bolshaya Nikitskaya ul.* ☎ *495/229–7446, 495/229–9401, 495/229–3957, or 495/229–7412* ⊕ *www.mosconsv.ru* Ⓜ *Okhotny Ryad or Arbatskaya.*

Tsaritsyno Museum. A music hall nestled among the remains of Catherine the Great's partially completed Moscow estate regularly holds classical-music concerts. ✉ *1 ul. Dolskaya, Southern Outskirts* ☎ *495/325–4844* Ⓜ *Orekhovo or Tsaritsyno.*

Opera & Ballet

Fodor'sChoice
★ **Bolshoi Opera and Ballet Theater.** The landmark building of this world-renowned theater is closed for restoration until 2009. Until then, performances are held on a second stage built in 2002. The quality of the Bolshoi's productions has been erratic at times, but recent guest foreign directors have made for more innovative shows. The Russian flair for set and costume design alone can be enough to keep an audience enthralled. Performances sell out quickly so order tickets far in advance. ✉ *1 Teatralnaya Pl.* ☎ *495/692–9986, 495/250–7317 tickets* ⊕ *www.bolshoi.ru* Ⓜ *Teatralnaya.*

★ **Helikon Opera.** In addition to delivering consistently appealing and critically acclaimed opera performances, the Helikon troupe is equally talented in space management: even the grandest of classics are fitted with ease onto the small stage. ✉ *19 Bolshaya Nikitskaya ul.* ☎ *495/290–6592* ⊕ *www.helikon.ru* Ⓜ *Pushkinskaya or Arbatskaya.*

Novaya Opera. As fresh as the name *Novaya* ("new") indicates, this opera house has quickly established itself as one of the best and most innovative in the city. The surrounding Hermitage Garden is a perfect place for a pre- or post-theater stroll. The choir is ranked as the best in the city. ⊠ *3 Karetny Ryad* ☎ *495/200–0868* ⊕ *www.novayaopera.ru* Ⓜ *Tverskaya.*

State Kremlin Palace. Formerly the hall where Soviet Communist Party congresses were held, this modern concert venue now hosts regular performances by opera and ballet troupes, including those from the Bolshoi. Of late it also has become the stage for international megastars such as Elton John, Bryan Adams, Cher, and Mariah Carey. Entrance is through the whitewashed Kutafya Gate. ⊠ *1 ul. Vozdvizhenka, in Kremlin, Kremlin/Red Square* ☎ *495/917–2336 or 495/928–5232* Ⓜ *Aleksandrovsky Sad.*

Theater

Even if you don't speak Russian, you might want to explore the intense world of Russian dramatic theater. The partial listings below cover Moscow's major drama theaters. Note that evening performances begin at 7 PM *sharp.*

Estrada Theater. The curtain goes up here for comedies starring some of Russia's best-known actors, along with a number of variety shows. ⊠ *20/2 Bersenyovskaya nab.* ☎ *495/959–0456* Ⓜ *Biblioteka Imeni Lenina.*

LenKom Theater. Good, often flashy productions are on the playbill here. Tickets are frequently very hard to get. ⊠ *6 Malaya Dmitrovka ul.* ☎ *495/299–0708 or 495/299–9668* Ⓜ *Pushkinskaya.*

Maly Theater. Moscow's first dramatic theater, opened in 1824, the Maly is famous for its staging of Russian classics, especially those of the 19th-century satirist Alexander Ostrovsky—his statue stands outside the building. ⊠ *1/6 Teatralnaya Pl.* ☎ *495/923–2621* Ⓜ *Teatralnaya.*

Fodor's Choice **Moscow Art Theater** (MKhAT). Founded in 1898, the MKhAT is the heart
★ of the Moscow theater scene. The theater is famous for its productions of the Russian classics, but it also stages plenty of modern and foreign performances. The American Studio at the Chekhov Art Theater presents performances, typically Russian classics, in English a few times a year. ⊠ *3 Kamergersky per.* ☎ *495/692–6748* ⊕ *www.chekhov.ru* Ⓜ *Okhotny Ryad.*

★ **Moscow Theater for Young Viewers.** Despite its name, this acclaimed theater mainly stages adult productions. It's famed for its dramatizations of Chekhov short stories, staged by director Kama Ginkas. ⊠ *10 Mamonovsky per.* ☎ *495/299–9917 or 495/299–5360* Ⓜ *Pushkinskaya.*

Mossoviet Theater. Contemporary drama shares the stage with comedies and musicals here. ⊠ *16 Bolshaya Sadovaya* ☎ *495/299–2035 or 495/200–5943* Ⓜ *Mayakovskaya.*

Operetta Theater. The Operetta stages lighthearted, and much humbler, versions of Western musicals, as well as the latest Russian musicals. ⊠ *6 ul. Bolshaya Dmitrovka* ☎ *495/692–1237* ⊕ *www.mosoperetta.ru* Ⓜ *Teatralnaya.*

Sovremennik Theater. This well-respected theater stages a mix of Russian classics and foreign adaptations. ⊠ *19a Chistoprudny bulvar* ☎ *495/921–6473* Ⓜ *Chistiye Prudy.*

★ **Taganka Theater.** Run by the legendary Yuri Lyubimov, the Taganka is one of the world's most famous theaters. The troupe's most redoubtable dramatization is of Mikhail Bulgakov's novel *The Master and Margarita*. Performances sell out far in advance. ⊠ *76 Zemlyanoy Val, Taganka* ☎ *495/915–1217 or 495/915–1015* ⊕ *www.taganka.theatre.ru* Ⓜ *Taganskaya.*

Tereza Durova Clown Theater. Attracting children and adults, the shows here are based on the commedia dell'arte, filled with music, dance, and acrobatics. ⊠ *6 Pavlovskaya ul., inside DK Zavoda Ilyicha, Southern Outskirts* ☎ *495/237–1689* Ⓜ *Serpukhovskaya.*

Nightlife

The *Moscow Times* (available at newsstands) and *Element* and *LifeStyle* (available for free at hotels, bars, and restaurants frequented by foreigners) publish up-to-date calendars of events in English.

Foreigners make easy crime targets, so you should take special precautions at night. You're safest venturing out with other people. Remember: the more vodkas you drink, the more vulnerable you can become. Do not drive under any circumstances if you drink; the laws here are strict, and traffic police can and do stop cars at will.

Bars

The quality of bars varies widely, from karaoke dives to posh Irish pubs filled with expatriates. Almost all the major hotels have upscale bars, but be aware that prostitution is still a thriving business at most of Moscow's low- to mid-range hotels. The National, Savoy, and Metropol have polished (generally prostitute-free) bars, but without much in the way of atmosphere. The Baltschug Kempinski, Ararat Park Hyatt, and Golden Ring are elegant and have majestic views of the city.

There are no cover charges for bars, unless perhaps live music is taking place there. At some clubs, there's a fee to be seated at a table.

Annushka. Housed on a tram that makes a constant and short loop around the picturesque Chistiye Prudy area, Annushka is a cozy bar and eatery. Wait outside the metro stration, where it stops every 10 to 15 minutes. ⊠ *Stops outside Chistiye Prudy metro station* ☎ *495/507–5770* Ⓜ *Chistiye Prudy.*

Glavpivtorg. Live musicians perform songs from the Soviet era at this enormous retro-styled eatery. It has a comprehensive choice of beers, including its own brand. The traditional Russian dishes are expensive, but served up with style. Book ahead, as it gets busy even on weeknights. ⊠ *5 Bolshaya Lubyanka ul.* ☎ *495/928–2591 or 495/924–1996* Ⓜ *Lubyanka.*

Hard Rock Cafe. It may be an international chain, but somehow the Moscow branch manages to maintain its own flavor. Locals come for the pop-music classics, and Westerners stop by for a taste of home. ⊠ *44 Arbat* ☎ *495/244–8973 or 495/244–8970* ⊕ *www.hardrockcafe.ru* Ⓜ *Smolenskaya.*

John Bull Pub. The food is excellent and there's a large selection of beers at this pricey, upscale, English-style pub. ⊠ *9 Karmanitsky per.* ☎ *495/ 241–0644* Ⓜ *Smolenskaya.*

Kitaiysky Lyotchik. Live music and tasty, affordable food draw a bohemian crowd to this cellar bar whose name translates into "Chinese Pilot." ⊠ *25 Lubyansky proyezd, Bldg. 1, Kitai Gorod* ☎ *495/924–5611* Ⓜ *Kitai Gorod.*

Krasny Bar. The views of the city from this upscale 27th-floor bar, open until the last customer leaves, are excellent. ⊠ *23a nab., Tarasa Shevchenko Krasnaya Presnya* ☎ *495/730–0808* Ⓜ *Kievskaya.*

Proyekt O. G. I. This was one of the city's first bohemian clubs, complete with a bookstore and live music. It has since evolved into an increasingly commercial, expanding chain of cheap restaurants. The original, however, is still authentic. ⊠ *8/12 Potapovsky per., Kitai Gorod* ☎ *495/ 927–5776* Ⓜ *Chistiye Prudy.*

Real McCoy's. A speakeasy theme pervades this bar. Weekend nights, the place explodes into an alcohol-fueled party with customers dancing on the bar. ⊠ *1 Kudrinskaya Pl.* ☎ *495/255–4144* Ⓜ *Barrikadnaya.*

Rosie O'Grady's. One of Moscow's oldest Irish pubs, Rosie O'Grady's is also one of the homiest. It's just a stone's throw from the Kremlin. ⊠ *9/12 Znamenka ul., Bldg. 1* ☎ *495/203–3822* ⊕ *www.rosie.ru* Ⓜ *Borovitskaya.*

Sally O'Brien's. Despite its habit of playing American country music, this is a pub with a definite Irish feel. It's a good place to meet other foreigners. ⊠ *1/3 Polyanka ul.* ☎ *495/959–0175* Ⓜ *Polyanka.*

Sixteen Tons. A popular pub with a club upstairs, this spot serves its own home-brewed beer. ⊠ *6 Presnensky Val, Krasnaya Presnya* ☎ *495/ 253–5300* ⊕ *www.16tons.ru* Ⓜ *Ulitsa 1905 Goda.*

Tinkoff. A futuristically styled beer restaurant run by Tinkoff brewery, this spot is popular with diplomats working in nearby embassies. ⊠ *11 Protochny per.* ☎ *495/777–3300* ⊕ *www.tinkoff.ru* Ⓜ *Smolenskaya.*

Casinos

Finding a place to gamble in Moscow is like shooting fish in a barrel. Every other metro station or kiosk has video poker and slot machines. However, most travelers skip the street-side gambling options in favor of one of Moscow's high-end casinos, with armed guards and armored Mercedes. Stick with some of the better-known places, including those listed below. Most big casinos arrange cab service to and from the city's major hotels and are open 24 hours. Come prepared with a wad of cash (just don't flash the money around) because Moscow's bigger and nicer venues are for the serious, not the curious.

The Metropol, Mezhdunarodnaya, Kosmos, Baltschug Kempinski, and National hotels all have their own casinos.

Golden Palace. A pink Cadillac and shotgun-toting guards give this gold-painted casino a great Wild West feel. ⊠ *15 Tretya (3rd) Yamskovo Polya ul., Kitai Gorod* ☎ *495/232–1515* ⊕ *www.goldenpalace.ru* Ⓜ *Belorusskaya.*

Kristall. This is a relatively upscale casino not far outside the city center. It's a popular spot for corny Russian pop acts. ⊠ *38 Marxistskaya* *ul., Bldg. 1, Southern Outskirts* ☎ *495/911–7711* ⊕ *www.crystal-casino.ru* Ⓜ *Proletarskaya.*

Metelitsa Cherry Casino. One of Moscow's oldest and most prominent clubs, the Metelitsa ("Blizzard") first gained notoriety as one of Moscow's early oligarch hangouts. It's still popular with high rollers. ✉ *21 Novy Arbat, Bldg. 1* ☎ *495/291–1170* ⊕ *www.metelitsa.ru* Ⓜ *Arbatskaya or Smolenskaya.*

Shangri-La. Shangri-La is by far the most gaudily decorated casino in town. This city-center casino looks after big spenders and ordinary customers, too. ✉ *2 Pushkinskaya Pl.* ☎ *495/209–6400* ⊕ *www.shangrila.ru* Ⓜ *Pushkinskaya.*

Clubs

Moscow's clubbing scene has finally grown up, with plenty of Western-quality places to go. However, *feis kontrol* (face control, or a velvet-rope mentality) is common at most high-end clubs. Most clubs don't get busy until between midnight and 2 AM. Live music is popular, and some larger clubs put on shows by famous foreign DJs and musicians.

B-2. One of the best places in Moscow for live rock performances, B-2 is an enormous five-story club that includes a sushi bar, a big-screen TV, a dance club, and several bars. ✉ *8 Bolshaya Sadovaya* ☎ *495/209–9909* ⊕ *www.b2club.ru* Ⓜ *Mayakovskaya.*

Club Che. This is a vibrant Latin American–themed club staffed by Cuban waiters. Drink service can be slow at night, when the staff often dances with the crowd. Show up early or you'll never get in. ✉ *10/2 Nikolskaya ul., Kitai Gorod* ☎ *495/921–7477* ⊕ *www.clubche.ru* Ⓜ *Lubyanka.*

Fabrique. Popular with expats and students, this two-story club features tasty food and sessions by top guest DJs. ✉ *2 Kosmodamianskaya nab.* ☎ *495/953–6576* ⊕ *www.fabrique.ru* Ⓜ *Novokuznetskaya or Paveletskaya.*

Garazh. Getting into this popular nightclub on the weekend isn't always easy, but if you make it you'll be among Moscow's most dedicated clubbers. Wednesday is hip-hop night. ✉ *16 Tverskaya ul., Bldg. 2/2* ☎ *495/209–1848* Ⓜ *Tverskaya or Chekhovskaya.*

Hungry Duck. Once famed as Moscow's wildest and most depraved place to spend a weekend night, the Duck has lost its edge since its mid-'90s heyday. Nevertheless, most visitors to Moscow still believe this sweaty, sticky dive is a must-see. Consider yourself warned. ✉ *9/6 Pushechnaya ul., Bldg. 1* ☎ *495/923–6158* ⊕ *www.hungryduck.com* Ⓜ *Kuznetsky Most.*

Karma Bar. Top 40 hits and a crew of die-hard regulars mean that hardly a weekend goes by without Karma's dance floor being packed wall to wall. Democratic face control also helps bring in the crowds. ✉ *3 Pushechnaya ul.* ☎ *495/924–5633* ⊕ *www.karma-bar.ru* Ⓜ *Kuznetsky Most.*

Keks. Housed in a former factory, this retro-theme café turns into a club at night with guest DJs and a small dance floor. ✉ *11/34 Timura Frunze ul.* ☎ *495/246–0864* ⊕ *www.cafekeks.ru* Ⓜ *Park Kultury.*

Papa's. Nights at Papa's are all about strip egg-and-spoon races, wet T-shirt contests, or any other silly games the management can think of. Dirt-cheap happy-hour drinks are a big draw for students. ⊠ *22 Myasnitskaya ul.* ☎ *495/755–9554* Ⓜ *Chistiye Prudy.*

★ **Propaganda.** This is probably the city's most reliable club for trendy, yet laid-back crowds and good DJs. It's *the* place to be on Thursday nights. On Sunday nights it turns into one of the city's most popular gay clubs. ⊠ *7 Bolshoi Zlatoustinsky per., Kitai Gorod* ☎ *495/924–5732* ⊕ *www.propagandamoscow.com/home.html* Ⓜ *Kitai Gorod.*

Vermel. Cheap drinks and affordable concerts have made Vermel a big hit with students and other young clubbers. ⊠ *4/5 Raushskaya nab., Zamoskvoreche* ☎ *495/959–3303* Ⓜ *Tretyakovskaya.*

Gay & Lesbian Clubs

No other part of Moscow's clubbing scene is more subject to closings than the tiny gay circuit, so these listings are far from definitive. Note also that the club Propaganda turns into a popular gay club on Sunday nights.

Three Monkeys. This gay club, a popular spot with students, is one of the most well-established in town, with a regular rotation of good DJs. Mostly men come here, but women are welcome. ⊠ *11 Nastavnichesky per., Bldg. 1 Zamoskvoreche* ☎ *495/916–3555* Ⓜ *Kurskaya or Chkalovskaya.*

12 Volt. This club for both men and women is tricky to find, but has a welcoming atmosphere. It has DJs, film screenings, karaoke, and cheap drink deals. ⊠ *12 Tverskaya ul., Bldg. 2, entrance in yard off Kozitsky per.* ☎ *495/933–2815* ⊕ *http://12voltclub.ru* Ⓜ *Tverskaya.*

Jazz & Blues

BB King Blues Club. The premiere opening featured the man himself, and visiting Western stars have continued to make appearances here, often for postconcert jams. ⊠ *4 Sadovaya-Samotyochnaya ul., Bldg. 2* ☎ *495/299–8206* Ⓜ *Tsvetnoy Bulvar.*

Blue Bird Jazz Café. Russian talent and the occasional odd foreign guest perform here, at one of Moscow's oldest jazz clubs. ⊠ *23/15 Malaya Dmitrovka ul., Kitai Gorod* ☎ *495/299–2225* Ⓜ *Mayakovskaya.*

Le Club. Firmly established as one of the city's leading jazz clubs, this is an upscale joint that always hosts some of the top names in town. ⊠ *21 Verkhnyaya Radishchevskaya, Taganka* ☎ *495/915–1042* ⊕ *www.le-club.ru* Ⓜ *Taganskaya.*

SPORTS & THE OUTDOORS

The Soviet Union may have been a sports superpower, but athletic activities were usually restricted to the pros, leaving the rest of the population to grow abysmally unfit. However, judo-loving president Vladimir Putin is doing his best to revive the nation's athletic glory, while simultaneously urging the general population to be more active. Access to Moscow's municipal athletic facilities is restricted, but new health clubs are opening all over the city (although they are usually expensive and discourage one-time users).

Rollerblading and mountain biking are increasingly popular, as is skate-boarding (with the younger generation). Although rare in the city center, joggers are common in parks; they are replaced in winter by cross-country skiers of all ages. Pickup soccer games can be found all over town and in some large parks, along with volleyball, table tennis, and even baseball. The public's steadily growing disposable income has also given rise to plenty of sporting-goods stores selling Western brands for only slightly higher prices than you'll find back home.

Tickets for sporting events can be purchased at the sports arena immediately prior to the game or at any of the numerous theater box offices (teatralnaya kassa) throughout the city. You can also ask your hotel's service bureau for assistance in obtaining tickets to sporting events, but the fee will probably far exceed the value of the ticket. Soccer is the most popular sport and Muscovites support local teams Dinamo and Lokomotiv.

On the banks of the Moskva River across from Sparrow Hills and Moscow State University, **Luzhniki Sports Palace** (⊠ 24 Luzhnetskaya nab., Southern Outskirts ☎ 495/201–1851, 495/788–1698 tennis, 495/201-0795 pool Ⓜ Sportivnaya) is probably the city's most easily recognized stadium. It has high-quality facilities for professional soccer, but its other facilities are a bit outdated. There's a nice pool (although you have to bring a medical certificate to use it), and tennis courts are available for rent by the hour.

Banyas

Of all Russia's traditions, perhaps none is more steeped in ritual than a trip to the steamy banya, a sauna-style bathhouse that is kept steamy by throwing a steady supply of water over heated rocks. In fact, for many banya lovers a trip to the bathhouse is almost a religious experience, complete with birch twigs for self-flagellation (to open pores and promote circulation). There's even a traditional garment—a peaked woolen hat (sold at numerous shops and sometimes at the banyas themselves) to keep the tips of your ears from burning. Manicures, pedicures, and massages are also often available, and some banyas are even attached to fitness centers. And for many, a jump in an icy-cold pool after a steam session is a must.

A few stores around the city sell banya goods, including hats, chamomile-soaked towels, and herb-enriched lotions. **Perekryostok Supermarket** (⊠ 1 Tishinskaya Pl. ☎ 495/254–3702 ⊕ www.perekrestok.ru Ⓜ Belorusskaya) stocks hats, aromatic oils, and ready-packed birch twigs at more than 50 branches around the city. **Novaya Zarya** (⊠ 4 Ulinka ul., in Gostiny Dvor, Kitai Gorod ☎ 495/298–0752 Ⓜ Ploshchad Revolyutsii) is one of Russia's oldest perfume manufacturers, which makes its own line of fragrant essences that you can add to banya water (you can get your own tub even at a public banya).

Unless otherwise indicated, the banyas listed below are open daily. Note that over the summer, most banyas close for two or three weeks when hot water is turned off for a few weeks at a time in different parts of the city.

CloseUp

RULES OF THE BANYA

If you plan to use the baths here, be aware of a few ground rules: men and women are separated in the general sections, although families can hire a private bath for use together. You'll be given towels, but this is a textile-free experience and acting shy about your nudity will only draw attention to yourself. Soap is strictly forbidden, as the steam is supposed to clean you. Thrashing yourself with soaked veniki (birch twigs) is said to open up the pores and increase circulation. Drinks and food can be bought whether you have rented a private banya or are simply relaxing in the public baths.

Try to avoid spending more than 10 to 15 minutes at a time in the steam, and limit your alcohol consumption. Remember to keep yourself hydrated. If you take it easy, the experience will be all the more relaxing. Those with low blood pressure and heart conditions may want to simply stay away. Otherwise, do as the Russians do and sit back and relax.

With a gym, salon, bar, pool, and massage, **Bani na Presne** (⊠ 7 Stolyarny per., Krasnaya Presnya ☎ 495/255–0115 Ⓜ Ulitsa 1905 Goda) is a popular, casual banya. It's fairly expensive at about 500R to 600R for a two-hour visit. **Russkie Bani** (⊠ 25A Bolshoy Strochenovsky per., Zamoskvoreche ☎ 495/236–3171 Ⓜ Dobrinskaya or Serpukhovskaya) is part of a fitness center across the street from the South African embassy. It's a truly Russian experience, staffed with beehive-haired female attendants. Two-hour sessions cost around 350R.

Fodor'sChoice ★ Dating to the late 1800s, the impeccably clean **Sandunovskiye Bani** (Сандуновские Бани) (⊠ 14 Neglinniy per. ☎ 495/925–4631 or 495/928–4633 ⊕ www.sanduny.ru ☉ Daily 8 AM–10 PM Ⓜ Teatralnaya) is probably the city's most elegant bathhouse, with a lavish interior. Prices depend on your gender and which section you visit, but range from 600R to 1000R. On-site facilities include a beauty parlor and, of course, massage. One of the better banya bargains in town, **Seleznyovskiye Banya** (⊠ 15 Seleznyovsky ul., Northern Outskirts ☎ 495/978–7521 Ⓜ Novoslobodskaya) combines quality service with low prices. Two hours cost around 400R, depending on what section you go into and the day of the week. Prices range from 300R to 700R. It's closed Monday.

Bowling

Bowling has become one of Moscow's most popular nightlife activities. Even outside the city center, lanes on weekend nights are booked until the wee hours of the morning. Reserve a lane in advance, or be prepared to wait for a long time.

A night club and bowling alley combined, **Apelsin** (⊠ 15 Malaya Gruzinskaya ☎ 495/253–0253 or 495/253–2121 ⊕ www.apelsinclub.ru Ⓜ Krasnopresnenskaya) has 30 lanes on two floors as well as Russian billiards and pool tables. Bowling and billiard balls collide at **Bou-Bol** (⊠ 2 Tretyaya [3rd] Yamskovo Polya ul., Kitai Gorod ☎ 495/257–

0048 ⊕ www.bowlball.ru Ⓜ Belorusskaya), where 16 lanes, 8 American pool tables, and 5 Russian billiards tables compete for your attention. One of the biggest and best bowling alleys in Moscow is at **B-69** (⊠ 69 ul. Vavilova, Southern Outskirts ☎ 495/935–0504 Ⓜ Profsoyuznaya), complete with its own health club. **Cosmic Bowling** (⊠ 18 ul. Lva Tolstovo, Zamoskvoreche ☎ 495/246–3666 ⊕ www.kosmik. ru Ⓜ Park Kultury) has 32 lanes, 20 billiards tables, and several restaurants. Sports fans can watch games on big screens. **Samolyot** (⊠ 14 Presnensky Val, Bldg. 1, Krasnaya Presnya ☎ 495/234–1818 Ⓜ Ul. 1905 Goda) has 34 lanes spread out over three stories, plus pool tables, karting, and a night club.

Ice Hockey

The NHL snaps up most of Russia's best players, but you can still catch some budding stars before the United States and Canada lure them away. Russians are passionate about their hockey, and the games are much more hooliganism-free than soccer matches. The season usually lasts from September through January.

Dinamo (⊠ 36 Leningradskoe shosse, Northern Outskirts ☎ 495/212–7092 or 495/201–0955 Ⓜ Dinamo), one of the city's larger hockey stadiums, with a seating capacity of 60,000, is home to the army's team, TsSKA. Spartak holds its home games at **Sokolniki Ice Palace** (⊠ 1b Sokolnicheski Val, Eastern Outskirts ☎ 495/268–6958 Ⓜ Sokolniki).

Ice-Skating

If you go ice-skating here, be prepared for some cultural differences. Russians do not skate in orderly circles or clean snow off the ice regularly, and rental skates can be rather shabby.

★ If you've packed your skates, head straight for **Gorky Park** (⊠ 9 Krymsky Val, Zamoskvoreche Ⓜ Oktyabrskaya), where in winter months the park's lanes are flooded to create ad hoc skating rinks. The park also has two large rinks where you can skate to piped-in Russian pop music. The park is open daily 10–10. Luzhniki's popular **Northern Lights rink** (⊠ Luzhnetskaya nab., Southern Outskirts ☎ 495/201–1655 Ⓜ Sportivnaya) is open to all skaters over the age of seven. There's a fee for entry and skate rental; the hours vary, so call ahead. You can rent skates at **Sokolniki Park** (⊠ 16 Sokolnichesky Val, Eastern Outskirts ☎ 495/268–8277 Ⓜ Sokolniki). Rink hours are daily 10–7 in cold weather.

Two picturesque downtown parks with natural ponds, **Patriarshiye Prudy** (⊠ 34 to 42 Malaya Bronnaya ul. Ⓜ Mayakovskaya) and **Chistiye Prudy** (⊠ Chistoprudny bulvar Ⓜ Chistiye Prudy) open skating rinks in winter.

Running

The best spots for jogging are along the path running from Gorky Park to **Vorobyovy Gory** (⊠ Vorobyovskaya nab. Ⓜ Vorobyovy Gory) near Moscow State University or on the trails through **Nyeskuchni Sad** (⊠ Entrances between 8 and 10 Leninsky pr. and 28 and 30 Leninsky pr. Ⓜ Leninsky Prospekt or Oktyabrskaya), **Filyovsky** (⊠ 24 to 26 Filyovskaya ul. Ⓜ Filyovsky Park), Izmailovsky, Kolomenskoye, or Sokolniki parks, where you can avoid most of Moscow's heavy traffic and accompanying noxious fumes. The Hash House Harriers, a social running and drinking club, meets weekly in front of the Ukraina hotel; meeting days and times are often listed in the *Moscow Times* community bulletin board section, published Wednesday. As in any city unaccustomed to joggers, it can be difficult to find a comfortable running route, and you probably will be in a conspicuous minority.

Skiing

On a crisp, clear winter day in Moscow, cross-country skiers take to the trails in the wooded parks that dot the city. Try Filyovsky, Izmailovsky, or **Bittsevsky** (⊠ Novoyasenevsky pr. Ⓜ Bittsevsky Park) parks, or near Novodevichy Monastery. You'll be in the good company of skiers of all abilities, from toddlers to grandparents.

For downhill skiing, there are several safe and reliable parks in Moscow and two facilities about an hour outside of the city. **Kant** (⊠ 7 Elektrolitny pr., Southern Outskirts ☎ 495/317–9577 Ⓜ Nagornaya) has its own snowmaking equipment, good rentals, several runs, and a snowboarding half pipe, plus three cafés where you can warm up. The **Krylatskoye Ski Center** (⊠ 2 Krylatskaya ul., Northern Outskirts ☎ 495/140–0307 Ⓜ Krylatskoye) brings skiers and snowboarders together on the 3,117-foot slope and rickety lift. In summer you can rent bikes here.

Ski Park Volen (⊠ 1 Troitskaya ul., Yakhroma ☎ 495/993–9502 ⊕ www. volen.ru) is a high-standard, often crowded park to the north of Moscow, along Dmitrovskoye shosse (about a one-hour drive). Thirteen snowboard and ski trails descend from the 230-foot summit in runs up to 1,476 feet long. Seven ski lifts and five baby lifts take you to the top. Ice skating, three cafés and a restaurant, a billiards bar, and accommodation in a 59-room hotel and wooden cottages (with and without sauna) tempt skiers from the slopes. Ski rentals are available. In summer the trails here are used for mountain biking, and bikes are available for rent. **Sorochany** (⊠ Dmitrovsky region, Kurovo Village ☎ 495/363–8961 ⊕ www.sorochany.ru), outside of Moscow, has taken some of the pressure off Volen's slopes with its 10 runs.

Sledding

In winter you may want to do as many young Muscovites do and buy cheap plastic sheets called *ledyanki* from any sports equipment or toy store and head for the hills. The best hills are in Kolomenskoye Park (a five-minute walk from the metro station of the same name) or Neskuchny Sad in Gorky Park.

Soccer

Footage of Russian teenagers rioting outside the Kremlin after Russia lost to Japan in the 2002 World Cup was a reminder to the world of how seriously this country takes its soccer (*futbol*). As a general rule, Russian soccer teams fare poorly in international events, but that doesn't seem to bother Russia's die-hard fans. Riots were once common at some of Moscow's larger stadiums, but an overwhelming police presence and the prohibition of alcohol sales at nearby stores have managed to quell the problem. Still, before games, neighborhoods surrounding the stadiums are often full of hooligans looking for any excuse for a fight. The season usually runs from early spring to late fall. During the off-season, Duma deputies and other politicians hold games that tend to be more comedic and less crowded. Moscow mayor Yuri Luzhkov is a huge fan and has been known to hold matches with players from city hall. You can buy tickets for the matches outside the stadiums or at the teatralnaya kassa.

Old and dilapidated but still in working order, **Dinamo** (✉ 36 Leningradskoe shosse, Northern Outskirts ☎495/212–7092 or 495/212–3132 Ⓜ Dinamo) is a favorite stadium for matches between Duma deputies and city hall officials. **Lokomotiv** (✉ 125a Bolshaya Cherkizovskaya, Eastern Outskirts ☎ 495/161–9060, 495/161–4283, or 495/161–9918 Ⓜ Cherkizovskaya), Moscow's newest and largest stadium, is probably the most comfortable place to watch a match. **Luzhniki** (✉ 24 Luzhnetskaya nab., Southern Outskirts ☎495/201–1536 or 495/201–1785 Ⓜ Sportivnaya), the city's flagship stadium and home of the Spartak, is fully up to European standards. It sometimes hosts international matches.

SHOPPING

Gone are the Cold War images of long lines and empty shelves, the uneven and unpredictable distribution of goods. These days, at least in Moscow, you can generally find most items you need, albeit in a more piecemeal way than at home. You will not go hungry or unclothed should you lose your shirt at one of Moscow's casinos. In fact, you'll find opportunities to buy something any which way you turn.

The proliferation of new stores is matched only by an escalation in prices. Stores can be roughly divided into two types: Western-style and Russian-style, though this differentiation is fast transforming into one of nice versus not-as-nice, as the Russian-owned shops upgrade their service and presentation. There's an ever-changing array of kiosks, tabletops, and wooden stalls, combined with nicer, underground glassware boutiques and stores. The Western-style stores are more likely to carry familiar brands from the United States and Europe, at high prices. Russian-owned establishments tend to stock a mix of local and imported products.

The high prices of consumer goods means it makes sense economically only to shop for souvenirs. If your schedule permits, it's interesting to browse in the shops that are frequented by locals, and it's a great way to take the pulse of a place, especially one in flux.

Keep in mind that you're forbidden to take some items out of the country. Customs regulations are vague and seem to change constantly, contingent upon who is checking your luggage. The law basically disallows the export of anything of "cultural value to the Russian nation." In practical terms, this means that anything older than 30 to 40 years is not allowed out without special permission from the Ministry of Culture or its local agent; the item will be confiscated at the border if you lack the necessary papers. Anything prerevolutionary is simply not let out at all. If you're buying paintings or art objects, it's important to consult with the seller regarding the proper documentation of sale for export. Keep receipts of your purchases.

Exercise caution when shopping. You'll stand out no matter what you do, and there are pickpocket and mugging rings, often operating in small bands. *Don't* be an easy target: don't flash your money and don't stop if you encounter bands of muggers. Swinging your arms or handbag and getting vocal often works to rout them.

Hours of operation can be capricious, but the general rule is Monday through Saturday 10 to 7 (occasionally closing for an hour sometime between 1 and 3). Food stores may open an hour earlier, and department stores may remain open later, with additional hours on Sunday (11 to 6). Most of the newer shopping malls stay open daily from 10 or 11 to 9 or 10.

Shopping Districts

Historically, the main shopping districts of Moscow have been concentrated in the city center, along Tverskaya ulitsa and Novy Arbat. Luxury designer stores like Cerutti, Versace, Hermès, Gucci, Armani, and Prada have settled along pedestrianized Stoleshnikov pereulok, Kuznetsky Most, and Tretyakovsky proyezd. On Kutuzovsky prospekt, off Novy Arbat, you'll find Dolce & Gabbana, Donna Karan, and Fendi boutiques. Along with Stary Arbat, which has been particularly spruced up for the tourist trade, these streets are your best bets. If you're willing to venture into distant regions outside the city, however, a brave new world of shopping awaits in Russia.

Department Stores & Malls

Atrium. A giant shopping mall in front of the Kursk Station, Atrium is yet another symbol of Mayor Yuri Luzhkov's Moscow. With everything under one roof, including numerous clothing stores, a perfumes supermarket, huge grocery store, casino, and the Formula Kino movie theater, this is one of the best places to shop. There's a great coffee shop in the lobby, where classical and jazz musicians give live concerts every night, as well as a trendy Italian café and a sushi bar. ⊠ *33 Zemlyanoi Val, Taganka* ☎ *495/927–3217* Ⓜ *Kurskaya.*

Detsky Mir. The famous "Children's World" department store now also hawks cars and a wide assortment of toys for grown-ups. The first and second floors are still a delight for kids. Grown-ups may appreciate the antiques market on the fifth floor. It's near Lubyanskaya Ploshchad. ⊠ *2 Teatralny proyezd* ☎ *495/974–2007* Ⓜ *Lubyanka.*

Gallery Aktyor. Next door to the high-end grocery Yeliseyevsky's, this space is smaller, more elegant, and often less crowded than GUM or Manezh. Popular brands like Naf Naf, Levi's, Chevignon, and Lacoste are on sale. The first floor houses a Swatch outlet and a Clinique cosmetics store. ⊠ *16/2 Tverskaya ul.* ☎ *495/290–9832* Ⓜ *Tverskaya or Pushkinskaya.*

★ **GUM.** A series of shops and boutiques inside a 19th-century arcade, this shopping emporium sits on Red Square, right across from the Kremlin. GUM, which stands for State Department Store, retains some of the Soviet feel in the upper-row stores. On the first floor you will find an arcade of boutiques, including MaxMara, Hugo Boss, and La Perla. Also here is the elegant Bosco restaurant, which overlooks Red Square and has a summer terrace. ⊠ *3 Red Sq., Kremlin/Red Square* ☏ *495/921–5763* ⊕ *www.gum.ru* Ⓜ *Ploshchad Revolutsii.*

Kalinka-Stockmann. This major Finnish chain store combines several departments under one roof at Smolensky Passazh on the Garden Ring. A grocery shop with a broad assortment of fresh fruits, vegetables, and fish is below ground. A vast men's and women's clothing shop occupies the first floor, and housewares, linens, electronics, footwear, and children's clothing are on the second floor. A separate store on Leninsky prospekt sells men's and women's clothing and footwear from last season's or year's collections. Two new Stockmann stores in MEGA Malls I and II on the city's outer ring road are the latest addition to the Moscow Stockmann family. ⊠ *3 Smolenskaya Pl., Bldg. 5* ☏ *495/785–2500* ⊕ *www.stockmann.ru* Ⓜ *Smolenskaya.*

Manezh. Although the proper name of this mall is Okhotny Ryad, everyone calls it Manezh for the square on which it sits. Inexpensive brands like Benetton, Tommy Hilfiger, Motivi, and MEXX along with gift items are the strong point of this shopping showcase. Set under the main square adjacent to the Kremlin, the Manezh attracts crowds of Russian out-of-towners, who stroll, photograph the intricate cupola that extends above ground, and window-shop. ⊠ *Trade Center Okhotny Ryad, 1 Manezhnaya Pl.* Ⓜ *Okhotny Ryad.*

Moskva Department Store. The aisles of this giant general store are filled with everything from tableware, chandeliers, clocks, and electronics to sports clothes and furs. ⊠ *54 Leninsky pr.* ☏ *495/137–0018* Ⓜ *Leninsky Prospekt.*

Petrovsky Passazh. MaxMara, Nina Ricci, Givenchy, Kenzo, and Bally boutiques and an antiques store bejewel this chic, glass-roof space, the most luxurious shopping *passazh* (arcade) in town. ⊠ *10 ul. Petrovka* ☏ *495/928–5047* Ⓜ *Kuznetsky Most.*

Ramstore. The huge outlets of this Turkish-owned superstore chain are the Russian version of Wal-Mart. The prices are slightly below normal Moscow levels. There are 22 Ramstore outlets in Moscow that differ only in size. ⊠ *31 Novinsky bulvar* ☏ *495/981–0797* Ⓜ *Barrikadnaya* ⊠ *60A Sheremetyevskaya ul., Northern Outskirts* ☏ *495/937–2600* Ⓜ *Rizhskaya or Belorusskaya* ⊠ *13 Chasovaya ul., Northern Outskirts* ☏ *495/937–0510* Ⓜ *Aeroport or Sokol* ⊠ *6 Komsololskaya Pl., Northern Outskirts* ☏ *495/207–3165* Ⓜ *Komsomolskaya.*

TsUM. TsUM, which stands for Central Department Store, has upgraded itself into an expensive store with collections of nearly all the top European designers. It's a two-minute walk down ulitsa Petrovka from Petrovsky Passazh. ⊠ *2 ul. Petrovka* ☏ *495/292–1157 or 495/292–7600* ⊕ *www.tsum.ru* Ⓜ *Kuznetsky Most.*

Specialty Stores

Arts & Crafts

Arbatskaya Kollektsia. This nice souvenir shop sells the best of locally produced folk art, including *palekh* (colorful, lacquered wood with folklore designs) chess sets, cocktail glasses, and coffee sets made of amber. ⊠ *12 Arbat* ☎ *495/291–9300* Ⓜ *Arbatskaya.*

Art boutiques of the Varvarka ulitsa churches. These boutiques are inside the Church of St. Maxim the Blessed, open daily 11–6, and the Church of St. George on Pskov Hill, open daily 11–7. Both carry a fine selection of handicrafts, jewelry, ceramics, and other types of native-Russian art. ⊠ *6 Varvarka ul., Kitai Gorod* Ⓜ *Kitai Gorod* ⊠ *12 Varvarka ul., Kitai Gorod* Ⓜ *Kitai Gorod.*

Ikonnaya Lavka. The Cathedral of Our Lady of Kazan, near Russian Museum World, houses this icon shop. In addition to icons, you can purchase religious books, silver crosses, and other Orthodox religious items. ⊠ *8 Nikolskaya ul., at Red Sq., Kitai Gorod* ☎ *495/298–3788* Ⓜ *Ploshchad Revolutsii.*

Russian Museum World. The Historical Museum's art shop deals in a wide gamut of souvenirs, from jewelry, T-shirts, handmade crafts, and replicas of museum pieces to Russian- and Ukrainian-style embroidered shirts, Gzhel ceramics, and more. Wooden bowls and spoons decorated in *khokhloma* style—with bright oils painted on a black-and-golden background—fill the shelves. The store is on the right-hand side of the museum as you enter Red Square through the Resurrection Gates. ⊠ *1/2 Red Sq., Kremlin/Red Square* ☎ *495/292–1320* Ⓜ *Ploshchad Revolutsii.*

Russkiye Uzory. The "Russian Patterns" for which the store is named are here in abundance. There's an extensive selection of traditional Russian craft objects, embellished with beautiful folkloric imprints and designs. ⊠ *16 ul. Petrovka* ☎ *495/923–1883* Ⓜ *Kuznetsky Most or Okhotny Ryad.*

Russky Suvenir. It's a long metro journey to the Novye Cheryomushki station in southwest Moscow, but a panoply of traditional Russian souvenirs awaits: this store delivers both good price and selection. ⊠ *3 ul. Namyotkina, Southern Outskirts* ☎ *495/424–0722* Ⓜ *Noviye Cheryomushki.*

Skazki Starovo Arbata. A popular place for souvenirs, this store sells amber, silver, crafts, nesting dolls, and lacquer boxes. ⊠ *29 Arbat* ☎ *495/ 241–6135* Ⓜ *Arbatskaya or Smolenskaya.*

Clothing

Adidas. The trendiness of this high-energy, German sportwear brand draws crowds to its concept stores within Atrium and Krasnaya Presnya, as well as to GUM, which has the biggest selection in town. ⊠ *GUM, 3 Red Sq., Kremlin/Red Square* ☎ *495/725–4125* Ⓜ *Ploshchad Revolutsii* ⊠ *23 Krasnaya Presnya, Krasnaya Presnya* ☎ *495/255–0706* Ⓜ *Krasnopresnenskaya* ⊠ *33 Zemlyanoi Val, Bldg. 2, Taganka* ☎ *495/927– 3217* Ⓜ *Kurskaya.*

Benetton. In addition to three outlets selling the trademark line of sweaters, skirts, pants, and jeans, the Italian-based clothing retailer has two megastores: one along the city's prime retail avenue, Tverskaya ulitsa, and one on Krasnaya Presnya. ⊠ *48/2 Krasnopresnenskaya nab., Krasnaya Presnya* ☎ *495/252–3765* Ⓜ *Ul. 1905 Goda* ⊠ *19 Tverskaya ul.*

☎ 495/299–7490 Ⓜ *Tverskaya or Pushkinskaya* ✉ *13 Novy Arbat*
☎495/291–1456 Ⓜ*Arbatskaya* ✉*1 Manezhnaya Pl.* ☎495/737–8397
Ⓜ *Okhotny Ryad* ✉ *GUM, pervaya liniya (1st), 3 Red Sq., Kremlin/
Red Square* ☎ 495/929–3217 Ⓜ *Ploshchad Revolutsii.*

Carlo Pazolini. At this giant store near Oktyabrskya metro, the merchandise
is mostly luxury and mid-price footwear. ✉ *52–54 Bolshaya Yaki-
manka ul., Zamoskvoreche* ☎ 495/238–9523 Ⓜ *Oktyabrskaya.*

Hugo Boss. This high-profile men's fashion label has two stores in
Moscow, one on the Arbat and the other on the main shopping avenue
of Tverskaya. Hugo Boss's women's line can be found in GUM. ✉ *15/
43 Arbat* ☎ 495/913–6978 Ⓜ *Arbatskaya* ✉ *13/1 Pervaya (1st) Tverskaya-Yamskaya ul., Krasnaya Presnya* ☎ 495/250–3323 Ⓜ *Belorusskaya.*

In Vogue. High-style fashion retail, an art gallery, and a homey bar combine to create an elegant shopping experience. ✉ *29/2 Kutuzovsky pr.,
Krasnaya Presnya* ☎ 495/249–4577 Ⓜ *Kievskaya.*

Levi's. Once a quasicurrency in the USSR, Levi's jeans and other clothing items are now sold in four company outlet stores. The most centrally located is in GUM. ✉ *GUM, pervaya liniya (1st), 1st fl., 3 Red
Sq., Kremlin/Red Square* ☎ 495/929–3152 Ⓜ *Ploshchad Revolutsii*
✉ *3 Sadovo-Spasskaya ul., Northern Outskirts* ☎ 495/208–3825
Ⓜ *Sukharevskaya* ✉ *14 Stoleshnikov per.* ☎ 495/733–9200 Ⓜ *Teatralnaya or Okhotny Ryad* ✉ *16/2 Tverskaya ul.* ☎495/935–7780 Ⓜ*Tverskaya or Pushkinskaya.*

Moskvichka. Although poorly laid out, this store purveys popular clothing brands like Guess?, Sisley, Esprit, and MEXX. It's just a few doors
down Novy Arbat from Novoarbatsky Gastronom. ✉ *15 Novy Arbat*
☎ 495/202–5250 Ⓜ *Arbatskaya.*

Naf Naf. Moscow has several outlets of this popular French retailer of
women's fashion, including one in GUM and one on Tverskaya ulitsa.
✉ *GUM, 3 Red Sq., Kremlin/Red Square* ☎495/929–3163 Ⓜ*Ploshchad
Revolutsii* ✉ *16/2 Tverskaya ul.* ☎ 495/935–7782 Ⓜ *Tverskaya or
Pushkinskaya* ✉ *11 Novy Arbat* ☎ 495/933–7288 Ⓜ *Arbatskaya.*

Nike. Nike fans can find footwear and sportswear right on the Garden
Ring and Novy Arbat, plus at the Manezh and GUM shopping malls.
✉ *GUM, 3 Red Sq., Kremlin/Red Square* ☎495/921–5763 Ⓜ*Ploshchad
Revolutsii* ✉ *Manezh, Trade Center Okhotny Ryad, 1 Manezhnaya Pl.*
☎ 495/737–8489 Ⓜ *Okhotny Ryad* ✉ *3 Smolenskaya ul.* ☎ 495/
244–7292 Ⓜ *Smolenskaya* ✉ *17 Novy Arbat* ☎ 495/203–4845 Ⓜ *Arbatskaya* ✉ *1 Kundrinsky per.* ☎ 495/255–4463 Ⓜ *Barrikadnaya.*

Reebok. This big, airy shop sells sports outfits, shoes, and equipment,
and is just across from the U.S. embassy. Two smaller stores operate in
GUM, vtoraya liniya (2nd line), first floor, and in the Manezh shopping
mall, middle level. ✉ *GUM, 3 Red Sq., Kremlin/Red Square* ☎ 495/
921–5763 Ⓜ *Ploshchad Revolutsii* ✉ *Manezh, Trade Center Okhotny
Ryad, 1 Manezhnaya Pl.* ☎ 495/737–8549 Ⓜ *Okhotny Ryad* ✉ *28/
35 Novinsky bulvar* ☎ 495/291–7873 Ⓜ *Barrikadnaya.*

Stockmann Discount. Those looking for high-fashion items from last year's collections should check out this store with clothes for men and women. ✉ *73 Leninsky pr., Southern Outskirts* ☎ *495/134–3546* Ⓜ *Universitet.*

Valentin Yudashkin Trading House. Make an appearance at Valentin Yudashkin for the latest Russian haute couture. The women's fashion designer is perhaps the only Russian designer known outside the country and many Russian celebrities prefer his work over that of Western designers. ✉ *19 Kutuzovsky pr., Krasnaya Presnya* ☎ *495/785–1051* Ⓜ *Kievskaya or Kutuzovskaya.*

Food & Spirits

Caviar in Russia? Who can resist? Especially when you can buy it at the bargain rates now being offered in Moscow. Unlike vodkas, there are few concerns about counterfeiting, and you can find authentic sturgeon caviar in any nice Russian food store. Expect to pay about $300 per kilo (nearly 3 pounds) of black caviar—it's best to purchase those already packed in export jars.

Buying liquor—especially vodka—in Russia is a de rigueur activity fraught with danger. Alcohol counterfeiting is a big problem; according to various estimates, illegally produced vodka accounts for 40% to 70% of what is available on the market. If you don't follow safe buying practices, you could end up with a severe case of alcohol poisoning. Your best bet on price and safety is to buy at outlet shops of vodka distilleries, such as Cristall, or at supermarkets. Note that every bottle of vodka sold in Russia must bear a white excise stamp, glued over the cap, and those sold in Moscow must also bear a bar-code stamp.

Western-style supermarkets are rapidly squeezing Soviet-style food stores such as bakeries out of business. Supermarket bakery counters have become the only options for bread in downtown Moscow. Some supermarkets have their own bakeries, others sell bread brought from one of the city's "khlebozavody" or bakeries. You'll still get good Russian bread for less than 20 rubles a loaf. *Podmoskovny* and *nareznoi* sell for about 15 rubles and are lighter than the white bread generally associated with Russia. Varieties of black rye bread (*borodinsky* and *khamovnichesky*) are the tastiest, and they still won't put you out more than 25 rubles. Branches of Sedmoi Kontinent and Perekryostok, often open 24 hours, have proliferated like underbrush below the high-rise canopies of Moscow's suburbs. Sedmoi Kontinent supermarkets offer probably the best borodinsky bread in town and great Ciabatta bread, both plain and with onions and herbs. The delicious and hugely popular Armenian lavash—soft, thin flatbread—is made with flour and water.

Cristall outlet. Cristall is Moscow's oldest and biggest vodka producer. In addition to about a dozen other unique brands, you can buy authentic Stolichnaya here in bottles that go for less than 150R. ✉ *41 Zamorenova ul., behind McDonald's restaurant, Krasnaya Presnya* Ⓜ *Ulitsa 1905 Goda.*

Danone. Health nuts take heart: this sleek shop on Tverskaya dishes out Dannon yogurt products—even six-packs. ✉ *4 Tverskaya ul.* ☎ *495/ 292–0512* Ⓜ *Okhotny Ryad or Teatralnaya.*

Globus Gourmet. Picky eaters will like this 24-hour grocery store that has been stocking its shelves with high-quality imported foodstuffs since its opening in 2005. Among the wide array of deli foods Globus offers is Italian raspberry-flavored balsamic vinegar, priced at $33 for a 250 milliliter jar. A kitchen run by Cuban chef Jose Sevilla churns out deli items and sells fresh produce from the owner's 20-hectare farm outside Moscow. The store's cheese department has to be seen to be believed. According to the staff, an average sales receipt at Globus runs $30–$40, making it reasonably priced compared to French competitor Fauchon. ✉ *22 Bolshaya Yakimanka, Zamoskvoreche* ☎ *495/995–2170* Ⓜ *Oktyabrskaya and Polyanka.*

Krasny Oktyabr chocolate factory. Russian-made chocolates make a great, unexpected souvenir from Russia. Those from Moscow's Krasny Oktyabr (Red October) factory are the best. You can buy both individual candies, of various names—*Krasnaya Shapochka* (Little Red Riding Hood), *Mishki* (Little Bears), and *Melodiya* (Melody)—and gift boxes. A nice box of *Nadezhda* (Hope) chocolates sells for just over 200R; a gift tin of Mishki for about 350R. The chocolates are widely available in stalls and kiosks as well as at the factory's corporate retail stores throughout Moscow (most are open 10–4). ✉ *22/24 Ovchinnikovskaya nab., Zamoskvoreche* Ⓜ *Borovitskaya* ✉ *12 Pervaya (1st) Tverskaya-Yamskaya ul., Krasnaya Presnya* Ⓜ *Mayakovskaya* ✉ *17 ul. Shabolovka* Ⓜ *Shabolovskaya.*

★ **Yeliseyevsky's.** Historic, sumptuous, gourmet—this turn-of-the-20th-century grocery store is the star of Tverskaya ulitsa. A late-18th-century classical mansion houses the store, and the interior sparkles with chandeliers, stained glass, and gilt wall decorations. Fine products abound, from cognac and Georgian wine (including Stalin's favorite Khvanchkara) to Russian chocolate and candy of all sorts. This is one of the best places to buy caviar or freshly baked goods. You'll find traditional favorite Russian rye breads such as Borodinsk and Stolichny, wheat Nareznoi, as well as a wide variety of croissants (including dark and multigrain), brioches, and seven-grain loaves that were virtually unknown to Muscovites a decade ago. Another plus: the store is open 24 hours. ✉ *14 Tverskaya ul.* ☎ *495/209–0760* Ⓜ *Tverskaya or Pushkinskaya.*

Street Markets

Food

Moscow's wave of reconstruction and renovation has benefited fresh-food markets *(rynok)*. At the same time many have been closed indefinitely, because of concerns over cleanliness and organized crime. Bargaining often takes place at food stalls. Suggest half the price of what the vendor asks, and if the offer is refused, pretend you are ready to move on. You'll likely receive a realistic price then.

Dorogomilovsky Rynok. This large covered hall is beyond the outdoor Veshchevoy Rynok (literally, "Market of Things," which is certainly an apt name). Inside are rows of vendors hawking homemade cheese and milk products, honey, flowers, and produce of all kinds. Against one wall are sellers of pickled goods, an understandably popular form of food preparation in this land of long winters; you may want to sample some of their cabbage and carrot slaws, salted cucumbers, or spiced eggplant or garlic. Tasting is free, but it's unlikely that you'll leave here without buying something. Remember to bargain. In another corner are tables of freshly cut meat, plucked chickens, and fish. The squeamish may want to avert their eyes from the whole suckling pigs and the occasional hare or goat, beheaded and proudly strung up for inspection. ⊠ *Off Mozhaisky Val ul., near Kiev Station, Krasnaya Presnya* Ⓜ *Kievskaya.*

Tishinka Rynok. Formerly an old-style chaotic market, the Tishinka has been turned into a huge trade center, combining the elements of a green grocer and a supermarket. The supermarket is open daily, 24 hours, the green market from 9 to 9 daily. The second floor houses boutiques and inexpensive Russian restaurants. ⊠ *50 Bolshaya Gruzinskaya ul.* ☎ *495/ 254–1572* Ⓜ *Belorusskaya.*

Souvenirs

For good souvenir hunting, you can certainly head straight to the Arbat. Stores here cater to tourists and Moscow's expatriate community, so you can expect good selection and service, but prices are on the high end. The Arbat's individual outdoor vendors invariably charge much more than they should, so stick to the stores.

Izmailovsky flea market. You could easily spend a whole day at Moscow's Izmailovsky Park, with its reasonably priced souvenirs, handicrafts, used books, and such Soviet memorabilia as authentic army belts and gas masks. *Matryoshky* (nesting dolls) come in both classic and nouveau styles: some bear likenesses of Soviet and Russian leaders; others depict American basketball stars and Monica Lewinsky. Nearby is the former royal residence of Izmailovo, situated in an old hunting preserve. The flea market is open weekends 9–6, but it's best to get here early. Many vendors close down by midday. Be sure to wrangle over prices: bargaining is expected here. You can pay in dollars if you come up short on rubles; this practice is technically illegal, but everybody does it. In fact, vendors are known to prefer hard currency and will usually offer a better price for *baksy* (New Russian lingo for "bucks"). ⊠ *Take the metro to Partizanskaya station and follow crowds as you exit, Eastern Outskirts.*

MOSCOW EXCURSIONS

Within easy reach of half-day excursions from the city await majestic old palaces, estates, and former noble residences, all set in emblematic Russian countryside. To see them to the best advantage you should try to make your visits in spring or summer.

All of these sights can be accessed by metro, though you may have to take a connecting bus or trolley.

Arkhangelskoye
Архангельское

26 km (16 mi) northwest of Moscow via Volokolamskoye shosse.

In addition to its fine location on the banks of the Moskva River, the town of Arkhangelskoye holds a beautiful example of a noble country palace of the late tsarist era, the imposing estate of Prince Yusupov. Yusupov's neoclassical palace forms the centerpiece of a striking group of 18th- and 19th-century buildings that make up the Arkhangelskoye Estate Museum. The main palace has been closed for restoration work for several years and will reopen in fall 2006 or later. In 1997 the estate was named one of the world's most endangered sites by the World Monuments Fund. Excursions can still be made to the estate grounds, but with the exception of the closed palace's ongoing reconstruction, a definite sense of disrepair pervades.

The main palace complex was built at the end of the 18th century for Prince Golitsyn by the French architect Chevalier de Huerne. In 1810 the family fell upon hard times and sold the estate to the rich landlord Yusupov, the onetime director of the imperial theaters and St. Petersburg's Hermitage Museum, and ambassador to several European lands.

The estate became home to Prince Yusupov's extraordinary art collection. The collection includes paintings by Boucher, Vigée-Lebrun, Hubert Robert, Roslin, Tiepolo, Van Dyck, and many others, as well as antique statues, furniture, mirrors, chandeliers, glassware, and china. Much of the priceless furniture once belonged to Marie Antoinette and Madame de Pompadour. There are also samples of fabrics, china, and glassware that were produced on the estate itself.

Allées and strolling lanes wind through the **French Park,** which is populated with statues and monuments commemorating royal visits. There's also a monument to Pushkin, whose favorite retreat was Arkhangelskoye. In the western part of the park is an interesting small pavilion, known as the Temple to the Memory of Catherine the Great, that depicts the empress as Themis, goddess of justice. It seems that Yusupov, reportedly a Casanova, had turned the head of Russia's empress, renowned herself for having legions of lovers. This "temple" was built as a compliment for a painting she had previously commissioned—one in which she was depicted as Venus, with Yusupov as Apollo.

Back outside the estate grounds on the right-hand side of the main road stands the **Estate (Serf) Theater,** built in 1817 by the serf architect Ivanov. Currently a museum, the theater originally seated 400 and was the home of the biggest and best-known company of serf actors in Russia. The well-preserved stage decorations are by the Venetian artist Pietrodi Gonzaga.

Prince Yusupov was a kindly, paternalistic man and often opened his home and gardens to the public, a tradition that continues today. The Arkhangelskoye Estate Museum can be reached by Bus 541 from the Moscow metro station Sokolniki, or by car from the Rublevskoye shosse (turn right at the Militia Booth toward Ilinskoye and take a right turn after you pass the Russkaya Izba restaurant). Check first with your hotel's service bureau or your tour agency for updated information on the renovation project. ✉ *Arkhangelskoye* ☎ *495/561–9660* ⊕ *www.arkhangelskoe.ru* ✉ *150R.*

Where to Eat

$ ✕ **Arkhangelskoye Restaurant.** A palekh motif—a traditional lacquer design depicting characters from Russian fairy tales—decorates this restaurant. The convenient location (directly across the road from the entrance to the Arkhangelskoye Estate Museum) adds value to the decent food. Try the borscht, followed by veal with mushrooms. Grilled salmon is also delicious. ✉ *Ilyinskoye shosse, across from main entrance to Arkhangelskoye Estate Museum* ☎ *495/562–0328* ▭ *AE, MC, V.*

$ ✕ **Russkaya Izba.** This wooden restaurant's rustic decor is patterned on the *izba*, a Russian country home. Caviar, blini, and other Russian dishes are served here. Reservations are recommended. ✉ *Ilyinskoye village, on road to Arkhangelskoye, near Moskva River* ☎ *495/561–4244* ▭ *No credit cards.*

Victory Park
Парк Победы

10 Km (6 mi) west of Moscow city center via Kutuzovsky pr.

This 335-acre park (Park Pobedy) near the landmark Triumphal Arch, on the western edge of the city, is historically linked to the defense of Moscow against invaders. Poklonnaya Gora, the hill that used to be here, is where Napoléon is said to have waited in vain for the keys to Moscow in 1812. Once the highest hill in Moscow, Poklonnaya Gora was razed in the 1970s to build Triumphal Arch, a World War II memorial, which was unveiled in 1995 in time for the 50th anniversary of the victory over Nazi Germany. Packed with all sorts of documentary evidence of the Soviet Army's victory, the memorial is the centerpiece of the park, but also here are a chapel and an outdoor display of vintage World War II arms. Victory Park is a popular spot for festivities on public holidays, including Victory Day, Orthodox Easter, and Christmas. On a warm day, expect to see strolling couples and hordes of rollerbladers, including whole families rollerblading together. The park is near the Park Pobedy metro station.

Kolomenskoye
Коломенское

★ *17 km (10½ mi) south of Moscow city center via Kashirskoye shosse, on west bank of Moskva River.*

If you want to spend an afternoon in the great Russian outdoors without actually leaving the city, Kolomenskoye, on a high bluff overlooking the Moskva River, is just the right destination. The estate was once a favorite summer residence of Moscow's grand dukes and tsars. Today it's a popular public park with museums, a functioning church, old Russian cottages, and other attractions. It's also the site of the city's main celebration of the holiday Maslenitsa, or Butter Week, which usually falls at the end of February or beginning of March. Traditional Russian amusements such as mock fist fights, bag races, and tug-of-war are held on the park's grounds, with heaps of hot blini served as round reminders of the spring sun. In September beekeepers from around the country set up a giant honey fair.

As you approach Kolomenskoye, the first sight you see are the striking blue domes of the **Church of Our Lady of Kazan,** a functioning church that is open for worship. It was completed in 1671. Opposite the church there once stood a wooden palace built by Tsar Alexei, Peter the Great's father. Peter spent much time here when he was growing up. Nothing remains of the huge wooden structure (Catherine the Great ordered it destroyed in 1767), but there's a scale model at the **museum,** which is devoted to Russian timber architecture and folk crafts. The museum lies inside the front gates of the park, at the end of the tree-lined path leading from the main entrance of the park.

The most remarkable sight within the park is the **Church of the Ascension,** which sits on the bluff overlooking the river. The church dates from the 1530s and was restored in the late 1800s. Its skyscraping tower is an example of the tent or pyramid-type structure that was popular in Russian architecture in the 16th century. The view from the bluff is impressive in its contrasts: from your 16th-century backdrop you can look north across the river to the 20th-century concrete apartment houses that dominate the contemporary Moscow skyline. In summer you'll see Muscovites bathing in the river below the church, and in winter the area abounds with cross-country skiers.

Examples of wooden architecture from other parts of Russia have been transferred to Kolomenskoye, turning the estate into an open-air museum. In the wooded area near the site of the former wooden palace you'll find a 17th-century prison tower from Siberia, a defense tower from the White Sea, and a 17th-century mead brewery from the village of Preobrazhenskaya. One of the most attractive original buildings on the site is the wooden cottage where Peter the Great lived while supervising the building of the Russian fleet in Arkhangelskoye. The cottage was relocated here in 1934.

To get to Kolomenskoye take the metro to Kolomenskaya station; a walk of about 10 minutes up a slight hill brings you to the park's entrance. ⊠ *39 Andropova pr.* ☎ *495/112–0416* 🖅 *Free* 🕓 *Tues.–Sun. 10–5.*

Tsaritsyno

Царицыно

21 km (13 mi) south of Moscow city center via Kashirskoye shosse.

This popular boating and picnicking spot is the site of the 18th-century summer palace that was started but never completed for Catherine the Great. Tsaritsyno was always an ill-favored estate. The empress pulled down the work of her first architect; the second building phase was never completed, probably for financial reasons. Her heirs took no interest in

Tsaritsyno, so the estate served all sorts of functions, from a wine factory to a testing ground for rock climbers. In 1984 the long-needed reconstruction began, and a museum was founded. By that time some buildings had been so neglected that tall trees grew inside the walls. The government allocated funds to restore the fabulous Opera House and the elegant Small Palace, but the funding dried up in 1996. In summer 2005 this most neglected of the Moscow estates was transferred to the control of the Moscow city government. Mayor Yury Luzhkov announced a plan to spend 410 million rubles ($14.38 million) on the ruins and surrounding park. Restoration is underway on the bread house (kitchens), the bridge, and other structures. The Gothic Revival architectural ensemble is still worth checking out, along with a collection of porcelain, paintings, and sculptures on display at the Opera House. Tsaritsyno is close to the metro station of the same name, three metro stops south of Kolomenskoye. ⊠ *1 ul. Dolskaya* ☎ *495/321–0743* ⌫ *Free* ⊙ *Wed.–Sun. 11–6.*

Kuskovo Estate & Palace Museum
Дворец-усадьба Кусково

18 km (11 mi) southeast of Moscow city center via Ryazansky pr.

In the 18th and 19th centuries the country estate of Kuskovo was the Moscow aristocracy's favorite summer playground. It belonged to the noble Sheremetyevs, one of Russia's wealthiest and most distinguished families, whose holdings numbered in the millions of acres. (Today, Moscow's international airport, built on land that once belonged to one of their many estates, takes their family name.)

The Sheremetyevs acquired the land of Kuskovo in the early 17th century, but the estate, often called a Russian Versailles, took on its current appearance in the late 18th century. Most of the work on it was commissioned by Prince Pyotr Sheremetyev, who sought a suitable place for entertaining guests in the summer. The park—one of the most beautiful spots in all of Russia—was created by Russian landscape artists who had spent much time in Europe studying their art. The French-style gardens are dotted with buildings representing the major architectural trends of Europe: the Dutch cottage, the Italian villa, the grotto, and the exquisite hermitage, where, in the fashion of the day, dinner tables were raised mechanically from the ground floor to the second-floor dining room.

The centerpiece of the estate is the **Kuskovo Palace,** built in the early Russian classical style by the serf architects Alexei Mironov and Fedor Argunov. Fronted by a grand horseshoe staircase and Greek-temple portico, this building is the absolute quintessence of Russian neoclassical elegance. The palace, which is made of timber on a white-stone foundation, overlooks a human-made lake. It has been a house museum since 1918, and its interior decorations, including fine parquet floors and silk wall coverings, have been well preserved. The bedroom, with its lovely canopy bed, was merely for show: the Sheremetyevs used the palace exclusively for entertainment and did not live here. The parquet floors, gilt wall decorations, and crystal chandeliers of the marvelous White Hall testify to the grandeur of the ballroom extravaganzas that once took place here. On display in the inner rooms are paintings by French, Italian, and Flemish artists; Chinese porcelain; furniture; and other articles of everyday life from the 18th and 19th centuries. The palace also houses a collection of 18th-century Russian art and a rather celebrated ceramics museum with a rich collection of Russian, Soviet, and foreign ceramics.

Pyotr Sheremetyev had more than 150,000 serfs, many of whom received architectural training and participated in the building of his estate. The serfs also constituted a theater troupe that gave weekly open-air performances, a common practice on nobles' estates—the crème de la crème of Moscow society made it a point to attend the Sheremetyev showings. Today, of course, only the setting for this spectacular lifestyle remains, but the dreamlike park and palace persist as mute and eloquent testimony to a royalty long vanished.

Kuskovo is just outside the ring road marking the city boundary, but you can reach it by public transportation. Take the metro to Ryazansky Prospekt station and then Bus 208 or Bus 133 six stops to Kuskovo Park. You may find it more convenient to book a tour that includes transportation. Whatever you do, be sure to phone ahead before making the trek, because the estate often closes when the weather is very humid or very cold. ⊠ 2 ul. Yunosti ☎ 495/370–0160 ⌦ 200R ⊙ Nov.–Apr., Wed. Sun. 10 4; May–Oct., Wed.–Fri. 11–7, weekends 10–6; closed last Wed. of month.

MOSCOW A TO Z

To research prices, get advice from other travelers, and book travel arrangements, visit www.fodors.com.

AIR TRAVEL

The Russian carrier Aeroflot operates flights from Moscow to just about every capital of Europe, as well as to Canada and the United States. The airline also serves numerous domestic destinations. Transaero, another Russian carrier, has a large network of domestic flights as well as several international routes. Among the international airlines with offices in Moscow are Air France, Alitalia, Austrian Airlines, British Airways, Delta, Finnair, Japan Airlines, KLM, Lufthansa, Malev, SAS, and Swiss.

🛈 Carriers **Aeroflot** ☎ 495/753-5555. **Air France** ☎ 495/937-3839. **Alitalia** ☎ 495/967-0110. **Austrian Airlines** ☎ 495/995-0995. **British Airways** ☎ 495/363-2525. **Delta** ☎ 495/937-9090. **Finnair** ☎ 495/933-0056. **Japan Airlines** ☎ 495/730-3070. **KLM** ☎ 495/258-3600. **Lufthansa** ☎ 495/737-6400. **Malev** ☎ 495/202-8416. **SAS** ☎ 495/775-4747. **Swiss** ☎ 495/937-7760 or 495/937-7767. **Transaero** ☎ 495/788-8080.

AIRPORTS

As the most important transportation hub in the Commonwealth of Independent States (CIS, a quasi-confederation of states including most of the former Soviet Union), Moscow has several airports. Most international flights arrive at Sheremetyevo II, north of the city center. One of the most modern airports in Russia when it was built in 1979, Sheremetyevo II is inadequate and old-fashioned these days. Be prepared for lines everywhere and a wait of up to an hour or two at passport control. Disembarked passengers descend a long staircase, then collect en masse in a large, dimly lighted chamber to vie for the three or four lines to the passport officials' booths. The baggage area is directly beyond passport control. Luggage carts are free, but they often go quickly. You can also hire a porter for a couple of dollars (agree on a price before you give your bags to the porter). There's a bank in the waiting area where you can exchange money or traveler's checks while you're waiting for your luggage. The bank is not always open, but there's also an ATM in the area. Beyond the baggage area is customs. If you have nothing to declare, you frequently can walk right through the green aisle to the waiting area, where you'll be greeted by mobs of Russians awaiting arriving passengers and eager gypsy cab drivers shouting, "*Taksi! Taksi!*"

In addition to its international airport, the city has four domestic terminals. Sheremetyevo I, some 30 km (19 mi) northwest of the city center, services domestic flights to St. Petersburg and the former Baltic republics (Estonia, Latvia, and Lithuania). It also handles the international flights of some of the newer Russian airlines. Domodedovo, one of the largest airports in the world (and perhaps the nicest in Russia), is some 48 km (30 mi) southeast of Moscow. British Airways, Swiss, and Transaero fly out of Domodedovo. Flights also depart from Domodedovo to the republics of Central Asia. Vnukovo, 29 km (18 mi) southwest of the city center, services flights to Georgia, the southern republics, and Ukraine. Bykovo, the smallest of the domestic terminals, generally handles flights within Russia and some flights to Ukraine.

For general information on arriving international flights, call the airline directly. Calling the airports usually takes longer and fewer people speak English.

🛈 Airport Information Bykovo ☎ 495/558-4933 or 495/558-4738. **Domodedovo** ☎ 495/933-6666 or 495/941-9999. **Sheremetyevo I Airport** ☎ 495/232-6565. **Sheremetyevo II Airport** ☎ 495/956-4666 or 495/578-9101 or 495/956-2372. **Vnukovo** ☎ 495/436-2813.

TRANSFERS   It's wise to make advance arrangements for your transfer from the airport. Most hotels will provide airport transfers (for a fee) upon request by prior fax (which you should confirm).

There are plenty of gypsy cabs available, but there's always a risk of being swindled. If you do take one, bargain, bargain, bargain. Even if you speak Russian, riding to the center may cost 1,000R. Anything more is a rip-off. Remember, though, that you will likely travel in an old, small, Soviet car with no guarantee of a smooth or safe ride. And don't get out of the taxi while the driver is still at the wheel and your luggage is in the trunk—he might just drive off with your belongings. It's better to use the services offered on the airport's ground floor. These private firms are less risky, can provide a receipt, and you may find their prices more reasonable than the gypsy cabs' prices. Traveling to the airport from the city is cheaper. You can hail a taxi on the street for about 700R or book a taxi in advance for 800R–1,000R.

All of the airports are served by municipal buses operating out of Aero-vokzal (City Airport Terminal) at 37 Leningradsky prospekt, near the Aeroport metro station. Even more convenient are the buses and the faster "marshrutka" minibuses that go from just outside the airport to the Rech-noy Vokzal metro station. From here it's about 25 minutes to the city center. Service is not very convenient, especially if you have a lot of lug-gage, but it's very inexpensive. Buses leave for Rechnoy Vokzal metro station every 5 to 10 minutes but are more erratic to the City Airport Terminal; service to Domodedovo and Vnukovo airports is more fre-quent. Domodedovo is the easiest airport, with a fast train running from the airport to Pavletsky train station (where you can check in immedi-ately with some airlines), although newly renovated Vnukovo also now has an express train service running from Kiev train station. Buses and marshrutka minibuses also run frequently from Domodedovo to the Do-modedovo metro station. A train runs from Bykovo airport to Kazan-sky train station.

BOAT & FERRY TRAVEL

Moscow has two river ports: Severny Rechnoy Vokzal (Northern River Terminal; used for long-distance passengers), on the Khimki reservoir, and Yuzhny Rechnoy Vokzal (Southern River Terminal). However, in-ternational cruise lines offering tours to Russia usually disembark in St. Petersburg and continue from there by land. It is possible, however, to book a two-way cruise, through Volga-Flot Tur, from Moscow along the Moscow-Volga canal, which makes for a pleasant way to see the Golden Ring town of Yaroslavl. Some 129 km (80 mi) long, the canal links the Russian capital with the Volga, which flows to the Caspian Sea, the Black Sea, the White Sea, and the Azov Sea.

⊞ **Severny Rechnoy Vokzal** ⊠ 51 Leningradskoye shosse, Northern Outskirts ☎ 495/459-7465. **Volga-Flot Tur** ⊠ 26 ul. Novoslobodskaya, Northern Outskirts ☎ 495/251-5757/4787 Ⓜ Novoslobodskaya. **Yuzhny Rechnoy Vokzal** ⊠ 11 Andropov pr., South-ern Outskirts ☎ 495/118-7955

BUS TRAVEL

🚩 **Bus Information Tsentralny Avtovokzal** (Central Bus Station) ⊠ 75 Schelkovskoe shosse, Moscow ☎ 495/468-0400 Ⓜ Schelkovskaya.

CAR RENTAL

Some hotels will make car-rental arrangements for you. Otherwise, sev-eral international car-rental agencies have offices in Moscow; be sure to reserve at least three days in advance. Avis rents several European and American makes. Budget rents various Fords and minivans. Hertz rents Fords and many other makes; for a fee you can have the car de-livered to you. Hertz and Budget also rent cars with drivers, which may be a better option unless you are an experienced driver; driving in Moscow is not unlike a big game of chicken.

🚩 **Agencies Avis** ⊠ 7/21 Meschanskaya ul., Northern Outskirts ☎ 495/744-0733 Ⓜ Sukharevskaya. **Budget** ⊠ 43 Volgogradsky pr., Southern Outskirts ☎ 495/737-0407 ⊠ Sheremetyevo II Airport, Northern Outskirts ☎ 495/578-7344. **Hertz** ⊠ 2 Tverskaya Zastava, Northern Outskirts ☎ 495/937-3274.

CAR TRAVEL

You can reach Moscow from Finland and St. Petersburg by taking the Helsinki–St. Petersburg Highway through Vyborg and St. Petersburg and continuing from there on the Moscow–St. Petersburg Highway. Be warned that driving in Russia is invariably more of a hassle than a pleasure. Roads are very poorly maintained, and many streets in the city center are one-way. In addition you face the risk of car theft, a crime that is on the rise.

EMBASSIES

Unless you have official business or are met by embassy personnel or a compound resident, the United States embassy is off-limits, even to Americans.

🔏 Canada ⊠ 23 Starokonyushenny per. ☎ 495/105-6000 Ⓜ Kropotkinskaya. **United Kingdom** ⊠ 10 Smolenskaya nab. ☎ 495/956-7200 Ⓜ Smolenskaya. **United States** ⊠ 19/23 Novinsky bulvar ☎ 495/728-5000 Ⓜ Barrikadnaya.

EMERGENCIES

The state medical system is plagued by poor service, low hygiene standards, and a lack of medicines and basic medical equipment. If you're ill, contact one of several Western clinics, which are used by the foreign community as well as Russians who can afford the higher fees. Some of these clinics are membership organizations, but all will provide service to tourists, though perhaps not with 24-hour access; costs will be higher than for members, too. Usually you must pay with rubles or a credit card, and you'll need to settle accounts up front.

In an emergency, you can also contact your country's consular section for help with the logistics of serious medical treatment. For U.S. citizens, contact American Citizens Services. British citizens can call their embassy, or during workdays get a referral from the embassy clinic. Canadian citizens should call the embassy number, where they will be connected to a duty officer.

🔏 Emergency Services Ambulance ☎ 03. **American Citizens Services** ☎ 495/728-5577 after-hours emergency. **British Embassy clinic** ☎ 495/956-7270. **Fire** ☎ 01. **Police** ☎ 02.

DENTISTS   Russian state dental facilities are as grim as their medical facilities. Of the general service clinics, the American Medical Center, European Medical Centre, International SOS Clinic, and Mediclub Moscow also provide dental services. The German Dental Clinic is open weekdays 9–9 and Saturday 9–3. U.S. Dental Care is a joint Russian–U.S. clinic offering all types of dental treatment. The clinic is open weekdays 9–9 and Saturday 9–3, and has after-hours emergency care.

🔏 German Dental Clinic ⊠ 2 Volochayevskaya ul., Bldg. 1, Western Outskirts ☎ 495/362-4902 Ⓜ Ploshchad Ilycha. **U.S. Dental Care** ⊠ 7/5 Bolshaya Dmitrovka ☎ 495/933-8686 Ⓜ Pushkinskaya.

HOSPITALS &   The American Medical Center offers full-range family practice and CLINICS   emergency services, including evacuation assistance. If treatment is needed outside the clinic, they use various hospitals. The office is open 24 hours, and doctors make house calls 24 hours a day. Medicine can be provided at the clinic. A tourist plan is available.

The European Medical Centre, which is not a membership group, offers a full range of services, including day and night house calls. Hospital referral is usually to the ZKB Presidential Hospital. English and French are spoken. Medicine can be provided at the clinic.

International SOS Clinic is a nonmember service that provides comprehensive care, hospitalization referral to the Kuntsevo (Kremlin VIP) Hospital, and evacuation via an in-house company (they are part of SOS International). English, French, and German are spoken, and there's a pharmacy on-site.

Mediclub Moscow is a Russian clinic that provides full medical service and hospital referral to Glavmosstroy Hospital. It's open weekdays 9–4, with last appointments at 3; you may call after hours for an emergency.

An English-language Alcoholics Anonymous meets six evenings a week at various locations. Check the *Moscow Times* community bulletin board listings, published Tuesdays.

🔳 **Clinics American Medical Center** ✉ 1 Grokholsky per., Northern Outskirts ☎ 495/933-7700 Ⓜ Prospekt Mira. **European Medical Centre** ✉ 5 Spiridonevsky per., Bldg. 1 ☎ 495/933-6655 Ⓜ Mayakovskaya or Pushkinskaya. **International SOS Clinic** ✉ 31 Grokholsky per., 10th fl., Northern Outskirts ☎ 495/937-5760 Ⓜ Prospekt Mira. **Mediclub Moscow** ✉ 56 Michurinsky pr., Southern Outskirts ☎ 495/931-5018 or 495/931-5318 Ⓜ Prospekt Vernadskovo.

🔳 **Hotlines Alcoholics Anonymous** ☎ 495/768-2551.

PHARMACIES Pharmacies are plentiful, and many stay open around the clock in the city center. One highly rated pharmacy is 36.6, which has many branches, including one in Central Telegraph (at 7 Tverskaya ulitsa) and a 24-hour branch near the Pushkin metro. Western-brand medicines may not be recognizable to you in their Russian packaging; however, you often can buy medicine over the counter that requires a prescription in the United States. For prescriptions, you can contact one of the foreign clinics' pharmacies, though prices will be high. Some hotels also have small pharmacies.

ENGLISH-LANGUAGE MEDIA

ENGLISH- You'll pay a premium for most imported books, though books in Rus-
LANGUAGE sian are remarkably inexpensive. Bright and comfortable Anglia British
BOOKSTORES Bookshop carries a good selection of literature and books about Russia—mostly books from Britain. It also holds readings and other events. The bookshop is open Monday through Friday 10–7, Saturday 10–6, and Sunday 11–5.

The Dom Inostrannikh Knig (House of International Books), a British oasis, is just around the corner from the Kuznetsky Most metro station. The staff can be very grumpy. It's open weekdays 10–9, Saturday 10–9, and Sunday 10-8.

Dom Knigi, open Monday through Friday 9–9 and weekends 10–9, is Russia's largest bookstore. It has a small foreign-literature section and a large section for students of Russian language. Be sure to examine the selection outside the front door, where individual sellers spread out their wares.

A cozy branch named after the famous Paris store, Shakespeare & Co. has crammed shelves, a helpful staff, and literary readings. You'll find a little of everything here, including used books; it's open daily 11–8. 🔽 **Anglia British Bookshop** ✉ 6 Vorotnikovsky per. ☎ 495/299-7766 Ⓜ Mayakovskaya. **Dom Inostrannikh Knig** ✉ 18 Kuznetsky Most ☎ 495/928-2021 Ⓜ Kuznetsky Most. **Dom Knigi** ✉ 26 Novy Arbat ☎ 495/789-3591 Ⓜ Arbatskaya. **Shakespeare & Co.** ✉ 5/7 Pervyi (1st) Novokuznetsky per., Zamoskvoreche ☎ 495/951-9360 Ⓜ Paveletskaya.

NEWSPAPERS & MAGAZINES
You can read up on world and local news in the city's English-language newspaper, the *Moscow Times* (⊕ www.themoscowtimes.com), published weekdays. It's available in just about any Western store, restaurant, or major hotel.

METRO TRAVEL

The Moscow metro, first opened in 1935, ranks among the world's finest public transportation systems. With more than 200 km (124 mi) of track, the Moscow metro carries an estimated 8 million passengers daily. Even in today's hard economic times, the system continues to run efficiently, with trains every 50 seconds during rush hour. It leaves New Yorkers green with envy.

If you're not traveling with a tour group or if you haven't hired your own driver, taking the metro is the best way to get around the Russian capital. You'll be doing yourself a great favor and saving yourself a lot of frustration if you learn the Russian (Cyrillic) alphabet well enough to be able to transliterate the names of the stations. This will come in especially handy at transfer points, where signs with long lists of the names of metro stations lead you from one major metro line to another. You should also be able to recognize the entrance and exit signs (⇨ English-Russian Vocabulary, at end of this book) because going the wrong way could earn you a scolding from one of the many red-hatted employees working in the stations.

Pocket maps of the system are available at newspaper kiosks and sometimes from individual vendors at metro stations. Be sure that you obtain a map with English transliterations in addition to Cyrillic. If you can't find one, try any of the major hotels (even if you're not a guest of the hotel they'll probably give you a map). Plan your route beforehand and have your destination written down in Russian and its English transliteration to help you spot the station. As the train approaches each station, the station name will be announced over the train's public-address system; the name of the next station is given before the train moves off. Reminders of interchanges and transfers are also given. Some newer trains do have the transliterated names of stations on line maps in the trains, which are very helpful for non-Russian speakers.

Stations are built deep underground (they were built to double as bomb shelters); the escalators are steep and run fast, so watch your step. If you use the metro during rush hour (8:30–10 AM, 4–6 PM), be prepared for a lot of pushing and shoving. In a crowded train, just before a station, you're likely to be asked, *"Vy vykhódite?,"* or whether you're getting off at the next station. If not, you're expected to move out of the way. Riders are expected to give up seats for senior citizens and small children.

Note that public displays of affection are frowned upon in the metro, and there's even talk of imposing fines for such behavior.

FARES &
SCHEDULES
The metro is easy to use and amazingly inexpensive. Stations are marked with a large illuminated "M" sign and are open daily 5:30 AM to 1 AM. The fare is the same regardless of distance traveled, and there are several stations where lines connect and you may transfer for free. You purchase a magnetic card (available at all stations) for 1, 5, 10, 20, or more journeys and insert it into the slot at the turnstile upon entering. The card will then appear again on the other side of the turnstile. Don't forget to take it. A single ride costs 7R, and discounts are available for multiple-journey cards. A card for 10 trips costs 50R.

You can also purchase a monthly pass (*yediny bilyet*), which is valid for all modes of public transportation (buses, trams, trolleys). The passes, which work like the magnetic cards, are on sale at the same windows as metro cards. At 500R, they are inexpensive and well worth the added expense for the convenience.

MONEY MATTERS

ATMS
You'll find ATMs all around the city center, though they're nowhere near as common as in U.S. cities.

CURRENCY
EXCHANGE
Most hotels have currency exchange bureaus, some operating 24 hours a day. Additionally, throughout the city you can find exchange bureaus bearing the OBMEN VALUTY/EXCHANGE sign—these are often in Cyrillic, but just look for the signs with daily rates posted in easy view, often on freestanding sidewalk signboards. Exercise reasonable caution when using them, and don't be surprised to find a security guard, who may let only one or two people inside at a time. By law it's required that you be issued a receipt, but you may find this erratic in practice; be sure to ask for one. You can also exchange currency or traveler's checks at the Russian banks; one of the most reliable is Sberbank, the Russian state bank. You can also try the Moscow Bank office in the Radisson Slavyanskaya hotel. The American Express office, listed under Travel Agencies, will cash American Express traveler's checks for rubles and, if it has cash available, for dollars.

🖪 Exchange Services **Moscow Bank** ✉ Radisson Slavyanskaya hotel, 2 Berezhkovskaya nab., Krasnaya Presnya ☎ 495/941–8020 Ⓜ Kievskaya. **Sberbank** ✉ 19 ul. Tverskaya ☎ 495/299–7995 Ⓜ Pushkinskaya.

SIGHTSEEING TOURS

Every major hotel maintains a tourist bureau that books individual and group tours to Moscow's main sights. In addition, there are numerous private agencies that can help with your sightseeing plans.

Patriarshy Dom Tours conducts unusual day and overnight tours in and around Moscow and St. Petersburg for groups or individuals. Among the tours are the Red October chocolate factory, the KGB museum, literature or architectural walks, and the space-flight command center. You can call for schedules or pick up copies in some hotels and Western stores.

Sputnik handles group and individual tours in Moscow and some day trips out of town. The company can tailor plans to suit your needs.
🚹 **Patriarshy Dom Tours** ✉ 6 Vspolny per. ☎ 495/795-0927, 650/678-7076 in U.S. **Sputnik** ✉ 15 Kosygina ul., Southern Outskirts ☎ 495/939-8374.

TAXIS

Exercise caution when using taxis. There are standard taxis of various makes and colors, but professional ones all have taxi lights on top and can easily be hailed in the city center. Official taxis have a "T" and checkered emblem on the doors (but there are not many of them). When you enter a cab, check to see if the meter is working; if it is not, agree on a price beforehand. Generally, everyone with a car is a potential taxi driver in Moscow; it's common for Muscovites to hail an ordinary car and negotiate a price for a ride. This is generally a safe practice, but it's best to avoid it, particularly if you don't speak Russian. If you do choose to take a ride in an ordinary car, take some precautions: never get in a car with more than one person inside, and if the driver wants to stop for another fare, say no or get out of the car.

You can also call cabs by phone or through your hotel's service bureau. Moscow has numerous cab companies, most with 24-hour service. There is sometimes a delay, but the cab usually arrives within the hour. If you order a cab in this way, you usually pay a set rate for the first 30 minutes (between 115R and 175R) and then a set rate per minute (usually 4R to 6R per minute). Always ask for an approximate price when you telephone for a cab. Moscow Taxi provides city cabs as well as airport service (from hotels or private residences) in vans or buses. Novoye Zhyoltoye Taksi (New Yellow Taxi) is a cab firm with a good reputation.
🚹 Taxi Companies **Moscow Taxi** ☎ 495/238-1001. **Novoye Zhyoltoye Taksi** ☎ 495/940-8888.

TRAIN TRAVEL

Moscow is the hub of the Russian railway system, and the city's several railway stations handle some 400 million passengers annually. There are several trains daily to St. Petersburg, and overnight service is available to Helsinki, Riga, and Tallinn. All the major train stations have a connecting metro stop, so they're easily reached by public transportation. Note that although there are phone numbers for each station, it's all but impossible to get through to them. If you have limited time, it's best to ask your hotel service bureau or a travel agent for railway information and schedules.

The most important stations are Belorussia Station (Belorussky Vokzal), for trains to Belorussia, Lithuania, Poland, Germany, and France; Kazan Station (Kazansky Vokzal), for points south, Central Asia, and Siberia; Kiev Station (Kievsky Vokzal), for Kiev and western Ukraine, Moldova, Slovakia, the Czech Republic, and Hungary; Kursk Station (Kursky Vokzal), for eastern Ukraine, the Crimea, and southern Russia; Leningrad Station (Leningradsky Vokzal), for St. Petersburg, northern Russia, Estonia, and Finland; Pavelets Station (Paveletsky Vokzal), for eastern Ukraine and points south; Riga Station (Rizhsky Vokzal), for Latvia;

and Yaroslav Station (Yaroslavsky Vokzal), for points east, including Mongolia and China. The Trans-Siberian Express departs from Yaroslav Station every day at 9:56 AM.

Both overnight trains and high-speed day trains (five hours) depart from Leningrad Station for St. Petersburg. Of the numerous overnight trains, the most popular is the *Krasnaya Strelka* (Red Arrow), which leaves Moscow at 11:55 PM and arrives the next day in St. Petersburg at 8:25 AM. The Nikolayevsky Express leaves Moscow at 11:30 PM and reaches St. Petersburg at 7 AM.

FARES & SCHEDULES

For information on train schedules, reservations, and ticket delivery, call the Moscow Railways Agency. You can also purchase tickets at the railway stations or at the ticket offices. Bring your passport.

🚆 Train Information **Main Ticket Offices** ✉ 6 Griboyedova ul. ☎ 495/266-9000 Ⓜ Chistiye Prudy ✉ 15/13 Petrovka ul. ☎ 495/929-8757 Ⓜ Teatralnaya. **Moscow Railways Agency** ☎ 495/266-9333 ⊕ www.mza.ru.

🚆 Train Stations **Belorussia Station** ✉ Northern Outskirts ☎ 495/251-6093 Ⓜ Belorusskaya. **Kazan Station** ✉ Northern Outskirts ☎ 495/264-6556 Ⓜ Komsomolskaya. **Kiev Station** ✉ Krasnaya Presnya ☎ 495/240-1115 Ⓜ Kievskaya. **Kursk Station** ☎ 495/916-2003 Ⓜ Kurskaya. **Leningrad Station** ✉ Northern Outskirts ☎ 495/262-9143. **Pavelets Station** ✉ Paveletsky Vokzal, Southern Outskirts ☎ 495/235-0522 Ⓜ Paveletskaya. **Riga Station** ✉ Northern Outskirts ☎ 495/971-1588 Ⓜ Rizhskaya. **Yaroslav Station** ✉ Northern Outskirts ☎ 495/921-5914 Ⓜ Komsomolskaya.

TRANSPORTATION AROUND MOSCOW

If you look at a map of Moscow, you'll see that the city consists of a series of distinct circles with the Kremlin and Red Square at its center. The most famous and important sights are clustered within the first circle, which was once enclosed by the fortification walls of Kitai Gorod, the city's oldest settlement outside the Kremlin. This area can be easily covered on foot. Beyond that, the sights are more spread out and are best reached by metro. To get a sense of the city's geographic layout, you might consider renting a car (possibly with a driver) for a few hours and traveling around the main roads encircling the city—the Boulevard and Garden rings.

Buses, trams, and trolleys operate on the honor system. Upon boarding, you validate your ticket by punching it in one of the machines attached to a wall of the vehicle. The buses and trolleys are often overcrowded, and you may not be able to reach the canceling machine. Ask the person next to you to pass your ticket along; the canceled ticket will make its way back to you, and you should hold on to it until you get off. On some routes, particularly out of the city center, you may be the only person to pay for your ride. However, inspectors do sometimes board buses and may detain or fine you if you cannot show a canceled ticket.

You can purchase strips of tickets at metro stations and at kiosks throughout the city. The ticket is valid for one ride only; if you change buses you must pay another fare. Buses, trams, and trolleys operate from 5:30 AM to 1 AM, although service in the late-evening hours and on Sunday day tends to be unreliable.

TRAVEL AGENCIES

The travel agents listed here can provide air (and sometimes train) ticketing for international travel and sometimes travel to other points within Russia and the CIS. (You can also call the airlines directly for plane tickets.) Call around to get competitive rates. They can vary widely, depending on the trip you want, the number of people you have, and your transportation needs.

American Express, open weekdays 9–5, handles arrangements for airplane tickets, trains, and hotel reservations. It's not necessary to be a member to receive these services. For members, American Express will replace lost traveler's checks and credit cards. The office has an ATM machine for its cardholders; a commission is charged (the amount depends on the type of card you possess).

Avantix.ru (Russian only) and Pososhok.ru (English page available) are two Internet-based agencies that provide competitive prices for international flights and flights within the CIS.

Intourist, formerly a behemoth Soviet tour company, is now private and can provide you with tickets and reservations, plus any tour you want in Moscow; the company also sets up trips elsewhere in the CIS.

Optima Travel can book air and train tickets, make hotel reservations, and arrange tours of Moscow.

In addition to booking air tickets on international charters and on Transaero and Aeroflot flights in the CIS, VIP Service can make hotel, plane, and train reservations for other CIS destinations. Numerous tours are also available.

🖪 Agencies **American Express** ✉ 33 Usacheva ul., Bldg. 1, Krasnaya Presnya ☎ 495/933-6633 Ⓜ Sportivnaya 🖥 495/933-6632. **Avantix.ru** ✉ 11/28 ul. Shchipok ☎ 495/787-7272 Ⓜ Serpukhovskaya ⊕ www.avantix.ru. **Intourist** ✉ 13/1 Milyutinsky per. ☎ 495/956-8844 ⊕ www.intourist.ru Ⓜ Turgenevskaya ✉ Hotel Kosmos, 150 Prospekt Mira, Northern Outskirts ☎ 495/753-0003 Ⓜ Prospekt Mira. **Optima Travel** ✉ 21/5 Kuznetsky Most, Moscow ☎ 495/926-0391 Ⓜ Kuznetsky Most 🖥 495/928-9837 Ⓜ Kuznetsky Most. **Pososhok.ru** ✉ 13 Komsomolsky pr. ☎ 495/234-8000 Ⓜ Frunzenskaya/Park Kultury ⊕ pososhok.ru. **VIP Service** ✉ 4/3 Myasnitsky proyezd, Office 309 ☎ 495/937-7075 Ⓜ Chistiye Prudy ✉ 4 Zubovsky proyezd, Krasnaya Presnya ☎ 495/247-0047 Ⓜ Park Kultury.

VISITOR INFORMATION

In addition to Moscow City Tourist Office, the service bureaus of all the major hotels offer their guests (and anyone else willing to pay their fees) various tourist services, including help in booking group or individual excursions, making a restaurant reservation, or purchasing theater or ballet tickets. You can also find help (as the hotels themselves often do) from Intourist, today's reincarnation of the old Soviet tourist service or from some of the tour agencies. For the latest on what's happening in Moscow, check the listings in the Friday edition of the *Moscow Times*.

🖪 Tourist Information **Moscow City Tourist Office** ✉ 21/5 Kuznetsky Most, Suite 2-022, Moscow ☎ 495/928-9837 Ⓜ Kuznetsky Most ⊕ www.moscowcity.com.

Moscow Environs
& the Golden Ring

By Paul E. Richardson and Mikhail V. Ivanov

Updated by Oksana Yablokova

THE RIVER VALLEYS EAST AND NORTH of Moscow hold a unique realm you might call Russia's Capital-That-Might-Have-Been—Suzdalia, the region that encompassed the historic centers of Rostov, Vladimir, Suzdal, and Yaroslavl. These small towns, all within easy striking distance of Moscow, witnessed nothing less than the birth of the Russian nation nearly a millennium ago and, consequently, are home to some of the country's most beautiful churches and monasteries, romantic kremlins (fortresses), and famous works of art, such as Andrei Rublyov's frescoes in the cathedral at Vladimir.

Many of these towns and districts have more than 10 centuries of history to share, but their story really begins early in the 12th century, when Prince Yuri Dolgoruky, son of Vladimir Monomakh, the Grand Prince of Kiev, was given control over the northeastern outpost of what was then Kievan Rus' (the early predecessor of modern-day Russia and Ukraine). Dolgoruky established his power and authority, and founded the towns that would become Pereslavl-Zalessky and Kostroma. He also built frontier outposts to guard against his neighbors, including one on the southwest border, called Moscow.

Yuri Dolgoruky's son, Andrei Bogolyubsky, amassed considerable power within Kievan Rus', centered on his inherited lands of Suzdalia. He made Vladimir his capital and built up its churches and monasteries to rival those of Kiev, the capital of Kievan Rus'. In 1169 unhappy with the pattern of dynastic succession in Kiev, Bogolyubsky sent his and allied troops to sack Kiev and placed his son on the throne as grand prince. From that point forward, political and ecclesiastical power began to flow toward the northeastern region of Rus'.

Had not the Mongol invasion intervened a century later in 1237, Vladimir might have continued to grow in power and be the capital of Russia today. But invade the Mongols did, and within three years every town in the region was nearly decimated; the region remained subjugated for more than 200 years. Moscow, meanwhile, with the cunning it's still known for today, slowly rose to prominence by becoming tax (or tribute) collector for the Mongols. Ivan Kalita ("Ivan Moneybags") was a particularly proficient go-between, and, as Mongol power receded in the 14th century, he began gathering together the lands surrounding Moscow, beginning with Vladimir.

The ancient Russian towns north and east of Moscow that make up what is most commonly called the "Golden Ring" seem quite unassuming now in comparison to the sprawling, bustling capital. Before the Mongol invasion, Rostov, Vladimir, Suzdal, and Yaroslavl were the centers of Russian political, cultural, and economic life. Although they may lack some of the amenities you can easily find in Moscow, they have a provincial charm and aura of history that make them an important stop for anyone seeking to become acquainted with Mother Russia.

Exploring Moscow Environs & the Golden Ring

With some exceptions, what you'll be traveling to see are churches and monasteries—the statement-making structures that princes, metropoli-

Be realistic about how long you have to explore and savor these rich, historic towns, allotting time to stop for a meal in a local restaurant or to linger in a historic monastery.

Numbers in the text correspond to numbers in the margin and on the Moscow Environs & the Golden Ring map.

If you have 1 or 2 days

The **Tchaikovsky's House Museum in Klin ❶**, **Leo Tolstoy's Museum in Yasnaya Polyana ❸**, **Sergiev-Posad ❹**, and **Abramtsevo Estate Museum ❺** can all be easily visited as separate day trips from Moscow.

If you have two days to explore the towns of the Golden Ring, drive or take a morning train to **Vladimir ❾**. Explore the town, being sure to take in the Church of the Intercession on the Nerl, then travel on to **Suzdal ❿** and overnight in the beautiful Convent of the Intercession. This will put you right in the thick of things to start exploring Suzdal early the next morning. Return to Moscow via Vladimir late in the day.

Alternatively, take a morning train to **Yaroslavl ❽** and spend the day and night there. The next morning catch a return train on the same route, stopping off in **Rostov ❼** (1½ hours from Yaroslavl) to spend the day before catching a late-afternoon train back to Moscow.

If you have 3 or 4 days

Follow any of the itineraries above. But for the Vladimir and Suzdal trip, devote another full day to Suzdal. For the Yaroslavl and Rostov trip, overnight in **Rostov ❼** and then stop for several hours in **Pereslavl-Zalessky ❻** before returning to Moscow.

tans, and merchants in old Russia built to display their largesse and power. And because most civil and residential buildings until the 18th century were constructed from wood, it turns out that these religious buildings, constructed of stone, have best survived the ravages of time, invading armies, and fire. Today, many are being returned to their original, ecclesiastical purposes, but most are still museums. In either instance, neglect and funding shortages have taken their toll on preservation and restoration efforts, and at times it can be difficult to imagine these historic monuments in their original glory.

A few of the attractions of the Moscow Environs section, such as the Abramtsevo Estate Museum and Sergiev-Posad, can be combined in one visit, but most of the sights of this region will require individual day trips. The towns of the Golden Ring lie on two main routes that most visitors travel as two separate excursions—north of Moscow to Sergiev-Posad, Pereslavl-Zalessky, Rostov, and Yaroslavl; and east of Moscow to Vladimir and Suzdal.

About the Restaurants

Although the tourist traffic to some towns near Moscow helps sustain a sufficient infrastructure, there are still few private restaurants, largely because Russians themselves do not dine out that frequently. The most reliable restaurants are in hotels catering to tourists or, occasionally, in downtown locations near main tourist sights. This is slowly changing, and some of the restaurants outside hotels can be quite cozy. Happily, restaurant prices here are considerably lower than in Moscow.

About the Hotels

None of the towns covered in this section has a long list of lodging options, let alone good, tourist-class hotels. Although basic amenities are not usually a problem, it will be some time before the hotels in these towns catch up with Moscow's two- and three-star hotels. As with restaurants, these hotels' prices are far below Moscow levels.

WHAT IT COSTS In U.S. dollars					
	$$$$	$$$	$$	$	¢
RESTAURANTS	over $25	$18–$25	$12–$18	$6–$12	under $6
HOTELS	over $60	$40–$60	$25–$40	$15–$25	under $15

Restaurant prices are for a main course at dinner. Hotel prices are for two people in a standard double room in high season, excluding tax.

Timing

To see the monasteries, churches, and kremlins of the region to the best advantage you should try to make your visits in spring or summer.

MOSCOW ENVIRONS

Within easy distance of Moscow are several sights of interest, including two monasteries: the New Jerusalem Monastery near Istra and the Troitse-Sergieva Lavra in Sergiev-Posad. Russian-culture buffs may want to explore Tchaikovsky's former home in Klin, Tolstoi's estate in Yasnaya Polyana, and the Abramtsevo Estate Museum, a beacon for Russian artists in the 19th century.

Tchaikovsky's House Museum in Klin
Дом-музей Чайковского в Клину

❶ *84 km (52 mi) northwest of Moscow via Leningradskoye shosse and M10.*

Visiting Tchaikovsky's home in Klin is simply a must for classical-music lovers, despite the town's relatively remote location. Pyotr Tchaikovsky (1840–93) spent a total of eight years in Klin, where he wrote Symphony Pathetique and two of his three ballets, *Sleeping Beauty* and *The Nutcracker.* He resided at a series of addresses, but this house was his last home. It's a typical, wooden residential building of the late 19th century, eclectic in style. It's standout features are the lantern-shaped balcony with stained-glass windows and a tower-shaped roof.

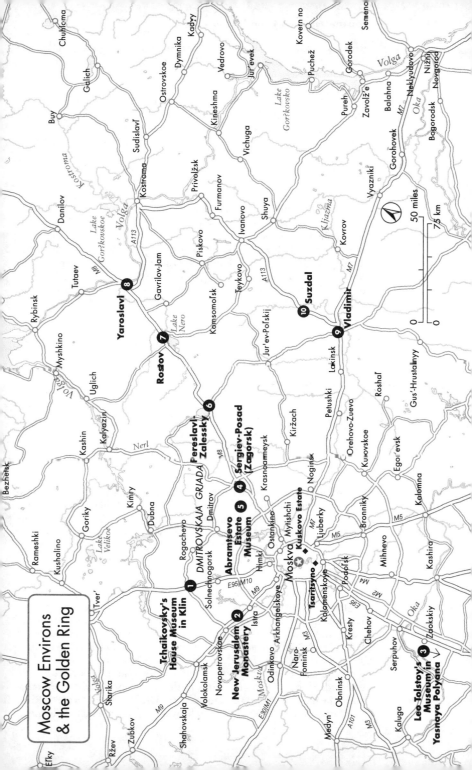

Moscow Environs & the Golden Ring

1 Tchaikovsky's House Museum in Klin

2 New Jerusalem Monastery

3 Leo Tolstoy's Museum in Yasnaya Polyana

4 Sergiev-Posad (Zagorsk)

5 Abramtsevo Estate Museum

6 Pereslavl-Zalessky

7 Rostov

8 Yaroslavl

9 Vladimir

10 Suzdal

50 miles

75 km

Russia's best-known composer departed from this abode on October 7, 1893, for St. Petersburg, where he performed his last concert before his death on November 6 of that year. Less than a year after his death, the composer's brother, Modest Tchaikovsky, transformed the house into a museum. A gifted playwright and translator, Modest also played an outstanding role in preserving his brother's heritage. He preserved the original appearance of the second-floor rooms, and secured personal belongings, photographs, and a unique library of some 2,000 volumes. Some of the original scores, drafts, and letters that Modest collected are now permanently displayed in Klin. The centerpiece of the museum is Tchaikovsky's Becker piano, on which only renowned musicians are permitted to play on special occasions. During World War II the house suffered major damage when the Nazis turned the first floor into a bike garage, and the second-floor rooms into soldiers' barracks. In the late 1940s the museum underwent major renovations, and a brick building with a concert hall was constructed next to the composer's house. The finalists of the annual Tchaikovsky International Competition of Young Musicians (held in May or June) perform in this Soviet-era hall. Additionally, on the anniversary of the composer's birth (May 7) and death (November 6) memorial concerts are held in the hall. Tchaikovsky's music plays continuously in the museum. The museum cafeteria serves a traditional Russian tea service from a samovar. ✉ *48 ul. Tchaikovskovo, Klin* ☎ *224/581–96* 💶 *80R* ✆ *Mon., Tues., Fri.–Sun. 10–6, ticket office closes at 5* ✆ *Closed last Mon. of month.*

New Jerusalem Monastery
Ново-Иерусалимский Монастырь

2 *65 km (40 mi) northwest of Moscow via Volokolamskoye shosse and the M9.*

Far from the crowds, the captivating Russian countryside surrounding the New Jerusalem Monastery (Novoierusalimsky Monastyr) is a marvelous setting for walks and excursions. This is not the most visited locale in Russia, and it's included in the standard offerings of tourist agencies only in summer. If you can't book a tour and are feeling adventurous, you could try an excursion on the commuter train. The monastery is near the town of Istra, at a bend in the river of the same name. Trains leave from Riga Station and take about an hour and a half. Be sure to pack your lunch—the best you'll find in Istra is an occasional cafeteria or outdoor café.

The monastery was founded in 1652 by Nikon (1605–81), patriarch of the Russian Orthodox Church. It lies on exactly the same longitude as Jerusalem, and its main cathedral, **Voskresensky Sobor** (Resurrection Cathedral), is modeled after the Church of the Holy Sepulchre in Jerusalem. Nikon's objective in re-creating the original Jerusalem in Russia was to glorify the power of the Russian Orthodox Church and at the same time elevate his own position as its head. It was Nikon who initiated the great church reforms in the 17th century that eventually led to the *raskol* (schism) that launched the Old Believer sects of the Russian Orthodox faith. As a reformer he was progressive and enlightened, but his lust for power was his eventual undoing. In 1658, before the monastery was even finished, the patriarch quarreled with Tsar Alexei Mikhailovich over Nikon's claim that the Church was ultimately superior to the State. Nikon was ultimately defrocked and banished to far-away Ferapontov Monastery, in the Vologda region, some 400 km (246 mi) north of Moscow. He died in virtual exile in 1681, and was then buried in the monastery that was supposed to have glorified his power. You can find his crypt in the Church of St. John the Baptist, which is actually inside the Resurrection Cathedral. Ironically, the same church commission that defrocked Patriarch Nikon later voted to institute his reforms. ⊠ *Near Istra* 🗺 *Monastery grounds free; small fees to exhibits* ☎ *8231/46549* ⊙ *Tues.–Sun. 10–4* ⊙ *Closed last Fri. of month.*

Leo Tolstoy's Museum in Yasnaya Polyana
Музей Льва Толстого в Ясной Поляне

❸ *190 km (118 mi) south of Moscow via Simferopolskoye shosse and M2.*

More than 50 years of Leo Tolstoy's life (1828–1910) passed at Yasnaya Polyana where he was born, wrote his most significant works, undertook social experiments, and was buried. Here he freed his serfs and taught peasant children at a school that he opened, attempting to transfer his ideal of a perfect world of universal equality to reality. Disappointed with his way of life and nobleman status, he decided at the age of 82 to depart from home forever, venturing out shortly before his death in October 1910.

In his home's upstairs dining room, you're greeted by numerous portraits of the Tolstoy aristocratic dynasty. Under their eyes Tolstoy held significant social discussions with his family and his many visitors. Next door is the study where Tolstoy wrote *Anna Karenina* and *War and Peace* at his father's Persian desk. Tolstoy seemed to prefer moving around his house to work on different books, however: another room downstairs was also used as a study. This is usually the last room on a visit to the main house. In November 1910 the writer's body lay here in state as some 5,000 mourners passed to pay their last respects.

The far wing of the building houses a literary museum dedicated to Tolstoy's writing career. Drawings and prints produced by Tolstoy's contemporaries, derived from the plots and characters of his novels, as well as Tolstoy's original manuscripts are displayed in the six halls. A path from the main house into the forest leads to Tolstoy's simple, unadorned grave. On the edge of a ravine in the Stary Zakaz forest, the site was a favorite place of Tolstoy and is now a popular pilgrimage destination for wedding parties. The walk to the grave takes about 20 minutes.

The estate-turned-museum is run by Tolstoy's great-great-grandson Vladimir Tolstoy, who is striving to turn it into a major cultural center. His concept is to purge the great author's home of modern technology (not that there's much modern technology there now) and turn the area back into a working 19th-century estate. Around this "living museum," however, Tolstoy plans to construct a tourist complex with a hotel, restaurants, and parking lots—none of which now exist.

A visit to the estate requires the whole day, because the trip from Moscow takes 2½ to 3 hours. If you plan to explore the grounds of Yasnaya Polyana independently you should strive to arrive there as early in the morning as possible, especially on Friday and weekends, to avoid busloads of tourists and crowds of newlyweds. A guided tour of the museums and the grounds, however, does give a better idea of all the important sights and Tolstoy's favorite spots. The cafeteria and the bookstore are directly opposite the main entrance.

Yasnaya Polyana is reached through the industrial town of Tula, some 170 km (105 mi) south of Moscow along Simferopolskoye shosse. After you pass through Tula's southern outskirts, Tolstoy's estate, only 14 km (9 mi) away, is easy to find thanks to clear signs in Russian and English; the roads, however, are notoriously bad. You can also get to Tula by commuter train from Moscow's Kursk Station; once in Tula, take a bus traveling to Shchyokino from the station at prospekt Lenina. ⊠ *Yasnaya Polyana, Near Tula* ☎ *0872/33–9118 or 0872/33–9832* ⊕ *www. yasnayapolyana.ru* ✉ *25R; foreign-language guided tours 200R* ⊙ *Tues.–Sun. 10–4* ⊙ *Closed last Wed. of month.*

Where to Stay & Eat

$–$$ ✕ **Voronka cafe.** Only 1½ km (1 mi) from Yasnaya Polyana on the way to Tula, Voronka is a good way to end a trip to Tolstoy's estate. The menu has an extensive selection of Russian dishes, including *solyanka* (a sharp-tasting soup of vegetables and meat or fish), borscht, *shashlyk* (kebabs), blini, and *ikra* (caviar). ⊠ *152 Orlovskoye shosse* ☎ *0872/38–3327* ⊟ *No credit cards.*

$$$$ ⊞ **Premiera.** The first western-style hotel in Tula opened in May 2004. The petite hotel, close to the center, has seven rooms and two suites. Air-conditioned rooms are clean and spacious, with rainbowlike striped curtains that match the bedspreads. Bathrooms have hair dryers and the huge wall mirrors gleam. ⊠ *3, ul. Maksimovskovo, Tula, 630114* ☎ *0872/49–0262 or 0872/49–9934* ⊕ *www.premieratula.ru* ⤷ *7 rooms, 2 suites* ⚭ *Bar, billiards, sauna* ⊟ *AE, MC, V.*

Sergiev-Posad (Zagorsk)
Сергиев Посад (Загорск)

❹ *75 km (47 mi) northeast of Moscow via Yaroslavskoye shosse and the*
Fodor'sChoice *M8.*
★

Sergiev-Posad is a comfortable and popular day trip from Moscow. The town's chief attraction is the Troitse-Sergieva Lavra, which for 500 years has been the most important center of pilgrimage in Russia and remains one of the most beautiful of all monasteries—the fairy-tale gold and azure onion domes of its Cathedral of the Assumption are among the most photographed in the country. Until 1930 the town was known as Sergiev, after the monastery's founder, and in 1991 it was officially renamed Sergiev-Posad. But the Soviet name of Zagorsk—in honor of a Bolshevik who was assassinated in 1919—has stuck, and you're as likely to hear the town and the monastery itself called one as the other.

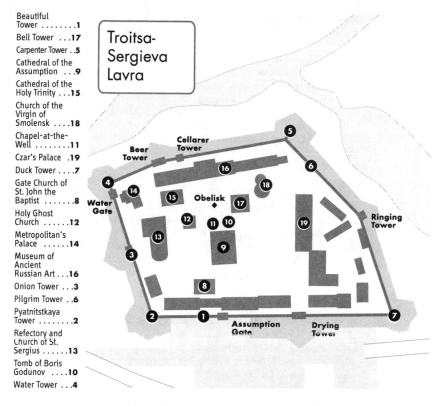

Beautiful
Tower 1

Bell Tower . . .17

Carpenter Tower . .5

Cathedral of the
Assumption . . .9

Cathedral of the
Holy Trinity . . .15

Church of the
Virgin of
Smolensk 18

Chapel-at-the-
Well 11

Czar's Palace .19

Duck Tower 7

Gate Church of
St. John the
Baptist 8

Holy Ghost
Church 12

Metropolitan's
Palace 14

Museum of
Ancient
Russian Art . . .16

Onion Tower . . .3

Pilgrim Tower . .6

Pyatnitstkaya
Tower 2

Refectory and
Church of St.
Sergius 13

Tomb of Boris
Godunov 10

Water Tower . . .4

The ride to Sergiev-Posad takes you through a lovely stretch of Russian countryside, dotted with colorful wooden cottages. As you approach the town, you see the sad and monolithic apartment buildings of the modern era. Then, peeking out above the hills, the monastery's golden cupolas and soft-blue bell tower come into view.

The best way to visit the town is to join an organized tour, because it's a full-day affair out of Moscow. The cost usually includes lunch in addition to a guided tour and transportation. You can also visit on your own by taking the commuter train from Moscow's Yaroslavsky Station. The ride takes about two hours. This is much less expensive than an organized tour, but far from hassle-free. If you choose this alternative, be sure to pack your own lunch, because Sergiev-Posad's only full-fledged restaurant fills up fast with prebooked tourist groups, especially in summer. Be sure to dress appropriately for your visit to the functioning monastery: men are expected to remove their hats, and women are required to wear below-knee-length skirts or slacks (*never* shorts) and bring something to cover their heads.

The heart of Holy Russia until 1920 (when the Bolsheviks closed down most monasteries and shipped many monks to Siberia), the **Trinity**

Monastery of St. Sergius (Troitse-Sergieva Lavra) was founded in 1340 by Sergius of Radonezh (1314–92), who would later become Russia's patron saint. The site rapidly became the nucleus of a small medieval settlement, and in 1550 the imposing white walls were built to enclose the complex of buildings, whose towers and gilded domes make it a smaller, but still spectacular, version of Moscow's Kremlin. The monastery was a Russian stronghold during the Time of Troubles (the Polish assault on Moscow in the early 17th century), and, less than a century later, Peter the Great (1672–1725) took refuge here during a bloody revolt of the *streltsy* (Russian militia), which took the lives of some of his closest relatives and advisers. After the Bolshevik Revolution, the monastery was closed and turned into a museum. During World War II, however, in an attempt to mobilize the country and stir up patriotism, the Soviet government gained the support of the Orthodox Church by returning to religious purposes some of the Church property that had been confiscated earlier, including the Trinity Monastery of St. Sergius. Today the churches are again open for worship, and there's a flourishing theological college here. Until the reopening in 1988 of the Danilovsky (St. Daniel) Monastery in Moscow, this monastery was the residence of the patriarch and administrative center of the Russian Orthodox Church.

You enter the monastery through the archway of the **Gate Church of St. John the Baptist,** which was erected in the late 17th century and is decorated with frescoes telling the life story of St. Sergius. One of the most important historic events in his life occurred prior to 1380, when the decisive Russian victory in the Battle of Kulikovo led to the end of Mongol rule in Russia. Before leading his troops off to battle, Prince Dmitri Donskoy sought the blessing of the peace-loving monk Sergius, a move that is generally thought to have greatly aided the Russian victory.

Although all of the monastery's cathedrals vie for your attention, the dominating structure is the massive, blue-domed, and gold-starred **Cathedral of the Assumption** (Uspensky Sobor) in the center. Built between 1554 and 1585 with money donated by Tsar Ivan the Terrible (1530–84)—purportedly in an attempt to atone for killing his own son in a fit of rage—it was modeled after the Kremlin's Uspensky Sobor. Its interior contains frescoes and an 18th-century iconostasis. Among the artists to work on it was Simon Ushakov, a well-known icon painter from Moscow. The cathedral is open for morning services.

The small building just outside the Cathedral of the Assumption (near the northwest corner) is the **tomb of Boris Godunov and his family.** Boris Godunov, who ruled as regent after Ivan the Terrible's death, died suddenly in 1605 of natural causes. This was during the Polish attack on Moscow led by the False Dmitri, the first of many impostors to claim he was the son of Ivan. The death of Godunov facilitated the invaders' victory, after which his family was promptly murdered. This explains why Godunov was not bestowed the honor of burial in the Kremlin normally granted to tsars.

Opposite Boris Godunov's tomb is a tiny and colorful chapel, the **Chapel-at-the-Well,** built in 1644 above a fountain that is said to work miracles. According to legend, the spring here appeared during the Polish Siege (1608–10), when the monastery bravely held out for 16 months against the foreign invaders (this time led by the second False Dmitri). You can make a wish by washing your face and hands in its charmed waters. Towering 285 feet next to the chapel is the five-tiered baroque belfry. It was built in the 18th century to a design by the master of St. Petersburg baroque, Bartolomeo Rastrelli.

Along the southern wall of the monastery, to your far left as you enter, is the 17th-century **Refectory and Church of St. Sergius.** The church is at the eastern end, topped by a single gilt dome. The long building of the refectory, whose colorful facade adds to the vivid richness of the monastery's architecture, is where, in times past, pilgrims from near and far gathered to eat on feast days. The pink building just beyond the refectory is the metropolitan's residence.

Across the path from the residence is the white-stone **Cathedral of the Holy Trinity** (Troitsky Sobor), built in the 15th century over the tomb of St. Sergius. Over the centuries it has received many precious gifts from the powerful and wealthy rulers who have made the pilgrimage to the church of Russia's patron saint. The icons inside were created by famous master Andrei Rublyov and one of his disciples, Danil Chorny. Rublyov's celebrated *Holy Trinity,* now on display at the Tretyakov Gallery in Moscow, originally hung here; the church's version is a copy. The interior's beauty is mainly due to its 17th-century gilded iconostasis (which separates the sanctuary from the altar and body of the church). The upper tier of the church was once used by monks as a manuscript library. A continual service in memoriam to St. Sergius is held all day, every day.

The vestry, the building behind the Cathedral of the Holy Trinity, houses the monastery's **Museum of Ancient Russian Art.** It's often closed for no apparent reason or open only to groups, which is yet another reason to visit Sergiev-Posad on a guided tour. The museum contains a spectacular collection of gifts presented to the monastery over the centuries. On display are precious jewels, jewel-encrusted embroideries, chalices, and censers. Next door to the vestry are two more museums, which are open to individual tourists. The first museum contains icons and icon covers, portrait art, and furniture. The other museum (on the second floor) is devoted to Russian folk art, with wooden items, toys, porcelain, and jewelry. There's also a gift shop here. ☎ 254/45–334 ⌨ 60R ☉ *Daily 10–5.*

The **Toy Museum** (Muzey Igrushki) is evidence of Sergiev-Posad's claim to fame as a center for toy making. The world's first *matryoshka* (the familiar colorful, wooden nesting doll) was designed here at the beginning of the 20th century, and most of the matryoshkas you see for sale in Moscow and St. Petersburg are made in Sergiev-Posad. The museum is rarely included on organized tours, but it's within walking distance of the monastery. With a collection of toys that amused, educated, and illuminated the lives of Russian children for generations, the museum is well worth an hour of your time, even if your interest is only casual. ✉ *136 pr. Krasnoy Armii* ☎ *254/44–101* ⌨ *90R* ☉ *Wed.–Sun. 10–5.*

Where to Stay & Eat

$–$$$ ✕ **Zolotoye Koltso.** The Golden Ring is considered the best restaurant in town. It caters to tour groups and has a good service record for preparing basic Russian fare: a selection of salads, soups, and (mostly) meat dishes.   ✉ *121 ul. Krasnoy Armii* ☎ *254/41–517* ▭ *No credit cards.*

$–$$ ✕ **Russky Dvorik.** A pleasant downtown café popular with tourist groups, the Russky Dvorik is right across from the Lavra. Be prepared for slow service.   ✉ *134 ul. Krasnoy Armii* ☎ *254/45–114* ▭ *AE, MC, V.*

$ 🏨 **Hotel Aristorkrat.** This newly built, redbrick hotel is in the town center on Blinnaya Gora (Pancake Hill), a five-minute walk from the Lavra. Cozy guest rooms that overlook the Lavra have all the amenities, such as televisions and refrigerators. Aristokrat restaurant serves traditional Russian food and has a great view as well. ✉ *1A ul. Sergiyevskaya, 141300* ☎ *254/725–94 or 254/480–21* 📞 *18 rooms* ↺ *Restaurant, refrigerators, pool, sauna* ▭ *No credit cards.*

Abramtsevo Estate Museum
Музей-усадьба Абрамцево

❺   *61 km (38 mi) northeast of Moscow via Yaroslavskoye shosse and the M8.*

The 18th-century, wooden Abramtsevo estate served as the center of Russia's cultural life in two different periods of the 19th century. In 1918 it was nationalized and turned into a museum. Its guest list from different years includes writers Nikolai Gogol and Ivan Turgenev, opera singer Fyodor Chaliapin, and theater director Konstantin Stanislavsky. The artists Valentin Serov, Mikhail Vrubel, Ilya Repin, Viktor Vasnetsov, and Vasily Polenov were just a few of the luminaries who frequented the estate. It's easier to name those cultural figures of the 19th and early 20th centuries who have not visited Abramtsevo than all of those who have.

Until 1870 Abramtsevo belonged to Sergei Aksakov, a Slavophile who advocated the exportation of Orthodox Christianity to the West. A very religious man, Aksakov chose Abramtsevo as his residence because it was close to the Trinity Monastery of St. Sergius. He opened his home to sympathetic writers and intellectuals of the 1840s. Nowadays only two rooms in the main house—Aksakov's dining room and study with his memorabilia—recall his presence. The rest of the house is dedicated to luminous Abramtsevo guests and the next (and final) private owner.

After Aksakov's death, railway tycoon Savva Mamontov purchased the estate in 1870 and turned it into an artists' colony. Here Mamontov and a community of resident artists tried to revive traditional Russian arts, crafts, and architecture to stimulate interest in Russian culture and make arts more accessible to the people.

In the 1880s half a dozen resident artists participated in the construction of the prettiest structure on Abramtsevo's grounds, the diminutive **Tserkov Ikony Spasa Nerukotvornovo** (Church of the Icon of the Savior Not Made by Hands). The idea to build a church was born when a flood prevented the local community from attending the festive Easter church service. The artist Polenov chose a 12th-century church outside Novgorod as a model. He and fellow artists Repin and Nesterov painted the gilt iconostasis; Vasnetsov laid the mosaic floor he had designed in the shape of a giant blooming flower. Some of the resident artists created their finest works in Abramtsevo. Serov painted his *Girl with Peaches,* an 1870 portrait of Mamontov's daughter, Vera, which now decorates Mamontov's dining room. Vasnetsov worked on his 1898 *Bogatyri* (Russian epic heroes) in Abramtsevo as well. Other structures on Abramtsevo's grounds include the wooden Izbushka Na Kuryikh Nozhkakh (House on Chicken Legs), the residence of the witch Baba-Yaga from Russian fairy tales; Polenov's dacha; and an artists' workshop. In 1889 the troubled artist Mikhail Vrubel joined the Abramtsevo colony to participate in the ceramics workshop, where his provocative grotesque designs are still evident in the tile stoves, ceramic inlay, and furniture.

The estate can easily be visited on the way back from Sergiev-Posad. For Russian art aficionados, however, it may be worth a single one-day trip. You can visit the estate on a tour or head there yourself by commuter train; take the train from Yaroslavsky Station to Sergiev-Posad or Alexandrov and get off at the Abramtsevo station. ✉ *Sergiev-Posad district, Abramtsevo station* ☎ *8254/306–68 or 8254/302–78* 💰 *90R* 🕙 *Wed.–Sun. 10–6* 🕙 *Closed last Thurs. of month.*

Where to Eat

$$$–$$$$ ✕ **Galereya.** The extensive menu of traditional Russian food served at this restaurant, which is right across the street from the central gate of the estate, makes it a solid lunch option. If you don't feel like dining in, order a few *pirozhki* (small pies of cabbage, apple, or potatoes) to go. They're particularly delicious with *mors,* a traditional Russian cranberry drink. ✉ *3 Muzeynaya ul.* ☎ *8254/350–53* 💳 *No credit cards.*

THE NORTHERN GOLDEN RING

Within this historic region northeast of Moscow are ancient towns, venerable churches, and the magnificent Rostov kremlin and Monastery of St. Ipaty. There are plenty of guided-tour options, ranging from one-day outings to 1,000-km (620-mi) bus tours. And if you want to visit this region on your own, you're in luck: these towns are tourist-friendly, even if the transition to the market economy has them straining to keep their streets clean and museums open.

Pereslavl-Zalessky
Переславль-Залесский

 127 km (79 mi) northeast of Moscow via the M8.

Pereslavl-Zalessky was founded in 1157 by Yuri Dolgoruky for two very important reasons. The first was political: he sought to draw parallels between the power base he was building in northeast Rus' and the center of power in Kiev, to the southeast. So he named this town Pereyaslavl (meaning "to achieve glory"; the "ya" was later dropped) after a town outside of Kiev, and he named the river alongside the town Trubezh, just as in the Kievan Pereyaslavl. The "Zalessky" appellation, added in the 15th century, means "beyond the forests" and was used to distinguish the town from many other Pereyaslavls (not least the one near Kiev).

The second reason was economic. The location of the town on the southern shore of Lake Pleshcheyevo was ideal for defending the western approaches to vital trade routes along the Nerl River to the Klyazma, Oka, and Volga rivers. The topography only accentuates this role. From the hills, the impressive Danilovsky and Goritsky monasteries peer down on the low wooden and stone buildings of town.

As the birthplace of Alexander Nevsky (1220–63), Pereslavl-Zalessky has yet another claim to fame. Nevsky entered the pantheon of Russia's great heroes when, as Prince of Novgorod, he beat back invading Swedes in 1240 at the Battle of the Neva (thus his last name). For his victory, the Mongol Khan awarded Nevsky the title of Grand Prince of Vladimir. There's a small church in town honoring Nevsky.

Note that the town can be reached by bus or car, but not by train.

The fortresslike **Goritsky Monastyr,** high on a hill south of the town center, was founded in the first half of the 14th century and is now an art and history museum. It displays ancient manuscripts and books found in this area, jewelry, and sculptures. An impressive collection of icons includes the 15th-century treasure, *Peter and Paul Apostles,* the oldest icon in the region, and a small collection of paintings with works of Konstantin Korovin. Outside the entrance to the museum is a proud monument to the T-34 tank, which was the tank that saved Russia from the Germans in World War II. Inside is the large Uspensky Sobor (Cathedral of the Assumption), built in 1544. ☎ *08535/381-00* 🖾 *100R* ⊙ *Wed.–Mon. 10–4:30* ⊙ *Closed last Mon. of month.*

In the center of town, along Sovetskaya ulitsa, is the 12th-century limestone **Cathedral of the Transfiguration** (Spaso-Preobrazhensky Sobor). Construction began on this church in the same year as the Church of Saints Boris and Gleb in Kideksha, near Suzdal, making it one of the oldest stone buildings standing in Russia. ⊠ *Sovetskaya ul.* ☎ *No phone* 🖾 *Free* ⊙ *May–Oct., Wed.–Mon. 10–6.*

Pereslavl-Zalessky was the birthplace of the Russian navy. The **Botik museum,** a few miles outside of town, houses the only remaining boat of the more than 100 Peter the Great built for the fleet he sailed on Lake Pleshcheyevo. The *botik,* a small sailboat, usually single-mast, is often called the grandfather of the Russian fleet. The museum also displays several naval guns, a triumphal arch, and a monument to Peter the Great. To get to the museum (3 km [2 mi] away), you take a narrow-gauge train running south and west along the lake from the bus station, which is on ulitsa Kardovskovo, just below the Goritsky Monastery. It departs the bus station at 9 AM, 1 PM, and 4:30 PM and returns from the museum at 12:30 PM, 4 PM, and 8:30 PM. ⊠ *Near Veslevo village* ☎ *08535/ 22–788* 🖾 *16R, 180R for guided tours in English* ⊙ *Tues.–Sun. 10–5* ⊙ *Closed last Thurs. of each month.*

Where to Stay & Eat

$$ ✕⊞ **Botik Tourist Complex.** A café and six pretty wooden houses that accommodate two people each are down the path from the Botik museum on the bank of Pleshcheyevo Lake. Houses need to be booked in advance. Besides accommodation, the complex also has a sauna, beach, and pub. The Botik Café, designed in the shape of a ship, serves moderately priced traditional Russian cuisine. ⊠ *Near Veslevo village, 152020* ☎ *08535/98–085* 🖷 *08535/98–865* 🍴 *6 houses* ⚒ *Café, sauna, beach, pub* ⊟ *No credit cards.*

$$ ✕⊞ **Hotel Pereslavl.** The Pereslavl is a Soviet-style provincial hotel, redeemed by its convenient downtown address. Bar Rita ($), which serves Russian food, has a staff that prides itself on service—the owner, as it turns out, learned quite a few things on his trips to the United States. The Russian flavored-vodkas, perhaps *pertsovka* (hot pepper) or *zubrovka* (bison grass), are worth sampling. ⊠ *27 Rostovskaya ul., 152020* ☎ *08535/21–788 hotel, 08535/21–633 restaurant* 🍴 *59 rooms* ⚒ *Restaurant, bar* ⊟ *No credit cards.*

$$$$ ⊞ **Hotel Zapadnaya.** On the bank of the Trubezh River, this hotel has a superb, picturesque location in the historical center of town. Rooms are clean and spacious, and the staff is friendly. ⊠ *1a Pleshcheyevskaya ul., 152020* ☎ *08535/34–378 or 08535/34–380* 🍴 *11 rooms* ⚒ *Restaurant, cable TV, in-room data ports* ⊟ *No credit cards.*

Rostov

Ростов

❼ *225 km (140 mi) northeast of Moscow via the M8, 58 km (36 mi) southwest of Yaroslavl.*

Rostov, also known as Rostov-Veliky ("the Great") so as not to confuse it with Rostov-on-the-Don, is one of the oldest towns in Russia. Founded even before Riurik, a semilegendary Viking prince, came to rule Russia in the 9th century, Rostov is first mentioned in historical chronicles in 862. It became an independent principality at the beginning of the 13th century and soon became one of the most prosperous and influential political centers of ancient Rus. However, the city was destroyed when the Mongols invaded in 1238. In the 15th century Rostov ultimately lost its political independence but retained its influence as a major religious center. It became the seat of the metropolitan in the late 16th century.

Fodor'sChoice ★ The small town, with a population of 36,000, is beautifully situated on the edge of Lake Nero, with earthen ramparts and radial streets. At the center of Rostov is the incomparable **Rostov kremlin,** a fortress with 6-foot-thick white-stone walls and 11 circular towers topped with wood-shingled cupolas. The kremlin dates from 1631, but it was built to its current glory between 1670 and 1690 by Rostov Metropolitan Jonah. Its main purpose was to serve as court and residence for the metropolitan, though Jonah saw himself as creating an ideal type of self-enclosed city focused on spiritual matters. As such, it was Russia's first planned city.

The huge, blue-domed **Cathedral of the Assumption** (Uspensky Sobor) stands just outside the walls of the kremlin—it was built about a century before. Inside are frescoes dating to 1675. But the truly memorable site is the adjacent four-towered **belfry**. The famous 13 bells of Rostov chime on the half hour and full hour and can play four tunes. It's said that the largest of the bells, which weighs 32 tons and is named Sysoi, for Jonah's father, can be heard from 19 km (12 mi) away.

You enter the kremlin through the richly decorated northern entrance, past the **Gate Church of the Resurrection** (Nadvratnaya Voskresenskaya Tserkov). Well-groomed pathways and a pleasant, tree-lined pond give the grounds a feeling of orderly solace. Just to the right of the entrance into the kremlin is the **Church of the Mother of God Hodegetria** (Tserkov Bogomateri Odigitrii), whose faceted baroque exterior rises to a single onion dome.

The **Church of John the Theologian** (Tserkov Ioanna Bogoslova), another gate church, is on the west side of the kremlin. Adjacent to this church is the two-story **Red Palace** (Krasnaya Palata), once known as the "Chamber for Great Sovereigns." Built first for Ivan the Terrible for his visits to the town, it was later used by Peter the Great and Catherine the Great. It's now a hotel known as the International Youth Tourism Center.

Adjacent is the **White Palace** (Belaya Palata; ☎ No phone 🎫 15R ⊙ May–Oct. 10–5)—the metropolitan's residence—most notable for its large hall (3,000 square feet) supported by a single column. Connected to the residence is the private church of the metropolitan, the Church of the Savior on the Stores, which was built over a food-storage shelter. This church has the most beautiful wall paintings in the entire complex, as well as gilded columns and handsome brass doors. The metropolitan's residence now houses a museum of icons and Rostov enamel (*finift*), a craft the town is famous for throughout Russia. The southern portion of the kremlin features the tall **Church of Grigory the Theologian** (Tserkov Grigoria Bogoslova). ☎ 08536/61–717 ⊕ *www. rostmuseum.ru* 🎫 *5R, plus small fees for individual churches and palaces inside kremlin* ⊙ *Daily 10–5, except Jan. 1. Churches: May–Oct., daily 10–5.*

On your way out of the kremlin complex, be sure to explore the shop arcade called **Torgoviye Ryady** (trade rows), across the square from Uspensky Sobor. In the early 19th century, after Rostov had lost its metropolitanate to nearby Yaroslavl, it became an extremely important trading center. Rostov's annual market was the third largest in Russia.

Along the lakefront and southwest of the kremlin is the rather eclectic **Yakovlevsky (Jacob) Monastery.** Dominating the ensemble is the huge, Romanesque Dmitriyev Church, crowned by a large spherical central dome and four smaller corner domes. The monastery was founded in 1389. Take the guided tour for access to the premises of the working monastery. ☎ 08536/743–69 🎫 *Monastery grounds free, guided tours 150R* ⊙ *Daily 9–5.*

The oldest monastery in Russia, **Avraamiyev (Abraham) Monastery** was founded at the end of the 11th century. Interestingly, it was erected on the site of a former pagan temple to Veles, god of cattle. The five-domed Epiphany Cathedral in the monastery complex dates from 1553 and is the oldest standing building in Rostov. The nuns' cloister, which is still working, is on the lakefront, northeast of the kremlin. ☎ *08536/637– 12 or 08536/740–05* ✉ *Free* ☉ *Daily 9–5.*

Where to Stay & Eat

$ ✗ **Krasnaya Palata.** Either a glorified cafeteria or site of provincial kremlin style, the large, single hall of this eatery within the kremlin brings those visiting the sights of historic Rostov together. ✉ *Rostov kremlin* ☎ *08536/31–717* ▭ *No credit cards.*

$ ✗ **Teremok.** Borscht, solyanka, and blini with caviar are among the good Russian dishes served at this cozy restaurant in front of the kremlin. ✉ *9 ul. Moravskovo* ☎ *08536/31–648* ▭ *No credit cards.*

$$$ ⊞ **Dom na Pogrebakh.** If you've ever wanted to stay overnight in a kremlin, here's your chance. Built over the food stores or *pogreba* of the kremlin, this modern hotel is in a two-story building of stone and wood. Although a bit Soviet in style and presentation, the wooden-wall rooms of varying sizes do have all the basic amenities. The hotel's great advantage is location as it allows you the privilege of wandering the grounds of the kremlin at night, though you should not be too loud. ✉ *Rostov kremlin, in Red Palace* ☎ *08536/61–244* 🖷 *08536/61–502* ⊕ *www.rostmuseum.ru/hotel/hotel.html* ⤶ *13 rooms with shared bath* ⌂ *Restaurant* ▭ *No credit cards.*

Yaroslavl

Ярославль

❽ *282 km (175 mi) northeast of Moscow on the M8.*

Yaroslavl has a very storied history, beginning with an apocryphal founding. It's said that local inhabitants set loose a bear to chase away Prince Yaroslav the Wise (978–1054). Yaroslav wrestled and killed the bear and founded the town on the spot. If true, these events happened early in the 11th century; Yaroslav decreed the town's founding as a fortress on the Volga in 1010. About 600 years later, in 1612, during the Time of Troubles, the town was the center of national resistance against the invading Poles, under the leadership of Kuzma Minin and Dmitri Pozharsky.

The town rests at the confluence of the Volga and Kotorosl rivers, which made it a major commercial center from the 13th century until 1937, when the Moscow-Volga canal was completed, allowing river traffic to proceed directly to the capital. This commercial heritage bequeathed the city a rich legacy that offers a glimpse of some of the finest church architecture in Russia.

In the town center, proceed northwest along Pervomaiskaya ulitsa, a favorite pedestrian area for locals that follows the semicircular path of the town's former earthen ramparts. Peruse the impressive, colonnaded **trade rows** and walk on to the Znamenskaya watchtower, which in the middle of the 17th century marked the western edge of the town—another watchtower stands on the Volga embankment. The yellow building directly across the square is the **Volkov Theater.** The theater and square are named for Fyodor Volkov, who founded Russia's first professional drama theater here in 1750—the theater was the first to stage *Hamlet* in Russia. Continue along Pervomaiskaya and it will take you to the banks of the Volga, which is 1 km (½ mi) wide at this point. Look for the monument to the great Russian poet Nikolai Nekrasov, who came from nearby Karabikha.

The mid-17th-century **Church of Elijah the Prophet** (Tserkov Ilyi Proroka) stands at the center of town on Sovetskaya Ploshchad (Soviet Square), some say on the site of Yaroslav's alleged wrestling match with the bear (though a monument down by the Volga commemorates the spot of the town's founding). Its tall, octagonal belfry and faceted green onion domes make the church the focal point of the town. Inside the ornamental church are some of the best-preserved frescoes (1680) by Gury Nikitin and Sila Savin, whose works also adorn Moscow Kremlin cathedrals, as well as churches throughout the region. The frescoes depict scenes from the Gospels and the life of Elijah and his disciple Elisha. ✉ *22 Sovetskaya pl.* ☎ *0852/3040–72* 🎟 *60R* 🕑 *Apr.–Oct., daily 10–1 and 2–6.*

The **Monastery of the Transfiguration of the Savior** (Spaso-Preobrazhensky Monastyr), surrounded by white, 10-foot-thick walls, was the site of northern Russia's first school of higher education, dating to the 13th century. It houses several magnificent churches and is where Ivan the Terrible took refuge in 1571, when the Mongols were threatening Moscow. Dating to 1516, the **Holy Gates** entrance to the monastery, on the side facing the Kotorosl River, is the oldest extant structure in the compound. A six-story **belfry** rises high above the round-domed Cathedral of the Transfiguration of the Savior, which was under restoration at this writing. Climb to the top of the belfry for a panoramic view of the city. The clock in the belfry hung in the famous Spasskaya Tower of Moscow Kremlin until 1624, when it was purchased by the merchants of Yaroslavl. ✉ *25 Bogoyavlenskaya pl.* ☎ *0852/3292–40* 🎟 *Free, small fee for individual museums within monastery* 🕑 *Tues.–Sun. 10–5* 🕑 *Closed 1st Wed. of month.*

A **statue of Yaroslav the Wise,** unveiled in 1993 by Russian president Boris Yeltsin and Ukrainian president Leonid Kravchuk, stands not far from the monastery. Yaroslav is depicted holding a piece of the kremlin and staring off in the direction of Moscow. To see the statue, walk away from the river down ulitsa Nakhimsona toward the monastery.

The large, redbrick, blue-cupola **Church of the Epiphany** (Tserkov Bogoyavleniya) is renowned for its fine proportions, enhanced by splendid decorative ceramic tiles and unusually tall windows. Inside are eight levels of wall paintings in the realistic style that began to hold sway in the late 1600s. The church is directly west of the Monastery of the Transfiguration of the Savior. ✉ *Bogoyavlenskaya pl.* ☎ *0852/3034–29 or 0852/7256–23* 🎟 *Free* 🕑 *Wed.–Mon. 10–1 and 2–5.*

The 100-foot-tall **"candle of Yaroslavl"** is actually a belfry for two churches, Ioann Zlatoust (St. John Chrysostom, 1649) and the miniature Tserkov Vladimirskoi Bogomateri (Church of the Vladimir Virgin,

1678). The former is a larger summer church, ornately decorated with colorful tiles; the latter is the more modest and easy-to-heat winter church. From the Monastery of the Transfiguration of the Savior, it's a 1-km (½-mi) walk (or two stops on Bus 4) across the bridge and along the mouth of the Kotorosl to the churches and belfry.

Although it looks as though it's made from wood, the 17th-century five-domed **Church of St. John the Baptist** (Tserkov Ioanna Predtechi) is actually fashioned from carved red brick. The church is on the same side of the Kotorosl River as the candle of Yaroslavl, but it's west of the bridge by about 1 km (½ mi). ⊠ *69 Kotoroslnaya nab.* ☎ *No phone.*

Where to Stay & Eat

$$ ✕ **Golden Bear Café.** In this pleasant café you'll find tasty Russian-style cooking, good service, and a modern interior. If the *salat* (salad) selection doesn't appeal, try the *buterbrod* (open-faced sandwich), a dependable choice. ⊠ *3 Pervomaiskaya ul.* ☎ *0852/328–532* ▭ *No credit cards.*

$ ✕ **Premiera.** St. Petersburg–brewed Baltika beer accompanies the moderately priced traditional Russian dishes (main courses cost $6 to $11) served at this café right behind the Volkov Theater. ⊠ *5 Pervomaiskaya ul.* ☎ *0852/728–601* ▭ *No credit cards.*

$$$ ✕▭ **Yubileynaya.** Located near the monastery, the Yubileynaya overlooks the Kotorosl River. The hotel restaurant's European-style cuisine is a nice plus. ⊠ *11a Kotoroslnaya nab., 150000* ☎ *0852/309–259* ⟳ *180 rooms* ⌂ *Restaurant, bar, meeting room* ▭ *No credit cards.*

$ ✕▭ **Kotorosl.** This decent, renovated, tourist-class hotel is not far from the city center, near the railway station. The restaurant serves basic Russian fare with little luster. ⊠ *87 Bolshaya Oktyabrskaya ul., 150000* ☎ *0852/211–581* ⟳ *184 rooms* ⌂ *Restaurant, gym, sauna, bar, meeting room* ▭ *No credit cards.*

$$$$ ▭ **Ring Premier Hotel.** Five minutes by foot from the Transfiguration monastery and just steps from Shinnik soccer stadium, this four-star hotel with the most luxurious accommodations in town opened in fall 2004. All guest rooms are reasonably large, nicely furnished, air-conditioned, and have satellite television and access to the Internet. The hotel's Sobinov restaurant serves European cuisine. ⊠ *55 ul. Svobody, 150040* ☎ *0852/5811–58 or 0852–5808–58* ⊕ *www.ringpremier-hotel.ru* ⟳ *122 rooms* ⌂ *Restaurant, minibars, cable TV, café, pub, gym, Internet, meeting room* ▭ *V, MC.*

$$ ▭ **Hotel Volga.** The only advantage of this 1920s-era hotel is its location in the very center of town. Many of the rooms, which have a bathroom, TV, and refrigerator, are worn, but some have been renovated. ⊠ *10 ul. Kirova, 150000* ☎ *0852/30–8131* ⟳ *120 rooms* ⌂ *Restaurant, refrigerators, sauna, bar, travel services* ▭ *No credit cards.*

THE EASTERN GOLDEN RING

Vladimir and Suzdal, which together make up a World Heritage Site, hold some of Russia's most beautiful medieval kremlins, churches, and monasteries. The towns lie to the east of Moscow.

Vladimir

Владимир

9 *190 km (118 mi) east of Moscow via the M7.*

Although this fairly peaceful city of 350,000 seems unassuming today, half a millennium ago it was the cultural and religious capital of northeastern Rus'. Several of the monuments to this time of prosperity and prestige remain, and a visit to this city, and nearby Suzdal, is vital to understanding the roots from which contemporary Russia grew.

Vladimir was founded in 1108 on the banks of the Klyazma by Vladimir Monomakh, grandson of Yaroslav the Wise and father of Yuri Dolgoruky. Yuri, as he increased his power en route to taking the throne in Kiev, preferred Suzdal, however, and made that town his de facto capital in 1152. Upon Yuri's death five years later, his son, Andrei Bogolyubsky, moved the capital of Suzdalia to Vladimir and began a massive building campaign.

Cathedral of the Assumption (Uspensky Sobor), a working church in the center of town, is an important city landmark from Andrei's time, completed in 1160. Its huge, boxy outline and golden domes rise high above the Klyazma River. After a fire in 1185, the cathedral was rebuilt, only to burn down again in 1237 when the Mongols attacked the city. The town's residents took refuge in the church, hoping for mercy. Instead, the invaders burned them alive. The cathedral was again restored, and in 1408 the famous artist Andrei Rublyov repainted the **frescoes of the** *Last Judgment,* which in themselves make this impressive monument worth a visit. Ivan the Great (1440–1505) had his architects use this cathedral as a model to build the Assumption Cathedral in the Moscow Kremlin. The cathedral also houses a replica of Russia's most revered icon, the Virgin of Vladimir; the original was moved from here to Moscow in 1390. Andrei Bogolyubsky is entombed here. ⊠ *Sobornaya Sq.* ☏ *0922/3242–63 or 0922/3252–01* 🎫 *100R* ☉ *Tues.–Sun. 1:30–4:45.*

Andrei Bogolyubsky was succeeded by Vsevolod III, also known as "the Great Nest" because of the great number of his progeny. Although he focused much of his energy in the neighboring regions of Ryazan and Murom, he was instrumental in rebuilding Vladimir's town center in 1185 after a fire caused much damage. He also built the remarkable **Cathedral of St. Dmitri** (Dmitriyevsky Sobor), finished in 1197. The cathedral stands adjacent to Vladimir's much larger Cathedral of the Assumption, where he is buried, and is covered in ornate carvings with both secular and religious images. The lower images are quite precise and detailed, the upper ones have fewer details but deeper grooves for better visibility. The Cathedral had been closed for a complex, five-year restoration and reopened its doors for visitors in summer 2005. ⊠ *Sobornaya Sq.* ☏ *0922/3242–63* 🎫 *80R* ☉ *Wed.–Sun. 11–5.*

Originally, Vladimir had four gates guarding the main approaches to the town. The 12th-century **Golden Gates** (Zolotye Vorota), which stand in the middle of Moskovskaya ulitsa, a few hundred yards west of the

Cathedral of the Assumption, guarded the western approach. The main road from Moscow to Siberia passed through these gates, which, starting in the 1800s, became a significant monument on the infamous "Vladimirka"—the road prisoners took east to Siberia.

Most of Andrei Bogolyubsky's construction projects were built in **Bogolyubovo,** 10 km (6 mi) east of Vladimir. Near the convergence of the Nerl and Klyazma rivers, he built an impressive fort and living compound. The dominant building in the compound today is the richly decorated **Cathedral of the Assumption** (Uspensky Sobor), rebuilt in the 19th century. Remnants of his quarters—a tower and an archway—still stand. It was on the stairs of this tower that Andrei, despised by many for his authoritarian rule, was stabbed to death by several members of his inner circle. In the 13th century, Bogolyubovo became a convent, which it remains today. In 1702 Andrei was canonized. ⊠ *Bogolyubovo village* ☎ *0922/3242–63 to book tour* ☏ *Free, fee for tour* ☉ *Daily 10–5.*

★ Andrei's greatest creation and, some feel, the most perfect medieval Russian church ever built, is the 1165 **Church of the Intercession on the Nerl** (Khram Pokrova Na Nerli), less than 2 km (1 mi) from Bogolyubovo. On a massive limestone foundation covered with earth, the church sits near the confluence of the Nerl and Klyazma rivers and appears to be rising out of the water that surrounds it. Andrei built the church in memory of his son Izyslav, who was killed in a victorious battle with the Bulgars. Look for the unique carvings of King David on the exterior, the earliest such iconographic carvings in this region. Inside, the high, narrow arches give an impressive feeling of space and light. To get to the church from Bogolyubovo, walk a few hundred yards west of the monastery, down ulitsa Frunze and under a railway bridge; then follow the path through a field to the church.

Where to Stay & Eat

$ ✕ **Stary Gorod.** This Old Town restaurant serving Russian and European cuisine is a good option for a meal, only steps away from the Sobornaya Square. The place is quiet, the staff is friendly. The summer terrace is open May through September. ⊠ *41, Bolshaya Moskovskaya ul.* ☎ *0922/3229–44* ▭ *No credit cards.*

$ ✕ **Tri Peskarya.** The Three Minnows is a cozy wood-lined place that resembles a beer cellar. The service is good, serving agreeable Russian cuisine, such as *ukha* (fish soup), grilled sturgeon, and fish *kulebyaka* (pie). ⊠ *88 ul. Tretyevo Internationala* ☎ *0922/2930–78* ▭ *No credit cards.*

$$$$ ▥ **U Zolotykh Vorot.** This elegant hotel is in a recently renovated 19th-century building, next to the Golden Gates. The hotel offers probably the best accommodation and service in town. Doubles and singles, tastefully decorated in beige and pink, are available along with one two-room suite. ⊠ *15, 17 Bolshaya Moskovskaya ul.* ☎ *0922/4208–23* ⊕ *www. golden-gate.ru* ☞ *13 rooms, 1 suite* ☼ *Bar, restaurant* ▭ *MC, V.*

$$$$ ▥ **Vladimir Hotel.** Although somewhat Soviet in atmosphere, this hotel offers decent service and standard amenities, like rooms with a bath, TV, and refrigerator. ⊠ *74 ul. Bolshaya Moskovskaya, 600006* ☎ *0922/ 3230–42* ☞ *45 rooms* ☼ *Restaurant, refrigerators, bar* ▭ *MC, V.*

$$ ⊞ **Zolotoye Koltso.** The Golden Ring is the biggest hotel in town and a landmark 15-story building. It provides all the basic amenities along with pleasant decor. The two floors of the hotel with standard double rooms are closed for renovation indefinitely; only upgraded rooms are available. The service, however, is not great. ✉ *27 ul. Chaikovskovo, 600000* ☎ *0922/2488–07* 📞 *127 rooms* ⚴ *Restaurant, refrigerators, sauna, bar, casino, nightclub* ⊟ *MC, V.*

Suzdal

Суздаль

★ ❿ *190 km (118 mi) east of Moscow on the M7 via Vladimir, then 26 km (16 mi) north on the A113.*

Suzdal is the crowning jewel of the Golden Ring, with more than 200 historic monuments and some of the most striking churches in Russia. This quiet tourist town of 12,000 on the Kamenka River is compact enough to be explored entirely on foot, but to do it justice, give it two days.

One of the earliest settlements in central Russia, Suzdal has been inhabited since the 9th century and was first mentioned in the *Russian Chronicle* (Russia's ancient historical record) in 1024. In 1152 Yuri Dolgoruky made Suzdal the capital of his growing fiefdom in northeastern Russia. He built a fortress in nearby Kideksha (the town, 4 km [2½ mi] to the east, is the site of the oldest stone church in northeastern Russia—the Church of Saints Boris and Gleb, built in 1152). His son, Andrei Bogolyubsky, preferred nearby Vladimir and focused much of his building efforts there. Still, Suzdal remained a rich town, largely because of donations to the many local monasteries and church building commissions. Indeed, medieval Suzdal had only about 400 families, but some 40 churches.

The **Suzdal kremlin,** which may have first been built in the 10th century, sits on an earthen rampart, with the Kamenka River flowing around all but the east side (demarcated by ulitsa Lenina). The dominant monument in the kremlin (and indeed the town) is the mid-13th-century **Sobor Rozhdestva Bogorodnitsy** (Cathedral of the Nativity of the Virgin), topped by deep-blue cupolas festooned with golden stars. It has been subjected to many calamities and reconstructions, and is closed to the public. Original limestone carvings can still be found on its corners and on its facade. Its exquisite bronze entry doors are the oldest such doors in Russia, having survived since the 13th century. Inside, the brilliant and colorful frescoes dating from the 1230s and 1630s are without compare.

The long, white, L-shape three-story building that the cathedral towers over is the **Archbishop's Chambers.** Behind its broad windows you'll find the superb "cross chamber" (named for its shape), which is a large hall without any supporting pillars—the first hall of its type in all Russia. The kremlin also holds museums of antique books and art. ✉ *Southern part of town* ☎ *09231/20–937* 💰 *22R* ⊙ *Wed.–Mon. 10–5* ⊙ *Closed last Fri. of month.*

The **Museum of Wooden Architecture** (Muzey Derevyannovo Zodchestva) contains interesting wooden buildings moved here from around the region. Of particular interest is the ornate **Church of the Transfiguration,** dating from 1756; it was moved here from the village of Kozlyatievo. The buildings can be viewed from the outside any time of year, but from the inside only from May to October. The museum is just below the kremlin and across the river to the south; to get here you'll need to go south on ulitsa Lenina, cross the river, and turn right on Pushkarskaya ulitsa. ⌨ *20R ⊙ May–Oct., Wed.–Mon. 9:30–4 ⊙ Closed last Fri. of month.*

Walking north from the kremlin on ulitsa Lenina, you'll pass several churches on your left and the pillared trading arcades. Just beyond the arcades are the beautiful **Churches of St. Lazarus and St. Antipy** (Tserkov Svyatovo Lazarya and Tserkov Svyatovo Antipiya), their colorful bell tower topping the unique, concave tent-roof design. This ensemble is a good example of Russian church architecture, where a summer church (St. Lazarus, with the shapely onion domes, built in 1667) adjoins a smaller, easier-to-heat, and more modest winter church (St. Antipy, built in 1745). ⌧ *Ul. Lenina* ☎ *No phone* ⌨ *Free.*

Rising 236 feet high, the bell tower in the **Monastery of the Feast of the Deposition of the Robe** (Rizopolozhensky Monastyr) complex is the tallest building in Suzdal. It was built by local residents in 1819 to commemorate Russia's victory over Napoléon. The monastery is on ulitsa Lenina, opposite the post office.

Fodor's Choice ★ The impressive **Monastery of St. Yefim** (Spaso-Yefimsky Monastyr) dates from 1350. The tall brick walls and 12 towers of the monastery have often been the cinematic stand-in for the Moscow Kremlin. The main church in the monastery, the 16th-century **Church of the Transfiguration of the Savior,** is distinctive for its extremely pointed onion domes and its New Testament frescoes by Gury Nikitin and Sila Slavin, the famous 17th-century Kostroma painters. A museum in the monastery is devoted to their life and work. The church also houses the tomb containing the remains of Dmitri Pozharsky, one of the resistance leaders against the Polish invaders in the Time of Troubles. Adjoining the church is a single-dome nave church, which is actually the original Church of the Transfiguration; it was built in 1509, constructed over the grave of St. Yefim, the monastery's founder. Every hour on the hour there's a wonderful chiming of the church's bells. The 16th-century **Church of the Assumption** (Uspenskaya Tserkov), next door to the larger Church of the Transfiguration of the Savior, is one of the earliest examples of tent-roof architecture in Russia.

In the middle of the 18th century, part of the monastery became a place for "deranged criminals," many of whom were in actuality political prisoners. The prison and hospital are along the north wall and closed to visitors. ⌧ *Ul. Lenina* ☎ *No phone* ⌨ *Monastery grounds 50R; museums in complex charge an additional 30R–90R each* ⊙ *Tues.–Sun. 10–4* ⊙ *Closed last Thurs. of month.*

In addition to being a religious institution, the **Convent of the Intercession** (Pokrovsky Monastyr) was also a place for political incarcerations.

Basil III divorced his wife Solomonia in 1525 and banished her here when she failed to produce a male heir. Basil may have chosen this monastery because, in 1514, he had commissioned the splendid octagonal, three-domed Cathedral of the Intercession here, as supplication for a male heir. Interestingly, local legend has it that Solomonia subsequently gave birth to a boy and then staged the child's death to hide him from Basil. Basil subsequently married Yelena Glinskaya, who did give him an heir: Ivan IV, who would be known as "the Terrible." Ivan, in turn, banished his wife Anna here. And when Peter the Great, after returning from Europe in 1698, finally decided that he wanted to rid himself of his wife, Yev-dokia, he forced her to take the veil and live out her life in this convent. A fine view of the monastery can be had from across the river, from the sparse remains of the Alexander Nevsky monastery. You can overnight in cozy *izbas* (wooden cabins) inside the convent, and dine in one of the town's best restaurants, here on the convent grounds. The convent sits across the Kamenka River from Spaso-Yefimsky, in an oxbow bend of the river. To get here, turn east off ulitsa Lenina onto ulitsa Stromynka and then go north on Pokrovskaya ulitsa. ☎ 09231/20–889 🖃 50R ☉ Wed.–Mon. 9:30–4 ☉ Closed last Fri. of month.

Where to Stay & Eat

$$ ✕ **Trapeznaya Kremlya.** Not to be confused with the restaurant of the same name in the Convent of the Intercession, this is an equally pleasant Russian-style eatery within the Suzdal kremlin. If you don't want to order a full meal, consider trying some tea and *keks* (cake) or *pirozhnoye* (pastry), all-day selections in Russia. ⊠ *Archbishop's Chambers, Suzdal kremlin* ☎ 09231/20–937 🖃 No credit cards.

$ ✕ **Trapeznaya.** Excellent, reputedly "authentic old-style" Russian fare such as grilled sturgeon and pancakes with red caviar is served in the Convent of the Intercession itself, making this place one of the best dining options around. ⊠ *Convent of the Intercession* ☎ 09231/20–889 🖃 No credit cards.

$$$$ 🏨 **GTK Tourist Complex.** The GTK, a large complex divided into separate functioning units, is a rather basic, Soviet-style hotel with middling service. The motel section has two-story rooms with separate street entrances; some even have garages. The Rezalit section offers 30 big rooms, plus winning personal service. A good way to explore the appealing grounds around Suzdal is to rent a snowmobile at GTK. ⊠ *7 ul. Korovniki, 601260* ☎ 09231/21–530 or 09231/20–908 🖶 09231/207–66 🛏 430 rooms ৬ Restaurant, pool, sauna, shops 🖃 No credit cards.

$$$$ 🏨 **Pokrovskaya.** These rustic accommodations are in 15 19th-century log cabins, also known as *izbas* (peasant wood cottages), on the grounds of the Convent of the Intercession. ⊠ *Pokrovsky Monastyr, 601260* ☎ 09231/20–889 🛏 30 rooms ৬ Restaurant 🖃 No credit cards.

$$$$ 🏨 **Sokol Hotel.** This newly opened hotel is in the historic part of the town, a pleasant 10-minute walk to the Kremlin. Guest rooms are clean, have all amenities, and great views of the churches. Buffet breakfast is a big plus to the hotel service. The hotel offers its customers excursions of Suzdal, horse-riding, and snowmobile trips around the town. ⊠ *2A, Tor-*

govaya pl., 601260 ☎ *095/925–1566 or 095/916–3364* ⊕ *www.hotel-sokol.ru* ⌷ *39 rooms* ⌂ *Restaurant, sauna* ⊟ *No credit cards.*

$$$ ⊡ **Dom Kuptsa Likhonina.** A cozy bed-and-breakfast option in a 17th-century house, this was formerly the abode of a rich merchant. It's best to reserve ahead, though the hotel charges a reservation fee of 25% of the room rate. ⊠ *34 Slobodskaya ul., 601260* ☎ *09231/21–901* ⌷ *5 rooms* ⊟ *No credit cards.*

MOSCOW ENVIRONS & THE GOLDEN RING A TO Z

To research prices, get advice from other travelers, and book travel arrangements, visit www.fodors.com.

BOAT & FERRY TRAVEL

Cruises from Moscow to St. Petersburg along the Moscow-Volga canal visit just one city of the Golden Ring, Yaroslavl. For more information, *see* Moscow A to Z *in* Chapter 1.

BUS TRAVEL

Though it's not as comfortable as traveling by train, the bus can be a decent way to travel as long as it's not the height of summer, when the vehicles can be exceedingly stuffy. Buses run on direct routes to all the towns of the Golden Ring. And, to get to two towns—Pereslavl-Zalessky and Suzdal—by public transport, you'll need to travel by bus at least part of the way.

For short-distance travel between towns, buses can't be beat. But buses are the most unreliable form of long-distance transport. Be sure to check schedules before you leave Moscow to make sure that there are plenty of return buses if you need one.

FARES & SCHEDULES Pereslavl-Zalessky is a three-hour journey from Moscow's Central Bus Station (Tsentralny Avtovokzal). There are four buses daily that run between the capital and Pereslavl-Zalessky; many other buses travel farther on and simply stop here. There are also four buses each day between Pereslavl-Zalessky and Sergiev-Posad (about a one-hour ride).

From Moscow it's a five-hour trip to Rostov and a 1- or 1½-hour trip to Sergiev-Posad. Vladimir is four hours and Yaroslavl is six hours from Moscow. Just one daily bus goes directly to Suzdal from Moscow, departing at 5 PM and taking five hours. It's best to take the train or bus to Vladimir and then change to a bus (running nearly every hour) between Vladimir and Suzdal.

🚌 **Bus Information Central Bus Station** ⊠ 75 Schelkovskoe shosse, Moscow ☎ 095/468–0400 Ⓜ Schelkovskaya.

CAR TRAVEL

For the towns of the Golden Ring, which lie relatively close to one another and are connected by some of Russia's better paved roads, travel by car is by far the most flexible option. There's no problem getting gas in these towns.

MONEY MATTERS

You'll find far fewer exchange points or ATMs in these smaller towns than in Moscow and St. Petersburg. Look for bureaus in the larger hotels or banks downtown.

TAXIS

You'll usually have no trouble getting a taxi at a train or bus station in these towns, which is important, because the stations are often far from the town center. Most of the towns are small enough to be navigated easily on foot, but a taxi may be a desirable alternative to short bus trips (e.g., from Vladimir out to Bogolyubovo, from Vladimir to Suzdal, or from Tula to Yasnaya Polyana).

TOURS

There are several local and international travel agents who specialize in tours to the Golden Ring and Moscow environs. Seattle-based Mir Corporation is particularly good for individual travelers and also conducts regular tours to Russia that include the Golden Ring. Moscow-based Patriarshy Dom Tours offers a variety of one-day and multiday tours throughout the Golden Ring at very reasonable rates.

🚩 **Mir Corporation** ☎ 800/424-7289 ⊕ www.mircorp.com. **Patriarshy Dom Tours** ☎ 095/795-0927 in Moscow ⊕ www.russiatravel-pdtours.netfirms.com.

TRAIN TRAVEL

There are plenty of trains running on the main routes (Moscow–Yaroslavl and Moscow–Nizhny Novgorod) on which most all the towns in this region lie, so it's quite easy to travel between towns here, as well as to and from Moscow. Two types of trains will get you to most of these towns: *elektrichkas* (suburban commuter trains) and normal long-distance trains. In addition to being cheaper, elektrichkas run more frequently. But they are also a bit less comfortable, and there's no reserved seating. Check with a local travel agent in Moscow or at the station itself for train schedules. With the exception of traveling by elektrichka at busy times (Friday evenings and weekends), you should not have trouble getting a ticket the same day you wish to travel.

FARES & SCHEDULES Most elektrichkas will stop in all the towns listed here; it's best to double-check, however, which stops your long-distance train makes.

Commuter trains to Klin, site of Tchaikovsky's House Museum, depart from Moscow's Leningrad Station. For the New Jerusalem Monastery, take an elektrichka from Riga Station and get off at Istra. From there take any local bus to the "muzey" (museum) stop. Rostov is four hours by long-distance train from Yaroslav Station in Moscow, and five hours by elektrichka (changing in Aleksandrov). Elektrichkas also run regularly between Rostov and Yaroslavl (originating in Moscow's Yaroslav Station); the trip lasts 1–1½ hours. Sergiev-Posad is 1½ hours by elektrichka from Yaroslav Station. Vladimir is a three- to four-hour train ride by long-distance train from Moscow's Kursk Station. You cannot take the train to Suzdal. Simply take the train to Vladimir, then catch one of the frequent buses to Suzdal. Although there's a train station near Yasnaya Polyana, the commuter trains departing from Moscow's Kursk

Station run only to Tula. The trip takes about three hours. Yaroslavl is five hours by long-distance train from Moscow's Yaroslav Station. For train station information, *see* Moscow A to Z *in* Chapter 1.

VISITOR INFORMATION

There's no regional tourist office dealing with the Golden Ring region. Any questions should be directed to travel agencies and guided tour companies in Moscow. The State Historical Architecture and Art Vladimir-Suzdal Museum-Reserve Web site (www.museum.vladimir.ru) has some interesting information on Vladimir and Suzdal.

St. Petersburg

WORD OF MOUTH

"[The State Hermitage Museum] is incredible. With a limited time schedule, do not try to see "everything"—a) it's impossible and b) you'll appreciate it less."

—katya_ny

"One of the best ways to see the city is to walk; it is a very walkable city if you are able."

—Garfield

"Do NOT miss the State Museum of Russian Art . . . as it is small enough to be seen in a couple of hours and is filled with Russian art that is amazing."

—vagabond65

By Lauri del Commune

Updated by Galina Stoylarova & Irina Titova

CONCEIVED IN THE SOUL OF A VISIONARY EMPEROR, St. Petersburg is Russia's adopted child. With its strict geometric lines and perfectly planned architecture, so unlike the Russian cities that came before it, St. Petersburg is almost too European to be Russian. And yet it's too Russian to be European. The city is a powerful combination of both East and West, springing from the will and passion of its founder, Tsar Peter the Great (1672–1725), to guide a resistant Russia into the greater fold of Europe, and consequently into the mainstream of history. That he accomplished, and more.

"The most abstract and intentional city on earth"—to quote Fyodor Dostoyevsky—became the birthplace of Russian literature, the setting for Dostoyevsky's Raskolnikov and Pushkin's *Eugene Onegin*. From here, Tchaikovsky, Rachmaninov, Prokofiev, and Rimsky-Korsakov went forth to conquer the world of the senses with unmistakably Russian music. It was in St. Petersburg that Petipa invented—and Pavlova, Nijinsky, and Ulanova perfected—the ballet, the most aristocratic of dance forms. Later, at the start of the 20th century, Diaghilev enthralled the Western world with the performances of his Ballets Russes. Great architects were summoned to the city by 18th-century empresses to build palaces of marble, malachite, and gold. A century later it was here that Fabergé craftsmen created those priceless objects of beauty that have crowned the collections of royalty and millionaires ever since.

The grand, new capital of the budding Russian empire was built in 1703, its face to Europe, its back to reactionary Moscow, which had until this time been the country's capital. Unlike some cities, it was not created by a process of gradual, graceful development but was forcibly constructed, stone by stone, under the might and direction of Peter the Great, for whose patron saint the city is named. Just as the U.S. capital, Washington, D.C., rose from a swamp, so did Peter's city. It was nearly an impossible achievement—so many men, forced into labor, died laying the foundations of this city that it was said to have been built on bones, not log posts. As one of 19th-century France's leading lights, the writer Madame de Staël, put it: "The founding of St. Petersburg is the greatest proof of that ardor of the Russian will that does not know anything is impossible."

But if Peter's exacting plans called for his capital to be the equal of Europe's great cities, they always took into account the city's unique attributes. Peter knew that his city's source of life was water, and whether building palace, fortress, or trading post, he never failed to make his creations serve it. Being almost at sea level (there is a constant threat of flooding), the city appears to rise straight up from its embracing waters. Half of the River Neva lies within the city's boundaries. As it flows into the Gulf of Finland, the river subdivides into the Great and Little Neva and the Great and Little Nevka. Together with numerous effluents, they combine to form an intricate delta. Water weaves its way through the city's streets as well. Incorporating more than 100 islands and crisscrossed by more than 60 rivers and canals, St. Petersburg is often compared, except for its northern appeal, to that other great maritime city, Venice.

Even during periods of economic hardship and political crisis, St. Petersburg's gleaming Imperial palaces emphasize the city's regal bearing, even more so in the cold light of the Russian winter. The colorful facades of riverside estates glow gently throughout the long days of summer in contrast with the dark blue of the Neva's waters. Between June and July, when the city falls under the spell of the White Nights, or *Belye nochy,* the fleeting twilight imbues the streets and canals with an even more delicate aura. During this time following the summer solstice (generally from June to early July), the gloom of night is banished, replaced by a twilight that usually lasts no more than 30 to 40 minutes. To honor this magical phenomenon, music festivals and gala events adorn the city's cultural calendar.

St. Petersburg is not just about its fairy-tale setting, however, for its history is integrally bound up in Russia's dark side, too—a centuries-long procession of wars and revolutions. In the 19th century, the city witnessed the struggle against tsarist oppression. Here the early fires of revolution were kindled, first in 1825 by a small band of starry-eyed aristocratic officers—the so-called Decembrists—and then by organized workers' movements in 1905. The full-scale revolutions of 1917 led to the demise of the Romanov dynasty, the foundation of the Soviet Union, and the end of St. Petersburg's role as the nation's capital as Moscow reclaimed that title. But the worst ordeal by far came during World War II, when the city—then known as Leningrad—withstood a 900-day siege and blockade by Nazi forces. Nearly 650,000 people died of starvation, and more than 17,000 were killed in air raids and as a result of indiscriminate shelling. Thousands more died from disease.

St. Petersburg has had its name changed three times during its brief history. With the outbreak of World War I, it became the more Russian-sounding Petrograd. After Lenin's death in 1924, it was renamed Leningrad in the Soviet leader's honor. Following the failed coup d'etat of August 1991, which hastened the demise of the Soviet Union and amounted to another Russian revolution, the city reverted to its original name—it was restored by popular vote, the first time the city's residents were given a choice in the matter. There were some who opposed the change, primarily because memories of the siege of Leningrad and World War II had become an indelible part of the city's identity. But for all the controversy surrounding the name, residents have generally referred to the city simply—and affectionately—as Peter.

In honor of the city's 300th anniversary in May 2003, the government spent more than 1 billion dollars restoring St. Petersburg to its prerevolutionary splendor—sprucing up mansions and palaces, polishing old monuments, repaving roads, and throwing festivals and celebrations. More than ever, busloads of tourists come to feast their eyes on pastel palaces, glittering churches, and that great repository of artwork, the Hermitage.

Exploring St. Petersburg

Commissioned by Peter the Great as "a window looking into Europe," St. Petersburg is a planned city whose elegance is reminiscent of Europe's

If you have 3 days

If you have only three days, begin your visit of the city on Vasilievsky Island and the left bank. Most of the city's historic sites are here, including the Rostral Columns, the Admiralteistvo (Admiralty), and St. Isaac's Cathedral. After lunch is the right time to tackle the gargantuan Hermitage, one of the world's richest repositories of art. Spend the rest of the afternoon wandering through its vast galleries. Devote the morning of your second day to visiting the Peter and Paul Fortress and the Petrograd Side. Spend the afternoon in the State Museum of Russian Art, one of the country's most important art galleries. On your third day, consider an excursion to Pushkin (formerly Tsarskoye Selo), south of St. Petersburg, once the summer residence of the Imperial family and a popular summer resort for the Russian aristocracy. The main attraction here is the Catherine Palace, with its magnificent treasures and the surrounding park filled with waterfalls, boating ponds, and marble statues. Should you choose to spend the whole day here, you can have lunch and then visit the Lyceum, formerly a school for the Russian nobility and now a museum.

3

If you have 7 days

Follow the three-day itinerary described above. Devote your fourth day to St. Petersburg's inner streets, squares, and gardens. Begin with the grandeur of Ploshchad Iskusstv, or Square of the Arts. Here you can visit the Ethnography Museum before moving on to the colorful Church of the Savior on Spilled Blood and Marsovo Pole (Field of Mars). Finish your walk at the Summer Garden with its famous railing designed by Yuri Felten in 1779. After lunch, visit the Kazan Cathedral. On the fifth day, head west of St. Petersburg to Peterhof (Petrodvorets), accessible by hydrofoil. The best time to visit is in summer, when the fountains, lush parks, and the magnificent Great Palace are at their best. Spend your sixth day at the Alexander Pushkin Apartment Museum, where the beloved poet Pushkin died, and at Menshikov Palace, the first stone building in St. Petersburg. Devote your seventh day to an excursion to the estate and Great Palace at Pavlovsk, only a few miles from the Catherine Palace in Pushkin and 30 km (18 mi) south of St. Petersburg.

If you have 10 days

Follow the seven-day itinerary above. On your eighth day, travel 39 km (24 mi) west of St. Petersburg to reach the town of Lomonosov, site of the only luxurious Imperial summer residence to have survived World War II intact. With its seaside location and splendid park, it's an ideal place to spend a summer's day. On your ninth day, visit Yusupov Palace, now a museum with a concert hall and a theater, on the banks of the Moika River. It was in this beautiful pre-revolutionary mansion that the "mad monk," Rasputin, was killed. You could also use this day (or part of this day) to return to the magnificent Hermitage. Devote your last day in St. Petersburg to the Piskaryevskoye Kladbische, a mass burial ground for half a million victims of the 900-day siege of Leningrad during World War II. Visit the museum and its collection of memoirs and photographs documenting that terrible time.

most alluring capitals. Little wonder it's the darling of today's fashion photographers and travel essayists: built on more than a hundred islands in the Neva Delta linked by canals and arched bridges, it was first called the "Venice of the North" by Goethe, and its stately embankments are reminiscent of those of Paris. An Imperial city of golden spires and gilded domes, of pastel palaces and candlelit cathedrals, it's filled with pleasures and tantalizing treasures.

The city's focal point is the Admiralteistvo, or Admiralty, a spire-topped golden-yellow building; a stone's throw away is the Winter Palace, the city's most-visited attraction. Three major avenues radiate outward from the Admiralty: Nevsky prospekt (St. Petersburg's main shopping street), Gorokhovaya ulitsa, and Voznesensky prospekt. Most visitors begin, however, at Palace Square, site of the fabled Hermitage. The square is one of the best starting points for exploring the city, and not just for geographical reasons: in a way it symbolizes the city's past, the transition years, and the present. The square housed not only the center of power—the tsar's residence and the great offices of state—but also the splendid art collections of the Imperial family. In the twilight of the tsar's empire, it was here that troops were ordered to disperse a workers' demonstration on Bloody Sunday in 1905—sealing the fate of the Imperial family and ushering in the Revolution of 1917.

Wherever you go exploring in the city, remember that an umbrella can come in handy. In winter be prepared for rather cold days that often alternate with warmer temperatures, often resulting in the famous Russian snowfalls. One note: as with most Russian museums, you will find that St. Petersburg's museums charge a small extra fee to entitle you to use your camera or video camera within their walls.

Prices in this chapter are provided in rubles for sightseeing attractions, but dollars for restaurants and hotels. In Russia prices are officially listed in rubles or "conditional units." Pricing in conditional units is a way of skirting a law that bans pricing items in foreign currencies. The "unit" is basically that day's dollar rate, or increasingly in St. Petersburg, that day's euro rate. Most attractions have small admission charges, and ruble conversions can be easily done in your head when they are listed in conditional units. Larger sums—hotel bills and restaurant meals—provide a greater challenge to convert on the spot, so to save some heavy-duty arithmetic, dollar sums are quoted for those prices. See the Money Matters section *in* Smart Travel Tips for more information.

Getting Your Bearings

The city can be divided into approximately nine neighborhoods. The City Center embraces Palace Square, the Hermitage, and the northern end of Nevsky prospekt, with the Fontanka River as its southeastern border. Most of St. Petersburg's major attractions are within this area. Within the City Center is the smaller neighborhood of the Admiralteisky, surrounding the Admiralty building.

Second in number of sights, including the Chamber of Art and the Rostral Columns, is Vasilievsky Island, opposite the Admiralty and set off from the City Center by the Little and Great Neva.

3

Culinary Delights

For years the dining scene was shamefully limited for such a large, cosmopolitan city, but today, several top-grade, privately owned restaurants and cafés have taken over from their jaded state-run predecessors. A common St. Petersburg dining establishment is the part-restaurant, part-bar—not quite one, not quite the other, but often very good at being both, combining menus found at more "formal" restaurants with the ambience of a warm and welcoming watering hole. Russian-style restaurants are most predominant; happily, those in search of traditional Russian cuisine will easily find many options for enjoying such delights as blini, caviar, *pelmeni* (tender meat dumplings), and beef Stroganoff. Keep in mind that eating out in St. Petersburg is often an all-night affair, with lots of drinking and dancing.

Farmers' Markets

The city's fresh-produce markets (*rynok*) are a true St. Petersburg experience that should not be missed. Inside these large covered halls you'll find rows of stalls packed with dairy products, honey, flowers, fresh and cured meats and fish, and fresh fruits and vegetables. Pickled goods are popular in St. Petersburg, and you'll most likely be invited to taste an array of pickled cabbage, salted cucumbers, vine leaves, and other herbs and spices by vendors from Georgia, Armenia, and Azerbaijan.

Palaces

During the 18th century, St. Petersburg was transformed into an Imperial city of dazzling palaces. Outstanding examples of Russian rococo and baroque architecture are, respectively, the Winter Palace (now the magnificent State Hermitage Museum) and the Stroganov Palace, both created by the Italian architect Rastrelli. The neoclassical style, which supplanted the baroque as the favored style of the city's greatest architects, is also well represented, with such mansions as the Mikhailovsky Palace (now the State Museum of Russian Art) and the Taurida Palace. Two suburban palaces, the Catherine Palace in Pushkin and the Great Palace in Peterhof, were the summer residences of the Imperial family from the days of Peter the Great. Though they lay in ruins after the 900-day siege of Leningrad, these magnificent palaces have been restored to their former splendor. Even more spectacular are the vast palace estates built in the suburbs of St. Petersburg—Pavlovsk, Lomonosov, and Gatchina are all reachable by commuter train and almost outshine Versailles for sheer grandeur.

Performing Arts

With countless museums, art galleries, and historic buildings, St. Petersburg has earned its reputation as Russia's cultural capital. Its rich musical heritage includes daily concerts and recitals; the month of June is particularly rich, as the city hosts an international festival of culture. The famous St. Petersburg Philharmonic has a history of collaborating with some of Russia's finest composers, including Rubinstein, Tchaikovsky, and Shostakovich. But it's ballet that the city is most famous for: the Mariinsky Theater (formerly the Kirov) has produced some of the world's greatest dancers. A night at the Mariinsky or Mussorgsky theater can be one of the highlights of your stay. St. Petersburg also has one of the best theater companies in Europe, the Maly Drama Theater, and some of Russia's best-known actors reside at the Bolshoi Drama Theater.

North of the City Center and the Neva River is the Petrograd Side, which holds Peter and Paul Fortress and the sights of Petrograd Island. Back on the mainland, Vladimirskaya is an area south of the Fontanka, taking in the lower part of Nevsky prospekt and bordered by the Obvodny Canal. The Liteiny/Smolny region lies to the northeast of Vladimirskaya and includes the Smolny cathedral. The Kirov Islands (north of the city), the Southern Suburbs, and the Vyborg Side (in the northeast corner of the city) have just a few sights.

St. Petersburg is a large city of 5 million inhabitants, which makes it as likely a place for petty crime as any other metropolis. As a foreigner, you're an even more likely target. Whatever you've heard about crime and poverty in Russia has probably been exaggerated, but you should still exercise caution if you wander too far off the beaten path.

Numbers in the text correspond to numbers in the margin and on the St. Petersburg map.

Imperial Splendor: Palace Square & the Hermitage
Дворцовая Площадь и Эрмитаж

The best place to get acquainted with St. Petersburg is the elegant Dvortsovaya Ploshchad, or Palace Square. Its scale alone can hardly fail to impress—the square's great Winter Palace was constructed to clearly out-Versailles Versailles—and within the palace is the best reason to come to St. Petersburg, the Hermitage. Renowned as one of the world's leading picture galleries, it also served as a residence of the Russian Imperial family, and provides a setting of unparalleled opulence for its dazzling collections, which include some of the greatest old master paintings in the world. As a relief from all this impressive glitz and grandeur, tucked away in the shadows of the great Imperial complex is the moving apartment museum of Alexander Pushkin, that most Russian of writers, set in a neighborhood that still enchantingly conjures up early-19th-century Russia.

a good walk

Begin at **Dvortsovaya Ploshchad** (Palace Square) ❶ ▶. Extending the length of the western side of the square, with its back to the river, is the **Winter Palace** ❷, which houses the legendary **State Hermitage Museum** ❸. In the center of the square is the **Alexander Column** ❹, commemorating the Russian victory over Napoléon in 1812. Dominating the eastern side of the square is the **General Staff Building** ❺, formerly the army's general staff headquarters and now part of the Hermitage. Next to it is the **Headquarters of the Guard Corps** ❻; leave by its right-hand side and cross the Pevchesky most, or Singing Bridge, to enter one of the most charming nooks of the city, enchantingly threaded by the Zimnaya Kanavka, or the Little Winter Canal. On the opposite side of the Moika River, head for the moving museum honoring the great Pushkin, the **Alexander Pushkin Apartment Museum** ❼, a short walk from the corner of Nevsky prospekt and naberezhnaya Moiki.

TIMING With more than 400 exhibit halls and gilded salons, the Hermitage cannot possibly be seen in a single day. It has been estimated that in order to spend one minute on each object on display, you'd have to devote several years to the museum. Official guided tours tend to be rushed, and you will probably want to return on your own. Also consider hiring a private guide from outside the museum: their licensing requires a year of study and training that will benefit your visit. If you have limited time, concentrate on the rooms dedicated to antiquities and Italian art, which will take at least a couple of hours to view properly. Devote another couple of hours to the extraordinary collection of impressionist and postimpressionist art on the third floor. It's best to begin your tour around 11:30, when the early-morning crowds have dispersed. During peak tourist season, or when there's a special exhibition, you may encounter long lines at the museum entrance. Note that the Hermitage is closed on Monday.

What to See

❹ Alexander Column (Aleksandrovskaya Kolonna, Александровская Колонна). The centerpiece of Palace Square is a memorial to Russia's victory over Napoléon. Approximately 156 feet tall, it was commissioned in 1830 by Nicholas I in memory of his brother, Tsar Alexander I, and was designed by August Ricard de Montferrand. The column was cut from a single piece of granite and, together with its pedestal, weighs more than 650 tons. It stands in place by the sheer force of its own weight; there are no attachments fixing the column to the pedestal. When the memorial was erected in 1832, the entire operation took only an hour and 45 minutes, but 2,000 soldiers and 400 workmen were required along with an elaborate system of pulleys and ropes. Crowning the column is an angel (symbolizing peace in Europe) crushing a snake, an allegorical depiction of Russia's defeat of Napoléon. ✉ *Dvortsovaya Pl., City Center* Ⓜ *Nevsky prospekt.*

★ ❼ Alexander Pushkin Apartment Museum (Muzey Kvartira Alexandra Pushkina, Музей-квартира Александра Пушкина). After fighting a duel to defend his wife's honor, the beloved Russian poet Alexander Pushkin died in a rented apartment in this building (which, at the end of the 18th century, had been the palace of Prince Volkhonsky) on January 27, 1837. The poet lived out the last act of his illustrious career here, and what a life it was. Pushkin (b. 1799) occupies in Russian belles lettres the position enjoyed by Shakespeare and Goethe in the respective literatures of England and Germany. He is most famous as the author of *Eugene Onegin,* the ultimate tale of unrequited love, whose Byronic hero is seen more as the victim than as the arbiter of his own fate (a new sort of "hero" who cleared the path for the later achievements of Tolstoy and Chekhov). At the heart of this story—which involves a young genteel girl who falls in love with Onegin only to be rejected, then years later winds up rejecting Onegin when he falls in love with her—is a sense of despair, which colored much of Pushkin's own life and death. The poet, alas, was killed by a dashing count who had openly made a play for Pushkin's wife, Natalya Goncharova, reputedly "the most beautiful woman in Russia."

Pushkin actually lived at this address less than a year (and could afford it only because of the palace owner, the noble Volkhonsky family, co-sympathizers with the poet for the Decembrist cause). The apartment

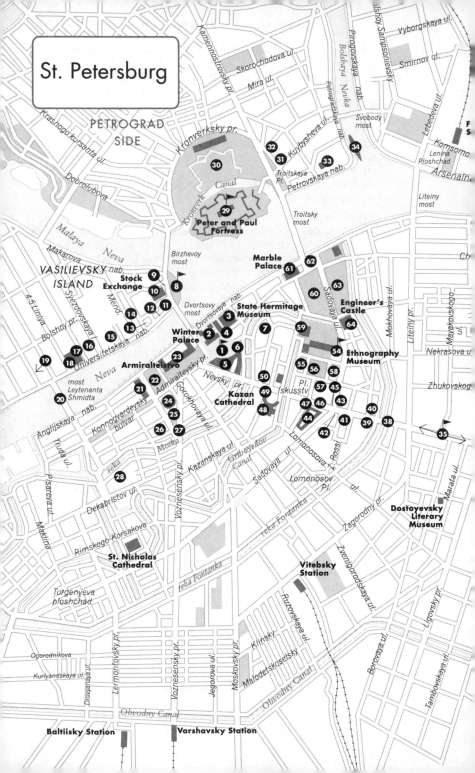

Palace Square & the Hermitage ▼

Alexander Column **4**

Alexander Pushkin
Apartment Museum **7**

Dvortsovaya Ploshchad . . .**1**

General Staff Building **5**

Headquarters of the
Guard Corps **6**

State Hermitage
Museum **3**

Winter Palace **2**

Vasilievsky Island & the Left Bank ▼

Admiralteistvo **23**

Chamber of Art **12**

Decembrists' Square **22**

Egyptian Sphinxes **18**

Maria's Palace **25**

Menshikov Palace **15**

Most Leytenanta
Shmidta **20**

Ploshchad
Rumyantseva **16**

Repin Institute of
Painting, Sculpture, and
Architecture **17**

Rostral Columns **9**

Russian Academy of
Sciences **13**

St. Isaac's Cathedral **24**

St. Petersburg Institute of
Mining Technology **19**

St. Petersburg State
University **14**

Senate and Synod **21**

Siniy most **27**

Stock Exchange **10**

Strelka **8**

Vladimir Nabokov
Museum-Apartment **26**

Yusupov Palace **28**

Zoological Museum **11**

The Petrograd Side ▼

Artillery Museum **30**

Avrora **34**

Mosque **32**

Peter and Paul
Fortress **29**

Peter the Great's
Cottage **33**

Russian Political History
Museum **31**

Nevsky Prospekt & the Inner City ▼

Alexander
Nevsky Lavra **36**

Alexander Pushkin
Drama Theater **41**

Anichkov most **38**

Anichkov Palace **39**

Armenian Church **45**

Church of
St. Catherine **46**

City Duma **47**

Dom Knigi **40**

Gostinny Dvor **44**

Kazan Cathedral **48**

Lutheran Church **49**

Nevsky prospekt **35**

Ploshchad Vosstaniya . . .**37**

Russian
National Library **42**

Smolny **51**

Smolnyi Institut **52**

Stroganov Palace **50**

Taurida Palace **53**

Yeliseyevsky
Food Emporium **43**

Square of Arts to Field of Mars ▼

Church of the Saviour on
Spilled Blood **59**

Engineer's Castle **64**

Ethnography
Museum **54**

Field of Mars
(Marsovo Pole) **60**

Isaac Brodsky
Museum **56**

Marble Palace **61**

Mussorgsky Theater of
Opera and Ballet **55**

Shostakovich
Philharmonia **57**

State Museum of
Russian Art **58**

Summer Garden **63**

Suvorovskaya
Ploshchad **62**

KEY

▶ *Start of walk/itinerary*

museum has been restored to give it the appearance of an upper-middle-class dwelling typical of the beginning of the 19th century. Pushkin had to support a family of six with his writing, so it's not surprising that his apartment was actually less luxurious than it looks now. Although few of the furnishings are authentic, his personal effects (including the waistcoat he wore during the duel) and those of his wife are on display. The library, where Pushkin actually expired, has been rebuilt according to sketches made by his friend and fellow poet Vasily Zhukovsky, who was holding vigil in his last hours. A moving tape-recorded account leads you through the apartment and retells the events leading up to the poet's death.

After you've seen Pushkin's deathbed, it's worth visiting the small **Konyushennaya church** (⊠ 1 Konyushennaya Pl., City Center) around the corner, where his funeral was held on February 1, 1837. Coming out of Moika 12, turn right, and right again at the bridge; the Imperial stables and Konyushennaya square are on your left. The door to the left of the passageway in the central portion of the stables is the entrance to the church. Pushkin's funeral was held here, some say, to keep a low profile (the church was too small for a big crowd to attend), and perhaps as a special favor from Emperor Nicholas I, since the church was attached to the palace and not open to the public. Its coziness, light, and warmth make the church, which was built between 1816 and 1823 by Stassov, a very tranquil stop. It's open daily 9 to 7. ⊠ *12 nab. Moika, City Center* ☎ *812/314–0006* ⊕ *www.museumpushkin.ru* 🖰 *210R; audioguide in English, German, or French 80R* ⊙ *Wed.–Mon. 10:30–5* ⊙ *Closed last Fri. of month* Ⓜ *Nevsky prospekt.*

> **need a break?**
>
> The **Pushka Inn** (⊠ 14 nab. Moika, City Center ☎ 812/314–0663 Ⓜ Nevsky prospekt), an eatery right next to the Alexander Pushkin Apartment Museum, is a great place to grab a refreshing drink and something to eat at any time of the day. The extensive menu includes Russian pancakes with caviar, homemade *pelmeni* (meat dumplings), *borscht* (beet soup), and *vareniki* (a Ukrainian dish—dumplings filled with all kinds of stuffing such as cabbage, cherries, and mushrooms). The name is both a play on Pushkin's name and the Russian word for cannon—which explains the military-theme paintings and the miniature cannon near the entrance. The spot is popular with members of the expatriate community.

★ ☙ ▶ **❶ Dvortsovaya Ploshchad** (Palace Square, Дворцовая Площадь). One of the world's most magnificent plazas, the square is a stunning ensemble of buildings and open space, a combination of several seemingly incongruous architectural styles in perfect harmony. It's where the city's Imperial past has been preserved in all its glorious splendor, but it also resonates with the history of the revolution that followed. Here, the fate of the last Russian tsar was effectively sealed, on Bloody Sunday in 1905, when palace troops opened fire on peaceful demonstrators, killing scores of women and children. It was across Palace Square in October 1917 that Bolshevik revolutionaries stormed the Winter Palace in a successful attempt to overthrow Kerensky's Provisional Government, an event

ST. PETERSBURG IN LITERATURE

"ON AN EXCEPTIONALLY HOT EVENING EARLY IN JULY, *a young man came out of the garret in which he lodged in S. Place and walked slowly, as though in hesitation, towards K. Bridge."* Thus opens Fyodor Dostoyevsky's Crime and Punishment, one of the greatest crime stories ever written, with the protagonist Rodion Raskolnikov making his way through 19th-century St. Petersburg. Both the grand landmarks and miserable details of St. Petersburg were so powerfully inspiring to the giants of Russian literature that the city became as much an inseparable part of their writing as it was of their lives.

The beloved Russian poet Alexander Pushkin (1799–1837) lived and died in St. Petersburg, and he honored the mighty capital in his works. In his epic Bronze Horseman, he immortalized the equestrian statue of Peter the Great on Decembrists' Square. In the poem, a poor clerk imagines that the rearing statue—which evokes the creative energy and ruthlessness of Peter, who used forced labor to build St. Petersburg—comes to life and chases him though the streets during one of the floods that regularly plagued the city. In his poetic novel Eugene Onegin, Pushkin writes of St. Petersburg's early-19th-century high society—of balls, receptions, theaters, and ballets.

In contrast, Dostoyevsky's St. Petersburg is a place of catastrophes, strange events, crimes, and dramas. His heroes live desperate lives in a dank city of slums, poverty, and hopelessness. Fyodor Dostoyevsky (1821–81) was born in Moscow but spent much of his life in St. Petersburg, and was so scrupulous about describing the city that you can find many of the places where his "brainchildren"—as he called his characters—lived. Dostoyevsky lived at 19 ulitsa Grazhdanskaya for a time, and

many believe this is the apartment he used as a model for Raskolnikov's home. Today, modern graffiti ("Rodya [short for Rodion]!" and "We are With You!") covers the dilapidated stairwell leading to his former apartment. Dostoyevsky wrote that on his way to murder the elderly pawnbroker, Raskolnikov took 730 steps from his lodgings to the victim's lodging at 104 Kanal Griboyedova/25 ulitsa Rimskovo-Korsakova. You can re-create this walk, though it requires more than 730 steps.

Nikolai Gogol (1809–52) also portrayed a shadowy St. Petersburg—a city of nonsensical businesslike character and ridiculous bureaucratic fuss. In Gogol's short story "The Nose," the protagonist, low-rank civil servant Kovalyov, mystically loses his nose and must search through St. Petersburg to find it. The nose starts boosting its own bureaucratic career, obtains a higher rank than its owner, and ignores the desperate Kovalyov. To mark Gogol's satirical story, a bas-relief nose is displayed at the corner of Voznesenskii prospekt and ulitsa Rimskogo Korsakova. The "memorial" regularly gets stolen.

The poetry of Anna Akhmatova (1889–1966) reflects the changing face of St. Petersburg (renamed Petrograd and then Leningrad) during her lifetime. Born in the St. Petersburg suburb of Tsarskoye Selo, Akhmatova wrote in her early years romantic and nostalgic verse about her beloved city. As the city changed, so did her poetry, based in part on her firsthand experience of Stalin's repression. Her son was imprisoned and her works were harshly denounced by government officials. Her poem "Requiem" describes the horrors of those times. During the siege of Leningrad, Akhmatova read on the city radio her poems of support for the hungry and dying city residents.

that led to the birth of the Soviet Union. Almost 75 years later, during tense days, huge crowds rallied on Palace Square in support of perestroika and democracy. Today, the beautiful square is a bustling hubbub of tourist and marketing activity, lively yet seemingly imperturbable as ever. Horseback and carriage rides are available for hire here. A carriage ride around the square costs 200R per person. A 20-minute tour of the city in the direction of your choosing costs 2,000R for up to six people. ⊠ *City Center* Ⓜ *Nevsky prospekt.*

⑤ General Staff Building (Glavny Shtab, Главный Штаб). The eastern side of Palace Square is formed by the huge arc of this building whose form and size give the square its unusual shape. During tsarist rule this was the site of the army headquarters and the ministries of foreign affairs and finance. Created by the architect Carlo Giovanni Rossi in the neoclassical style and built between 1819 and 1829, the General Staff Building is actually two structures connected by a monumental archway. Together they form the longest building in Europe. The arch itself is another commemoration of Russia's victory over Napoléon. Topping it is an impressive 33-foot-tall bronze of Victory driving a six-horse chariot, created by the artists Vasily Demut-Malinovsky and Stepan Pimenov. An errant flare partly melted the statue on New Year's Eve 2000, necessitating lengthy repairs. The passageway created by the arch leads from Palace Square to St. Petersburg's most important boulevard, Nevsky prospekt. Part of the Hermitage, the building has a permanent display on its history and architecture, plus temporary exhibits of local and international artwork. ⊠ *Dvortsovaya Pl., City Center* ☎ *812/311–3420* ⊕ *www.hermitagemuseum.org* ▱ *200R, 700R for multi-access ticket to several branches of State Hermitage Museum* ⊙ *Tues.–Sun. 10:30–6; kassa open until 5* Ⓜ *Nevsky prospekt.*

⑥ Headquarters of the Guard Corps (Shtab Gvardeiskovo Korpusa, Штаб Гвардейского Корпуса). This modest structure serves as an architectural buffer between the neoclassical General Staff Building to the left of it and the baroque Winter Palace. Designed by the architect Alexander Bryullov and built between 1837 and 1843, the building is noteworthy for the very fact that it easily goes unnoticed. Instead of drawing attention to itself, it leads the eye to the other architectural masterpieces bordering Palace Square. The restraint shown in Bryullov's creation was considered the ultimate architectural tribute to the masters who came before him. ⊠ *Dvortsovaya Pl., City Center* Ⓜ *Nevsky prospekt.*

③ State Hermitage Museum (Gosudarstvenny Ermitazh, Государственный Эрмитаж). Leonardo's *Benois Madonna* . . . Rembrandt's *Danaë* . . . Matisse's *The Dance* . . . you get the picture. As the former private art collection of the tsars, this is one of the world's most famous museums, virtually wallpapered with celebrated paintings. In addition, the walls are works of art themselves, for this collection is housed in the lavish Winter Palace, one of the most outstanding examples of Russian baroque magnificence. The museum takes its name from Catherine the Great (1729–96), who used it for her private apartments, intending them to be a place of retreat and seclusion. "Only the mice and I can admire all this," the empress once declared.

Fodor'sChoice
★

Between 1764 and 1775, the empress undertook, in competition with rulers whose storehouses of art greatly surpassed Russia's, to acquire some of the world's finest works of art. In doing so, sometimes acquiring entire private collections outright, she quickly filled her gallery with masterpieces from all over the world. This original gallery section of the Hermitage, completed in 1770 by Vallin de la Mothe, is now known as the Maly (Little) Hermitage. It's attached to the Stary (Old) Hermitage, which was built in 1783 by Yuri Felten to house the overflow of art, and also contained conference chambers for the tsarina's ministers. Attached to the Hermitage by an arch straddling the Winter Canal is the **Hermitage Theater** (built between 1783 and 1787), created for Catherine the Great by the Italian architect Giacomo Quarenghi. Yet another addition, the New Hermitage, was built between 1839 and 1852 under Catherine's grandson, Nicholas I; it became Russia's first public museum, although admission was by royal invitation only until 1866. Its facade is particularly striking, with 10 male figures cut from monolithic gray granite supporting the portico. Today's Hermitage is one of the world's richest repositories of art; it was continually enlarged with tsarist treasures and acquisitions, all later confiscated and nationalized, along with numerous private collections, by the Soviet government after the 1917 Bolshevik Revolution.

The entrance to the museum is through the main gates on Palace Square. When you first enter the Hermitage you'll see a *kassa* (ticket window) on both the right and left. Once you purchase your tickets, you can check your belongings and then return to enter the hall that was to your left as you entered the museum. Be forewarned that the ticket-takers are strict about oversize bags and about foreigners trying to enter on Russian-rate tickets.

Although the museum is divided into eight sections, they are not clearly marked, and the floor plans available are not very useful, though they are in English as well as Russian. Just after you have your ticket checked at the front entrance, head straight to the computer consoles in front of you (there are also some scattered throughout the museum)—the plans shown here are similarly short on information, but you can print them out, complete with instructions on how to get to various rooms. Click on the links to read more information on the history of the museum's collection. High technology notwithstanding, it's easy to get lost in the mazelike complex of the Hermitage, but do not despair. Enjoy your wander, and don't be shy about asking the special assistants placed throughout the museum to point you in the right direction. There's also a helpful information desk in the main hall, before you go into the museum, where you can ask specific questions.

There are three floors. The **ground floor** covers prehistoric times, displaying discoveries made on former Soviet territory, including Scythian relics and artifacts; art from the Asian republics, the Caucasus, and their peoples; and Greek, Roman, and Egyptian art and antiquities.

On the **second floor** you'll find many rooms that have been left as they were when the Imperial family lived in the Winter Palace. Through the entrance hall you can reach the second-floor galleries by way of the Jordan Staircase, a dazzling 18th-century creation of marble, granite, and gold. The staircase was once used by the Imperial family in processions down to the Neva River for christenings. The masterwork of Count Bartolomeo Rastrelli—Empress Elizabeth I's favorite architect—the Jordan Staircase shows how theatrical Russian taste could be. Art historians now point to the famous 17th-century scenographic engravings of the Bibiena brothers, famous designers of opera and theater presentations, as one of Rastrelli's main sources of inspiration.

One of the first rooms you pass through on the second floor is the Malachite Room, with its displays of personal items from the Imperial family. In the White Dining Room the Bolsheviks seized power from the Provisional Government in 1917. Balls were staged in the small Concert Hall (which now also holds the silver coffin, and just the coffin, of the hero Alexander Nevsky) and, on grand occasions, in the Great Hall.

A wealth of Russian and European art is also on this floor: Florentine, Venetian, and other Italian art through the 18th century, including Leonardo's *Benois Madonna* and *Madonna Litta* (Room 214), Michelangelo's *Crouching Boy* (Room 229), two Raphaels, eight Titians, and works by Tintoretto, Lippi, Caravaggio, and Canaletto. The Hermitage also houses a superb collection of Spanish art, of which works by El Greco, Velázquez, Murillo, and Goya are on display on the second floor. Its spectacular presentation of Flemish and Dutch art contains roomfuls of Van Dycks, including portraits done in England when he was court painter to Charles I. Also here are more than 40 canvasses by Rubens (Room 247) and an equally impressive number of Rembrandts, including *Flora, Abraham's Sacrifice,* and *The Prodigal Son* (Room 254). The famous *Danaë,* which was mutilated by a knife- and acid-wielding lunatic in 1985, is back on exhibition once again. A smattering of excellent British paintings, extending also to the next floor, includes works by Joshua Reynolds, Thomas Gainsborough, and George Morland.

Reflecting the Francophilia of the Empresses Elizabeth and Catherine, the museum is second only to the Louvre in its collection of French art. The scope is so extraordinary that the collection must be housed on both the second and third floors. Along with masterpieces by Lorrain, Watteau, and Poussin—including Poussin's *Tancrède et Herminie* (Room 279)—there are also early French art and handicrafts, including some celebrated tapestries.

On the **third floor,** you can start with the French art of the 19th century, where you'll find Delacroix, Ingres, Corot, and Courbet. You then come to a stunning collection of impressionists and postimpressionists, originally gathered mainly by two prerevolutionary industrialists and art collectors, Sergei Shchukin and Ivan Morozov. They include Monet's deeply affecting *A Lady in the Garden,* Degas's *Woman at Her Toilette* and *After the Bath,* and works by Sisley, Pissarro, and Renoir. Sculptures by Auguste Rodin and a host of pictures by Cézanne, Gauguin, and van Gogh are followed by Picasso and a lovely room of Matisse, including one of the amazing *Joys.* Somewhat later paintings—by the

Fauvist André Derain and by Cubist Fernand Léger, for example—are also here. Rounding out this floor is the museum's collection of Asian and Middle and Near Eastern art, a small American collection, and two halls of medals and coins.

Possibly the most prized section of the Hermitage—and definitely the most difficult to get into—is the first-floor's **Treasure Gallery,** also referred to as the Zolotaya Kladovaya (Golden Room). This spectacular collection of gold, silver, and royal jewels is well worth the hassle and expense of admission. The collection is divided into two sections. The first section, covering prehistoric times, includes Scythian gold and silver treasures of striking simplicity and refinement recovered from the Crimea, Ukraine, and Caucasus. The second section contains a dizzying display of precious stones, jewelry, and such extravagances as jewel-encrusted pillboxes and miniature clocks, all from the 16th through the 20th centuries.

The best deal is to buy a multi-access ticket, which allows you to visit the State Hermitage Museum and three other splendid museums: the original, wooden Winter Palace of Peter the Great, accessible through a tunnel (historians believe this is the site where Peter the Great died) from the museum; the General Staff Building; and Menshikov Palace. Tours in English (of several sections of the museum or just the Treasure Gallery) are available; call ahead for tour times. An exchange bureau, Internet café, and theater ticket office are on the premises. ⊠ 2, Dvortsovaya Pl., City Center ☎ 812/710–9625 or 812/571–3420, 812/571–8446 tours ⊕ www.hermitagemuseum.org ☜ State Hermitage Museum 350R (free 1st Thurs. of the month); multi-access ticket 700R; Treasure Gallery 300R, plus 160R for daily English-language tour, which takes place around noon ☉ Tues.–Sat. 10:30–6; Sun. 10:30–5; kassa open until 5, on Sun. until 4 Ⓜ Nevsky prospekt.

❷ Winter Palace (Zimny Dvorets, Зимний Дворец). With its 1,001 rooms swathed in malachite, jasper, agate, and gilded mirrors, this famous palace—the residence of Russia's rulers from Catherine the Great (1762) to Nicholas II (1917)—is the focal point of Palace Square. The palace, now the site of the State Hermitage Museum, is the grandest monument of that strange hybrid, the Russian rococo, in itself an eye-popping mix of the old-fashioned 17th-century baroque and the newfangled 18th-century neoclassical style (at the time of the palace's construction a chic import from France). Now "Russianized," the palace's neoclassic ornament lost its early gracefulness and Greek sense of proportion and evolved toward the heavier, more monumental, Imperial style. Still, the exterior—adorned with rows of columns and outfitted with 2,000 heavily decorated windows—is particularly successful and pleasing; note the way its enormous horizontal expanses of outer wall are broken up by vertical lines and variations of lines, pediments, and porches, all topped with a roof balustrade of statues and vases.

FodorsChoice
★

The palace, which was created by the Italian architect Bartolomeo Francesco Rastrelli, stretches from Palace Square to the Neva River embankment. It was the fourth royal residence on this site, the first having been a wooden palace for Peter the Great (today, a remnant of this palace exists and has been restored; it can be visited separately within the State Hermitage Museum). Oddly enough, the all-powerful tsar had to observe some bureaucratic fine print himself. Because it was forbidden to grant land from this site to anyone not bearing naval rank, Peter had to obtain a shipbuilder's license before building his palace. The current palace was commissioned in 1754 by Peter's daughter Elizabeth. By the time it was completed, in 1762, Elizabeth had died and the craze for the Russian rococo style had waned. Catherine the Great left the exterior unaltered but had the interiors redesigned in the neoclassical style of her day. In 1837, after the palace was gutted by fire, the interiors were revamped once again. The Winter Palace contains more than 1,000 rooms and halls, three of the most celebrated of which are the **Gallery of the 1812 War,** where portraits of Russian commanders who served against Napoléon are on display; the **Great Throne Room,** richly decorated in marble and bronze; and the **Malachite Room,** designed by the architect Alexander Bryullov and decorated with columns and pilasters of malachite. These rooms and parts of the Winter Palace that encompass the State Hermitage Museum are the only bits of the palace on view to the public. When touring the museum, you must therefore think of portions of it as the Imperial residence it once was. ⊠ *Dvortsovaya Pl., City Center* ⊕ *www.hermitagemuseum.org* Ⓜ *Nevsky prospekt.*

Vasilievsky Island & the Left Bank
Васильевский Остров и Левый Берег

Peter the Great wanted his city center to be on Vasilievsky Ostrov (Vasilievsky Island), the largest island in the Neva Delta and one of the city's oldest developed sections. His original plans for the island called for a network of canals for the transport of goods from the main sea terminal to the city's commercial center at the opposite end of the island. These plans to re-create Venice never materialized, although some of the smaller canals were actually dug (and later filled in). These would-be canals are now streets, and are called "lines" (*liniya*). Instead of names they bear numbers, and they run parallel to the island's three main thoroughfares: the Great (Bolshoi), Middle (Sredny), and Small (Maly) prospects. Now the island is a popular residential area, with most of its historic sites concentrated on its eastern edge. The island's western tip, facing the Gulf of Finland, houses the city's main sea terminals. Also on the island are the city's most renowned academic institutions, including the St. Petersburg branch of the Academy of Sciences; St. Petersburg University; the Repin Institute of Painting, Sculpture, and Architecture (formerly St. Petersburg Academy of Arts); and the city's oldest institute of higher learning, Gorny Institut, or the St. Petersburg Institute of Mining Technology.

Begin your tour of Vasilievsky Island at its easternmost tip, which is known colloquially as the **Strelka** ❽ ▶, or "arrow." It's most easily reached by crossing the Dvortsovy most (Palace Bridge), the one in front of the Hermitage, or by taking Trolley 1 or 7 from any stop on Nevsky prospekt. As you stand in Birzhevaya Ploshchad, as the park on the Strelka is called, you'll be between two thick, brick-red columns, known as the **Rostral**

Columns ❾. The columns frame the most significant architectural sight on this side of the river, the **Stock Exchange ❿**. Flanking the Stock Exchange are the almost identical Dokuchayev Soil Museum and, to the southwest, the **Zoological Museum ⓫**.

Walk along Universitetskaya naberezhnaya, which leads away from the Strelka (the Neva River will be on your left). The next buildings you encounter are the **Chamber of Art ⓬** and **Russian Academy of Sciences ⓭**. Continue along the embankment, crossing Mendeleyevskaya liniya and passing an imposing statue of the 18th-century Russian scientist Mikhail Lomonosov. You soon come to the main campus of **St. Petersburg State University ⓮**. Farther up the embankment, after passing on the left a monument that marks the location of the first (floating) bridge of the city, stands one of St. Petersburg's grandest—and oldest—buildings, the **Menshikov Palace ⓯**. After visiting this palace, cross Syezdovskaya liniya and you'll come upon **Ploshchad Rumyantseva ⓰** on your right. Another notable building farther up the embankment is the **Repin Institute of Painting, Sculpture, and Architecture ⓱**. On the landing in front of the institute are the **Egyptian Sphinxes ⓲**, among the city's most memorable landmarks. **St. Petersburg Institute of Mining Technology ⓳** lies at the end of the embankment, at the corner of 21 liniya. It can be reached either by walking (quite a distance) or by taking any of the trams that stop at the corner of 11 liniya and the embankment. At this point you conclude your tour of Vasilievsky Island by retracing your steps along the embankment and crossing the bridge called **most Leytenanta Shmidta ⓴**, which will take you back across the Neva and toward the city center. Once across, you can explore **English Embankment,** the left bank of the Neva. Continue down the embankment with the Neva on your left. You pass the former **Senate and Synod ㉑**. Across the street from it, if you continue going straight, is **Ploshchad Dekabristov ㉒**, a large open square on your right. The golden-yellow building on the other side is the famous **Admiralteistvo ㉓**, or Admiralty.

Proceed through the park in front of the Admiralty and you'll come out on Admiralteisky prospekt, the eponymous avenue running parallel to the building. Ahead of you is the back of massive **St. Isaac's Cathedral ㉔**. To reach the entrance, go right on Admiralteisky prospekt a bit to take a left and go around the cathedral's side. Where Admiralteisky meets Konnogvardeisky bulvar is the gracefully designed Manège. On the opposite side of the square is a palace, **Maria's Palace ㉕**. From here, off to the right on Bolshaya Morskaya is the **Vladimir Nabokov Museum-Apartment ㉖**. To the left, past the Nicholas Statue and in front of the palace, is the short **Siniy most ㉗**. Passing over the Moika on this bridge, you will spot a stone column. Its marks show the different water levels of the many floods that have plagued the city over the years. November 19, 1824, when the water level rose 13 feet and killed at least 200 people, is still a sad and memorable day in the history of St. Petersburg. Turn to the right and continue down the Moika embankment. The elegant yellow building ahead is the **Yusupov Palace ㉘**. You can end your tour at this palace, perhaps choosing to return to the nearby Astoria hotel for coffee or a snack. If you have time, continue along the Moika and turn left at the next bridge. Ahead of you is **St. Nicholas Cathedral,** also well worth a visit. From here, you can head back downtown using public transportation. Walk 100 yards south to Sadovaya ulitsa, where any tram except the 11 will take you back to Nevsky.

TIMING   This is a long walk, divided into two sections (Vasilievsky Island and the Left Bank), though there is (literally) a bridge between them. If you have the time and want to linger in each place, it's best to break this tour up into two separate days. Otherwise, pick and choose the sights in which you'd like to linger, and plan a lunch break midway.

What to See

㉓ **Admiralty** (Admiralteistvo, Адмиралтейство). The Admiralty is considered the city's architectural center, and its flashing spire—visible at various points throughout the city—is one of St. Petersburg's most renowned emblems. To get the picture-perfect first impression, walk around to the front of this lovely golden-yellow building.

A series of important constructions, all related to the naval industry, predate the current building. The first was a shipyard of Peter the Great's, followed by an earthen fortress that guarded the port; after these came the first Admiralty, made of stone and topped by the famous spire that has endured to grace each successive structure.

The current building was designed by Andrei Zakharov and was built between 1806 and 1823, after it was decided that the city required a much grander Admiralty to match its more impressive buildings. It's adorned with classical sculptures glorifying Russia's naval prowess, including a frieze of Neptune handing his trident to Peter. Used as a shipbuilding center through the 1840s, it has belonged to the Higher Naval Academy since 1925 and is closed to the public.

An Admiralty Lawn once adorned its front expanse, but in Tsar Alexander I's time it was turned into a small park bearing his name (to which it has been returned, after having been named for Maxim Gorky under the Communists). As you walk through the park, you'll see various statues, mostly of artists such as the composer Mikhail Glinka and the writer Mikhail Lermontov; the one accompanied by the delightful camel is of Nikolai Przhevalsky, a 19th-century explorer of Central Asia. ✉ *Admiralteisky pr., Admiralteisky* Ⓜ *Nevsky prospekt.*

⑫ **Chamber of Art** (Kunstkammer, Кунсткамера). The Chamber of Art, also called the Chamber of Curiosities, is a fine example of the Russian baroque. Painted bright azure with white trim, the building stands out from the surrounding classically designed architecture. Its playful character seems to reflect its beginnings; it was originally commissioned in 1718 to house Peter the Great's collection of oddities, gathered during his travels. Completed by 1734, the Kunstkammer (from the German *Kunst,* "art," and *Kammer,* "chamber") was destroyed by fire in 1747 and almost entirely rebuilt. Today it houses the **Museum of Anthropology and Ethnography** but still includes a room with Peter's original collection, a truly bizarre assortment ranging from rare precious stones to preserved human organs and fetuses. The museum is enormously popular, so purchase entrance tickets early in the day. ✉ *3 Universitetskaya* *nab., Vasilievsky Island ☎ 812/328–1412 💰 200R ⊙ Tues.–Sun. 11–6, kassa open until 4:45 ⊙ Closed last Tues. of month Ⓜ Vasileostrovskay.*

㉒ **Decembrists' Square** (Ploshchad Dekabristov, Площадь Декабристов). This square, which was originally called Senatskaya Ploshchad (Senate Square), holds one of St. Petersburg's best-known landmarks: the gigantic equestrian statue of Peter the Great. The name "Decembrists' Square" refers to the dramatic events that unfolded here on December 14, 1825, when, following the death of Tsar Alexander I (1777–1825), a group of aristocrats staged a rebellion on the square in an attempt to prevent the crowning of Nicholas I (1796–1855) as the new tsar, and perhaps do away with the monarchy altogether. Their coup failed miserably, as it was suppressed with much bloodshed by troops already loyal to Nicholas, and those rebels who were not executed were banished to Siberia. Although the Decembrists, as they came to be known, did not bring significant change to Russia in their time, their attempts at liberal reform were often cited by the Soviet regime as proof of deep-rooted revolutionary fervor in Russian society. In 1925 the square was renamed in their honor; it has since reverted to its original name of Senate Square, but nobody uses this title.

In the center of the square is the grand statue called the **Medny Vsadnik** (Bronze Horseman), erected as a memorial from Catherine the Great to her predecessor, Peter the Great. The simple inscription on the base reads, TO PETER THE FIRST FROM CATHERINE THE SECOND, 1782. Created by the French sculptor Etienne Falconet and his student Marie Collot, the statue depicts the powerful Peter, crowned with a laurel wreath, astride a rearing horse that symbolizes Russia, trampling a serpent representing the forces of evil. The enormous granite rock on which the statue is balanced comes from the Gulf of Finland. Reportedly, Peter liked to stand on it to survey his city from afar. Moving it was a Herculean effort, requiring a special barge and machines and nearly a year's work. The statue was immortalized in a poem of the same name by Alexander Pushkin, who wrote that the tsar "by whose fateful will the city was founded beside the sea, stands here aloft at the very brink of a precipice, having reared up Russia with his iron curb." ⊠ *Admiralteisky* Ⓜ *Sennaya Ploshchad.*

English Embankment (Anglijskaya naberezhnaya, Английская набережная). Before the Revolution of 1917 this was the center of the city's English community. Here you can find some of St. Petersburg's finest aristocratic estates–cum–overcrowded communal apartments. No. 28 (east of most Leytenanta Shmidta), for example, was formerly the mansion of Grand Duke Andrei Vladimirovich Romanov. Today it's called the **Palace of Marriages** and was once the only place under Communism where marriages could be performed; the state-run, secular ceremonies, still the usual type held here, are perfunctorily recited with assembly-line efficiency. Its baroque-style interiors are decorated with marble stairwells, statuary, golden candelabra, and huge mirrors. Many of the mansions on the embankment have been renovated and have become once again luxury real estate, whether office space or housing. ⊠ *City Center* Ⓜ *Nevsky prospekt.*

★ ⓲ **Egyptian Sphinxes** (Yegipetskiye Sfinksy, Египетские Сфинксы). On the landing in front of the Repin Institute, leading down to the Neva, stand two of St. Petersburg's more magnificent landmarks, the famous Egyptian Sphinxes. These twin statues date from the 15th century BC and were discovered during an excavation at Thebes in the 1820s. They were apparently created during the era of Pharaoh Amenhotep III, whose features they supposedly bear. It took the Russians more than a year to transport the sphinxes from Thebes. ⌧ *Universitetskaya nab., Vasilievsky Island* Ⓜ *Vasileostrovskaya.*

Herzen Pedagogical University (Pedagogicheskii Universitet imeni Gertsena, Педагогический Университет имени Герцена). The grounds of this institution belonged to Count Razumovsky, who had his three-story palace built here in the late 18th century. It was built in the transition style—from baroque to classicism. Its facade has a colonnade made of six Corinthian columns that carry a steep attic. The adjacent house, dating from the early 1750s, belonged to the merchant Stegelmann, who was in charge of selling supplies to the royal court. Both houses were later taken over, linked, and made into a foundling hospital and orphanage. Today they house the Pedagogical University. ⌧ *48 nab. Moika, City Center* Ⓜ *Gostinny Dvor.*

㉕ **Maria's Palace** (Mariinsky Dvorets, Мариинский Дворец). Completed in 1844 by Andrei Stakenschneider for the eldest and favorite daughter of Nicholas I, Grand Duchess Maria Nikolayevna, this palace was subsequently used briefly as the residence of the Provisional Government and as the seat of the Leningrad Soviet's Executive Committee. Today, it houses the St. Petersburg City Council. In August 1991 it was on this square, in front of the palace, that citizens put up barricades and held all-night vigils to demonstrate their commitment to democracy. The facade is still adorned with Soviet regalia, although the flag and the double eagle above it are actually reclaimed Russian emblems. At night, this is a particularly impressive building, benefiting from a program to illuminate the city with money from the World Bank. Since this is a working government building, public access is restricted; however, by special request group tours can be arranged after 6 PM on weekdays or during the day on weekends. ⌧ *6 Isaakievskaya Pl., Admiralteisky* ☎ *812/319–9418 for tours* ⊟ *35R per person for groups of 10 or more; fee includes a guide; surcharge applies to groups of fewer than 10* Ⓜ *Sennaya Ploshchad.*

> **need a break?**

The **restaurant Idiot** (⌧ 82 nab. Moika, City Center ☎ 812/315–1675 Ⓜ Sennaya Ploshchad), halfway between Maria's Palace and the Yusupov Palace, is a favorite among St. Petersburg expatriates. Its entrance is marked by a discreet white globe with IDIOT inscribed on it. The cozy café would be at home in New York's East Village and serves hearty vegetarian Russian food, good seafood, and a nice cappuccino. The background music leans heavily on Charles Aznavour, Louis Armstrong, and Ella Fitzgerald. Add occasional art exhibits, chess and backgammon sets, and a small library, and you have several excuses to linger here for a while.

⓯ Menshikov Palace (Menshikovsky Dvorets, Меншиковский Дворец). Alexander Menshikov (1673–1729), St. Petersburg's first governor, was one of Russia's more flamboyant characters. A close friend of Peter the Great (often called his favorite), Menshikov rose from humble beginnings as a street vendor, reportedly getting his start when he sold a cabbage pie to the tsar—or so the legend goes. He eventually became one of Russia's most powerful statesmen (he was granted all of Vasilievsky Island outright for a while), but Menshikov was famous for his corruption and political maneuvering. He is said to have incited Peter the Great against his son Alexei, and later attempted to take power from Peter the Second by arranging the young tsar's engagement to his daughter. The marriage did not take place and the young tsar exiled Menshikov and his family to Siberia.

His palace, the first stone building in St. Petersburg, was, at the time of its completion in 1720, the city's most luxurious building. Although only a portion of the original palace has survived, it easily conveys a sense of Menshikov's inflated ego and love of luxury. Particularly noteworthy are the restored bedrooms: the walls and ceilings are completely covered with handcrafted ceramic tiles. It's said that Peter had them sent home from Delft for himself, but that Menshikov liked them and appropriated them. After Menshikov's exile to Siberia in 1727, his palace was turned over to a military training school and was significantly altered over the years. In June 1917 it served as the site of the First Congress of Russian Soviets. The Menshikov Palace is today a branch of the Hermitage Museum. In addition to the restored living quarters of the Menshikov family, there's an exhibit devoted to early-18th-century Russian culture. ☒ *15 Universitetskaya nab., Vasilievsky Island* ☏ *812/ 323–1112* ☒ *200R, includes guided tour; 700R for multi-access ticket to State Hermitage Museum; guided tour for up to 15 people in English or French 1,500R; order by phone 1–2 days in advance* ☉ *Tues.–Sun. 10:30–4:30* Ⓜ *Vasileostrovskaya.*

⓴ Most Leytenanta Shmidta (Lieutenant Schmidt Bridge, Мост Лейтенанта Шмидта). Built between 1842 and 1850 this was the first stationary bridge to connect Vasilievsky Island with the left bank of the Neva; it was renamed in honor of the naval officer who was a leader of the Black Sea Fleet mutiny during the 1905–07 Revolution. The bridge will close in spring 2006 for about a year for major renovation work. The bridge will be widened to accommodate the city's expanding traffic, but maintain its historic form. A temporary bridge will replace it during construction. ☒ *Vasilievsky Island* Ⓜ *Vasileostrovskaya.*

⓰ Ploshchad Rumyantseva (Rumyantsev Square, Площадь Румянцева). This square was established in honor of the 18th-century general who led Russia to victory in the Russo-Turkish wars of 1768–74. Its obelisk, designed by Vikenty Brenna, originally stood in the Marsovo Pole (Field of Mars) and was moved to its current site in 1818. The new site was chosen for its proximity to the military school in the former Menshikov Palace, where Rumyantsev once studied. ☒ *Vasilievsky Island* Ⓜ *Vasileostrovskaya.*

⑰ Repin Institute of Painting, Sculpture, and Architecture (Institut Zhivopisi, Skulptury i Arkhitektury imeni Repina, Институт Живописи, Скульптуры и Архитектуры имени Репина). During the reign of Peter the Great, artists, like architects, began equally abruptly—and perhaps still more slavishly—to imitate Western models. In order to enforce the "right" Western standards, Peter set up a school of drawing in St. Petersburg, which was later elevated by Catherine the Great to the Russian Academy of Fine Arts in 1757. The success of this Westernizing policy was complete—excessively so. Russian artists started painting portraits in the Gainsborough mode and imitated the French and German Romantics, but unlike native architects, Russian painters failed to put their own stamp on the foreign styles they had imported. Finally, in 1863, several talented painters broke away from the academy and began to foster the idea that art should serve a social purpose. The supreme artist among this group was Ilya Repin (1844–1930), whose most famous works, such as the *Volga Bargemen,* hang in Moscow museums. Along with Repin, other famous graduates of the institute include Dmitri Levitsky and Orest Kiprensky.

Today the Repin Institute maintains a public museum of graduation works from the original academy. The rarest thing to be seen in the academy, however, is probably a foreign tourist. Don't expect any kind of sign in English, except the one that tells you to pay six times more than a Russian to gain admission to this temple of culture. You might just as well go all the way and spend an extra 70R for a guided tour, because the names and significance of the artists may be unknown to you. This place is one of the last to display Socialist Realist art (most famously seen in the graduation works of the current academicians and authorities of the institute). It's also bustling with the activity of aspiring artists. As you make your way to the museum, on the second floor, take a peek through the balcony to the interior circular courtyard. The building itself, a fine example of early Russian classicism, was built between 1764 and 1788 and designed by Alexander Kokorinov and Vallin de la Mothe. ✉ *17 Universitetskaya nab., Vasilievsky Island* ☎ *812/323–6496, 812/323–3578 guided tour in foreign language* 🎫 *200R* ☽ *Wed.–Sun. 11–6, kassa open until 5:30* Ⓜ *Vasileostrovskaya.*

need a break?

Kalinka (✉ 9 Syezovskaya liniya, Vasilievsky Island ☎ 812/323–3718 Ⓜ Vasileostrovskaya), a small, popular, local establishment, serves hearty Russian food such as *solyanka* (a spicy, thick stew made with vegetables and meat or fish), borsch, and blini. Stuffed wild animals decorate the dining room, and in the evenings you can eat to the strains of live folk bands. It's a short walk away from the embankment and up from the Repin Institute; the street runs parallel to the 1st liniya.

❾ Rostral Columns (Rostralnyie Kolonny, Ростральные Колонны). Swiss architect Thomas de Thomon designed these columns, which were erected between 1805 and 1810 in honor of the Russian fleet. The monument takes its name from the Latin *rostrum,* meaning "prow." Modeled on similar memorials in ancient Rome, the columns are decorated with ships' prows; sculptures at the base depict Russia's main waterways, the Dnieper, Volga, Volkhov, and Neva rivers. Although the columns originally served as lighthouses—until 1855 this was St. Petersburg's commercial harbor—they are now lit only on special occasions, such as City Day on May 27. They were designed to frame the architectural centerpiece of this side of the embankment—the old Stock Exchange, which now holds the Naval Museum. ⊠ *Birzhevaya Pl., Vasilievsky Island* Ⓜ *Vasileostrovskaya.*

⓭ **Russian Academy of Sciences** (Rossiiskaya Akademiya Nauk, Российская Академия Наук). Erected on strictly classical lines between 1783 and 1789, this structure, the original building of the Russian Academy of Sciences, is considered Giacomo Quarenghi's grandest design, with an eight-column portico, a pediment, and a double staircase. The administrative offices of the academy, founded in 1724 by Peter the Great, were transferred to Moscow in 1934. This building, which stands next to the Chamber of Art, now houses the St. Petersburg branch of the Russian Academy of Sciences and is not open to the public. ⊠ *Universitetskaya nab., Vasilievsky Island* Ⓜ *Vasileostrovskaya.*

㉔ **St. Isaac's Cathedral** (Isaakievsky Sobor, Исаакиевский Собор). Of the
Fodor's Choice grandest proportions, St. Isaac's is the world's third-largest domed
★ cathedral and the first monument you see of the city if you arrive by ship. Its architectural distinction is a matter of taste; some consider the massive design and highly ornate interior to be excessive, whereas others revel in its opulence. Tsar Alexander I commissioned the construction of the cathedral in 1818 to celebrate his victory over Napoléon, but it took more than 40 years to actually build it. The French architect Auguste Ricard de Montferrand devoted his life to the project, and died the year the cathedral was finally consecrated, in 1858.

Tickets, which can be bought at the kassa outside, are sold both to the church ("the museum") and to the outer colonnade; the latter affords an excellent view of the city. Follow the signs in English. The interior of the cathedral is lavishly decorated with malachite, lazulite, marble, and other precious stones and minerals. Gilding the dome required 220 pounds of gold. At one time a Foucault pendulum hung here to demonstrate the axial rotation of the earth, but it was removed in the late 20th century. The church can hold up to 14,000 people. After the Revolution of 1917 it was closed to worshippers and in 1931 was opened as a museum; services have since resumed. St. Isaac's was not altogether returned to the Orthodox Church, but Christmas and Easter are celebrated here (note that Orthodox holidays follow the Julian calendar and fall about 13 days after their Western equivalents).

When the city was blockaded during World War II, the gilded dome was painted black to avoid its being targeted by enemy fire. Despite efforts to protect it, the cathedral nevertheless suffered heavy damage, as bullet holes on the columns on the south side attest.

Opening up in front of the cathedral is **Isaakievskaya Ploshchad** (St. Isaac's Square), which was completed only after the cathedral was built. In its center stands the **Nicholas Statue.** Unveiled in 1859, this statue of Tsar

Nicholas I was commissioned by the tsar's wife and three children, whose faces are engraved (in the allegorical forms of Wisdom, Faith, Power, and Justice) on its base. It was designed, like St. Isaac's Cathedral, by Montferrand. The statue depicts Nicholas mounted on a rearing horse. Other engravings on the base describe such events of the tsar's reign as the suppression of the Decembrists' uprising and the opening ceremonies of the St. Petersburg–Moscow railway line.

To one side of the cathedral, where the prospect meets Konnogvardeisky bulvar, is the early-19th-century **Konnogvardeisky Manège,** gracefully designed by Giacomo Quarenghi and decorated with marble statues of the mythological twins Castor and Pullox. This former barracks of the Imperial horse guards is used as an art exhibition hall. Every January it hosts an exhibition of new works by St. Petersburg artists. ⊠ *1 Isaakievskaya Pl., Admiralteisky* ☎ *812/315–9732* ✉ *Cathedral 270R, colonade 120R* ⊙ *Cathedral: May–Sept., Thurs.–Tues. 11–6, kassa closes at 6. Colonnade 11–10 PM, kassa closes at 10; Oct.–Apr., Thurs.–Tues. 11–6, kassa closes at 5* Ⓜ *Sennaya Ploshchad.*

St. Nicholas Cathedral (Nikolsky Sobor, Никольский Собор). This turquoise-and-white extravaganza of a Russian baroque cathedral was designed by S. I. Chevakinsky, a pupil of Bartolomeo Francesco Rastrelli. It's a theatrical showpiece, and its artistic inspiration was in part derived from the 18th-century Italian prints of the Bibiena brothers, known for their opera and theater designs. The church's wedding-cake silhouette, marked by a forest of white Corinthian pilasters and columns, closes ulitsa Glinki and makes the area a natural pole of attraction if you find yourself in the vicinity. Canals and green spaces surround the cathedral, which is also flanked by an elegant campanile. Inside are a lower church (low, dark, and warm for the winter) and an upper church (high, airy, and cool for the summer), typical of Russian Orthodox sanctuaries. The interior is no less picturesque than the outside. This is one of the few Orthodox churches that stayed open under Soviet power. It's also of special significance to the Russian navy; as such, the cathedral held the memorial service in honor of those who died aboard the *Kursk* nuclear submarine, which sank in 2000. If you go during a service, you'll likely hear the beautiful choir. ⊠ *1/3 Nikolskaya Pl., City Center* ☎ *812/714–6926* ⊙ *Daily, usually 6:30 AM–7:30 PM; morning services at 7 and 9 AM, vespers at 6 PM* Ⓜ *Sennaya Ploshchad.*

⑲ St. Petersburg Institute of Mining Technology (Gorny Institut, Горный Институт). Founded in 1773 by Catherine the Great, this is St. Petersburg's oldest technical institution of higher learning and well worth the visit if you have time. The current building, in the neoclassical style, was built between 1806 and 1811 by Andrei Voronikhin, architect of the Kazan Sobor on Nevsky prospekt. Twelve Doric columns support the main entrance, which is lined with statues designed by Demut-Malinovsky and Pimenov (creators of the bronze sculpture above the General Staff Building). The institute has an unusual museum of precious stones and minerals, including a piece of malachite weighing more than a ton and an iron meteorite. ⊠ *21 liniya, Vasilievsky Island* ☎ *812/328–8429* ⊙ *Call for tour arrangements and fees* Ⓜ *Vasileostrovskaya.*

⓮ St. Petersburg State University (Sankt-Peterburgskii Gosudarstvenny Universitet, Санкт-Петербургский Государственный Университет). In 1819 Tsar Alexander I founded this university, today one of Russia's leading institutions of higher learning, with an enrollment of more than 20,000. Its campuses date from the time of Peter the Great. The bright-red baroque building on the right (if you're walking west along the embankment) is the **Twelve Colleges Building**, named for the governmental administrative bodies established during Peter's reign. The building, which was designed by Domenico Trezzini and completed in 1741, 16 years after Peter's death, was transferred to the university at the time of its establishment and today houses the university library and administrative offices. It's not officially open to the public, but no one will stop you from looking around.

The next building in the university complex is the **Rector's Wing**, another red building in the yard of the Twelve Colleges Building, where a plaque on the outside wall attests that the great Russian poet Alexander Blok (d. 1921) was born here in 1880. The third building along the embankment is a former **palace** built for Peter II (1715–30), Peter the Great's grandson, who lived and ruled only briefly. Completed in 1761, the building was later given to the university. The palace is connected to the Twelve Colleges Building via a gate and its facade faces the Neva River. It's a three-story rectangular building with two-story wings. The three blocks together with the palace form a large inner courtyard. The palace houses one of the University's most prestigious departments of Philology where dozens of foreign languages are taught. ☒ *7 Universitetskaya nab., Vasilievsky Island* Ⓜ *Vasileostrovskaya.*

㉑ Senate and Synod (Senat i Synod, Сенат и Синод). Before the Revolution of 1917, this long, light-yellow building, built along classical lines, housed Russia's highest judicial and administrative bodies, the Senate and the Synod. It was designed by Carlo Rossi and erected between 1829 and 1834. It now contains state historical archives and is closed to the public. ☒ *Dekabristov Pl., City Center* Ⓜ *Sennaya Ploshchad.*

㉗ Blue Bridge (Siniy most, Синий мост). This bridge spanning the Moika River is so wide (328 feet) and stubby that it seems not to be a bridge at all but rather a sort of quaint raised footpath on St. Isaac's Square. It's named for the color of the paint on its underside. ☒ *Admiralteisky* Ⓜ *Sennaya Ploshchad.*

❿ Stock Exchange (Birzha, Биржа). Erected between 1804 and 1810, the neoclassical Thomas de Thomon–designed Stock Exchange was modeled on one of the Greek temples at Paestum. It was intended to symbolize St. Petersburg's financial and maritime strength. Since 1940, the building has housed the **Voenno-Morskoy Muzey** (Naval Museum), which was itself founded in 1805. Its collections date from Peter the Great's reign and include, in accordance with his orders, a model of every ship built in Russian shipyards since 1709. On display are exhibits of Russia's naval history; the more modern exhibits (of submarines and entire missiles) are clearly meant to awe the visitor with a display of military might. The collections also contain a 3,000-year-old dugout found on the bottom of the Bug River as well as Peter's personal belongings, including his first boat and the ax he used in building it. Engravings and posters bearing the political slogans of the Communist regime pertaining to the "American aggressor" have been left on the walls, making this a museum not just of the navy, but of the Cold War days of "them versus us." ⊠ *4 Birzhevaya Pl., Vasilievsky Island* ☎ *812/ 328–2502* 🖾 *320R; free last Wed. of month* ⊙ *Wed.–Sun. 11–6, kassa open until 5:15* ⊙ *Closed last Thurs. of month* Ⓜ *Vasileostrovskaya.*

⏵ **⑧** **Strelka** (Стрелка). The Strelka ("arrow" or "spit") affords a dazzling Fodor'sChoice view of both the Winter Palace and the Peter and Paul Fortress. This bit ★ of land also reveals the city's triumphant rise from a watery outpost to an elegant metropolis. Seen against the backdrop of the Neva, the brightly colored houses lining the embankment seem like children's toys—the building blocks of a bygone aristocracy. They stand at the water's edge, seemingly supported not by the land beneath them but by the panorama of the city behind them. Gazing at this architectural wonder is a great way to appreciate the scope of Peter the Great's vision for his country. The view is also revealing because it makes clear how careful the city's founders were to build their city not despite the Neva but around and with it. The river's natural ebb and flow accord perfectly with the monumental architecture lining its course. ⊠ *Vasilievsky Island* Ⓜ *Vasileostrovskaya.*

㉖ **Vladimir Nabokov Museum-Apartment** (Musei Kvartira Vladimira Nabokova, Музей-квартира Владимира Набокова). Vladimir Nabokov (1899–1977), author of the famous novel *Lolita,* was born and lived in this apartment until his 18th year. Judging from Nabokov's novels, in which the author often describes his building in detail or at least mentions it, one can say that the writer always kept warm memories about his first home. When in exile, Nabokov lived in hotels or rented apartments in different cities but never had his own house. When asked why he didn't want to buy his own, he would answer, "I already have one in St. Petersburg." Although the museum has no restored interiors of the writer's apartment, it presents family photos; the writer's drawings and various editions of his books; some of his belongings; and his collection of butterflies, which was previously kept at Harvard University. All these exhibits are in one room on the first floor. The museum is very close to the Manège. ⊠ *47, ul. Bolshaya Morskaya, Admiralteisky* ☎ *812/315–4713* 🖾 *100R* ⊙ *Tues.–Fri. 11–6. Weekends 12–5* Ⓜ *Sennaya Ploshchad.*

★ **㉘** **Yusupov Palace** (Yusupovsky Dvorets, Юсуповский Дворец). On the cold night of December 17, 1916, this elegant yellow palace, which belonged to one of Russia's wealthiest families, the Yusupovs, became the setting for one of history's most melodramatic murders. Prince Yusupov and others loyal to the tsar spent several frustrating and frightening hours trying to kill Grigory Rasputin (1872–1916), who had strongly influenced the tsarina, who in turn influenced the tsar, during the tumultuous years leading up to the Bolshevik Revolution. To their horror, the courtiers found the "mad monk" nearly invincible: when he did not succumb to the arsenic-laced cake given to him, the conspirators proceeded to shoot him several times (thinking him dead after the first shot, they had left the room, only to return and find he'd staggered outside—whereupon they shot him again). They then dumped him, still living, into the icy waters of an isolated section of a nearby canal, where he finally succumbed after becoming trapped under a floe of ice.

On display in the palace, which is set on the bank of the Moika River, are the rooms in which Rasputin was (or began to be) killed, as well as a waxworks exhibit of Rasputin and Prince Yusupov (who was forced to flee the country when the monk's murder was uncovered). They are visible only on an organized tour given once daily in the late afternoon. Another organized tour (given several times daily during the afternoon) takes you through the former reception rooms of the second floor. As for the scenes where the final acts of the drama were played out—the palace's underground tunnel and Turkish bath—they're ostensibly off-limits, but you may be able to view them if you can avail yourself of the bathroom facilities on the lower level of the mansion. It's essential that you phone ahead at least a week in advance to arrange an English-language tour.

On a lighter note, the showpiece of the palace remains the jewel-like rococo theater, whose stage was once graced by Liszt and Chopin; today, concerts are still presented here, as well as in the palace's august and elegant White-Columns Room (concert tickets usually have to be purchased just before performance time). ⊠ *94 nab. Moika, City Center* ☎ *812/314–9883, 812/314–8893 tours* 🖃*400R, extra 150R includes tour in Russian to Rasputin Rooms* ☉ *Mon.–Sun. daily 10:45–5, tour in Russian Mon. 1:45* ☉ *Closed 1st Wed. of month* Ⓜ*Sennaya Ploshchad.*

🐣 ⑪ **Zoological Museum** (Zoologichesky Muzey, Зоологический Музей). The prize of this zoological museum's unusual collection, which contains more than 40,000 species, is a stuffed mammoth recovered from Siberia in 1901. The museum also has impressive skeletons of whales and large fish, but no dinosaur fossils. The other stuffed animals, posed in natural compositions, run the gamut of world fauna: tigers, foxes, bears, goats, and many kinds of birds. A few families of penguins seem to proudly pose with their countless funny nestlings on a piece of artificial ice; a moose walks along a fading fall forest. The museum also has a large collection of butterflies and other insects. ⊠ *1 Universitetskaya nab., Vasilievsky Island* ☎ *812/328–0112* 🖃*60R* ☉ *Sat.–Thurs. 11–6, kassa until 4:50* Ⓜ *Vasileostrovskaya.*

The Petrograd Side
Петроградская Сторона

St. Petersburg was born in the battles of the Northern Wars with Sweden, and it was in this area, on Hare Island (Zayachy Ostrov), that it all began: in 1703 Peter laid the foundation of the first fortress to protect the mainland and to secure Russia's outlet to the sea. Ever since, the small hexagonal island forms, as it were, the hub around which the city revolves. The showpiece of the island is the magnificent Peter and Paul Fortress, the starting point for any tour of this section of the city, which actually consists of a series of islands, and is commonly referred to as the Petrograd Side (Petrogradskaya Storona). Hare Island and the fortress are almost directly across the Neva from the Winter Palace. Cut off from the north by the moatlike Kronverk Canal, the island is connected by a footbridge to Trinity Square (Troitskaya Ploshchad, sometimes still referred to by its Soviet name, Revolution Square) on Petrograd Island (Petrogradsky Ostrov). Along with its famous monuments, this part of the city is also one of its earliest residential areas, and Troitskaya Ploshchad, named for the church that once stood here (demolished in 1934), is the city's oldest square.

a good walk

You can reach Hare Island, site of the **Peter and Paul Fortress** ㉙ ▶, by crossing the Troitsky most from the Palace embankment. It's also easy to reach from the metro station Gorkovskaya. After exiting the station, bear to your right and walk through the small park in front of you, heading in the direction of the Neva. The fortress will emerge through the trees to your right. To make your visit to this famed monument complete, head across the Kronverk Canal to the north of the fortress to the horseshoe-shape **Artillery Museum** ㉚. If you leave the fort by its western end and cross the footbridge there, bear right; if you leave by the way you came in and cross the footbridge there, bear left. The large museum will soon be visible.

Coming out of the Artillery Museum, turn left and walk toward Troitskaya Ploshchad. At the northern edge of the square, at the corner of Kuybysheva ulitsa and Kamennoostrovsky prospekt, stands the **Russian Political History Museum** ㉛. As you leave the museum, take a right, and then turn right again onto Kronversky prospekt. It's hard to miss the bright azure domes of St. Petersburg's only **Mosque** ㉜—above the trees. After visiting the mosque, head back (left) in the direction of the Neva River. When you reach the waterfront, turn left again to walk along Petrovskaya naberezhnaya. After a few minutes of walking you'll encounter **Peter the Great's Cottage** ㉝. Keep walking east along the embankment. When you reach the corner where the Petrovskaya and Petrogradskaya embankments meet (and the Great Nevka converges with the Neva River), you'll be in front of a blue-and-white building in the Russian baroque style (although it was built only in 1911 by Alexander Dmitriev). This is the Nakhimov Academy of Naval Officers, in front of which is anchored the cruiser **Avrora** ㉞. Across the river stands the enormous St. Petersburg Hotel (Gostinitsa Sankt-Petersburg). Built in the monotonous style of a Brezhnev-era high-rise, the concrete-and-steel structure seems horribly out of place among the prerevolutionary architecture lining the embankment. From here you can return to your starting point by retracing your steps along the embankment.

If you want to see more of the Petrograd Side's residential areas, take the longer route back via Kuybysheva ulitsa. Walk down to the bridge to your left (as you face the cruiser *Avrora*) and turn left onto Kuybysheva. This will take you back to Troitskaya Ploshchad. From here Troitsky most is to your left and the Gorkovskaya metro stop is a short walk to your right. The straight avenue opening up to your right is Kamennoostrovsky prospekt, the most fashionable and modern avenue at the end of the 19th century; it runs all the way to Stone Island (Kamenny

Ostrov), where the well-to-do families of the day built their dachas. If you're an architecture buff and want a delicious feast of northern art nouveau, walk to the next metro station (Petrogradskaya) along the avenue and pay attention on the way to buildings Nos. 1–3, 9, 13, 16, 20, 24, and 26–28 (where Sergei Kirov, the former head of the city's Communist Party, once lived). Your effort will be rewarded by the sight of the "house with towers," which gives shape to the intersection of Kamennoostrovsky and Bolshoi prospekts, on Ploshchad Lva Tolstovo (Leo Tolstoy Square), and which is also where you should take the metro back to downtown and enjoy some well-deserved rest.

TIMING Simply walking this entire route requires two or three hours—more time will be needed if you plan to visit the sights. The main attraction, the Peter and Paul Fortress, can easily eat up an afternoon. Note that the cathedral within the fortress is closed on Wednesday.

What to See

30 **Artillery Museum** (Artilleriysky Muzey, Артиллерийский Музей). Formerly the city's arsenal, this building was turned over to the Artillery Museum in 1872. You can't miss it—just look for the hundreds of pieces of artillery on the grounds outside. The museum itself dates from the days of Peter the Great, who sought to present the entire history of weaponry, with a special emphasis on Russia. Today the Artillery Museum is St. Petersburg's main army museum. Like the Naval Museum in the old Stock Exchange, it still has exhibits with a distinctly Soviet feel—if you're interested in circuit boards inside ballistic missiles, for example, this is the place to come. It also contains plenty of military curiosities both modern and ancient. ⊠ *7 Alexandrovsky Park, Petrograd Side* 🕾 *812/232–0296* 💳 *200R* 🕑 *Wed.–Sun. 11–5, kassa open until 5* 🕑 *Closed last Thurs. of month* Ⓜ *Gorkovskaya.*

need a break? The **Evropa** (⊠ 3 nab. Mytninskaya, Petrograd Side 🕾 812/230–9162 or 812/972–3447 Ⓜ Gorkovskaya) is on a ship permanently moored (the third in the row) in the Kronverk Canal, just south of the Artillery Museum. It may look gloomy, particularly if the weather is bad, but down below is a snug bar where you can enjoy a cup of strong coffee, a pastry, or even a shot of cognac. The restaurant on the second floor offers three different halls, two of which have magnificent views of the Hermitage Museum over the Neva River.

🕐 **34** *Avrora* (Аврора). This historic cruiser is permanently moored in front of the **Nakhimov Academy of Naval Officers.** Launched in 1903, it fought in the 1904–05 Russo-Japanese War as well as in World War II, but it's best known for its role in the Bolshevik Revolution. At 9:40 PM on November 7, 1917, the cruiser fired the shot signaling the storming of the Winter Palace. The revolution it launched brought itself under fire in the end. A cherished relic in the Soviet era—it was scuttled during the siege of Leningrad to keep it from being hit by a German shell, and resurfaced later—the *Avrora* was carefully restored in the 1980s and opened as a museum. The cruiser is a favorite of families, and on weekends you may encounter long lines. On display are the crew's quarters and the radio room used to broadcast Lenin's victory address. ✉ *4 Petrograd-skaya nab., Petrograd Side* ☎ *812/230–8440* 💰 *Free, tours usually 200R per person, price depends on group size* ☉ *Tues.–Thurs. and weekends 10:30–4; last tour at 3* Ⓜ *Gorkovskaya.*

Botanical Gardens (Botanichesky Sad, Ботанический Сад). Founded as an apothecary garden for Peter the Great, the grounds here display millions—literally—of different forms of plant life. The gardens are near the cruiser *Avrora.* ✉ *2 ul. Professora Popova, Petrograd Side* ☎ *812/ 234–1764* 💰 *90R* ☉ *Hothouses Sat.–Thurs. 11–4; grounds mid-May–Sept., daily 10–6* Ⓜ *Petrogradskaya.*

Kirov Museum (Muzey Kirova, Музей Кирова). This is the home of the former head of the city's Communist Party, Sergei Kirov, whose murder by Stalin in 1934 marked the beginning of the infamous purges. Look for a red sign marked MUSEI KIROVA, and take the elevator to the fourth floor. You can see the restored interiors of Kirov's five-room apartment including his study, library, dining room, bedroom, kitchen, maid's room. The kitchen and bedroom were for a long time closed to visitors because in Soviet times, museum workers tended not to show the everyday life of almost sacred Communist leaders. The kitchen features such real objects as a stove, white enamel-lined copper sink, and utensils typical of the last century, as well as plaster casts of Kirov's favorite dishes. They say Kirov preferred unpretentious food such as baked potatoes, pickles, pelmeni, and buckwheat. In the corridor is an imported refrigerator from the early 20th century, which was ordered especially for Kirov at two times the cost of a Ford automobile. A special part of the exhibition is dedicated to Kirov's hobby of hunting. The rest of the building is occupied by the administration of the Petrograd district. ✉ *26/28 Kamennoostrovsky pr., Petrograd Side* ☎ *812/346–0217* 💰 *50R* ☉ *Thurs.–Tues. 11–6* Ⓜ *Petrogradskaya.*

㉜ Mosque (Mechet, Мечеть). Built between 1910 and 1914 to serve St. Petersburg's Muslim community, the Mosque was designed after the Gur Emir in Samarkand, Uzbekistan, where Tamerlane, the 14th-century conqueror, is buried. The huge dome is flanked by two soaring minarets, and covered with sky-blue ceramics. In the style of St. Petersburg's northern architecture, the walls of the mosque are lined with rough, dark-gray granite. The inside the columns, which support the arches under the dome, are faced with green marble. In the center of the praying hall is a huge chandelier upon which sayings from the Koran are engraved. It's open only during services. ✉ *7 Kronversky pr., Petrograd Side* ☎ *812/233–9819* ☉ *Services daily at 2:20* Ⓜ *Gorkovskaya.*

▶ ㉙ Peter and Paul Fortress (Petropavlovskaya Krepost, Петропавловская
FodorsChoice   Крепость). The first building in Sankt-Piter-Burkh, as the city was then
★   called, the fortress was erected in just one year, between 1703 and 1704, during the Great Northern War against Sweden. It was never used for its intended purpose, however, as the Russian line of defense quickly moved farther north, and, in fact, the war was won before the fortress was mobilized. Instead, the fortress served mainly as a political prison, primarily

under the tsars. The date on which construction began on the fortress is celebrated as the birth of St. Petersburg.

Cross the footbridge and enter the fortress through **St. John's Gate** (Ioannovskyie Vorota), the main entrance to the outer fortifications. Once inside, you'll need to stop at the ticket office, which is inside the outer fortification wall on the right.

Entrance to the inner fortress is through **St. Peter's Gate** (Petrovskiye Vorota). Designed by the Swiss architect Domenico Trezzini, it was built from 1717 to 1718. After you pass through St. Peter's Gate, the first building to your right is the **Artilleriisky Arsenal**, where weaponry was stored. Just to your left is the **Engineer's House** (Inzhenerny Dom), which was built from 1748 to 1749. It's now a branch of the Museum of the History of St. Petersburg (as are all exhibits in the fortress) and presents displays about the city's prerevolutionary history.

As you continue to walk down the main center lane, away from St. Peter's Gate, you soon come to the main attraction of the fortress, the **Cathedral of Sts. Peter and Paul** (Petropavlovsky Sobor). Constructed between 1712 and 1733 on the site of an earlier wooden church, it was designed by Domenico Trezzini and later embellished by Bartolomeo Rastrelli. It's highly unusual for a Russian Orthodox church. Instead of the characteristic bulbous domes, it's adorned by a single, slender, gilded spire whose height (400 feet) made the church for more than two centuries the city's tallest building. The spire is identical to that of the Admiralty across the river, except that it's crowned by an angel bearing a golden cross. The spire remained the city's highest structure—in accordance with Peter the Great's decree—until 1962, when a television tower was erected (greatly marring the harmony of the city's skyline).

The interior of the cathedral is also atypical. The baroque iconostasis, designed by Ivan Zarudny and built in the 1720s, is adorned by freestanding statues. Another uncommon feature is the pulpit. According to legend, it was used only once, in 1901, to excommunicate Leo Tolstoy from the Russian Orthodox Church for his denouncement of the institution. Starting with Peter the Great, the cathedral served as the burial place of the tsars. You can identify Peter's tomb—a spot he chose himself, to the far right as you face the iconostasis—by the tsar's bust on the railing. Nearly all of Peter's successors were buried ceremoniously in the cathedral as well, with a few notable exceptions: Peter II, Ivan VI, and the last tsar, Nicholas II, who was executed with his family in Ekaterinburg in 1918. In 1992, in recognition of Russia's Imperial past, the most recent Romanov pretender, Grand Duke Vladimir, had been bestowed the honor of burial here, although not in the royal crypt. In 1998, what were thought to be the remains of Nicholas II and his family were identified (with Alexei, the tsarevich, and one of the three daughters still missing) and were solemnly given a final resting place in the cathedral on July 17. Scientific doubts have since been raised, however, about whether or not these remains really belong to members of the Imperial family. You can exit the cathedral through the passageway to the left of the iconostasis. This leads to the adjoining **Grand Ducal Crypt** (Usypalnitsa), built between 1896 and 1908. It contains an exhibit on the architectural history of the fortress.

As you leave the cathedral, note the small classical structure to your right. This is the **Boathouse** (Botny Domik), built between 1762 and 1766 to house Peter the Great's boyhood boat. The boat has since been moved to the Naval Museum on Vasilievsky Island, and the building is not open to the public.

The long pink-and-white building to your left as you exit the cathedral is the **Commandant's House** (Komendantsky Dom), erected between 1743 and 1746. It once housed the fortress's administration and doubled as a courtroom for political prisoners. The Decembrist revolutionaries were tried here in 1826. The room where the trial took place forms part of the ongoing exhibits, which deal with the history of St. Petersburg from its founding to 1917. Across the cobblestone yard, opposite the entrance to the cathedral, stands the **Mint** (Monetny Dvor), which was first built in 1716; the current structure, however, was erected between 1798 and 1806. The mint is still in operation, producing coins, medals, military decorations, and *znachki,* or Russian souvenir pins. The coins that were taken along on Soviet space missions were made here.

Take the pathway to the left of the Commandant's House (as you're facing it), and you'll be headed right for **Neva Gate** (Nevskiye Vorota), built in 1730 and reconstructed in 1787. As you walk through its passageway, note the plaques on the inside walls marking flood levels of the Neva. The most recent, from 1975, shows the river more than 9 feet above normal. The gate leads out to the **Commandant's Pier** (Komendantskaya Pristan). Up above to the right is the **Signal Cannon** (Signalnaya Pushka), fired every day at noon. From this side you get a splendid view of St. Petersburg. You may want to step down to the sandy beach, where even in winter hearty swimmers enjoy the Neva's arctic waters. In summer the beach is lined with sunbathers, standing up or leaning against the fortification wall.

As you return back to the fortress through the Neva Gate, you'll be following the footsteps of prisoners who passed through this gate on their way to their execution. Several of the fortress's bastions, concentrated at its far western end, were put to use over the years mainly as political prisons. One of them, **Trubetskoi Bastion,** is open to the public as a museum. Aside from a few exhibits of prison garb, the only items on display are the cells themselves, restored to their chilling, prerevolutionary appearance. The first prisoner confined in its dungeons was Peter the Great's own son, Alexei, who was tortured to death in 1718 for treason, allegedly under the tsar's supervision. The prison was enlarged in 1872, when an adjacent one, Alexeivsky Bastion, which held such famous figures as the writers Fyodor Dostoyevsky and Nikolai Chernyshevsky, became overcrowded with dissidents opposed to the tsarist regime. A partial chronology of revolutionaries held here includes some of the People's Will terrorists, who killed Alexander II in 1881; Lenin's elder brother Alexander, who attempted to murder Alexander III (and was executed for his role in the plot); and Leon Trotsky and Maxim Gorky, after taking part in the 1905 Revolution. The Bolsheviks themselves imprisoned people here for a short period, starting with members of the Provisional Government who were arrested and "detained for their own safety" for a few days, as well as sailors who mutinied against the Communist regime in Kronstadt in 1921. They were apparently the last to be held here, and in 1925 a memorial museum (to the prerevolutionary prisoners) was opened instead. Some casements close to the Neva Gate have been converted into a printing workshop (**pechatnya**), where you can buy good-quality graphic art in a broad range of prices. Original late-19th-century presses are used to create lithographs, etchings, and linocuts depicting, most often, urban St. Petersburg landscapes, which make nice alternatives to the usual souvenirs. In the basement, the original foundations were excavated; different layers of the history of the fortress can thus be seen. ☒ *3 Petropavlovskaya Krepost, Petrograd Side* ☎ *812/238–4511* 🎫 *120R* ⊙ *Thurs.–Tues. 11–6, kassa open until 5 Thurs.–Mon., until 4 on Tues.; Cathedral of Sts. Peter and Paul closed Wed.; fortress closed last Tues. of month* Ⓜ *Gorkovskaya.*

㉝ **Peter the Great's Cottage** (Domik Petra Pervovo, Домик Петра Первого). Built in just three days in May 1703, this cottage was home to Peter the Great during construction of the Peter and Paul Fortress. It's made of wooden logs painted to resemble bricks. The stone structure enclosing the cottage was erected in 1784 by Catherine the Great to protect it from the elements. Inside, 18th-century furniture is on display, arranged as it might have been in Peter's day, along with a few of Peter's personal effects. The cottage consists of just three rooms, whose ceilings are surprisingly low—considering that Peter the Great was nearly 7 feet tall. In the courtyard in front of the cottage stands a bronze bust of the tsar. The large stone sculptures of the Shi-Tsza (Lion-Frog) flanking the stair well leading down the embankment side were brought to Russia from Manchuria in 1907. ☒ *6 Petrovskaya nab., Petrograd Side* ☎ *812/232–4576, 812/314–0374 tours* 🎫 *150R* ⊙ *Wed.–Sun. 10–6, Mon. 10–5* ⊙ *Closed last Mon. of month* Ⓜ *Gorkovskaya.*

㉛ **Russian Political History Museum** (Gosudarstvenny Muzey Politicheskoi Istorii Rossii, Государственный Музей Политической Истории России). "From Sublime to Ridiculous," the most popular permanent display at this museum, traces the history of Russia in 20th century through paintings, posters, flags, and porcelain. Socialist realism is featured prominently in the collections. There are always several theme exhibitions on political figures, spies, and controversial historical personages such as Rasputin. The elegant house itself, which was built in the art nouveau style in 1905 by Alexander Goguen, is the former mansion of Mathilda Kshesinskaya, a famous ballerina and the mistress of the last Russian tsar, Nicholas II, before he married Alexandra. She left Russia in 1917 for Paris, where she married a longtime lover, Andrei Vladimirovich, another Romanov. One of Kshesinskaya's pupils was the great English ballerina Margot Fonteyn. The mansion served as Bolshevik committee headquarters in the months leading up to the October Revolution (an exhibit at the museum that reconstructs Lenin's study is a nod to this period). In 1957 it was linked to the adjoining town house by a rather nondescript central wing and turned into the Museum of the Great October Socialist Revolution; in 1991 it was given its current name. All that is left of the original interiors is the reception hall. Call in advance to arrange a guided tour. ✉ *2/4 ul. Bolshaya Dvoryanskaya, ul. Kuybysheva, Petrograd Side* ☎ *812/233–7052* ✎ *150R; 200R per person with Russian-speaking guide; 300R with English-speaking guide, per person up to four people, 240R per person for 5–15 people* ☉ *Fri.–Wed. 10–6, kassa open until 5* Ⓜ *Gorkovskaya.*

Nevsky Prospekt & the Inner City
Невский Проспект и Центр Города

"There is nothing finer than Nevsky prospekt, not in St. Petersburg at any rate, for in St. Petersburg it is everything . . ." wrote the great Russian author Nikolai Gogol more than 150 years ago. Today Nevsky prospekt may not be as resplendent as it was in the 1830s, when noblemen and ladies strolled along the elegant avenue or paraded by in horse-drawn carriages, but it's still the main thoroughfare, and remains the pulse of the city. Through the 18th century it was built up with estates and manors of the gentry, most of which still stand as testimony to the city's noble past. The next century saw a boom of mercantile growth that added sections farther south as centers for commerce, finance, and trade. Under the Communists, few new sites were planned on the prospekt. Instead, old structures found new uses, and the bulk of the Soviets' building was directed outside the city center. Today, Nevsky is once more a retail center, complete with souvenir shops, clubs, neon lights, and young hipsters sporting some outrageous clothes.

a good tour

To explore the inner city and St. Petersburg's most famous avenue, **Nevsky prospekt** ㉟ ▶, start at the relatively peaceful monastery of **Alexander Nevsky Lavra** ㊱, at the southeastern end of Nevsky prospekt. You can reach the monastery by taking the metro to the Ploshchad Alexandra Nevskovo station, which comes out at the foot of the gargantuan Moskva hotel. The entrance to the Lavra is across Ploshchad Alexandra Nevskovo (Alexander Nevsky Square) from the metro exit. After visiting the monastery, return to the square. The bridge to your right, also named for Alexander Nevsky, is the city's longest; it leads to some of St. Petersburg's main bedroom communities, where, these days, most of the city's residents live. Take the metro one stop north to the Mayakovskaya station; at that stop, follow the signs for the adjacent Vosstaniya exit. It's at this point that the avenue's most interesting architecture begins, starting at **Ploshchad Vosstaniya** ㊲, or Insurrection Square. Head west, away from the monastery and the railway station, and after three blocks you'll reach the Fontanka River and one of the city's most beautiful bridges, the **Anichkov most** ㊳; over the river, on the opposite corner, stands the **Anichkov Palace** ㊴. Across from it is the city's largest bookstore, **Dom Knigi** ㊵. Farther along on Nevsky prospekt you'll come to Ploshchad Ostrovskovo, dominated by the city's oldest theater, the **Alexander Pushkin Drama Theater** ㊶. Before moving beyond the square, step around to the back of the theater, where **ulitsa Zodchevo Rossi**—a street whose every proportion has been carefully detailed—begins.

Back on Ploshchad Ostrovskovo, take note of the neoclassical building on the west side of the square. This is the **Russian National Library** ㊷, the nation's largest library after the Russian State Library in Moscow. You may want to cross Nevsky at this point to peek inside the **Yeliseyevsky Food Emporium** ㊸. As you pass Sadovaya ulitsa, taking up the entire block on the other side of the street is the huge **Gostinny Dvor** ㊹ department store. Sadovaya ulitsa also leads to Sennoi Rynok, the city's cleanest and most efficient farmers' market. On the same side of Nevsky prospekt as Yeliseyevsky, between Nos. 40 and 42, is the blue-and-white **Armenian Church** ㊺. At the corner of Mikhailovskaya ulitsa is the Grand Hotel Europe. No. 34 is another recessed church, the **Church of St. Catherine** ㊻. Across the street, on the corner, at No. 33, stands the former city hall under the tsars, the **City Duma** ㊼. Cross the short Kazan Bridge over the Griboyedov Canal to reach one of the city's more resplendent works of religious architecture, the **Kazan Cathedral** ㊽. Cross the street and continue one block down Nevsky; you'll soon reach the **Lutheran Church** ㊾, yet another church on a recessed lot, at Nos. 22–24.

Return now to the other side of the street. Before you cross the little bridge spanning the Moika Canal, you'll be at a magnificent green palace overlooking the embankment. This is the **Stroganov Palace** ㊿. Ahead, the golden building of the Admiralty marks the end of Nevsky prospekt. To return to the metro, take Trolley 1, 5, 7, 10, or 22 one stop to Nevsky prospekt station; however, you might prefer to walk, as trolleys on Nevsky are notoriously overcrowded. But if you have time, head to **Smolny** (51), the great convent and cathedral on the left bank of the Neva; the **Smolnyi Institut** (52); and the **Taurida Palace** (53) on Shpalernaya ulitsa. You can reach all of these sights from Nevsky prospekt by Trolley 5 or 7 (get off at Tulskaya ulitsa).

TIMING To really explore the sights on this tour you should devote a full day to it. Your best bet to avoid the crowds that pack the trolleys and the metro is to do this tour in the morning. However, if you take the metro or trolley instead of walking from one sight to the next, you'll save at least a couple of hours—hours that you can then devote to a little shopping. Most of the souvenir shops are on and around Nevsky prospekt.

What to See

㊱ **Alexander Nevsky Lavra** (Александро-Невская Лавра). The word *lavra* in Russian is reserved for a monastery of the highest order, of which there are just four in all of Russia and Ukraine. Named in honor of St. Alexander Nevsky, this monastery was founded in 1710 by Peter the Great and given lavra status in 1797. Prince Alexander of Novgorod (1220–63), the great military commander, became a national hero and saint because he halted the relentless eastward drive for Russian territory by the Germans and the Swedes. Peter chose this site for the monastery, thinking that it was the same place where the prince had fought the battle in 1240 that earned him the title Alexander of the Neva (Nevsky); actually, the famous battle took place some 20 km (12 mi) away. Alexander Nevsky

Fodor'sChoice ★

had been buried in Vladimir, but in 1724, on Peter's orders, his remains were transferred to the monastery that was founded in his honor.

Entrance to the monastery is through the archway of the elegant **Gate Church** (Tserkovnye Vorota), built by Ivan Starov between 1783 and 1785. The walled pathway is flanked by two cemeteries—together known as the Necropolis of Masters of Arts—whose entrances are a short walk down the path. To the left lies the older **Lazarus Cemetery** (Lazarevskoye kladbische). The list of famous people buried here reads like a who's who of St. Petersburg architects and includes Quarenghi, Rossi, de Thomon, and Voronikhin. The cemetery also contains the tombstone of the father of Russian science, Mikhail Lomonosov. The **Tikhvinskoye kladbische** on the opposite side, is the final resting place of several of St. Petersburg's great literary and musical figures. The grave of Fyodor Dostoyevsky, in the northwestern corner, is easily identified by the tombstone's sculpture, which portrays the writer with his flowing beard. Continuing along the walled path you'll soon reach the composers' corner, where Rimsky-Korsakov, Mussorgsky, Borodin, and Tchaikovsky are buried. The compound includes an exhibition hall with temporary exhibits of "urban sculpture."

After this look at St. Petersburg's cultural legacy, return to the path and cross the bridge spanning the quaint **Monastyrka River.** As you enter the monastery grounds, the **Church of the Annunciation** (Tserkov Blagovescheniya), under renovation at this writing, greets you on your left. The red-and-white rectangular church was designed by Domenico Trezzini and built between 1717 and 1722. It now houses the Museum of City Sculpture (open daily 9:30–1 and 2–5), which contains models of St. Petersburg's architectural masterpieces as well as gravestones and other fine examples of memorial sculpture. Also in the church are several graves of 18th-century statesmen. The great soldier Generalissimo Alexander Suvorov, who led the Russian army to numerous victories during the Russo-Turkish War (1768–74), is buried here under a simple marble slab that he purportedly designed himself. It reads simply: "Here lies Suvorov." Opposite the church, a shop sells religious items and souvenirs.

Outside the church and continuing along the same path, you'll pass a millennial monument celebrating 2,000 years of Christianity on your right, before reaching the monastery's main cathedral, the **Trinity Cathedral** (Troitsky Sobor), which was one of the few churches in St. Petersburg allowed to function during the Soviet era. Designed by Ivan Starov and completed at the end of the 18th century, it stands out among the monastery's predominantly baroque architecture for its monumental classical design. Services are held here daily, and the church is open to the public from 6 AM until the end of the evening service around 8 PM. The magnificent interior, with its stunning gilded iconostasis, is worth a visit. The large central dome, adorned by frescoes designed by the great architect Quarenghi, seems to soar toward the heavens. The church houses the main relics of Alexander Nevsky.

As you leave the church, walk down the steps and go through the gate on the right. A door on the left bears a simple inscription, written by hand: SVEZHY KHLEB (fresh bread). Here you can buy delicious bread baked on the premises. After the gate comes a courtyard and, at the back of the church, a gate to yet another burial ground: St. **Nicholas Cemetery** (Nikolskoye Kladbishche), opened in 1863 and one of the most prestigious burial grounds of the time; it's open daily 9–8 (until 7 in winter). In 1927 the cemetery was closed and the remains of prominent people buried here, including novelist Goncharov and composer Rubinstein, were transferred over the course of several years to the Volkovskoye Cemetery and the Necropolis of Masters of Arts. This pilferage of the tombs went on until the 1940s, by which time valuable funeral monuments had been irretrievably lost. As you reach the steps of the little yellow-and-white church in the center (which gave its name to the graveyard), turn right and walk to a derelict chapel of yellow brick, which has been turned into a makeshift **monument to Nicholas II**. Photocopies stand in for photographs of the Imperial family; pro-monarchy white, yellow, and black flags hang from the ceilings; and passionate adherents have added primitive frescoes to the scene. Nearby, in front of Trinity Cathedral, is yet another final resting place on the lavra's grounds—the **Communist Burial Ground** (Kommunisticheskaya Ploshchadka), where, starting in 1919, defenders of Petrograd, victims of the Kronshtadt rebellion, old Bolsheviks, and prominent scientists were buried. The last to receive that honor were people who took part in the Siege of Leningrad.

Entrance to the monastery grounds is free, although you are asked to make a donation, but you must purchase a ticket for the two cemeteries of the Necropolis of Masters of Arts and the museum, and (as with most Russian museums) it costs extra to take photos or use a video camera. There are ticket kiosks outside the two paying cemeteries, after the gate, and inside the Tikhvin Cemetery, on the right side. ⊠ *1 Pl. Alexandra Nevskovo, Vladimirskaya* ☎ *812/274 1612* ☐ *60R donation, Museum of City Sculpture 30R* ☉ *Fri.–Wed. 9:30–5:30* Ⓜ *Ploshchad Alexandra Nevskovo.*

㊶ Alexander Pushkin Drama Theater (Alexandrinskyi Pushkinsky Teatr, Александринский (Пушкинский) Театр). It might be closed for renovation, but the most imposing building on Ploshchad Ostrovskovo (also referred to as Alexandrinskaya Ploshchad) is this theater built in classical style between 1828 and 1832. Six Corinthian columns adorn the Nevsky facade. Apollo's chariot dominates the building, with statues of the muses Terpischore and Melpomene to keep him company. In the small garden in front of the theater stands the **Catherine Monument**, which shows the empress towering above the principal personalities of her famous reign. Depicted on the pedestal are Grigory Potemkin, Generalissimo Alexander Suvorov, the poet Gavril Derzhavin, and others. Among the bronze figures is Princess Dashkova, who conspired against her own sister's lover—who just happened to be Catherine's husband, Peter III—to help the empress assume the throne. ⊠ *2 Pl. Ostrovskovo, City Center* ☎ *812/312–1545 or 812/710–4103* Ⓜ *Gostinny Dvor or Nevsky prospekt.*

㊳ Anichkov Bridge (Anichkov most, Аничков мост). Each corner of this beautiful bridge spanning the Fontanka River (the name means "fountain") bears an exquisite equestrian statue designed by Peter Klodt and erected in 1841; each bronze sculpture depicts a phase of horse taming. Taken down and buried during World War II, the beautiful monuments were restored to their positions in 1945. The bridge was named for Colonel Mikhail Anichkov, whose regiment had built the first wooden drawbridge here. At that time, early in the 18th century, the bridge marked the city limits, and the job of its night guards was much the same as that of today's border guards: to carefully screen those entering the city. As you cross the bridge, pause for a moment to look back at No. 41, on the corner of Nevsky and the Fontanka. This was formerly the splendiferous **Palace of Prince Beloselsky-Belozersky**—a highly ornate, neobaroque pile designed in 1848 by Andrei Stackenschneider, who wanted to replicate Rastrelli's Stroganovsky Dvorets. The facade of blazing red stonework and whipped-cream stucco trim remains the most eye-knocking in St. Petersburg. The lavish building, once opulent inside and out, housed the local Communist Party headquarters during the Soviet era. Today it is the setting for classical music concerts. The interiors have been largely destroyed and are no longer as magnificent as the facades.

The **St. Petersburg Tourist Information Center** (Gorodskoi Turistichesky Tsentr Informatsii ot Soveta po Turismu; ✉ 14/52 Ul. Sadovaya, City Center ☎ 812/310–2822 Ⓜ Nevsky prospekt) is at the corner of Nevsky Prospect. It's open weekdays 10–7. ✉ *City Center* Ⓜ *Nevsky prospekt.*

㊵ Anichkov Palace (Anichkov Dvorets, Аничков Дворец). This palace, which was named for the colonel whose regiment constructed the nearby Anichkov most, was built by Empress Elizabeth for her lover, Alexei Razumovsky, between 1741 and 1750. As if to continue the tradition, Catherine the Great later gave it to one of her many favorites, Grigory Potemkin. An able statesman and army officer, Potemkin is famous for his attempts to deceive Catherine about conditions in the Russian south. He had fake villages put up for her to view as she passed by during her 1787 tour of the area. The term "Potemkin village" has come to mean any impressive facade that hides an ugly interior.

The palace's neoclassical ensemble was originally designed by Mikhail Zemtsov and completed by Bartolomeo Francesco Rastrelli; it has undergone numerous changes, and little now remains of the elaborate baroque facade. The shady garden has two pavilions—the pearls of Carlo Rossi's architecture. This was once a suburban area, which explains why the main entrance faces the Fontanka rather than Nevsky, where there's only a side entrance. Today, its role as a Youth Palace (once the Pioneer Palace), a kind of recreation center, combined with the fact that it hosts the occasional business conference makes for a strange mix. ✉ *Nevsky pr., City Center* Ⓜ *Nevsky prospekt.*

Anna Akhmatova Literary Museum (Muzey Anny Akhmatovoy, Музей Анны Ахматовой). This museum occupies the former palace of Count Sheremetyev and is accessible either from 53 Liteiny prospekt or from the Fontanka embankment, through the palace hall and the garden. The famous St. Petersburg poet lived for many years in a communal apartment in a wing of the palace. She was born in 1888 in Odessa and was published for the first time in 1910. Akhmatova did not leave Petrograd after the October Revolution, but remained silent between 1923 and 1940. She died in 1966 and is remembered as one of the greatest successors to Pushkin. Her museum is also the venue for occasional poetry readings, other literary events, and temporary exhibitions—in short, a slice of the old-style Russian intelligentsia. Tours are available in Russian only. ⊠ *34 nab. Fontanki or 53 Liteiny pr., City Center* ☎ *812/ 272–2211 or 812/272–5895* ⊕ *www.akhmatova.spb.ru* ✉ *200R, tours 300R for group up to 10 people* ⊗ *Tues.–Sun. 10:30–6, kassa until 5:30* Ⓜ *Nevsky prospekt.*

㊺ Armenian Church (Armyanskaya Tserkov, Армянская Церковь). A fine example of the early-classical style, this blue-and-white church set back from the street was built by Yuri Velten between 1771 and 1780. It's known as "the blue pearl of Nevsky prospekt." This is a quiet, soothing spot to catch your breath before you head back out onto the main Nevsky thoroughfare. ⊠ *Nevsky prospekt, between Nos. 40 and 42, City Center* ☎ *812/318–4108* ⊗ *Daily 9–9* Ⓜ *Nevsky prospekt.*

need a break?

The **Grand Hotel Europe** (⊠ 1/7 Mikhailovskaya ul., City Center ☎ 812/329–6000 Ⓜ Nevsky prospekt) has a lovely mezzanine café, where you can enjoy a pot of tea or a glass of champagne, served with bowls of strawberries. Take a peek at the art nouveau lobby, replete with stained-glass windows and antique furnishings.

off the beaten path

CHESMA CHURCH, CHESMA PALACE (Chesmenskaya Tserkov, Chesmensky Dvorets, Чесменская Церковь и Чесменский Дворец) – Surrounded by dreary Soviet high-rises in a remote residential area, the bright red-and-white-striped Chesma Church is a delightful surprise. A rare example of pseudo-Gothic Russian architecture, the church was built to accompany the Chesma Palace (across the street), which served as a romantic staging post for the Imperial court en route to the summer palaces of Tsarskoye Selo (now Pushkin) and Pavlovsk. The palace was originally called Kekerekeksinensky, which means "frog swamp" in Finnish, but Catherine the Great renamed it to commemorate the Russian naval victory at Chesma in the Aegean in 1770. Both the church and the palace were constructed between 1774 and 1780 by Yuri Felten, designer of the famous fence at the Summer Garden in Liteyny. The palace was rebuilt as a hospice in the 1830s by A. E. Shtaubert, upon instructions from Nicholas I, to house invalid veterans of the Patriotic War of 1812 (against Napoléon's forces). The two wings that he attached to the main building destroyed the charm of the original equilateral triangle, and the rare toothed parapets were demolished. Today it's a unique training school for aircraft designers, but it's in dire disrepair—another example of what happens when a city has too many moldering landmarks on its hands. The church had been made into a branch of the city's Naval Museum, but is once again a place for services. Not far from the Pulkovskaya hotel, the buildings are within walking distance of the Moskovskaya metro stop. You can enter the church, but the palace remains closed to the general public. ✉ *12 ul. Lensoveta, Southern Suburbs* ☎ *812/443–6114, 812/373–6114 church* ⊘ *Daily 9–7; services Tues.–Sun. at 10 AM, Sat. also at 6* Ⓜ *Moskovskaya.*

46 **Church of St. Catherine** (Tserkov Svyatoi Yekateriny, Церковь Святой Екатерины). Built between 1763 and 1783 by Vallin de la Mothe and Antonio Rinaldi, this Catholic church incorporates the baroque and classical styles that were converging at the time in Russia. The grave of Stanislaw Poniatowski, the last king of Poland and yet another lover of Catherine the Great, is here. As with so many churches in the city, services stopped here during the Soviet period, but St. Catherine's is once again fully operational. The small square outside is a favorite haunt of St. Petersburg's street artists. ✉ *34 Nevsky pr., City Center* ☎ *812/717– 5795* ⊘ *Daily 8–8* Ⓜ *Nevsky prospekt.*

47 **City Duma** (Gorodskaya Duma, Городская Дума). This building with a notable red-and-white tower served as the city hall under the tsars. Its clock tower, meant to resemble those in European cities, was erected by Ferrari between 1799 and 1804. It was originally equipped with signaling devices that sent messages between the Winter Palace and the royal summer residences. ✉ *1 ul. Dumskaya, City Center* Ⓜ *Nevsky prospekt.*

40 **Dom Knigi** (House of Books, Дом Книги). This is where you'll find Petersburgers in a favorite pursuit: perusing and buying books. The city's largest bookstore still goes by its generic Soviet name. You may be pleasantly surprised by the prices for classic Russian literature in the original language. Some English-language books are also sold. The store has several branches around the city. ✉ *62 Nevsky pr., City Center* ☎ *812/ 570–6546* ⊘ *Daily 9–10* Ⓜ *Gostiny Dvor.*

F. M. Dostoyevsky Literary-Memorial Museum (Literaturno Memorialnyi Muzey Fyodora Dostoyevskovo, Литературно-мемориальный Музей Ф.М. Достоевского). Here, at the last place in which he lived, Fyodor Dostoyevsky (1821–81) wrote *The Brothers Karamazov*. Dostoyevsky preferred to live in the part of the city inhabited by the ordinary people who populated his novels. He always insisted that the windows of his workroom overlook a church, as they do in this simple little house that has been remodeled to look as it did at the time Dostoyevsky and his family lived here. Perhaps the most interesting section of the museum deals with the writer's stay in prison in the Peter and Paul Fortress, and his commuted execution. ✉ *5/2 Kuznechny per., Vladimirskaya* ☎ *812/571–4031* ⊕ *www.md.spb.ru* ✉ *90R* ⊘ *Tues.–Sun. 11–5* Ⓜ *Dostoyevskaya or Vladimirskaya.*

off the beaten path

FREE ARTS FOUNDATION (Tovarischestvo Svobodnaya Kultura, aka Pushkinskaya Desyat, Товарищество Свободная Культура) – Although the Free Arts Foundation is officially located at 10 Pushkinskaya ulitsa, the entrance is actually nearby at 53 Ligovsky prospekt, an arrangement that gives you some idea of the quirkiness of this bohemian arts collective. Founded in 1989, as glasnost and perestroika were in full cry, this collective brought together St. Petersburg's many underground artists, poets, rock musicians, and other cultural dissidents and gave them a home. Although some of the art produced here is of dubious quality, it's worth dropping in to get a taste of the city's bohemian spirit. Without its artists, St. Petersburg wouldn't be St. Petersburg. This arts collective is also twinned with the club Fish Fabrique, where many of the city's best-known bands play. Opening hours vary (though many studios in the collective are open Wednesday through Sunday from 3 to 7), so the best way to visit is to show up and hope for the best—phone numbers and opening hours mean little here. To find this place, walk down Nevsky prospekt (with the Admiralty behind you) until you reach Ploshchad Vosstaniya, then turn right along Ligovsky prospekt (the Moscow Railroad Station is on the other side of the road) until you reach No. 53; head through the archway, and don't be put off by the shabby door straight ahead—down the stairs, all is artistic wonder and light. The address is also known for housing one of Russia's most famous fans of the legendary Beatles, Kolya Vasin. Vasin, who is now in his early 60s, has never worked and never gotten married because, as he says, he only had time for the Beatles. The little apartment he lives in at 10 ul. Pushkinskaya is called Office of John Lennon's Temple. Vasin dreams of building a temple to John Lennon in St. Petersburg, where thousands of people can worship the Liverpool Four. ☒ *10 Pushkinskaya ul., Vladimirskaya* ☏ *812/764-5371* ☉ *Generally Wed.–Sun. 3–7* ⊕ *www.pushkinskaja-10.spb.ru* Ⓜ *Ploshchad Vosstaniya.*

44 **Gostinny Dvor** (Гостиный Двор). Taking up an entire city block, this is St. Petersburg's answer to the GUM department store in Moscow. Initially constructed by Rastrelli in 1757, it was not completed until 1785, by Vallin de la Mothe, who was responsible for the facade with its two tiers of arches. At the time the structure was erected, traveling merchants were routinely put up in guesthouses (called *gostinny dvor*), which, like this one, doubled as places for doing business. This arcade was completely rebuilt in the 19th century, by which time it housed some 200 general-purpose shops that were far less elegant than those in other parts of the Nevsky. It remained a functional bazaar until alterations in the 1950s and 1960s connected most of its separate shops into St. Petersburg's largest department store. Today Gostinny Dvor houses fashionable boutiques, and you can also find currency-exchange points and ATMs here. Virtually across the street, at 48 Nevsky prospekt, is the city's other major "department store," also an arcade, called **Passazh,** built in 1848. ☒ *35 Nevsky pr., City Center* ☏ *812/710–5408* ☉ *Daily 10–10* Ⓜ *Gostinny Dvor.*

need a break?

40 Nevsky prospekt (☒ 40 Nevsky pr., City Center ☏ 812/312–2457 Ⓜ Nevsky prospekt), a German venture with a restaurant and a coffee bar, is a soothing place to take a break. The wood-panel interior and parquet ceilings have been restored to their original, prerevolutionary appearance. Coffee, ice cream, and scrumptious cakes are available in a no-smoking environment (in the restaurant part, through the left entrance), and it's open noon to midnight.

Zhyly-Byly (✉ 52 Nevsky pr., City Center ☎ 812/314–6230 Ⓜ Nevsky prospekt) takes its name from the phrase used to open every Russian folktale (something like "Once upon a time"), and the clean, cool interior displays a smattering of folk-related objects. It's open around the clock, and serves mainly excellent salads, as well as pastries, and the most delicious and beautiful cakes (some hot food is available). Most surprising is its lengthy wine list. Zhyly-Byly is on the corner of Sadovaya ulitsa.

❽ Kazan Cathedral (Kazansky Sobor, Казанский Собор). After a visit to Rome, Tsar Paul I (1754–1801) commissioned this magnificent cathedral, wishing to copy—and perhaps present the Orthodox rival to—that city's St. Peter's. It was erected between 1801 and 1811 from a design by Andrei Voronikhin. You approach the huge cathedral through a monumental, semicircular colonnade. Inside and out, the church abounds with sculpture and decoration. On the prospect side the frontage holds statues of St. John the Baptist and the apostle Andrew as well as such sanctified Russian heroes as Grand Prince Vladimir (who advanced the Christianization of Russia) and Alexander Nevsky. Note the enormous bronze front doors—exact copies of Ghiberti's Gates of Heaven at Florence's Baptistery.

In 1932 the cathedral, which was closed right after the revolution, was turned into the Museum of Religion and Atheism, with emphasis on the latter. The history of religion was presented from the Marxist point of view, essentially as an ossified archaeological artifact. The museum has since moved to 14 Pochtamtskaya ulitsa, not far from St. Isaac's Cathedral and opposite the main post office (the *pochtamt*). Kazan Cathedral is once again a place of worship.

At each end of the square that forms the cathedral's front lawn are statues of a military leader—at one end, one of Mikhail Barclay de Tolly, at the other, Mikhail Kutuzov. They reflect the value placed in the 19th century on the cathedral as a place of military tribute, especially following Napoléon's invasion in 1812. Kutuzov is buried in the cathedral's northern chapel, where he's supposed to have prayed before taking command of the Russian forces. ✉ 2 *Kazanskaya Pl., City Center* ☎ 812/314–4663 ⊙ *Open daily 8:30–8; services weekdays at 10 AM and 6 PM, weekends at 7 and 10 AM and 6 PM* Ⓜ *Nevsky prospekt.*

off the beaten path

TSPKiO (ЦПКиО) – The commonly used acronym of this park stands for "Central Park of Culture and Leisure named after Kirov." It covers most of Yelagin Ostrov, an island named after its 18th-century aristocratic owner. Within the park are an open-air theater, boating stations, a beach, and Yelagin Palace, designed by Carlo Rossi in the 18th century for Alexander I, who then presented it to his mother, Catherine the Great. The palace contains several fine rooms, including the Porcelain Room, beautifully decorated with painted stucco by Antonio Vighi, and the Oval Hall. If you walk along Primorsky prospekt for about 1 km (½ mi) to the *strelka* (spit), you can catch a view of the sunset over the Gulf of Finland. To reach the park, which is popular year-round with city residents, head south from the Staraya Derevnya metro station along Lipovaya alleya. As you reach the embankment, you'll see a bridge to the island. ✉ *4 Yelagin Ostrov, Vyborg Side* ☎ *812/430–0911* ✉ *Free* ☉ *Park daily 8 AM–10 PM, palace Wed.–Sun. 11–5* Ⓜ *Staraya Derevnya.*

㊾ Lutheran Church (Lyuteranskaya Tserkov, Лютеранская Церковь). Designed by Alexander Bryullov in 1833 to replace an older church that had become too small, this church follows the Romanesque tradition of rounded arches and simple towers. It suffered the same fate as the giant Cathedral of Christ Our Savior in Moscow: during the years in which religion was repressed, the church was converted into a municipal swimming pool. Now, the upper floor is once again a church full of light. Farther down, at No. 20, is the **Dutch Church** (currently a library), yet another reminder of the many denominations that once peacefully coexisted in old St. Petersburg. ✉ *22–24 Nevsky pr., City Center* ☎ *812/ 717–2423* ☉ *Services Sun. at 10:30 AM and 6 PM* Ⓜ *Nevsky prospekt.*

★ ▸ ㉟ Nevsky prospekt (Невский проспект). St. Petersburg's Champs-Élysées, Nevsky prospekt was laid out in 1710, making it one of the city's first streets. Just short of 5 km (3 mi) long, beginning and ending at different bends of the Neva River, St. Petersburg's most famous street starts at the foot of the Admiralty building and runs in a perfectly straight line to the Moscow Station, where it curves slightly before ending a short distance farther at the Alexander Nevsky Lavra. Because St. Petersburg was once part of the larger lands of Novgorod, the road linking the city to the principality was known as Great Novgorod Road; it was an important route for trade and transportation. By the time Peter the Great built the first Admiralty, however, another major road clearly was needed to connect the Admiralty directly to the shipping hub. Originally this new street was called the Great Perspective Road; later it was called the Nevskaya Perspektiva, and finally Nevsky prospekt.

On the last few blocks of Nevsky prospekt as you head toward the Neva are some buildings of historic importance. No. 18, on the right-hand side, was once a private dwelling before becoming a café called Wulf and Beranger; it's now called **Literary Café**. It was reportedly here that Pushkin ate his last meal before setting off for his fatal duel. **Chicherin's House**, at No. 15, was one of Empress Elizabeth's palaces before it became the Nobles' Assembly and, in 1919, the House of Arts. Farther down, at No. 14, is one of the rare buildings on Nevsky prospekt built *after* the Bolshevik Revolution. The blue sign on the facade dates from World War II and the siege of Leningrad; it warns pedestrians that during air raids the other side of the street is safer. The city was once covered with similar warnings; this one was left in place as a memorial, and on Victory Day (May 9 in Russia) survivors of the siege lay flowers here. ✉ *City Center* Ⓜ *Nevsky prospekt, Gostinny Dvor, Mayakovskaya, Ploschad Vosstaniya, or Ploshchad Alexandra Nevskovo.*

off the beaten path

PISKARYEVSKOYE CEMETERY (Piskaryevskoye Kladbische, Пискаревское кладбище) – The extent of this city's suffering during the 900-day siege by the Nazis between 1941 and 1944 becomes clear after a visit to the sobering Piskaryevskoye Cemetery. Located on the northeastern outskirts of the city, the field here was used, out of necessity, as a mass burial ground for the hundreds of thousands of World War II victims, some of whom died from the shelling, but most of whom died from cold and starvation. The numbingly endless rows of common graves carry simple slabs indicating the year in which those below them died. In all, nearly 500,000 people are buried here, and individual graves were an impossibility. The cemetery, with its memorial monuments and an eternal flame, serves as a deeply moving historical marker. Inscribed on the granite wall at the far end of the cemetery is the famous poem by radio personality Olga Bergholts, which ends with the oft-repeated phrase, "No one is forgotten, nothing is forgotten." The granite pavilions at the entrance house a small museum with photographs and memoirs documenting the siege. (Start with the one on the right side; the pavilions are open until 5 and admission is free.) On display is Tanya Savicheva's diary, scraps of paper on which the young schoolgirl recorded the death of every member of her family. The last entry reads, "May 13. Mother died. Everyone is dead. Only I am left." (Later, she, too, died as a result of the war.) A moving context for a visit to this cemetery is provided by the *Blockade Diary* of Lidya Ginzburg (Harvill Press, 2003). Visiting this cemetery today gives you a taste of what the current rupture of the metro Line 1 means for the locals: go to Lesnaya stop, then follow the crowd and take the free shuttle, Bus 80, to Ploshchad Muzhestva metro station (which the transit authority has been promising to reconnect to the line for years); from there, walk back 20 yards to the other side of the avenue and take Bus 123 to the cemetery. On the way back, Bus 123 will leave you at the exact same bus stop where you will board Bus 80 to Lesnaya. ⊠ *74 Nepokorennykh, Vyborg Side* ☎ *812/247–5716* 🎫 *Free* ☉ *Daily 10–6* Ⓜ *Ploshchad Muzhestva via shuttle from Lesnaya.*

㊲ **Ploshchad Vosstaniya** (Insurrection Square, Площадь Восстания). Originally called Znamenskaya Ploshchad (Square of the Sign) after a church of the same name that stood on it, the plaza was the site of many revolutionary speeches and armed clashes with military and police forces—hence its second name. Like Decembrists' Square, the plaza has reverted to its original name, though people still generally call it Insurrection Square (the metro station of the same name hasn't changed). The busy Moscow Railroad Station is here, and this part of Nevsky prospekt is lined with almost every imaginable kind of shop, from fruit markets to art salons to bookstores—although as with elsewhere in the city, some of this area is being cleaned up and put on a semiofficial footing. A stroll here is not a casual affair, for Nevsky is almost always teeming with bustling crowds of shoppers and street artists. Budding entrepreneurs, who sell their wares on the sidewalk on folding tables, further obstruct pedestrian traffic. Here you will also see an increasingly rare sight, the old men of the

Great Patriotic War (the Russian name for World War II), still proudly wearing their medals. ✉ *Vladimirskaya* Ⓜ *Ploschad Vosstaniya.*

Rimsky-Korsakov Museum (Muzei Rimskovo-Korsakova, Музей Римского-Корсакова). Classical concerts are held twice a week in the small concert hall of the composer's former home. On display are many of his personal effects. To get to this small museum from Insurrection Square go south and west to Vladimirsky, then to Zagorodny prospekt. ✉ *28 Zagorodny pr., Apt. 39, Vladimirskaya* ☎ *812/113–3208* 💰 *50R* 🕐 *Wed.–Sun. 11–6* 🕐 *Closed last Fri. of month* Ⓜ *Dostoyevskaya.*

㊷ Russian National Library (Rossiiskaya Natsionalnaya Biblioteka, Российская Национальная Библиотека). Opened in 1814 as the Imperial Public Library, this was Russia's first public library, and today it's still known fondly as the "Publichka." It holds more than 20 million books and claims to have a copy of every book ever printed in Russia. Among its treasures are Voltaire's personal library and the only copy of *Chasovnik* (1565), the second book printed in Russia. The building comprises three sections. The main section, on the corner of Nevsky prospekt and Sadovaya ulitsa, was designed by Yegor Sokolov and built between 1796 and 1801. Another wing, built between 1828 and 1832, was designed by Carlo Rossi as an integral part of Ploshchad Ostrovskovo. True to the building's purpose, the facade is adorned with statues of philosophers and poets, including Homer and Virgil, and the Roman goddess of wisdom, Minerva. You can see the facilities if you bring your passport and ask very nicely. Using the library requires a passport, registration note, and two photos. ✉ *18 Sadovaya ul., City Center* ☎ *812/ 310–7137* 🕐 *Weekdays 9–9, weekends 11–7* 🕐 *Closed last Tues. of month* Ⓜ *Nevsky prospekt.*

★ ㊿ Smolny (Смольный). Confusion abounds when you mention the Smolny, for you can mean either the beautiful baroque church and convent or the classically designed institute that went down in history as the Bolshevik headquarters in the Revolution of 1917. The two architectural complexes are right next door to each other, on the Neva's left bank. Construction of the Smolny convent and cathedral began under Elizabeth I and continued during the reign of Catherine the Great, who established a school for the daughters of the nobility within its walls. The centerpiece of the convent is the magnificent five-domed **Cathedral of the Resurrection**, which was designed by Bartolomeo Rastrelli and which is, some historians say, his greatest creation. At first glance, the highly ornate blue-and-white cathedral seems to have leapt off the pages of a fairy tale. Its five white onion domes, crowned with gilded globes supporting crosses of gold, convey a sense of magic and power. Begun by Rastrelli in 1748, the cathedral was not completed until the 1830s, by the architect Vasily Stasov. Though under renovation it's now open to the public, but few traces of the original interior have survived. It's currently used for concerts, notably of Russian sacred music, and rather insignificant exhibits. The cathedral tower affords beautiful views of the city. ✉ *3/1 Pl. Rastrelli, Liteiny/Smolny* ☎ *812/271–9421 guided tours, 812/271–9182 box office* 💰 *Cathedral 200R, cathedral tower 100R* 🕐 *Wed.–Mon. 10–5* Ⓜ *Chernyshevskaya.*

52 **Smolnyi Institut** (Смольный Институт). The institute, just south of the Cathedral of the Resurrection at Smolny, is a far different structure. Giacomo Quarenghi designed the neoclassical building between 1806 and 1808 in the style of an imposing country manor. The Smolnyi Institute will long be remembered by the Russian people as the site where Lenin and his associates planned the overthrow of the Kerensky government in October 1917. Lenin lived at the Smolnyi for 124 days. The rooms in which he resided and worked are now a memorial museum; to visit the museum you must call for an appointment at least a day in advance and you must bring your passport. Today the rest of the building houses the offices of the governor of St. Petersburg and can be visited only by special request. ⊠ *1 Proletarskoy Diktatury, Liteiny/Smolny* ☎ *812/276–1321* ⊠ *Museum 100R* ⊗ *Museum weekdays 10–5 by appointment* Ⓜ *Chernyshevskaya.*

50 **Stroganov Palace** (Stroganovsky Dvorets, Строгановский Дворец). Even by the regal standards of Russia's aristocratic past, the Stroganovs were the richest of the rich, so it's not surprising that their palace, completed in 1754, is an outstanding example of the Russian baroque and one of Rastrelli's finest achievements. Above the archway of the entrance facing Nevsky prospekt is the family coat of arms: two sables holding a shield with a bear's head above. It symbolizes the Stroganovs' source of wealth—vast holdings of land, with all its resources, including furs—in Siberia. This was, by the way, the birthplace of beef Stroganoff, and it's therefore fitting that the palace courtyard is now the site of the Stroganoff Yard restaurant. The palace, a branch of the State Museum of Russian Art, is open to the public. It houses temporary exhibits, plus a permanent exhibit of exquisite Russian porcelain. ⊠ *17 Nevsky pr., City Center* ☎ *812/571–8238* ⊠ *300R* ⊗ *Mon. 10–4, Wed.–Sun. 10–5:30* Ⓜ *Nevsky prospekt.*

53 **Taurida Palace** (Tavrichesky Dvorets, Таврический Дворец). Built between 1783 and 1789 on the orders of Catherine the Great for her court favorite, Count Grigory Potemkin, the palace is one of St. Petersburg's most magnificent buildings. Potemkin had been given the title of the Prince of Taurida for his annexation of the Crimea (ancient Taurida) to Russia. The Taurida Palace is a splendid example of neoclassicism, the main trend in Russian architecture in the late 18th century. The luxurious interior contrasts with the palace's modest exterior. The palace was inhabited for a long period after Potemkin's death, but in 1906 it was partially rebuilt for the State Duma, Russia's parliament. During the February Revolution of 1917 the Taurida Palace became a center of revolutionary events. Today the palace is used for international conferences and meetings; it also houses the Interparliamentary Assembly of the Commonwealth of Independent States (CIS). It's not open to the public. ⊠ *47 Shpalernaya ul., Liteiny/Smolny* Ⓜ *Chernyshevskaya.*

Ulitsa Zodchevo Rossi (Улица Зодчего Росси). This thoroughfare, once world famous as "Theater Street" (because it meets with the Alexandrinsky Theater), has extraordinary proportions: it's bounded by two buildings of exactly the same height, its width (72 feet) equals the height of the buildings, and its length is exactly 10 times its width. It reminds one of a big dancing hall without a roof. A complete view unfolds only at the end of the street, where it meets Lomonosov Ploshchad. The perfect symmetry is reinforced by the identical facades of the two buildings, which are painted the same subdued yellow and decorated with impressive white pillars. One of the buildings here is the legendary **Vaganova Ballet School** (founded in 1738), whose pupils included Karsavina as well as Pavlova, Nijinsky, Ulanova, Baryshnikov, and Nureyev. ⊠ *City Center* Ⓜ *Nevsky prospekt.*

❹❸ **Yeliseyevsky Food Emporium** (Елисеевский Магазин). Officially called Gastronome No. 1 under the Communists, this famous store directly across the street from the Catherine Monument is known once again by its original name. Built at the turn of the 20th century for the immensely successful grocer Yeliseyev, the store is decorated in the style of early art nouveau. The interior, with its colorful stained-glass windows, gilded ceilings, and brass chandeliers, is worth a look. Before the revolution Yeliseyevsky specialized in imported delicacies, and after several lean decades, goods again overflow its shelves—this is a particularly good place to find wines and spirits from all over the former Soviet Union. ⊠ *56 Nevsky pr., at Malaya Sadovaya, City Center* ☎ *812/312–1865* ⊙ *Weekdays 10–9, weekends 11–9* Ⓜ *Nevsky prospekt.*

From the Square of the Arts to the Field of Mars
От Площади Искусств до Марсова Поля

This area introduces you to some of St. Petersburg's prettiest inner streets, squares, and gardens, starting at Ploshchad Iskusstv (Square of the Arts). Along the route are several squares and buildings of historic interest: it was in this part of the city that several extremely important events in Russian history took place, including the murder of Tsars Paul I, who was assassinated in the Engineer's Castle by nobles opposed to his rule, and of Alexander II, killed when a handmade bomb was lobbed at him by revolutionary terrorists as he was riding in a carriage along Kanal Griboyedova.

a good walk

Start by heading down Nevsky prospekt to Mikhailovskaya ulitsa, opposite Gostinny Dvor. Walking up this short street will take you past the handsome Grand Hotel Europe, built in the 1870s and given its art nouveau facade in 1910. Nearby is the start of a large pedestrian zone that extends through much of the historic center of the city, running from the Academic Kapella on the Moika embankment all the way south to Manezhnaya Ploshchad. Straight up Mikhailovskaya ulitsa is Mikhailovsky Dvorets, now the site of the magnificent State Museum of Russian Art, at the far end of Ploshchad Iskusstv. The building to the right of the palace appears to be an extension of its right wing but is a different building entirely—the **Ethnography Museum** ❺❹ ▶.

If you stand in front of the palace and turn to survey the entire square, the first building on your right, with old-fashioned lanterns adorning its doorways, is the **Mussorgsky Theater of Opera and Ballet** ❺❺. Next door, at No. 3, is the **Isaac Brodsky Museum** ❺❻. Bordering the square's south side, on Mikhailovskaya ulitsa's east corner, is the former Nobles'

Club, now the **Shostakovich Philharmonia** 🔂, home to the St. Petersburg Philharmonic. The buildings on the square's remaining side are former residences and school buildings. One of the entrances to the **State Museum of Russian Art** 🔂 is around the corner, through Korpus Benois. To find it, leave Ploshchad Iskusstv and go down ulitsa Inzhenernaya toward the Kanal Griboyedova. Take a right and you'll find the entrance a few steps away. Go right when you leave the museum; straight ahead is the almost outrageously colorful **Church of the Savior on Spilled Blood** 🔂.

To the right as you walk past the church is a small park behind a lovely wrought-iron fence. Known as Mikhailovsky Sad (Mikhail Garden), it forms the back of Grand Duke Mikhail's former estate. On the other side of this pleasant park runs Sadovaya ulitsa. Follow the street you're on, however, as it curves around gently to the right. Opposite the gardens, across the street, spreads **Marsovo Pole** 🔂, the Field of Mars (you'll have to cross the Moika River to get here). The buildings flanking the left side of the field are the former barracks of the Pavlovsky Guards Regiment. They were completed in 1819, in tribute to the regiment's victories in the war against Napoléon. Walk down this side of the street to reach Millionaya ulitsa (Millionaire's Street), which, as the name implies, was once one of St. Petersburg's swankiest addresses.

On this street, in front of you, is the **Marble Palace** 🔂. Take a right and walk down Millionaya ulitsa the length of the Field of Mars. On the left you pass **Suvorovskaya Ploshchad** 🔂. Walk up to the river and continue going east (right). Very soon you'll find yourself in front of the marvelous grille that marks the entrance to **Summer Garden** 🔂, once Peter the Great's private garden. You enter the garden at the far left end of the railing. Exiting at the south end of the park will bring you out in front of the former castle of Tsar Paul I, across the street, the **Engineer's Castle** 🔂. The tour ends here. From the castle, you can walk down Sadovaya ulitsa until it intersects with Nevsky prospekt. If you take the first right off Sadovaya ulitsa, you'll return to Ploshchad Iskusstv. If you like, you can stop in the Mikhail Garden now; there's an entrance on this side, to the right.

Starting from its originating point, the Grand Hotel Europe, this walk can also be done in the opposite direction, taking in a few additional sights along the way. This time, as you face the square, instead of going past the Mussorgsky Theater you should instead turn right and walk along Italianskaya ulitsa past the Philharmonia. As you continue you'll pass the Theater of Musical Comedy and a bright orange building on your right, which is the official Currency Exchange. Straight ahead you'll enter the Manezhnaya Ploshchad pedestrian zone, which has a pleasant little park in the middle with a fountain and bright flower beds. It's a great place to sit under a tree and cool off on a hot summer day. In warmer weather, you can also find several outdoor cafés and glorified beer tents here. Just as you enter the square, you may want to take a short side trip down Malaya Sadovaya ulitsa, another pedestrian zone to your right. As you take the short walk toward Nevsky prospekt be sure to look up at the buildings on both sides of the street, where you'll find a number of statues of cats—a reminder of the inhuman conditions brought on by the 900-day siege of Leningrad during World War II, during which many starving residents resorted to eating their pets to stay alive.

Head back to the park in Manezhnaya Ploshchad. Opposite you can see a large yellow building in front of which sits a statue of one of Russia's great 19th-century writers, Ivan Turgenev. Leaving the square, follow Karavannaya ulitsa north until you reach the **St. Petersburg Circus.** From here take a left and keep walking until you see two pink buildings on Inzhenernaya ulitsa; take a right between the two buildings and enter the park behind the Engineer's Castle. Once you reach the castle, it's time to jump back on the path of the walk mentioned above. You can go left entering the Mikhail Garden and cross the street in front of the castle to enter the Letny Sad, or you can enter the Field of Mars and head toward the Neva.

TIMING Including stops, this walk should take between two and three hours, unless you want to linger at the State Museum of Russian Art, in which case you might want to plan an entire day for this tour. Outdoor attractions on this tour, such as the Summer Garden, are worth visiting at any time of the year. Note that the Neva is very close here and that it's windy year-round.

What to See

★ ⑤⑨ **Church of the Savior on Spilled Blood** (Khram Spasa na Krovi, Храм Спаса на Крови). The highly ornate, old-Russian style of this colorful church seems more befitting to Moscow than St. Petersburg, where the architecture is generally more subdued and subtle; indeed, the architect, Alfred Parland, was consciously aiming to copy Moscow's St. Basil's. The drama of the circumstances leading to the church's inception more than matches the frenzy of its design, however. It was commissioned by Alexander III to memorialize the shocking death of his father, Alexander II, who was killed on the site in 1881 by a terrorist's bomb.

The church opened in 1907 but was closed by Stalin in the 1930s. It suffered damage over time, especially throughout World War II, but underwent meticulous reconstruction for decades (painstaking attempts were made to replace all original components with identically matched materials) and finally reopened at the end of the 20th century. The interior is as extravagant as the exterior, with glittering stretches of mosaic from floor to ceiling (70,000 square feet in total). Stone carvings and gold leaf adorn the walls, the floors are made of pink Italian marble, and the remarkable altar is constructed entirely of semiprecious gems and supported by four jasper columns. Blinded by all this splendor, you could easily overlook the painted scenes of martyrdom, including one that draws a parallel between the tsar's death and the crucifixion of Christ. Across the road there's an exhibit that takes a compelling look at the life of Alexander II. ✉ *2a Kanal Griboyedova, City Center* ☎ *812/315–1636* 🎫 *270R* ☉ *Thurs.–Tues. 11–6* Ⓜ *Nevsky prospekt.*

⑥④ **Engineer's Castle** (Inzhenerny Zamok, Инженерный Замок). This orange-hue building belonged to one of Russia's stranger and more pitiful leaders. Paul I grew up in the shadow of his powerful mother, Catherine the Great, whom he despised; no doubt correctly, he held her responsible for his father's death. By the time Paul became tsar, he lived in terror that he, too, would be murdered. He claimed that, shortly after ascending the throne, he was visited in a dream by the Archangel Michael, who instructed him to build a church on the site of his birthplace (hence the other name of this landmark: Mikhailovsky Castle, not to be confused with the Mikhailovsky Palace). Paul then proceeded to erect not just a church but a castle, which he tried to make into an impenetrable fortress. Out of spite toward his mother, he took stones and other materials from castles that she had built. The Fontanka and Moika rivers cut off access from the north and east; and for protection everywhere else, he installed secret passages, moats with drawbridges, and earthen ramparts. All of Paul's intricate planning, however, came to naught. On March 24, 1801, a month after he began living there, he was murdered—suffocated with a pillow in his bed. Historians speculate that his own son Alexander I knew that such a plot was underway and may even have participated. After Paul's death, the castle stood empty for 20 years, then was turned over to the Military Engineering Academy. One of the school's pupils was Fyodor Dostoyevsky, who may have absorbed something of the castle while he studied here: as a novelist he was preoccupied with themes of murder and greed. The castle is now part of the State Museum of Russian Art; it houses temporary exhibits from the museum, plus an exhibit on the history of the castle. ⊠ *2 Sadovaya ul., City Center* ☎ *812/313–4112, 812/313–4173 private tours* ⊕ *www.rusmuseum.ru* ✉ *300R; 1,200R for group tour in Russian* ☉ *Mon. 10–4, Wed.–Sun. 10–5; tours weekends at 2 and 4* Ⓜ *Nevsky prospekt.*

▶ **54** **Ethnography Museum** (Etnograficheskii Muzey, Этнографический Музей). This museum contains a fascinating collection of applied art, national costumes, weapons, and many sociological displays about peoples of the 19th and 20th centuries, including the various ethnic groups of the former Soviet Union. On Sunday the museum offers very interesting Russian crafts workshops where you can learn to paint on wood or clay, model something out of clay or birch bark, or make a folk doll. ⊠ *4/1 Inzhenernaya ul., City Center* ☎ *812/313–4421* ✉ *300R, 450R for craft workshop* ☉ *Tues.–Sun. 11–6, kassa until 5; closed last Fri. of month. Crafts workshop Sun. 11–5* Ⓜ *Nevsky prospekt.*

56 **Isaac Brodsky Museum** (Muzey Isaaka Brodskovo, Музей Исаака Бродского). This structure was built in the 1820s for the Golenishchev-Kutuzovs, a high-ranking military family. The painter Isaac Brodsky (1884–1939) lived here from 1924 to 1939, and it's now a memorial museum to him. On view are some of his works as well as items from his private collection, which included pieces by Ilya Repin and Valentin Serov. ⊠ *3 Pl. Iskusstv, City Center* ☎ *812/314–3658* ✉ *200R, guided tour 500R* ☉ *Wed.–Sun. 11–6, kassa open until 5* Ⓜ *Nevsky prospekt.*

need a break? No. 5 Ploshchad Iskusstv had a famous café–cum–art salon, the "Stray Dog," in its basement from 1911 to 1915. A diverse group of painters, writers, and musicians—including the poets Anna Akhmatova, Nikolai Gumilev, and Osip Mandelstam—used it as a creative meeting point. The restaurant is now open again under the same name, **Brodyachaya Sobaka** (✉ 5 Pl. Iskusstv, City Center ☎ 812/315–7764 Ⓜ Nevsky prospekt). It valiantly tries to re-create some of the original "arty" ethos. The attendant results, however, are bizarre: quasi-postmodernist dog sculptures made of wood, newspapers, and various fabrics by local artists are scattered through a gleaming white interior. At the bar you'll find a selection of pamphlets of poetry hot off the press, as well as paintings by local artists on the walls. The restaurant also has a café and a third hall, which was host to all those celebrities of the early 20th century. The hall is mainly used for concerts. On the menu are dishes that were served during the restaurant's first epoch, such as Dogs Rissoles, cutlets made of pork and beef.

⑥ **Marble Palace** (Mramorny Dvorets, Мраморный Дворец). One of Catherine the Great's favorite palaces, this was designed for Count Grigory Orlov, one of the empress's more famous amours, by Arnoldo Rinaldi and built between 1768 and 1785. However, Count Orlov never lived in the palace because he died two years before the end of its construction. Later the palace belonged to members of Russian royal family. Its name derives from its pale pink-purple marble facing. From 1937 to 1991 it housed the Lenin Museum; in the courtyard was the armored automobile from which he made his revolutionary speech at the Finland Station. Today, instead of Lenin's automobile you can see an equestrian statue of Tsar Alexander III first erected in 1909 on Znamenskaya Ploshchad (by the Moscow Station). The statue survived under the Soviets, hidden in the State Museum of Russian Art's courtyard. The palace now belongs to that noted museum and houses three main collections: on the second floor are pieces by foreign artists who worked in Russia in the 18th and early 19th centuries, as well as a collection of contemporary art by 33 artists (including Rauschenberg, Lichtenstein, and Warhol), donated to the museum by the noted German collectors Peter and Irene Ludwig.

You may also wish to have a look at the Marble Hall, covered with lazurite and marbles from the Urals, northern Russia, and Italy; enjoy the superb views of the Peter and Paul Fortress and the Engineer's Castle; check out the curious *Peter the Great as a Child, Saved by His Mother from the Fury of the Streltsy* by Steuben; and then head to the third floor. The gallery here is called "a museum in the museum"; it houses paintings and drawings by such avant-garde Constructivists as Puni, Altman, Tatlin, Malevich, and Matiushin, put together between 1918 and 1922 for the Museum of Fine Arts, which belongs to the palace and is included in the admission price. The Constructivists' work, which developed on a par with that of the French Cubists in the early 20th century, was deemed unacceptable under the Soviets and was kept in storage until perestroika. A separate ticket (100R) is required for a guided tour of Grand Duke Konstantin Konstantinovich Romanov's private quarters (groups of 10 people maximum). This grand duke (1858–1915), uncle of the last Russian tsar, was also known as a writer and was head of Emperor's Academy of Science. He was the last owner of Marble Palace. ✉ *5/1*

Millionaya ul., City Center ☎ *812/312–9054* ⊕ *www.rusmuseum.ru* ☞ *300R* ☉ *Mon. 10–5, Wed.–Sun. 10–6, kassa open until 1 hr before closing* Ⓜ *Chernyshevskaya or Nevsky prospekt.*

★ ⑥⓪ **Marsovo Pole** (Field of Mars, Марсово Поле). The site was once a marsh, from which both the Mya and the Krikusha rivers began. Peter the Great had it drained (and the rivers linked by a canal), and the space was subsequently used for parades and public occasions. The field acquired its current name around 1800, when it began to be used primarily for military exercises. Shortly after 1917 it was turned into a burial ground for Red Army victims of the revolution and ensuing civil war. The massive granite **Monument to Revolutionary Fighters** was unveiled here on November 7, 1919, with an eternal flame lit 40 years later, on the revolution's anniversary. Keep an eye out for newlyweds, who come here (among other famous city landmarks) immediately after their weddings for good luck. ✉ *City Center* Ⓜ *Chernyshevskaya or Nevsky prospekt.*

⑤⑤ **Mussorgsky Theater of Opera and Ballet** (Театр Оперы и Балета имени Мусоргского). This historic theater built in 1833 is also known as the Maly, or Little Theater, the name given it during the Communist era, but a nomenclature that makes the theater itself bridle. Before the revolution it was the Mikhailovsky Theater, but French companies performed here so often that it was more commonly referred to as the French Theater. After the Mariinsky (formerly the Kirov), this is St. Petersburg's second-most important theater. ✉ *1 Pl. Iskusstv, City Center* ☎ *812/595–4305* Ⓜ *Nevsky prospekt.*

🎪 **St. Petersburg Circus** (Tsirk Sankt-Peterburga, Цирк Санкт-Петербурга). Though perhaps not as famous as the Moscow Circus, the St. Petersburg Circus, dating from 1867, remains a popular treat for children. Avid young circus fans get a kick out of its adjacent **Circus Art Museum,** as well, with displays about the world of the circus. ✉ *3 nab. Fontanki, City Center* ☎ *812/313–4198 circus, 812/313–4413 museum* ☉ *Performances Fri. 7 PM, Sat. 3 and 7 PM, Sun. 1 and 5 PM; museum weekdays noon–5* ☞ *100R–400R* Ⓜ *Chernyshevskaya or Nevsky prospekt.*

⑤⑦ **Shostakovich Philharmonia** (Филармония имени Шостаковича). Once part of the private Nobles' Club, the Philharmonia, or Philharmonia Hall, is now home to the **St. Petersburg Philharmonic.** Its main concert hall, the Bolshoi Zal, with its impressive marble columns, has been the site of many celebrated performances, including in 1893 the first presentation of Tchaikovsky's Sixth (*Pathetique*) Symphony, his final masterpiece, with the composer conducting. (He died nine days later.) More recently, in 1942, when Leningrad was completely blockaded, Dmitri Shostakovich's Seventh (*Leningrad*) Symphony premiered here, an event broadcast in the same spirit of defiance against the Germans in which it was written. Later the concert hall was officially named for this composer. A smaller hall, the **Maly Zal** (Glinka Hall; ✉ 30 Nevsky pr., City Center ☎ 812/579–8333), around the corner, is also part of the complex. ✉ *2 Milkhailovskaya ul., City Center* ☎ *812/710–4257 kassa, 812/710–4290 directory service* Ⓜ *Nevsky prospekt.*

58 **State Museum of Russian Art** (Gosudarstvenny Russky Muzey,

Fodor'sChoice Государственный Русский Музей). In 1898 Nicholas II turned the stu-

★ pendously majestic neoclassical **Mikhailovsky Palace** (Mikhailovsky
Dvorets) into a museum that has become one of the country's most important art galleries. He did so in tribute to his father, Alexander III,
who had a special regard for Russian art and regretted, after seeing
Moscow's Tretyakov Gallery, that St. Petersburg had nothing like it.

The collection at the museum, which is sometimes just referred to as
the Russian Museum, is four times greater than Moscow's Tretyakov
Gallery, with scores of masterpieces on display. Outstanding icons include the 14th-century *Boris and Gleb* and the 15th-century *Angel Miracle of St. George.* Both 17th- and 18th-century paintings are also well
represented, especially with portraiture. One of the most famous 18th-
century works here is Ivan Nikitin's *The Field Hetman.* By far the most
important cache, however, comprises 19th-century works—huge canvases by Repin, many fine portraits by Serov (his beautiful *Countess
Orlova* and the equally beautiful, utterly different portrait of the dancer
Ida Rubinstein), and Mikhail Vrubel's strange, disturbing *Demon Cast
Down.* For many years much of this work was unknown in the West,
and it's fascinating to see the stylistic parallels and the incorporation of
outside influences into a Russian framework. Painters of the World of
Art movement—Bakst, Benois, and Somov—are also here. There are several examples of 20th-century art, with works by Kandinsky and Kaz-
imir Malevich. Natan Altman's striking portrait of the poet Anna
Akhmatova is in Room 77. The museum usually has at least one excellent special exhibit in place, and there's a treasure gallery here as well
(guided tours only; you need a special ticket that you can get before noon).
The Marble Palace, Engineer's Castle, and Stroganov Palace are all
branches of the museum.

The square in front of the palace was originally named Mikhailovsky
Ploshchad for Grand Duke Mikhail Pavlovich (1798–1849), the younger
brother of Alexander I and Nicholas I and resident of the palace. The
square's appearance is the work of Carlo Rossi, who designed the facade of each building encircling it as well as the Mikhailovsky Palace.
Each structure, as well as the plaza itself, was made to complement
Mikhail's residence on its north side. The palace, which was built between 1819 and 1825, comprises a principal house and two service wings.
The central portico, with eight Corinthian columns, faces a large courtyard now enclosed by a fine art nouveau railing, a late (1903) addition.
The statue of Alexander Pushkin in the center of the plaza was designed
by Mikhail Anikushin and erected in 1957. ⊠ *4/2 Inzhenernaya ul., City
Center* ☎ *812/595–4248* ⊕ *www.rusmuseum.ru* 🎫 *300R* ⊙ *Mon.
10–5, Wed.–Sun. 10–6, kassa open until 1 hr before closing* Ⓜ *Nevsky
prospekt.*

★ **63** **Summer Garden** (Letny Sad, Летний Сад). Inspired by Versailles, the Summer Garden was one of Peter the Great's passions. When first laid out
in 1704, it was given the regular, geometric style made famous by Louis
XIV's gardener, Andre Le Nôtre, and decorated with statues and sculptures as well as with imported trees and plants. Grottoes, pavilions, ponds,

fountains, and intricate walkways were placed throughout, and the grounds are bordered on all sides by rivers and canals. In 1777, however, disastrous floods did so much damage (entirely destroying the system of fountains) that the Imperial family stopped using the garden for entertaining. When they decamped for environs farther afield, they left the Summer Garden for use by the upper classes. Today it's a popular park accessible to everyone, but you'll have to imagine the first formal garden, for it's no longer there. The graceful wrought-iron fence that marks the entrance to the garden was designed in 1779 by Yuri Felten; it's supported by pink granite pillars decorated with vases and urns.

Just inside this southeastern corner is Peter's original **Summer Palace**, Letny Dvorets. Designed by Domenico Trezzini and completed in 1714, the two-story building is quite simple, as most of Peter's dwellings were. The walls are of stucco-cover brick, painted primrose yellow. Open since 1934 as a museum, it has survived without major alteration. Two other attractive buildings nearby are the **Coffee House** (Kofeinyi Domik) built by Carlo Rossi in 1826 and the **Tea House** (Tchainyi Domik) built by L. I. Charlemagne in 1827, neither of which, alas, serves the beverage for which it is named.

As you walk through the park, take a look at some of its more than 80 statues. *Peace and Abundance,* sculpted in 1722 by Pietro Baratta, is an allegorical depiction of Russia's victory in the war with Sweden. Another statue, just off the main alley, is of Ivan Krylov, a writer known as "Russia's La Fontaine." Peter Klodt, who also did the Anichkov Bridge horse statues, designed this sculpture, which was unveiled in 1855. Scenes from Krylov's fables, including his version of "The Fox and the Grapes," appear on the pedestal. As in many other parks and public places, the sculptures are protected from the harsh weather by wooden covers from early fall to late spring. There's a small admission fee (15R) to the park on weekends in summer. ⊠ *City Center* Ⓜ *Chernyshevskaya or Nevsky prospekt.*

62 **Suvorovskaya Ploshchad** (Suvorov Square, Суворовская Площадь). In the middle of this square stands a statue of the military commander Alexander Suvorov, cast as Mars, god of war. Appropriately enough, when first unveiled in 1801, the statue stood in the Field of Mars, but in 1818 it was moved to its current location. ⊠ *City Center* Ⓜ *Chernyshevskaya or Nevsky prospekt.*

WHERE TO EAT

The new restaurants and cafés of the burgeoning scene stand in sharp contrast to the traditional, sometimes uninspired, Russian-style eateries of the former Soviet Union. Of course, the old-style restaurants can still be found in abundance—the places that insist on bottles of vodka on every table, the synthesizer-accompanied singer droning Russian chansons, and long, often pricey meals in settings designed to evoke the luxury of the Imperial past. Although it's certainly worth experiencing Russian-style dining during your stay—and discovering the French underpinnings of Russian cuisine that become apparent at some of the finer establishments—know that you have plenty of options, and you don't have to pay an exorbitant price to eat well.

At the new breed of Russian eateries, you almost feel you could be anywhere in Europe. Although originality is still rare, the food is often reasonably priced and almost always good. Old habits die hard, however, so even when the chef ventures into new territory, say, with Asian-influenced dishes, you tend to still find traditional standbys like borscht on the same menu.

Hotels often house excellent restaurants and foreign chefs, who used to be a rarity even in top-flight hotels, have become an integral part of the city's culinary scene. The Grand Hotel Europe is filled to the brim with reliable places, including Chinese and Western restaurants, as well as the elegant L'Europe, in a category all its own. At the restaurants of the Astoria and Radisson SAS Royal you will find top-notch service, some imaginative chefs, and often good views. Most leading hotels and finer restaurants offer tempting three-course or generous buffet business lunches for $10–$15. They are normally advertised or reviewed in dining sections of *The St. Petersburg Times* and *St. Petersburg In Your Pocket,* and are a fantastic value, so be sure to check them out.

It's not necessary to plan ahead if you want to land a table in a nice establishment on weekdays, but it's generally a good idea to reserve ahead for weekend dining or for a large party. Ask your hotel or tour guide for help making a reservation. Note that few restaurants in St. Petersburg have no-smoking sections; in fact, some places have cigarettes listed on the menu. Most restaurants stop serving food around 11 PM or midnight, although more and more 24-hour cafés are opening.

Homey and jovial little budget eateries serving quick, substantial, and good meals for under $10 have mushroomed around the city. You can opt for a Russian pancake cafeteria, an authentic Italian pizzeria, a Greek taverna, or a lively Caucasian inn. What has also boomed across the city are stands selling Russian bliny, the hearty Russian cousin of the French crepe. The dish seems easy to make but it's actually even easier to ruin, so to avoid a pale, bland, glutinous mass with an indiscernible filling, our advice is to stick to the best purveyor, Teremok.

The selection of reviews that follows is a sampling of old-era restaurants that have managed to maintain a high level of quality, new places of international standards, eateries that cater to tourists and expats, and a few bargain, off-the-beaten-path spots. It's cause to rejoice that it's no longer possible to enumerate all of the good dining spots in the city. At one time the only place to find a decent espresso was at one of the city's upscale hotels. The situation has changed drastically, with numerous true Western-style coffee shops opening up all over the city.

Prices

Don't assume credit cards are accepted, even when you see them listed at the entrance; it's best to double-check with the staff. Many restaurants list their prices in dollars or "conditional units" (YE in Cyrillic), which are pegged to an exchange rate of their own devising (usually the

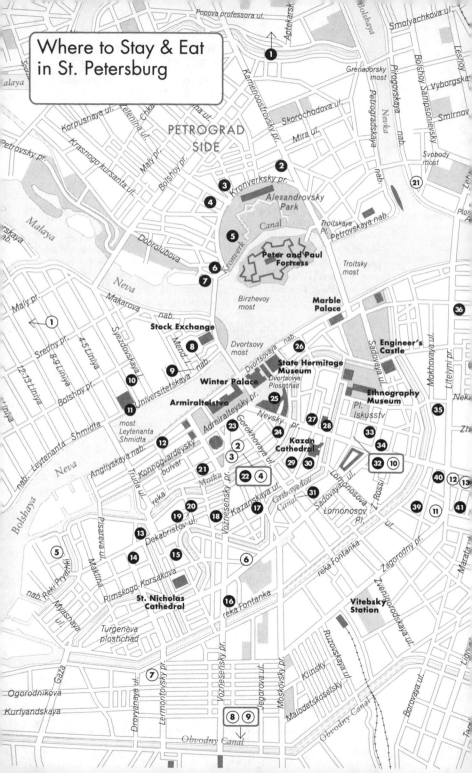

Where to Stay & Eat in St. Petersburg

Restauraunts ▼

Akvarium **2**
Aquarel **7**
Bagrationi **36**
Bessonnitsa **6**
Bistro Garçon **44**
Bliny Domik **41**
Canvas **21**
Caravan **16**
Che **42**
Da Albertone **26**
Dvoryanskoye Gnezdo . .**19**
Ermitazhniy Restoran . . .**25**
Gorniy Orel **5**
Idealnaya Chashka **27**
Il Grappolo **35**
James Cook **12**
Kilikia **31**
Kvareli **4**
Laima Bistro **28**
LeChaim **14**
L'Europe **32**
Macaroni **39**
Mechta Molokhovets . . .**37**
New Island **11**
1913 . . . .**18**
Oliva **22**
Onegin **33**
Palkin **40**
Pirozhkovaya
Mr. Baker **38**
Pirozhkovaya
Stolle **10, 13, 20**
Restoran **9**
Russkaya Rybalka **1**
Staraya Tamozhnya **8**
Sukawati **30**
Taleon **24**
Tandoor **23**
Teremok **34, 43**
Tinkoff **29**
Volshebniy Vkus **3**
Za Stsenoi **15**
Zov Ilicha **17**

Hotels ▼

Ambassador **6**
All Seasons **8**
Astoria **3**
Casa Leto **4**
City Realty **2**
Corinthia Nevsky
Palace Hotel **13**
Deson-Ladoga **15**
Dostoyevsky **11**
Grand Emerald Hotel **18**
Grand Hotel Europe **10**
Matisov Domik **5**
Moskva **16**
Okhtinskaya-Victoria **19**
Oktyabrskaya **14**
Pribaltiskaya **1**
Pulkovskaya **9**
Radisson SAS Royal **12**
Rus **20**
Sovietskaya **7**
St. Petersburg **21**
St. Petersburg
International Hostel **17**

dollar or euro). Even when prices are listed in conditional units, cash payment is only accepted in rubles.

WHAT IT COSTS In U.S. dollars				
$$$$	**$$$**	**$$**	**$**	**¢**
AT DINNER over $35	$25–$35	$18–$25	$10–$18	under $10

Prices are per person for a main course at dinner.

City Center (Palace Square, the Hermitage)
American/Casual
¢–$$ ✗ **Tinkoff.** The crowded, loftlike Tinkoff is St. Petersburg's first microbrewery. People come to enjoy good beer and tasty comfort food in a relaxed, almost clublike dining room. There's a sushi bar, too, but you're better off sticking with the beer and burgers. ✉ *7 Kazanskaya ul., City Center* ☎ *812/718–5566* ▭ *AE, DC, MC, V* Ⓜ *Nevsky prospekt.*

Armenian
¢ ✗ **Kilikia.** A haven for the local Armenian diaspora, Kilikia, named after its namesake Armenian region in Turkey, has a strong reputation for its ethnic cuisine. Sizzling beef stew is a hit, and expertly cooked kebabs are available in tempting variety. There are six halls in this sprawling, dimly lighted eatery but seating only expands to them as space is needed. The seemingly endless menu may confuse the non-initiated, but the staff are competent and are a great help with orientation. Budget travelers will be thrilled by Kilikia's business lunch at $4. ✉ *26/40 Gorokhovaya ul.* ☎ *812/327–2208* ▭ *MC, V* Ⓜ *Sennaya Ploshchad.*

Cafés & Coffee Shops
¢–$ ✗ **James Cook.** Upon entering James Cook you have a choice: turn right for the pub with a decent menu or left for one of the finest coffee shops in town. Choose from 40 kinds of coffee, elite teas, various coffee cocktails, and desserts. The breakfast deal at the coffee shop is one of the best in town: $5 will buy you a hot dish plus coffee or tea, toast, and a choice of yogurt or fruit salad. ✉ *2 Svedsky per., City Center* ☎ *812/312–3200* ▭ *DC, MC, V* Ⓜ *Nevsky prospekt.*

¢ ✗ **Idealnaya Chashka.** "Ideal Cup" is St. Petersburg's answer to Starbucks, with new branches popping up all over the city. Serving more than three dozen kinds of coffee and fine desserts at good prices and in comfortable surroundings, these are nice spots to take a break. Take a look at the Web site so you'll recognize the logo around town. ✉ *15 Nevsky pr., City Center* ☎ *No phone* ⊕ *www.chashka.ru* ▭ *No credit cards* Ⓜ *Nevsky prospekt.*

¢ ✗ **Laima Bistro.** Just off Nevsky, this central, bright, 24-hour café is not far from the colorful Church of the Savior on Spilled Blood. Laima serves tasty, inexpensive, Russian fast food—if you can call kebabs, salads, and beef Stroganoff fast food. The extensive menu on the wall is in English and Russian. ✉ *16 Kanal Griboyedova, City Center* ☎ *812/318–9219* ▭ *No credit cards* Ⓜ *Nevsky prospekt.*

★ ¢ ✕ **Teremok.** Don't be intimidated by the café's Spartan setting and plastic plates. Teremok's owners penny pinch only on furnishings and presentation. Cooked in front of your eyes, their famous bliny—priced at 40R–100R—are deservedly rated the best in town. Stuffed with mushrooms, ham, pork, grilled chicken, cream, honey, and a dozen of other fillings, the bliny, rich in flavor and never over- or underdone, taste just as if a Russian mom cooked them. A single bliny is so rich and hefty, it may leave you stuffed. Be conservative when you order unless you are absolutely starving. Aside from this café, Teremok encompasses a huge chain of street stands. The most central addresses include 5 ulitsa Marata; 52 Zagorodny pereulok; 27 Bolshaya Konyushennaya ulitsa; and 22 Chkalovsky pereulok. ✉ *60 Nevsky pr.* ☎ *No phone* ▤ *No credit cards* Ⓜ *Nevsky Prospect.*

French

$$–$$$$ ✕ **Palkin.** The Premiere Casino's grand restaurant envokes the name of
Fodor$Choice a great restaurant established on this spot in 1785. With white table-
★ cloths and candelight, the interior is formal and elegant, and you'll be treated like royalty the moment you enter. Already renowned for its fine and original cuisine and courteous service, Palkin has recently launched its own wine and introduced an à la carte menu. Look for poularde with morels sauce, venison with pine nuts marmalade, fillet of turbot served with pistachio nuts and curry sauce, and salad of smoked salmon with fresh oysters and beluga caviar. Palkin would be worth a visit for the window seats looking out onto Nevsky prospekt alone. ✉ *47 Nevsky pr., at Vladirmirsky pr., City Center* ☎ *812/703–5371* 🗐 *Reservations essential* ▤ *AE, MC, V* Ⓜ *Mayakovskaya or Nevsky prospekt.*

Greek

¢–$ ✕ **Oliva.** The cavernous size of this Greek taverna, seating more than 200 people, illustrates the confidence of its cooks, and the venue is almost always full. Feta cheese is delivered directly from Greece, and the house specialties get high marks in the city. Try *mussaka* (minced-meat baked with potatoes and spices) and kefal fish baked with tarragon. No one even tries to finish their enormous business lunch ($7.50), which includes soup, unlimited salad bar, main course, dessert, hot drinks, and even a glass of good house wine. ✉ *31 Bolshaya Morskaya ul.* ☎ *812/ 314–6563* ▤ *AE, MC, V* Ⓜ *Nevsky Prospect.*

Indian

$–$$ ✕ **Tandoor.** One of the best ethnic restaurants in town, Tandoor has a great location across the street from St. Isaac's Cathedral. With its succulent curries and spicy oven specialties, this place wouldn't do badly in a much more established culinary Mecca. Every meal is a gastronomic delight, and you can trust finding your Indian favorites here. Waiters, dressed in ethnic costumes and soft embroidered shoes, move soundlessly in this comfortable and quiet little place. Tandoor is not cheap, at least by Russian standards, and a dinner for two people with alcohol can come to about $50, but the food is worth every dime. The restaurant serves a generous business lunch for $12. ✉ *2 Voznesensky pr.* ☎ *812/ 312–3886* ▤ *AE, DC, MC, V* Ⓜ *Sennaya Ploshchad.*

Indonesian

¢–$ ✕ **Sukawati.** The first Indonesian restaurant in Russia, Sukawati has trendy beige interiors and good, reliable cuisine. The coexistence of Indonesian and Japanese dishes on the menu is bizarre, but if quality is the issue, nobody is complaining. If you feel like a big meal, order one of the rice platters as well as the renowned Indonesian dessert, *gendar bali* (a warm black rice pudding served with coconut cream, fruit, and vanilla ice cream). The Herculean four-course business lunch ($7) includes a drink and a dessert. ⊠ *8 Kazanskaya ul.* ☎ *812/312–0540* ▭ *MC, V.*

Italian

★ $–$$$$ ✕ **Il Grappolo.** Easily the city's best Italian restaurant, the comfortable, elegant Grappolo is a culinary treat, a place for people who know and appreciate good food. The chef and owners are knowledgeable and use only the best ingredients available—it's the only place in town with true buffalo mozzarella, which makes the delicious Caprese salad a house specialty. The menu includes fresh arugula salad, mushroom risotto, veal with mushroom sauce (or just about anything with porcini mushrooms), and an excellent tiramisu. Downstairs at the sister wine bar Probka, you can order wines by the glass from the well-chosen list and eat the only real Caesar salad in town. ⊠ *5 ul. Belinskovo, City Center* ☎ *812/273–4904* ▭ *AE, DC, MC, V* Ⓜ *Gostinny Dvor.*

¢–$ ✕ **Da Albertone.** Get your cheap and scrumptious pizza here. This cheerful pizzeria serves more than 40 kinds of pizza prepared by Italian cooks who are very good at what they do. Although clearly not a gastronomic palace, Da Albertone has a diverse choice of traditional dishes. Though it's busy, the service is friendly and prompt. The children's play room is an added draw for families. ⊠ *23 Millionnaya ul.* ☎ *812/315–8673* ▭ *AE, MC, V* Ⓜ *Nevsky Prospect.*

Russian

$$$–$$$$
Fodor'sChoice
★

✕ **Taleon.** An opulent mansion houses an ultra-exclusive restaurant, private club, and casino, all connected with the Yeliseyev Palace Hotel. You'll find the usual array of fun for the bodyguard-protected high-society set—gambling, cigars, $230 glasses of cognac—in a glittering setting, with marble fireplaces and gilded ceilings. The Russian and European menus are full of hearty, classic options, including caviar, oven-baked partridge in coriander sauce, veal cutlet with sage sauce, and carre d'agneau in rosmarine sauce. The most expensive dish is baked dorade with ragout of spinach and snails with mascarpone ($67). The Sunday brunch ($45) includes black and red caviar as well as lobster and champagne. Be sure to tour the casino, with its lush cigar lounge with walnut-covered walls and leather sofas. ⊠ *59 nab. Moika, City Center* ☎ *812/312–5373 or 812/315–7645* ⌖ *Reservations essential* ⌂ *Jacket and tie* ▭ *AE, DC, MC, V* Ⓜ *Nevsky prospekt.*

$–$$$$
Fodor'sChoice
★

✕ **L'Europe.** In a category all its own, this elegant restaurant in the Grand Hotel Europe serves fine Russian and Continental cuisine. The breathtaking interior—complete with an art nouveau stained-glass roof, shining parquet floors, and private balconies—is fit for a tsar, as are the prices. The menu is simply mouthwatering, with some dishes inspired by authentic royal recipes. Try the venison marinated in vodka and juniper berries, or the lobster, sturgeon, and salmon *à la Russe.* If you're not up to an expensive dinner, consider the buffet breakfast or popular Sunday champagne-and-caviar brunch. Reserve well ahead, particularly in summer. ⊠ *Grand Hotel Europe, 1/7 Mikhailovskaya ul., City Center* ☎ *812/329–6000* ⚿ *Reservations essential* 🎩 *Jacket and tie* ⊟ *AE, DC, MC, V* Ⓜ *Nevsky prospekt or Gostinny Dvor.*

$–$$$$ ✕ **Onegin.** Chic or pretentious, it's your call, but Onegin exemplifies the latest in St. Petersburg's dining and social scene, with the restaurant turning into an exclusive dance club late at night. Seeing and being seen are the main reasons to come, but it also happens to have an outstanding kitchen. The duck, fish, and arugula salad (a rare find in this city) are flavorful, but pricey, as are most of the dishes. The design of this underground refuge is a modern twist on Imperial St. Petersburg style, down to the ceiling reliefs finessed by the artisans who keep the Hermitage's baroque details looking spectacular. It all feels like a private party at an aristocratic Russian's home. ⊠ *11 Sadovaya ul., City Center* ☎ *812/ 571–8384* ⊟ *AE, MC, V* Ⓜ *Gostinny Dvor.*

¢–$$ ✕ **Ermitazhniy Restoran.** Although it differs greatly in style from the Hermitage's General Staff Building in which it's housed, this modern, stylish restaurant maintains subtle connections to the museum; for example, the green throughout the museum appears everywhere here, from the fresh apple juice to the staff uniforms. Each dining "hall" is different; the Music Salon hosts live music, while the Cameo Room is romantic with amber lamps and tables for two. Paintings by local artists line the walls of the hall connecting these dining rooms. There are two menus—one European, one Russian—with many reasonably priced options. Try any of the salads, soups, or blini. ⊠ *General Staff Bldg., 8 Dvortsovaya Pl., City Center* ☎ *812/314–4772* ⊟ *AE, DC, MC, V* Ⓜ *Nevsky prospekt.*

¢–$ ✕ **Zov Ilyicha.** If you can laugh at the images of Lenin, Stalin, and Dzerzhinsky, "Lenin's Mating Call" is something to experience. The place mixes Soviet icons and raunchy jokes (which you won't get unless you know Russian); you have to see it to believe it. And all the attention is not focused on the decor: the menu, divided into "Soviet" and "anti-Soviet" listings, has some tempting choices. Try the ostrich carpaccio, mushroom *pelmeni* (dumplings), or the definitely non-Soviet sauerkraut with sausage. Wash it all down with an infused vodka, such as juniper berry. The weekday business lunch from 1 to 4 is an affordable option. ⊠ *34 Kazanskaya ul., City Center* ☎ *812/311–8641* ⊟ *AE, DC, MC, V* Ⓜ *Sadovaya or Sennaya Ploshchad.*

Admiraltisky

Cafés

¢ ✕ **Pirozhkovaya Stolle.** The two branches on the same street combine the best of the old and new: the fashionable surroundings are comfortable, clean, and spacious, while the kitchen turns out fresh pirogi. Choose from sweet or savory fillings, including fish, vegetables, and fruits. The apricot is a must, but they are all mini-masterpieces. ⊠ *19 ul. Dekabritsov, Admiralteisky* ☎ *812/315–2383* Ⓜ *Sennaya Ploshchad* ⊠ *33 ul. Dekabristov, Admiralteisky* ☎ *812/714–2571* ⊟ *No credit cards* Ⓜ *Sennaya Ploshchad.*

Continental

★ $$$–$$$$ ✕ **Dvoryanskoye Gnezdo.** At the Noble Nest, tucked away in the garden pavilion of the Yusupov Palace, formal attire matches the service, decor, and Continental food. There are two set menus: the "Turgenev" is very Russian, and the "Nobleman" has more of a French touch. Try the fillet of venison, baked pheasant, or a selection from the small vegetarian menu. The wine list is extensive and includes Lafite, Latour, and Margaux at extraordinary prices, but there are some more reasonable choices. With the Mariinsky just around the corner, the restaurant attracts a post-theater crowd as well as foreign dignitaries and businesspeople (an expense account helps). ✉ *21 ul. Dekabristov, Admiralteisky* ☎ *812/312–0911* ⚐ *Reservations essential* ⛨ *Jacket and tie* ☐ *AE, DC, MC, V* Ⓜ *Sadovaya or Sennaya Ploshchad.*

¢–$ ✕ **Za Stsenoi.** Just steps from the Mariinsky Theater, with windows overlooking the pretty Kryukova Canal, "Backstage" has a dramatic setting. Its scrubbed floorboards were taken from the old Mariinsky stage, and the exposed-brick walls are bedecked with ornate mirrors and theater props. The menu fuses French and Russian influences. Venison carpaccio and crème lobster soup with cognac make good overtures for beluga fillet baked with mushrooms and béchamel sauce or grilled salmon with caviar sauce. The wine list has reasonably priced wines. All in all, this is a great choice for a post-theater dinner, but be sure to plan ahead as this small place fills up quickly. You can read the full menu and make a reservation at the Mariinsky theater Web site, www.mariinsky.ru. ✉ *18/10 Teatralnaya Pl., Admiraltsky* ☎ *812/327–0684* ⚐ *Reservations essential* ☐ *AE, DC, MC, V* Ⓜ *Sadovaya or Sennaya Ploshchad.*

Kosher

¢–$ ✕ **LeChaim.** This new, spacious, and welcoming kosher restaurant has been a hit with cosmopolitans and a nonreligious crowd since it opened in the spring of 2005. In a spacious basement of the St. Petersburg Great Choral Synagogue, LeChaim serves generous portions of high-standard Jewish cuisine at modest prices and is an excellent value for the money. Try chicken schnitzel or trout fillet wrapped in grape leaves. The lemon and orange sponge cake for dessert is not to be missed. A disadvantage is the closing time: 10 PM. ✉ *2 Lermontovsky pr.* ☎ *812/972–2774.*

Middle Eastern

$ ✕ **Caravan.** The stuffed camel, Turkish carpets, and food cooking in the middle of the room leave you in little doubt as to the theme of this spacious restaurant, a leading contender for the best Mideastern eatery in town. You can lounge in separate cabins at one end of the restaurant, or sit at the more orthodox chairs and tables nearer the entrance. The *kutab,* a lightly fried pocket filled with shrimp, pumpkin, or cheese, makes a good starter. From there move on to any of the more than 30 varieties of kebabs on offer. ✉ *46 Voznesensky pr., City Center* ☎ *812/310–5678* ☐ *AE, DC, MC, V* Ⓜ *Sadovaya or Tekhnologichesky Institut.*

Russian

★ $$–$$$$ ✕ **Canvas.** Serving innovative Russian cuisine with a modern twist, Canvas, on the first floor of the St. Petersburg Renaissance Baltic Hotel, is a member of the Chaine des Rotisseurs, a prestigious international association promoting the culinary arts. This cozy little restaurant designed in warm, bright colors juxtaposes traditional Russian ingredients with a European approach and artistic presentation. A perfect example is beetroot jelly with herring fillet and Laredo apple served on toasted black bread with potatoes and dill-mustard sauce. Try sturgeon roulade with spinach and the excellent game solyanka, filled with bear, elk, and wild boar meat. Your dinner can also be served on the hotel's sixth-floor terrace, where the shiny golden cupola of St. Isaac's Cathedral, set against charming crumbling rooftops, makes for an unrivaled view. Canvas offers an excellent three-course business lunch at $11. Reservations are recommended. ⊠ *4 Pochtamtskaya ul.* ☎ *812/380–4000* ▤ *AE, DC, MC, V* Ⓜ *Sadovaya.*

¢–$$$ ✕ **1913.** With its name, this restaurant recalls Russia's best year in history. Low-key, comfortable elegance combines with affordable prices, a giant menu, and giant portions. It's a fine alternative to the stuffier, more touristy dining options, and it's convenient to the Mariinsky Theater. The menu's traditional Russian cuisine emphasizes game and fish, plus there are European dishes. Try the mushroom soup or borscht for a starter, followed by sturgeon or salmon. ⊠ 13/2 Voznesensky pr., Admiralteisky ☎ 812/315–5148 ⌕ Reservations essential ▤ AE, DC, MC, V Ⓜ Sadovaya or Sennaya Ploshchad.

Vasilievsky Island

Cafés & Coffee Shops

¢ ✕ **Pirozhkovaya Stolle.** This spot near the Repin Institute combines the best of the old and new: the fashionable surroundings are comfortable, clean, and spacious, while the kitchen turns out fresh pierogi. Choose from sweet or savory fillings, including fish, vegetables, and fruits. The apricot is a must, but they are all mini-masterpieces. ⊠ *50 1st liniya, Vasilievsky Island* ☎ *812/328–7860* ▤ *No credit cards* Ⓜ *Vasileostrovskaya.*

Continental

★ $$$–$$$$ ✕ **Staraya Tamozhnya.** Considered for many years the best restaurant in St. Petersburg, the Old Customs House has been surpassed, but it's still pretty impressive and a good time. The restaurant's greatest advantage is that it has class without being snobbish. Comfortable elegance and pizzazz come together here—the open brickwork and neon lights sound grim, but they actually work well with the immaculately presented tables. Much of the food is exquisitely prepared, the wine list is excellent, and the service is top-notch and friendly. You can even watch the chefs at work in the open kitchens as they create such dishes as salmon with coconut sauce and spinach, and roast veal with figs and a pumpkin-morel puree. ⊠ *1 Tamozhenny per., Vasilievsky Island* ☎ *812/327–8982* ⌕ *Reservations essential* ▤ *AE, MC, V* Ⓜ *Nevsky prospekt or Vasileostrovskaya.*

Russian

★ ¢–$$$ ✕ **New Island.** In summer this ship-turned-restaurant has a stunning view as it sails along the Neva River, past the rows of colorful palaces lining its banks. New Island sets sail promptly at 2, 6, 8, and 10:30 PM. In winter, when the river is frozen, glitzy fairy lights adorn the ship, and the boat stays put (and prices go down significantly). Inside, all is simple but refined, including the menu; try the duck carpaccio as a starter. The fried fillet of trout with almonds and the various blini are good. The wine list is extensive and pricey. ⊠ *Universitetskaya nab., between Lieutenant Schmidt and Palace bridges, across road from Repin Institute, Vasilievsky Island* ☎ *812/963–6765* ⚠ *Reservations essential* ⊟ *AE, MC, V* Ⓜ *Vasileostrovskaya.*

¢–$ ✕ **Restoran.** Spacious, with soft lighting and earth tones, Restoran (lit-
Fodor'sChoice erally "Restaurant") is at once stylish and traditional, and it bustles with
★ tour groups and locals who know the *Russkiy stol* (Russian table) is the real thing—and a real bargain at $11. It's an all-you-can-eat smorgasbord of Russian *zakuski,* or small dishes: soups, salads (such as tuna), and pickled treats like garlic, green tomatoes, and cucumber. The main courses are as minimalist as the decor; try the simple veal with broccoli and cauliflower in a cheese sauce. For dessert, return to the Russian table for teas, cakes, and other Russian delights. ⊠ *2 Tamozhenny per., Vasilievsky Island* ☎ *812/327–8979* ⚠ *Reservations essential* ⊟ *AE, DC, MC, V* Ⓜ *Vasileostrovskaya.*

Vladimirskaya (Lower Nevsky Prospect)

Russian

$–$$$$ ✕ **Mechta Molokhovets.** A refined and intimate restaurant with prerev-
Fodor'sChoice olutionary flair, "Molokhovets' Dream" has a tantalizing menu entirely
★ based on a famous 19th century cookbook by the Russian Mrs. Beaton, *Yelena Molokhovets* ("A Gift to Young Housewives"), which inspired many culinary episodes in works by Russian writers. Cooking is state-of-the-art here. Try venison fillet accompanied by baked pears filled with cranberries and soaked in chanterelle sauce, foie gras with hot saffron sauce and iced apples, or pike-perch soaked in a piquant sauce made with red caviar. The restaurant's solid waiters show reverence to the guests, serving them in a pleasant ceremonial, but not at all artificial, manner. The cuisine is grand yet the place itself is relaxing. With only six tables, booking is recommended. ⊠ *23/10 Kovensky per.* ☎ *812/279–2247* ⊟ *MC, V* Ⓜ *Ploshchad Vosstania.*

¢ ✕ **Bliny Domik.** This homey, pocket-size place is all about blini. Everything served here is tasty, filling, and inexpensive—try the mushroom soup, followed by pork, cheese, or jam blini. *Blinchiki* are also available; they differ from blini (at least at this place) in that while blini resemble pancakes with toppings, blinchiki are wrapped around fillings and sometimes fried. Bliny Domik is no longer the secret it once was, but that only means it's even more foreigner-friendly. You sit at communal picnic tables, giving you a chance to meet other travelers and strike up conversation. ⊠ *8 Kolokolnaya ul., Vladimirskaya* ☎ *812/327–8979* ⊟ *AE, MC, V* Ⓜ *Vladimirskaya.*

¢ ✕ **Pirozhkovaya Mr. Baker.** With a choice of two dozen expertly cooked rich and filling pies priced between 40R and 80R a piece, this place is a budget traveler's dream. Fish and mushroom pies are particular favorites. Accompanied by traditional Russian soups (40R–50R) served in hearty portions, the meal provides a substantial refuel. ✉ *33 ul. Vosstania* ☎ *812/279–6410* 🚫 *No credit cards* Ⓜ *Ploshchad Vosstania.*

¢ ✗ **Teremok.** Don't be intimidated by the café's Spartan setting and plastic plates. Teremok's owners penny pinch only on furnishings and presentation. Cooked in front of your eyes, their famous bliny—priced at 40R–100R—are deservedly rated the best in town. Stuffed with mushrooms, ham, pork, grilled chicken, cream, honey, and a dozen of other fillings, the bliny, rich in flavor and never over- or underdone, taste just as if a Russian mom cooked them. A single bliny is so rich and hefty, it may leave you stuffed. Be conservative when you order unless you're absolutely starving. Teremok encompasses a huge chain of street stands. The most central addresses include 5 ulitsa Marata; 52 Zagorodny perulek; 27 Bolshaya Konyushennaya ulitsa; and 22 Chkalovsky perulek. ✉ *93 Nevsky pr.* ☎ *812/277–0881* 🚫 *No credit cards* Ⓜ *Ploshchad Vosstania.*

Liteiny/Smolny

Cafés

¢ ✗ **Che.** A trendy 24-hour café, Che is a popular stop for many clubbers. It has live music in the evenings, good coffee and tea, and even better desserts. ✉ *3 Poltavskaya ul., Liteiny/Smolny* ☎ *812/277–7600* 🚫 *No credit cards* Ⓜ *Ploshchad Vosstania.*

French

$–$$$$ ✗ **Bistro Garçon.** This comfortable, Parisian-style bistro on Nevsky prospekt may not have the timeworn quality of the real thing, but from the first bite of baguette, it doesn't matter—the food is the real treat here. The menu changes every three months but you can always expect delicious onion soup, mussels, salad roquefort, quiche, and crème brûlée from its distinguished French chef. Fresh oysters are flown in from Cancale, France, on Monday and Thursday. With omelets starting at $3, real croissants on offer at $5, and continental breakfast with good coffee, this is one of the best places for breakfast in the city (it opens at 9 AM). The excellent Boulangerie Garcon is virtually next door, at 103 Nevsky prospect. ✉ *95 Nevsky prospekt, Liteiny/Smolny* ☎ *812/277–2467* 🚫 *AE, MC, V* Ⓜ *Ploshchad Vosstania.*

Georgian

¢–$$$ ✗ **Bagrationi.** The dining room may be a little sterile and the live music droning, but they take their Georgian cooking seriously here. Everything is prepared fresh and very slowly, but it's worth the wait. Start with the *adjarsky khachapuri,* a Georgian calzone topped with egg. The fish and the *shashlyk* (grilled kebabs) are sure bets. Ask for the *tkemali* (plum) sauce with your meat. The dishes are heavy, but you can order half-portions, which will do less damage to your heart and purse. Bagrationi also owns the simple next-door café, which serves many of the same dishes at one-third the price and half the wait. ✉ *5 Liteiny pr., at ul. Chaikovskovo, Liteiny/Smolny* ☎ *812/272–7448* ⌛ *Reservations essential* 🚫 *MC, V* Ⓜ *Chernyshevskaya.*

¢–$ ✗ **Macaroni.** A sister restaurant of the excellent Il Grappolo, this trattoria serves simple Italian fare with an emphasis on fresh ingredients.

The risotto primavera, pastas, pizzas, and salads are delicious and reasonably priced. The plush booths and muted shades of red, orange, brown, and green give this trattoria a unique look that sets it apart from other restaurants in the city. All and all, Macaroni is a comfortable, casual break from the hectic city. A 20% discount is offered for weekday dining between noon and 5 PM. ⊠ 23 ul. Rubinshteyna, City Center ☎ 812/315–6147 ▭ No credit cards Ⓜ Dostoevskaya, Vladimirskaya, or Mayakovskaya.

Petrograd Side

Chinese

$$–$$$ ✕ **Akvarium.** Chinese restaurants are easy to find all over the city, but this spacious, sophisticated spot, not far from the Peter and Paul Fortress and right next to the famed LenFilm movie studio, is particularly worth seeking out. Start with the meat-and-vegetable rolls in bean paper, or the wonton soup, which is pricey ($9) but full of flavor. Any of the dishes cooked in clay pots, such as the five-spice pork in garlic sauce or the duck, are good choices. The back of the menu has a curious "food tonic menu"—one for men, one for women—that's touted as being "good for health." ⊠ 10 Kamennoostrovsky pr., Petrograd Side ☎ 812/326–8286 ▭ MC, V Ⓜ Gorkovskaya.

Contemporary

$–$$$$ ✕ **Aquarel.** With three stories of floor-to-ceiling windows overlooking Vasilievsky Island's Rostral Columns and Stock Exchange, this restaurant-boat docked on the Neva River may have the best dining views in the city. The fusion menu, combining European and Asian influences, is superb. Try the terrine of foie gras with cognac-scented winter fruits, Thai lobster hot pot, or Asian brined veal chops. The spicy Thai coconut soup with shrimp and black mushrooms makes a good starter. The third floor houses Aquarelissimo, where modern Italian and Mediterranean cuisine is served. The tapas menu is a tempting option, while pasta papardelle and *vitello tonnato* (fillet of veal and fresh bluefin tuna with extra-virgin olive oil) are among the restaurant's signature dishes. ⊠ Near Birzhevoy most, entrance from Petrograd Side, Petrograd Side ☎ 812/320–8600 ▭ AE, DC, MC, V Ⓜ Sportivnaya.

¢–$$ ✕ **Bessonnitsa.** An alert, friendly looking owl greets guests at this new classy restaurant named "Insomnia," where innovative Russian chefs creatively interpret European and Asian dishes. Veal fillet is served with fried grapefruit and blackberry sauce. The Vietnamese noodle soup Fo Bo arrives sizzling hot, leaving you to put the finishing touches on it by dropping in thin slices of meat to cook. Pasta farfalle with mushrooms and cedar nuts is fresh and aromatic. Consider carrot cutlets and the French omelette for breakfast. Beige linen, terra-cotta lamps, and chocolate-color walls define the comfortable interior that overlooks the Winter Palace. The owl, by the way, is served raw meat according to the staff. Reservations are recommended. ⊠ 3 Mytninskaya nab. ☎ 812/973–3577 ▭ AE, MC, V Ⓜ Sportivnaya.

Georgian

¢–$ ✕ **Gorniy Orel.** Try to eat on the terrace of this friendly, casual eatery in Alexandrovsky Park; this will place you away from the tacky interior, and closer to the grill, where you can smell the *shashlyk* (shish-kebab) cooking to perfection. One of the few St. Petersburg restaurants not afraid to use spices, Gorniy Orel is considered by many to serve the most authentic Georgian food in the city. Try the *lobio* (vegetarian chili) or a cheesy *khachapuri* (cheese bread), accompanied by a plate of fresh greens, the ubiquitous tomatoes and cucumbers, or pickled garlic. A clay jug of Georgian wine—*sladkoe* (sweet) or *sukhoe* (dry)—complements your meal. ⊠ *1 Alexandrovsky Park, off Kronverkskiy pr. and near zoo entrance, Petrograd Side* ☎ *812/232–3282* ⊟ *No credit cards* Ⓜ *Gorkovskaya.*

¢ ✕ **Kvareli.** In contrast to the miniscule size of the place—there are only six tables—the food arrives in enormous amounts in this congenial and hugely popular Georgian café. It's tucked away in a back street, a stone's throw from the Peter and Paul Fortress and the city Zoo. The place immediately wins you over with its lively atmosphere and cordial service, and when you try their gorgeous juicy Georgian kebabs, spicy *satsivi* (chicken in thick nut sauce), rich khachapuri, hot lobio, and other Caucasian delights, you'll just melt. It gets addictive quickly. The prices are most appealing: the entrées are all less than $10. ⊠ *22 ul. Lizy Chaikinoi* ☎ *812/947–7878* ⧆ *Reservations essential* ⊟ No credit cards Ⓜ *Gorkovskaya.*

Russian

¢ ✕ **Volshebniy Vkus.** Usually filled with clued-in locals, Magical Taste—or, as it's more simply known, Pelmeni Bar—does one thing and does it better than anywhere else in the city: dumplings, whether they be Russian pelmeni, Ukrainian *vareniki* (usually sweet), Uzbekistani *manti* (meat dumplings, sometimes in broth), or Georgian *khenkali* (made with lamb). You can order sauces, such as the traditional *smetana* (sour cream), on the side. Prices are ridiculously low; the most expensive pelmeni, filled with salmon, costs less than $3. Do as the locals do and order a half-liter of vodka; the $4 chilled carafe of Gzhelka Kristal is a good choice. The place is no-frills but clean, and service is fast. ⊠ *53a Kronverkskiy pr., entrance around corner on ul. Markina, Petrograd Side* ☎ *812/238–0977* ⊟ *No credit cards* Ⓜ *Gorkovskaya.*

Kirov Islands

Russian

¢–$$ ✕ **Russkaya Rybalka.** The gimmick at Russian Fishing is that you catch your own dinner. It's set in a charming wooden house overlooking a lake full of trout, sturgeon, and beluga sterlet. Tackle, bait, and expert advice are provided, and your catch is prepared before you on the grill. There are several other options on the menu as well, including a baked eggplant dish that is quite good. ⊠ *Primorsky Park Pobedy, 11 Yuzhnaya doroga, Kirov Islands* ☎ *812/323–9813* ⊟ *No credit cards* Ⓜ *Krestovsky Ostrov.*

CloseUp

VODKA: A TASTE OF RUSSIA

THE NATIONAL DRINK IS AN INSEPARABLE PART of Russian social life. Vodka is drunk everywhere, with the intention of breaking down inhibitions and producing a state of conviviality Russians refer to as dusha-dushe (soul-to-soul). When a Russian taps his throat, beware: it's impossible to refuse this invitation to friendship. If you have a cold, sore throat, or any such minor ailment, don't be surprised if someone prescribes a shot of vodka—even for a hangover. Russians' belief in the curative and preventative powers of this drink is almost limitless.

Vodka is often flavored and colored with herbs and spices. Limonnaya, lemon-flavored vodka, is particularly popular with American tourists, as is pertsovka, pepper-flavored vodka. Other varieties include starka (a dark, smooth "old" vodka), pshenichnaya (made from wheat), ryabinovka (in which ashberries have been steeped), and tminnaya (caraway-flavored vodka). Be wary of krepkaya vodka, which at 110 proof is the strongest variety.

There are hundreds of brands of vodka in Russia, as a glance into any store will show. Some of these are rough and best left alone; two of the best are Flagman and Russky Standart, although there are many acceptable cheaper brands. Alcohol counterfeiting, which can lead to alcohol poisoning, is a big problem, so you should always purchase vodka from a reputable-looking store, and never from a kiosk.

When you're drinking vodka, there is some etiquette involved. In North America and Great Britain, vodka is generally associated with cocktails and martinis. In Russia, mixing vodka with anything else is considered a waste, unless the mixer is beer, which produces a fearsome beverage known as yorsh. Vodka is meant to be gulped down in one go, not sipped. Since this can give you a bit of a kick, Russians always have some zakuski, or snacks (including pickles, herring, boiled potatoes, and black bread) to chase the shot. You may witness something called the "vodka procedure," which, if you want to try it yourself, goes roughly as follows. Prepare a forkful of food or chunk of bread. Inhale and exhale quickly, bringing the food to your nose. Breathe in and tip the vodka down your throat. Now breathe out again, and eat your food.

Vodka shots (unlike beer and wine) are downed collectively, and always preceded by a toast. You'll score points if you propose toasts—it doesn't matter if they are in English, particularly if you wax long and eloquent. Drinking before a toast is considered a faux pas of the first order. Although you're expected to gulp down the first couple of shots, no one will mind if you take it a little easier after that—saying choot'-choot', pozhaluista (just a little, please) is a polite way of asking for a smaller refill. Vodka is also considered predominantly a man's drink, so it's more acceptable for women to take things easier.

If all this sounds like an ordeal, rest assured that vodka drinking can be an extremely pleasurable experience, involving good food, great company, and a unique sense of mild inebriation that can last for hours. Vodka is, and always has been, a social leveler, drunk by everyone from tramps to top-ranking politicians. It's a memorable taste of Russia in more ways than one.

WHERE TO STAY

The city's capacity for overnight visitors is rather small: 139 hotels can accommodate 36,000 people. By 2010 St. Petersburg plans to have added dozens of new hotels, yet with tourism projected to bring 5 million visitors a year by 2010, some unfortunate tourists will be well exposed to the White Nights in the high season of May and June. What the city especially lacks are two- and three-star hotels, which would be a welcome alternative to the predominance of expensive ones.

On an organized tour, you're likely to land in one of the old Intourist standbys, which used to belong to the Soviet tourist agency that enjoyed a monopoly. Most U.S. and British tour operators take advantage of the discounted rates at the Moskva, the Pribaltiyskaya, the Pulkovskaya, or the St. Petersburg. These hotels were built in the late '70s and early '80s, and though they are dated, many of them were spruced up in time for St. Petersburg's 300th anniversary celebrations. The facilities at these hotels are fairly uniform and generally include several restaurants and perhaps business services and pools; many hotels are slowly improving their facilities to meet Western standards. The service, though mildly unpredictable, is perfectly acceptable—provided you don't expect royal treatment. The main reason to choose one of these hotels is their lower rates; note that many of them are not convenient to the major attractions.

If you want insulation from the uglier side of life here, however, plan to shell out a substantial sum for a higher level of accommodation. Almost all of the hotels with Web sites have online booking facilities, though you should follow up such applications with phone calls.

An expanding number of realty agents can organize a suitable and safe apartment rental, usually in the center of the city. The prices for such apartments usually run the level of three-star hotels, but they often have much more space and you can also share the expenses with your traveling companions.

Prices

You can get a room at one of the former Intourist hotels for less than $200 a night, and sometimes closer to $100. The finer hotels, such as the Astoria, Grand Hotel Europe, and Radisson SAS Royal, charge several hundred dollars a night.

WHAT IT COSTS In U.S. dollars					
	$$$$	**$$$**	**$$**	**$**	**¢**
FOR 2 PEOPLE	over $275	$200–$275	$150–$200	$75–$150	under $75

Prices are for a standard double room in high season, excluding taxes and service charge.

City Center (Palace Square, the Hermitage)

$$$$ ▦ **Astoria.** The Astoria is actually two hotels: it connects with the older,
Fodor'sChoice slightly less luxurious Angleterre, whose enduring "fame" is thanks to
★ the beloved poet Sergei Yesenin's suicide there in 1925. Built in art nouveau style between 1910 and 1912, the Astoria was one of St. Petersburg's most renowned hotels before the Revolution of 1917; despite
protests by residents, the original structure was torn down in the early
1990s during the renovation that connected it to the Angleterre. Nevertheless, it's a magnificent hotel in downtown St. Petersburg, near the
Hermitage. Antiques retrieved from various museums decorate the
splendid interior. The restaurant Borsalino at the Angleterre affords memorable views of St. Isaac's Cathedral and a mere breakfast at the Astoria's Davidov restaurant costs $33. ⊠ *39 Bolshaya Morskaya ul., City
Center, 190000* ☎ *812/313–5757* 🖷 *812/313–5133* ⊕ *astoria.spb.ru*
🛏 *223 rooms in Astoria, 213 rooms in Angleterre* ♿ *2 restaurants, cable
TV, pool, gym, sauna, bar, library, shop, business services, meeting
rooms, travel services* ▭ *AE, MC, V* Ⓜ *Sennaya Ploschad or Sadovaya.*

$$$$ ▦ **Corinthia Nevsky Palace Hotel.** This spacious and light-filled hotel is
a complete reconstruction of two 19th-century buildings. The main
building, facing Nevsky Prospect, was built in 1861 in neoclassic style.
Before the October revolution the house belonged to the actors' dynasty
of the Samoilovs, who starred on the stages of St. Petersburg for more
than 150 years. A museum within the hotel honors the family. Behind
the historical facade, huge glass doors reveal the most modern of interiors, full of glass. The central location means no time lost in the city's
traffic jams. At the same time, the view of busy Nevsky Prospect may
not appeal to romantics. The hotel is also known for its fine restaurant
complex, which serves just about any cuisine you might crave. Service
is personable and the hotel's prices lower if the hotel is not full. ⊠ *57
Nevsky pr., City Center, 191025* ☎ *812/380–2001* 🖷 *812/380–1937*
⊕ *www.corinthia.ru* 🛏 *283 rooms, 22 suites* ♿ *4 restaurants, café, lobby
bar, satellite TV, fitness center, sauna, open terrace for sun bathing, massage, laundry, shop, hair salon, 7 conference halls, business center, fax,
printer, Internet, meeting rooms, currency exchange, parking, deposit
safe at reception, order taxi service and car rent, travel services, medical service* ▭ *AE, DC, EC, MC, V* Ⓜ *Mayakovskaya.*

$$$$ ▦ **Grand Hotel Europe.** Combining the elegance of prerevolutionary St.
Fodor'sChoice Petersburg with every modern amenity, this luxurious 1875 hotel has
★ earned the unofficial and uncontested title of the finest accommodation
in town. Behind the stunning baroque facade lies an art nouveau interior, complete with stained-glass windows and antique furnishings.
Pleasing shades of mauve, cream, and gold decorate the stylish and comfortable rooms. The Russian staff upholds European standards of excellence, and the service shines. And Nevsky prospekt, the Hermitage,
and Ploshchad Iskusstv are all within walking distance. If money is no
object (breakfast alone costs $38), this is the place to stay. ⊠ *1/7
Mikhailovskaya ul., City Center, 191011* ☎ *812/329–6000* 🖷 *812/
329–6002* ⊕ *www.grand-hotel-europe.com* 🛏 *212 rooms, 65 suites* ♿ *5
restaurants, café, room service, cable TV, health club, hair salon, mas-*

sage, sauna, bar, nightclub, shops, dry cleaning, laundry service, Internet, business services, meeting rooms, no-smoking floor ⊟ *AE, MC, V* Ⓜ *Nevsky prospekt or Gostinny Dvor.*

★ $$$$ 🏨 **Radisson SAS Royal.** Originally built in 1765, this grand historic structure first became a hotel in 1879; the writer Anton Chekhov stayed here during his first visit to the city. In Soviet times the building housed Café Saigon, the noted hangout for city dissidents and rock-and-rollers. Once again it's a sumptuous hotel, with antique reproductions, soft cream walls and navy carpets in the guest rooms, and heated floors in the bathrooms. On the corner of Nevsky prospekt and Vladimirsky prospekt, it's in the heart of St. Petersburg. The hotel can also offer visa support (via previous fax arrangements). Check the Web site for special rates. Guide dogs for blind guests are allowed. ✉ *49 Nevsky prospekt, City Center, 191025* ☎ *812/322–5000* 🖷 *812/322–5002* ⊕ *www.radisson. com* 🛏 *147 rooms, 17 suites* 🍴 *Restaurant, café, room service, in-room safes, minibars, cable TV, in-room data ports, health club, sauna, bar, dry cleaning, laundry service, Internet, business services, meeting rooms* ⊟ *AE, DC, MC, V* Ⓜ *Mayakovskaya.*

$$$–$$$$ 🏨 **Casa Leto.** Next to the Hermitage and St. Isaac's Cathedral, Casa Leto has a mere five rooms. With high ceilings, stucco work, and neutral tones, rooms are spare, but larger than average for the city. Complimentary extras include breakfast, light refreshments, local telephone calls (and international to most destinations), and high-speed Internet. The staff can organize tickets to performances and tours beyond the usual, such as mushroom picking, ice fishing, or visiting the vaults of the Hermitage. The hotel not only provides airport transfers, but if you need a translator or a member of the hotel staff to meet you, they'll do so, too. Visa help, translators, a local mobile phone—this small casa seems to stop at nothing when it comes to service. The building shares a late-night sushi restaurant and a hair salon. ✉ *34, ul. Bolshaya Morskaya, City Center, 190000* ☎ *812/314–6622 or 812/600–1096* 🖷 *812/314–6639* ⊕ *www.casaleto.com* 🛏 *5 rooms* 🍴 *Cable TV, in-room broadband, airport transfer* ⊟ *AE, DC, MC, V* ❧| *BP* Ⓜ *Sadovaya/Sennaya.*

$$ 🏨 **Oktyabrskaya.** It's hard to miss this Soviet monolith in the city center. Directly opposite the Moscow Station, the Oktyabrskaya hits you right between the eyes with its huge sign, LENINGRAD–GOROD GEROI (Leningrad–Hero City), set on top. The location, near Nevsky prospekt, is great. The hotel opened in 1851 in conjunction with Russia's first railroad between then capital of St. Petersburg and Moscow. In those times it was known as one of the city's best hotels. The hotel no longer has that reputation but has undergone extensive renovations and has added dark-wood furniture and cream accents in the rooms. There's an annex across the street and breakfast is included in the room rate. ✉ *10 Ligovsky pr., City Center, 193036* ☎ *812/717–6330* 🖷 *812/315–7501* 🛏 *555 rooms in main hotel, 108 rooms in annex* 🍴 *Restaurant, cable TV, in-room data ports, hair salon, billiards, 5 bars, business services; no a/c* ❧| *BP* ⊟ *AE, DC, MC, V* Ⓜ *Ploshchad Vosstaniya.*

$ 🏨 **Matisov Domik.** If you're looking for homey accommodations, consider this small, quiet hotel, a cozy blue cottage with a tiled roof. Most of the rooms overlook the Pryazhka River and the small, pleasant yard with maple and chestnut trees, flowers, and benches. Though the halls are narrow, the pleasant pastel colors, wood paneling, and smiling staff are welcoming. Avoid rooms on the third floor, which have thin walls. Though it's only a 10-minute walk to the Mariinsky, Matisov Domik is far from a metro stop; the hotel, however, provides shuttles to the airport and railway stations. Rooms have showers instead of tubs, and there's no air-conditioning (a fan is available for a small fee). Continental breakfast is included. ⊠ *3/1 nab. Reki Pryazhki, Admiralteisky, 190121* ☎ *812/318–5445 or 812/318–7051* 🖨 *812/318–7419* ⊕ *www.matisov. spb.ru* ⇆ *46 rooms, 2 suites, 7 apartments* ♿ *Café, refrigerators, cable TV, sauna, shop, Internet, meeting rooms, airport shuttle, travel services, free parking; no a/c* ☰ *MC, V* ⦿ *CP.*

$ 🖫 **Moskva.** The main attraction here is location: this enormous, visibly aging hotel is literally on top of the metro and faces the entrance to the 18th-century Alexander Nevsky Lavra, which is at one end of Nevsky prospekt, but still in the center of town. The lackluster service can make even paying your bill a frustrating experience. Though the rooms are hardly sophisticated, they are neat and clean, as are the public areas with their flowers and greenery. This is a popular option for tour groups. ⊠ *2 Pl. Alexandra Nevskovo, City Center, 193317* ☎ *812/274–0022 or 812/274–4001* 🖨 *812/274–2130* ⊕ *www.hotel-moscow.ru* ⇆ *770 rooms* ♿ *2 restaurants, snack bars, hair salon, billiards, 6 bars, shops, dry cleaning, laundry service, Internet, business services, car rental, travel services, parking (fee)* ☰ *AE, DC, MC, V* Ⓜ *Ploshchad Alexandra Nevskovo.*

¢ 🖫 **St. Petersburg International Hostel.** One of the first projects to freshen up the entrepreneurial landscape of the city, this joint Russian-American enterprise was launched in the early '90s. The converted dormitory has rooms holding three to five beds; breakfast and linens are included. The staff is friendly, and the location near the Moscow Station is excellent. An in-house Sindbad Travel caters to budget travelers, facilitates visa support, and is the starting point of walking tours. There's a curfew from 1 AM to 8 AM. The hostel fills up quickly in summer. ⊠ *28 3rd Sovietskaya ul., City Center* ⊕ *Box 8, SF-53501, Lappeenranta, Finland* ☎ *812/329–8018* 🖨 *812/329–8019* ⊕ *www.ryh.ru* ⇆ *55 beds with shared bath* ☰ *No credit cards* Ⓜ *Ploshchad Vosstaniya or Mayakovskaya.*

Vasilievsky Island

$$$ 🖫 **Pribaltiskaya.** This huge '70s-era skyscraper is frequently booked by tourist groups and international conferences. The modest furnishings in the clean rooms are adequate, although slightly worn. The views of the Gulf of Finland from rooms on the western side of the hotel are phenomenal, especially at sunset, but otherwise the location is a drawback: on the western tip of Vasilievsky Island, it's far from the metro and it's a good 20-minute drive from downtown St. Petersburg. The predominantly residential area has a combination of endless Soviet-era high-rises and modern elite apartment buildings, but few shops and restaurants. The hotel's many facilities include 24-hour medical assistance and breakfast is included. ⊠ *14 ul. Korablestroitelei, Vasilievsky Island, 199226*

☎ *812/356–0158 or 812/356–3001* 🖷 *812/356–4496* ⊕ *www.*
pribaltiyskaya.ru 🛏 *1,180 rooms, 20 suites* ♨ *11 restaurants, room ser-*
vice, cable TV, pool, hair salon, sauna, bowling, 5 bars, shop, dry clean-
ing, laundry facilities, Internet, convention center, meeting rooms, travel
services, parking (fee) 🖃 *AE, DC, MC, V* ⦿ *BP* Ⓜ *Vasileostrovskaya,*
accessible from hotel by bus.

Vladimirskaya (Lower Nevsky Prospekt)

$$$$ 🖾 **Ambassador.** This central, nine-story hotel opened in 2005 next to
Yusupovsky Garden, a seven-minute walk from the metro station. The
opulent entrance hall in white and cream has marble floors, leather sofas,
and sparkling Czech glass chandeliers. The focus of the interior is the
atrium that houses the Ambassador restaurant and allows romantic views
of the city. Guest rooms are furnished with light brown alder tree furniture, plasma TV sets, and high-standard bath facilities. The restaurant on an upper floor offers not only exquisite à la carte cuisine but
also a panoramic view of St. Petersburg. The hotel is seeking to add a
helicopter landing to its roof, pending city permission. The hotel also
has comfortable rooms equipped for disabled guests. ✉ *5–7 Pr. Rim-*
skovo-Korsakova, Vladimirskaya, 190068 ☎ *812/331–8844* 🖷 *812/331–*
9300 ⊕ *www.ambassador-hotel.ru* 🛏 *255 rooms* ♨ *2 restaurants,*
café, lobby bar, cable TV, Internet, in-room safes, minibars, business cen-
ter, fitness center, indoor pool, sauna, hair salon, laundry service, park-
ing 🖃 *AE, DC, MC, V* Ⓜ *Sadovaya/Sennaya.*

$$$ 🖾 **Dostoyevsky.** This modern hotel, named after famed writer Fyodor Dos-
toyevsky, who used to live close by, presents the new standard among
St. Petersburg three-star hotels. Directly in the trade and hotel complex
of Vladimirsky Passage (with 200 shops), the decor combines classic style
with modern comfort. Rooms have heated floors and Internet access. Some
are equipped for hosting disabled travelers. A 24-hour supermarket and
currency exchange in the complex can save you precious time. Breakfast
is included. ✉ *19 Vladimirsky pr., City Center, 191002* ☎ *812/331–3200*
🖷 *812/331–3200* ⊕ *www.dostoyevsky-hotel.ru* 🛏 *207 rooms* ♨ *Restau-*
rant, bar, fitness center, pool, sauna, laundry service, shops, business cen-
ter, Internet, meeting rooms, car rental, travel services, parking 🖃 *AE,*
DC, MC, V ⦿ *BP* Ⓜ *Vladimirskaya/Dostoyevskaya.*

Liteyny/Smolny

$$$$ 🖾 **Grand Emerald Hotel.** A dark-glass exterior with a modern turret
fronts this luxurious, high-tech hotel built in 2003. Inside, marble floors
and chandeliers made of Swarovski crystal decorate the elegant public
spaces. The airy atrium café has wicker chairs, old-fashioned street
lamps, and plenty of natural light. Italian wood furniture fills the bright,
spacious guest rooms, some of which have parquet floors. Most rooms
overlook one the city's oldest streets—Suvorovsky prospect—or offer
an enchanting view into the atrium. Some standard rooms have a bay
window where comfortable arm chairs and coffee table are arranged.
Bathrobes, towels, slippers, and amenities are at the guests' disposal.
Breakfast and tax are included in the room price. ✉ *18 Suvorovsky pr.,*
Liteiny/Smolny, 193036 ☎ *812/740–5000* 🖷 *812/740–5001 or 812/740–*

5006 🌐 *www.grandhotelemerald.com* 📠 *59 rooms, 34 suites* ⚐ *Restaurant, café, room service, in-room safes, minibars, cable TV, gym, hair salon, sauna, spa, bar, casino, laundry service, Internet, business services, meeting rooms, airport shuttle, no-smoking floors* 🖃 *AE, MC, V* 🍴 *BP* Ⓜ *Ploschad Vosstaniya or Chernyshevskaya.*

¢ 🕾 **Rus.** The name of this hotel refers to the first medieval Russian state, but forget about onion domes and Tartary trim. Many Petersburgers say this is the most hideous building in town—and that the architect should be banished for creating an eyesore in an otherwise charming and quiet neighborhood (home to many consulates and cultured expatriates). Yet the hotel's location (two steps away from Liteiny prospekt and near the metro) and its prices, which include a Swedish breakfast, make it an excellent option. Inside, a helpful staff awaits. Book early, especially if you're visiting during the White Nights. An exchange office is on the premises. ✉ *1 Artilleriyskaya ul., side entrance at 26 Liteiny prospekt, Liteiny/ Smolny, 191104* ☎ *812/273–4683* 🖷 *812/279–3600* 📠 *170 rooms* ⚐ *Restaurant, café, cable TV, hair salon, sauna, bar, shop, business services, travel services; no a/c* 🖃 *AE, DC, MC, V* 🍴 *BP* Ⓜ *Chernyshevskaya.*

Vesyolyi Posyolok

$ 🕾 **Deson-Ladoga.** This three-star hotel, built in the 1960s and renovated in the 1990s to European standards, sits on the right bank of the Neva. The location may look slightly inconvenient compared to the centrally located hotels, but it's a five-minute walk from a metro station. The hotel specializes in hosting foreign tourists, most often from Scandinavia and Europe. The personnel of the hotel speaks English and is particularly attuned to the needs of foreign guests. The rooms are modest, but fresh and comfortable, with light colors and dark-brown furniture. The lobby, which also houses a souvenir shop, is small but cozy. The price includes a Swedish breakfast and sauna. The restaurant serves European and Chinese food. ✉ *26 Shaumyana pr., Vesyolyi Posyolok, 195213* ☎ *812/ 528–5393* 🖷 *812/528–5448* 🌐 *www.deson-ladoga.ru* 📠 *101 rooms* ⚐ *Restaurant, hair salon, sauna, bar, nightclub, Internet, business services, no-smoking rooms, parking; no a/c* 🖃 *AE, DC, MC, V* 🍴 *BP* Ⓜ *Novocherkasskaya.*

★ $ 🕾 **Okhtinskaya-Victoria.** You get a nice view of Smolny cathedral across the river here, and though St. Petersburg's main attractions and the metro are some distance away, a hotel shuttle bus runs to Nevsky prospekt. Service at this modern hotel is unusually friendly, and the reasonable rates include breakfast. Marble and chrome adorn the interior, and the public areas are cheery and bright. Imported furnishings and pretty flowered wallpaper decorate the clean rooms. Most have balconies, but only suites have full bathtubs. Although only a handful of rooms face the cathedral, the views of the urban landscape here are more refreshing than most. Swedish breakfast is included. ✉ *4 Bolsheokhtinsky pr., Okhta, 195027* ☎ *812/227–4438 or 812/227–3767* 🖷 *812/227–2618* 🌐 *www.okhtinskaya.spb.ru* 📠 *204 rooms* ⚐ *2 restaurants, café, snack bar, cable TV, sauna, 2 bars, shops, meeting rooms, travel services* 🖃 *AE, DC, MC, V* 🍴 *BP* Ⓜ *Novocherkasskaya, accessible from hotel by bus.*

Vyborg Side

¢–$ 🏨 **St. Petersburg.** Although this is not the luxury hotel it once was, if
FodorśChoice you can land a waterfront room, the St. Petersburg is the place to stay
★ for ultimate White Nights vistas. If you can't get a room with magnificent vistas of the Neva and the waterfront architecture, you'll likely have
a depressing city view, which costs slightly less than the rooms with the
view. The Finnish-decorated interior is faded and the furnishings are a
bit worn, but the rooms and public areas are clean. The Congress Hall
makes the hotel popular with international conference planners. The Finland Station and metro are within walking distance, but the route is unpleasant and takes you along a busy highway. Swedish breakfast is
included. ✉ *5/2 Pirogovskaya nab., Vyborg Side, 194044* ☎ *812/380–
1919* 🖶 *812/380–1920* ⊕ *www.hotel-spb.ru* ➴ *410 rooms* ⚿ *2 restaurants, in-room data ports, hair salon, sauna, 2 bars, shops, business services, meeting rooms, travel services; no a/c* ▭ *AE, DC, MC, V* ⫶◉⫶ *BP*
Ⓜ *Ploshchad Lenina.*

Southern Suburbs

$$$ 🏨 **Pulkovskaya.** The attractive, Scandinavian-designed interior of this
hotel is in decent condition, thanks partly to renovations for the city's
300th-anniversary celebrations in 2003. Unusual for a Russian hotel,
the curtains and bedspreads actually match the upholstery, and the
bathrooms are relatively large. Far from the city center, the hotel is con-
venient only to the airport, but it's also handy for travelers who wish
to visit the imperial palaces of Pushkin, Pavlovsk, and Peterhof. The metro
is a 10-minute walk away, and the ride into town takes 20 minutes. The
surrounding residential area has plenty of shops and a restaurant or two.
The views from the rooms—of gloomy high-rises and smokestacks or
of the severe, very Soviet Victory Square monument—can be depress-
ing. Breakfast is included. ✉ *1 Pobedy Pl., Southern Suburbs, 196240*
☎ *812/140–3900* 🖶 *812/140–3913* ⊕ *www.pulkovskaya.ru* ➴ *840
rooms, 17 suites* ⚿ *4 restaurants, 2 snack bars, cable TV, in-room data
ports, 2 pools, hair salon, sauna, 3 bars, shops, business services, travel
services; some pets allowed* ▭ *AE, DC, MC, V* ⫶◉⫶ *BP* Ⓜ *Moskovskaya.*

$ 🏨 **Sovietskaya.** The recent renovation (be sure to ask for a renovated
room) has done much to improve the once-decaying interiors of this 1960s
concrete-and-steel monstrosity in an unattractive section of downtown.
Although the location allows for some good views of St. Petersburg's
canals and sights, it's still a long walk to just about anywhere, includ-
ing the metro. A currency-exchange office, taxi and transfer service, and
visa support are all available. The room rate includes a Swedish break-
fast, and if you book through the Web site you can get a discount. ✉ *43/
1 Lermontovsky pr., Vladimirskaya, 190103* ☎ *812/740–2640* 🖶 *812/
251–8890* ⊕ *www.sovetskaya.com* ➴ *1,000 rooms* ⚿ *2 restaurants,
café, pizzeria, some in-room safes, some minibars, some in-room data
ports, hair salon, sauna, 5 bars, business services, travel services; no a/c
in some rooms* ▭ *AE, MC, V* ⫶◉⫶ *BP* Ⓜ *Baltiyskaya.*

¢ ⊞ **All Seasons.** Travelers on a budget will appreciate this hostel in one of the city's oldest and most prestigious districts—Moskovsky, though it's south of the city center. It takes about 10 minutes to walk to the metro Park Pobedy and another 15 minutes by metro to reach the city center. The area's big and beautiful park, also called Park Pobedy (Victory Park), is seen from the hostel's windows. The simple rooms have from five to eight beds, and individual ones are available ($50). The place recalls a good, safe college dormitory. The location is also very convenient for getting to the airport. ⊠ *11 Yakovlevsky Pereulok, Southern Suburbs, 196105* ☎ *812/327–1070* 🖷 *812/327–1033* ⊕ *www.hostel. ru* 🛏 *100 dorm beds with shared bath* ♨ *Kitchen, TV* ▤ *MC, V* Ⓜ *Park Pobedy.*

Apartments

City Realty. This American-owned company will find whatever type of accommodation you're looking for, be it a minihotel or B&B or a selection of central apartments, which it normally owns. During low season you can rent a one- or two-room apartment for $80–$95 per night; high season can demand $125–$150 per night. It's better to make a reservation a week or two in advance in order to choose from a wider range of apartments. City Realty also offers visa support for $25, and registration for $35. ⊠ *35 ul. Bolshaya Morskaya, City Center* ☎ *812/ 312–7842* 🖷 *812/710–6457* ⊕ *www.cityrealtyrussia.com* ☒ *Weekdays 9:30–6:30* Ⓜ *Nevsky prospect.*

NIGHTLIFE & THE ARTS

The Arts

St. Petersburg's cultural life is one of its top attractions. Except for the most renowned theaters, tickets are easily available and inexpensive. You can buy them at the box offices of the theaters themselves, at *teatralnaya kassa* (theater kiosks) throughout the city—Central Box Office No. 1 is at 42 Nevsky prospekt (☎ 812/571–3183) and is open daily from 11 to 7—and at service bureaus in hotels, most of which post performance listings in their main lobby. Note that some theaters charge different prices for Russians and foreigners.

The very efficient online service www.kassir.ru is available in English: go to http://spb.kassir.ru to reach the page with an English-language option on the upper right-hand side. The Mariinsky theater also sells tickets online through its Web site www.mariinsky.ru. The tickets can either be bought or reserved.

Bear in mind, too, that theater tickets purchased through hotels are the priciest of all, as most hotels tend to charge a markup on the foreigner price. All in all, your best option is to go in person to the theater concerned and buy the ticket there.

Your best source of information is the *St. Petersburg Times* (www. sptimes.ru), a free, local, independent English-language newspaper. It comes out on Tuesday and Friday and is widely distributed. The Friday edition has a calendar of events in the "All About Town" section, with theater and concert listings, and a restaurant column. *Pulse,* a glossy, advertising-driven paper published monthly in English and Russian editions, also has extensive listings. Copies of both papers can be found at Western airline offices, bars, clubs, hotels, cafés, and other places generally patronized by foreigners.

Most major theaters close down between mid-July and early August and start up again in mid-September or early October. However, summer is also the time for touring companies from other regions in Russia to come to town, so it's a rare day that there are no shows on at all. Sumptuous balls are thrown in the most famous palaces and concert halls in winter; the top two events are the Mariinsky Ball and the Temirkanov Ball on New Year's Eve.

Festivals

St. Petersburg's premier arts event is the Mariinsky Theater's **Stars of the White Nights** (☎ 812/714–4344 ⊕ www.mariinsky.ru), which stretches from the end of May until the middle of July or longer. The event's founder and driving force is Mariinsky's indefatigable artistic director Valery Gergiev, who puts on a pantheon of international stars and orchestras that any other Russian festival can only dream of inviting. It helps that Gergiev, a principal guest conductor with the New York's Metropolitan Opera, is a regular with the world's most acclaimed orchestras. The festival interweaves opera, ballet, symphonic, and chamber music in almost equal proportions and provides a rare opportunity to see the Mariinsky's most renowned soloists—who spend most of their time between La Scala, Opera Bastille, and the Met—perform on home soil. Don't miss mezzo-soprano Olga Borodina, tenor Vladimir Galuzin, bass Ildar Abdrazakov, baritone Nikolai Putilin, and soprano Anna Netrebko.

Prices soar up during the festival and may reach $150 or more. Pricing policy ranges wildly at the Mariinsky, sometimes not following any apparent logic.

Another attractive event is the **Musical Olympus** (⊕ www.musicalolympus. ru) festival organized by acclaimed Russian pianist Irina Nikitina at the Philharmonic in May and June. The festival assembles winners and laureates of each year's most respected musical contests from all over the globe. Each musician is handpicked by Nikitina herself or members of the festival's honorary committee, ranging from Placido Domingo to Claudio Abbado and Mstislav Rostropovich. What is especially precious about this festival is that the audiences get to see the rising talent immediately after they have claimed the fame but haven't yet been booked up for years to come.

The Arts Square Festival (⊕ www.artsquarewinterfest.ru), brainchild of Yury Temirkanov, artistic director of the St. Petersburg Philharmonic, runs between Catholic and Orthodox Christmas and showcases classical concerts and ballets with top-notch international stars. A complete and, more importantly, reliable program is available from its Web site a year in advance. The State Russian Museum organizes special exhibitions and hosts receptions for the festival, which culminates on New Year's Eve with a luxurious ball in Yusupovsky palace.

The **Palaces of St. Petersburg** (☎ 812/572–2226 ⊕ www.palacefest.spb. ru) festival presents an impressive series of classical concerts in more than two dozen magnificent palaces and mansions year-round. Remarkably enough, in the heyday of imperial Russia, the social season, with its grand balls, masquerades, and concerts, occurred in winter. White nights or not, during the stuffy summers the pillars of high society abandoned the heat and dust of the city to enjoy a relaxing escape in their country estates and summer residences. A century later, St. Petersburg is trying to restore the glories of the past.

Also of interest is the city's **Early Music Festival** (⊕ www.earlymusic.ru), which attracts international soloists and ensembles; it's usually held late September through early October. Every fall, vibrant performances of its refined ensembles evoke, embody, and revive the long-lost noble spirit of St. Petersburg.

Art Galleries

St. Petersburg may have one of the world's great museums, but it's not known for its contemporary art. The paradox of St. Petersburg is that although originally designed as a cosmopolitan metropolis, it has evolved into a place remarkably resistant to foreign influences. Reclusive and trapped in endless reflection, the city makes it difficult for young, experimental, and unorthodox artists to get exposure, let alone recognition. That said, the Iron Curtain played a weird trick with modern Russian artists. When the borders fell, they were so eager to catch up with what they had been missing that many of them somehow lost their own ideas, direction, and identity in the process. A new work of art is generally judged according to whether it fits in with the city's venerable artistic traditions. The issue is taken so seriously that the installation of every new monument, especially in the city center, provokes a massive debate. There's a history of modern artworks being removed because of public protests and pressure from cultural circles. The temptation to preserve the historical center in its original state is so strong that contemporary sculpture is nonexistent in the streets of St. Petersburg.

The Russian Museum is home to the largest collection of Russian art in the world but not much of Russian art is sold in the city's art galleries, and there isn't a single art auction house. Three to four dozen private galleries make up St. Petersburg's modest art market and we list the most worthy in this chapter. Stylistic variety corresponds with the size of the market.

If you buy any artwork in St. Petersburg other than a standard souvenir, ask the shop to provide you with the necessary documentation to let you take it out of the country. Anything more than 100 years old or of significant cultural value cannot leave the country. Art stores and antiques shops should be able to handle the paperwork, but if you're in any doubt, take the item to the **Board for the Preservation of Cultural Valuables** (Upravlenie po sokhraneniu kulturnikh tsennostei; ✉ 17 Malaya

Morskaya ul., City Center ☎ 812/571–5196 Ⓜ Nevsky prospekt) for assessment and to receive the relevant certificate. This can cost anywhere from $15 to $40, depending on the item and how quickly you need the paperwork to be processed.

Borey. On display here are the works of avant-garde and academic artists, including paintings, graphics, and applied art. ⊠ *58 Liteiny pr., Liteiny/Smolny* ☎ *812/273–3693* Ⓜ *Mayakovskaya.*

Exhibition Center of the St. Petersburg Artists Union. There's an exhibition hall on the ground floor, and art by theatrical artists for sale upstairs. ⊠ *38 Bolshaya Morskaya, City Center* ☎ *812/315–7414* Ⓜ *Nevsky prospekt or Gostinny Dvor.*

Free Arts Foundation. As far as St. Petersburg's art galleries are concerned, this collective is the leader of the pack, with artwork of all different media and quality. ⊠ *10 Pushkinskaya ul., entrance at 53 Ligovsky pr., Vladimirskaya* ☎ *812/764–5371* ⊕ *www.pushkinskaja-10.spb.ru* Ⓜ *Ploschad Vosstaniya.*

Guild of Masters. You'll find paintings, graphics, applied art, and various jewelry items here. ⊠ *82 Nevsky pr., City Center* ☎ *812/279–0979* Ⓜ *Nevsky prospekt or Gostinny Dvor.*

Lion's Bridge. Soviet art with an emphasis on social realism is represented here, with most works dating from 1920–1970. You'll find masterpieces of propaganda art, landscapes, still lifes, and some examples of Soviet impressionism. ⊠ *96 Kanal Griboedova, Admiralteisky* ☎ *812/31–0795 or 812/380–7458* ⊕ *www.lionsbridge.ru* Ⓜ *Sadovaya/Sennaya Ploshchad.*

Maria Gisich's Private Art Gallery. One of the best small galleries in St. Petersburg, Maria Gisich hosts local and national Russian artists and exhibitions. ⊠ *121 Fontanka, No. 13, City Center* ☎ *812/314–4380* ⊕ *www.gisich.com* Ⓜ *Tekhnologichesky Institute.*

Matiss Club. Underground art is the main focus of this gallery, which represents a number of well-known local artists. ⊠ *104 Kanal Griboedova, Admiralteisky* ☎ *812/310–6722* ⊕ *www.matissclub.com* Ⓜ *Sadovaya/Sennaya Ploshchad.*

★ **Mitki-VKhUTEMAS.** Occupying a spacious attic, the gallery exhibits works of the legendary nonconformist group Mitki, famous for their use of blue-and-white striped sailors shirts that they wear and often portray in their artworks. Their style fuses deliciously twisted social realism with a touch of primitivism. The group pulled through the Communist era, when they were oppressed for mocking social realism and portraying tipsy sailors rather than heroes of labor. Artists were often kept down for ideological reasons, with the police breaking in and destroying works. In an ironic and eccentric fashion, Mitki paintings touch on the issues of human happiness, social injustice, or Russia's eternal pains like alcoholism or poverty. The main characters of their works are best described as philistines. The city of St. Petersburg is vividly present in almost every work. It's best to call to make an appointment. ⊠ *36–38* *ul. Marata, Vladimirskaya* ☏ *812/764–6462* Ⓜ *Dostoyevskaya/ Vladimirskaya.*

The Russian Icon. This gallery exhibits and sells contemporary Russian Orthodox icons. It's possible to order customized icons. ✉ *15 Bolshaya Konyushennaya ul., City Center* ☏ *812/314–7040* Ⓜ *Nevsky Prospect.*

★ **Sol-Art.** Next to the prestigious Mukhina Academy for Arts and Design and in the same building as the magnificent and crumbling Baron Stieglitz Museum, this wonderful gallery exhibits St. Petersburg's young artistic talents. The gallery showcases some of the big names in the local contemporary art scene as well. ✉ *15 Solyanoy per., Liteiny/Smolny* ☏ *812/327–3082* Ⓜ *Nevsky Prospect.*

S.P.A.S. This spacious gallery exhibits a good collection of contemporary artists. ✉ *93 nab. Moiki, Admiralteisky* ☏ *812/571–4260* Ⓜ *Sadovaya.*

Music

St. Petersburg oozes musical history, and there's a fascinating and thrilling concentration of the brightest names in classical music here. The spiritual presence of Tchaikovsky, Mussorgsky, Prokofiev, and Shostakovich is strong in their alma mater. But unlike Salzburg that made Mozart a successful, well-selling brand, or Bonn that organizes a rapidly expanding Beethoven Festival every year, the city hasn't ventured far into building an infrastructure or even a regular festival around any of its biggest classical names.

With its 18th-century heritage, St. Petersburg makes the perfect setting to hear Russia's sometimes-forgotten early music. The Early Music Festival spawned the Catherine the Great Orchestra, Russia's first baroque orchestra, which launched its own recording label and plays year-round at various venues.

Only the St. Petersburg Philharmonic is capable of programing its schedule well in advance, and other places are much more spontaneous. A detailed program of a festival at the Mariinsky is usually available three weeks before the event, while confirmed cast for premieres is normally announced a week prior to the performance. Last-minute changes and cancellations aren't uncommon for any venue. St. Petersburg's concert halls and theaters have been slow starters on the Web, not least because of the old chestnut—money. The two exceptions are the Philharmonic (⊕ www.philharmonia.spb.ru) and the Mariinsky (⊕ www.mariinsky. ru). You can find information on musical events around town at ⊕ www. classicalmusic.spb.ru.

Fodor'sChoice When scanning the listings, don't miss **Terem Quartet** (⊕ www. ★ terem-quartet.com), the famous local four who have adapted "inviolable" classical jewels such as Oginsky's "Polonaise" or Schubert's "Ave Maria" for balalaika, bayan, domra, and alto domra to superb effect. Virtuosi in their instruments, and highly interactive in their performing style, which critics have branded "instrumental theater," they freely mix J. S. Bach's "Toccata and Fugue in D Minor" with Russian folk songs, and make every concert a fun and overwhelming experience.

★ Another must-see is the marvleous **St. Petersburg Male Choir** (Peterburgsky Muzhskoi Khor) led by artistic director Vadim Afanasiev. Their favorite venues are the Capella and Petropavlovsky Cathedral in Peter and Paul Fortress, where the choir performs Orthodox chants and choral works by Russian composers. The sound is mesmerizing, and their bottomless yet velvet profoundo basses make an extraordinary asset.

The **St. Petersburg Horn Capella** (Rogovaya Kapella; ⊕ www.horncapella. ru) revives the traditions of 18th-century Russian horn music, and is the only ensemble of its kind in Russia. Apart from baroque pieces written specifically for horn, the musicians perform a wide repertoire of charming arrangements of well-known classical works.

For a relaxing evening of classical music in a prerevolutionary setting, try the concert halls in some of St. Petersburg's museums, mansions, palaces, and churches. Performances are held regularly at the following venues.

Academic Kapella Chamber Hall (Osobnyak Bosse; ⊠ 15 4th liniya, Vasilievsky Island ☎ 812/323–4029). **Kochneva's House** (Dom Kochnevoi; ⊠ 41 nab. Fontanki, City Center Ⓜ Nevsky prospekt ☎ 812/710–4062). **Palace of Prince Beloselsky-Belozersky** (Beloselsky-Belozersky Dvorets; ⊠ 41 Nevsky pr., City Center ☎ 812/315–5236 or 812/319–9790 Ⓜ Nevsky prospekt). **St. Catherine Lutheran Church** (⊠ 1a Bolshoi prospekt, Vasilievsky Island ☎ 812/323–1852 Ⓜ Vasileostrovskaya). **Samoilovs Family Museum** (⊠ 8 Stremyannaya ul., entrance from back side of Nevsky Palace Hotel, City Center ☎ 812/764–1130 ⊕ www.theatremuseum.ru/ eng/expo/sam.html Ⓜ Mayakovskaya). **Sheremetev Palace** (Sheremetev Dvorets; ⊠ 34 nab. Fontanki, City Center ☎ 812/272–4441 ⊕ www. theatremuseum.ru/eng/expo/sher.html Ⓜ Mayakovskaya). **Smolny** (⊠ 3/ 1 Pl. Rastrelli, Liteiny/Smolny ☎ 812/271–9182 Ⓜ Chernyshevskaya). **Yusupov Palace** (⊠ 94 nab. Moiki, Admiralteisky ☎ 812/314–8893 Ⓜ Sennaya Ploshchad); tickets available only on the spot.

Many of the concerts organized at St. Petersburg's most historic venues are run by **Peterburg-Concert** (In Kochnevaya's House ⊠ 41 nab. Fontanki, City Center ☎ 812/710–4032 ⊕ www.petroconcert.spb.ru/ Ⓜ Nevsky prospekt). These concerts are not of the highest standard found at other musical events in the city—although there are some exceptions—but they are a much better bet than most of the events organized especially for tourist groups. Tickets can be bought right at the Peterburg-Concert offices. The entrance is rather inconspicuous: look for a door on the right side in the passageway at 41 Fontanka (after the Mexican restaurant La Cucaracha, coming from Nevsky).

Academic Kapella. One of St. Petersburg's best-kept secrets is also its oldest concert hall, dating to the 1780s. It presents not only choral events but also symphonic, instrumental, and vocal concerts. Many famous musicians, including Glinka and Rimsky-Korsakov, have performed in this elegant space along the Moika, just near the Alexander Pushkin Apartment Museum and the Winter Palace. The main entrance and the surrounding courtyards have been beautifully restored. ⊠ *20 nab. Moiki, City Center* ☎ *812/314–1153* Ⓜ *Nevsky prospekt.*

Fyodor Chaliapin Museum. If you want to hear the next generation of opera stars even before the Mariinsky Theater snaps them up, head to the former apartment of the legendary opera singer, Fyodor Chaliapin (1873–1938). The best of the conservatory's opera students give frequent performances. ⊠ *2b ul. Graftio, Petrograd Side* ☎ *812/234–1056* ⊕ *www.theatremuseum.ru/eng/expo/sha.html* Ⓜ *Petrogradskaya.*

Glinka Hall. For chamber and vocal music, head to this small hall, part of the Shostakovich Philharmonia (it's just around the corner from the Philharmonia). It's also known as the Maly Zal. ⊠ *30 Nevsky pr., City Center* ☎ *812/571–8333* Ⓜ *Nevsky prospekt.*

Hermitage Theater. This glorious and highly unusual theater in the Hermitage mainly hosts the St. Petersburg Camerata, a rather fine and often overlooked chamber ensemble. Note that the theater doesn't have a box office, so purchase tickets at a theater kiosk or via your concierge. ⊠ *32 Dvortsovaya nab., City Center* ☎ *812/579–0226 or 812/966–3776* ⊕ *www.hermitagemuseum.org* Ⓜ *Nevsky prospekt.*

House of Composers (Dom Kompozitorov). Lovers of contemporary music flock here for the concerts of music written by its members—look out for names such as Sergei Slonimsky, Boris Tishchenko, and Andrey Petrov—and their students at the conservatory. ⊠ *45 Bolshaya Morskaya ul., City Center* ☎ *812/571–3548* Ⓜ *Nevsky prospekt.*

Shostakovich Philharmonia. Two excellent symphony orchestras perform in the Philharmonia's famous, grand concert hall: the St. Petersburg Philharmonic Orchestra and the Academic Philharmonic (a fine outfit, although it's officially the B-team). Both troupes have long, illustrious histories of collaboration with some of Russia's finest composers, and many famous works have premiered in this hall. The venue will be closed for renovation until November 2006. ⊠ *2 Mikhailovskaya ul., City Center* ☎ *812/710–4257 or 812/710–4290* Ⓜ *Nevsky prospekt.*

Opera & Ballet

Russian classical ballet was born in St. Petersburg. The Imperial Ballet School was founded here on May 4, 1738, by the order of Empress Anna Ioannovna, to be run by Frenchman Jean-Baptiste Lande. French and Italian masters taught the first class of 12 boys and 12 girls. Works of another Frenchman, Marius Petipa, who arrived at the academy in 1847 to shape up the Russian classical ballet together with his Russian counterpart Lev Ivanov, still dominate the repertoire of the Mariinsky theater. Today the school is called the Vaganova Ballet Academy in honor of Agrippina Vaganova, who radically changed the way ballet was taught in Russia. The best students traditionally appear on the venerable Mariinsky stage around Christmas in *The Nutcracker* and then in May and June in graduation performances.

During the high tourist season, *Swan Lake,* a signature production for the Russian classical ballet, appears by the dozen each day on various stages. If purity is important to you, go to either the Mariinsky or Mussorgsky theaters, and beware of the clones: not all stages are fit for such a grand ballet and there's a high risk of being served a brutally circumcised version, with difficult bits omitted, a few swans missing, and even no live orchestra.

Contemporary dance doesn't really flourish in the cradle of classical tradition but the dance company and school Kannon Dance (⊕ www.kannondance.ru) organizes several modern dance festivals during the year.

Russian opera is much less known and much less appreciated abroad. Many potential spectators are frightened merely by the sound of them. There's always a peasant riot, a doomed tsar, much chaos and insanity, and a lack of tuneful, languid, and tender belcanto heroines. St. Petersburg opera singers, who have long been complaining about a lobby against Russian operas in the West, and who are all convinced that Tchaikovsky's *The Queen of Spades* is the greatest-ever dramatic opera, are eager to make you change your mind. The Mariinsky's artistic director, Valery Gergiev, has declared it the company's policy to reveal the obscure masterpieces of Russian operatic legacy to the audiences. Opera in Russia is about power, drama, depth, and philosophy. And among those most likely to convert you are the philosophical and spiritual renditions of Rimsky-Korsakov's *The Legend of the Invisible City of Kitezh* or Glinka's *A Life For the Tsar.*

FodorsChoice ★ **Boris Eifman Ballet Theater** (☎ 812/232–0235). Psychological drama reigns here. Most of the ballets in the repertoire of this internationally acclaimed troupe—the only professional contemporary ballet company in St. Petersburg—have been inspired by biographies of extraordinary Russians with a tragic fate or are based on Russia's literary gems. A must-see is *Red Giselle,* which tells the story of the great Russian ballerina Olga Spessivtseva, who fled Russia after the Bolshevik Revolution and spent 20 years in a psychiatric ward in New York. Also highly recommended are *Anna Karenina, Tchaikovsky,* and *The Russian Hamlet,* devoted to the doomed life of Russian tsar Paul I, who was murdered by plotters in Mikhailovsky castle. The troupe, founded in the late 1970s, has no permanent home, and spends most of its time abroad. When here, the company usually performs at the Alexander Pushkin Drama Theater, the Mariinsky, or Mussorgsky.

Konservatoria. The Konservatoria is directly opposite the Mariinsky, but the opera and ballet performances are nothing like the level of its famous neighbor—partly because the Mariinsky is so good at siphoning off the conservatory's brightest talent. ⊠ *3 Teatralnaya Pl., Admiralteisky* ☎ *812/312–2519* Ⓜ *Sadovaya.*

FodorsChoice ★ **Mariinsky Theater of Opera and Ballet** (Mariinsky Teatr Opery I Balleta). Formerly known as the Kirov, the world-renowned Mariinsky is one of Russia's finest artistic institutions, a definite must-see. The names Petipa, Pavlova, Nijinsky, and Nureyev—and countless others associated with the theater and the birth of ballet in St. Petersburg—are enough to lure ballet lovers to an evening here. The Mariinsky is without doubt one of the best ballet companies in the world, with a seemingly inexhaustible supply of stars.

While maintaining its reputation as a citadel of classical ballet, the works of George Balanchine, Kenneth MacMillan, Michel Fokine, John Neumeier, and William Forsythe are winning greater prominence on the playbill. However, audiences are slow to change their expectations and modern ballets almost always perform to a half-empty auditorium. Between February and March, the company runs the **Mariinsky International Ballet Festival,** an impressive and tantalizing one that features at least one premiere and an array of guest performers from other renowned companies such as London's Royal Ballet, Opera Bastille, and the American Ballet Theater.

The Mariinsky is also at the forefront of the world's opera companies, thanks largely to the achievements of the Mariinsky's artistic director Valery Gergiev (who now also masterminds many productions at New York City's Metropolitan Opera). The company's best operatic repertoire centers on Russian opera of all centuries: Tchaikovsky's *The Queen of Spades,* Prokofiev's *Semyon Kotko,* Shostakovich's *The Nose,* Rimsky-Korsakov's *The Legend of the Invisible City of Kitezh,* and *The Snow Maid* are particularly recommended.

Wagner is sung in German, Puccini in Italian, and Saint-Saens in French. Russian operas are all provided with English subtitles, while Russian subtitles are given for foreign operas. Verdi can be hit-or-miss but Wagner is one of Gergiev's greatest passions, and the company now feels very much at home with the composer. Basses Yevgeny Nikitin and Viktor Chernomortsev have excellent Wagnerian voices and technique. The orchestra's rapport with the conductor is amazing, the sound is nuanced and powerful. Be sure to see *Parsifal* and *Tristan und Isolde,* and of course, if you have the stamina, the whole of Wagner's Ring Cycle.

Ballet and opera mix freely in the calendar schedule throughout the year; the opera and ballet companies both tour, but at any given time one of the companies is performing in St. Petersburg. The Mariinsky's main venue will be closed for renovation for two years starting August 2006. The second stage, just across Kryukov Canal, is scheduled to open in 2008. In the summer of 2006, the company opens its third concert venue on nearby ulitsa Pisareva to host most of its shows during the years of renovation and construction. ✉ *1/2 Teatralnaya Pl., Admiralteisky* ☎ *812/714–1211* ⊕ *www.mariinsky.ru/en* Ⓜ *Sadovaya.*

Mussorgsky Theater of Opera and Ballet. This lesser known venue has raised its prices for foreigners considerably, but it's still cheaper than the Mariinsky, and the best of its productions rivals its bigger and richer cousin. As far as opera is concerned, the Russian repertoire is the theater's strong point, but it occasionally strikes gold with Italian works as well. Although the company hosted the world premieres of Shostakovich's *Lady Macbeth of Mtsensk* in 1934 and Prokofiev's *War and Peace* in 1946, the works of these composers are now absent from the repertoire, which focuses heavily on 19th-century classics. Highlights include Mussorgsky's *Boris Godunov,* Rimsky-Korsakov's *The Tsar's Bride,* Borodin's *Prince Igor,* and Tchaikovsky's *Iolanta.*

The company's strong dance division is deservedly rated the second-best in town. The classical fare includes *Swan Lake, Giselle, La Esmeralda,* and *Don Quixote* as well as some jewels of Soviet-era choreography, like Rodion Schedrin's *The Little Humpbacked Horse* and Prokofiev's *Romeo and Juliet.*

The opera season usually opens in early September, traditionally with a gala performance of Mussorgsky's famous opera, *Boris Godunov*. Ballet and opera are both generally performed September through June or July. ✉ *1 Pl. Iskusstv, City Center* ☎ *812/595–4305* ⊕ *www. mikhailovsky.ru* Ⓜ *Nevsky prospekt.*

St. Petersburg Chamber Opera (Opera Sankt Peterburg). Until 2003 this company, founded in 1987 by former Mariinsky stage director Yuri Alexandrov as an "opera laboratory," had no permanent home. The company is now based in the former mansion of Baron Derviz, a place with a rich musical history. Vsevolod Meyerhold staged productions here at the end of the 19th century, before it was turned into a concert hall. The company's repertoire is small and dominated by Russian classics and light Italian operas, with occasional experimental performances. ✉ *33 Galernaya ul., Admiralteisky* ☎ *812/312–3982 or 812/312–0815* ⊕ *www.opera.spb.ru.*

Theater

St. Petersburg has some excellent drama theaters, but performances are almost exclusively in Russian. Cutting-edge productions are a missing link in local repertoires, mainly because too many directors feel that there's so much modern language and depressing social malaise on television, that it's best kept off the stage. This widespread escapist approach means you have a choice of three renditions of *Antigona*, while Gogol's *Marriage* and Chekhov's *Uncle Vanya* are served up by the dozen, in renditions that vary from enthralling to downright dull.

Alexander Pushkin Drama Theater (Alexandrinsky Teatr). Russia's oldest theater, opened in 1756, is also one of its most elegant. Its repertoire is dominated by 19th-century classics (and the productions can be as musty as the costumes). With prominent Moscow director Valery Fokin taking the helm in 2004, the company is enjoying a renaissance. Fokin's interpretations of Dostoyevsky's *The Double* and Gogol's *Government Inspector* are thought-provoking and engaging. The theater reopens on August 30, 2006, after a massive renovation. ✉ *2 Pl. Ostrovskovo, City Center* ☎ *812/312–1545 or 812/710–4103* Ⓜ *Gostinny Dvor or Nevsky prospekt.*

Baltiisky Dom Theater-Festival. An umbrella venue for a dozen experimental companies of various genres, Baltiisky Dom holds performances in its large hall and a variety of basements, attics, and back rooms. Once a full-fledged theater, it has turned into a modern art polyhedron, where aspiring directors play with material from Luigi Pirandello to Ivan Turgenev to the Presnyakov Brothers. This is the only venue in town staging plays written in the past five years. To get a sense of experimental Russian theater, look out for the shows of "Farces" theater and productions directed by Andrei Moguchy as well as one-man shows by local actors. In October the theater hosts an impressive four-week Baltic Theater Festival, attracting the best talent from the Baltic Sea region. ✉ *4 Alexandrovsky park, Petrograd Side* ☎ *812/232–3539* Ⓜ *Gorkovskaya.*

Bolshoi Drama Theater (Bolshoi Dramatichesky Teatr). The legendary Bolshoi has some of the best-known names in Russian drama and film on its stage. The only problem is that most of its stars are well beyond retirement age. The company had its golden age between the 1960s and tge 1980s under the directorship of Georgy Tovstonogov, who died in 1990. No adequate replacement was found, and it was decided to concentrate on "preserving the legacy" of the famous director. Now, the house that the director built is aged and rickety. Excellent actors Alisa Freindlikh, Kirill Lavrov, and Oleg Basilashvili carry most of the repertoire on their shoulders, and any production with them on the list isn't going to be a disappointment. But after so many years of being denied any fresh influence and experiment, the troupe finds itself in a crumbling state.

In addition to Russian classics, the theater stages works by Shakespeare, Molière, Harwood, Miller, and Stoppard. Two productions—"The Pickwick Papers" and "Uncle Vanya"—have survived from Tovstonogov's day and miraculously even feature almost entirely the same cast as 30 years ago. An interesting theatrical phenomenon, it still leaves the viewer with a lingering feeling of sadness, as though looking at a dried butterfly. ⊠ *65 nab. Fontanki, City Center* ☎ *812/310–0401* Ⓜ *Nevsky prospekt.*

FodorśChoice **Maly Drama Theater** (Maly Dramatichesky Teatr). Even if you can't un-
★ derstand the dialogue, any performance at the MDT—home to one of the best theater companies in the world—is a must-see. The repertoire includes productions of Chekhov, Dostoyevsky, Shakespeare, and Oscar Wilde. Maly is also nearly the only company in town that continues to stage the finest plays from the Soviet era. Seeing their whole repertoire has been compared to living through the entire 20th-century history of Russia. If you have a whole day to spare and lots of stamina, the nine-hour performance of Dostoyevsky's *The Possessed* makes for an incredible theatrical experience, although it can be a bit hard on the posterior. It takes two consecutive evenings to sit through the company's veteran show, Fyodor Abramov's "Brothers And Sisters," but nobody is known to have regretted doing that. Order tickets well in advance because it's rare that the Maly plays to a less than packed house. ⊠ *18 ul. Rubinshteina, Vladimirskaya* ☎*812/712–2078* ⊕*www.mdt-dodin.ru* Ⓜ *Vladimirskaya.*
Molodezhny Theater. Although most troupes in town tend to work their most seasoned players to the bone, this theater is brave enough to have younger talent figure prominently in the troupe. Shows are bursting with youthful energy and romanticism yet there's no amateur student feel to them. Not really catering to intellectuals, the troupe appeals directly to one's heart, and this approach has found the company many admirers among the city's younger crowd. Most of the shows are expertly staged by artistic director Semyon Spivak, a professor at the renowned St. Petersburg Academy for Theatre Art. The company's signature show is Alexei Tolstoy's "The Swallow." Isaac Babel's "Cries From Odessa" and Alexander Ostrovsky's "Love Lace" are also among its hits. ⊠ *2 Fontanka Embankment, Admiralteisky* ☎ *812/316–6870* Ⓜ *Tekhnologichesky Institute.*

CHILDREN'S The following St. Petersburg puppet theaters perform regularly for chil-
THEATER dren. **Bolshoi Puppet Theater** (⊠ 10 ul. Nekrasova, Liteiny/Smolny ☎ 812/ 273–6672 Ⓜ Mayakovskaya). **Puppet-Marionette Theater** (⊠ 52 Nevsky pr., City Center ☎ 812/310–5879 Ⓜ Gostinny Dvor).

Children's Philharmonic. The Children's Philharmonic stages children's musicals and even "adult" operas that kids can enjoy. ✉ *1/3 Dumskaya ul., City Center* ☎ *812/315–7222* Ⓜ *Nevsky prospekt.*

🔾 **Zazerkalye Theater** (Through the Looking Glass Theater). This is perhaps the best musical choice for children. Captivating shows masterfully blend dramatic and musical elements and are famous for daring direction experiments. The company is good at winning children over to opera with entertaining yet unabridged versions of serious repertoire such as Donizetti's "L'elisir d'amore"—during which Nemorino sings his famous aria while riding a bike—or Offenbach's "Les contes d'Hoffmann" and Puccini's "La Boheme." It's open Friday through Sunday. ✉ *13 ul. Rubinshteina, Vladimirskaya* ☎ *812/764–1895 or 812/712–5000* Ⓜ *Vladimirskaya or Dostoevskaya.*

Nightlife

After the fall of Communism, St. Petersburg became the first Russian city to adopt club culture. The underground and rock scene here is thriving and a number of the first clubs and musical heavyweights are still around. Most of Russia's living rock patriarchs live here and make regular appearances at venues.

The city's nightclubs and discos don't compete with Moscow's glamorous establishments in terms of grand scale, pomp, exorbitant prices, and attitude, but they do offer a more relaxed environment and laid-back feel, very much in tune with the city's chamber spirit. Even popular spots, however, are well hidden and you need to know where to look. At night, the town's quiet and serene historical center evokes associations with "Sleeping Beauty" so don't expect much of a seething street life. Notoriously conservative, the city guards its architectural treasures and even advertising banners were removed from Nevsky Prospect for aesthetic reasons. Thus nightclubs and casinos have to think of ways other than neon lighting to advertise themselves discreetly.

It's also an ever-changing scene, so it's always best to consult current listings. The most reliable English-language sources are the Friday edition of the free *St. Petersburg Times* (www.sptimes.ru) or the monthly English-language issue of *St. Petersburg In Your Pocket* (www. inyourpocket.com). These publications include excellent unbiased club guides in addition to detailed listings. There are more comprehensive sources in Russian, such as the magazines *Afisha* (⊕ spb.afisha.ru) and *Time Out/Kalendar.*

A good rule of thumb for tourists with little or no experience in Russia is to stick to the city center, where you have plenty of options: bohemian art clubs, trendy dance clubs, live-music venues, and simple pubs. Locals in the city center are friendly and more than a few speak English—and foreigners are not the novelty they once were. If you're seeking the company of expats, you'll find them in centrally located Irish and British pubs or at low-key artsy bars such as *Dacha*. The historical center is abundant with expensive strip-clubs but these are meant for deep-pocketed foreign tourists and ravenous Russian beauties hunting for them.

The city's red-light district is the part of Nevsky prospect farther north from Ploshchad Vosstaniya, where prostitutes stand at every other corner and can be rather aggressive. Beware that if you venture to a place beyond the historical center, the risk of being robbed or attacked by one of the city's many skinhead and hooligan gangs increases significantly. During the months when the rivers and canals are not frozen (generally April–November), watch the clock: bridges start to go up around 1:30 AM. If you get stuck on the wrong side, you'll have to wait until 5 AM or so to cross.

Bars

The line separating bars, clubs, and restaurants in St. Petersburg is often not clear. For that reason, many establishments listed here could also be found under restaurants—though they may have the look and feel of bars, they also offer seating and a full menu. Bars and cafés regularly host live concerts, parties, and DJs, but prefer not to advertise themselves in the club section.

City Bar. One of the city's few true expat hangouts is a few minutes walk from the Hermitage. The American-owned bar-restaurant draws a lively bunch of mostly foreign students and long-term expats who can't seem to leave the city—maybe owner Ailene's "just-like-Mom-makes-it" daily specials (a bargain at $4) help them feel at home. It's also the only place in town where you'll find blueberry pancakes smothered in maple syrup for breakfast. ⊠ *10 Millionnaya ul., City Center* ☎ *812/314–1037 or 812/315–8575* Ⓜ *Chernyshevskaya or Nevsky prospekt.*

Cynic. This haven for young expats and local bohemians off St. Isaac's Square has a big, three-room basement to accommodate spontaneous performances by some of the city's best underground musicians, or just random dancing on the tables. Don't miss the delicious *grenki* (fried garlic bread). ⊠ *4 per. Antonenko, Admiralteisky* ☎ *812/312–8779* ⊕ *www. cynic.spb.ru* Ⓜ *Sennaya Ploshchad.*

Dacha. A tremendously popular haunt of expats, bohemians, students, and night owls, Dacha is influenced by the merry joints of the Reeperbahn in Hamburg (the owner is German). The galvanizing spirit of this friendly and eclectic art bar is hugely addictive—despite its claustrophobic size, low ceilings, shabby setting, and no food service except for peanuts. The music, mainly rock and ska, is so loud that an intimate chat is out of the question. Reckless dance parties sometimes get out of hand and spill into the street. ⊠ *9 Dumskaya ul., City Center* ☎ *No phone* Ⓜ *Nevsky Prospect.*

Krasniy Lev. The closest thing to a British pub in St. Petersburg, the Red Lion is a welcoming place with live music, dancing, and a full menu—with a shepherd's pie as authentic as you could hope to find outside the United Kingdom. It's open 24 hours a day. ⊠ *4 Alexandrovksy Park, next to Baltisky Dom Theater, Petrograd Side* ☎ *812/233–9391* ⊕ *www. redlion.ru* Ⓜ *Gorkovskaya.*

Sadko. The premier bar of the Grand Hotel Europe screens live sporting events from the United States—such as the Super Bowl—and occasionally hosts live music. There's outdoor seating in summer. The hotel's suave Lobby Bar is a relaxed and spacious setting with plenty of room for a private conversation. ✉ *1/7 Mikhailovskaya ul., City Center* ☎ *812/329–6000* ⊕ *www.grandhoteleurope.com/restaurants/sadko* Ⓜ *Nevsky prospekt or Gostinny Dvor.*

Fodor'sChoice ★ **Shamrock Irish Pub.** A long-standing favorite of the local foreign community, this jolly inn with great pub food, cozy wooden furnishings, and two dozen types of beer stands across the street from the Mariinsky theater. The company's younger talent can be often spotted having a quick bite or beers here at any time of day. Live Irish music is played every night, except Tuesday and Friday. ✉ *27 ul. Dekabristov, Admiralteisky* ☎ *812/318–4625* Ⓜ *Sadovaya.*

Stirka. A peculiar hybrid of bar and launderette, informal and homey Stirka ("laundry") was originally a graduation project of a German design student. Catering to a young crowd, Stirka features underground rock DJs once or twice a week. Guests are welcome to make use of one of its three washing machines and two dryers. It costs 100R to use one machine, and a cup of tea or coffee is included. The place doesn't serve hard liquor. ✉ *26 Kazanskaya ul., City Center* ☎ *812/314–5371* ⊕ *www.40gradusov.ru* Ⓜ *Sennaya Ploshchad or Nevsky Prospect.*

★ **Tschaika.** This legendary Russian-German establishment serving good beer, authentic bratwurst, sauerkraut, and other German specialties was one of the first foreign bars to open in town after the fall of communism. It has remained an unbeatable expat hangout since (President Vladimir Putin dined with former German chancellor Gerhard Schroeder here). Inspired by the pubs of Hamburg, Tschaika gets especially noisy on weekends. Live music gets started every night at 9 PM. ✉ *14, nab. Kanala Griboyedova, City Center* ☎ *812/312–4631* ⊕ *www.tschaika.ru* Ⓜ *Nevsky Prospect.*

Cabaret

The genre is barely present in town, and most attempts fail miserably. Variety shows in restaurants usually strike out with vulgarity and lack of taste or coherent concept. For many years in Russia entertainment was considered "low culture" as opposed to "high art" and the consequences are still felt. There are, however, two genuine gems.

★ **Comic-Trust.** Theater troupe "Comic-Trust," which consists of three actors led by director Vadim Fisson exercises various forms of visual comedy, be it cabaret, parody, clownage, puppetry, or pantomime. The resulting theatrical fusion, spiced up with black humor, farce, and the grotesque, is a rather shaking theatrical experience. The troupe, which produced a sensation during the Fringe Festival in Edinburgh in 2001, is vagrant but mostly performs at the Lensoviet Palace of Culture. The hits include "Second Hand," "Naphtalene," "White Side Story," and Shakespeare's "Antony and Cleopatra." ✉ *42 Kamennoostrovsky pr., Petrograd Side* ☎ *812/328–1619* ⊕ *www.comic-trust.com* Ⓜ *Petrogradskaya.*

Chaplin Club. The name describes the spirit of this, one of the few cabarets in town. From Friday to Sunday, the small stage is most often occupied by the Litsedeyi, a pantomime troupe that has established its home base here but also fills up the biggest concert halls of the city. There's a cover charge of 50R or more when there's a performance, and prices for food and beverages are reasonable. Small bands play live music when Litsedeyi isn't performing. ✉ *59 ul. Chaikovskovo, Liteiny/Smolny* ☎ *812/272–6649* Ⓜ *Chernyshevskaya.*

Casinos

There are plenty of casinos in St. Petersburg, but don't expect to find a strip of neon lights to lead the way. Instead, many of them are barely discernible as they're ensconced in historic buildings in the center of the city.

Adamant. This casino is housed in the building where the sale of Alaska to the United States was finalized—perhaps you'll have your own Klondike gold rush here. It's just a little farther down the Moika embankment from the Taleon. ✉ *72 nab. Moiki, off St. Isaac's Sq., Admiralteisky* ☎ *812/311–0409.*

Papanin. The place's name and inventive design make a reference to the famous Papanin's drift. In 1937–38 Russian polar researchers led by Ivan Papanin completed a dramatic expedition to the North Pole. The risky enterprise involved more than 270 days of working on the drifting ice, but it doesn't mean you have to stay that long. The casino, one of the newest and less pretentious in town, has a free bar and breakfast for gamblers. There's a big bowling club and a disco in the same building. Going there means a little detour from the center, but the neighborhood is safe. ✉ *111 Moskovsky prospekt* ☎ *812/389–3575* ⊕ *www.papaninclub.ru* Ⓜ *Moskovskie Vorota.*

Premier Casino-Club. Distinction and taste define one of the most luxurious casinos in town. It belongs to the owners of the Palkin restaurant and is in the same building. Stakes are high. ✉ *47 Nevsky prospekt, City Center* ☎ *812/703–5370* ⊕ *www.club-premier.ru* Ⓜ *Nevsky prospekt.*

Taleon Club. In the former mansion of one of the entrepreneurial Yeliseyev brothers (the building once housed the Institute of Marxism-Leninism), Taleon caters to the rich and famous from both Russia and abroad. Unless you're dressed immaculately (jacket and tie for men), you won't get in. ✉ *59 nab. Moiki, City Center* ☎ *812/312–5373 or 812/315–7645* ⊕ *www.taleon.ru/* Ⓜ *Nevsky prospekt.*

Vegas. The two-story Vegas is a huge gambling center that attracts both locals and visitors. Its nearly 50 TVs and big screens make it a great place to catch sports events from around the world. It's a short walk from Nevsky prospekt. ✉ *6 Manezhnaya pl., City Center* ☎ *812/710–5000* ⊕ *www.vegas.ru* Ⓜ *Nevsky prospekt.*

Clubs

St. Petersburg is hardly hip, but it's waking up to what hip really is. The city's vibrant and evolving club scene is diverse enough to incorporate funky theme clubs, bunker-style techno venues, cozy artsy basements, run-down discos, cool alternative spots, and elegant hedonist establishments to keep the clubbers up all night. There are still several chic nightclubs opened only to its members but more and more elitist venues are canceling its memberships, so most of the places are generally accessible.

Griboedov. The best underground (literally) club in the city, this small bomb shelter–turned–club is usually packed with friendly, down-to-earth hipsters. It's owned and operated by a local band. In addition to decent live music, there's a mix of talented DJs spinning house, techno, and funk; check listings for different nights. ☒ *2a Voronezhskaya ul., at intersection with ul. Konstantina Zaslonova, Vladimirskaya* ☏ *812/ 164–4355* ⊕ *www.griboedovclub.ru* Ⓜ *Ligovsky prospekt.*

Hali Gali. Trying to capture the feel of a risqué Berlin cabaret, this isn't much more than a well-performed strip show, with an energetic host who uses as much foul language as he can; if you don't understand Russian, you'll miss most of the jokes. It's not for everyone, of course, but it remains a popular spot. There's dancing after the show. ☒ *23 Lanskoye shosse, Vyborg Side* ☏ *812/246–9910* Ⓜ *Chyornaya Rechka.*

Havana. Welcoming and nonaggressive, this is the place to go if you have a craving for salsa, merengue, and other sensual Latin dances. A friendly and cosmopolitan crowd of diverse ages comes here. There are three dance floors at this bright and smart spacious club, plus a restaurant and pool tables. ☒ *21 Moskovsky prospekt, City Center* ☏ *812/259–1155* ⊕ *www.havanaclub.ru* Ⓜ *Tekhnologichesky Institute.*

Konyushenny Dvor. It's widely known that foreigners get in free here, and, well, you get what you pay for. Pop music and strip shows are the usual order, and there's no attitude. Also known as Marstall, it's a bit of an institution at this point. ☒ *5 Kanal Griboyedova, City Center* ☏ *812/ 315–7607* Ⓜ *Nevsky prospekt.*

★ **Magrib.** Designed in ornate, Moroccan style, fashionable, and glamorous, small Magrib has dance parties every night, belly dancers, a hugely popular striptease show, and a very good but pricey restaurant with European and Middle Eastern dishes. DJs play a mixture of European disco, Latin, and Russian popular music. Dimly lit and relaxed, Magrib was initially aimed at the nouveau riches and "gilded youth" but eventually became much more democratic. ☒ *84, Nevsky Prospect, Liteiny/Smolny* ☏ *812/275–1255* Ⓜ *Mayakovskaya.*

Metro. An old standard as far as dance clubs are concerned, Metro is frequented mostly by young teenagers from all over the city and the suburbs. Each of the three floors plays different music. Chewing gum is banned for reasons the owners keep to themselves and the door policy is very strict. ☒ *174 Ligovsky pr., Vladimirskaya* ☏ *812/766–0204* ⊕ *www. metroclub.ru* Ⓜ *Ligovsky prospect.*

Plaza. Some of the biggest names in Russian pop music and the DJ circuit perform at this pretentious club in a 19th-century building on the Strelka, overlooking Neva River and Peter and Paul Fortress. Boasting spacious dance floors, a casino, and a fine restaurant, Plaza is the recipient of several "Best Nightclub of St. Petersburg" awards. Guests arrive in fancy cars and designer dress. There's more than enough space to show off: the venue accommodates up to 600 people or more. ☒ *Naberezhnaya Makarova, City Center* ☏ *812/323–9090* Ⓜ *Nevsky prospect/Sportivnaya.*

Purga. They celebrate the New Year every night here, and it's still as engaging as ever. Whatever season and the weather outside, you get the full holiday package in Purga, complete with decorated Christmas tree, Father Frost, and Snow Maid, champagne, dance party, and festive atmosphere. It's archived an enviable collection of season's greetings recordings delivered by Soviet and Russian leaders, which is broadcast and mocked all through the night. The food is good and inexpensive, the beer cheap, and the droll staff is dressed in white rabbit costumes. Each table has its own original design. Be sure to get there and fill your glass before midnight. Purga's clone next door throws wedding parties with the same regularity and similar comic bent. ⊠ *11–13, nab. Reki Fontanki, City Center* ☎ *812/313–4123* Ⓜ *Mayakovskaya.*

Tunnel. A cool military-theme spot in a former bunker and almost exclusively devoted to electronic dance music, Tunnel is one of the oldest and most popular techno clubs in town. ⊠ *At Zverinskaya ul. and Lyubansky per., Petrograd Side* ☎ *812/233–4015* ⊕ *www.tunnelclub. ru* Ⓜ *Gorkovskaya.*

Gay & Lesbian Clubs

Unlike much of Europe and North America, Russia has not yet opened up to the idea of alternative sexual orientations. The gay scene in St. Petersburg is in its embryonic stage and the few friendly and unpretentious venues that are available keep a low profile. It's wise to exercise caution, and for personal safety, you would be best off sticking to the known gay clubs.

Club Mono. This tiny club is nothing special, but it's friendly. The staff are most efficient and the intimate, vest-pocket dance floor is proportional to the club's elfin size. Even so, there's room to arrange a private dancer. Mostly men frequent Club Mono, but women are welcome. ⊠ *4 Kolomenskaya ul., Vladimirskaya* ☎ *812/764–3678* Ⓜ *Ligovsky prospekt.*

Greshniki. No matter how much they complain about this crowded, central spot, people still come in droves to Sinners, even if it's their last stop of the night. There are go-go boys and a sometimes-amusing drag show. The third floor is for men only. Beware of hustlers. Also, note that the club uses a pay-as-you-leave system, so don't lose the card they give you on entry (you'll need it to buy drinks). ⊠ *28 Kanal Griboyedova, City Center* ☎ *812/318–4291* ⊕ *www.greshniki.ru* Ⓜ *Nevsky prospekt.*

Tri El. The only lesbian club in town, also known as LLL, this laid-back, smart venue with a big dance floor, is managed by a lesbian team with substantial experience in the clubbing field. The drinks are cheap, staff helpful, and there's a strip-room and some pool tables. ⊠ *45 ul. 5-ya Sovetskaya, Liteiny/Smolny* ☎ *812/710–2016* ⊕ *www.triel.spb.ru* Ⓜ *Ploshchad Vosstaniya.*

Jazz, Rock & Country

Russia's rock movement was born in St. Petersburg and almost all key names in the country's rock culture come from the city. The first bands emerged in the 1970s, when rock and roll was branded alien music and rock culture was repressed by the Soviet culture bosses. Underground musicians and artists refrained from contacts with state-run music organizations. They worked as night guards, boiler-room operators, or street cleaners and expressed their protest in rock ballads, which reached a wider audience only with the arrival of perestroika.

Some of the most famous bands still play regular gigs—look for veteran bands like Akvarium, DDT, and Tequilajazzz. The strongest point of Russian rock ballads are the meaningful lyrics but even without knowledge of the language, you can still feel the drive.

Fish Fabrique. This is a favorite haunt of locals and expats who enjoy drinking and listening to local alternative musicians, or who just want to play Foosball. ⊠ *10 Pushkinskaya ul., entrance through courtyard of 53 Ligovsky pr., Vladimirskaya* ☎ *812/764–4857* ⊕ *www.fishfabrique. spb.ru* Ⓜ *Ploshchad Vosstaniya.*

Jazz Philharmonic Hall. Russia's top jazz musicians, including the famous Leningrad Dixieland Band and the David Goloshchokin's Ensemble, regularly appear at this venue in a turn-of-the-20th-century building. ⊠ *27 Zagorodny pr., Vladimirskaya* ☎ *812/764–8565* ⊕ *www.jazz-hall.spb. ru* Ⓜ *Dostoyevskaya.*

Jazz Time. The music starts at 9 PM nightly at this cozy, welcoming jazz club. It's in a neighborhood that is fast becoming a dining hot spot; the best Italian restaurant in the city, Il Grappolo, is just around the corner on Belinskovo. ⊠ *41 Mokhovaya ul., Liteiny/Smolny* ☎ *812/273–5379* Ⓜ *Chernyshevskaya.*

JFC Jazz Club. They know good jazz here. The most popular jazz venue in town, the club attracts top musicians performing all styles of jazz from acid funk to swing and blues to avant-garde to mainstream jazz or improvisation. The only disadvantage is its modest size, so you may want to reserve a seat ahead of time. ⊠ *33 ul. Shpalernaya, Liteiny/Smolny* ☎ *812/272–9850* ⊕ *www.jfc.sp.ru* Ⓜ *Chernyshevskaya.*

Moloko. The biggest names in the local rock scene perform at Moloko, the city's premier underground venue with a long-standing reputation. One of the oldest clubs, it has changed location but kept its direction, clientele, and flair. ⊠ *2/3 3-ya Sovetskaya ul. Liteiny/Smolny* ⊕ *www. molokoclub.ru* ☎ *812/274–9467* Ⓜ *Ploshchad Vosstaniya.*

Money Honey Saloon. If rockabilly is your thing, or if you simply want to see a country-western saloon in Russia, head to this always-crowded bar for dancing and lots of fun. The live music usually starts at 8 PM. The upstairs City Bar attracts a slightly older crew and often has live music, too. There's a 40R cover charge. ⊠ *13 Apraksin Dvor, enter courtyard at 28–30 Sadovaya ul., City Center* ☎ *812/310–0549* ⊕ *www. moneyhoney.org* Ⓜ *Gostinny Dvor or Sadovaya.*

Platforma. This modern, mini art complex is a leading St. Petersburg's alternative venue hosting gigs by top musicians from Russia and abroad. The club has a good café and a cozy library and often hosts highbrow literary events and film screenings. Platforma is open around the clock, seven days a week. ⊠ *40 ul. Nekrasova Liteiny/Smolny* ☎ *812/719–6123* ⊕ *www.platformaclub.ru* Ⓜ *Ploshchad Vosstaniya.*

Red Club. Civilized and comfortable, this former warehouse close to Moscow Station attracts the best local rock bands and some good international alternative acts, such as Marc Ribot and Solex. The downstairs level has a stage and dance floor; upstairs, there are tables, a bar, and billiards. ⊠ *7 Poltavskaya ul., Vladimirskaya* ☎ *812/277–1366* ⊕ *www.clubred.ru.*

Sunduk. This is an intimate and quiet little art café in the colonial style offering live jazz, blues, or rock. The menu is varied and food commendable yet inexpensive, so Sunduk is a popular eatery during the day as well. The toilet, with its many large decorative but defunct locks, is designed to confuse the guests. ✉ *42 Furshtatskaya ul. Liteiny/Smolny* ☎ *812/272–3100* Ⓜ *Chernyshevskaya.*

SPORTS & THE OUTDOORS

Tickets for sporting events can be purchased at the sports arena immediately prior to the game or at one of the many teatralnaya kassa throughout the city, notably on Nevsky prospekt at Nos. 22–24, 39, 42, and 74. Alternatively, use http://spb.kassir.ru to order tickets online.

Banyas

A word of warning: going to just any banya is not recommended. Many municipal banyas are free on certain days for the poorest and most deprived people. In central St. Petersburg there are still apartments without bath or shower, where the only sources of running water are the toilet and a sink in the kitchen. If you don't feel like facing the naked truth of Russian life up close and personal (in the general section everyone walks through the same water), consider sticking to the places we recommend. And opt for a private cabin, rather than the general section.

Kazachi Bani (✉ 11 Kazachii per. ☎ 812/315–0734 Ⓜ Pushkinskaya). **Posadskie Bani** (✉ 28/2 Malaya Posadskaya ul. ☎ 812/233–5092 Ⓜ Gorkovskaya). **Yamskie Bani** (✉ 9 ul. Dostoyevskovo ☎ 812/713–3580).

Ice Hockey & Figure Skating

The **Ice Palace** (Ledovy Dvorets; ✉ 1 pr. Pyatiletok, Southern Suburbs ☎ 812/718–2157 or 812/718–6620 ⊕ www.newarena.spb.ru Ⓜ Prospekt Bolshevikov) hosts ice-hockey and figure-skating events. **SKA Sports Palace** (✉ 2 Zhdanovskaya nab., Petrograd Side ☎ 812/230–7819 or 812/237–0073 ⊕ www.ska.spb.ru Ⓜ Sportivnaya) is used for ice hockey. SKA, St. Petersburg's hockey team, plays at the **Yubilyeiny Sports Palace** (✉ 18 pr. Dobrolyubova, Petrograd Side ☎ 812/323–9315 Ⓜ Sportivnaya). Check any of the city's teatralnaya kassa for tickets.

Running

In the center, a good option is **Tavrichesky Gardens,** about a five-minute walk east of the Chernyshevskaya metro station, in the direction of Smolny. For a more serious run, you should head outside the city center to **Primorsky Park Pobedy,** on Krestovsky Island. The park has both gravel and paved pathways, as well as a lake and beautiful views. To get here, take the metro to Krestovsky Ostrov or Staraya Derevnya station. **Kirovsky Park,** covering most of the island of Yelagin Ostrov, is one of the most beautiful parks in the city and a good option for running. To get here take the metro to Staraya Derevnya station; walk south along Lipovaya alleya. When you reach the embankment, you will see a bridge to the island. You might also stick to the Neva embankments or head for the Summer Garden or the Field of Mars.

Skating

You can skate at several rinks in the city. The open hours change frequently. **Ice Palace** (Ledovy Dvorets ✉ 1 pr. Pyatiletok, Southern Suburbs ☎ 812/718–4117 ⊕ www.newarena.spb.ru Ⓜ Prospekt Bolshevikov). **Ledovy Mir** (✉ 16 Aptekarsky pr., Petrograd Side ☎ 812/234–6542 Ⓜ Petrogradskaya). **Moskovsky Park Pobedy** (✉ 25 ul. Kuznetsovskaya, Southern Suburbs ☎ 812/388–3249 Ⓜ Park Pobedy), open daily 2–9 in winter. **Yubileyny Sports Palace** (✉ 18 ul. Dobrolyubova, Petrograd Side ☎ 812/323–9315 Ⓜ Sportivnaya), by advance booking only.

Soccer

Zenit, St. Petersburg's soccer team, plays at **Petrovsky Stadium** (✉ 2g Petrovsky Ostrov, Petrograd Side ☎ 812/328–8902 Ⓜ Sportivnaya). Check any of the city's teatralnaya kassa for tickets. Another important venue is **Kirov Stadium** (✉ 25 Yuzhnaya Doroga, Petrograd Side ☎ 812/235–5452 Ⓜ Krestovsky Ostrov), located in Primorsky Park Pobedy.

SHOPPING

Pick up a copy of Russian *Vogue* and you may be surprised to see that it nearly outdoes its Parisian and American counterparts for sheer gloss, glitz, and elegant, trendy garb. And all those nifty threads that the models are wearing—Versace, Hugo Boss, Gucci, Kenzo, Prada, Armani—are fully stocked in the international boutiques around the city. The days of basic items being scarce are long gone. And to make room for all these new shoppers, stores have considerably extended their opening hours—many stay open until 8 or 9 PM, or on Sunday.

The same sense of a two-tiered system of stores exists in St. Petersburg as in Moscow. "Western-style" shops taking credit-card payment have replaced the old Beriozkas (Birch Trees) emporiums, which were stocked only for foreigners. With increased competition, some of the prices at these shops have gone down, and they are open to anyone who can afford them. State-run shops are better stocked now than before, and if you aren't looking for anything fancy you might be interested in some of these groceries and department stores. Only rubles (as opposed to credit cards) are accepted here, however, and you'll have a tough time maneuvering through the cashiers if you don't speak some Russian.

Kiosks, street tables, and impromptu markets sell a colorful jumble of junk most of the time. You'll see women lined up selling socks, scarves, and who-knows-what near Sennaya Ploshchad, and if you're lucky you might pick up some great old books (watch in particular the corner of Nevsky and Fontanka, across the street from the Palace of Prince Beloselsky-Belozersky). But this mini-industry of individual entrepreneurs, which mushroomed wildly in the first years of glasnost, is on the wane. Everything is being tidied up and taken back inside. You may also be surprised to find a plethora of "24 chasa" stores (i.e., open 24 hours a day). They vary from smallish to big, but there will always be one near you, stocked with alcohol, cigarettes, and groceries.

Shopping Districts

The central shopping district is Nevsky prospekt and the streets running off it. Don't expect too many bargains beyond the bootlegged CDs and videos (which could be confiscated at customs in the United States), however, because prices for items such as clothes and electronic goods are just as high as in the West, and in the chic stores in hotels they are even higher.

Department Stores

Outside the large department stores of Nevsky prospekt, you'll find some boutiques and lots of "variety shops"—part souvenir-oriented, part practical—which can be a bit bewildering. Check them out if you have time; you never know what you may find.

DLT. Just off Nevsky is Dom Leningradskoi Torgovly, once considered the poorer cousin to the other department stores, but now considerably spruced up. It's a good bet for the patient shopper to find some tremendous bargains in the way of souvenirs; fluffy toys and children's games are also big here, and caviar is a little cheaper than at the shops on Nevsky. ✉ *21/23 Bolshaya Konyushennaya ul., City Center* Ⓜ *Nevsky prospekt.*

Gostinny Dvor. The city's oldest and largest shopping center, built in the mid-18th century, has upscale boutiques, but it's still a good place to find souvenirs, such as *matryoshka* (nesting dolls), at some of the best prices in the city (look upstairs). The second floor houses a string of multibrand designer boutiques selling women's and men's clothes from famous European designers. *Gostinka,* as it's also known, also has some stores with cheaper prices; it can be a good place to buy winter clothing, such as a fur hat. The store, open daily from 10 until 10, is smack in the center of town and easily reached by the metro—the metro station right outside its doors is named in its honor. ✉ *35 Nevsky pr., City Center* ☎ *812/710–5408* ⊕ *www.bgd.ru* Ⓜ *Gostinny Dvor.*

Grand Palace. Reigning at the top end of the boutique market and serving shoppers with the deepest pockets, this brand-new consumer temple carries Woolford lingerie, Escada dresses, and Trussardi suits as well as perfume and jewelry at knock-out prices. The café on the ground floor offers irresistible desserts crafted by a sophisticated French chef who knows his art. ✉ *44 Nevsky pr./15 Italyanskaya ul., City Center* ☎ *812/449–9344* ⊕ *www.grand-palace.ru* Ⓜ *Gostinny Dvor.*

Passazh. Passage, a mid-19th-century shopping arcade across the street from Gostinny Dvor, caters primarily to locals. The souvenir sections, however, are worth visiting, as prices, in rubles, are significantly lower here than in the souvenir shops around hotels and in other areas frequented by tourists. You can also pick up fine table linens at bargain prices. The porcelain section at the far end of the ground floor is worth a look, too, and there's a large supermarket in the basement. ✉ *48 Nevsky pr., City Center* ☎ *812/312–2210* ⊕ *www.passage.spb.ru* Ⓜ *Gostinny Dvor.*

Stockmann. This branch of the Finnish company tries hard to bring some Scandinavian efficiency and style to Russian commerce. Its wares include quality clothes, lingerie, toys, kitchen gadgets, linens, and bathroom goods, mainly by Finnish and Scandinavian producers. The Atrium café is a quiet place to take a break. ⊠ *25 Nevsky pr., City Center* ☎ *812/ 329–7448* Ⓜ *Nevsky prospekt.*

Vladimirsky Passazh. This modern and spacious four-story store, just outside Dostoyevskaya metro station, has numerous small boutiques selling jewelry, clothes, shoes, bags, lingerie and cosmetics at less than exorbitant prices. The basement houses a large, 24-hour supermarket, and there's a great bakery on the ground floor—an excellent budget choice for a quick refuel. ⊠ *19 Vladimirsky pr., Vladimirskaya* ☎ *812/331– 3232* ⊕ *www.vladimirskiy.ru* Ⓜ *Dostoyevskaya/Vladimirskaya.*

Specialty Stores

Clothing

Defile. Devoted entirely to Russian designers, this boutique offers diverse and innovative collections from some of the biggest names in the country's fashion industry, including St. Petersburger Lilia Kissilenko. The boutique's owner is a co-organizer of the St. Petersburg's premier fashion event, the annual Defile on the Neva. ⊠ *27 nab. Griboyedov Canal, City Center* ⊕ *www.defilenaneve.ru* ☎ *812/571–9010* Ⓜ *Nevsky prospekt.*

Lena. A wide selection of furs is sold at this store across the street from Gostinny Dvor. Here's some help with the Russian: rabbit (*krolik*), sheep (*caracul*), raccoon (*yenot*), white fox (*pisets*), silver fox (*chernoburka*), sable (*sobol*), and, of course, mink (*norka*). Note that some furs from protected species, such as seals, cannot be brought into the United States. ⊠ *50 Nevsky pr., at Malaya Sadovaya, City Center* ☎ *812/312–3234* Ⓜ *Gostinny Dvor.*

SELA. Russia's answer to the Swedish giant H & M, SELA is unbeatable in the casual chic category, offering trendy and durable clothes for pennies. The brand primarily targets youth but people of all ages shop there. This rapidly expanding chain has several dozen branches around town. ⊠ *77 Nevsky pr., City Center* ☎ *812/764–6577* Ⓜ *Nevsky prospekt.*

St. Petersburg Clothing Factory (FOSP). The leading label for menswear, FOSP produces well-made jackets, trousers, suits, and coats at great prices. The FOSP factory itself is at 75 Moika, but there are branches in other department stores. ⊠ *75 nab. Moika, Admiralteisky* ☎ *812/315–1873* Ⓜ *Nevsky prospekt.*

★ **Tatyana Kotegova Fashion House.** Kotegova creates stylish and romantic collections with a note of restraint. Her soaring classical silhouettes are believed to capture the essence of St. Petersburg. The designer uses only natural materials, with an emphasis on wool, silk, and cashmere. Kotegova's velvet evening dresses, simple yet exquisite, are the dream of a good half of the local female population. ⊠ *44 Bolshoi pr., Petrograd Side* ⊕ *www.kotegova.com* ☎ *812/346–3467* Ⓜ *Petrogradskaya.*

Crafts & Souvenirs

Angel. This embroidery fashion house produces stunning silk scarves, luxurious tablecloths, and bright-colored blouses, all beautifully embroidered by hand. Visits are by appointment. ✉ *40-B1 11-ya Linia, Vasilievsky Island* ☏ *812/321–2199* Ⓜ *Vasileostrovskaya.*

★ **Armeisky Magazin.** All army surplus—belts, flasks, caps, pins, and marine shirts with Russian and Soviet army symbols—is a much better bargain here, at this state-run store, than in touristy markets. You'll find a huge variety. ✉ *24 Kirochnaya ul., Liteiny/Smolny* ☏ *812/279–2907* Ⓜ *Chernyshevskaya.*

Farfor. For china and porcelain made at the Lomonosov Porcelain Factory (LFZ), once a purveyor to the tsars, go to this noted porcelain resource. ✉ *32 Kondratyevsky pr., Vyborg Side* ☏ *812/542–3055* ⊕ *www. farfor.spb.ru/* ✉ *7 Vladimirsky pr., Vladimirskaya* ☏ *812/713–1513* Ⓜ *Vladimirskaya.*

Galereya Stekla. At this glass gallery the city of St. Petersburg is reflected in carved Easter eggs, stained glass, vases, and candlesticks. Each work is handmade, and many are one-of-a-kind. ✉ *1/28 ul. Lomonosova, City Center* ☏ *812/312–2214* Ⓜ *Nevsky prospekt.*

Guild of Masters. Jewelry, ceramics, and other types of Russian traditional art, all made by members of the Russian Union of Artists, are sold here. ✉ *82 Nevsky pr., City Center* ☏ *812/279–0979* Ⓜ *Mayakovskaya.*

Nasledie. There are art and antiques shops like this one all over the city, but Nasledie has a convenient location on Nevsky prospekt, and the staff is used to tourists. It's a reliable place to find *palekh* and *khokhloma* (different types of hand-painted lacquered wood), samovars, nesting dolls, amber, and hand-painted trays. ✉ *116 Nevsky pr., City Center* ☏ *812/ 279–5067* Ⓜ *Ploshchad Alexandra Nevskovo.*

Slavyansky Style. This is a good source for linen goods created in the traditional Russian style of the 19th century. There are several branches throughout the city. ✉ *151 Nevsky pr., City Center* ☏ *812/277–5164* ⊕ *www.linorusso.ru/* Ⓜ *Ploshchad Alexandra Nevskovo* ✉ *3 Pushkinskaya ul., City Center* ☏ *812/764–5455* Ⓜ *Mayakovskaya.*

Stanni Cast. This is the perfect place to get tin soldiers and other miniature masterpieces made by local craftsmen in bronze, tin, and pewter. ✉ *9 nab. Reki Volkhovki, City Center* ☏ *812/712–8047* Ⓜ *Nevsky prospekt.*

Vernisazh. At this open-air market outside the Church of the Savior on Spilled Blood, more than 100 vendors sell nesting dolls, paintings, Soviet icons, and miscellaneous trinkets. Never accept the first price quoted. ✉ *1 Kanal Griboyedova, City Center* ☏ *812/167–1628* Ⓜ *Nevsky prospekt.*

Farmers' Markets

The farmers' markets (rynok) in St. Petersburg are lively places in which a colorful collection of goods and foods are sold by individual farmers, often from out of town and sometimes from outside the Russian republic. In addition to the fine cuts of fresh and cured meat, dairy products, and homemade jams and jellies, piles of fruits and vegetables are sold here, even in winter. Try some homemade pickles or pickled garlic, a tasty local favorite. You can also find many welcome surprises such as hand-knitted scarves, hats, and mittens. The markets are much cleaner and better lit here than in Moscow, so it can be fun just to visit and browse. In general, the markets are open daily from 8 AM to 7 PM (5 PM on Sunday).

Apraksin Dvor. Locals come here by thousands to shop for cheap clothes, shoes, videos, household items, and whatever else you can think of. As to where most of the stuff was produced and how long it will last—prices are too low to raise any questions. ✉ *28–30 Sadovaya ul., City Center* Ⓜ *Nevsky Prospect.*

Kuznechny Rynok. This is the best and most expensive of St. Petersburg's farmers' markets. It's just outside the metro station. ✉ *3 Kuznechny per., Vladimirskaya* Ⓜ *Vladimirskaya.*

Polyustrovsky Rynok. On the weekend you can find a pet market, with puppies, kittens, chickens, and more. In a somewhat chilling twist, the market boasts an impressive fur department with some good bargains on things like rabbit winter hats. ✉ *45 Polyustrovsky pr., Vyborg Side* Ⓜ *Ploshchad Lenina.*

Sennoi Rynok. Once a huge, sprawling flea market, this is now perhaps the cleanest and most organized farmers' market in the city; the entrance is just a short walk from Sennaya Ploshchad. ✉ *4 Moskovsky pr., City Center* Ⓜ *Sadovaya or Sennaya Ploshchad.*

Udelnaya. Scrap-artists and theater designers looking for Soviet-era paraphernalia frequent this place, St. Petersburg's largest flea market. The sight of Russian babushkas selling their home furnishings, clocks, gadgets, vases, and porcelain figurines can be somewhat heartbreaking, but if you have a keen interest in this kind of merchandise, there's much to be found. Cross Udelny prospect outside the metro Udelnaya. ✉ *Vyborg Side* Ⓜ *Udelnaya.*

Food

There are several supermarket chains in town expanding at lightning speed but almost every store has had a history of selling outdated dairy products, and some survived a major outburst of hepatitis at least once. The two biggest chains, Pyaterochka and Paterson, with dozens of branches around town, have a good reputation but you're still advised to look at everything closely, the expiration date in particular. Buying food from kiosks means courting a stomach bug and should be avoided.

Kalinka-Stockmann. If you're looking for a big Western-style supermarket that takes credit cards, try Kalinka-Stockmann. It's open daily 9 AM–10 PM. ✉ *1 Finlandsky pr., Vyborg Side* ☎ *812/542–2297* Ⓜ *Ploshchad Lenina.*

Paterson. You'll find this well-stocked supermarket inside the large shopping mall "Sennaya." ✉ *3 ul. Efimova, Admiralteisky* ☎ *812/740–4706* Ⓜ *Sennaya Ploshchad.*

Super Babylon. This superstore is open 24 hours a day. ✉ *54/56 Maly pr., Petrograd Side* ☎ *812/233–8892* Ⓜ *Chkalovskaya.*

Supermarket. Within the Passage shopping arcade, Supermarket sells cheese and fresh fruits and vegetables. It opens daily at 10 (11 on Sunday) and closes at 9. ✉ *48 Nevsky pr., City Center* ☎ *812/312–4701* Ⓜ *Gostinny Dvor.*

Vladimirsky Supermarket. In the spacious basement of Vladimirsky Passazh, this good, well-stocked supermarket is conveniently open 24 hours a day. ✉ *19 Vladimirsky pr., Vladimirskaya* ☎ *812/331–3232* Ⓜ *Vladimirskaya.*

★ **Yeliseyevsky Food Emporium.** If for no other reason than to see its beautiful art nouveau interior, be sure to stop by Yeliseyevsky, across from Gostinny Dvor. The smaller shop on the right is a good place to buy caviar or a tasty fish snack. Otherwise, check out the local *dieta* (dairy-food store), *gastronom* (food store), and *produkty* (selling nonperishable products). It's open daily 10–10. ✉ *56 Nevksy pr., at Malaya Sadovaya, City Center* ☎ *812/312–1865* Ⓜ *Nevsky prospekt.*

Jewelry

Jewelry used to be an unlikely reason to come to St. Petersburg, but there are some good places to explore these days, particularly on Nevsky prospekt.

Ananov. Head and shoulders above the jewel meccas in town, this quiet, dim store is owned by former sailor and theater director Andrei Ananov, now internationally famous as a jeweler following in the traditions of the great Peter Fabergé. Ananov is as much a gallery as a shop, and no one here would ever be vulgar enough to list prices; if you have to ask, you probably can't afford it. ✉ *31 Nevsky pr., City Center* ☎ *812/314–1952* ⊕ *www.ananov.com/* Ⓜ *Gostinny Dvor.*

Etalon-Jenavi. The detour necessary to get here will be well rewarded: the best costume jewelry in town is fashionable, sophisticated, and original, embracing everything from fine replicas of museum artworks to children's collections of enameled pendants in the shapes of insects, toys, and balloons. It certainly won't empty your wallet. ✉ *172 Moskovsky pr.* ☎ *812/371–2722* Ⓜ *Elektrosila.*

Russian Jewelry House. This is a good bet for jewelry, particularly amber pieces. ✉ *27 Nevsky pr., City Center* ☎ *812/312–8501* Ⓜ *Nevsky prospekt.*

★ **Russkie Samotsvety.** Many items in these collections were inspired by St. Petersburg's architecture, history, literature, and its immense artistic legacy. Jewelers play with well-familiar visual images, like ballet or shipbuilding, and incorporate city symbols in their designs. ✉ *1 ul. 1-ya Krasnoarmeiskaya, Admiralteisky* ☎ *812/316–7646* Ⓜ *Tekhnologichesky Institut.*

Treasure Island. Creations from the St. Petersburg School of Jewelry and Stone-Cutting Art are sold here. Visits are by appointment only. ✉ *37 nab. Leytenanta Shmidta, Vasilievsky Island* ☎ *812/232–1908* Ⓜ *Vasileostrovskaya.*

Music Stores

Classica. This is the best shop for classical music. The oldest store of its kind in St. Petersburg, it sells a good choice of recordings as well as folk and religious music with an emphasis on Russian composers and performers. You can also find rare recordings on vinyl LPs here. ✉ *2 Mikhailovskaya ul., City Center* ☎ *812/710–4428* Ⓜ *Nevsky prospekt.*

Kailas. This shop obviously has someone on staff who pays attention to new and interesting music emerging around the world. You'll find the Flaming Lips or the White Stripes here before any other shop in the city, plus a vast selection of electronica, world music, jazz, and classical music. ✉ *10 ul. Pushkinskaya, City Center* ☎ *812/320–9147* ⊕ *www. kailas.sp.ru* Ⓜ *Mayakovskaya or Ploshchad Vosstaniya.*

Otkryty Mir. For classical music, the choice is surprisingly poor for a city that prides itself on its cultural legacy. Although no one could accuse this store of being overstocked, it does hold the occasional hidden classical delight, particularly when it comes to Russian composers and artists and recordings on the old Melodiya label. Hunt around. ✉ *13 Malaya Morskaya ul., Admiralteisky* ☎ *812/715–8939* Ⓜ *Nevsky prospekt.*

Titanik. The delights of megastores such as Virgin have yet to hit St. Petersburg, and even the best shops have a rather scruffy look about them, not to mention a cavalier attitude toward copyright law. But among the best sources is this chain, which sells a motley collection of Western and Russian rock and pop, plus DVDs and videos (the DVDs usually have an English track available, and many are without regional-zone coding). ✉ *63 Nevsky pr., City Center* ☎ *812/336–5745* ⊕ *www.titanik-spb. ru* Ⓜ *Mayakovskaya* ✉ *10 Zagorodny pr., Vladimirskaya* ☎ *812/ 315–5843* Ⓜ *Dostoevskaya* ✉ *Saigon club, 9 Nevsky pr., City Center* Ⓜ *Nevsky prospekt* ✉ *158 Nevsky pr., Liteiny/Smolny* ☎ *812/277– 3034* Ⓜ *Ploshchad Vosstaniya* ✉ *57 Liteiny pr., Liteiny/Smolny* ☎ *812/ 275–4445* Ⓜ *Vladimirskaya.*

ST. PETERSBURG A TO Z

To research prices, get advice from other travelers, and book travel arrangements, visit www.fodors.com.

AIR TRAVEL

St. Petersburg air carrier Pulkovo, Russia's second-largest airline after Aeroflot, offers direct flights to more than 20 countries out of Pulkovo II. Aeroflot and its tough competitor Transaero fly from St. Petersburg only to Moscow, where the passengers have to get a connecting flight to other destinations.

Other international airlines with offices in St. Petersburg include Air France, Austrian, Alitalia, SN Brussels Airlines, Air Malta, Air Baltic, Korean Air Lines, Armenian Airlines, British Airways, CSA (Czech Airlines), Delta, El Al, Finnair, KLM, LOT, Lufthansa, Malev, and SAS. Note that there are no direct flights from the United States to St. Petersburg. Korean Air and Air Baltic don't have offices in town and sell tickets via tour operators, including Infinity Travel and Sindbad travel (see Travel Agencies).

🛪 **Carriers Aeroflot** ☎ 812/327-3872. **Air France** ☎ 812/325-8252 or 812/336-2900. **Air Baltic** ⊕ www.airbaltic.com. **Air Malta** ☎ 812/740-3820. **Alitalia** ☎ 812/336-9131.

Armenian Airlines ☎ 812/388-3054. Austrian ☎ 812/331-2005. British Airways ☎ 812/329-2565 or 812/380-0626. CSA ☎ 812/315-5259. Delta ☎ 812/571-5820. El Al ☎ 812/380-6880. Finnair ☎ 812/303-9898. KLM ☎ 812/346-6868. Korean Air Lines ⊕ www.koreanair.com. LOT ☎ 812/272-2982. Lufthansa ☎ 812/320-1000. Malev ☎ 812/922-0662. Pulkovo ☎ 812/303-9268. SAS ☎ 812/326-2600. SN Brussels Airlines ☎ 812/723-8691. Transaero ☎ 812/279-6463.

AIRPORTS

St. Petersburg is served by two airports, Pulkovo I (domestic) and Pulkovo II (international), just 2 km (1 mi) apart and 17 km (11 mi) south of central St. Petersburg. The runways of the two Pulkovos interconnect, so it's possible you could land at Pulkovo I and taxi over to Pulkovo II. Compared with Moscow's Sheremetyevo II, Pulkovo II is a breeze. It's compact and well lit, with signs in both Russian and English.

However, the airport's toy size—there are only eight gates and one landing line in Pulkovo II—prevents it from receiving more airlines and developing into a venue fit for a large European city. Remember that on departure you'll need to fill out a final customs declaration (available at all the long tables) before proceeding through the first checkpoint. If you have nothing to declare, just head through the "green channel" of the customs area. Try to arrive at the airport at least 1½ hours in advance. Bear in mind that check-in stops 40 minutes before departure, so don't count on making the plane at the last minute without some frantic pleading.

🛈 Airport Information **Pulkovo I Airport** ☎ 812/704-3822 ⊕ www.pulkovo.ru. **Pulkovo II Airport** ☎ 812/704-3444 ⊕ www.pulkovo.ru

TRANSFERS From Pulkovo I, Municipal Bus 39 (in Russian, the word to look for is "avtobus") will take you to the Moskovskaya metro stop on Moskovsky prospekt; the stop at the airport is right outside the terminal. Tickets are sold on the bus, which runs every 20 minutes during the day. From Pulkovo II, the service is less reliable and more inconvenient. If you have any luggage, the only realistic way to reach downtown St. Petersburg is by car. If you are traveling with a tour package, all transfers will have been arranged. If you're traveling alone, you're strongly advised to make advance arrangements with your hotel. There are plenty of taxis available, but for safety reasons you should not pick up a cab on your own if you don't speak Russian. Foreign tourists, especially passengers arriving at train stations and airports, are prime crime targets. Cab fare from the airport will depend entirely on your negotiating skills; the range is $30 to $50. The airport is about a 40-minute ride from the city center. When you return to the airport, a regular cab that you order by phone will cost you only $15. The operator for Taxi Million tells you the fare in advance.

Public transportation to Pulkovo II is also more reliable than from it— take bus No. 13 from outside the Moskovskaya metro stop (you may have to buy an extra ticket for your luggage if it takes up what the conductor considers to be too much room). There are also *marshrutki* taxi vans outside the metro stop; these are clearly marked, but difficult to squeeze your suitcases into. Marshrutkas No. 213 and K-3 go along Moskovsky prospect down to Sennaya Ploshchad in the city center, and a single fare costs 17R. Marshrutka No. 350 follows the same route until Sennaya Ploshchad, and then continues up to Primorskaya metro station via Teatralnaya Ploshchad. Full fare costs 30R.

🚹 **Central Taxi** (Tsentralnoye Taksi) ☎ 812/312–0022. **Petersburg Taxi** (Petersburgskoye Taxi) ☎ 068. **Taxi Million** ☎ 812/700-0000.

BOAT & FERRY TRAVEL

Sea travel is on the rise in St. Petersburg. Leading Baltic Sea shipping company Silja Line (www.silja.com) operates a route between St. Petersburg and Rostock via Tallinn, and a direct St. Petersburg–Helsinki route. Estonian ferry operator Tallink (www.tallink.com) runs regular ferry service between St. Petersburg and Tallinn via Helsinki.

Traveling by boat between St. Petersburg and the Kotlin border is 1½ hours of sheer enjoyment: a pleasure cruise passes the island of Kotlin (Kronstadt), then travels along the coastline where Lomonosov, Peterhof, and Strelna can be seen with the aid of binoculars. Finally, it arrives into the huge city harbor, with St. Isaac's Cathedral as a constant focus. Make arrangements at the sea passenger terminal, which is on Vasilievsky Island at Ploshchad Morskoi Slavy. For inland trips to places such as Valaam Island, Kizhi Island, or even Moscow, boats depart from the river passenger terminal.

🚹 **Baltic Line** ☎ 812/322–1616 ⊕ www.balticline.ru. **River passenger terminal** 🚊 195 pr. Obukhovskoi Oborony Vladimirskaya ☎ 812/262–0239 Ⓜ Proletarskaya. **Sea passenger terminal** ✉ Pl. Morskoi Slavy, Vasilievsky Island ☎ 812/322-6052.

BUS TRAVEL

Several firms operate bus routes between St. Petersburg and central Europe. A bus trip can be a reasonably comfortable way to connect with the Baltic states, Scandinavia, and Germany, although as with train travel in and out of the country, it entails a two- to three-hour wait at the border for everyone to clear customs. The Gorodskoi Avtobusny Vokzal (City Bus Station), open from 6:30 AM until 11:30 PM sells tickets for international and domestic routes. It takes about 15 minutes to walk to the station from Ligovsky Prospect metro station.

Among the most reliable of the bus companies is Eurolines, which runs coaches to Tallinn, Riga, Stuttgart, and Tbilisi. The Finnish bus company Finnord runs coaches between Helsinki and St. Petersburg via the border town of Vyborg. The service runs twice daily, leaving from the Pulkovskaya hotel, stopping at the Astoria hotel and at Finnord's offices at 37 Italyanskaya ulitsa, and then at half a dozen Finnish towns before reaching Helsinki. The Russian firm Sovavto St. Petersburg offers daily departures to Helsinki from the following hotels: Astoria, Grand Hotel Europe, Pulkovskaya, and St. Petersburg.

🚹 **Bus Information** **The City Bus Station** ✉ 36, Obvodnovo kanala nab. ☎ 812/766–5777 Ⓜ Ligovsky Prospect. **Eurolines** ☎ 812/380-5245 ⊕ www.eurolines.ru. **Finnord** ✉ 37 Italyanskaya ul. ☎ 812/314-8951 Ⓜ Nevsky prospect. **Sovavto St. Petersburg** ☎ 812/702-2550 ⊕ www.sovavto.com.

CAR TRAVEL

You can reach St. Petersburg from Finland via the Helsinki–St. Petersburg Highway through the border town of Vyborg; the main street into and out of town for Finland is Kamennoostrovsky prospekt. To reach Moscow, take Moskovsky prospekt; at the hotel Pulkovskaya roundabout, take Mosvoskoye Shosse (M–10/E–95), slightly to the left of the road to the airport. Bear in mind that it will take at least two hours to clear customs and immigration at the border, and on occasions (e.g., Friday night and weekends) the lines can be lengthy, increasing your wait considerably.

CONSULATES

In case of emergency, the U.S. and U.K. consulates have consular officers on call at all times. This can be useful if a shakedown on the part of the local police goes too far, and—heaven forbid—if you land in the cells for a spell. Insist on your right to call your consulate. There's a Canadian Consulate in St. Petersburg; Australians and New Zealanders should check with the U.K. consulate in the first instance and the Canadian one if that doesn't work. A word of warning: phone lines to the U.S. consulate are constantly busy. It may take hours of persistent dialing to get through.

Canada ⊠ 32 Malodetskoselsky pr., Vladimirskaya ☎ 812/325–8448 🖷 812/325–8393 ⊕ www.dfait.gc.ca Ⓜ Tekhnologichesky Institut. **United Kingdom** ⊠ 5 Pl. Proletarskoi Diktatury, Liteiny/Smolny ☎ 812/320–3200 🖷 812/325–3211 ⊕ www.britain.spb.ru Ⓜ Ploshchad Vosstaniya. **United States** ⊠ 15 Furstadtskaya ul., Liteyny/Smolny ☎ 812/331–2600 or 812/274–8689, 812/271–6455 off-hours emergencies 🖷 812/331–2852 ⊕ www.stpetersburg-usconsulate.ru Ⓜ Chernyshevskaya.

EMERGENCIES

Most staff at police stations don't speak foreign languages, which makes it impossible or painstakingly long to report a crime. Travel agencies often arrange a translator and driver for their clients who have been victims. If you're on your own and need to report a theft or another crime committed against you, head to the central City Tourism Information Office. Staff there have been trained and can competently assist foreigners in preparing and filing a police report, which in case of theft of valuables is necessary for insurance claims. The center operates only during business hours and is closed on weekends.

A lost-and-found office operated by the police is available in English as well. The St. Petersburg chapter of the American Chamber of Commerce and the city police have developed very helpful and detailed list of safety recommendations, which is available on the chamber's Web site at www.amcham.ru (click on St.Petersburg chapter and then go to Important Links section).

Emergency Services Ambulance ☎ 03 for Russian speakers only. **City Tourism Information Center** ⊠ 14 Sadovaya ul., City Center ☎☎ 812/310–8286 or 812/310–2822 ⊕ www.spb.ru/eng ☉ Weekdays 10–6 Ⓜ Sennaya Ploshchad. **Fire** ☎ 01. **Lost and Found** ☎ 812/578–3690, English speakers available. **Police** ☎ 02 for Russian speakers only, 812/278–3018 foreigner hotline, 812/764–9798 task force for crimes against foreigners.

DENTISTS In an emergency, you could ask your hotel for a referral, or try one of several private clinics in the city. Besides highly qualified doctors, the American Medical Center also has a dentist on staff, and even offers 24-hour emergency services; this place is not cheap, however. Another option is the chain of Medi clinics with 11 different locations; the clinics listed below are the most central ones. Other clinics that offer dental services include the Clinic Complex, Dental Polyclinic No. 3, and Normed.

🔓 **American Medical Center** ✉ 78 nab. Moiki, City Center ☎ 812/740-2090 ⊕ www. amcenters.com Ⓜ Sennaya Ploshchad. **Clinic Complex** ✉22 Moskovsky pr., Vladimirskaya ☎ 812/316-6272 Ⓜ Tekhnologichesky Institut. **Medi** ✉ 82 Nevsky pr., Vladimirskaya ☎ 812/324-0021 Ⓜ Nevsky Prospect ✉ 31 Italianskaya ul., City Center ☎ 812/324-0006 Ⓜ Nevsky Prospect ✉13 10th Sovietskaya, Liteiny/Smolny ☎ 812/324-0002 ⊕ www.mam.ru Ⓜ Ploshchad Vosstania. **Nordmed** ✉ 12/15 ul. Tverskaya, Liteiny/Smolny ☎ 812/710-0401 Ⓜ Chernyshevskaya.

HOSPITALS & Public medical facilities in St. Petersburg are poorly equipped. However,
CLINICS as with dentistry, private clinics, which offer a higher level of treatment, are proliferating. Several Russian clinics offer quality health services, but they rarely have English speakers available to assist you. In case of emergency, it's best to seek help from a Western-style clinic.

The American Medical Center is open weekdays 8:30 to 6, and offers 24-hour comprehensive care. The Clinic Complex has been around for years (formerly as the St. Petersburg Polyclinic No. 2); it's open weekdays 9–9, Saturday 9–3. The largest and most impressive clinic with an en-suite hospital is MEDEM, where multilingual staff can provide more than 2,000 medical tests and services. The clinic works 24 hours, and is certainly the best-equipped in town. The central Euromed clinic provides high-quality medical services and is recognized by all major European insurance companies. Another possibility in the same neighborhood is Emergency Medical Consulting, a European medical center. If you're unfortunate enough to be hospitalized while in St. Petersburg, you'll probably be placed in Hospital No. 20.

🔓 Clinics **American Medical Center** ✉ 78 nab. Moiki, City Center ☎ 812/740-2090 ⊕ www.amcenters.com Ⓜ Sennaya Ploshchad. **Clinic Complex** ✉ 22 Moskovsky pr., Vladimirskaya ☎ 812/316-6272 Ⓜ Tekhnologichesky Institut. **Emergency Medical Consulting** ✉ 78 Moskosvky pr., Vladimirskaya ☎ 812/325-0880 Ⓜ Frunzhenskaya. **Euromed** ✉ 60 Suvorovsky pr., Liteiny/Smolny ☎ 812/327-0301 Ⓜ Nevsky Prospect. **MEDEM International Clinic & Hospital** ✉ 6 ul. Marata, Liteiny/Smolny ☎ 812/336-3333 Ⓜ Mayakovskaya.

🔓 Hospital **Hospital No. 20** ✉ 21 ul. Gastello, Southern Suburbs ☎ 812/708-4808 or 812/708-4066 Ⓜ Moskovskaya.

PHARMACIES You can find pharmacies all over St. Petersburg, and, unlike in the West, just about everything is available without a prescription. Most pharmacies close by 8 or 9 PM, though there are several dozen places operating round the clock. Below are a choice of late-night pharmacies.

🔓 Late-Night Pharmacies **Pervaya Pomoshch** (First Aid) ✉ 27 Moskovsky pr., Vladimirskaya ☎ 812/324-4400 Ⓜ Nevsky prospect. **PetroFarm** ✉ 22 Nevsky pr., City Center ☎ 812/314-5401 Ⓜ Nevsky prospekt ✉ 83 Nevsky pr., City Center ☎ 812/277-7966 Ⓜ Mayakovskaya. **Natur Produkt** ✉ 68 Sadovaya ul., Admiralteisky ☎ 812/714-

2024 Ⓜ Sennaya Ploshchad. **Pharmacy Doctor** ✉ 7 Liteiny pr., Liteiny/Smolny ☎ 812/273-6135 Ⓜ Chernyshevskaya. **Pharmacy MEDEM** ✉ 6 ul. Marata, Liteiny/Smolny ☎ 812/336-3333 Ⓜ Mayakovskaya. **Pharmacy Doctor** ✉ 61-building 3, Lesnoi pr., Vyborg Side ☎ 812/245-7434 Ⓜ Lesnaya. **Natur Produkt** ✉ 47 Sredni pr., Vasilievsky Island ☎ 812/327-0990.

ENGLISH-LANGUAGE MEDIA

ENGLISH-LANGUAGE BOOKSTORES

Anglia is St. Petersburg's only true English-language bookstore, with a large selection of Russian literature in translation, popular fiction, and classic English literature, as well as sections on photography, history, biography, and foreign languages. The friendly English-speaking staff is ready to assist you with all your literary needs. Though it doesn't have nearly the same selection, you could also try St. Petersburg's largest bookstore, Dom Knigi (House of Books). A limited selection of outdated English-language guidebooks on various parts of the former Soviet Union is available at Akademkniga. Iskusstvo, like Akademkniga, stocks English-language guidebooks.

🚩 Bookstores **Akademkniga** ✉ 57 Liteiny pr., Liteiny/Smolny Ⓜ Mayakovskaya. **Anglia** ✉ 38 nab. Fontanki (Turgenev House), City Center ☎ 812/279-8284 ⊕ www.anglophile.ru. **Dom Knigi** ✉ 62 Nevsky pr., City Center ☎ 812/570-6546 Ⓜ Nevsky prospekt ✉ 62 Nevsky pr., City Center Ⓜ Nevsky prospekt.

NEWSPAPERS & MAGAZINES

American and British paperbacks, newspapers, and magazines are on sale in hotel gift shops. The *St. Petersburg Times* (www.sptimes.ru), a free, local, English-language newspaper, is a good source for happenings around town. It's published Tuesday and Friday and is available at hotels, cafés, and clubs around town.

METRO TRAVEL

Although St. Petersburg's metro does not have the elaborate design and decoration of Moscow's metro system, its good qualities are still substantial. Despite economic hardships, St. Petersburg has managed to maintain efficient, inexpensive service; the only drawback is that the stops tend to be far apart.

Stations are deep underground—the city's metro is the deepest in the world—necessitating long escalator rides. Some of them have encased landings so that entry is possible only after the train has pulled in and the secondary doors are opened.

A word of warning: avoid Sportivnaya station on Saturdays, because it leads to the city's main soccer stadium and trains will likely be full of rowdy fans of the local club, Zenit. All central stations are infamous for theft and rank high in the city's list of pickpocket hot spots. Although the city police regularly trumpet successes and report arrests of more gangs, it doesn't seem to get any safer.

FARES & SCHEDULES

To use the metro, you must purchase a token or a magnetic card (available at stations) and insert it, upon entering, into the slot at the turnstile. The fare (10R) is the same regardless of distance. Alternatively, you may purchase a pass valid for an entire month (600R) and good for transport on all modes of city transportation. You can also opt for a two-week all-inclusive pass (300R). The cost is insignificant and well worth the convenience if you plan to use the metro often.

There's a monthly pass for metro only (460R), and a choice of magnetic cards for 10 trips (82R) or 25 trips (194R). The metro operates from 5:30 AM to midnight, but is best avoided during rush hours. The nicer hotels often give out metro maps printed in English.

MONEY MATTERS

Exchange bureaus can be found throughout the city. ATMs, with access to Cirrus, Visa, MasterCard, and Plus, although not as plentiful as in a typical North American or European city, can be found on any of the main streets in the city center. You can also look for them in metro stations and in exchange bureaus. For withdrawing money late at night, your safest option is one of the city's nicer hotels. ATMs and exchange offices work around-the-clock at both the Angleterre (connected to the Astoria) and the Grand Hotel Europe.

SIGHTSEEING TOURS

In addition to the private agencies, every major hotel has a tourist bureau through which individual and group tours can be booked. Explorer-Tour arranges city tours. The Modern travel agency offers incoming tour services for groups and individuals, arranges excursions around St. Petersburg and Moscow, and can also arrange wedding and business tours. Mir Travel Agency can custom-design tours.

🇮 **Explorer-Tour** ✉ 50 ul. Marata, Vladimirskaya ☎ 812/320-0954 🖷 812/712-1967 ⊕ www.explorer-tour.ru Ⓜ Mayakovskaya. **Mir Travel Agency** ✉ 11 ul. Marata, Liteiny/Smolny ☎🖷 812/325-7122 Ⓜ Mayakovskaya. **Modern** ✉ 3 Torzhovskaya ul., Office 236, Vyborg Side ☎ 812/246-9533 Ⓜ Chernaya Rechka.

BOAT TOURS   A float down the Neva or through the city's twisting canals—*Exkursii na katere po rekam i kanalam*—is always a pleasant way to spend a summer afternoon. For trips through the canals, take one of the boats at the pier near Anichkov Bridge on Nevsky prospekt. Boats cruising the Neva leave from the pier outside the State Hermitage Museum. Both boat trips have departures early morning to late afternoon from mid-May through mid-September.

St. Petersburg's aquatic infrastructure is still a far cry from the developed waterways of Amsterdam or Venice but six local cruise operators have joined with the city to create the City Water Bus project. Four routes circulate between the main tourist sights and theaters. Each departs once an hour and takes from 1 to 1 ½ hours to complete. One stop on any route costs 30R, while the entire journey is a bargain at 150R–200R. Another option is an all-day ticket for 350R.

River and canal cruises are slightly more expensive than water buses (they cost 200R–500R depending on route, time of day, and day of the week) but departures are far less regular. You can hop on and off at various stops. Route A starts and ends at the Peter and Paul Fortress. Route B begins and ends by Kazan Cathedral. Route C starts near the Russian Museum's Stroganov Palace on Nevsky Prospekt and ends at St. Isaac's Cathedral. Route D begins by the Admiralty and circulates between the Hermitage, Smolny Cathedral, the Okhtinskaya Hotel, the cruiser *Avrora,* and the Peter and Paul Fortress before ending at St. Isaac's Cathedral.

Smaller boats that you can hire on demand for 1,200R–1,800R per hour—without the running commentary, making for an extremely peaceful ride—also leave from the Moika River, opposite the Field of Mars, two steps away from the Church of the Savior on Spilled Blood. Perhaps best of all, you can negotiate with the owners of the smaller boats to take you out at almost any time of the night, which can be a magical way of seeing the city during the White Nights. This is likely to cost your party a total of 2,100R–2,300R.

WALKING TOURS If you prefer to plunge into city life instead of observing it from the window of your tour bus, the best bet is to take an excursion (400R) with the sole walking tour company, Peter's Walking Tours. Founded by inveterate local backpacker Peter Kozyrev, the company turns walks and pub crawls into a real experience. The guides masterfully interweave history, current affairs, mystery, and gossip. The most popular walk is the five-hour-long Original Walking Tour: express your wishes and the guide tailors the route. There's no need to book a tour, just be sure to check the schedule on the company's Web site at www.peterswalk.com, choose a walk, and show up about 15 minutes before the start. There's no telephone number for the company, and all private tours have to be made via e-mail.

🛈 Peter's Walking Tours ⊕ www.peterswalk.com.

TAXIS

Take the same precautions when using taxicabs in St. Petersburg as in Moscow. Although taxis roam the city quite frequently, it's far easier—and certainly safer—to order a cab through your hotel. Fares vary according to the driver's whim; you're expected to negotiate. Foreigners are always charged much more than Russians, and oblivious tourists tend to be gouged. Make sure that you agree on a price before getting into the car, and try to have the correct money handy. If you speak Russian, you can order a cab by dialing one of the numbers listed below. There's sometimes a delay, but usually the cab arrives within 20–30 minutes; the company will phone you back when the driver is nearby. If you order a cab this way, you pay the official state fare, which turns out to be reasonable in dollars, plus a fee for the reservation. No tip is expected beyond rounding up the amount on the meter. If you hail a cab or a private car on the street, expect to pay the ruble equivalent of $5 for most usual trips.

🛈 Taxi Companies **Central Taxi** (Tsentralnoye Taksi) ☎ 812/312-0022. **Petersburg Taxi** (Peterburgskoye Taxi) ☎ 068. **Taxi Million** ☎ 812/700-0000.

TRAIN TRAVEL

St. Petersburg has several train stations, the most important of which are Baltic Station (Baltiysky Vokzal), for trains to the Baltic countries; Ladozhsky Station (Ladozhsky Vokzal), for trains to Finland; Moscow Station (Moskovsky Vokzal), at Ploshchad Vosstania, off Nevsky prospekt, for trains to Moscow and points east; and Vitebsk Station (Vitebsky Vokzal), for trains to Ukraine and points south. Only suburban trains depart from Finland Station (Finlandsky Vokzal). All the major train stations have a connecting metro stop, so they're easily reached by public transportation.

For information on train arrival and departure schedules, call the train-information number below. Train tickets may be purchased through the tourist bureau in your hotel or at the Central Railway Agency Office (Tsentralnoye Zheleznodorozhnoye Agenstvo) off Nevsky prospekt, adjacent to the Kazan Cathedral. The agency is open 8–8 Monday through Saturday and 8–4 on Sunday. The office has three information points that can point you in the direction of the correct desks. Even better is the Central Airline Ticket Agency on Nevsky, which has two train-ticket desks and is a far quieter option. It's possible to buy tickets at the stations themselves, but this is best attempted only by the brave or bilingual.

FARES & SCHEDULES Several trains run daily between Moscow and St. Petersburg, the most popular of which is the *Krasnaya Strela* (Red Arrow), a night train that departs from one end at 11:55 PM and arrives at the other at 8:25 AM the next day. Its new rival, *Nikolayevsky Express,* departs the city at 11:24 AM and gets to Moscow at 7:10 PM. Designed to resemble a typical early-20th-century train and named after Russia's last tsar, Nicholas II, this romantic train has staff dressed in turn-of-the-twentieth-century costumes, oak settings in its restaurant, and brass details in compartments. You pay less than $100 round-trip for a berth in a four-person compartment. The most sumptuous way to travel between the two cities is the *Grand Express*: the most luxurious cabin has an LCD-TV, DVD-player, air-conditioning, toilet and shower, and bathrobe and slippers (12,500R [$440] per person, one-way).

During the day travelers can choose between the *Avrora,* which makes the trip in less than six hours, or the high-speed ER–200 trains, which leave twice a day and take a lightning-quick 4 hours and 45 minutes. There are two trains daily to and from Helsinki from Ladozhsky station; the trip takes 6½ hours.

🚆 Train Information **Central Airline Ticket Agency** ✉ 7/9 Nevsky pr., City Center Ⓜ Nevsky prospekt. **Central Railway Agency Office** ✉ 24 Kanal Griboyedova, City Center ☎ 812/201 Ⓜ Nevsky prospekt. **Train information** ☎ 812/768–3344.

TRANSPORTATION AROUND ST. PETERSBURG

Although St. Petersburg is spread out over 650 square km (250 square mi), most of its historic sites are concentrated in the downtown section and are best explored on foot. These sites are often not well served by the extensive public transportation system, so be prepared to do a lot of walking. Bilingual city maps with bus routes marked on them are sold at the bookstore Dom Knigi (62 Nevsky prospect), while *St. Petersburg In Your Pocket* prints valuable info about marshrutki routes in every issue.

When traveling by bus, tram, or trolley, you must purchase a ticket from the conductor. At this writing, a ticket valid for one ride costs 10R, regardless of the distance you intend to travel; if you change buses, you must pay another fare. Buses, trams, and trolleys operate from 5:30 AM to midnight, although service in the late evening hours and on Sunday tends to be unreliable.

Note that all public transportation vehicles tend to be extremely overcrowded during rush hours; people with claustrophobia should avoid them. It's very much the Russian philosophy that there's always room for one more passenger. Make sure you position yourself near the exits well before the point at which you want to disembark, or risk missing your stop. Buses tend to be newer and reasonably comfortable. Trolleys and trams, on the other hand, sometimes give the impression that they're held together with Scotch tape and effort of will, and can be extremely drafty. In winter the windows tend to ice up to the point where it's impossible to see where you are, so ask the conductor to tell you if in doubt.

TRAVEL AGENCIES

Even though the various forms of travel and assorted companies have their own official outlets—airline offices, or the Central Railway Agency Office, for example—perhaps your best bet to avoid lines and bureaucratic hassle is to head to the Central Airline Ticket Agency. This is mainly for air travel, but its international department, on the right as you go in, can also book domestic and international sea and bus tickets as well. Additionally, in the main hall there are two desks (Nos. 9 and 10) that offer domestic and international train tickets for a negligible additional fee. In fact, you could say that this is a haven for the troubled traveler because it can deal with most major travel questions under one roof.

For international travel help, American Express operates an office in the Grand Hotel Europe. Besides ticketing, the office replaces lost traveler's checks and credit cards. For international bookings, try Infinity Travel, in the Angleterre hotel (connected to the Astoria). In addition to providing tickets on all major domestic and international airlines, Infinity also offers last-minute reservations and a free ticket-delivery service. Sindbad Travel, at the Russian International Hostel, is friendly and helpful. There are many more agencies, and it would be impossible to list them all. For other options, you could always ask at your hotel, or flip through a copy of the St. Petersburg Yellow Pages, which has all of its listings in both Russian and English. Yellow pages are also available online at www.yell.ru.

🚩 Agencies **American Express** ✉ 1/7 ul. Mikhailovskaya, off Nevsky pr., City Center ☎ 812/329-6060 ⊙ Weekdays 9–5 ⊕ www.americanexpress.com Ⓜ Nevsky prospect. **Avista Tours** ✉ 7 Millionnaya ul., City Center ☎ 812/275-6635 🖨 812/275-3488 Ⓜ Nevsky prospect. **Central Airline Ticket Agency** ✉ 7/9 Nevsky pr., City Center ☎ 812/717-8093 for flights in Russia and former Soviet Union, 812/315-0072 for international flights ⊙ Weekdays 9–9, weekends 9–6 Ⓜ Nevsky Prospect. **Infinity Travel** ✉ 39 Bolshaya Morskaya ul., City Center ☎ 812/313-5085 🖨 812/313-5084 ⊕ www.infinity.ru Ⓜ Sennaya Ploshchad. **Sindbad Travel** ✉ 28 3rd Sovietskaya ul., Vladimirskaya ☎ 812/327-8384 🖨 812/329-8019 ⊕ www.sindbad.ru Ⓜ Ploshchad Vosstaniya.

VISITOR INFORMATION

The staff members of the City Tourist Information Center (Gorodskoi Turistichesky Tsentr Informatsii ot Soveta po Turismu) are generally friendly, although they have a tendency to thrust maps and booklets at you in the absence of any great ideas themselves. The center has a database on cultural and sports events, hotels, major tourist attractions, and so on. You may also consult the St. Petersburg Tourism and Excursions Council (Soviet po Turismu i Ekskursiyam). You can also call the Infoline 24 hours a day; the operators may not have the answer to your question, but they will tell you so nicely.

Your best bet for information and assistance is your hotel, for virtually all of the hotels have established tourist offices for their guests. These offices, which provide many services, can help you book individual and group tours, make restaurant reservations, or purchase theater tickets. Even if you're not a hotel guest, you're usually welcome to use these facilities, provided you are willing to pay the hefty fees for their services.

If you plan on spending a great deal of time in the city, it might be worthwhile to invest about $5 in the *Traveller's Yellow Pages for Saint Petersburg* (⊕ www.infoservices.com), a compact telephone book and handbook written in English, with indexes in several languages, including English. You can pick one up at most of the bookstores that carry English-language books.

🚹 Tourist Information **City Tourist Information Center** ⊠ 14 Sadovaya ul., City Center ☎📠 812/310-8286 or 812/310-2822 ⊕ www.spb.ru/eng ⊙ Weekdays 10-6 Ⓜ Sennaya Ploshchad. **Infoline** ☎ 812/325-9325. **St. Petersburg Tourism and Excursions Council** ⊠ 3 Italianskaya ul., City Center ☎ 812/110-6739, 812/314-8786 office, 812/710-6690 foreign section 📠 812/710-6824.

Summer Palaces & Historic Islands

4

"[Tour] Peterhof, nicknamed the "Russian Versailles," with its impressive rooms and remarkable . . . acres of gorgeous flowers and fountains."

—rudy

"Catherine Palace and its star attraction, the fabulous Amber Room, [was] one of the highlights of our recent trip."

—Kristi

"You have to fit in at least two of the summer palaces as well. They are wonderful. I enjoyed Pushkin and Peterhof the most."

—shandy

By Barnaby
Thompson &
Lauri del
Commune

Updated by
Irina Titova

IF ST. PETERSBURG IS THE STAR OF THE SHOW, then its suburbs are the supporting cast without which the story could not be told. For every aspect of the city's past—the glamour and glory of its Imperial era, the pride and power of its military history, the splendor of its architecture, the beauty of its waterways—there's a park, a palace, a playground of the tsars somewhere outside the city limits with a corresponding tale to tell. From the dazzling fountains of Peterhof on the shores of the Gulf of Finland, to the tranquil estate of Pavlovsk to the south, to the naval stronghold of Kronstadt—a quiet town with a turbulent history and a still-Soviet feel (and once completely closed to foreigners)—what surrounds St. Petersburg is as important to its existence and identity as anything on Nevsky prospekt. It might seem odd to exhort you to get out of the city almost as soon as you have arrived, but you'll understand why once you have seen the suburbs for yourself, wandered through the palaces imagining what it would be like to call them home, and strolled through the grounds in the footsteps of the aristocrats and officers who made Russia a world power.

Of all the palaces in Russia, the one that generally makes the most distinct and lasting impression on visitors is Peterhof, on the shore of the Baltic Sea, some 29 km (18 mi) west of St. Petersburg. More than a mere summer palace, it's an Imperial playground replete with lush parks, monumental cascades, and gilt fountains. In tsarist times, Tsarskoye Selo, now renamed Pushkin, was a fashionable haunt of members of the aristocracy who were eager to be near the Imperial family and to escape the noxious air and oppressive climate of the capital to the north. After the Revolution of 1905, Nicholas II and his family lived here, more or less permanently. Pavlovsk, the Imperial estate of Paul I, is some 30 km (19 mi) south of St. Petersburg and only 5 km (3 mi) from Pushkin and the magnificent Catherine Palace. Because of the proximity of the two towns, tours to them are often combined. If you decide to do both towns in one visit, make sure to give yourself enough time to do justice to each of them. The estate of Lomonosov, on the Gulf of Finland, some 40 km (25 mi) west of St. Petersburg and about 9 km (5½ mi) northwest of Peterhof, is perhaps the least commanding of the suburban Imperial palaces. It is, however, the only one to have survived World War II intact.

Exploring Summer Palaces & Historic Islands

The area around St. Petersburg is one big monument to the city's history as Russia's Imperial capital, from the time of Peter the Great (1672–1725) to the ill-fated Nicholas II, whose execution in Ekaterinburg in 1918 brought the Romanov dynasty to an end. The palaces at Lomonosov, Peterhof, Pushkin, and Pavlovsk—the status symbols of the royal elite—are at the heart of any trip outside St. Petersburg. But even Russians who have already visited these tsarist residences in the suburbs find themselves returning time and time again, drawn by the acres of beautiful parks and gardens, which are wonderful places to wander through and relax. Unlike Moscow's Golden Ring, monasteries and churches are not much in evidence, with the exception of Valaam on Lake Ladoga, which is dominated by the 14th-century Transfiguration of the Savior Monastery.

Except for Kronshtadt and Valaam, all of the destinations in this section can be reached by commuter train (*elektrichka*), but the simplest way to see the palaces is to book an excursion (available through any tour company). The cost is reasonable and covers transportation, a guided tour, and admission fees. An organized excursion to any of the suburban palaces will take at least four hours; if you travel on your own, it's likely to take up the entire day. But whichever plan you opt for, you'll enjoy numerous sights filled with splendor and magic.

Note that the sights in this region do not make up one easy circuit. In a few cases—notably Gatchina—you have to return to St. Petersburg to find direct rail transport. Of all the places, the ones that make the most sense to do in tandem would be: Pushkin and Pavlovsk, Peterhof and Lomonosov, Peterhof and Kronshtadt, or Lomonosov and Kronshtadt.

Because this region is so close to St. Petersburg, hotels are few and far between, and are completely unnecessary for the typical day-tripper.

About the Restaurants

Because most of the suburbs involve only a short trip from St. Petersburg, there has not been any real demand for quality restaurants and cafés, and some of the eateries you may stumble across serve truly execrable food. There are some exceptions, notably in Pavlovsk and Pushkin, but on the whole it's best to pack some sandwiches if you want to be sure of a decent meal. You will, however, find plenty of beer tents and ice-cream vendors, which at least offer temporary sustenance.

WHAT IT COSTS In U.S. dollars					
	$$$$	$$$	$$	$	¢
AT DINNER	over $25	$18–$25	$12–$18	$6–$12	under $6

Prices are per person for a main course at dinner.

Timing

To see the palaces and estates to their best advantage, you should try to time your visits to coincide with spring or summer. Peterhof in particular is best visited in summer, so you can fully appreciate the fountains, gilt statues, monumental cascades, and lush parks. A winter trip can be quite disappointing, as from late September to early June the fountains and cascades are closed down and take on the depressing look of drained pools. Autumn can also be a pleasant time for viewing the palaces. Note also that the waterway along the Neva River and Lake Ladoga to Valaam is only open from June through September.

If you're traveling in the extreme cold of winter or the hottest days of summer, dress carefully, as much of your time may well be spent outdoors.

You don't need to see every town to get a feel for the life of the tsars, and it would be against the luxurious and laid-back spirit of the region to make an exhausting attempt to do so. For example, it's possible to combine Pushkin and Pavlovsk in one day, or to do the same with Peterhof and Kronshtadt, but these towns offer such individual delights that it's worth lingering for a full day in each. Hotels are few and far between in this region, so it's best to make nearby St. Petersburg your home base.

Numbers in the text correspond to numbers in the margin and on the Summer Palaces & Historic Islands map.

4

If you have 1 or 2 days

You can take your pick of the suburbs for any day trip, although your choice of destination will be influenced by the time of year. In summer, **Peterhof ❷** is a must. At this time of year, **Pushkin ❹** and **Pavlovsk ❺** are at their most attractive, and can be seen in a single day or, better still, over two days. For a destination with a completely different historical feel, head for the naval town of **Kronshtadt ❼**. If you have two days to see the summer palaces, you could also strike out for **Gatchina ❻** or **Lomonosov ❶** on the second day.

If you have 3 or 4 days

In summer head to **Peterhof ❷** and **Pushkin ❹** on your first two days. On your third day, take a break from the palaces and visit the unforgettable **Valaam Archipelago ❽**. To get to Valaam, catch the boat on the evening of your second day down the Neva River and up into Lake Ladoga. Spend the third day admiring the secluded monasteries and natural beauty of the islands, and return to the city overnight. On your final day, head for **Gatchina ❻**, **Lomonosov ❶**, or the **Konstantine Palace ❸**.

THE SUMMER PALACES

A visit to this region takes you through a lavish trail of evidence of the Imperial spirit. These majestic old palaces, estates, and former nobles' residences—all set on lovingly tended grounds—are within easy reach of St. Petersburg.

Lomonosov (Oranienbaum)
Ломоносов (Ораниенбаум)

 39 km (24 mi) west of St. Petersburg's city center on the southern shore of the Gulf of Finland.

This was the property of Alexander Menshikov (circa 1672–1729), the first governor of St. Petersburg and Peter the Great's favorite, who, following Peter's example, in 1710 began building his own luxurious summer residence on the shores of the Baltic Sea. Before construction was complete, however, Peter died and Menshikov was stripped of his formidable political power and exiled, leaving his summer estate half finished. The palace reverted to the crown and was given to Peter III, the ill-fated husband of Catherine the Great. Most of the buildings on

the grounds were erected during his six-month reign, in 1762, or completed later by Catherine.

Many suburbs of St. Petersburg had names of German origin and this property was given the German name Oranienbaum after the orangery attached to its palace. During World War II, Stalin was understandably irritated by the many Germanic names. A few years after the liberation of Leningrad, Oranienbaum was renamed for the 18th-century scientist Mikhail Lomonosov, who had conducted a number of experiments at his nearby estate. Oranienbaum was the only imperial residence to have survived World War II entirely intact.

Menshikov's Great Palace (Bolshoi Menshikovskii Dvorets), the original palace on the property, is also Lomonosov's biggest. It stands on a terrace overlooking the sea. Built between 1710 and 1725, it was designed by the same architects who built Menshikov's grand mansion on St. Petersburg's Vasilievsky Island, Giovanni Fontana and Gottfried Schaedel. Currently closed to the public, the Great Palace is in need of renovation, but you can see its decaying interiors when visiting the palace's annually changing exhibits on everything from the Orthodox church in St. Petersburg to Japanese artwork. Nearby is **Peterstadt Dvorets,** the modest palace that Peter III used, a two-story stone mansion built between 1756 and

1762 by Arnoldo Rinaldi. Its interior is decorated with handsome lacquered wood paintings. That it seems small, gloomy, and isolated is perhaps appropriate, as it was here, in 1762, that the tsar was arrested, then taken to Ropsha and murdered in the wake of the coup that placed his wife, Catherine the Great, on the throne.

The building that most proclaims the estate's Imperial beginnings, however, is unquestionably Catherine's **Chinese Palace** (Kitaisky Dvorets) also designed by Rinaldi. Intended as one of her private summer residences, it is quite an affair—rococo inside, baroque outside. Lavishly decorated, it has ceiling paintings created by Venetian artists, inlaid-wood floors, and elaborate stucco walls. The small house outside served as the kitchen. Down the slope to the east of the Great Palace is the curious **Katalnaya Gorka.** All that remains of the slide, which was originally several stories high, is the pavilion that served as the starting point of the ride, where guests of the empress could catch their breath before tobogganing down again. Painted soft blue with white trim, the fanciful, dazzling pavilion looks like a frosted birthday cake; it was, however, closed for extensive renovations at this writing. Also on the premises, near the pond, is a small amusement park offering carnival rides. When taking a commuter train here, be careful to exit at Oranienbaum-I (not II). ✉ *48 ul. Yunovo Lenintsa* ☎ *812/422–4796* ✉ *Exhibition at Menshikov's Great Palace 185R; Chinese Palace 370R; Peterstadt Dvorets 260R; Oriental exhibition at Japanese pavilion 185R* ☉ *Estate Wed.–Sun. 11–5, Mon. 11–4; Chinese Palace late May–late Sept., Wed.–Mon. 11–5. Some buildings are closed on Mon. Estate closed last Mon. of month.*

Peterhof (Petrodvorets)
Петергоф (Петродворец)

★ ❷ *29 km (18 mi) west of St. Petersburg on the southern shores of the Gulf of Finland.*

Visiting Peterhof and other Imperial palaces nearby, you may find it difficult to believe that when the Germans were finally driven out of the area toward the end of World War II, almost everything was in ruins. Many priceless objects had been removed to safety before the Germans advanced, but a great deal had to be left behind and was consequently looted by the invaders. Now, after decades of painstaking work, art historians and craftspeople, referring to photographs and records of descriptions, have returned the palaces to their former splendor. Peterhof and its neighboring palaces are so vast, however, that renovation work will be ongoing for many years to come.

The complex of gardens and residences at Peterhof was masterminded by Peter the Great, who personally drew up the original plans, starting around 1720. His motivation was twofold. First, he was proud of the capital city he was creating and wanted its evolving Imperial grandeur showcased with a proper summer palace. Second, he became attached to this spot while erecting the naval fortress of Kronshtadt on a nearby island across the Gulf of Finland; because it lay in easy view, he often stayed here during the fort's construction. When the fort was finished,

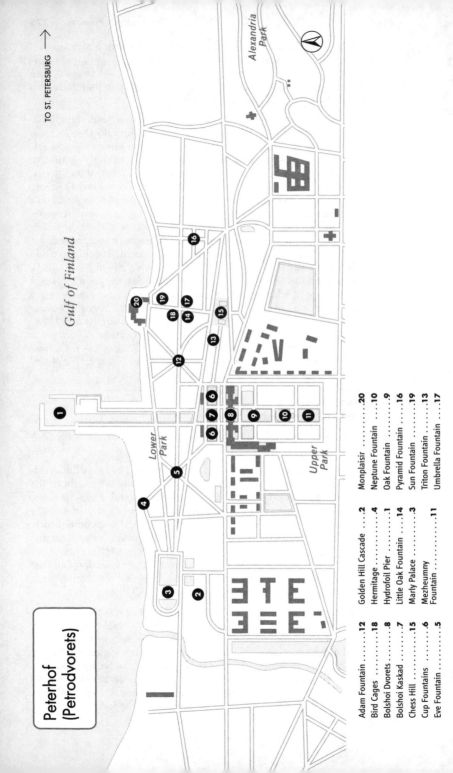

Peterhof
(Petrodvorets)

TO ST. PETERSBURG →

Gulf of Finland

Alexandria Park

Lower Park

Upper Park

Adam Fountain **12**
Bird Cages **18**
Bolshoi Dvorets **8**
Bolshoi Kaskad **7**
Chess Hill **15**
Cup Fountains **6**
Eve Fountain **5**

Golden Hill Cascade . . .**2**
Hermitage **4**
Hydrofoil Pier **1**
Little Oak Fountain **14**
Marly Palace **3**
Mezheumny
Fountain **11**

Monplaisir **20**
Neptune Fountain **10**
Oak Fountain **9**
Pyramid Fountain **16**
Sun Fountain **19**
Triton Fountain **13**
Umbrella Fountain **17**

by which time he had had a series of naval victories (including the Northern War against the Swedes), he threw himself into establishing many parts of the grounds that would be called Peterhof (Peter's Court), a German name that was changed to Petrodvorets after World War II.

If you travel by hydrofoil, you'll arrive at the pier of the Lower Park, from which you work your way up to the Great Palace. If you arrive by land, you'll simply go through the process in reverse. Either way, the perspective always emphasizes the mightiness of water. Half-encircled by the sea, filled with fountains and other water monuments, and with the Marine Canal running straight from the foot of the palace into the bay, Peter's palace was also intended as a loving tribute to the role of water in the life, and strength, of his city. The **Lower Park** was designed as a formal baroque garden in the French style, adorned with statues, fountains, and cascades. Peter's playful spirit is still very much in evidence here. The fun-loving tsar installed "trick fountains"—hidden water sprays built into trees and tiny plazas and brought to life by stepping on a certain stone or moving a lever, much to the surprise of the unsuspecting visitor and the delight of the squealing children who love to race through the resulting showers on hot summer days.

Located in the eastern half of Lower Park is the oldest building at Peterhof, **Monplaisir** (literally "My Pleasure"), completed in 1721. This is where Peter the Great lived while overseeing construction of the main Imperial residence. As was typical with Peter, he greatly preferred this modest Dutch-style villa to his later, more extravagant living quarters. The house is open to the public and makes for a pleasant tour. Some of its most interesting rooms are the Lacquered Study, decorated with replicas of panels painted in the Chinese style (the originals were destroyed during World War II); Peter's Naval Study; and his bedroom, where some personal effects, such as his nightcap and a quilt made by his wife, are on display. Attached to Peter's villa is the so-called Catherine Wing, built by Rastrelli in the mid-18th century in an utterly different style. The future Catherine the Great was staying here at the time of the coup that overthrew her husband and placed her on the throne; the space was later used mainly for balls.

In the western section of the Lower Park is another famous structure, the **Hermitage,** built in 1725. It claims to be the first of the great Imperial hermitages (the most famous, of course, still stands in St. Petersburg), or retreats, in Russia. This two-story pavilion gives new meaning to the concept of a movable feast. The building, which was used primarily as a banqueting hall for special guests, was at one time equipped with a device that would hoist the dining table area—diners and all—from the ground floor to the private dining room above. A slightly different system was put in place after Tsar Paul I's chair broke during one such exercise. The center part of the table could be lifted out, and guests would write down their dinner preferences and then signal for their notes to be lifted away. Shortly thereafter, the separated section would be lowered, complete with the meals everyone had ordered. The only way to the Hermitage was over a drawbridge, so privacy was ensured.

Almost adjacent to the Hermitage is the **Marly Palace,** a modest Peter the Great construction that is more of a country retreat than a palace. As with Monplaisir, it's mostly Petrine memorabilia on display here. The four ponds around the back are where Catherine the Great used to stock fish.

A walk up the path through the center of the Lower Park (along the Marine Canal) leads you to the famous **Great Cascade** (Bolshoi Kaskad). Running down the steep ridge separating the Lower Park and the Great Palace towering above, the cascade comprises three waterfalls, 64 fountains, and 37 gilt statues. The system of waterworks has remained virtually unchanged since 1721. The ducts and pipes convey water over a distance of some 20 km (12 mi). The centerpiece of the waterfalls is a gilt Samson rending the jaws of a lion, out of which a jet of water spurts into the air. The statue represents the 1709 Russian victory over the Swedes at Poltava on St. Samson's day. The present figure is a meticulous replica of the original, which was carried away by the Germans during World War II. A small entrance halfway up the right-hand staircase (as you look at the palace above) leads to the grotto, where you can step out onto a terrace to get a bit closer to Samson before going inside to have a look under the waterworks.

Crowning the ridge above the cascade is the magnificent **Bolshoi Dvorets.** Little remains of Peter's original two-story house, built between 1714 and 1725 under the architects Leblond, Braunstein, and Machetti. The building was considerably altered and enlarged by Peter's daughter, Elizabeth. She entrusted the reconstruction to her favorite architect, Bartolomeo Rastrelli, who transformed the modest residence into a sumptuous blend of medieval architecture and Russian baroque. Before you begin your tour of the palace interiors, pause for a moment to enjoy the breathtaking view from the marble terrace. From here a full view of the grounds below unfolds, stretching from the cascades to the Gulf of Finland and on to the city horizon on the shore beyond.

As for the main palace building, the lavish interiors are primarily the work of Rastrelli, although several of the rooms were redesigned during the reign of Catherine the Great to accord with classicism, the prevailing architectural style of her day. Of Peter's original design, only his **Oak Study Room** (Dubovy Kabinet) survived the numerous reconstructions. The fine oak panels (some are originals) lining the walls were designed by the French sculptor Pineau. The entire room and all its furnishings are of wood, with the exception of the white-marble fireplace, above whose mantel hangs a long mirror framed in carved oak.

One of the largest rooms in the palace is the **Throne Room** (Tronny Zal), which takes up the entire width of the building. Classically designed, this majestic room—once the scene of great receptions and official ceremonies—has exquisite parquet floors, elaborate stucco ceiling moldings, and dazzling chandeliers. The pale-green and dark-red decor is bathed in light, which pours in through two tiers of windows (28 in all) taking up the long sides of the room. Behind Peter the Great's throne at the eastern end of the room hangs a huge portrait of Catherine the Great.

The empress, the epitome of confidence after her successful coup, is shown astride a horse, dressed in the uniform of the guard regiment that supported her bid for power.

Next to the Throne Room is the **Chesma Hall** (Chesmensky Zal), whose interior is dedicated entirely to the Russian naval victory over the Turks in 1770. The walls are covered with 12 huge canvases depicting the battles; they were created by the German painter Phillip Hackert at Empress Catherine's behest. According to legend, the artist explained that he could not paint a burning ship, since he had never seen one. Catherine arranged to have ships blown up for him to use as models. Such were the privileges of divine right. Arguably the most dazzling of the rooms is the **Audience Hall** (Audients Zal). Rastrelli created the definitive baroque interior with this glittering room of white, red, and gold. Gilt baroque bas-reliefs adorn the stark white walls, along which tall mirrors hang, further reflecting the richness of the decor.

Other notable rooms include the **Chinese Study Rooms** (Kitaiskye Kabinety), designed by Vallin de la Mothe in the 1760s. Following the European fashion of the time, the rooms are ornately decorated with Chinese motifs. Finely carved black-lacquered panels depict various Chinese scenes. Between the two rooms of the study is the **Picture Hall** (Kartinny Zal), whose walls are paneled with 368 oil paintings by the Italian artist Rotari. The artist used just eight models for these paintings depicting young women in national dress.

Following a tour of the palace interiors (they are offered regularly in English), a stroll through the Upper Park, on the south side of the palace, is in order. This symmetrical formal garden is far less imaginative than the Lower Park, with its playful fountains and cascading waterfalls. Its focal point is the **Neptune Fountain,** made in Germany in the 17th century and bought by Paul I in 1782. During the war this three-tiered group of bronze sculptures was carried away by the Germans, and eventually recovered and reinstalled in 1956.

You can reach the palace by commuter train from St. Petersburg but, minimal fog permitting, the best way to go is by hydrofoil (June–September only), from which your first view is the panorama of the grand palace overlooking the sea. The lines to get into the palace can be excruciatingly long in summer, and sometimes guided tours get preferential treatment. The ticket office for foreigners is inside the palace, which means admission is more expensive than it is for Russians but the lines are significantly shorter. Some park pavilions are closed Wednesday and others on Thursday; visiting on the weekend is the best chance to see everything.

An integral part of visiting any museum-palace in Russia is encountering the autocratic *babushki* (a colloquial term for museum caretakers, often hearty grandmothers). In this, Peterhof is no exception. No matter how irksome, they deserve respect, for many survived the 900-day siege of Leningrad, witnessed the palaces' destruction, and saw them rise again, almost miraculously, from the ashes. As you enter the palace, you'll be given tattered shoe covers to wear, so as to protect the highly polished floors of the splendid halls. One cautionary note: on most occasions, flash photography is not allowed, although for a fee, fast film and videotape may be used. Sometimes the babushki aren't aware of the difference. So hang on tight to your equipment to avoid having it confiscated by an overzealous custodian of Peter's treasures. ✉ *2 ul. Razvodnaya* ☎ *812/427–9527* ⊕ *www.peterhof.org* ✉ *Palace 430R; 300R; separate admission fees (100R–150R) for park pavilions* ☉ *Great Palace Tues.–Sun. 10:30–5; some park pavilions are closed Wed. and others on Thurs.; closed last Tues. of month.*

Where to Eat

$$–$$$$ ✕ **Imperatorsky Stol.** The best option on the grounds of the palace itself is in the palace's old *oranzhereya*, or garden house. A comfortable, quaint spot for a snack and cup of tea, it also serves full meals of Continental cuisine featuring various kinds of fish and meat, including venison and duck courses. Traditional Russian borscht (beet soup) or solyanka (slightly spicy meat soup with pickles) are also very popular. The restaurant is open from 10 to 6. ✉ *Peterhof palace grounds, near Triton fountain* ☎ *812/427–9106* ▭ *MC, V* ☉ *Closed early Oct.–Apr.*

Konstantine Palace

Константиновский Дворец

❸ *19 km (12 mi) south of St. Petersburg on the southern shores of the Gulf of Finland.*

Once one of the most neglected jewels in the dazzling necklace of St. Petersburg's historical suburbs, the Konstantine Palace (Konstantinovsky Dvorets), which was nearly destroyed in World War II, has been restored to its original splendor. After years of renovation, based on old photographs and plans, the Italian-baroque, coffee-color palace and grounds reopened in 2003. It's now officially the Palace of Congress, used to host government functions, such as the Russia-EU Summit.

Proudly waving the Russian flag, the castle stands on a hill surrounded by vast green lawns, ponds, and lime trees. Its northern facade overlooks the windy Gulf of Finland, which is connected to the palace by canals with drawbridges and fountains. In 1720 Peter the Great commissioned work on this maritime country residence that was to be a "Russian Versailles." Italian architect Nicolo Micketti designed not only the palace, but also beautiful fountains and waterworks meant to draw water from the Gulf of Finland. However, the fountains never worked, and the palace itself underwent several fires, was redesigned, and had its name changed from Big Strelna Palace to Konstantine Palace. (Although at different periods the palace belonged to at least three members of the Russian royalty bearing the name Konstantine, it was not renamed until the 19th century, when Tsar Nicholas I presented the palace to his four-year-old son, Konstantine.)

The palace offers three different tours. One is a regular, 90-minute excursion to the eastern, historical part of the palace and includes narration about the tsar's family and its members who used to live here. The "VIP" tour covers the western part of the palace, which is used for official occasions and summits. You'll also see a part of the Russian president's apartments and the boudoir of the first lady. The third tour is a 90-minute amble through the vast park, which frankly doesn't have as many attractive sights as the parks of Peterhof and Pushkin. Join this one only in summer or on warm days since the location on the bank of the Gulf of Finland can make for very windy and chilly conditions in fall, winter, and spring.

Of the palace's 50-odd rooms, several are open to the public when no state functions are taking place. Both the VIP and historic tours visit the Marble Hall and Oval Hall. The central **Marble Hall,** used to host official events, lives up to its name with yellow marble pilasters framed by bluish marble walls. A balcony here affords a breathtaking view of the huge park and canals leading to the Gulf of Finland. Next door is the large, pink **Oval Hall,** also used for official meetings. The VIP tour goes on to visit the **Blue Hall,** opposite the Marble Hall, with blue walls, high mirrors, and gilt ornamentation. A **wine cellar** has been reconstructed; it holds Hungarian Tokay wines, as it did when this was a royal residence. The third-floor **belvedere** is a new addition. Styled as a ship's hold, it's made of oak, with a spiral staircase leading to an observation deck with lovely views of the grounds. In addition to the rooms themselves, you can see various permanent exhibits, such as Russian state symbols from the Hermitage, and naval memorabilia from St. Petersburg's Naval Museum.

The grounds are worth exploring, particularly the Upper (English) Park, Big Pond, canals, drawbridges, and the monument to Peter the Great, which stands just in front of the palace. Also on the property are 20 new, luxurious cottages, each named for a different Russian city that contributed objects to the decor; they were initially built to house visiting heads of state, but they are available for private rent at exorbitant prices. Visiting officials now tend to stay in the Baltic Star hotel, also on the grounds.

Before visiting, be sure to call ahead to make sure the palace will not be closed for state functions. A great option is to join a special tourist bus (labeled "To Konstantine Place") that leaves from Beloselsky-Belozersky Palace (located at Nevsky Prospect) in St. Petersburg. You can purchase a ticket from any theater box office. The excursion departs weekdays at 2 PM and at 11 AM and 3 PM on weekends, and includes a visit to the eastern part of the palace and the return trip. ⊠ *3 Beryozovaya alleya, Strelna* ☎ *812/438–5360* ⊕ *www.konstantinepalace.ru* ✉ *Eastern palace tour: weekdays 150R, weekends 200R; VIP tour of western palace 280R; grounds tour 100R. Bus excursion from St. Petersburg 500R* ☉ *Thurs.–Tues. 10–6, ticket office open until 5* ☉ *Closed for official events.*

Pushkin (Tsarskoye Selo)
Пушкин (Царское Село)

❹ *24 km (15 mi) south of St. Petersburg's city center via commuter train* **Fodor'sChoice** *from the Vitebsk Station, 40 km (25 mi) southeast of Peterhof.*
★

The town of Pushkin was a summer residence of the Imperial family from the days of Peter the Great right up to the last years of the Romanov dynasty. Pushkin was initially known as Tsar's Village (Tsarskoye Selo), but the town's name was changed after the Revolution of 1917, first to

Pushkin
(Tsarskoye Selo)

Alexander Park

Catherine Park

Great Pond

Aleksandrovsky
Dvorets . . . . **.4**
Cameron Gallery . . . . . . **.9**
Cameron's Pyramid . . . . **.10**
Canal . . . . **.16**
Chapel . . . . **.1**
Chesma Column . . . . . **.11**
Chinese Theater . . . . . . **.2**

Chinese Village . . . . **.3**
Concert Hall . . . . **.8**
English Garden . . . . . . **.17**
Great Pond . . . . **.14**
Grotto . . . . **.15**
Lyceum . . . . **.7**
Marble Bridge . . . . . . **.12**

Pushkin Monument . . . **.6**
Ruined Tower . . . . **.13**
Yekaterininsky Dvorets
(Catherine Palace) . . . . **.5**

THE STORY OF THE AMBER ROOM

THE ORIGINAL AMBER ROOM PANELS, a unique masterpiece of amber carving once referred to as the "Eighth Wonder of the World," were presented to Peter the Great in 1716 by Prussian king Friedrich Wilhelm I in exchange for 55 "very tall" Russian soldiers (that was Friedrich's request). The panels were eventually incorporated in one of the numerous halls of Yekaterininsky Dvorets (Catherine Palace) in Tsarskoye Selo. After the Revolution of 1917, Catherine Palace was turned into a museum, and the public had its first chance to see the Amber Room. The Nazis looted the palace in 1941 and moved the contents of the Amber Room to what was then the German town of Konigsberg. That town (soon to become the Russian town of Kaliningrad) was captured by the Soviets in 1945, but by the time the Soviet troops entered the city, the amber panels had disappeared.

There are two major theories on the fate of the amber: the panels were either destroyed by Allied bombing or were somehow hidden by the Nazis. For obvious reasons, the second theory has held the most appeal, and over the years it has given hope to eager treasure seekers. Some postulated that the amber could have been buried in a silver mine near Berlin, hidden on the shores of the Baltic Sea, or secreted as far away as South America. Explorers have searched caves, jails, churches, salt mines, tunnels, bunkers, and ice cellars. There's even a club devoted to uncovering the hiding place of the Amber Room (the late Belgian novelist Georges Simenon was a member). For some, the quest was an obsession: Georg Stein, a former German soldier, was one of the Amber Room's most dedicated hunters. He searched for more than two decades, spent almost all his fortune, and in the end was found

mysteriously murdered in a Bavarian forest in 1987. In 1991 the German magazine Der Spiegel organized its own ultimately unsuccessful archaeological expedition to search for the amber in the ruins of Lochstedt Castle in the Kaliningrad region.

In 1979 the Soviet government gave up all hope of relocating the panels and initiated the reconstruction of the Amber Room, allocating about $8 million for the project. It would take another $3.5 million donation from the German company Ruhrgas AG in 1999 to complete the restoration work. More than 30 craftspeople worked tirelessly, some dedicating up to 20 years of their lives to the project. Using microscopes to make the tiniest engravings in the amber, many lost their vision over the years or suffered illness from inhaling amber dust. Ironically, most of the amber came from the world's biggest deposit of the fossil resin, in Kaliningrad—the very place where the original amber panels had disappeared. After 25 years of work and 6 tons of amber (though 80% of this amber was waste product), the replica of the Amber Room was unveiled in 2003 in time for St. Petersburg's 300th-anniversary celebrations.

Covered with more than a ton of amber, the room embraces you with the warm glow of more than 13 hues of this stone, ranging from butter yellow to dark red. Also here are copies of the Florentine mosaic panels (representing the five senses), also stolen, that originally adorned the room. However, one panel, Smell and Touch, is an original, found in Bremen, Germany, in 1997; a German pensioner whose father had fought in the Soviet Union was caught trying to sell the panel.

Children's Village (Detskoye Selo) and then to Pushkin, in honor of the great Russian poet who studied at the lyceum here. During the 18th and 19th centuries, Tsarskoye Selo was a popular summer resort for St. Petersburg's aristocracy and well-to-do citizens. Not only was the royal family close by, but it was here, in 1837, that Russia's first railroad line was opened, running between Tsarskoye Selo and Pavlovsk, to be followed three years later by a line between here and St. Petersburg.

Fodor'sChoice
★ Pushkin's main attraction is the dazzling 18th-century **Catherine Palace** (Yekaterininsky Dvorets), a perfect example of Russian baroque. The bright-turquoise exterior has row after row of white columns and pilasters with gold baroque moldings running the entire length (985 feet) of the facade. Although much of the palace's history and its inner architectural design bears Catherine the Great's stamp, it's for Catherine I, Peter the Great's second wife, that the palace is named. Under Empress Elizabeth, their daughter, the original modest stone palace was completely rebuilt. The project was initially entrusted to the Russian architects Kvasov and Chevakinsky, but in 1752 Elizabeth brought in the Italian architect Bartolomeo Rastrelli. Although Catherine the Great had the interiors remodeled in the classical style, she left Rastrelli's stunning facade untouched.

You enter the palace grounds through the gilded black-iron gates designed by Rastrelli. The *E* mounted atop is for Catherine ("Ekaterina" in Russian). To your right, a visual feast unfolds as you walk the length of the long blue-and-gold facade toward the museum entrance. Sparkling above the palace at the northern end are the golden cupolas of the Palace Church. The interiors are just as spectacular, and many of the rooms are famous in their own right. Although little of Rastrelli's original design remains, the many additions and alterations made between 1760 and 1790 under Catherine the Great do; these were carried out by a pair of noted architects, the Scottish Charles Cameron and the Italian Giacomo Quarenghi.

Entering the palace by the main staircase, which was not added until 1861, you will see displays depicting the extent of the wartime damage and of the subsequent restoration work. Like Peterhof, the palace was almost completely destroyed during World War II. It was used by occupying Nazi forces as an army barracks, and as the Germans retreated, they blew up what remained of the former Imperial residence. Today the exterior of the palace again stands in all its glory, and work on the interior is ongoing.

The largest and arguably most impressive room is the **Great Hall** (Bolshoi Zal), which was used for receptions and balls. The longer sides of the hall are taken up by two tiers of gilt-framed windows. Tall, elaborately carved, gilded mirrors have been placed between them. Light pouring in through the windows bounces off the mirrors and sparkles on the gilt, amplifying the impression of spaciousness and brilliance. The huge ceiling painting, depicting Russian military victories and accomplishments in the sciences and arts, makes the room seem even larger. Here it's easy to imagine the extravagant lifestyle of St. Petersburg's prerevolutionary elite.

On the north side of the State Staircase is one of the palace's most famous rooms, the **Amber Room** (Yantarnaya Komnata), so named for the engraved amber panels that line its walls (⇨ *See* Close Up: The Story of the Amber Room). The room owes much of its fame to this mysterious disappearance in World War II. In 1979 the Soviet government finally gave up hope of ever retrieving the panels and began the costly work of restoring the room. After 25 years of restoration a nearly exact replica of the room opened in 2003.

Leaving the Amber Room, you'll come to the large **Picture Gallery** (Kartinny Zal), which runs the full width of the palace. The paintings are all from Western Europe and date from the 17th to the early 18th century.

Highlights among the other splendid rooms on the north side include the Blue Drawing Room, the Blue Chinese Room, and the Choir Anteroom, all of which face the courtyard. Each has pure silk wall coverings. The Blue Chinese Room, originally designed by Cameron, has been restored on the basis of the architect's drawings. Despite its name, it's a purely classical interior, and the only thing even remotely Chinese is the Asian motif on the silk fabric covering the walls. The fine golden-yellow silk now on the walls of the Choir Anteroom is from the same bolt used to decorate the room in the 18th century. When the postwar restoration began, this extra supply of the original silk was discovered tucked away in a storage room of the Hermitage.

Having savored the treasures inside the palace, you can now begin exploring the beautiful **Yekaterininsky Park** outside, with its marble statues, waterfalls, garden alleys, boating ponds, pavilions, bridges, and quays. The park is split into two sections. The inner, formal section, known as the French Garden, runs down the terraces in front of the palace's eastern facade. The outer section encloses the Great Pond and is in the less-rigid style of an English garden. If you follow the main path through the French Garden and down the terrace, you'll eventually reach Rastrelli's Hermitage, which he completed just before turning his attention to the palace itself. The hermitage was closed at this writing for extensive renovation. Other highlights of the French Garden include the Upper and Lower Bath pavilions (1777–79) and Rastrelli's elaborate blue-domed Grotto.

There is much to be seen in the English-style garden, too. A good starting point is the **Cameron Gallery** (Galereya Kamerona), which actually forms a continuation of the palace's park-side frontage. It's off to the right (with your back to the palace). Open only in summer, it contains a museum of 18th- and 19th-century costumes. From its portico you get the best views of the park and its lakes—which is exactly what Cameron had in mind when he designed it in the 1780s. The double-sided staircase leading majestically down to the Great Pond is flanked by two bronze sculptures of Hercules and Flora. From here, descend the stairs to begin your exploration of the park. Just beyond the island in the middle of the Great Pond, actually an artificial lake, stands the Chesma Column, commemorating the Russian naval victory in the Aegean in 1770.

At the far end of the pond is Cameron's Pyramid, where Catherine the Great reportedly buried her beloved greyhounds. If you walk around the pond's right side, you'll come to the pretty blue-and-white Marble Bridge, which connects the Great Pond with a series of other ponds and small canals. At this end, you can rent rowboats. Farther along, up to the right, you come to the "Ruined Tower." It's neither authentic nor ancient, having been built in the late 18th century merely to enhance the romantic ambience of these grounds.

Outside the park, just north of the Catherine Palace, stands yet another palace, the **Alexander Palace** (Alexandrovsky Dvorets), a present from Catherine to her favorite grandson, the future Tsar Alexander I, on the occasion of his marriage. Built by Giacomo Quarenghi between 1792 and 1796, the serene and restrained classical structure was the favorite residence of Russia's last tsar, Nicholas II. The left wing of the building is open to the public and hosts topical exhibits. Most of the interior was lost, with the notable exception of Nicholas's cabinet, a fine example of art nouveau furniture and design. A visit is most interesting in the context of the ongoing rehabilitation of Nicholas II's reputation in Russia.

Built in 1791 and originally intended for the education of Catherine the Great's grandchildren, the **Lyceum** later became a school for the nobility. Its most famous student, enrolled the first year it opened, was the beloved poet Alexander Pushkin. The building now serves as a museum; the classroom, library, and Pushkin's bedroom have been restored to their appearance at the time he studied here. In the school's garden is a statue of the poet as a young man, seated on a bench, presumably deep in creative meditation. The building is attached to the Catherine Palace. ⊠ 7 ul. Sadovaya ☎ 812/465–2024 or 812/466–6669 ⬛ Park 100R, group tour 600R; Catherine Palace 500R; Alexander Palace 260R; Lyceum 200R ☉ Park and palaces Wed.–Mon. 10–5; Catherine Palace closed last Mon. of month; Alexander Palace closed last Wed. of month.

Where to Eat

$$–$$$$ ✕ **Staraya Bashnya.** Tucked away in a clutch of buildings known as the Fyodorovsky Gorodok (a short walk north of Alexander Palace) is the Old Tower, a tiny restaurant that serves Russian and European cuisine. The European dishes are perhaps more expensive than they should be, so stick to Russian items such as the *pelmeni* (tender meat dumplings) with garlic or beef Stroganoff. The portions are very generous. ⊠ 14 Akademichesky per. ☎ 812/466–6698 ⚃ Reservations required ☰ MC, V.

$–$$$$ ✕ **Admiralteistvo.** This charming land-friendly little restaurant is on the second floor of an old redbrick pavilion just across the lake from the Catherine Palace. Its nostalgic, retro-style interiors are furnished with antique furniture and a number of partially enclosed seating areas give you some isolation for a private dinner. The restaurant specializes in European and excellent Russian cuisine. For a genuine Russian delight, go for fish such as baked sturgeon or sterlet, which was very popular at the tsars' tables. The restaurant also serves Italian pastas and has a sushi bar run by a Korean. It indeed offers not only the widest variety of dishes, but also a wide range of prices. ⊠ 7 Sadovaya ul., in Yekaterininsky Park ☎ 812/465–3549 ☰ DC, MC, V.

Pavlovsk

Павловск

★ ❺ *30 km (19 mi) south of St. Petersburg's city center, a 5-min train jour-*
ney from Tsarskoye Selo, 6 km (4 mi) south of Pushkin.

The estate grounds of Pavlovsk had always been the royal hunting grounds, but in 1777 Catherine the Great awarded them to her son Paul I (Pavlovsk comes from "Pavel," the Russian for Paul) upon the birth of his first son, the future tsar Alexander I. Construction of the first wooden buildings started immediately, and in 1782 Catherine's Scottish architect Charles Cameron began work on the Great Palace and the landscaped park. In contrast to the dramatically baroque palaces of Pushkin and Peterhof, Pavlovsk is a tribute to the reserved beauty of classicism. Paul's intense dislike of his mother apparently manifested itself in determinedly doing exactly what she would *not*—with, most visitors agree, gratifying results. The place is popular with St. Petersburg residents, who come to stroll through its beautiful 1,500-acre park, full of woods, ponds, tree-lined alleys, and pavilions.

Begin a tour of Pavlovsk with the golden yellow **Great Palace** (Bolshoi Dvorets), which stands on a high bluff overlooking the river and dominates the surrounding park. (If you walk the grandious park first, you risk being too tired or too late for touring the palace, whose rooms begin closing after 4 PM.) Built between 1782 and 1786 as the summer residence of Paul and his wife, Maria Fyodorovna, the stone palace was designed in imitation of a Roman villa. The architect Vincenzo Brenna enlarged the palace between 1796 and 1799 with the addition of a second story to the galleries and side pavilions. Despite a devastating fire in 1803 and further reconstruction by Andrei Voronikhin in the early 19th century, Cameron's basic design survives. The building is crowned with a green dome supported by 64 small white columns. Its facade is currently under renovation. In front of the palace stands a statue of the snub-nosed Paul I, a copy of the statue at Gatchina, Paul's other summer residence.

Many rooms are open for viewing, and you may start on either the first or the second floor. The splendid interiors, with their parquet floors, marble pillars, and gilt ceilings, were created by some of Russia's most outstanding architects. Besides Cameron, Brenna, and Voronikhin, the roll call includes Quarenghi, who designed the interiors of five rooms on the first floor, and Carlo Rossi, who was responsible for the library, built in 1824. The state apartments on the first floor include the pink-and-blue **Ballroom**; the formal **Dining Hall,** where the full dinner service for special occasions is set out; and the lovely **Corner Room,** with walls of lilac marble and doors of Karelian birch. On the first floor, on the way from the central part of the palace to the southern section, are the **Dowager Empress Rooms** (Komnaty Vdovstvuyuschei Imperatritsy), six rooms that were designed for Maria Fyodorovna after the death of Paul I. The most impressive of these is the Small Lamp Study (Kabinet Fonarik), a light-green room that overlooks Tsar's Little Garden. The empress's library and other belongings are on display here.

Among the lavishly decorated state rooms on the second floor is the famous **Greek Hall,** with a layout like that of an ancient temple. Its rich green Corinthian columns stand out against the white of the faux-marble walls. The hall, which also served as a small ballroom, linked the state chambers of Paul I to those of his wife, Maria. The last room on his side, leading to the Greek Hall, was the **Hall of War.** Maria's **Hall of Peace,** was designed to correspond to it. The gilt stucco wall moldings of her suite are decorated with flowers, baskets of fruit, musical instruments, and other symbols of peace. Beyond Maria's apartments is the light-filled **Picture Gallery,** with floor-length windows and an eclectic collection of paintings. From the gallery, via a small, pink, marble waiting room, you reach the palace's largest chamber, **Throne Hall.** It once held the throne of Paul I, which was removed for a victory party after Napoléon's defeat and somehow never returned.

Like the palace, the design of the park was shared by the leading architects of the day—Brenna, Cameron, Voronikhin, and Rossi. The park differs greatly from park designs of other Imperial palaces, where the strict rules of geometrical design were followed; at Pavlovsk nature was left unfettered, with simple beauty the splendid result.

The combined length of the park's paths and lanes is said to equal the distance between St. Petersburg and Moscow (656 km [407 mi]). Because you can't possibly cover the entire territory in one day anyway, you might just want to follow your whim. If you walk down the slope just behind the palace to the **Tsar's Little Garden** (Sobstvenny Sadik), you can see the Three Graces Pavilion, created by Cameron. The 16-columned pavilion encloses a statue of Joy, Flowering, and Brilliance. Directly behind the palace, a stone staircase, decorated with lions, will take you to the Slavyanka Canal. On the canal's other side, down to the left, is the graceful **Apollo Colonnade,** built in 1783, whose air of ruin was not entirely human-made: it was struck by lightning in 1817 and never restored. If you bear right at the end of the stairs, you come to the **Temple of Friendship,** meant to betoken the friendship between Empress Maria and her mother-in-law, Catherine the Great. Beyond it is a monument from Maria to her own parents; the center urn's medallion bears their likenesses. Of the other noteworthy pavilions and memorials dotting the park, the farthest one up the bank is the **Mausoleum of Paul I,** set apart on a remote and overgrown hillside toward the center of the park. Maria had the mausoleum built for her husband after he was murdered in a palace coup. Paul was never interred here, however, and though Maria is portrayed as inconsolable in a statue here, historical evidence indicates that she was well aware of the plot to kill her husband. ⊠ *20 ul. Revolutsii* ☎ *812/470–2156* ⊕ *www.pavlovsk.org* ✉ *Palace and grounds 370R; park 60R; additional 30R for Dowager Empress Rooms; Sobstvennyi Sadik 60R* ۞ *Sat.–Thurs. 10–5* ۞ *Closed 1st Mon. of month.*

Where to Eat

★ **$–$$$$** ✕ **Podvoriye.** Past guests at this unmissable wooden restaurant built in the *terem* (folk- or fairy-tale) style include the presidents of France and Russia. Inside a stuffed bear greets you with samplings of vodka. Traditional Russian fare includes pickled garlic and mushrooms, excellent sturgeon dishes, and cutlets of wild boar, bear, or elk. Among the less expensive traditional main courses are *pelmeny* (meat dumplings) and *golubtsy* (a mixture of rice and meat wrapped in cabbage or grape leaves). An expensive course of a frying pan filled with homemade sausage, pork and beef, or with sturgeon and trout, can be enough for three or even four people. Drinks to try are *kvas* (a sweet, lightly fermented drink made from bread or grains) and *mors* (a sour-sweet cranberry juice). It's best to make a reservation. ⊠ *16 Filtrovskoye shosse* ☎ *812/465–1399* ⊟ *AE, DC, MC, V.*

$$ ✕ **Great Column Hall.** The former servants' quarters inside Pavlovsk house this Russian restaurant with both cafeteria-style and full-menu service. The European offerings include different kinds of salads and well-prepared trout and pike-perch. If you want to try Russian cuisine you can order traditional national dishes, such as pancakes with caviar, or fish or meat in aspic, by phone beforehand. You can also order picnic items here to eat on the palace's extensive grounds. Keep in mind that the restaurant closes by 6 PM. ⊠ *Pavlovsk Palace* ☎ *812/470–9809* ⊟ *MC, V.*

Gatchina

Гатчина

❻ *45 km (28 mi) southwest of St. Petersburg's city center.*

The main attractions of Gatchina, the most distant of St. Petersburg's palace suburbs, are an expansive park with a network of bridges for island-hopping, and a grim-looking palace—actually more like a feudal English castle—that has unfortunately been allowed to deteriorate over the years. Perhaps because Gatchina doesn't hold the Imperial splendor that's available in excess at the other suburbs, it's usually not included in prearranged excursions, and thus is rarely visited by foreign tourists. Because it does offer a chance to escape from the crowds for a while, however, it's worth a visit. Keep in mind that fine dining is not widely available, so be sure to bring along a lunch that you can enjoy on the shores of the Silver Lake.

The name Gatchina itself is of questionable origin. One popular suggestion is that it comes from the Russian expression *gat chinit,* meaning "to repair the road." Others believe it comes from the German phrase *hat schöne,* meaning "it is beautiful." In its current state, both expressions could apply. Gatchina, which is the name of both the city and the park-palace complex, dates to the 15th century, when it was a small Russian village. In 1712, following the final conquest of the area by Russia, Peter I gave Gatchina to his sister, the tsarevna Natalya Alexeyevna. The land changed hands several times over the years, eventually ending up as a possession of Catherine the Great. She gave it to one of her favorites, Count Grigory Orlov, in 1765. Orlov maintained possession of the complex until 1783. It was during this period that the architect Antonio Rinaldi designed and built the palace and laid out the park, which was eventually decorated with obelisks and monuments in honor of the Orlovs.

In 1783 Orlov died, and Gatchina passed to Catherine's son Paul I and his wife. While Gatchina was in Paul's possession, the architect Vincenzo Brenna produced plans for the construction of the Eagle and Venus pavilions, the Birch House, and the Constable Column, which are scattered throughout the park. But at various times, Gatchina Palace was a residence of Nicholas I, Alexander II, and Alexander III, and it bears witness to many important historic events, as well as the political and personal secrets of the Romanov dynasty.

In contrast to the pastel colors and flashiness of the palaces of Pushkin and Peterhof, Gatchina Palace has the austere look of a military institution, with a restrained limestone facade and a blocklike structure almost completely bereft of ornamentation. The palace, which is built on a ridge, is also surrounded by a deep moat, which emphasizes the castle design of the facade. Its northern side faces a green forest tract stretching for some distance. The southern facade opens up to the main parade grounds, which were once used for military displays. Along the outer edge of the parade grounds runs a short bastion with parapets cut out with embrasures for firing weapons. The palace is also accentuated by two five-sided, five-story towers, the Clock Tower, and the Signal Tower.

Construction on the palace was carried out in three main phases. The first period began in 1766 under the guidance of Rinaldi. He built the three-story central part of the palace, as well as the service wings and the inner courtyards, known as the Kitchen Block and the Stable Block (later called the Arsenal Block). The second stage of construction began in 1783, when Brenna made the side blocks level with the galleries and installed cannons, adding to the palace's image as a feudal castle. Brenna also integrated new palatial halls, thus turning Rinaldi's chamberlike interiors into ceremonial rooms.

The third stage took place under the watchful eye of Nicholas I. He hired the architect Roman Kuzmin to reconstruct both side blocks between 1845 and 1856. He also built a new chapel, and living rooms were arranged in the Arsenal Block. Kuzmin's work also eventually led to the restoration of the 18th-century rooms, the construction of a new main staircase in the central section, and the reshaping of the bastion wall in front of the palace.

The palace was badly damaged during World War II, and restoration is still in progress (though you can still visit the palace). Fortunately, a collection of watercolors by the artists Luigi Premazzi and Edward Hau survived. Painted during the 1870s, these watercolors are accurate depictions of the state- and private-room interiors, and have provided the information necessary for workers to restore the palace to its prewar condition. Within the palace you can see some partially restored rooms and exhibits of 19th-century arms and clothing.

A 10-minute walk from Gatchina Palace will bring you to Black Lake and the white **Prioratsky Palace,** a unique construction made of rammed earth. It was built at the end of the 18th century by architect Nikolai Lvov, the first person in Russia to introduce cheap, fireproof, rammed-earth construction. The palace was meant for the great French prior Prince Conde (though he never lived here). The southern part of the palace resembles a Gothic chapel, but the rest resembles a fortification. On the first floor are exposed samples of the rammed earth; the second floor has displays on the palace's construction.

After touring the palaces, you may want to consider heading down to the lakes for a little relaxation. Rowboats and catamarans are available at a cost of 50R for 30 minutes—just look for the bare-chested, tattooed men standing along the lake (you may also be asked to provide your passport as a deposit, just to make sure you actually return the boat instead of fleeing to Finland). The Gatchina park is laid out around a series of lakes occupying about one-third of its entire area. One of the largest sections of the park is called the **English Landscape Gardens** (Angliiskiye Sady), built around the White and Silver lakes. On a clear day the mirrorlike water reflects the palace facade and pavilions. The park is dotted with little bridges, gates, and pavilions, among which several are dedicated to the state and military deeds of the Orlov brothers. These include the Eagle (Orliny) Pavilion, built in 1792 on the shores of the Long Island, and the so-called Chesma Column, built by Rinaldi in honor of the Orlovs' military deeds. Keep in mind that the signs in the park are in Russian and point to eventual destinations, such as Berlin, but if you keep to the lakeshore at all times, you shouldn't have any trouble. ⊠ *1 Krasnoarmeisky Pr.* ☎ *81371/13492 Gatchina Palace, 81371/76467 Prioratsky Palace* 🖃 *Gatchina Palace and park 360R, Prioratsky Palace 100R* ☺ *Park, Gatchina Palace, and Prioratsky Palace Tues.–Sun. 10–5* ☺ *Closed 1st Tues. of month.*

KRONSHTADT & VALAAM

Two islands, one to the west and one to the northeast of St. Petersburg, set a different tone than the palace suburbs but are still of historic significance. The town of Kronshtadt, on Kotlin Island, has a long and proud naval tradition, while the monasteries of Valaam Archipelago hark back to the earliest days of Christianity, more than a millennium ago, in the land of Rus'.

Kronshtadt

Кронштадт

❼ *30 km (19 mi) west of St. Petersburg.*

Kronshtadt, on Kotlin Island to the west of St. Petersburg, was built between 1703 and 1704 by Peter the Great as a base from which to defend St. Petersburg or to attack the long-standing enemy of the Russian Empire, the Swedish navy. For a long time it was the only military harbor of the empire, which is why it was off-limits to all but its permanent residents; visitors were stopped at special checkpoints as late as 1996. Today anyone can visit, either by boarding Bus 510 or the hydrofoil *Meteor* (both depart from St. Petersburg), or by taking an excursion from one of the agencies on St. Petersburg's Nevsky prospekt (between Gostinny Dvor and the old City Duma). If you take the bus you'll be traveling on a huge dike erected in 1979 where the Finnish border was until 1939.

In the first half of the 20th century the Kronshtadt "Commune" aimed to break the monopoly of the Communist Party and to give back to peasants the right to use their land freely; the revolt lasted two weeks, seriously jeopardizing Lenin's hold on power, but was finally bloodily repressed. Tellingly, the streets of Kronshtadt are still named after Marx and Lenin, and the town still seems to live in the past, as if to hold on to the mighty era of the Soviet military machine. Despite being in dire condition, Kronshtadt is proud of its naval pedigree. Its significance was gradually diminished by the development of St. Petersburg throughout the 19th century, but there are still military and scientific vessels using its harbors. Off the shore of Kotlin Island are several forts that were constructed during the Crimean War (1853–56). The most interesting of these is **Fort Aleksandr,** which in the 19th century was turned into a laboratory to research the bubonic plague. These days it's a favorite stop-off point for yachters sailing either from Kotlin Island or St. Petersburg; it also hosts the occasional evening dance in summer. One of Kronshtadt's highlights is its **Church of Seamen** (Morskoi Sobor), built between 1902 and 1913 by Vassili Kosyakov—the finest example of neo-Byzantine architecture in Russia. Other sights include the Gostinny Dvor (one of Kronshtadt's first buildings and now a department store in need of renovation), the Summer Garden, and the Menshikov Palace, now a club for the island's sailors.

Valaam Archipelago
Валаамский Архипелаг

★ ❽ *170 km (105 mi) north of St. Petersburg, east along the Neva River, and up into Lake Ladoga.*

An overnight trip by boat from St. Petersburg delivers you out of the bustle of the city and into the Republic of Karelia. The republic is one of the 88 federal subjects of the Russian Federation and though it's language is Russian, it has close cultural ties to its neighbor, Finland. One of its most tranquil and beautiful settings is Valaam, a cluster of island jewels in the northwestern part of Lake Ladoga, Europe's largest freshwater lake, which is completely frozen over in winter. The southern part of the lake borders Russia. The archipelago consists of Valaam Island and about 50 other isles.

Valaam Island is the site of an ancient monastery said to have been started by Saints Sergey and German, missionaries who came to the region (probably from Greece) some time in the second half of the 10th century—perhaps even before the "official" conversion of the land of the Rus' to Christianity. The next 1,000 years are a sorry story of Valaam and its monks battling to survive a regular series of catastrophes—including plague, fire, invasion, and pillage—only to bounce back and build (and rebuild) Valaam's religious buildings and way of life. In 1611 the monastery was attacked and razed by the Swedes; it languished for a century until Peter the Great ordered it rebuilt in 1715. Valaam was also to pass into the hands of Finland on more than one occasion, the longest period being from the end of World War I to 1940. After World War II, during which the islands were evacuated and then occupied by Finnish and German troops, the monasteries fell into almost total disrepair, and it was only in 1989 that monks returned to Valaam.

A guided tour of Valaam takes about six hours, although with a break for lunch this is not at all as arduous as it might sound. You can also buy a map of the island (easy to find at any of the many tourist shops here) and strike out on your own. But the tour guides, most of whom live on the island throughout the summer, have an enormous amount of interesting information to impart about Valaam (most, however, don't speak English). The guides also know where the best shady spots to sit and relax are, and while you catch your breath they will tell you everything about Valaam's history, prehistory, wildlife, geology and geography, religious life, and gradual renaissance as a monastic center. The island's beauty has also inspired the work of many Russian and foreign artists, composers, and writers; the second movement of Tchaikovsky's First Symphony is said to be a musical portrait of the island, and you will hear it played over loudspeakers as your ferry departs.

Most tours to Valaam spend the first half day on a small selection of the *skity,* a monastery in seclusion. Only four *skity* are currently used as places of worship, and some of them are in the archipelago's most remote areas. Closest to where the ferries dock is the **Voskresensky (Resurrection) Monastery,** consecrated in 1906. In the upper church, you can hear a performance of Russian liturgical music (for an extra 20R) performed by a rather good male quartet. Another monastery within easy walking distance is the **Getsemanskii (Gethsemene) monastyr** consisting of a wooden chapel and church built in a typically Russian style, and monastic cells, which are inaccessible to the public. The squat construction next door is a hostel for pilgrims, some of whom you may see draped in long robes on your walk.

After lunch, buy a ticket (100R for a round-trip ticket) for the ferry that will take you to the 14th-century **Spaso-Preobrazhensky Valaamskii (Transfiguration of the Savior) Monastyr,** the heart of the island's religious life. You can walk the 6 km (4 mi) from the harbor in either direction, but if you choose to walk back from the monastery, make sure you give yourself enough time to catch the ferry back to St. Petersburg (about 1¼ hours should be enough time to walk back). As you reach the monastery, you'll see tourist stands and beer kiosks—something about which the monks themselves have mixed feelings. The walk up the hill past the bric-a-brac, however, is well worth it, as you reach the splendid Valaamskii Monastyr cathedral (under ongoing restoration). The cathedral's lower floor is the **Church of St. Sergius and St. German,** finished in 1892, and is in the best condition. It's a living place of worship, as you'll see from the reverence of visitors before the large icon depicting Sergey and German kneeling before Christ. The upper **Church of the Transfiguration of the Savior,** consecrated in 1896, is still in a terrible state, although the cavernous interior, crumbling iconostasis, and remaining frescoes are still impressive in their own right.

Although drinking and smoking are freely permitted in most areas of the island, you'll be asked to refrain while on the territory of the monasteries. Visitors are also required to observe the dress code on the grounds of the cathedral: women must wear a long skirt and cover their heads (scarves and inelegant black aprons are provided at the entrance for those who need appropriate garb), and men must leave their heads uncovered and wear long trousers—shorts are strictly forbidden.

You can only visit Valaam from June through September, when the waterway along the Neva River and Lake Ladoga is open. Note that the level of luxury on the 10-hour ferry journey to Valaam is not high. Nevertheless, you'll be witnessing a real throwback to the Soviet era. The rooms are clean, if spartan, and are perfectly manageable for two nights' sleep. In any case, you can spend much of the journey sitting on the sundeck; watch the industrial south of St. Petersburg give way to the rural setting of the lower Neva, before the ancient fort of Petrakrepost ghosts past on your right as the ferry sails into Lake Ladoga. The return journey is just as magical, as the golden spires and cupolas of the monasteries poke out of the tree line and glint in the setting sun.

One crucial piece of advice, however, is to take some food with you. Although three meals are included in the price of most tours, they are best avoided. Instead, pack some sandwiches, fresh fruit, and perhaps some wine. You might want to poke your head into the incredibly Soviet bar on the island, but you are unlikely to want to linger. ⊕ *www.valaam.ru.*

SUMMER PALACES & HISTORIC ISLANDS A TO Z

To research prices, get advice from other travelers, and book travel arrangements, visit www.fodors.com.

BOAT TRAVEL

June–September, the *Meteor* hydrofoil is the best way of getting from St. Petersburg to Peterhof, and it's also one of the options for traveling to Kronshtadt.

For Kronshtadt and Lomonosov, boats depart from St. Petersburg's naberezhnaya Makarova (Makarova Embankment), near the Tuchkov bridge joining the Petrograd Side with Vasilievsky Island. For Peterhof, hydrofoils depart from the pier just outside the State Hermitage Museum in summer; they leave approximately every 30–40 minutes, and the journey time is about a half hour. June–September, ferries to the Valaam Archipelago leave from 195 prospekt Obukhovskoy Oborony, not far from Proletarskaya metro station in the south of St. Petersburg. The journey takes around 10 hours.

BUS TRAVEL

Though not as convenient and comfortable as train travel, travel by bus from St. Petersburg can be a good way to go as long as it's not the height of summer, when buses can be exceedingly stuffy. Buses or minibuses run on direct routes to almost all of the suburbs, as well as to Kronshtadt. Tour companies also operate their own, rather scruffy, coaches to Kronshtadt.

Although all the palaces are theoretically within walking distance from their respective train stations, there are often buses linking the two. Buses 1, 5, 7, 431, or 525 will take you to Gatchina from the station for 10R. You can also get to Gatchina Palace taking Buses 18 or 100 from the city's Moskovsky metro station for 30R. For Pavlovsk, should you for some reason not want to walk from the station through the lovely park to the palace, Buses 370 or 383 will take you directly there for 10R.

Minibuses (called *marshrutka*) from the city to the suburbs are more convenient than by commuter trains (called elektrichka) because they usually take you directly to the sights. Minibuses 299, 286, and 545 will take you from St. Petersburg's Moskovskaya metro station to Pavlovsk for 30R. The same buses can take you to Pushkin for 30R. Bus 287 leaves Moskovskaya for Pushkin as well. Yellow double-decker buses marked "Peterhof" and minibuses 340 and 404 leave from outside St. Petersburg's Baltic Station for Peterhof, charging 40R. From Avtovo metro station you get to Peterhof train station by minibuses 424, 420, 300, 224 (for 30R); then take buses 350, 351, 351a, 352, 353, 354, or 356 to the palace park for 10R. The ride lasts 10 minutes. Minibus 300 will take you to Lomonosov/Oranienbaum from Avtovo metro station and bus 340 from Baltiisky railway station (also metro station) for 30R.

To catch a bus to Kronshtadt, take the subway to St. Petersburg's Chernaya Rechka metro station; walk across ulitsa Savushkina to the embankment of the River Chernaya Rechka and catch Bus 405 or 406 for 30R to the very end. Buses leave every 3–5 minutes from 5:40 AM through 12 AM and take about an hour.

TAXIS

You'll usually have no trouble getting a taxi at a train or bus station in these towns. Most of the towns are small enough to be navigated easily on foot, but a taxi is an alternative to short bus or train trips (e.g., from Pushkin to Pavlovsk). In an emergency, it's also possible to take a taxi all the way back to St. Petersburg from most of these towns (about $20–$25), if you speak Russian.

TOURS

There are several local tour groups congregated on St. Petersburg's Nevsky prospekt, and although they operate out of somewhat flea-bitten kiosks, they are good enough to get you to where you want to go in the suburbs. Usually, it's enough simply to step up and buy a ticket, the price of which includes coach seating and a guided tour, but you can also book in advance by visiting or phoning the tour-company offices.

Two of the most reliable excursion companies are Mir and Davranov-Travel. Mir, which specializes in serving foreign tourists, offers excursions to the whole list of St. Petersburg suburbs. For groups of less than six people Mir organizes a mini-van (for more than six people, a microbus) that will take you to a suburb you choose. For instance, a mini-van trip to Peterhof, which includes excursion to the palace and park, costs $76 per person; an excursion to Lomonosov, $64; Kronshtadt, $69; Gatchina, $56; Pushkin, $64; and Pavlovsk, $58. You can also make a deal if ordering a combined trip to Pushkin and Pavlovsk for $89. The company can also take you to Valaam and even to the old Russian town of Novgorod, known for its fascinating Kremlin, and located 200 km from St. Petersburg (for $144). Trips by a micro-bus cost slightly less. Everything can be organized by phone. Davranov Travel also offers excursions to all suburbs. You can buy tickets to their travel bus at their kiosk at the corner of Nevsky Prospect and ulitsa Sadovaya (it's outside Gostinni Dvor metro station). Usually they take you on the bus with Russian tourists but provide you with a guide who speaks your language. It's less expensive if you're not alone. Thus, an excursion to Peterhof for an individual tourist costs $73, for four people $47 per person. Tickets to other suburbs cost approximately the same. Buses of Davranov Travel leave four times a day to each suburb from 10 AM through 2 PM. Eklektika Gid has been a leading tour outfitter for years. Today it offers micro-bus excursions for foreign tourists to Peterhof ($63) at 2 PM on Tuesday, Wednesday, Friday, and Monday; and Pushkin ($63) also at 2 PM on Monday, Thursday, and Saturday. You can buy tickets to their excursions at their kiosk outside Gostinni Dvor metro station and take the excursion bus from that very location, too.

🛈 **Mir** ☒ Office 1, 11 Nevsky prospekt, City Center ☎ 812/325-7122 or 812/380-68-67. **Davranov-Travel** ☒ 17 Italianskaya ul., City Center ☎ 812/571-8694 or 812/312-4662. **Eklektika Gid** ☒ 1 Ligovsky pr., No. 310, City Center ☎ 812/710-5529.

TRAIN TRAVEL

Do not be discouraged by the chaos of St. Petersburg's train stations, for traveling by elektrichka is not only to a certain extent a convenient way to get to the suburbs, it also provides a slice of authentic Russian life all on its own. Given the astonishingly low fares, the less than 45-minute journey time to most suburbs, and infrequent delays, train travel is well worth the minor discomforts of the press of humanity and hard wooden seats.

Check with a local travel agent or at the station for schedules. With the exception of traveling by elektrichka at busy times (Friday evenings and weekends), you should not have trouble getting a ticket on the same day you wish to travel. For the most part, ticket booths are easy to find; if you don't speak Russian, just say the name of your destination and hold up as many fingers as there are passengers. Bear in mind that there's a lull in departures between 10 AM and noon.

The elektrichka to Gatchina leaves from Baltic Station (42R); the trip lasts around 45 minutes. For Lomonosov, catch the elektrichka from Baltic Station to Oranienbaum-I (not II), approximately one hour from St. Petersburg (35R). For Pavlovsk (28R) and Pushkin (21R), take the elektrichka from Vitebsk Station to Detskoye Selo; the trip to Pavlovsk lasts approximately 30 minutes, and it's another five minutes to Pushkin (from which you'll have to walk 15–20 minutes to the palace). For Peterhof, take the elektrichka from Baltic Station to Novy Peterhof (28R) station, approximately 40 minutes from St. Petersburg; from the station take one of many buses (numbers 350, 351, 351a, 352, 353, 354, or 356) to the palace.

VISITOR INFORMATION

Any questions about the suburbs should be directed to officials at St. Petersburg's City Tourism Information Center (where operators are very helpful and speak English, French, and German) or private travel agencies and guided-tour companies. St. Petersburg's City Tourism Information Center also has an information kiosk at Palace Square.

🛈 **City Tourist Information Center** ☒ 14/52 ul. Sadovaya, at Nevsky Prospect and ul. Sadovaya, City Center ☎🖨 812/310-2822 Ⓜ Nevsky Prospekt.

UNDERSTANDING MOSCOW & ST. PETERSBURG

RUSSIA AT A GLANCE

ENGLISH-RUSSIAN VOCABULARY

RUSSIA AT A GLANCE

Understanding Russia

Type of government: Federation
Capital: Moscow
Administrative divisions: 89 administrative regions, broken down into 49 *oblastey* (districts), 21 *respubliky* (republics), 10 *avtonomnykh okrugov* (autonomous regions), 6 *krayev* (regions), 2 *goroda* (federal cities), 1 autonomous region
Independence: August 24, 1991 (following the collapse of the Soviet Union)

I cannot forecast to you the action of Russia. It is a riddle wrapped in a mystery inside an enigma.
— Winston Churchill, 1939

Constitution: December 12, 1993
Legal system: Based on civil law, with judicial review of legislative acts
Legislature: Bicameral parliament: Duma (lower house) and Federation Council (upper house)
Population: 143,420,309

Fertility rate: 1.27 children per woman
Language: Russian is the official state language; other languages are spoken by limited numbers of ethnic minorities, including Bashkir, Tatar, Yevnik, Chuvash, Buryat, and numerous languages in the Caucuses.
Ethnic groups: Russian 81.5%, Tatar 3.8%, Ukrainian 3%, Chuvash 1.2%, Bashkir 0.9%, Belarusian 0.8%, Moldavian 0.7%, other 8.1%
Life expectancy: Female 74, male 61
Literacy: Total population 99.7%; male 99.7%, female 99.5%
Religion: Russian Orthodox, Muslim, Other (Jewish, Buddhism, Shamanism, various other Christian sects)
Inventions: Ice slide (precursor to the roller coaster, 17th century), periodic table (invented by Dmitry Mendeleev, 1869), Kalashnikov Assault Rifle (AK-47; invented by Mikhail Kalashnikov, 1947), magnetohydrodynamic power generator (1972)

Economy

The Soviet Union is a long-forgotten memory for Russia's capitalists as the country's economy continues to surge ahead, despite the slowdown from the 1998 financial crisis. The economy is largely dependent on commodities exports—mostly oil.

To believe that Russia has got rid of the evils of capitalism takes a special kind of mind. It is the same kind of mind that believes that a Holy Roller has got rid of sin.
— Henry Louis Mencken, mid-20th century

Annual growth: 5.9%
Inflation: 12.9%
Unemployment: 7.6%

Per capita income: $9,700
GDP: $1.535 trillion
Services: 59.6%
Agriculture: 5.8%
Industry: 34.6%
Work force: 74.22 million; agriculture 10.3%, industry 21.4%, services 68.3%
Currency: Ruble
Exchange rate: 28 rubles per U.S. dollar
Major industries: Petroleum, natural gas, coal, chemicals, steel, mining, lumber, transportation equipment (aircraft, ships, railways), communications equipment, medical and scientific instruments, consumer goods, textiles
Agricultural products: Wheat, potatoes, livestock, sugar beets
Exports: $245 billion

Major export products: Crude oil and refined oil products, natural gas, wood and wood products, metals, chemicals, military equipment
Export partners: Netherlands 9.1%, Germany 8%, Ukraine 6.4%, Italy 6.2%, China 6%, United States 5%

Imports: $125 billion
Major import products: Machinery, medicine, meat, sugar, consumer goods, metal products
Import partners: Germany 15.3%, Ukraine 8.8%, China 6.9%, Japan 5.7%, Kazakstan 5%, United States 4.6%

Disputes

A guerilla conflict with militants in the Chechen Republic continues to dominate headlines, despite government claims that the situation is under control. Other unresolved conflicts include a dispute with Japan over the Kuril Islands south of Sakhalin in the Pacific Ocean. The biggest dispute between Russia and the European Union is over travel and visa regulations for Kaliningrad residents (Kaliningrad, formerly Konigsberg, was captured from Germany by the Soviet Union in World War II). A 1990 maritime boundary agreement between the United States and the Soviet Union regarding the Bering Sea has yet to be ratified by Russia.

A Russian is wise after the event.
— Russian proverb

Fast Facts

• Russia contains the greatest mineral reserves of any country in the world.

• The world's only freshwater seals live in Russia, at Lake Baikal in Siberia.

• Russia's population density is a mere eight people per square mile.

• More than 100 languages are spoken in Russia.

• In the Soviet Union, the richest 10% of the population earned only four times more than the poorest 10%. By the mid-1990s, the richest 10% earned as much as 15 times more than the poorest 10%.

• More than 20 million Russian civilians died as a result of World War II.

ENGLISH-RUSSIAN VOCABULARY

Although we have tried to be consistent about the spelling of Russian names in this book, we find the Russian authorities are not consistent about transliteration of the Cyrillic alphabet into our familiar Latin letters. We've tried to stick to internationally recognized U.S. and British systems of transliteration, but don't be surprised if you occasionally come across differences like Chekhov and Tchekov, Tolstoy and Tolstoi, Baykal, and Baikal, Tartar and Tatar, rouble and ruble—to say nothing of icon and ikon!

We give here some hints on the vital matter of reading Russian signs and on pronunciation, as well as a general English-Russian tourist vocabulary. Reading street names is probably the most important use for even a small knowledge of the Cyrillic alphabet. There are a few things you should know about Russian street names. Many Russian streets and squares are named after *people,* but the people's names may appear in different spellings—often they are made into adjectives. Suppose we have a street called Pushkin Street, after the poet. The word street, *ultisa* in Russian, is feminine (all Russian nouns have a gender; masculine nouns usually end in consonants, feminine nouns in "a," and neuter nouns in "o" or "e"). So you will see the street name as *Pushkinskaya ulitsa,* a feminine form of Pushkin. Pushkin Avenue would be *Pushkinsky prospekt* in Russian (the word for avenue is masculine). Pushkin Highway would be *Pushkin-skoye shosse* (shosse is neuter). Don't be worried if you see one of these signs when our guide tells you you are on *Pushkin* street, avenue, etc.—it's the same thing! As a general rule, once you have deciphered the first few letters, you will recognize the name—don't worry about the ending!

Another common way of naming streets is to say, for example, "Street of Pushkin," "Avenue of Tolstoy," etc.—*ultisa pushkina, prospekt Tol-stovo* and so on. Here again, the *name* is easy to spot—its ending is not a spelling mistake, just a genitive case form of Pushkin, Tolstoy, etc. If you do get lost, most passersby will understand if you ask for a street by its English name.

We owe a debt of gratitude to the Government Affairs Institute, Washington, D.C., for their permission to reproduce the Tables of the Russian Alphabet that follow.

THE RUSSIAN ALPHABET

А а	И и	С с	Ъ ъ
Б б	Й й	Т т	Ы ы
В в	К к	У у	Ь ь
Г г	Л л	Ф ф	Э э
Д д	М м	Х х	Ю ю
Е е	Н н	Ц ц	Я я
Ё ё	О о	Ч ч	
Ж ж	П п	Ш ш	
З з	Р р	Щ щ	

The Sound of Russian

English-Russian Vocabulary

The Russian Vowels

Russian Letter (Capital)	Russian Letter (Small)	Sound
А	а	ah
Я	я	yah
Э	э	eh
Е	е	yeh
Ы	ы	ih
И	и	i (ee)
О	о	oh
Ё	ё	yo
У	у	u (oo)
Ю	ю	yu

Category 3: Russian Consonants that Have No English Equivalents

Russian Letter (Capital)	Russian Letter (Small)	Sound
Ч	ч	ch
Х	х	kh
Ш	ш	sh
Щ	щ	shch
Ц	ц	ts
Ж	ж	zh
	ь	soft sign

Category 2: Russian Consonants that Look Different from Their English Equivalents

Russian Letter (Capital)	Russian Letter (Small)	English Letter
Д	д	d
Ф	ф	f
Г	г	g
Л	л	l
Н	н	n
П	п	p
Р	р	r
С	с	s
В	в	v
Й	й	y

Category 1: Russian Consonants that Look and Sound like English

Russian Letter (Capital)	Russian Letter (Small)	English Letter
Б	б	b
К	к	k
М	м	m
Т	т	t
З	з	z

EVERYDAY WORDS AND PHRASES

The most important phrase to know (one that may make it unnecessary to know any others) is: "Do you speak English?" — *Gavaree'te lee vy pa anglee'skee?* If the answer is "Nyet," then you may have recourse to the lists below:

Please	Пожалуйста	pazhah'lsta
Thank you	Спасибо	spasee'ba
Good	Хорошо	kharasho'
Bad	Плохо	plo'kha
I	Я	ya
You	Вы	vy
He	Он	on
She	Она	anah'
We	Мы	my
They	Они	anee'
Yes	Да	da
No	Нет	nyet
Perhaps	Может быть	mo'zhet byt
I do not understand	Я не понимаю	ya ne paneemah'yoo
Straight	Прямо	pryah'ma
Forward	Вперёд	fperyo't
Back	Назад	nazah't
To (on) the right	Направо	naprah'va
To (on) the left	Налево	nale'va
Hello!	Здравствуйте!	zdrah'stvooite!
Good morning!	Доброе утро!	do'braye oo'tra!
Good day (evening)!	Добрый день (вечер)!	do'bree den (ve'cher)!
Pleased to meet you!	Очень рад с вами познакомиться!	o'chen rat s vah'mee paznako'meetsa!
I am from USA (Britain)	Я приехал из США (Англии)	ya preeye'khal eez sshah' (ah'nglee ee)
I speak only English	Я говорю только по-английски	ya gavaryoo' to'lka pa anglee'skee
Do you speak English?	Говорите ли вы по-английски?	gavaree'te lee vy pa anglee'skee?
Be so kind as to show (explain, translate)	Будьте добры покажите (объясните, переведите)	boo'te dobry' pakazhee'te (abyasnee'te, perevedee'te)
Excuse my poor pronunciation	Извините моё плохое произношение	eezveenee'te mayo'plakho'ye praeeznashe'nye
I beg your pardon	Простите	prastee'te
I want to post a letter	Мне нужно отправить письмо	mne noo'zhna atprah'veet peesmo'
Postcard	Открытка	otkrytka

DAYS OF THE WEEK

Monday	Понедельник	panede'lneek
Tuesday	Вторник	fto'rneek
Wednesday	Среда	sredah'
Thursday	Четверг	chetve'rk

Friday	Пя́тница	pyah'tneetsa
Saturday	Суббо́та	soobo'ta
Sunday	Воскресе́нье	vaskrese'nye
Holiday, feast	Пра́здник	prah'zneek
Today	Сего́дня	sevo'dnya
Tomorrow	За́втра	zah'ftra
Yesterday	Вчера́	vcherah'

NUMBERS

How many?	Ско́лько?	sko'lka?
1	оди́н	adee'n
2	два	dva
3	три	tree
4	четы́ре	chety're
5	пять	pyat
6	шесть	shest
7	семь	sem
8	во́семь	vo'sem
9	де́вять	de'vyat
10	де́сять	de'syat
11	оди́ннадцать	adee'natsat
12	двена́дцать	dvenah'tsat
13	трина́дцать	treenah'tsat
14	четы́рнадцать	chety'rnatsat
15	пятна́дцать	pyatnah'tsat
16	шестна́дцать	shesnah'tsat
17	семна́дцать	semnah'tsat
18	восемна́дцать	vasemnah'tsat
19	девятна́дцать	devyatnah'tsat
20	два́дцать	dvah'tsat
30	три́дцать	tree'tsat
40	со́рок	so'rak
50	пятьдеся́т	pyadesyah't
60	шестьдеся́т	shezdesyah't
70	се́мьдесят	se'mdesyat
80	во́семьдесят	vo'semdesyat
90	девяно́сто	deveno'sta
100	сто	sto
1000	ты́сяча	ty'syacha

INFORMATION SIGNS

Toilet (Gentlemen) (Ladies)	Туале́т (М) (Ж)	tooale't
No smoking!	Не кури́ть!	ne kooree't!
Taxi rank	Стоя́нка такси́	stayah'nka taksee'
Entrance	Вход	fkhot
Exit	Вы́ход	vy'khat
No exit	Вы́хода нет	vy'khada net
Emergency exit	Запасно́й вы́ход	zapasnoi' vy'khat
Stop!	Стоп!	stop!

Drinks

cold water	холо́дной воды́	khalo'dnoi vady'
mineral water	минера́льной воды́	meenerah'lnoi vady'
grape, tomato juice	виногра́дного, тома́т- ного со́ка	veenagrah'dnava, tamah'tnava so'ka
whisky, vodka	ви́ски, во́дка	vee'skee, vod'ka
liqueur	ликёр	leekyo'r
lemonade	лимона́д	leemanah't
beer	пи́во	pee'va
tea, coffee, cocoa, milk	чай, ко́фе, кака́о, молоко́	chai, ko'fe, kakah'o, malako'
fruit juice	сок	so'kee

Meat

steak	бифште́кс	beefshte'ks
roast beef	ро́стбиф	ro'stbeef
veal chops	отбивну́ю теля́чью котле́ту	atbeevnoo'yoo telyah- chyoo katle'too
pork chops	свину́ю котле́ту	sveenoo'yoo katle'too
ham	ветчину́	vecheenoo'
sausage	колбасу́	kalbasoo'

Poultry

chicken	цыплёнка	tsyplyo'nka
hazel-grouse	ря́бчика	ryah'pcheeka
partridge	куропа́тку	koorapah'tkoo
duck	у́тку	oo'tkoo

Fish

soft caviar	зерни́стой икры́	zernee'stoi eekry'
pressed caviar	па́юсной икры́	pah'yoosnoi eekry'
salmon	лососи́ны	lasasee'ny
cold sturgeon	холо́дной осетри́ны	khalo'dnoi asetree'ny

Vegetables

green peas	зелёный горо́шек	zelyo'nee garo'shek
radishes	реди́ску	redee'skoo
tomatoes	помидо́ры	pameedo'ry
potatoes	карто́шка	karto'shka

Desserts

cake	пиро́жное	peero'zhnaye
fruit	фру́ктов	froo'ktaf
pears	груш	groosh
mandarines	мандари́нов	mandaree'naf
grapes	виногра́ду	veenagrah'doo
bananas	бана́нов	banah'naf

white and rye bread	бе́лый и чёрный хлеб	be'lee ee cho'rnee khlep
butter	ма́сло	mah'sla
cheese	сыр	syr
soft-boiled eggs	яйца всмя́тку	yai'tsa fsmyah'tkoo
hard-boiled eggs	яйца вкруту́ю	yai'tsa fkrootoo'voo
an omelette	омле́т	amle't

SHOPPING

Description

good	хоро́ший	kharo'shee
bad	плохо́й	plakhoi'
beautiful	краси́вый	krasee'vee
dear	дорого́й	daragoi'
cheap	дешёвый	desho'vee
old	ста́рый	sta'ree
new	но́вый	no'vee

Colors

white	бе́лый	be'lee
black	чёрный	chyo'rnee
red	кра́сный	krah'snee
pink	ро́зовый	ro'zavee
orange	ора́нжевый	arah'nzhevee
yellow	жёлтый	zho'ltee
brown	кори́чневый	karee'chnevee
green	зелёный	zelyo'nee
light blue	голубо́й	galooboi'
blue	си́ний	see'nee
violet	фиоле́товый	feeale'tavee
grey	се́рый	se'ree
golden	золото́й	zalatoi'
silver	сере́бряный	sere'bryance

In the shop

Baker's	Бу́лочная	boo'lachnaya
Confectioner's	Конди́терская	kandee'terskaya
Food Store	Гастроно́м	gastrano'm
Grocer's	Бакале́я	bakale'ya
Delivery Counter	Стол зака́зов	stol zakah'zaf
Wine and Spirits	Ви́на—коньяки́	vee'na — kanyakee'
Fruit and Vegetables	Овощи—фру́кты	o'vashshee — froo'kty

INDEX

A

Abramtsevo Estate Museum, 142–143
Addresses, F20
Admiralteistvo ✕, 286
Admiralty, 176
Air travel, F20–F24
    airports, F23–F24
    luggage, F42–F43
    Moscow, 121–123
    St. Petersburg, 259–261
Akvarium ✕, 224
Alexander Column, 165
Alexander Garden, 11
Alexander Nevsky Lavra, 193–195
Alexander Palace, 286
Alexander Pushkin Apartment Museum, 165, 168
Alexander Pushkin Drama Theater, 195
All Seasons 🏨, 234
Almazny Fond, 16
Ambassador 🏨, 231
Amber Room (Catherine Palace), 283, 285
American Bar and Grill ✕, 37, 77
Andrei Bely Apartment Museum, 48
Andrei Rublyov Museum of Ancient Russian Culture and Art, 68
Andronikov Monastery, 68–69
Anichkov Bridge, 196
Anichkov Palace, 196
Anna Akhmatova Literary Museum, 196–197
Annunciation Cathedral, 12
Apartment rentals, F38
    St. Petersburg, 234
Apollow Colonnade, 288
Aquarel ✕, 224
Ararat Park Hyatt 🏨, 88
Arbat, 46–51
Arbatskaya Ploschad (Moscow), 48
Archbishop's Chambers, 152
Arkhangelskoye, 117–118
Arkhangelskoye Estate Museum, 117–118
Arkhangelskoye Restaurant ✕, 118
Arkhangelsky Sobor, 14–15
Armeisky Magazin (store), 256
Armenian Church, 197

Armory Palace, 12–14
Arsenal, 14
Art galleries and museums
    Moscow, 19, 36, 44, 55–56, 59, 60, 61–63, 68, 97–98, 111–112, 119, 120–121
    Moscow environs and the Golden Ring, 141
    St. Petersburg, 170–173, 180, 182, 198–199, 208, 210, 211, 236–238
Art Park, 59
Arte 🏨, 94
Artillery Arsenal, 189
Artillery Museum, 187
Arts and crafts shops
    Moscow, 111–112
    St. Petersburg, 255–256
Assumption Cathedral, 14
Astoria 🏨, 228
ATMs, F40
Avraamiyev (Abraham) Monastery, 146–147
Avrora (ship), 187–188

B

Bagrationi ✕, 223
Balls, F12
Ballet, F12–F13
    Moscow, 99–100
    St. Petersburg, 240–243
Banyas (bathhouses), F11
    Moscow, 31, 105–106
    St. Petersburg, 252
Bars and lounges
    Moscow, 101–102
    St. Petersburg, 246–247
Bavarius ✕, 79
Bell Tower, 71
Beloye Solntse Pustyni ✕, 73
Bely Dom (White House), 40
Bessonnitsa ✕, 224
Birzha (Stock Exchange), 183–184
Bistro Garçon ✕, 223
Blagoveschchensky Sobor, 12
Bliny Domik ✕, 222
Blue Bridge, 183
Boat and ferry travel
    Moscow, 123
    Moscow environs and the Golden Ring, 155
    St. Petersburg, 261
    Summer Palaces and Historic Islands, 294
Boathouse, 190

Bochka ✕, 85
Bogolyubovo, 151
Bogoyavlensky Sobor, 25–27
Bolshaya Nikitskaya Ulitsa, 38–46
Bolshaya Ordinka ulitsa (Moscow), 58–59
Bolshoi Dvorets, 278
Bolshoi Kremlyovsky Dvorets, 16
Bolshoi Opera and Ballet Theater, 99
Bolshoi Theater, 26
Bookstores
    Moscow, 49
    St. Petersburg, 198
Boris Eifman Ballet Theater, 241
Borovitskaya Tower, 14
Bosco ✕, 73
Botanical Gardens, 188
Botik Museum, 144
Botik Tourist Complex ✕🏨, 145
Botny Domik, 190
Bowling, 106–107
Brioche ✕, 78
Brodyachaya Sobaka ✕, 209
Bronze Horseman statue, 177
Bulvar ✕, 73, 76
Bulvarnoye Koltso (Moscow), 44
Bus travel, F24
    Moscow, 123
    Moscow environs and the Golden Ring, 155
    St. Petersburg, 261
    Summer Palaces and Historic Islands, 294–295
Business hours, F24

C

Cabaret, 247–248
Café des Artistes ✕, 78
Café Kranzier ✕, 54
Cafe Margarita ✕, 80
Café Pushkin ✕, 79–80
Cameras and photography, F24–F25
Cameron Gallery, 285–286
"Candle of Yaroslavl," 148–149
Canvas ✕, 220–221
Car travel and rental, F25–F27
    Moscow, 123–124

Moscow environs and the
Golden Ring, 155–156
St. Petersburg, 262
Caravan ✕, 220
Carré Blanc ✕, 84
Casa Leto ⬚, 229
Casinos
Moscow, 102–103
St. Petersburg, 248
Cathedral of Christ Our Savior,
54
Cathedral of Our Lady of
Kazan, 27
Cathedral of St. Dmitri, 150
Cathedral of Sts. Peter and
Paul, 189
Cathedral of the Archangel,
14–15
Cathedral of the Assumption
(Rostov), 145–146
Cathedral of the Assumption
(Sergiev-Posad), 140
Cathedral of the Assumption
(Vladimir), 150, 151
Cathedral of the Deposition of
the Virgin's Robe, 15–16
Cathedral of the Epiphany,
26–27
Cathedral of the Holy Trinity,
141
Cathedral of the Resurrection,
203
Cathedral of the Sign, 27
Cathedral of the
Transfiguration, 144
Cathedral of the Twelve
Apostles, 15
Catherine Monument, 195
Catherine Palace, 283,
284–286
CDL ✕, 82
CDL: Central House of Writers,
40
Cemeteries
Moscow, 64–66
St. Petersburg, 194, 195, 202
Central Armed Forces Museum,
34
Central House of Artists, 59
Central Telegraph, 33–34
Chaliapin House Museum, 40,
42
Chamber of Art, 176–177
Chapel-at-the-Well, 140–141
Che ✕, 223
Chekhov House Museum, 42
Chesma Church and Chesma
Palace, 197–198

Children, attractions for
Moscow, 26, 46, 59–60
St. Petersburg, 168, 170, 185,
187–188, 210, 244–245
Children, traveling with,
F27–F28
Chinese Palace, 275
Church of All-Saints in
Kulishki, 27
Church of Elijah the Prophet,
148
Church of Grigory the
Theologian, 146
Church of John the Theologian,
146
Church of Our Lady of Kazan,
119
Church of St. Catherine, 198
Church of St. George on Pskov
Hill, 27
Church of St. John the Baptist,
149
Church of St. Martin the
Confessor, 69
Church of St. Maxim the
Blessed, 27
Church of St. Nicholas in
Pyzhi, 58
Church of St. Nicholas of the
Weavers, 59
Church of St. Sergius and St.
German, 293
Church of St. Simon the Stylite,
49
Church of Seamen, 292
Church of the Annunciation,
194
Church of the Archangel, 64
Church of the Ascension, 119
Church of the Assumption, 153
Church of the Epiphany, 148
Church of the Great Ascension,
42
Church of the Icon of the
Savior Not Made by Hands,
142–143
Church of the Intercession on
the Nerl, 151
Church of the Mother of God
Hodegetria, 146
Church of the Resurrection, 34
Church of the Resurrection in
Kadosh, 59
Church of the Savior on Spilled
Blood, 207
Church of the Transfiguration,
153
Church of the Transfiguration
of the Savior, 293

Church of the Transfiguration
on the Sands, 49
Church of the Trinity in
Nikitniki, 27–28
Church of the Virgin of All
Sorrows, 58–59
Churches
Moscow, 5, 12, 14–16, 20,
26–28, 29, 30, 34, 42, 49,
54, 58–59, 64, 66–67, 68–70,
71–72, 119
Moscow environs and the
Golden Ring, 140–141, 144,
145–146, 148–149, 150, 151,
152, 153
St. Petersburg, 168, 181–182,
189, 194, 197–198, 200,
201, 203, 207
Summer Palaces and Historic
Islands, 292, 293
Churches of St. Lazarus and
St. Antipy, 153
Circus Art Museum, 210
Circuses, 210
City Duma, 198
City Grill ✕, 37
City Realty ⬚, 234
Climate, F16
Clothing shops
Moscow, 112–114
St. Petersburg, 255
Clubs
Moscow, 103–104
St. Petersburg, 248–252
Coffee Bean ✕, 78, 84
Coffeehouse ✕, 78
Coffeemania ✕, 81
Colleges and universities
Moscow, 43
St. Petersburg, 178, 180, 182,
183
Comic-Trust (cabaret), 247
Commandant's House, 190
Commandant's Pier, 190
Communist Burial Ground,
195
Communist legacy, F13
Computers, traveling with,
F28
Concierges, F28
Conservatory ✕, 73
Consulates and embassies,
F34
Moscow, 124
St. Petersburg, 262
Consumer protection, F28
Convent of the Intercession,
153–154

Convents
Moscow, 30, 58, 63–67
Moscow environs and the Golden Ring, 153–154
St. Petersburg, 203
Cook Street (Moscow), 44
Corinthia Nevsky Palace Hotel ⚏ , 228
Correa's ✕ , 81–82, 84
Courtyard Marriott ⚏ , 89
Credit cards, F6, F32, F40
Cruise travel, F29
Cuisine, F11, F33, 163
Currency, F40–F41
Customs and duties, F29–F31

D

Da Albertone ✕ , 218
Decembrists' Square (St. Petersburg), 177
Department stores and malls
Moscow, 110–111
St. Petersburg, 254–255
Deson-Ladoga ⚏ , 232
Diamond Fund, 16
Dining. ⇨ *See* Restaurants
Disabilities and accessibility, F31–F32
Discounts and deals, F32
Dom Druzhby (Friendship House), 49
Dom Knigi (bookstores), 49, 198
Dom Kuptsa Likhonina ⚏ , 155
Dom na Pogrebakh ⚏ , 147
Donna Klara ✕ , 78
Donskoy Monastery, 63–67
Dostoyevsky ⚏ , 231
Dostoyevsky Memorial Apartment, 35
Drugs, prescription, F36
Duties, F29–F31
Dvortsavaya Ploschad (St. Petersburg), 164–168, 170–174
Dvoryanskoye Gnezdo ✕ , 220
Dzhagannat Express ✕ , 77

E

Eastern Golden Ring, 149–155
Egyptian Sphinxes, 178
Electricity, F34
Embassies and consulates, F34
Moscow, 124
St. Petersburg, 262
Emergencies, F34

Moscow, 124–125
St. Petersburg, 262–264
Engineer's Castle, 207–208
Engineer's House, 189
English Court, 28
Engish Embankment, 177
English Landscape Gardens, 291
English-language media, F34
Moscow, 125–126
St. Petersburg, 264
Episcopal Church, 42
Ermitazhniy Retoran ✕ , 219
Estate (Serf) **Theater**, 117
Ethnography Museum, 208
Etiquette and behavior, F34–F35
Evropa ✕ , 187

F

F. M. Dostoyevsky Literary-Memorial Museum, 198
Farmers' markets, 163, 256–257
Festivals, F10–F11, F17–F19
St. Petersburg, 235–236
Field of Mars, 210
Five Spices ✕ , 83
Food and spirits, shopping for
Moscow, 114–116
St. Petersburg, 257–258
Fort Aleksandr, 292
40 Nevsky prospekt ✕ , 199–200
Free Arts Foundation, 198–199
French Park, 117
Friendship House, 49

G

Galereya (Abramtsevo Estate Museum) ✕ , 143
Galereya (Moscow) ✕ , 79
Gamma-Delta Izmailovo ⚏ , 96
Gardens. ⇨ *See* Parks and gardens
Gatchina, 289–291
Gate Church, 194
Gate Church of St. John the Baptist, 140
Gate Church of the Resurrection, 146
Gay and lesbian clubs
Moscow, 104
St. Petersburg, 250
Gay and lesbian travelers, tips for, F35
Genatsvale VIP ✕ , 83

General Staff Building, 170
Getsemanskii (Gethsemene) **monastyr**, 293
Godunov family tomb, 140
Gogol statue, 49–50
Golden Apple ⚏ , 89
Golden Bear Café ✕ , 149
Golden Gates, 150–151
Golden Ring. ⇨ *See* Moscow environs and the Golden Ring
Golden Ring ⚏ , 89–90
Goodman's Steakhouse ✕ , 77, 81
Goritsky Monastyr, 144
Gorky Literary Museum, 42–43
Gorky Park, 59–60, 107
Gorniy Orel ✕ , 225
Gostinny Dvor (department store), 199
Gostinny Dvor, 29
Gosudarstvenny Ermitazhniy Muzey, 170–173
Gosudarstvenny Kremlyovsky Dvorets, 21
Gosudarstvenny Muzey Politicheskoi Istorii Russii, 191–192
Gosudarstvenny Russky Muzey, 211
Grand Ducal Crypt, 189
Grand Emerald Hotel ⚏ , 232
Grand Hotel Europe ⚏ , 228–229
Grand Imperial ✕ , 83–84
Granovitaya Palata, 16
Great Cascade, 278
Great Column Hall ✕ , 289
Great Kremlin Palace, 16
Great Palace, 287–288
GTK Tourist Complex ⚏ , 154
Guelman Gallery, 97
Guardhouse, 189
GUM (department store), 16, 110–111

H

Headquarters of the Guard Corps, 170
Health concerns, F35–F36
Helikon Opera, 99
Hermitage (Peterhof), 277
Hermitage Museum, 170–173
Hermitage Theater, 171
Herzen Museum, 50
Herzen Pedagogical University, 178

Historic islands. ⇨ *See*
  Summer Palaces and
  Historic Islands
Historical Museum, *16–17*
Hola Mexico ✕, *26*
Holiday Inn Lesnaya 🏨, *92*
Holidays, *F37*
Hostels, *F38*
Hotel Aristorkrat 🏨, *142*
Hotel Budapest 🏨, *89*
Hotel Danilovskaya 🏨, *92*
Hotel Pereslavl ✕🏨, *145*
Hotel Volga 🏨, *149*
Hotel Zapadnaya 🏨, *145*
Hotels, *F6, F38–F39*
Moscow, 87–96
*Moscow environs and the
  Golden Ring, 134, 138, 142,
  145, 147, 149, 151–152,
  154–155*
price categories, 87, 134, 227
St. Petersburg, 227–234

I

Ice hockey
Moscow, 107
St. Petersburg, 252
Ice skating, *F13*
Moscow, 107
St. Petersburg, 252, 253
Idealnaya Chashka ✕, *216*
Il Grappolo ✕, *218*
Il Patio ✕, *79, 83*
Imperatorsky Stol ✕, *280*
Imperial balls, *F12*
Insurance, *F26, F36, F37*
Inzhenerny Dom, *189*
Inzhenerny Zamok, *207–208*
Ioannnovskyie Vorota, *188*
Iris 🏨, *95*
Isaac Brodsky Museum, *208*
Isaakievkaya Ploshchad (St.
  Petersburg), *181–182*
Isaakievsky Sobor, *181–182*
Itineraries, *F14–F15*
Moscow, 3
*Moscow environs and the
  Golden Ring, 133*
St. Petersburg, 161
*Summer Palaces and Historic
  Islands, 273*
Ivan the Great Bell Tower, *17*

J

James Cook ✕, *216*
Jean Jacques ✕, *82*
Jewelry stores, *258*

K

Kalinka ✕, *180*
Karetny Dvor ✕, *81*
Katalnaya Gorka, *275*
Katerina 🏨, *91*
Kazan Cathedral, *200*
Khrushchev's grave, *65–66*
Kiliklia ✕, *216*
Kirov Museum, *188*
Kitai Gorod, *22–31*
Kolomenskoy, *118–119*
Konnogvardeisky Manège,
  182
Konstantine Palace, *280–281*
Konyushennaya Church, *168*
Kosmos 🏨, *95*
Kotorosl ✕🏨, *149*
Krasnaya Palata ✕, *147*
Krasnaya Ploshchad (Red
  Square), *6–22*
Krasny Bar ✕, *85*
Krasny Oktyabr (Red
  October) candy factory, *55*
Kremlin (Moscow), *6–22*
Kronshtadt, *291–292*
Kropotkinsky District
  (Moscow), *51–57*
Krutitskoye Ecclesiatical
  Residence, *69–70*
Kudrinskaya Ploshchad
  (Moscow), *43*
Kunstkammer, *176–177*
Kuskovo Estate and Palace
  Museum, *120–121*
Kutafya Tower, *17*
Kvareli ✕, *225*

L

Laima Bistro ✕, *216*
Language, *F37, 300–305*
Last Judgement frescoes, *150*
Lazarus Cemetery, *194*
LeChaim ✕, *220*
Left Bank (St. Petersburg),
  174–185
Lenin Mausoleum, *17–18*
Lenin Museum, *31*
Leo Tolstoy's Museum in
  Yasnaya Polyana, *137–138*
Lermontov House Museum, *50*
Letny Dvorets, *212*
Letny Sad, *211–212*
L'Europe ✕, *218–219*
Libraries
Moscow, 56
St. Petersburg, 203
Lieutenant Schmidt Bridge,
  179

Literature, *169*
Literaturny Muzey Gorkovo,
  42–43
Lobnoye Mesto, *18*
Lodging. ⇨ *See* Hotels
Lomonosov (Oranienbaum),
  273–275
Lower Park (Peterhof), *277*
Lubyanskaya Ploshchad
  (Moscow), *28*
Luggage, *F42–F43*
Lutheran Church, *201*
Lyceum, *286*

M

Macaroni ✕, *223–224*
Magrib (nightclub), *249*
Mail and shipping, *F39*
Maly Drama Theater, *244*
Maly Theater, *28*
Maly Zal, *210*
Manezhnaya Ploshchad
  (Moscow), *43*
Marble Palace, *209–210*
Marco Polo Presnya 🏨, *90*
Maria's Palace, *178*
Mariinsky Theater of Opera
  and Ballet, *241–242*
Mario's ✕, *84–85*
Marly Palace, *278*
Marriott Grand 🏨, *90*
Marriott Royal Aurora 🏨, *90*
Marriott Tverskaya 🏨, *92–93*
Marsovo Pole, *210*
Martha and Mary Convent, *58*
Matisov Domik 🏨, *229–230*
Mausoleum of Paul I, *288*
Mavzolei Lenina, *17–18*
Mayakovskaya metro station,
  37
Mayakovsky Museum, *28–29*
Meal plans, *F6*
Mechta Molokhovets ✕, *222*
Medny Vsadnik (Bronze
  Horseman statue), *177*
Melnikov House, *50*
Menshikov Palace, *179*
Menshikov's Great Palace,
  274
Merchants' Arcade, *29*
Mesto Vstrechi ✕, *80*
Metro travel
Moscow, 37, 126–127
St. Petersburg, 264–265
Metropol ✕🏨, *26, 29, 76,
  88*
Mezhdunarodnaya 🏨, *93*
Mikhailovsky Palace, *211*

Minin and Pozharsky statue,
18–19
Mint (Moscow), 29
Mint (St. Petersburg), 190
Mitki-VKhUTEMAS (gallery),
237–238
Monasteries
Moscow, 5, 29, 54–55, 63–72
Moscow environs and the
Golden Ring, 136–137,
140–141, 144, 146–147, 148,
153
St. Petersburg, 193–195
Summer Palaces and Historic
Islands, 293
Monastery of St. Sergius,
140–141
Monastery of St. Yefim, 153
Monastery of the Conception,
54–55
**Monastery of the Feast of the
Deposition of the Robe,** 153
**Monastery of the Savior
Behind the Icons,** 29
**Monastery of the
Transfiguration of the
Savoir,** 148
Monastyrka River, 194
Monetny Dvor, 29
Money matters, F39–F41
Moscow, 127
Moscow environs and the
Golden Ring, 156
St. Petersburg, 265
Monplaisir, 277
**Monument to Revolutionary
Fighters,** 210
Moscow, F8, 2–130
Arbat, 46–51
Bolshaya Nikitskaya Ulitsa,
38–46
children, attractions for, 26, 46,
59–60
Donskoy Monastery and New
Maiden's Convent, 63–67
embassies, 124
emergencies, 124–125
English-language media,
125–126
excursions from, 116–121
Gorky Park to the Tretyakov
Gallery, 57–63
hotels, 87–96
itineraries, 3
Kitai Gorod, 22–31
Kremlin and Red Square area,
6–22
Kropotkinsky District, 51–57
monasteries southeast of, 67–72

money matters, 127
nightlife and the arts, 5, 96–104
price categories, 72–73, 87
restaurants, 5, 26, 48, 54, 61,
67, 72–87, 118
shopping, 109–116
sports and the outdoors,
104–109
tours, 127–128
transportation, 121–124,
126–127, 128–129
travel agencies, 130
Tverskaya Ulitsa, 31–38
visitor information, 130
Moscow Art Theater, 34, 100
Moscow City Council, 34
**Moscow environs and the
Golden Ring,** F8, 132–157
Eastern Golden Ring, 149–155
hotels, 134, 138, 142, 145, 147,
149, 151–152, 154–155
itineraries, 133
money matters, 156
Northern Golden Ring,
143–149
price categories, 134
restaurants, 134, 138, 142, 143,
145, 147, 140, 151, 154
timing the visit, 134
tours, 156
transportation, 155, 156–157
visitor information, 157
Moscow State University, 43
**Moscow Theater for Young
Viewers,** 100
Moskva 🖼 , 230
Moskva Cinema, 37
Mossoviet Theater, 37
Most Leytenanta Shmidta, 179
Movies, 98–99
**Museum of Ancient Russian
Art,** 141
**Museum of Anthropology and
Ethnology,** 176–177
Museum of Private Collections,
56
**Museum of 17th-Century
Applied Art,** 19
**Museum of the Contemporary
History of Russia,** 35
**Museum of the History of
Moscow,** 29–30
**Museum of Wooden
Architecture,** 153
Museums
Abramtsevo Estate Museum,
142–143
Akhmatova, 196–197

Alexander Pushkin Apartment
Museum, 165, 168
Andrei Bely Apartment
Museum, 48
Andrei Rublyov Museum of
Ancient Russian Culture and
Art, 68
Anna Akhmatova Literary
Museum, 196–197
anthropology, 176–177
architectural, 51, 119, 153, 180
Arkhangelskoye Estate
Museum, 117–118
Artillery Museum, 187
Bely, 48
Botik museum, 144
Brodsky, 208
Cameron Gallery, 285–286
Central Armed Forces Museum,
34
Central House of Artists, 59
Chaliapin House Museum, 40,
42
Chekhov House Museum, 42
circus, 210
Circus Art Museum, 210
costumes, 285–286
Diamond Fund, 16
Dostoyevsky, 35, 198
ethnography, 176–177, 208
Ethnography Museum, 208
F. M. Dostoyevsky Literary-
Memorial Museum, 198
folk art, 36, 119
fortress, 188–191
Free Arts Foundation, 198–199
Gorky, 42–43, 45
Gorky Literary Museum, 42–43
Herzen Museum, 50
historical, 16–17, 29–30, 35,
191–192, 204
Historical Museum, 16–17
houses as, 35, 40, 42, 45, 48,
50–51, 56–57, 60–61,
117–118, 120–121, 134, 136,
137–138, 142–143, 165, 168,
184, 191, 198, 203, 208
Isaac Brodsky Museum, 208
Kirov Museum, 188
Kolomenskoye, 119
Konnogvardeisky Manège, 182
Kuskovo Estate & Palace
Museum, 120–121
Lenin, 31
Leo Tolstoy's Museum in
Yasnaya Polyana, 137–138
Lermontov House Museum, 50
Lyceum, 286
Mayakovsky Museum, 28–29

military, 34, 187
mineral, 182
Moscow, 16–17, 19, 28–30, 31,
    34, 35, 36, 40, 42–43, 44,
    45, 46, 48, 50–51, 55–57, 59,
    60–63, 68, 120–121
Moscow environs and the
    Golden Ring, 134, 136,
    137–138, 141, 142–143, 144,
    153
Museum of Ancient Russian
    Art, 141
Museum of Anthropology and
    Ethnography, 176–177
Museum of the Contemporary
    History of Russia, 35
Museum of the History of
    Moscow, 29–30
Museum of Private Collections,
    56
Museum of 17th-Century
    Applied Art, 19
Museum of Wooden
    Architecture, 153
Nabokov, 184
naval, 144, 183–184, 187–188
New Tretyakov Gallery, 60
Oriental Art Museum, 44
Peter and Paul Fortress,
    188–191
Peter the Great's Cottage, 191
Polytechnical Museum, 30
Pushkin, 50, 55–56, 165, 168
Pushkin Apartment Museum, 50
Pushkin Memorial Museum, 55
Pushkin Museum of Fine Arts,
    55–56
Repin Institute of Painting,
    Sculpture, and Architecture,
    180
Rimsky-Korsakov Museum, 203
Russian Folk Art Museum, 36
Russian Political History
    Museum, 191–192
Ryabushinsky Mansion, 45
St. Petersburg, 165, 168,
    170–173, 176–177, 180, 182,
    183–184, 185, 187–188–192,
    196–197, 198–199, 203, 204,
    208, 210, 211, 236–238
St. Petersburg Institute of
    Mining Technology, 182
Scriabin Museum, 50–51
Shchusev Architecture Museum,
    51
Smolnyi Institut, 204
Stanislavsky Museum, 36
State Hermitage Museum,
    170–173

State Museum of Russian Art,
    211
Summer Palaces and Historic
    Islands, 285–286
Tchaikovsky's House Museum
    in Klin, 134, 136
technology, 30
Tolstoy, 56–57, 60–61,
    137–138
Tolstoy House Estate Museum,
    60–61
Tolstoy Memorial Museum,
    56–57
toys, 141
Tretyakov Gallery, 61–63
Tsvetaeva House Museum, 45
V.I. Lenin Museum, 31
Vladimir Nabokov Museum-
    Apartment, 184
Voenno-Morskoy Muzey,
    183–184
zoological, 46, 185
Zoological Museum (Moscow),
    46
Zoological Museum (St.
    Petersburg), 185
Music
Moscow, 104
St. Petersburg, 238–240,
    248–252
Music stores, 258–259
**Mussorgsky Theater of Opera
    and Ballet,** 210
Muzey Anny Akhmatovy,
    196–197
Muzey V.I. Lenina, 31

N

Nadmogilnaya Chasovnya,
    71–72
**Nakhimov Academy of Naval
    Officers,** 187–188
National Hotel ⬚ , 43–44,
    90–91
Neptune Fountain, 279
Neva Gate, 190
Nevsky prospect (St.
    Petersburg), 201
New Island ✕ , 221–222
New Jerusalem Monastery,
    136–137
New Maiden's Convent,
    63–67
New Savior Monastery, 71–72
New Tretyakov Gallery, 60
Nicholas II monument, 195
Nicholas Statue, 181–182
Nightlife and the arts
Moscow, 5, 96–104

St. Petersburg, 163, 234–252
Nikitskiye Vorota (Moscow),
    44
1913 ✕ , 221
Northern Golden Ring,
    143–149
Novodevichy cemetery, 64–66
Novodevichy Monastyr, 63–67
Novoierusalimsky Monastyr,
    136–137
Novotel Moscow Center ⬚ ,
    93
**Novetel Sheremetyevo 2
    Moscow Airport** ⬚ , 94–95

O

Okhtinskaya-Victoria ⬚ , 233
Oktyabrskaya ⬚ , 229
Oliva ✕ , 217
Onegin ✕ , 219
Opera
Moscow, 99–100
St. Petersburg, 240–243
Oranienbaum, 273–275
Oriental Art Museum, 44
Oruzheynaya Palata, 12–14

P

Packing, tips for, F41–F43
Palace of Marriages, 177
**Palace of Prince Beloselsky-
    Belozersky,** 196
Palace Square (St.
    Petersburg), 164–168,
    170–174
Palaces, F9, F12. ⟳ Also
    Summer Palaces and
    Historic Islands
Moscow, 12, 16, 19, 21, 30,
    120–121
Moscow environs and the
    Golden Ring, 146
St. Petersburg, 163, 173–174,
    177, 178, 179, 184–185,
    196, 197–198, 200–201, 204,
    209–210, 211, 212
**Palaty Romanovych v
    Zaryadye,** 30
Palkin ✕ , 217
Parks and gardens
Moscow, 11, 35, 37–38, 59–60,
    117, 118
St. Petersburg, 188, 200–201,
    211–212
Summer Palaces and Historic
    Islands, 277, 285–286, 288,
    291
Pashkov House, 55

Passazh (shopping arcade), 199
Passports and visas, F43–F44
Patriarch's Palace, 19
Patriarch's Pond, 35
Pavlovsk, 287–289
Peace Wall, 48
Peking Hotel, 37
Pereslavl-Zalessky, 143–145
Pertsov House, 55
Peter and Paul Fortress, 188–191
Peter the Great statue, 60
Peter the Great's Cottage, 191
Peterhof (Petrodvorets), 275–280
Peterstadt Dvorets, 274–275
Petrodvorets, 275–280
Petrograd side (St. Petersburg), 185–192
Petrovich ✕, 80
Photographers, tips for, F24–F25
Pirogi na Nikolskoy ✕, 76–77
Pirozhkovaya Mr. Baker ✕, 222–223
Pirozhkovaya Stolle ✕, 219, 221
Piskaryevskoye Cemetery, 202
Ploshchad Revolutsii metro station (Moscow), 37
Ploshchad Rumyantseva (St. Petersburg), 179
Ploshchad Vosstaniya (St. Petersburg), 202–203
Podvoriye ✕, 288–289
Pokrovskaya 🏨, 154
Pokrovsky Tserkov, 72
Polytechnical Museum, 30
Porcelain, F10
Poslednyaya Kaplya ✕, 80
Poteshny Dvorets, 19
Praga ✕, 82
Premiera (Yaroslavl) ✕, 149
Premiera (Yasnaya Polyana) ✕, 138
Preobrazhensky Tserkov, 66–67
Pribaltiskaya 🏨, 230–231
Price categories
dining, 72–73, 134, 213, 216, 272
lodging, 87, 134, 227
Prioratsky Palace, 290
Project O.G.I. ✕, 81
Propaganda (nightclub), 104
Propaganda ✕, 76
Pulkovskaya 🏨, 233–234

Pushka Inn ✕, 168
Pushkin (Tsarskoye Selo), 281–286
Pushkin Apartment Museum, 50
Pushkin Memorial Museum, 55
Pushkin Museum of Fine Arts, 55–56
Pushkin Square (Moscow), 36
Pyramida ✕, 79

R

Radisson SAS Royal 🏨, 229
Radisson Slavyanskaya 🏨, 94
Rector's Wing, 183
Red Palace (Rostov), 146
Red Square (Moscow), 6–22
Refectory and Church of St. Sergius, 141
Renaissance Moscow 🏨, 95–96
Repin Institute of Painting, Sculpture, and Architecture, 180
Restaurant Idiot ✕, 178
Restaurants, F6, F32–F34
Moscow, 5, 26, 48, 54, 61, 67, 72–87, 118
Moscow environs and the Golden Ring, 134, 138, 142, 143, 145, 147, 140, 151, 154
price categories, 72–73, 134, 213, 216, 272
St. Petersburg, 163, 168, 178, 180, 187, 197, 199–200, 208–209, 212–225
Summer Palaces and Historic Islands, 272, 280, 286, 288–289
Restoran ✕, 222
Restrooms, F44
Resurrection Gates, 19–20
Rimsky-Korsakov Museum, 203
Ring Premier Hotel 🏨, 149
Rizopolozhensky Monastyr, 153
Romanov Palace Chambers in Zaryadye, 30
Rostov, 145–147
Rostov kremlin, 145
Rostral Columns, 180–181
Running
Moscow, 107–108
St. Petersburg, 252
Rus 🏨, 232
Russian Academy of Sciences, 181

Russian Folk Art Museum, 36
Russian National Library, 203
Russian Political History Museum, 191–192
Russian State Library, 56
Russian vocabulary, 300–305
Russkaya Izba ✕, 118
Russkaya Rybalka ✕, 225
Russkie Samotsvety (store), 258
Russky Dvorik ✕, 142
Ryabushinsky Bank, 30
Ryabushinsky Mansion, 45
Rytzarsky Klub ✕, 86–87

S

Safety, F44–F45
St. Barbara's Church, 30
St. Basil's Cathedral, 20
St. Catherine's Church, 58
St. Clement's Church, 58
St. Isaac's Cathedral, 181–182
St. John's Convent, 30
St. John's Gate, 188
St. Nicholas Cathedral, 182
St. Peter's Gate, 188–189
St. Petersburg, F8–F9, 159–269
children, attractions for, 168, 170, 185, 187–188, 210, 244–245
consulates, 262
cuisine, 163
emergencies, 262–264
English-language media, 264
farmers' markets, 163, 256–257
hotels, 227–234
itineraries, 161
literature, 169
money matters, 265
Nevsky Prospekt and the Inner City, 192–205
nightlife and the arts, 163, 234–252
Palace Square and the Hermitage, 164–168, 170–174
Petrograd side, 185–192
price categories, 213, 216, 227
restaurants, 163, 168, 178, 180, 187, 197, 199–200, 208–209, 212–225
shopping, 163, 253–259
sports and the outdoors, 252–253
Square of the Arts to the Field of Mars, 205–212
tours, 265–266

transportation, 259–262, 264–265, 266–268
travel agencies, 268
Vasilievsky Island and the Left Bank, 174–185
visitor information, 196, 269
St. Petersburg ⌂ , 233
St. Petersburg Circus, 210
St. Petersburg Institute of Mining Technology, 182
St. Petersburg International Hostel ⌂ , 230
St. Petersburg Male Choir, 239
St. Petersburg Philharmonic, 210
St. Petersburg State University, 183
St. Petersburg Tourist Information Center, 196
Sandunovskaya Bani, 31, 106
Satire Theater, 36–37
Savoy ⌂ , 88
Scandinavia ✕ , 81
Scriabin Museum, 50–51
Senate and Synod, 183
Senior-citizens, tips for, F45
Sergiev-Posad (Zagorsk), 138–142
Seven Gothic Sisters, 41
Shamrock Irish Pub, 247
Shchusev Architecture Museum, 51
Sheraton Palace Moscow ⌂ , 93
Shinok ✕ , 85
Shopping, F45–F46
Moscow, 109–116
St. Petersburg, 163, 253–259
Shostakovich Philharmonia, 210
Shtab Gvardeiskovo Korpusa, 170
Signal Cannon, 190
Siniy Most, 183
Sirena ✕ , 86
Skating
Moscow, 107
St. Petersburg, 252, 253
Skiing, 108
Sledding, 108
Smolenskoy Bogomateri, 67
Smolny, 203
Smolnyi Institut, 204
Sobakina Tower, 20–21
Sobor Rozhdestva Bogorodnitsy, 152
Sobor Spasa Preobrazheniya, 71

Sobornaya Ploshchad (Moscow), 21
Soccer
Moscow, 107–108
St. Petersburg, 253
Sokol Hotel ⌂ , 154–155
Sol-Art (gallery), 238
Souvenirs, shopping for
Moscow, 116
St. Petersburg, 255–256
Sovietskaya ⌂ , 233
Spaso House, 51
Spaso-Preobrazhensky Valaamskii (Transfiguration of the Savior) Monastyr, 293
Spassky Sobor (Kitak Gorod, Moscow), 29
Spassky Sobor (Southeast Moscow), 68–69
Sports and the outdoors
Moscow, 104–109
St. Petersburg, 252–253
Sretenskaya ⌂ , 88–89
Stanislavsky Museum, 36
Staraya Bashnya ✕ , 286
Staraya Tamozhnya ✕ , 221
Starlite Diner, ✕ , 77–78, 84
Stary Gorod ✕ , 151
State Hermitage Museum, 170
State Kremlin Palace, 21
State Museum of Russian Art, 211
Stella Art (gallery), 98
Stella Art Russian (gallery), 98
Stock Exchange, 183–184
Stena Mira (Peace Wall), 48
Street markets, 115–116
Strelka, 184
Stroganov Palace, 204
Student travelers, tips for, F46
Sukawati ✕ , 218
Summer Garden, 211–212
Summer Palace (St. Petersburg), 212
Summer Palaces and Historic Islands, F9, 271–296
itineraries, 273
Kronshtadt and Valaam, 291–294
price categories, 272
restaurants, 272, 280, 286, 288–289
timing the visit, 272
tours, 295–296
transportation, 294–295, 296
visitor information, 296
Suvorovskaya Ploshchad (St. Petersburg), 212

Suzdal, 152–155
Suzdal kremlin, 152
Swissôtel ⌂ , 92
Symbols, F6

T

Taganka Theatre, 101
Taleon ✕ , 218
Tandoor ✕ , 217
Tatyana Kotegova Fashing House (store), 255
Taurida Palace, 204
Taxes, F46
Taxis
Moscow, 128
Moscow environs and the Golden Ring, 156
St. Petersburg, 266
Summer Palaces and Historic Islands, 293
Tchaikovsky Concert Hall, 36
Tchaikovsky Conservatory, 45, 99
Tchaikovsky's House Museum in Klin, 134, 136
Telephones, F46–F47
Temple of Friendship, 288
Terem, 16
Terem Quartet, 238
Teremok (Gate Tower), 70
Teremok (Rostov) ✕ , 147
Teremok (St. Petersburg) ✕ , 217, 223
Theater
Moscow, 100–101
St. Petersburg, 243–245
Theater buildings
Moscow, 16, 28, 34, 36–37, 38, 45, 51, 117
Moscow environs and the Golden Ring, 147–148
St. Petersburg, 171, 195, 210
Tiflis ✕⌂ , 83, 91
Tikhvinskoye kladbische, 194
Time zones, F47–F48
Timing the visit, F16
Moscow environs and the Golden Ring, 134
Summer Palaces and Historic Islands, 272
Tinkoff (Moscow) ✕ , 82
Tinkoff (St. Petersburg) ✕ , 216
Tipping, F48
Tolstoy House Estate Museum, 60–61
Tolstoy Memorial Museum, 56–57

Tomb of the Unknown Soldier, 21

Tours and packages, F48–F49
Moscow, 127–128
*Moscow environs and the
Golden Ring,* 156
St. Petersburg, 265–266
*Summer Palaces and Historic
Islands,* 295–296

Tower of the Savior, 21–22

Toy Museum, 141

Trade rows, 146, 147

Train travel, F49–F51
Moscow, 128–129
*Moscow environs and the
Golden Ring,* 156–157
St. Petersburg, 266–267
*Summer Palaces and Historic
Islands,* 296

**Transfiguration of the Savior
Monastery,** 293

Transportation, F51
Moscow, 121–124, 126–127,
128–129
*Moscow environs and the
Golden Ring,* 155, 156–157
St. Petersburg, 259–262,
264–265, 266–268
*Summer Palaces and Historic
Islands,* 294–295, 296

Trapeznaya ✕, 154

Trapeznaya Kremlya ✕, 154

Travel agencies, F32, F51
Moscow, 130
St. Petersburg, 268

Traveler's checks, F41

Travelers Guest House Moscow
🖫, 96

Tretyakov Gallery, 61

Tri Peskarya ✕, 151

Trinity Cathedral, 194

Triumphal Square (Moscow),
36–37

Troitskaya Tower, 22

Trubetskoi Bastion, 190–191

Tsar Bell, 22

Tsar Cannon, 22

Tsaritsyno, 119–120

Tsar's Hunt, The ✕, 86

Tsar's Little Garden, 288

Tsarskoye Selo, 281–286

Tschaika (bar), 247

Tsentralny Detsky Teatr, 26

Tserkov Archangela Mikhaila,
69

Tserkov Znamenia, 72

TSPKIO (park), 200–201

Tsvetaeva House Museum, 45

Tverskaya Ploshchad
(Moscow), 37–38

Tverskaya Ulitsa, 31–38

Tverskaya-Yamskaya ulitsa
(Moscow), 38

Twelve Colleges Building, 183

U

U Pirosmani ✕, 67, 86

U Zolotykh Vorot 🖫, 151

Ukraina 🖫, 94

Ulitsa Zodchevo Rossi (St.
Petersburg), 204–205

Uspensky Sobor, 70

Uspensky Tserkov, 67

Usypalnitsa (Grand Ducal
Crypt), 189

V

V. I. Lenin Museum, 31

Vaccinations, F36

Vakhtangov Theater, 51

Valaam Archipelago, 291,
292–294

Vasilievsky Island, 174–185

Victory Park, 118

Visas, F43–F44

Visitor information, F51
Moscow, 130
*Moscow environs and the
Golden Ring,* 157
St. Petersburg, 196, 269
*Summer Palaces and Historic
Islands,* 296

Vladimir, 150–152

Vladimir Hotel 🖫, 151

**Vladimir Nabokov Museum-
Apartment,** 184

Vodka, 226

Voenno-Morskoy Muzey,
183–184

Vogue Café ✕, 76

Volkov Theater, 147–148

Volshebniy Vkus ✕, 225

Voronka cafe ✕, 138

Voskresenskiye Vorota, 19–20

Voskresensky (Resurrection)
Monastery, 293

W

Waterfalls, 278

Weather, F16

Web sites, F52

White House (Bely Dom), 40

White Palace, 146

Winter Palace, 173–174

Women travelers, tips for, F45

Y

Yakitoria ✕, 76, 83, 85

Yakovlevsky (Jacob)
Monastery, 146

Yaroslav the Wise statue, 148

Yaroslavl, 147–149

Yekaterininsky Park, 285

Yelagin Palace, 200–201

Yeliseyevsky Food Emporium,
205, 258

Yeliseyevsky's (store), 38,
115

Yermolava Theater, 38

Yolki-Palki Po . . . ✕, 79

Yubileynaya ✕🖫, 149

Yuspov Palace, 184–185

Z

Za Stsenoi ✕, 220

Zachatievsky Monastyr, 54–55

Zagorsk, 138–142

Zaikonospassky Monastyr, 29

Zhiguli ✕, 48

Zhyly-Byly ✕, 200

Zimny Dvorets (Winter
Palace), 173–174

Znamensky Sobor, 27

Zolotoye Koltso ✕, 142

Zolotoye Koltso 🖫, 152

Zoo, 46

Zoological Museum
(Moscow), 46

Zoological Museum (St.
Petersburg), 185

Zov Ilicha ✕, 219

PHOTO CREDITS

Cover Photo (Old Soviet Union era posters for sale in Moscow): *Iain Masterton/Alamy*. F8, *Dmitry Aremaev/viestiphoto.com*. F9 (left), *Jon Arnold/Agency Jon Arnold Images/age fotostock*. F9 (right), *Jon Arnold/Agency Jon Arnold Images/age fotostock*. F10, *Russian Look/viestiphoto.com*. F11, *Konstantin Tarusov/viestiphoto.com*. F12, *Peter Titmuss/Alamy*. F13 (left), *Russian Look/viestiphoto.com*. F13 (right), *Konstantin Kokoshkin/viestiphoto.com*. F17, *P. Narayan/age fotostock*. F18, *Russian Look/viestiphoto.com*. F19 (left), *P. Narayan/age fotostock*. F19 (right), *Walter Bibikow/viestiphoto.com*.

ABOUT OUR WRITERS

Moscow-based journalists Nathan Toohey and Jennifer Chater handled Smart Travel Tips. They have been living in Russia for eight years, and they write and edit on a wide range of subjects having to do with life in Russia, from restaurants to real estate. They have also traveled extensively around the country.

Anna Malpas contributed to the Moscow chapter. She moved to Moscow in 2003 to take up the post of deputy editor of the Arts & Ideas section of the *The Moscow Times*. Previously she lived for a year in Vladivostok, working as a reporter on the Vladivostok News web site.

Kevin O'Flynn, who moved to Moscow in 1995, is a journalist with *The Moscow Times*, the capital's leading English-language newspaper. He is also a cofounder of the Moscow Architecture Preservation Society (www.map-moscow.com), an organization which works to save the city's historic buildings. He contributed to the Moscow chapter.

St. Petersburg contributer, Galina Stolyarova is a chief reporter at *The St. Petersburg Times*. She started out as a theater, opera, and dining reviewer, but she now covers politics as well. She has covered opera and arts festivals in Russia and Europe.

Irina Titova worked on the St. Petersburg and Summer Palaces & Historic Islands chapters. A reporter at *The St. Petersburg Times*, she has written everything from daily-news articles to unusual feature stories. She also studied for a year at St. Michael's College in Vermont, which first introduced her to American journalism.

A native Muscovite, Oksana Yablokova is a journalist at the news desk of the *Moscow Times*. She has covered a wide range of topics, including regional elections, dog hotels, the Kursk salvaging operation, and Formula One racing in Moscow. Before working at the *Times* Oksana was a freelance interpreter. She worked on the Moscow and Moscow Environs & the Golden Ring chapters.

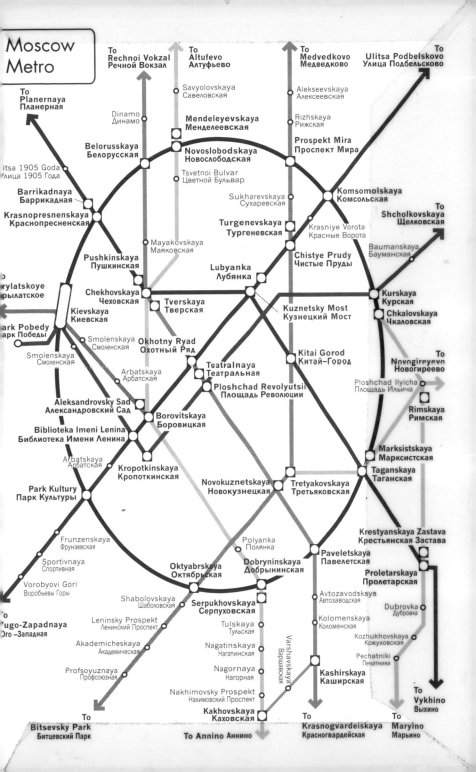

Get inside
Moscow & St. Petersburg

Explore everywhere

Ride a hydrofoil to an imperial playground of parks and palaces ⇨p.275.

Count the onion domes on Ivan the Terrible's cathedral ⇨p.20.

Make a pilgrimage to the monastery at the heart of Holy Russia ⇨p.140.

Eat well and often

Taste bliny prepared just the way Russian moms make them ⇨p.217.

Savor venison or beluga caviar with a view of Nevsky prospekt ⇨p.217.

Travel back to Pushkin's time whenever you want at a 24-hour eatery ⇨p.79.

Soak up the culture

Watch the company of Nijinsky and Nureyev perform *Swan Lake* ⇨p.241.

Sweat out the toxins at the most lavish banya in town ⇨p.106.

Get lost in the awesome art collection that belonged to the tsars ⇨p.170.

Upgrade with Fodor's

> ### Rely on the Freshest Facts

We frequently update our Moscow &
St. Petersburg guide, and we make
every effort to bring you the most
accurate and thorough book. Plus we
provide timely updates about the area
at Fodors.com.

> ### Get the Inside Scoop

Unlike some other travel books, Fodor's
guides rely heavily on local experts—
so you know you're seeing the real
Moscow & St. Petersburg.

> ### Travel with Confidence

We give you all the planning tools you
need to tailor your trip. We give options
for all budgets. You make the choices.

...RIENCE
VISIT WWW.FODORS.COM
Research and book airlines
and hotels. Link quickly to
other travel sites. Talk to your
fellow Fodor's travelers.

ISBN 1-4000-1669-X

51995

9 781400 016693

US $19.95   CAN $26.95   UK £12.99